Praise for *Lawrence and Aaronsohn*

"Ronald Florence . . . has created a revealing narrative about the territorial conflicts in the Middle East." —*The Boston Globe*

"Florence's well-written and frequently surprising work sheds light on usually neglected aspects of Middle Eastern history." —*Booklist*

"There are so many fascinating stories in *Lawrence and Aaronsohn*, and Ronald Florence has done marvelous work. . . . Lawrence and Aaronsohn, their times and places, positively come alive. . . . Masterful . . . history as drama, and it makes for compelling reading."

—*Chicago Jewish Star*

"There's suspense and pathos in Florence's saga of the war-torn Middle East." —*Publishers Weekly*

"It would be hard for a playwright to juxtapose two characters more out of tune with each other and with the world they inhabited than T. E. Lawrence and Aaron Aaronsohn. Yet Ronald Florence engagingly shows how Aaronsohn worked in an odd sort of tandem with Lawrence, spokesman for the Arab tribes. The unpredictable Lawrence and the often obnoxious Aaronsohn may not have been regarded as good company by their contemporaries, but in this dual biography they are as fascinating as their turbulent times."

—Brian Garfield, author of *Hopscotch*, *Death Wish*, and *The Meinerzhagen Mystery*

"Two colleagues in British intelligence had conflicting obsessions that presaged the Arab-Israeli conflict. . . . Historian and novelist Florence tells their story well." —*Harvard Magazine*

"T. E. Lawrence and Aaron Aaronsohn are, in many ways, the fathers of the modern Middle East and its myriad woes. Their disputes anticipated the religious and political battles that continue to tear that region apart. With dramatic flair, Florence reconstructs these two men in fine . . . detail." —*Washington CEO*

PENGUIN BOOKS

LAWRENCE AND AARONSOHN

Ronald Florence is a historian and novelist and the author of eight previous books, including *The Gypsy Man*, *The Perfect Machine*, and *Blood Libel: The Damascus Affair of 1840*. He lives in Providence, Rhode Island.

T. E. Lawrence, Aaron Aaronsohn,
and the Seeds of the Arab-Israeli Conflict

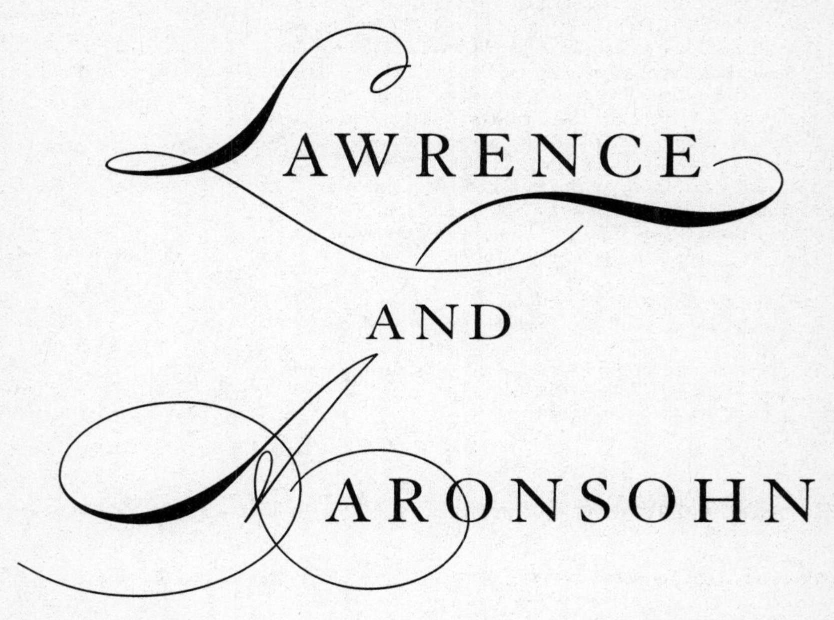

RONALD FLORENCE

PENGUIN BOOKS

PENGUIN BOOKS
Published by the Penguin Group
Penguin Group (USA) Inc., 375 Hudson Street, New York, New York 10014, U.S.A.
Penguin Group (Canada), 90 Eglinton Avenue East, Suite 700, Toronto,
Ontario, Canada M4P 2Y3 (a division of Pearson Penguin Canada Inc.)
Penguin Books Ltd, 80 Strand, London WC2R 0RL, England
Penguin Ireland, 25 St Stephen's Green, Dublin 2, Ireland (a division of Penguin Books Ltd)
Penguin Group (Australia), 250 Camberwell Road, Camberwell,
Victoria 3124, Australia (a division of Pearson Australia Group Pty Ltd)
Penguin Books India Pvt Ltd, 11 Community Centre,
Panchsheel Park, New Delhi – 110 017, India
Penguin Group (NZ), 67 Apollo Drive, Rosedale, North Shore 0632,
New Zealand (a division of Pearson New Zealand Ltd)
Penguin Books (South Africa) (Pty) Ltd, 24 Sturdee Avenue,
Rosebank, Johannesburg 2196, South Africa

Penguin Books Ltd, Registered Offices:
80 Strand, London WC2R 0RL, England

First published in the United States of America by Viking Penguin,
a member of Penguin Group (USA) Inc. 2007
Published in Penguin Books 2008

10 9 8 7 6 5 4 3 2 1

Photograph credits appear on page 513.

THE LIBRARY OF CONGRESS HAS CATALOGED THE HARDCOVER EDITION AS FOLLOWS:
Florence, Ronald.
Lawrence and Aaronsohn : T. E. Lawrence, Aaron Aaronsohn, and
the seeds of the Arab-Israeli conflict / by Ronald Florence.
p. cm.
Includes bibliographical references and index.
ISBN 978-0-670-06351-2 (hc.)
ISBN 978-0-14-311382-9 (pbk.)
1. World War, 1914–1918—Palestine. 2. World War, 1914–1918—Military intelligence—Palestine. 3. Jews—Palestine—History. 4. Zionism. 5. Palestine—History—1799–1917. 6. Aaronsohn, Aaron, 1876–1919. 7. Lawrence, T. E. (Thomas Edward), 1888–1935. I. Title.
DS125.5.F56 2007
940.4'15—dc22 2006034931

Printed in the United States of America
Designed by Carla Bolte
Maps by Jeffrey L. Ward

FOR JUSTIN AND MAYA

CONTENTS

Two important phenomena, of the same nature though opposed, to which nobody has drawn attention, manifest themselves at this moment in Asiatic Turkey; they are, the awakening of the Arab nation, and the hidden efforts of the Jews to reconstruct on a very large scale the ancient monarchy of Israel. These two movements are destined to combat each other continually until one of them takes it [Palestine] from the other.

—Négib Azoury, 1905[1]

I'll be frank with you. During the world war they gave the Arabs and the Jews conflicting assurances. We sold the same horse twice.

—Lloyd George[2]

Lawrence and Aaronsohn

Prologue

Everyone had been so enthusiastic in August 1914. As the inconceivable war became inevitable, rulers and ruled alike watched the bellicose parades, crossing the boulevards from apprehension to enthusiasm. Military bands played lusty martial airs like the "Marseillaise" and the "Radetsky March." Young men talked of duty, honor, and glory as they flocked to recruiting offices, lying about their height, eyesight, experience, and health. A few mothers and fathers and wives schemed to keep sons and husbands from the war effort, but they and their poems, like "I Didn't Raise My Boy to Be a Soldier," were shouted down by the crowds cheering the marching recruits.

Priests blessed the departing warriors and proclaimed that God was on their side. Women kissed their husbands, fiancés, and sons among the departing troops; some kissed strangers. The horrible photographs of the prolonged and brutal American Civil War were long forgotten as both sides counted on swift victories: the Germans trusting the strategic brilliance of the Schlieffen plan, while the Entente counted on the peerless British navy, the vaunted élan of the French troops, and the seemingly limitless Russian geography and army. When the mighty German Social Democratic Party voted for war credits, even the threat of socialist opposition to the war collapsed in an orgy of nationalism and jingoism, as pundits in every capital predicted that in a few short months the troops would return home with honor and glory.

For many, the war was a solution. A swift, glorious victory would miraculously bring an end to the personal, social, and economic woes that had ruffled the complacency of the emerging twentieth century. War would cure not just the economic inequalities, threats of revolution, and pressures of competition, but the private woes of unfaithful wives, thoughtless bosses, unruly children, sexual frustration, and troubled romance. This would be a war like no other, a collision that could only end in changes too earthshaking to predict.

In living rooms and ministries alike, once-distant place names were suddenly the stuff of everyday conversations. British diplomats and generals began thinking anew about their sprawling empire, contemplating the spoils and a redrawing of the maps that victory would bring. For some, the strategic needs of the empire, like overland and sea routes to India and control of the Suez Canal, were absolute. Years of intelligence skirmishes and the diplomatic battles of the Great Game with Russia had also persuaded many British strategists that access to the vast spaces between the Mediterranean and Persia were essential for the security of the empire. The war was made of dreams.

But by October 1916 the war showed no signs of ending. No one called it a world war yet, but armies faced one another on battlefields across Europe, the Middle East, the Caucasus, and on the frontiers of colonial empires. Fleets blockaded whole coasts, submarines mercilessly stalked merchant ships on the seas. Trench warfare and the machine gun had created deadly killing fields where whole generations fell in futile charges while the battle lines scarcely moved. With the end of the war nowhere in sight, attentions turned to the fates of the great empires that ruled much of Eastern Europe, Asia, and the Middle East, where the failed promises of the war seemed to open the way for postponed colonial ambitions and the long-stifled aspirations of subject peoples. Even while the fighting raged on the battlefields and general staffs planned for another year of war, secret diplomatic agreements parceled up the faltering empires, and the minorities within began earnest talk and dedicated action toward founding new nation-states.

The Ottoman Empire—the sick man of Europe in diplomatic circles—was especially vulnerable. Internal weaknesses, bumbling diplomacy, and disastrous wars had already lost the sultans Greece, Egypt, Montenegro, Serbia, Romania, Cyprus, and Tunisia; only the intervention of the Great Powers in 1840 had prevented the loss of Syria and Palestine. Turkey had imported European military bandmasters in an effort to catch up with the military in the West,[1] but there was no joy at the coming of war in the streets of Constantinople. And by the second year of the Great War, despite the unexpected Turkish victories at Gallipoli and at Kut in Mesopotamia, the Young Turk government in Constantinople, or Istanbul, as they preferred to call it, faced formidable British and French forces in the Mediterranean, Russian forces in the Caucasus, and an incipient revolt among the Arabic-speaking populations. Café rumors talked of the diplomatic maneuvering of the Entente allies and secret treaties that would dismantle the empire. Even a deliberate and brutal campaign against the Armenians was not enough to keep other subject peoples of the empire—Arabs, Jews, Circassians, Kurds—from talking about "rights" and "national aspirations," and from contemplating actions that bordered on outright revolt.

For the Jewish settlers of Palestine and the Arabs of the Ottoman Empire, both chafing under deeply resented Turkish rule, it was a time of terror and opportunity. If many lived in fear of the insecurity and chaos of war and change, others saw the conflicting promises from the Great Powers and the sudden collapse of what had seemed a timeless empire as a seed ground for new ideas and new nations, a political and social chaos ripe for charlatans, adventurers, and profiteers—and for men and women of audacity and passionate conviction. It was a time when a young second lieutenant from Oxfordshire named T. E. Lawrence, with no frontline or command experience of war, and a Palestinian scientist named Aaron Aaronsohn, renowned as an agronomist but only an observer of the war, could rise to unlikely positions of leadership. They were novices to politics, but their ideas about the future were too bold, their self-confidence too compelling, to ignore. Where others saw only the chaos of collapse, Lawrence and Aaronsohn saw clear futures for the Arabs and the Jews; they saw new nations overcoming centuries of inertia by harnessing long-dormant energies to long-suppressed ideas. Where others wavered, hesitant in the face of the complexities of diplomacy and strategy, they were driven men, sure of their convictions.

It was a time when both the Arabs and the Jews of Palestine looked to the heavens for guidance. Lawrence and Aaronsohn streaked across the desert skies like blazing meteors—unexpected, blinding in their brilliance, demanding attention as they turned heads from the everyday to the sudden exception, from the workaday to startling plans for the future. And like meteors they disappeared all too quickly, leaving behind only their ionized trails across the sky. For some those trails resembled rainbows, illusionary paths to pots of gold. The rainbows met in the land some called Palestine, and others would one day call Israel.

1

The Road to the Savoy Hotel

You will arrive and you will find no one there.
—Avshalom Feinberg[1]

So I went down to Arabia to see its great men. The first, the Sherif of Mecca, we knew to be aged. Abdulla I found too clever. Ali too clean, Zeid too cool. . . . Then I rode up-country to Feisal and found in him the leader with the needful fire, and yet with reason to give effect to our science.
—T. E. Lawrence[2]

A tall blond man watched the passengers board the *Oscar II*. It was October 1916, the third year of the world war, and the port and steamship offices in Copenhagen were generously posted with notices warning of spies and the dangers of German submarines, but he seemed oblivious to the warnings. He was imposing in his well-tailored but rumpled suit, broad-shouldered and muscular, with the paunch and thick neck of a man who watched his weight. Anyone who looked his way would notice his towering brow and piercing blue eyes, and find him hard to place.

The Scandinavian-American liner was scheduled to stop for coal in the Orkney Islands en route to New York, and the British authorities in Copenhagen were checking each passenger for a laissez-passer. With his Turkish papers, the tall blond man had needed weeks to be cleared by the British consulate, and even then it had taken a last-minute flurry of phone calls to get his papers right. He wondered about the odd British gallantry that allowed so many German women on board. They were enemy aliens too. Was it "English hypocrisy," he wondered, or "mid-Victorian sentimentality"? Whatever the explanation, he was delighted. Once the ship left Copenhagen he met the most beautiful woman on board, a charming German named Olga Bernhardt, who was traveling without her husband. He spoke French with her and called her "Mademoiselle Bernhardt."

The weather was perfect. After a stop in Christiania (Oslo) the *Oscar II* sailed into bright sunshine and a calm sea, with just a touch of morning frost and the crisp feel of autumn in the air. The newspapers carried reports of nonbelligerent ships that had "mistakenly" been torpedoed by German U-boats, and even ships from neutral countries, like the *Oscar II,* had to maintain a constant lookout for German submarines, so most of the passengers were content to stay in their cabins or in the common rooms below. The tall blond man stayed topside, pacing, not a casual stroll around the deck but a deliberate, forceful stride, as if he were on a mission or thinking through a problem. He paced thirteen miles that day. He also found time to talk to Mlle. Bernhardt. When she discovered that he shared her dislike of England, Mlle. Bernhardt "honored" him with unexpected "confidences."[3] She was one of the few people on board to learn his name: Aaron Aaronsohn.

Aaronsohn had been traveling in secrecy for five months, crossing and recrossing enemy lines, hiding his purpose with sham papers and outrageous if authentic-sounding stories as he bluffed his way through belligerent and neutral countries from Palestine* to Denmark. He was an Ottoman subject, an enemy alien to the British, and his audacious plan had worked so far, but he had grown up in the early Jewish settlements in Palestine, where openness, informality, and brusque directness were prized; he was acutely uncomfortable in the closed spaces of conspiracy. When he had finally gotten permission to board

*The Great Powers used the name of a Roman province, Palestine. The Turks called it South Syria; the Jews called it Eretz Israel, the Land of Israel.

the *Oscar II* in Copenhagen, two Americans he had met, Rabbi Judah Magnes and Dr. Alexander Dushkin, offered him the third bunk in their cabin. Finding the shared cabin stuffy and confining, Aaronsohn escaped to the deck to think. He had always paced when he thought.[4] And he had much to think about. He had bet everything on his plan: his family, his colleagues, his own future, and the future of a nation.

When the ship docked at Kirkwall, in the Orkney Islands, British customs officials boarded. Their interrogations and inspections of the passengers, beginning with the Americans and Scandinavians, were cursory until they came to Aaronsohn. The inspecting officer gave him an odd look, then in front of the other passengers ordered Aaronsohn to his stateroom and told him that he would be searched and questioned after lunch. A guard was posted outside his cabin. After lunch an officer from shore came to the stateroom and escorted Aaronsohn back to the deck, where the other passengers were waiting. In a loud voice the officer announced that Aaronsohn's cabin was full of German "stuff" and that he was being detained. As Aaronsohn was escorted off the ship, his fellow passengers, especially Mlle. Bernhardt, appeared moved by his fate.[5]

On shore, Sergeant T. H. Bond of the Orkney Reserve Force took Aaronsohn into custody. Captain Brims and another officer interviewed him over tea, and he was taken to a room to sleep. Sergeant Bond slept in the same room, assuring Aaronsohn that he was not under arrest, but that as his status was "irregular" he would be escorted to London.

Early the next morning Captain Brims escorted Aaronsohn around the edge of Scapa Flow to Stromness, where they could catch the mail steamer to Thurso. From the shore they could see row upon row of the dreadnoughts and cruisers of the British Grand Fleet in the vast anchorage at Scapa Flow. A few of the warships were licking their wounds from the great naval battle against the German High Seas Fleet at Jutland months before, but the Grand Fleet was still the mightiest naval force in the world, an awesome display of British military power. From Stromness they caught the mail steamer to Scrabster Pier, near Thurso, in the extreme north of Scotland, where they boarded the train that would take them south to London. The long train ride gave Aaronsohn plenty of time to think about the elaborate scheme that had gotten him this far.

Boarding the ship to the United States in Copenhagen, telling a fellow passenger that he disliked England, the discovery of German "stuff" in his cabin, and his escort off the ship under guard had all been a ruse. After long negotiations in Copenhagen, Aaronsohn and the British consul had arranged the details of the journey so fellow passengers, including any Turkish, Austrian, or German sympathizers who might have been aboard, would think Aaronsohn had been arrested as a Turkish spy. That would spare Aaronsohn's family and friends in Palestine the consequences of his being identified as a traitor who had gone over to the British.

Once he was safely on British soil Aaronsohn wrote in his diary: "The trick was played."[6]

~

While Aaron Aaronsohn was in a railcar on his way to London, four thousand miles away a young second lieutenant from Oxfordshire was riding up the Wadi Safra, a rugged valley near the coast of Arabia north of Rabegh. The valley was named for the mustard-yellow goatgrass that grew with spring rains (*safra* means yellow), but in late October there was no grass, only scattered tamarisk and thorn trees, jagged flintstone outcroppings, and endless expanses of sharp pebbles, a stark landscape that stretched as far as the eye could see under a cobalt blue sky and a fierce desert sun.[7]

It was the lieutenant's first long ride on a camel.[8] His legs and back ached from the unfamiliar position and the jolting gait, and his fair skin blistered in the painful heat. An Arab cloak and headdress concealed his short stature and unusually large head, but his eyes still recoiled from the harsh sunlight glinting off the stones. He had read that the Arab headdress was practical in the desert, and that the Christian habit of wearing a hat between their "weak eyes and the uncongenial sight of God" was an unwelcome reminder to Muslims that "God was miscalled and misliked" by Christians,[9] and had learned the practicality of Arab headdress in earlier travels in Syria. Under the cloak, his khaki uniform, army-issue boots, pink complexion, and heavily accented Arabic gave him away as an Englishman. He was about to be the first Christian to visit Emir Faisal and the Army of the Arab Revolt at their desert camp.

Only a week before, T. E. Lawrence had been at a desk in the intelligence section of the British general headquarters (GHQ) at the Savoy Hotel in Cairo, reading dispatches, translating obscure Arabic newspapers, drawing maps, analyzing policy options, and designing postage stamps for the Arab ruler of the Hejaz, the coastal province of the Arabian Peninsula along the Red Sea, home to the Muslim holy places of Mecca and Medina. Lawrence had traveled in Syria and Palestine before the war, read widely about Arab culture and history, and had participated for years in a major archaeological dig near the border of Turkey and Syria. The closest he had come to combat had been a quasi-diplomatic mission to Mesopotamia. His experience and knowledge of Arabic were welcome skills at British GHQ, where there were no recent authoritative descriptions of the social and political conditions of the area in any European language, and the only recent map of Palestine was of a wild area near the Gaza frontier. But Lawrence's occasionally uppity manner and borderline insubordination toward his colleagues and superiors—"I took every opportunity to rub into them their comparative ignorance and inefficiency (not difficult!) and irritated them yet further by literary airs, correcting split infinitives and tautologies in their reports"[10]—earned him little respect. He had a few good friends among his fellow officers, men he had worked with on archaeological digs and who were accustomed to his sarcasm, wit, and pranks. But no one seemed to know him well. If he had dreams, no one in Cairo knew about them.

And despite his extensive reading and ready disquisitions on the tribes and customs of Arabia, Lawrence had never been to the Arabian Peninsula. He was entitled to a leave in the fall of 1916, and was quietly asked by General Gilbert Clayton, the head of military intelligence in

Cairo, to accompany Ronald Storrs, the oriental secretary to Lord Kitchener, on a diplomatic mission to Jidda, where Lawrence's Arabic and his observational experience might be of use.[11] There they would meet with Emir Abdullah, the youngest son of Sherif Hussein of Mecca.

Sherif Hussein ibn Ali of the Hashemite clan of the Quraish was the ruler of the Hejaz, official guardian of the holy places of Mecca and Medina, and a direct descendant of the Prophet, revered by his loyal followers as a man of uncommon piety. He was also an ambitious man and contemptuous of Turkish rule over Arabia. There was no Arabian state, but for Hussein and his contemporaries Arabia was a vivid concept, encompassing the vast geographic basin south of the line of mountains that ran from the Aegean across southern Turkey to Persia, an area that today includes Saudi Arabia, Iraq, Israel, Jordan, Lebanon, Syria, Gaza, Sinai, Kuwait, the gulf states, and the edges of bordering countries. The term was also sometimes used to describe the collective Arabic-speaking peoples of southwest Asia. Hussein saw his own Hejaz with its Islamic holy places of Medina and Mecca at the center of that vast Arab world, and resented the Ottoman bureaucrats sent from Constantinople: their ignorance of Arabic was not only an inconvenience, forcing the Arabs to petition in Turkish, but to Sherif Hussein a token of Turkish disdain for the Qur'an and other Arabic holy books. He resented the recent construction of the Hejaz Railway from Damascus to Medina, which threatened the lucrative local business of providing camel and donkey-cart transport for pilgrims on the annual hajj, and allowed too easy access to the Hejaz for unwelcome Turkish troops. Hussein was particularly incensed when he returned from an expedition against mutinous factions in the Arabian Peninsula in 1910, which he had conducted in the name of the sultan and government in Constantinople, only to find that the Turks had made Medina an independent *muhafaza* bound directly to Constantinople and no longer part of the *vilayet* he ruled.[12] By 1914 Sherif Hussein's patience with the Ottoman rulers had been sorely tried.

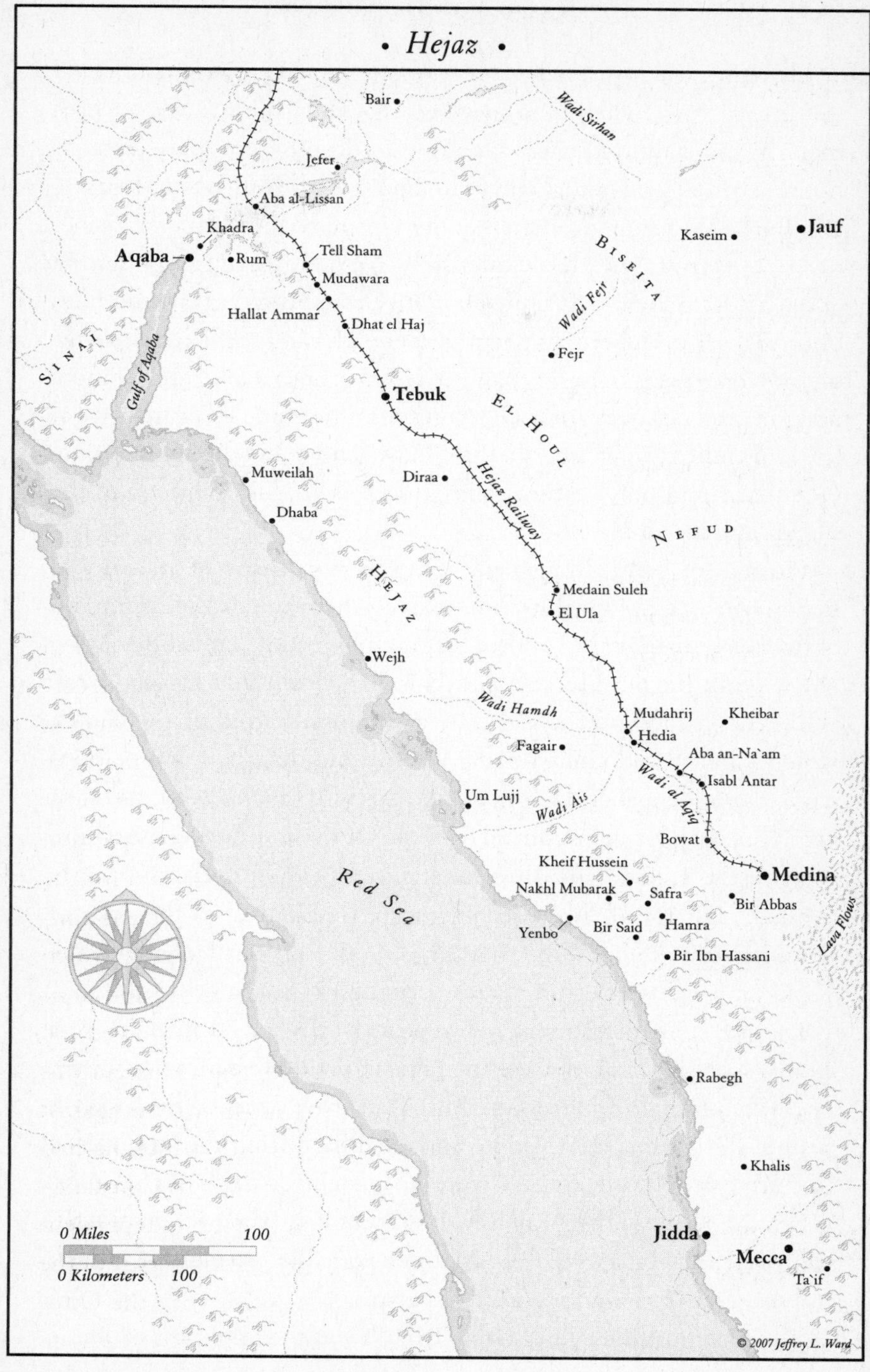
• Hejaz •
Bair
Wadi Sirhan
Jefer
Aba al-Lissan
Khadra
Aqaba
Rum
Tell Sham
Mudawara
Hallat Ammar
Dhat el Haj
Kaseim
Jauf
Biseita
Wadi Fejr
Fejr
Sinai
Gulf of Aqaba
Tebuk
El Houl
Muweilah
Diraa
Hejaz Railway
Dhaba
Nefud
Hejaz
Medain Suleh
El Ula
Wejh
Wadi Hamdh
Mudahrij
Kheibar
Hedia
Fagair
Aba an-Na`am
Wadi al Aqiq
Isabl Antar
Um Lujj
Wadi Ais
Bowat
Kheif Hussein
Medina
Red Sea
Nakhl Mubarak
Safra
Bir Abbas
Yenbo
Bir Said
Hamra
Lava Flows
Bir Ibn Hassani
Rabegh
Khalis
0 Miles 100
0 Kilometers 100
Jidda
Mecca
Ta`if
© 2007 Jeffrey L. Ward

Hussein's worst suspicions of Ottoman intentions were confirmed in January 1915, when he discovered that the Young Turk government in Constantinople was planning to depose him, that Arab nationalists in Beirut and Damascus had been executed, and that a handpicked force of 3,500 men under German commanders was being sent deep into the Hejaz, ostensibly to establish a telegraph station at the tip of the Arabian Peninsula. The Germans were wartime allies of the Turks, and German generals were advising the Turkish army, but the force was far larger than needed to protect a telegraph station, and the presence of a senior German staff officer and a German wireless detachment suggested that the Turks had a more ambitious purpose that could only be threatening to Hussein, his dominion in the Hejaz, and his ambitions.

Hussein responded by encouraging the formation of an army of Bedouin irregulars loyal to him, placing them under the command of his son Emir Faisal in a force he grandiloquently named the Army of the Arab Revolt. Hussein and Faisal expected that 100,000 Arab volunteers, drawn to the cause by a common hatred of the Turks, would join the Bedouin irregulars. Some said that their expectations were too modest, that the army could attract as many as a quarter of a million Arab recruits from all over the Ottoman Empire, the equivalent of the entire Turkish combat force.[13] There were no clearly defined goals for an Arab revolt, except freedom from the yoke of Ottoman rule, but a force that large would seriously threaten the Turks and their war effort against Britain, France, and Russia.

Despite colorful banners and repeated calls for Arab unity, few Arabic speakers from outside the Hejaz joined Hussein's new army. And when Faisal and the makeshift Arab army attacked the Turkish positions at Mecca, Taif, Jidda, and Medina during the summer of 1916, the Bedouin irregulars were no match for the Turkish guns. When the Army of the Arab Revolt was easily driven back in humiliating defeats, Hussein temporarily put aside his wariness of infidels and turned to Britain for funds and arms.

To Hussein and his sons, Great Britain was the mightiest nation in the world, with a navy that could roam the seas unchallenged and armies that had been victorious on every continent and on every manner of terrain. Yet two years after Britain and Turkey had declared war on each other, Syria, Palestine, Gaza, and Mosul were still in Turkish hands, and it was the Turks who could brag about a glorious victory at Gallipoli and the surrender of the British garrison at Kut, in Mesopotamia. The British, with French help, had repelled two thrusts of the Turkish army toward the Suez Canal, but Constantinople celebrated even those battles after Djemal Pasha, the commander of the Turkish Fourth Army, described his failed attack as a successful "offensive reconnaissance against the canal" and pointed out that the British army was still stuck in Egypt. It seemed that the British needed help with their war effort as much as Hussein needed arms and funds for the Army of the Arab Revolt. In early negotiations the British promised funds and air support, and paid former prisoners of war in British-held territory to join up with the Arab army. The meeting in Jidda had been set up to discuss new requests for British support.[14]

When Storrs and Lawrence met with Hussein's son Emir Abdullah, Abdullah spoke of his concern about the Turkish advance into the Hejaz and asked about the possibility of landing British troops to fight alongside the Bedouin army. Storrs, an able and cautious diplomat, explained that the British could not send troops to Arabia, and that because of the changing war situation and other commitments, there were complications relating to their earlier promise to send aircraft and a payment of £10,000.* Abdullah was furious. He and his father did not understand that the British considered their wartime promises tentative and fluid commitments that could be modified and restructured as the diplomatic and military situation ebbed and flowed. To Sherif Hussein and Emir Abdullah each broken agreement with the British was another breach of infidel promises.

*In 1914–19, a pound sterling was worth approximately U.S. $10; five French francs was worth approximately one U.S. dollar.

A French military mission had arrived in Jidda only a month earlier, headed by a veteran of North Africa, Colonel Édouard Brémond, who had brought £1.25 million in gold francs to sweeten his own negotiations with Hussein. Abdullah, aware of the British-French rivalry in the Middle East, angrily threatened to take his case to Colonel Brémond. But even as he threatened, Abdullah was impressed with the young lieutenant who sat at Storrs's side, the back of his jacket streaked with bright scarlet from the leather backs of the gun-room chairs on board the steamer they had taken to Jidda. When Abdullah said that the Arabs would have to disperse if the two Turkish planes that were harassing them were not driven off, Lawrence assured him that "very few Turkish aeroplanes last more than four or five days." And when they discussed the disposition of the Turkish forces, including Syrian, Circassian, Anatolian, and Mesopotamian units, Lawrence snapped off exactly which Turkish unit was in each position.

Abdullah turned in amazement to Storrs. "Is this man God," he asked, "to know everything?"[15]

Lawrence did not reciprocate the admiration. Abdullah had shown up for the meeting wearing a yellow silk headcloth, a camel's hair cloak, a white silk shirt, and knee-high patent-leather boots. The emir was short and stocky, with a round, smooth face, full but short lips, a brown beard, and an affectedly open and charming manner. In their talks he came across as a "keen dialectician" who could choose his words carefully, but Lawrence thought Abdullah was "probably not so much the brains as the spur of his father: he . . . has large ideas, which no doubt include his own particular advancement." Abdullah seemed foppish and soft, too comfortable in city ways, too clever, sophisticated, and extroverted to be the leader of a successful Arab Revolt.[16]

Lawrence also disagreed with Abdullah's ideas of how to conduct the war. Bringing in British troops, Lawrence thought, would make the Arab Revolt one more front in a British war: if the British fought the battles for the Arabs, or if British officers led the Arab army, the Arabs would have little claim to their own independence.

The British had often shown a fondness for desolate places, especially those on the routes to India. If they came to Arabia, they wouldn't leave easily. To be truly free, Lawrence thought, the Arabs would have to fight, or at least seem to fight, for their own independence.

Lawrence's thinking wasn't exactly treasonous—Ronald Storrs had been sent to Jidda to turn down Hussein's requests for British troops—but Lawrence's ideas about Arab independence were an uneasy fit with the British imperial vision shared comfortably among many military and diplomatic officers in London and Cairo. Lawrence was careful not to voice his views at the meeting with Emir Abdullah. After Storrs presented the bad news about the impossibility of the British command sending troops or airplanes, Lawrence obsequiously suggested that the decisions might not be final, and that perhaps if he had an opportunity to ride up-country and speak to Abdullah's brother Faisal at his command post with the Arab army, he might more convincingly be able to give his backing to Abdullah's case.

Abdullah liked the idea, and the young lieutenant. He also knew that as guardian of the holy places, his father was adamantly against infidels visiting the interior of his domain, fearing it would compromise his position in the Muslim world.[17] When Abdullah telephoned for permission to authorize the visit, the answer from Sherif Hussein was a predictable and resolute no! Abdullah and Storrs took turns on the phone, pleading their case, before Sherif Hussein finally granted the young lieutenant the coveted permission to ride to a region few Christians had ever visited.

~

The ride up Wadi Safra was exhausting but exhilarating. The scenery ranged from rugged shingled stone to vast sandy wadis bordered by sheer hills of brown granite and porphyry, streaked with garish pink and resting on hundred-foot-high pillows of green cross-grained stone that looked like moss. After two years in Cairo, writing and thinking all day in an overcrowded, noisy room, with a hundred pressing tasks and no bodily exertion except the walk or bike ride each day between the headquarters office and a hotel, the silence and emptiness of the desert, the "pestilent beating of the Arabian sun, and the long monotony of camel pacing,"[18] was a dramatic and severe change. When Lawrence reached Hamra, where Emir Faisal was camped with his army of camel-mounted Bedouin, the remoteness and edgy excitement of the camp made Lawrence feel involved in the war for the first time.

The Bedouins at Faisal's camp were small, dark men, spare, fit, clad in loose dishdashas, baggy sirwals, and headcloths, their shoulders slung with cartridge belts. They lived sparsely, close to the desert, carrying rations of flour and killing an occasional sheep or camel for meat. From reading C. M. Doughty's *Arabia Deserta*, and from his own rich imagination, Lawrence had romanticized the Bedouin as the last pure people, the nobility of their desert life a stark contrast to the Victorian and Edwardian society in which he had grown up. Now, up close for the first time, their lives seemed pure and unspoiled. "They were absolute slaves of their appetite," he wrote, "with no stamina of mind, drunkards for coffee, milk or water, gluttons for stewed meat, shameless beggars of tobacco. They dreamed for weeks before and after their rare sexual exercises, and spent the intervening days titillating themselves and their hearers with bawdy tales. Had the circumstance of their lives given them opportunity they would have been sheer sensualists."[19]

And if Prince Abdullah had been disappointingly foppish, his brother Faisal was exactly Lawrence's image of an Arab leader. Lawrence had already studied intelligence reports characterizing Faisal as "a good leader" who had "immense authority" with the tribes.[20] The emir was tall, and he posed like a pillar, with a long face, black beard, and penetrating eyes. Dressed in elegant white silk robes and a brown headcloth bound with a brilliant scarlet-and-gold cord, his hands crossed on his dagger, he looked like a prince of the desert, "ambitious; full of dreams, and the capacity to realize them, with keen personal insight, and very efficient." He reminded Lawrence of the monument of Richard I, one of his personal heroes, at Fontevrault. Lawrence later admitted that even at this early meeting he realized that Faisal was a timid man, but felt compelled to portray him as courageous because "it was the only way to get the British to support the Arabs—physical courage is the essential demand of a typical British officer."[21]

But just as Lawrence had not reciprocated Abdullah's admiration, Faisal was skeptical of the young second lieutenant. Although he and his father distrusted the English less than other Christian nations, and still harbored expectations that the British navy would transport the Bedouin army up and down the coast of the Hejaz, to Faisal all Westerners were infidels. In earlier negotiations he, his father, and his brother Abdullah had found the British fickle and duplicitous: the officials and generals in Cairo had already reneged on promises of transport, supplies, and arms. As their frustrations built, Hussein and his sons had begun to question British motives. "I am not a Hejazi by upbringing," Faisal said. "And yet, by God, I am jealous for it. And though I know the British do not want it, yet what can I say, when they took the Sudan, also not wanting it? They hunger for desolate lands, to build them up; and so, perhaps, one day Arabia will seem to them precious."[22] Faisal was also sufficiently familiar with Western military ranks to be distinctly unimpressed by the arrival of a second lieutenant. He and Lawrence spent much of an evening and the next day arguing.

Faisal knew his irregular Bedouin troops were ill trained, ill organized and ill supplied: the Bedouin army had been no match for the entrenched Turkish forces at Medina, and their retreat toward Yenbo had been prolonged and humiliating. He also knew that in a culture that prizes victory in battle the Bedouin army's lack of success on the battlefields was not winning followers. What he and his father and brother called the Arab Revolt enjoyed little support beyond Sherif Hussein's own subjects in the Hejaz. The problem, Faisal explained, was that their forces were ill equipped. What they needed, he told Lawrence, was for the British to supply them with artillery to match the Turkish guns at Medina.

Lawrence explained that he had come to assess their needs, but could only do so if he fully understood the general situation. He asked

Faisal to tell him the history of the Arab Revolt. It was a sad story of Arab shock at the brutality of Turkish war measures, the rape and slaughter of civilians, and Turkish soldiers slitting the throats of prisoners as if they were sheep. The Turkish superiority in armaments kept the attacking Arabs at a distance, so much of the fighting had taken place at night, when the guns were effectively blinded. Under the cover of darkness both sides had resorted to hurling frenzied insults at their enemies: the Turks called the Arabs "English" and the Arabs screamed back "German" at the Turks.[23] There were few Germans in the Hejaz, and Lawrence was the first Englishman in the interior, but cursing was a creative art and much admired by the Arabs.

Lawrence was experienced enough in the Middle East to recognize Arab pride. Careful not to praise the Turks directly, he noted that the Turkish army was adept at defending fortified positions, and that in pitched battles the Bedouin army would be no match for the Turkish superiority in numbers and experience. He had also read Karl von Clausewitz, and knew that cultural and historical knowledge of the enemy could be more important than technology. What had been an advantage for the Turks at Medina, he suggested, might in a different situation be a fatal disadvantage. The Turkish defensive mentality was not easily adaptable to desert warfare. Perhaps the Bedouin could take advantage of their knowledge of the desert and their mobility to play to the Turkish weaknesses.

Though instinctively suspicious of Lawrence's motives, Faisal was intrigued enough to hear him out. The young lieutenant wore a British uniform, but he wasn't like the other British soldiers and diplomats Faisal had encountered. Lawrence understood and spoke Arabic, and if he had the distinct accent of a foreigner, he seemed to know the Qur'an, and he spoke of Islam and Arab culture with a respect Faisal had never before heard from a Christian. Lawrence's suggestion that the Bedouin troops might be more effective as a guerrilla raiding force seemed to reflect an understanding of desert warfare and Bedouin values. Indeed, the quiet yet strangely ambitious lieutenant seemed openly sympathetic to the Arab cause.

When Faisal asked Lawrence how he liked the Arab camp at Wadi Safra, Lawrence said, "Well, but it is far from Damascus." It was a comment Emir Faisal could welcome, not only for the politeness and enigmatic terseness of Lawrence's words—treasured manners in a culture that reveres poetry and hospitality—but especially because the phrase signaled that Lawrence grasped the complex diplomatic situation in the Middle East as Faisal and his father saw it. Damascus, the fourth most important city in Islam, was for the Arabs the key to Jerusalem and Palestine. The lieutenant's words suggested that he might be sympathetic to the Arab need to advance into Syria and take the great cities—Damascus, Homs, Hama, and Aleppo—if they were to achieve their real ambitions. Faisal held his breath for a silent but poignant minute before he answered Lawrence: "Praise be to God, there are Turks nearer us than that."[24]

Emir Faisal prided himself on being a judge of men. He was shrewd enough to realize that Lawrence—young, articulate, romantic, an admirer of the Arabs, and a man who showed he understood the Arabs' need to be more than an auxiliary force to the British—could provide to the Bedouin army what British arms, the support of the British navy, and even British money could not buy. Lawrence could be a voice for the Arabs in British command circles. If he was heard and respected, his articulation of Arab goals and needs could provide a legitimacy that the Arabs had desperately sought. He could generate favorable publicity not only at British GHQ in Cairo, but at the baize-covered tables of the foreign offices in Europe and America, where the Great Powers would someday carve nations out of the empires that were waging war. It was a dream, and still inchoate while the Turks fought on under the flag of the Ottoman Empire, but Faisal, who had traveled to Paris and London as well as Constantinople and Damascus, could imagine what the fulfillment of that dream would mean to him, to his father and brothers, to his father's subjects in the Hejaz, and, indeed, possibly to the entire Arabic-speaking world. If Lawrence pressed the Arab case it might lend credibility and gravitas to what had until then been an obscure revolt in a remote corner of the Ottoman Empire.

Lawrence's official assignment was to make an appraisal of Faisal's Bedouin force, and to assess whether the Arab army was capable of harassing the Turkish forces in Arabia sufficiently to divert personnel and matériel from the Turkish main front against the British. But he also had a private agenda. He had studied Arab culture for years, and had spent enough time visiting crusader castles and on prewar archaeological digs in Syria to have a stronger sense of the desert and the Arabs than most of the British command. He often spoke admiringly at GHQ of "the Arabs"—to the annoyance of his fellow officers—but he knew that there were no strong sentiments of nationalism among the Arabic-speaking peoples of the Ottoman Empire. Café intellectuals in Damascus and Cairo might talk of an Arab empire, but neither they nor the conspiratorial groups like the Society for Arab Union and the Arab Revolutionary Society had a widely shared notion of distinctly Arab nationalism. "There is no national feeling," Lawrence had written in 1915. "Between town and town, village and village, family and family, creed and creed, exist intimate jealousies, sedulously fostered by the Turks to render a spontaneous union impossible."[25]

He had written those sentences about Syria, which he knew close-up. Arabia he thought of as a pure Arab culture, untainted by Western or Turkish civilization or by the corruptions of industrial and urban development. Arabia could be different: "Their idea of nationality is the independence of tribes and parishes, and their idea of national union is episodic combined resistance to an intruder."[26] The men he met on a tour of Faisal's camp seemed "entirely tribal" in their loyalties, and he didn't think much of the desert tribesmen. But the men from hill tribes were lean and tough-looking: "I doubt whether men were ever harder. . . . I have had them running and walking with me in the sun through sand and over rocks for hour after hour without their turning a hair. Those I saw were in wild spirits, as quick as hawks, keen and intelligent, shouting that the war may last for ten years." Those men struck him as "good material for guerrilla warfare. They are hard and fit, very active; independent, cheerful snipers." They had "suspended their blood feuds for the period of the war, and will fight side by side with their old blood enemies, if they have a Sherif in supreme command."[27] If he had seen no traces of Arab nationalism or of the institutions of a modern state, in the fierce loyalty of the Bedouin warriors and their unfaltering allegiance to Emir Faisal, Lawrence saw the potential for an army and a movement that could extend its notions of allegiance beyond the traditional bonds to tribe and clan, perhaps enough to make a reality out of the grandly named Arab Revolt.

Another British intelligence officer, sent on the same mission, might have seen it as one more tiresome negotiation with the intractable Arabs, the ride into the desert thrilling for a day, but ultimately exhausting, dirty, hot, and frustrating, a much too long distraction from the delights of a comfortable billet in Alexandria or Cairo. Lawrence had no experience as a field officer, but the Arab Revolt with Faisal as leader loomed as an opportunity to break away from an establishment that he had cautiously skirted since childhood. The difficult and dramatic camel ride, the nearness of Turkish guns, the sight of the Bedouin troops, and the imposing presence of Faisal with his remarkable resemblance to Lawrence's crusader hero Richard I were enough to inspire Lawrence's imagination of what could be, a future that could bring a triumph for himself as well as for the Arabs. The spectacular skies and endless expanse of the desert hinted at an epic life like those he had long admired in literature. He saw the possibility of going beyond intelligence reports, maps, Arabic newspapers, and designs for postage stamps, the possibility of playing a role in an epic adventure. He had found a chance to make history, and the opportunity was irresistible.

Even at that first meeting, Lawrence and Faisal understood each other enough to make an unspoken Faustian bargain.

~

Aaron Aaronsohn's train ride from the tip of northern Scotland, via Inverness and Perth to London, was uneventful. The British railroads were a wartime marvel—smooth, reliable, and still mostly on time, even as they had to meet the deployment schedules for the troops and matériel that were being swallowed up on the battlefields of the western front. Only a few months before Aaronsohn had ridden the famed Berlin–Baghdad Railway from Damascus to Constantinople and on to Germany. The German-built railroad had been a nightmare—days in stifling, cramped cars, without food, water, or sanitary facilities, waiting out breakdowns and delays. Sometimes the passengers were transferred to rude carts while the roadbed was repaired, or they had to detrain and walk alongside as the locomotive struggled up slopes. The differences between the railroads, like the impressive Grand Fleet at anchor in Scapa Flow, left little question which side should win the war.

Aaron Aaronsohn was already an experienced traveler. He was self-educated as an agronomist and geologist, except for two years at a French institute, and had been exploring the flora and geology of the slopes of Mount Hermon in 1906 when he discovered wild emmer (*Triticum dicoccoides*), a primitive form of wheat that appeared to be unchanged from biblical times. Aaronsohn's identification of what seemed to be the mother of all wheats, a varietal unchanged for thousands of years, earned him sudden worldwide recognition. He gave talks and seminars in Europe, and spent two years in the United States as a guest of the U.S. Department of Agriculture (USDA). When he traveled in those heady days, hosts had met him at the docks and train stations, and prebooked accommodations and fine dinners awaited him. Now he was traveling as an enemy alien, with a military escort.

They arrived at King's Cross Station on a dark, foggy night, the lights of automobiles shining through the mist and their horns making an "extremely sad impression." There were posted warnings about the danger of bombings from zeppelins, and more soldiers on the streets than Aaronsohn had seen even in Berlin. Captain Brims took Aaronsohn to Scotland Yard, where he was told to come back the next day "at twelve sharp" to appear before Assistant Commissioner Basil Thomson. Captain Brims was eager to return to Scotland, and left Aaronsohn on his own for the night. There were no rooms at the Cecil Hotel or the Waldorf, and Aaronsohn finally checked into the First Avenue Hotel in High Holborn, using a false name. The name he signed in the register was Mack: Judge Julius Mack of Chicago was a friend and supporter he had met in the United States.[28]

The High Holborn, like the rest of London, was posted with notices of the curfew in effect for enemy aliens. Only a few weeks before, in Berlin, he had been acutely aware of the wartime shortages: no vegetables in the shops except turnips, eggs limited to one per person per week, milk available only with a prescription for those over six years old, even the German staple of pork missing from the butcher shops. Aaronsohn was so eager to compare conditions in London that he ignored the curfew signs, walking the streets of London until 12:30 A.M. No one even asked for his identification.

The next day, Sir Basil Thomson, the head of the Criminal Investigation Division, was waiting for him at Scotland Yard. Papers Thomson had received in advance from the consulate in Copenhagen identified Aaronsohn as a special assistant to Djemal Pasha, commander of the Turkish Fourth Army in Syria and Palestine. That was enough to guarantee Sir Basil's attention. Djemal Pasha was Britain's chief foe in the Palestine theater: his unpredictable and inscrutable strategy and tactics had resulted in one disaster after another for the British forces. British intelligence in Cairo and London knew little about Djemal, except that he was one of the three powerful men at the top of the Young Turk government, and he had been head of the Ottoman navy before being given command of the Fourth Army and a virtual dictatorship over Palestine and Syria. In photographs Djemal was short, almost hunchbacked, with a forbidding black beard and darting black eyes. Despite his frightening appearance, he had a reputation for charm. Supposedly, when he was awarded a minor decoration after watching a destroyer sink in maneuvers during a prewar visit to Toulon, he had said, "It's a pity I didn't see a cruiser sunk; they might then have given me the Grand

Croix."[29] Testimony from Turkish prisoners of war captured on the Gaza front and the occasional intelligence reports that dribbled into British GHQ in Cairo told a different story: in Palestine and Syria Djemal had a reputation for impulsiveness and cruelty toward the enemy, the local population, and even to his own troops.

Aaronsohn explained to Sir Basil that Djemal fed and equipped the Turkish army with requisitioned crops and supplies, and that the army levies fell especially hard on the Jewish settlers in Palestine, who had the most productive farms. The Turks had demanded baksheesh from the Jewish settlers to avoid conscription, and under special wartime regulations had seized the crops from productive cropland and orchards. They had also taken draft animals, carts, wagons, farm tools, and irrigation pumps, crippling the farms. As if those woes had not been enough, the spring of 1915 had brought the worst infestation of locusts anyone in the Holy Land could remember. The locusts devoured the meager crops that had survived the lack of irrigation and the Turkish requisitions, until many Jewish settlers were on the verge of starvation, awaiting the next pitiful harvest with dread.

Because of his reputation as an agronomist, Aaronsohn explained, Djemal Pasha had recruited him to lead a campaign against the locusts. He could not refuse the pasha, and had hoped that his official position would enable him to ameliorate the conditions of the Jewish settlers. With his travel privileges as a member of the pasha's staff he was able to observe much of the country under wartime conditions, and had found the food and fuel supplies even more meager than he had supposed; the impact of the requisitions on the settlers had been aggravated by the needless cruelty of the Turkish authorities and their German allies. Aaronsohn told Thomson that he and his colleagues at his research institute at Athlit, on the coast south of Haifa, were able to divert enough foodstuffs and contributions to the institute to keep a few settlers from starvation, but that they were increasingly convinced that if the war continued there was little hope for the Jews of Palestine as a minority under Turkish rule.

As Aaronsohn spoke, Sir Basil realized that along with an encyclopedic knowledge of the terrain, climate, and economic situation in Palestine, Aaronsohn was exceedingly well informed on the disposition, equipment, and preparations of the Turkish army. The British had little recent intelligence on Palestine. Aaronsohn had surveyed so much of the countryside, both in his scientific studies and through his efforts at locust eradication, that he could describe the placement of Turkish positions, their equipment shortages and training deficiencies, and the Turkish defense plans for Palestine and Gaza.

Aaronsohn explained that he had investigated the Turkish defenses because he represented a secret group in Palestine, men and women, mostly young, all trustworthy, and all committed to opposing the Turks. Some of them had originally organized themselves to defend the Jewish settlements from Arab bandits and marauding youth who harassed the settlers. Later the group had been recruited to the staff of Aaronsohn's agricultural experimental station to work on the locust eradication program. As part of their work they had traveled throughout Palestine, visiting Turkish military sites to train soldiers in locust eradication procedures and supervise the battle against the locusts. They had made detailed observations of the roads, railways, and supply depots, the armaments and supplies available to the troops, and the training levels of the Turkish army. Many in Aaronsohn's group knew Turkish or German, and spent enough time with the Turkish soldiers and the officers at various military facilities to overhear and elicit information on the Turkish order of battle, logistic plans, and defenses.

Aaronsohn told Sir Basil that the group had previously sent someone to Cairo to offer their information to British intelligence, but for reasons they didn't understand the offer had been rejected. They had later briefly established a connection and had waited for ships to land swimmers who would pick up the information they had gathered, but the ships had never come. By late 1915 they had confirmed an even more terrifying threat to the very existence of the Jewish communities in Palestine. Although wartime communications in the Ottoman

Empire were poor, and people in one province often could not verify the rumors they heard from other provinces, reports of massacres of Armenians and the destruction of Armenian villages in Anatolia had begun to filter into Palestine. Aaronsohn said that they had firsthand reports of the massacres, eyewitness accounts of orphans scavenging in the ruins of smoldering villages, dogs gnawing on unburied corpses, and women who had been raped wandering around dazed. It was impossible to escape the stench of death.[30]

Aaronsohn said that Djemal Pasha had the same fate in mind for the Jews of Palestine. The only difference was that Djemal seemed to prefer to deal with what he called the "undesirable minorities" of "Christian dogs, Jewish dogs and unfaithful Arabs" through deliberate starvation rather than open massacre.[31] Whenever the forces under his command suffered a setback against the British or the Russians, he would evict the Jews from a city like Jaffa or Haifa, as if they had somehow been responsible for his battlefield losses. The homeless urban Jews suffered even more than the farmers.

In the midst of an answer to one of Sir Basil's questions, Aaronsohn turned the tables. "Why do you bring water for the Army from Egypt?" Aaronsohn asked. "It slows your progress. There is water right there in the desert, 300 feet down. All you have to do is drill for it."

"How do you know that?" Sir Basil said.

"The rocks indicate it. And Flavius Josephus corroborates it. He wrote that he could walk for a whole day south from Caesarea and never leave flourishing gardens. Today the desert sands reach to the walls of Caesarea. Where there were gardens there must have been water. Where is that water now?"[32]

Aaronsohn knew the area around the site of the Roman city of Caesarea, on the Galilee coast, well. It was an easy horseback ride from Zichron Ya'aqov, where he had grown up. As a botanical and geological researcher he had surveyed much of Palestine on horseback or on foot. From plants and rock strata he had mapped areas that had turned to desert but which almost certainly were over aquifers. The Roman wells that had once tapped those aquifers had been lost in one thousand years of Arab subsistence agriculture. There was enough underground water, he told Sir Basil, to turn the whole of the Sinai into flourishing fields of wheat.

"And what can you do?" Sir Basil asked.

"If I were with the British Army, I could show the engineers where to drill. I guarantee that they would find enough water for the Army without having to bring a single drop from Cairo."[33]

If Aaronsohn was right it could change British strategy and fortunes dramatically. The British army had been reluctant to go on the offensive against the Turks because of the elaborate logistics needed to supply water for the troops, who were dependent on the water they carried or what they could draw from shallow wells with spear-point pumps.[34] The increased mobility would give the British a huge advantage against the fixed Turkish defenses, and allow the British command to speed up the timetable for an assault on the Turkish strongholds. The French, Britain's ally, were also jockeying for position in the Middle East, specifically in Syria and Lebanon; their expectations overlapped British aspirations, and accelerating the timetable for a British advance would have the additional advantage of preempting the French. Ultimately, progress against the Turks would let Britain focus more assets on the western front, maybe enough to win what most of the generals and the politicians thought of as the *real* war, the one against Germany.

But could he believe this man and his stories? Aaronsohn had displayed dazzling erudition. His knowledge of the terrain and conditions in Palestine and Syria and the Turkish order of battle, training, logistics, and defense plans seemed too good to be true. How could any outsider know that much? His story of his journey from Palestine to Britain—across hostile borders, under the noses of Turkish and German authorities, tricking even the fellow passengers on a ship to the United States—was even harder to believe.

Aaronsohn's wasn't the first bizarre story Sir Basil had heard. By 1917 MI5 held dossiers on more than 38,000 individuals and Scotland Yard's Special Branch had investigated 28,000 suspicious aliens; from the beginning of the war they had sent wild-eyed dreamers and schemers to Sir Basil's office. It fell to him to separate the rare kernels of useful information from the chaff of preposterous propositions and incredible stories. Even after years of oddball cases, Aaronsohn's story stood out. Sir Basil concluded that Aaronsohn's journey from Palestine to Copenhagen, then secretly on to England, thousands of miles of dangerous travel across enemy lines, was the most extraordinary and romantic tale he had yet heard.

Why did you do it? Sir Basil asked him. Why risk everything to come to Britain?

Aaronsohn had thought about the question. Sir Basil wasn't the first to discover that Aaron Aaronsohn had thought about most questions. Aaronsohn knew that crossing the battle lines to an enemy nation would make him an outcast, a man who had bet everything—family, friends, home, and career—on the outcome of the war. Once he was safely in England he had no problem explaining his motives. He was determined not to see the Jews of Palestine follow the destiny of the Armenians. The only way to prevent that, Aaronsohn told Sir Basil, was for the British to win the war.

Sir Basil was no fool. He was well aware of Britain's wartime goals in the Middle East. From his position at Scotland Yard he knew about the wartime organizing and propaganda efforts of the Zionists in England and elsewhere. He knew about Chaim Weizmann, the chemist who had invented a method of producing acetone, essential for the production of explosives, in his Manchester laboratory. In gratitude for Weizmann's discovery the British had tolerated and even supported his continuing propaganda efforts as a leader of the international Zionist movement. Sir Basil probably guessed that Aaronsohn shared Weizmann's long-term goals for the Jews in Palestine. They did not discuss Aaronsohn's expectations and aspirations for the Jews that day, but Sir Basil had dealt with intelligence sources often enough to know that any offer of information, at least of *good* information, would not come for free. In return for helping the British,

Aaronsohn and his colleagues would expect support, or at least cooperation, in building a Jewish homeland in Palestine.

But that was all left unsaid in October 1916. The two men did not talk about Zionism. Instead, Aaron Aaronsohn told Sir Basil only that he and his colleagues and friends knew that their spying efforts were dangerous, that if they were found out by the Turks they would be hanged and their families would suffer reprisals. But after what they had heard and seen in the Jewish communities of Palestine, and what they knew about the fate of the Armenians, they were prepared to collect secret information for the British command on the Turkish military preparations and plans. It was for that, Aaronsohn said—to work for a British victory—that he had come to England to offer his services as a spy.

Only a few months after Aaronsohn's arrival in London and Lawrence's meeting with Faisal at his desert camp, the two men met in a hallway at the British GHQ in the Savoy Hotel in Cairo. By then their separate plans to reshape the Middle East were already in motion, and the two ambitious and strong-willed men would discover that the futures they had planned for Palestine were on a collision course.

Romania, Romania

I could have chosen cheaper farmers, but instead I chose Jewish ones.
—Edmond de Rothschild, 1930

It is better to dwell in the deserts of Palestine than in palaces abroad.
—Rabbinic saying

The story was sometimes told that only three men understood the 1878 Treaty of Berlin: a professor in Berlin who went mad, Chancellor Otto von Bismarck, who wasn't about to explain it to anyone else, and no one remembers what happened to the third man. However obscure the terms of the separation of the Balkan provinces from the Ottoman Empire, the Jews of Romania quickly felt the consequences. Article 44 of the treaty provided that none of the polyglot population was to be discriminated against on the basis of religion, but the new government in Romania, citing an 1877 court ruling that "the Jews do not have a country of their own and therefore do not belong to any state," systematically denied the rights of citizenship to the 100,000 Jews living in Romania.[1] Every instance of a Jew seeking citizenship required individual legislation; in the next twenty years only two hundred Romanian Jews were nationalized. The remainder were officially aliens, a pariah people, systematically evicted from the countryside, openly targeted for violence and mob assaults, their inns and shops confiscated, their synagogues pillaged and burned. From their impoverished shtetls the Jews fled to urban slums, but even in the cities they were prohibited from professions and the civil service, and subject to relentless harassment and attacks.

Many elected to leave. Romanian intellectuals had traditionally looked toward France, but few of the Jews knew French or considered themselves intellectuals. From 1881 to 1910, 20 percent of the Jews in Romania emigrated to the United States. Others, rejecting the promises of capitalist freedom in America (or believing the letters about sweatshops and tenement slums from landsmen who had already emigrated), chose the age-old dream of a return to Zion, an aspiration filled with both lofty hopes and the terrifying perils of settlement in a strange land. Jews had lived in what came to be known as Palestine from biblical times; Jews all over the world had collected donations in blue-and-white tin *pushkes* to support the ancient Jewish communities of Jerusalem and Safad. Those tiny communities had been tolerated by the Ottoman Empire; indeed, in much of the Ottoman Empire the Jews were a favored minority, even recruited as tax collectors and financial advisers, as long as they remained a well-behaved minority community, scrupulously respecting the authority of the sultan's bureaucrats and deferring to the primacy of Islam. The idea that Jews would uproot themselves from their diaspora homes and "return" to Zion was a nineteenth-century notion that gained sudden attention only in the wake of the Treaty of Berlin and the pogroms of the early 1880s. It was a frightening prospect for both the Jews contemplating the journey and for the Ottoman Empire contemplating an influx of Jews into Palestine.

In newly founded Lovers of Zion societies the Jews of Romania and the Russian empire articulated their dreams of a new life in the Promised Land: by providing work "in field and vineyard" they would remove the stain of gentile accusations that Jews would not work, regain "national honor," and reawaken in the hearts of Jews those "holy feelings which the sheer weight of pain, want, and poverty had put to sleep for thousands of years." With the obsessive attention to detail of those who had never known self-governance, the societies debated the countless choices of utopians: Who should go first to the Promised Land—the rich who could provide a livelihood for the poor, or the poor, who were after all the ones suffering? Where would they obtain the funds to establish themselves in a faraway land? What kind of central committee should be established? How many members should it have, and by what rules would it govern? What would each prospective settlement require—synagogue, school, bathhouse, hospital? Which professions would need to be represented—doctor, midwife, schoolmaster, ritual slaughterer, agricultural expert? They occasionally debated practical questions: Where would they live until a settlement was ready? How many would go? By what criteria would the first settlers be selected?[2]

The Romanian group decided to start with one hundred families, that they would live in a hostel in Jaffa or Haifa until a permanent settlement was ready, and that they would choose those to go on the basis of moral standards, age span, family status, needed trades, and the personal resources the volunteers could commit to the venture. The wealthy Jews of Jassy donated 60,000 francs to fund the venture. When other contributions followed, two delegates were sent ahead to Palestine to choose land for a settlement. Following the recommendation of their advance representatives, the group purchased land in an Arab village called Samarin, on a hilltop fifteen miles south of Haifa. In August 1882, 228 souls set off for the Promised Land on the *Thetis,* sailing across the perennially rough Black Sea, through the Bosporus and Dardanelles, and down to the coast of Palestine. For those who had never ranged far from their shtetls and towns in Romania, it was like sailing to the end of the world.

For all their far-ranging debates, the pioneers from Romania hadn't paid attention to Ottoman regulations and the need for applications, authorizations, and baksheesh to placate the Ottoman bureaucracy. When their ship reached Palestine the pioneers found the ports posted with notices from the local authorities: "Jewish immigrants are forbidden to cross the coast of Syria and in all circumstances forbidden to live in Palestine. This ban is permanently binding." Barred from landing at either Jaffa or Haifa, they sailed up and down the coast, in squalid conditions of deteriorating sanitation, until the authorities were finally persuaded to allow the ship to dock at Jaffa. The families were then locked up in the town jail for weeks before enough baksheesh was collected and paid to get them released.[3]

One of the chosen settlers on that early adventure was Ephraim Fishel Aaronsohn, a grain seller from Bacau, 185 miles north of Bucharest. By all accounts he was a hardworking man with little formal education, more interested in grain than selling. His golden-haired wife, Malka, also had no formal education. They brought two sons with them: Aaron was six, his brother Zvi younger. Like so many families in Romania, they had personally experienced vicious and uncloaked anti-Semitism at the hands of the gentile majority. Aaron's grandfather had been accused of murdering a gentile child to take his blood for ritual purposes—the age-old "blood libel"[4]—and had been hanged upside down from a tree by a mob.

When they reached Palestine Ephraim and the other men settled their families in a caravansary in Haifa while they went to their newly acquired hilltop land on the coast of Galilee. They learned that a pair of petty speculators in Haifa, a watchmaker and a merchant of bric-a-brac, had sold the parcel to the central committee in Galata, Romania. Along with the spectacular views of the Mediterranean and the hills of Galilee they had been promised, the newly arrived settlers found a few tired oxen and horses, one or two wooden Arab plows, remnants of some mud-and-wattle huts, a few sacks of grain, and an accumulation of centuries of stones. Few of the settlers had any agricultural experience. They had dreamed of verdant, bucolic fields. Instead, when shifts of the wind brought thick swarms of mosquitoes from the swamps along the coast, they learned the origins of the term "malaria" (*mal area,* bad air). Some, convinced that their grand experiment was destined to be stillborn, sought passage back to Romania.

Those who stayed set to work clearing stones from the neglected fields, building huts on the mud-and-stone foundations left behind by former Arab inhabitants, and draining some of the low areas where the mosquitoes bred. They planted wheat, barley, and vetch, and once the winter rains eased, set up a small nursery and planted the slopes with olive trees purchased from a nearby Arab settlement. The work was exhausting. The former artisans, merchants, shopkeepers, and peddlers had not anticipated the difficulty of clearing land, and hadn't been prepared for the malaria, yellow fever, and trachoma; the challenges of dealing with the Ottoman authorities and bureaucracy; the intractability of their Arab neighbors; or the cost of building materials, seed, supplies, and transport. Some who had promised funds for the project had already defaulted, and anticipated additional funds from the central committee in Galata never arrived. They labored harder than they had imagined was possible for a full year, but the crops they were able to eke from the old seed and exhausted soil were meager; the living conditions—the women and children in the caravansary in Haifa and the men five to ten in each hut in Samarin—were far harsher than they had imagined; their funds had dwindled to nothing; and no matter how much stone they cleared from the fields, more seemed to grow.[5] Some cursed the entire venture and left to return to Romania, choosing a known evil over the terrifying uncertainty and unwelcome surprises of the new land.

Those who stayed were close to despair when a French Jew named Veneziani, touring Palestine on behalf of the eccentric German Jewish philanthropist Baron de Hirsch, came across the Samarin colonists picking stones from a field. The baron had contributed huge sums from railroad concessions he had been granted in the Ottoman Empire to promote Jewish colonization in Argentina, and was always looking for more settlers. "Why are you growing stones in this desert?" Veneziani asked the colonists from his horse. "Come to the Pampas, the true land of milk and honey."

Malka Aaronsohn answered him: "Monsieur, if we have to eat stones, we will eat them, but we will not budge from this place."[6]

They did not leave, but they could not eat pride, defiance, or stones, and by June 1883 the settlers in Samarin were reduced to pawning the Torah scrolls they had brought from Romania on Shavuot, the spring holiday that celebrates the receiving of the law on Mount Sinai. No Jew could have missed the irony. The desperate settlers cabled the Alliance Israélite Universelle in Paris, an organization that had been founded to help Jews in the Middle East: "If we do not receive assistance as soon as possible, we are lost." Their funds and spirits exhausted, there was nothing left but to pray for a miracle.

This time their prayers were answered. A special-delivery letter from Veneziani in Paris reached the Lovers of Zion society in Romania, announcing,

> It is my pleasure to inform you that I have been able to interest a most distinguished and well-positioned gentleman in the plight of the colony of Samarin and its inhabitants. At the present moment I am not at liberty to disclose the name of this estimable personage, whose dear wish it is to support your colony and to enlist it in the great enterprise we have before us, namely, the resettlement of the land of Israel. His one condition is that he alone shall be the colony's sole lord and that all things in its domain be under his rule, no other person having the right or privilege to interfere in its affairs or howsoever to challenge his will or pleasure.[7]

The terms of the offer were harsh, but the colonists had no other option. They agreed to the conditions, and received relief funds that would get them through another season, letting them bring their wives and children from Haifa to join the pioneering men, and funding the purchase of prefabricated wooden houses from Romania.[8] They began talking of orchards and vineyards, a school, and a synagogue. They could finally dream of milk and honey. If a few thanked God for the answers to their prayers, others were content to learn that their benefactor was a man many in late-nineteenth-century Europe would have ranked a close second in power and wealth to God: Baron Edmond Rothschild.

~

Around the time the group departed Romania for Palestine, shortly after a wave of pogroms in 1881–82, Rabbi Samuel Mohilever of

Bialystok had called upon Baron Rothschild in Paris, seeking a commitment to help Jews from the Pale of Settlement in Russia to settle in Palestine. Rothschild was reluctant to get involved, sympathetic to the plight of the Jews but more interested in his art collection than in what he saw as the risky venture of Zionism. But Rabbi Mohilever was a persuasive man, and from a modest initial investment the baron soon found himself taking an active interest in an ever-growing list of new colonies in Palestine. His initial investments in settlements like Samarin were deliberately anonymous: "The Baron wishes that there should be no public recognition for that would be bound to harm the great work to which we are all committed with our whole heart."[9] As his commitments increased Rothschild applied the fabled family business acumen to the project, appointing agents to report in detail on the status and activities of the Jewish settlers, and to make his own wishes known to them. "Naturally," his chief representative in Palestine, Elie Scheid, wrote to Paris, "I was received like a god; virtually carried in triumph and showered with congratulations and compliments." Scheid compared the group at Samarin to "shipwrecks thrown on a desert island without means, resources or guidance . . . lost in the middle of a population who regarded them as intruders, and of whose customs and language they were ignorant." If they could be supported, Scheid wrote, the pioneers would be a demonstration that the Jew could conquer rather than be conquered by his environment.[10]

The baron was sufficiently persuaded to commit more money, agents, and attention to the settlement, and the Zionists began calling him the "Well-Known Benefactor" (*hanadiv hayadua*). The settlers at Samarin got permission to rename their settlement Zichron Ya'aqov in memory of Baron Edmond Rothschild's father, James Jacob Rothschild. With his identity out in the open, Rothschild sent architects, agronomists, administrators, and agents to Palestine. His representatives explored chinks in the Ottoman laws that would allow land to be registered in the baron's name, and quietly bought surrounding land to add to Zichron Ya'aqov, moving the settlement from the hilltop of Samarin down to the intersection of two new streets, Founders Street and Street of the Benefactor. The baron had not been active in the business side of the Rothschild holdings in France, but he applied to his eleemosynary commitments the same standards his brothers applied to the family investments in railroads and loans to foreign governments. Before long Rothschild had appointed a vast bureaucracy, from a director-general and an agricultural director in Paris to Rothschild agents in pith helmets at the Palestine colonies.

Legally, the colonists owned the original land they had purchased while still in Romania, but they were now stipendiary laborers, receiving twelve francs per month each. They were told what crops could be grown on which allotments of land, and what irrigation, cultivation, and harvesting techniques to use for each crop; they had to queue daily for quotas of animal fodder and inputs for their fields. The French agents specified which plows, fruit trees, and grapevines the colonists would import from Europe and the dimensions, architecture, and construction details of residences and public buildings the colonists were to build. The baron would have preferred dormitories, but the colonists were allowed to live in two-room houses modeled after native Arab dwellings but with materials and construction details specified in France. Rothschild officials told the settlers what kind of services to hold in their synagogue, hired a doctor and the teachers for the schools, dictated dress and conduct standards, and decided which colonists had shown sufficient evidence of discipline and hard labor to be allowed to marry. Carts and carriages were ruled luxuries, and women settlers were upbraided for adopting coiffure or couture the Rothschild agents considered inappropriate for the wives of peasant cultivators. Bells rang in the village each day to signal the time to wake up, the noon lunch break, the end of the lunch break, and the end of the workday.

"The Baron provides us with whatever is needed and required," the wife of one settler wrote home to relatives. "We will be getting 54 francs a month. . . . We don't have to pay fees for *shechita* [kosher slaughter], nor do we have to pay for the synagogues or tuition for schooling. . . . If God forbid, someone gets sick—the doctor will treat him without charge, and medicines are also free and the midwife is available for those who need her without cost. We have to pay bath-house fees only." If a woman had twins, the Rothschild agents would provide both a second wet nurse and an extra bed for the household. "We live in the shadow of the Baron, who feels the pain of his sons, may God be merciful on him, and we know no want."[11]

A few settlers were clever enough to escape the paternalism by dissembling: after Rothschild protested the Paris fashions in the general store on his first visit to Zichron in 1887, the women learned to put their good clothes away and dress in smocks and work shifts for the baron's infrequent visits. Those who chose open protest against the regime had a portion of their stipends withheld, leading many to speculate that Rothschild was a Social Darwinist—then a fashionable philosophy—and that the regime was structured to select those settlers who lived quiet, well-regulated, nondisruptive lives, and willingly shared in communal responsibilities. For men who had grown up in a world where the only opportunities for Jews were as self-employed craftsmen or merchants, the rules demanded a dramatic and disrupting shift in perspectives and values.

It didn't take long for the settlers to fear as much as respect Rothschild. More from hunch than any practical research or experience, the baron believed that one hundred *dunams* of land (a little more than twenty-two acres), a team of oxen, a crude Arab plow and harrow, a few chickens, and a mule was enough for each pioneer family in Palestine to become self-supporting.[12] In pursuit of the baron's vision, the Zichron Ya'aqov settlers were directed to traditional unirrigated crops like olives, grapes, almonds, mulberries, and figs, and discouraged from the orange export business they had glimpsed elsewhere in Palestine. After a few seasons it was clear that to succeed with the "hot," or tropical, crops the Rothschild agents wanted the settlers to grow they would need two hundred to three hundred *dunams* per family. Since the total holdings of Zichron were around twenty-five *dunams* of arable land per family, the Rothschild directives were totally unworkable unless much more land were acquired or the number of settlers was sharply reduced. When they weren't answering the tempo of the bells, the settlers debated their futures and their relationship with the baron's agents.

~

For an inquisitive young boy like Aaron Aaronsohn, with few memories to which he could compare the hardships of pioneering in a strange land, Zichron Ya'aqov was a child's paradise. Open fields, Arab neighbors with exotic dress and customs, roads lined with thorny acacia trees with tiny yellow blossoms that smelled sweeter than honey, ancient ruins, mountains, desert, and the seashore were all within an easy walk or a horseback ride. Aaron hiked and later rode his horse, Knight, into the desert, down to the great ruins of the Roman city of Caesarea, to the nearby ruins of an Ottoman villa,[13] and up the slopes of Mount Carmel, collecting stones and plant specimens. Two brothers (Alexander and Samuel) and two sisters (Sarah and Rivka) were born in Palestine. His sisters remembered that Aaron would involve the entire family in classifying and storing his collections of botanical and geological specimens.[14]

He was sent to the original school at Samarin, a *kheyder* modeled after the Jewish day schools the settlers had known in Romania, which provided basic instruction in Yiddish and a smattering of Hebrew at an elementary school level. With the influx of Rothschild funds, the school became a "Talmud Torah," the equivalent of a middle school. Classrooms for the new school were in a public building instead of at the home of the *melamed,* and French educational specialists set the new curriculum: Hebrew, French, Arabic, and a smattering of history, religion, science, and agronomy, based in part on the programs of the Alliance Israélite Universelle, which had set up schools for Jewish children in Sephardic communities in Egypt, Turkey, and other Middle Eastern countries after the Damascus Affair of 1840. The Jews were a tiny minority in the Ottoman Empire, but they enjoyed prestigious connections to the government as tax collectors or financial advisers, and ran businesses in cities of the empire, so even a few thousand French-speaking students could increase French influence. In the wake of the humiliating defeat in the Franco-Prussian War of 1870, France was eager to compete with Germany in science, sports, art, industry, and culture. Advocacy of the French language, pedagogy, science, and culture became a nationalistic duty, especially where German-funded and -inspired institutions like the Hilfsvereinschule in Palestine were visible competition.

Aaron spoke Yiddish with his parents at home, but in school he and his brothers and sisters learned French and Hebrew. In 1887 the schools were further reformed with classes for women, immersion programs to teach Hebrew, qualifications specified for the teachers, the appointment of headmasters and school inspectors, and above them a Rothschild-administered educational hierarchy.[15] Baron Edmond took a personal interest in the schools: on his first visit to Zichron Ya'aqov he had the schoolmaster dismissed because he thought, wrongly, that the children had not been taught elementary prayers. For Aaron, the French he learned in school became a second mother tongue, the language he would use all his life for his diaries, science, and much of his correspondence. The stress on logic, discipline, style, and precise grammatical and rhetorical constructions that are second nature in French may have held the same appeal for him as the precision of the classification systems for the stones and plant specimens he collected.

At the age of eleven students normally ended their formal education and went to work for the baron, sometimes with a few months of supplementary training at the agricultural school at Metulla to qualify them as agronomist's aides. Aaron, a bright boy, fawned over by his family, with his father's love of the land and appetite for hard work, and an insatiable curiosity about the natural world, had thrived on a curriculum focused on the practical education of agricultural workers. A year after he graduated, at twelve, he was appointed a supervisor under the Rothschild-appointed managers, which required him to ride his horse to working locations all over the settlement, giving him the opportunity to study every aspect of the local agriculture.

On his days off he went on geological and botanical explorations or camping with friends. The children of Zichron weren't as isolated as their parents: some of his friends on the trips and in his explorations were Arabs.

Intelligent, engaged, and relentlessly curious, Aaron would have found it difficult to avoid the lively debates going on at Zichron about the future of the settlement. The earliest agricultural efforts of the settlers had been modeled on the native Arab agriculture, plowing with primitive wooden plows, applying few inputs, and relying on a fallow year after one or two years of production to restore the exhausted soils. The colonists debated whether to follow the biblical and Talmudic imperatives for *shmitta,* which called for leaving the land fallow for a sabbatical year after six years of tilling. Rothschild adamantly opposed the proposal as archaic and a waste of valuable resources. The issue was finally settled by an arrangement in which the land was perfunctorily leased to Arab "owners" for the sabbatical year. In time the settlers, though all nominally Orthodox, discovered that the tempo of farming life was ill-matched to the demanding schedules of religious observance. The festivals and holidays of Passover, Shavuot, Sukkoth, Rosh Hashanah, and Yom Kippur still punctuated the yearly calendar, and the sabbath was observed on Saturdays, but for most of the colonists the daily details of the religiously observant life were turned under by their plows.

Once Zichron survived the challenges of the early years, it became clear that if the settlement was ever to wean itself from the baron's subsidies, the field crops and low-yielding olive and fig cultivation would have to be supplemented or replaced by crops with the potential for export sales. Other early colonies had been successful growing oranges, which they exported under the Jaffa brand name. The Rothschild agricultural experts rejected oranges for Zichron in favor of a more challenging export crop: viticulture, grapes grown for wine. The timing seemed right. In the 1880s phylloxera and mildew had taken a heavy toll on the French wine industry, North American and North African producers had already geared up to take advantage of the market opportunity, and experiments showed that grapes grew well in the dry Palestine climate. The soil seemed suited to growing grapes for a robust *vin ordinaire,* a relatively easy to produce red wine that could be brought to market quickly. The Zionists had a ready market for traditional sacramental wines in the Jewish communities of Central and Eastern Europe, and inexpensive wine would be tolerant of the learning curves of the settlers.

Baron Edmond had a different idea. "In Algeria it is all very well to make a great deal of poor quality wine," he wrote to his local agents in Palestine. "It enters France without paying [duty]. We, for our part, must make *good* wine." He wanted the settlement to produce *vins de marque,* fine wines modeled after the great wines of Bordeaux, like those from his brothers' famed estates. Viticulturists were sent to join the Rothschild agents in Palestine, and the settlers at Zichron were sent off into newly planted vineyards to apply the techniques that had been successful for so long in France.

It proved maddeningly impossible to produce fine wine in the near-desert climate of coastal Galilee. The temperature of the fermenting must would reach 100 degrees Fahrenheit, sometimes even 110, hot enough to turn the wine into vinegar. They installed enormous and complex cooling and refrigeration equipment, but the resulting wines were inconsistent and not competitive with their French counterparts. Rothschild persisted, building large wineries at Rishon le Zion and Zichron Ya'aqov, and introducing American-grafted seedlings when phylloxera—the parasite that had already devastated many of the great vineyards of France—was discovered on the local grapevines. But the Palestinian wines were still not competitive in world markets, and as long as the settlers' energies and grapes were devoted to the futile effort to produce fine wines, the vineyards could not supply the ready market in Russia for cheap sacramental wines.

The often angry debates about viticulture were coupled to political developments. After five years Ephraim Aaronsohn and a few other hardworking settlers at Zichron were able to wean themselves from the Rothschild subsidies to become independent farmers.

Most of the other settlers remained dependent on their monthly stipends, which left them under the authority of the Rothschild agents and resentful of the overbearing attitude and impositions of the pith-helmeted men who micromanaged the colony. Especially for the zealous Zionists, who had come to Palestine with a vision of leading a new life and restoring the dignity of the biblical Jewish kingdoms, the baron's tepid commitments seemed "back door" Zionism—piecemeal, furtive, and "shame-faced."[16] The efforts of the PICA (Palestine Jewish Colonial Association), which the baron supported, were similarly criticized. Some settlers complained that they had given up one form of oppression in Romania only to find another under the French in Palestine.

~

After his success in school and as a young supervisor, in 1893, at the age of fifteen, Aaronsohn was singled out by the Rothschild agents to be sent to France to study agronomy and botany at the famed Grignon Institute. Grignon, west of Versailles, had begun as a model farm. Following the war with Prussia in 1870, it was transformed into a research institute and school for agronomy as part of the effort to compete with German science.[17]

For a young man who had grown up in Zichron, France in the 1890s was eye-opening. Paris was the capital of literature, music, art, café society, and the celebrated boulevard culture. The famed French institutes of science enjoyed incomparable reputations: by 1900 an astounding 87 percent of world congresses were held in Paris.[18] The new Eiffel Tower, built for the International Exposition of 1889, was the tallest structure in the world, a stark, elegant symbol of French engineering prowess. The glories of French science and culture were paired with an increasingly virulent world of politics. When Aaronsohn arrived in France, the Panama scandal had just broken as investors, rich and poor alike, discovered that the 1.5 billion francs they had poured into Ferdinand de Lessep's Panama Company had been squandered in what appeared to be a giant swindle. Two years before, on May Day 1891, troops had fired on a crowd of demonstrating workers at Fourmies, killing women and children and providing graphic images of class warfare and headlines of MASSACRE! for the left-wing press. In the years when Aaronsohn was at the Grignon Institute, the Chambre de Députés was bombed, and anarchist followers of Michael Bakunin and Prince Peter Kropotkin attempted assassinations of the president of the republic and visiting monarchs. The arrest of Captain Alfred Dreyfus, charged with treason for allegedly giving General Staff secrets to a German military attaché, awakened the nation and the world to the fundamental political splits in French society and the power of anti-Semitism as an idea and movement. The premise has been challenged recently, but Theodor Herzl, then a feuilletonist and Paris reporter for the *Neue Freie Presse* of Vienna, claimed that gradual disillusionment as he followed the Dreyfus case led him to the idea of political Zionism.[19]

For two years at Grignon Aaronsohn was exposed to world-class botanists and agronomists, a superb library and specimen collections, and a demanding curriculum focused on laboratory work, the accumulation of data from experiments, and explorations and lectures by famed experts. As a young man he had collected books on botany and geology as avidly as he had combed the hills and deserts for specimens to add to his collections. At Grignon he refined his curiosity and collecting with the rigors of scientific methods. The formal training at the school focused on temperate grains, fruits, vegetables, forage, and flowers, many unfamiliar to Aaronsohn and ill adapted to the climate and soils of Palestine. But the underlying principles of science, the absolute precision of identification and classification schemes, the demonstrable and seemingly immutable logic that underlay the processes of nature, engrossed a bright young man hungry for knowledge. That so much knowledge could be structured into towering frameworks of categorization and the unassailable precision of science as it was practiced at Grignon was a striking contrast to the vagaries of the politics that dominated so much of the life and discourse at Zichron Ya'aqov. That precision of science, so different from the ebb and flow of political debate, became a lifelong obsession for Aaron Aaronsohn. His letters home were mostly about the excitement of learning, though he raised the question of how a nation that could produce a Zola and a Clemenceau could also produce a vicious anti-Semite like Edouard Drumond.[20]

The financial and educational discipline of Grignon was harsh: Aaronsohn could not afford the theater or concert halls, and spent the few francs he could save on books. His monthly stipend at Grignon was paid through a Rothschild agency, and he had opportunities during his two-year stay in France to meet with Baron Edmond. Rothschild was a remarkably generous, dedicated, and hardworking philanthropist, but there was no concealing the strong sense of class, privilege, and birthright that separated him from the recipients of his beneficence. He required the settlers in his Palestine colonies to dress and deport themselves in a manner appropriate to "cultivators and peasants," while on his own visits to Palestine he appeared in the jodhpurs, pith helmet, collar, and tie of a Victorian gentleman on safari. The same distance separated the Well-Known Benefactor from the chosen few who had been selected to receive advanced education in France. Rothschild wasn't much of a listener, and his comments to a caller like Aaronsohn were tainted with the noblesse oblige that characterized his relations with the settlers at Zichron Ya'aqov. Before Aaronsohn left France to return to Palestine, he was told that in recognition of the excellence of his work he would be appointed an instructor at Metulla, a showcase settlement in the northern Galilee that included an agronomy training center designed to prepare a generation of young workers by introducing French scientific methods. The baron had purchased the land for Metulla from the Druze in 1895, with plans for a new settlement that would prove Jewish farmers could be self-sufficient without Arab laborers.

Eighteen years old, a confident, even cocksure young man, trusting his knowledge of the land, his familiarity with the resources and management of Zichron Ya'aqov, and the scientific methods he had learned at Grignon, Aaronsohn reported to Metulla in August 1896, only to discover that the management of the settlement was overcharging the baron's agents and underpaying the Druze workers. When his questions to the managers went unanswered, he wrote to Baron Rothschild, not realizing that the Rothschild agents added comments to his letters questioning Aaronsohn's loyalty and competence and accusing him of stealing wheat from the school. When the baron finally answered the letters, he called Aaronsohn a kid just out of school who already thinks he knows everything and is trying to change the world, and he wrote that if Aaronsohn came to Paris the baron would not meet with him, would fire him from any position he held, and that Aaronsohn should save his money to deal with his own problems, a reference to the accusations that Aaronsohn had stolen grain. Unaccustomed to bureaucratic infighting when the "facts" were so clear, Aaronsohn resigned after less than ten months at the job. He was given no recommendation.[21]

His next job was managing a huge family estate in southern Anatolia. Managing the vast Kuzinry estate was an opportunity to study the soils, climate, and crops of the arid southwest Asian plains; to learn Turkish and the mentalities and interactions of the peasants, landowners and bureaucrats in the Ottoman Empire; and to get a close-up view of the inertia of agricultural production and the lagging infrastructure of Anatolia, which lacked the roads, transport, water distribution, electrical power, and communications that had been so important in the pioneering Jewish settlements in Palestine. From Zichron the nominal Turkish rulers of the Ottoman Empire had seemed distant, insulated by layers of bureaucracy and the Rothschild agents. In Anatolia Aaronsohn encountered up-close the inefficiency of the Ottoman bureaucracy, the structural weaknesses of the economy, and the primitive level of its agriculture and trade. After he had managed the estate for two years, he hired a friend named Ben Dano as assistant manager. Dano promptly criticized Aaronsohn's management to the owners. Aaronsohn, homesick and lacking the patience for another bureaucratic battle, resigned.

He had a hard time finding a new job. The end of the century had brought a sudden shift in fortunes to the Jewish settlements in Palestine. After years of continuing subsidies and the close management of the Rothschild agents, Zichron and the other Rothschild colonies in Palestine were still not self-supporting, and in 1900 the baron transferred control and ownership of the settlements he had supported to the ICA (Israelite Colonization Association), a Palestine-based agency with a long title and little funding. The Rothschild officials needed ten wagons to move their furniture from Zichron. Pundits blamed the baron's decision on the laziness of the farmers (using Yiddish terms like *shnorer* and *luftmenschen*) and their overreliance on the subsidies, claiming that the whole enterprise was an expensive welfare society, with the farmers doing little except paying hired Arab labor.

The uproar in the settlements was immediate. As much as the settlers had resented their quasi-serf status and the heavy-handed Rothschild agents, they had grown accustomed to the subsidies and had persisted with the understanding that ultimately the farmers themselves would own the land. Now, after years of Rothschild micromanagement, the ownership of the land and control of the settlements was being transferred not to the farmers but to another bureaucracy, this one lacking the funds that had at least subsidized the start-up losses at Zichron and other settlements. When they sent a delegation to try to convince Rothschild to change his mind, the ICA answered with the suggestion that half the farming families of Zichron should leave. The colonists refused, and somehow survived by pitching in to support those who were most in need, later proudly calling those years "the time of the commune."[22] Rothschild ultimately agreed to purchase additional large tracts to the south of Zichron that were divided to allocate each farmer hillside slopes for olives and orchards and lowlands for grain. For years the farmers had to pay off the loans for the land from their meager crops.

If some of the accusations of laziness had been true, it was not a charge that fit Aaron Aaronsohn. More often than not in Zichron, Metulla, and Anatolia he had been criticized for working too hard, taking problems and issues too seriously, relentlessly pursuing the perfect solution until everyone around him was exhausted. He typically slept no more than four to five hours per night, getting up before dawn to read or do research.[23] His perfectionism was as absolute with people as with his carefully classified collections of botanical and geological specimens, and it combined with his brazen self-confidence, strikingly quick intelligence, and often unconcealed impatience in a personality that friends would characterize as one that "does not suffer fools gladly." Others, including Baron Rothschild, called him arrogant.

~

In the new climate of economic and social dislocation, when what once seemed an assured future was suddenly insecure, Aaronsohn had one absolute conviction: the future of Palestine depended as much on science, on a carefully researched and planned development of agriculture and industry, as on the dedicated and backbreaking labor that was so celebrated in the early days of the settlements.

He went into business with a German named David Haim to import agricultural equipment; they established branches all over Palestine, and Aaronsohn got Hillel Yaffe, the doctor in Zichron, to intervene to get equipment orders from the ICA, but the partnership collapsed over differences and ended up in court. Aaronsohn began consulting on farms owned by absentee landowners, working with Dr. Zalig Suskin, a German-educated friend he had met at Metulla. "His [Aaronsohn's] talent for botany was incredible," Suskin remembered. "He also had an incredible understanding of geology. He sensed the relationship between the plants and the ground that is the final product of geologic activities. It seemed as if his very personality was invested in plants and the ground, as if he became part of them."[24] Together they published articles on agricultural development and the potential for a silk industry in Palestine. They were joined by a German hydrology engineer named Josef Traydle, forming the Agronomisch-Kultur-Technische Büro für Palastina, with an office in one room of Aaron's father's house in Zichron. The three men collaborated on research on water resources and consulted on large farms until Suskin went to Germany for medical treatment, and Traydle, despairing of making a living in Palestine, first tried the United States, then finally returned to Germany. Aaronsohn took over the consulting alone, but soon found himself in trouble for his relentless candor. When the owners of a large farm sought funds to start another farm in the north of Palestine, Aaronsohn questioned their priorities, telling them they should invest in more irrigation instead of trying to expand. The chairman of the farm called in another consultant from Rishon le Zion, and Aaronsohn resigned in protest, convinced his analysis was right even if it wasn't what the farm owner wanted to hear.[25]

Aaronsohn did not have an academic degree, but when his articles on olive and sesame oil, silk production, tobacco, and cotton, some written with Suskin and Traydle, appeared in German, French, Russian, and English journals, they attracted agricultural investments in Palestine and scientific recognition for Aaronsohn, even among the "Professor Doctors" of the famed German research institutes. Otto Warburg, professor of chemistry and medicine at Humboldt University in Berlin, admired Aaronsohn's dogged and solitary research and invited him to visit Berlin, where he received a warm welcome from distinguished scientists, including the geologist Max Blankenhorn.

These were the years when Theodor Herzl's much publicized writings and energetic efforts to negotiate a future for the Jews in Palestine elevated Zionism into a large-scale political movement. After the first Zionist congress in Basel in 1897, the movement built up a central bureaucracy, developed lobbying forces in European countries and the United States, and appointed commissions to explore issues important for the future. In 1911 Otto Warburg was elected president of the Zionist organization and named Max Blankenhorn head of a newly established Zionist commission for research on Palestine. Aaronsohn was named Blankenhorn's assistant in charge of researching the economic and political program. It was an ideal appointment for Aaronsohn, giving him responsibility and the authority for independent research in the policy areas that interested him, along with time to pursue the private research in botany and geology that had fascinated him since childhood.

There was no end of subjects that needed research. What crops and exactly which cultivars would prove economically productive in the Palestinian climate and soils? What cultivation, irrigation, and harvesting techniques, and what fertilizer or manure inputs would produce profitable crops? Were there untested cultivars that warranted experimentation with new management regimes? As tools Aaronsohn had his observing acumen, familiarity with the soils and terrain of Palestine, an awareness of the latest scientific literature, and deep knowledge of the Bible and other ancient sources. From Roman and biblical references he knew where the land had once been fruitful. He was a good rider, capable of covering many miles on horseback in a day of exploration. He scrimped to buy himself a camera, a magnifier, and other observing and cataloging tools, although he could not afford the first-class instruments he considered essential for serious research.[26] The more he explored what had become desert or swampland, the more he asked himself: What happened to the water supplies that made crops and gardens flourish at Caesarea in Roman times? Where are the rich croplands mentioned in the Bible and other ancient sources?

At the turn of the twentieth century these were not academic questions. Despite the vast grain farms of Canada, the United States, Russia, the Ukraine, Prussia, and Argentina, and the burgeoning development of harvesting and threshing machinery, world wheat yields were declining. Most agronomists attributed the drop in yield to overbreeding that left the cultivars susceptible to rust and drought; they speculated that if an untainted cultivar—an *ur-wheat* that had not been bred and rebred for millennia—could be found, it would hold the secret to increasing yields of the world's most important food crop. Wheat and bread made from wheat are mentioned frequently in the Bible. Where better to look for that original wheat than Palestine?

Rachel Yaffe, the sister of the Zichron physician Hillel Yaffe, encouraged Aaronsohn in his research. Aaron agreed to mentor Rachel in her studies of botany, and later admitted that if it had not been for her encouragement he would not have continued to pursue his research. From her letters Rachel seems to have been in love with him. Her love was unrequited: Aaronsohn's only passion seemed to be for his research. Hillel Yaffe and his wife took Aaron's lack of feelings for Rachel personally, and eventually broke off their friendship with him.

Rachel was not the only woman in Aaronsohn's life. Around 1900, at the time of his first trip to Berlin, he met the wife of his colleague Zalig Suskin. Sonia Suskin was an accomplished pianist, and Aaron fell in love with her the first time he saw her play.[27] Before each of Aaronsohn's visits to Europe she made plans to spend time with him, and they became increasingly close. Zalig was aware of Aaronsohn's friendship with Sonia, and perhaps for that reason Sonia seems to have been reluctant to allow the relationship to go too far, although she was fiercely jealous of even Aaronsohn's male friendships. When he considered the offer of a position in Germany she urged him not to accept, arguing that he would find it impossible to earn a living. Aaron, normally reticent when it came to talking about his feelings, seems to have held nothing back from Sonia, including his relationship with Rachel. He wrote poetry for Sonia, and while his letters to her seem not to have survived, her letters to him convey the intensity of their relationship. "I deserve the cruel letter," she wrote in one, "but you are insulting me in a great way. I pity you, my miserable friend. How much pain you must feel if you can say those things. We live to make each other suffer. As if those we love were made to hurt us."[28]

Aaronsohn's official research for Blankenhorn and the Zionists was a complicated mission. The Turkish authorities were suspicious of Jewish ambitions in Palestine, which put a premium on secrecy—not easy for geological and botanic research over huge areas like the Judean Desert, the Jordan valley, and the Dead Sea. Aaronsohn thought there was a good chance of economic success for mining ventures, and encouraged Warburg to apply to Constantinople for permission to mine. But in the wake of Herzl's death in 1904, and the exhausting debates around a proposal that Zionist energies be shifted to a project to settle Jews in Uganda, the Zionist movement was too preoccupied with governance issues to consider a major new economic initiative. Otto Warburg rejected Aaronsohn's idea, but Max Blankenhorn was sufficiently impressed with Aaronsohn's research to invite him to present a doctoral thesis to a German university, and offered to be his mentor.[29]

Aaronsohn declined the offer in order to pursue his botanical research independently, exploring alone to map the flora of the Galilee and Syria. He soon became a familiar figure in remote areas, on horseback or tramping on foot with a copy of the Ordinance Survey of Palestine that Kitchener had worked on as a lieutenant in the 1870s,[30] a compass, hammer, his Hastings magnifying glass and a .577/.450 Martini-Henry rifle. In a Druze village in the north the natives told visitors about a Jew "who had been gathering wild grasses of no value."[31] Oblivious to the comments, Aaronsohn kept exploring, and in 1906, while collecting wild grasses on the slopes of Mount Hermon, close to the settlement at Rosh Pinah, he discovered patches of wild wheat growing in the crevice of a rock. On close examination he determined that it was a previously unidentified emmer, a primitive form of wheat with a large head and a long beard that appeared to be unchanged from biblical times. Aaronsohn hurriedly published his findings in European journals. The articles were read widely. The wild wheat he had discovered, which later received the scientific name *Triticum dicoccoides,* seemed to be what the huge world wheat industry had been searching for, an untainted cultivar that could be bred into existing wheat stocks to rejuvenate them and produce greater resistance to rust and drought.[32]

Overnight, Aaron Aaronsohn became famous.

3

Bastard

They thought always that they were living in sin, and that we would some day find out. Whereas I knew it before I was ten, and they never told me.

—T. E. Lawrence[1]

By the time he was ten years old, Thomas Edward Lawrence—he was called "Ned" as a boy—noticed that, unlike the other families he encountered, his family moved often, always to a place near the coast, with neighbors who seemed to be of a different social class. He overheard hush-hush discussions between his parents, and sometimes between his father and strangers, and as young as four years old he heard his father talking with a solicitor about an estate in Ireland. His brothers paid no notice to these details, but Ned put the bits and pieces together and concluded that his mother had been a governess in the family of a man of some position who was his real father, and that the man who lived in their household as his father had married his mother only later and had adopted Ned and his brothers, which meant that Ned and his brothers were illegitimate.[2]

Out-of-wedlock birth wasn't just odd in late Victorian England; it was unspeakable. There were routes around the other strictures of Victorian society. Havelock Ellis wrote openly about alternatives to restrictive sexual mores. Social climbers used money and skillfully arranged marriages to transcend humble origins and present themselves as proper society. The ambitious could rise from the misfortune of poverty by taking advantage of the opportunities offered by empire, the industrial revolution, and dislocations from the land. But in a fundamentally patriarchal society, where titles, class, fortunes, and social position were inherited, illegitimacy was a social brand that neither marriage nor wealth nor accidental or even planned good fortune could eradicate. Sunday sermons preached ferociously on the wages of sin, identifying an illegitimate child as both the just deserts for the sinners and a public advertisement of their trespass. Even as a secret, the illegitimacy of Ned's birth was a heavy psychological burden that would remain with him throughout his life. It may also have been strangely liberating, provoking him to defy Victorian culture and mores, to create his own world as an outsider.

The truth about his parents, which Ned would not learn until after the Great War, was even stranger than what he had imagined. The man who lived in the house as his father, and who went by the name Thomas Lawrence, *was* his father and the father of his brothers. Thomas Lawrence was the adopted name of Sir Thomas Robert Tighe Chapman, a distant relative of Sir Walter Raleigh's. He had once lived somewhat grandly on an estate in County Westmeath, northwest of Dublin, married to a cousin, with four daughters and a reputation for moroseness. Sometime between 1878 and 1880 he brought an attractive and capable young woman named Sarah into the household to be a companion and governess for his daughters. One of Sir Thomas's daughters recalled that whenever Sarah entered a room, her father's dour manner brightened and he became "all gay."[3] In time Sarah became pregnant. Sir Thomas took lodgings for her in Dublin, and began dividing his time between the two households. After a son was born to Sarah, a butler from the Chapman estate overheard her give her name in a grocery store as "Mrs. Chapman," and followed her home. An angry quarrel at the Chapman household followed when Lady Chapman refused to give Sir Thomas a divorce. Thomas and Sarah moved to Tremadoc, in North Wales, and took the surname Lawrence. Their second son, Thomas Edward Lawrence, was born there in 1888.

The new family spent a little more than a year in Tremadoc before moving to Kirkcudbright, Scotland, then, in succession, to Dinard on the Brittany coast, the Isle of Wight, and the New Forest in Hampshire. As young Ned noticed, each new home was near the sea, which facilitated communications with Ireland and the estates from which Thomas still drew an income, and in locales where their English neighbors were not of Thomas's landowning class, and hence were unlikely to recognize him as Sir Thomas Chapman or to be suspicious of the new family. The Lawrences lived modestly enough to call little attention to themselves. In 1896, with their sons old enough that education was a concern, they moved to Oxford, where Ned and his older brother, Bob, were enrolled in the City of Oxford High School for Boys, a school with a good reputation and modest fees.

Ned was always different. His four brothers (three others died during childbirth or as infants) were tall and athletic; Ned stopped growing at less than five feet five inches. Perhaps because of his shortness, or because he was a middle son without the attention fawned on the first and last born, or because of his awareness of his illegitimacy, he often behaved eccentrically, playing pranks, proposing bizarre ideas or actions, experimenting with self-imposed tests of physical endurance, or forcing himself to go for periods without food or sleep. He avoided organized athletics but took exaggeratedly long walks and cycle rides, setting off in search of medieval ruins on his bicycle or on explorations of the Trill Mill Stream, which ran under Oxford. He was adventurous enough to be prone to injuries. As early as age six he could be "frightfully bossy" and exert a "quiet authority" with friends.[4] A ready sense of humor saved him from schoolyard bullying, but he also had a mischievous streak, defiantly keeping his hat on in church. His imagination and acute powers of observation were unique in the family: his brothers were content with athletic games and more typical childhood adventures, and none of them seems to have perceived anything unusual about the family or to have concluded that their parents weren't properly married.

Although they could not live in the style to which Sir Thomas

Chapman had once been accustomed, Thomas Lawrence received sufficient income from Irish estates—£200 to £1,000 per year, the equivalent of a midlevel professional income—to live at leisure and spend his time at home with the boys. He was a skilled photographer, taught his sons carpentry, played word games with them, bought fashionably new bicycles, and liked riding one hundred miles per day. He hunted, knew properly grammatical French, was interested in current affairs and medieval architecture, and even in old age could quote Horace and Homer. Ned seems to have picked up a knack for photography and cycling and an admiration for medieval architecture from his father, and perhaps his love of Greek and Roman authors. Yet Thomas Lawrence remained emotionally distant and detached from his second-oldest son, the emotional reticence typical of many British fathers of his generation perhaps accentuated by a reaction to Ned's misperception that this man was not his real father.

His mother, whom Ned later learned was also illegitimate, had been raised in modest circumstances and had worked hard to achieve her position as a governess. She worked even harder to maintain her family at what she considered proper moral standards. She was strong-willed, insistent, demanding, and relentlessly probing. Many years later Ned still carried scars from their intense relationship. "Mother is rather wonderful," he wrote, "but very exciting. She is so set, so assured in mind. . . . I have a terror of her knowing anything about my feelings, or convictions, or way of life. If she knew they would be damaged: violated: no longer mine. You see, she would not hesitate to understand them: and I do not understand them, and do not want to."[5]

Perhaps as remorse for her own sins, Sarah Lawrence was puritanically strict. She referred to Thomas Lawrence as "Tom" or "the boys' father," never as "my husband," and staunchly disapproved of dancing or the theater, with the exception of Shakespeare. People who knew her well found her overpowering, "a terror" who devoured people and had to be treated accordingly: "If you know what to say it won't eat you up. Better to step out of the way."[6]

Sarah was harsh in enforcing her demanding standards, and as the prankster of the family, Ned got the brunt of the severe whippings on the buttocks that were administered as punishments for disciplinary infractions. Thomas Lawrence was too gentle to deal out the punishments; Sarah applied the whip. Physical punishment of children was not unusual in late Victorian homes, and by most accounts the Lawrence household was not especially unhappy, but by 1905 the tension and frustrations were enough that Ned ran away from home. With no relatives to take him in, he chose one of the few options open to a young man without means or a place to stay: he enlisted.

The local recruiting office placed him in the Royal Garrison Artillery as a boy soldier. Boys between fourteen and eighteen were recruited as trumpeters, and when competent were allowed to blow the regular bugle calls of regimental life. Ned was posted to the Falmouth Garrison, and soon found the constant fistfights and barracks bullying—men and boys showed up at every parade with black eyes—terrifying. An appeal to his father got Lawrence out of the regiment. The brief enlistment and the defiance of running away seemed to end his emotional dependence on his mother.

He was a voracious reader, and later claimed to have read "every book which interested me in the Library of the Oxford Union (best part of 50,000 fols. I expect) in 6 years." The claim was certainly an exaggeration, but he sometimes read eighteen hours a day, and claimed he could "tear the heart out of the soberest book in half an hour."[7] His father would borrow the volumes for him, and seems to have encouraged his enthusiasm for medieval brass rubbing, archaeology, and history. He had earlier studied mathematics, but medieval history and archaeology suited both his disinclination for theoretical studies and his imagination. Like many boys who feel a bit odd or different, Ned's fantasies had already begun to venture widely and creatively, although his later recollections—"I fancied to run up in my own life that new Asia which inexorable time was slowly bringing upon us. The Arabs made a chivalrous appeal to my young instinct, and when still at the High School in Oxford, already I thought to remake them into a nation, client and fellow of the British Empire"[8]—are probably informed by his wartime experiences.

After taking the senior Oxford local examinations, the equivalent of the current A level exams, he set off at the age of eighteen, in the summer of 1906, on a bicycle tour of Brittany to explore medieval architecture and archaeology. His letters home from France that summer, the earliest record of his feelings and interests, are by turns impersonal chronicles of his adventures, detailed observations of archaeological and architectural sites, and gossipy commentaries on people and current affairs. He is reticent about revealing his own feelings, but was a compulsive listener and observer, readily penning provocative comments about old acquaintances and people he met. He had learned about cycling and photography from his father, but did not bring a camera, relying on commercial picture postcards to document the places he had visited. When he returned home in the fall, he entered the university.

Looking back Lawrence saw his childhood as "miserable wasted years of unwilling work: and when after them I suddenly went to Oxford, the new freedom felt like heaven. I don't think men ever work as hard as boys are made to work . . . nor do I think the miseries of grown-up feelings are as bad as those of boys."[9]

~

He entered Oxford in 1906, the year Aaron Aaronsohn discovered wild emmer on a slope of Mt. Hermon. The cost of education for five sons was a growing burden for the Lawrence family, and the scholarship T.E. received at Oxford was small, so he continued to live at home. He made some friends at Jesus College, but it was not until the summer term of 1908 that he moved into rooms at the college and began to participate in undergraduate life.

Already an outsider, Lawrence remained a loner and an eccentric at Oxford, testing himself with long bicycle rides, fasts, strict vegetarian diets, and by staying awake for extended periods. Contemporaries remembered seeing Lawrence "almost always late at night, walking in the quadrangle at Jesus [College]. I do not know when he went to bed; some nights, I am pretty sure, not at all, certainly seldom till well on in the small hours." He would sit cross-legged on the floor, "explaining that he never sat on chairs if he could help it, that he never indulged in the meals known as breakfast, lunch, tea and dinner, nor smoked or took drinks; in fact he did nothing which qualified him to be an ordinary member of society."[10] On one occasion he wandered into the rooms of a friend "and began to fire a revolver, blank cartridge fortunately, out of the windows . . . one glance at his eyes left no doubt at all that he told the truth when he said that he had been working for forty-five hours at a stretch without food, to test his powers of endurance."[11]

Without close friends or regular social activities, Lawrence seems to have lost himself in his studies, eschewing what was a more typical concentration for an undergraduate in the early years of the twentieth century. He was not a scholar by temperament, but read voraciously, especially out-of-the-way and oddball books, and his work struck at least some observers as "unusual without the effort to be unusual."[12] His official field was modern history, which at Oxford meant everything after the Greeks and Romans. He was continually drawn to medieval history, and in 1908, when the examiners offered the new option of a thesis on a special subject as part of their examination, Lawrence opted for "Military History and Strategy," which would allow him to present a thesis on medieval military architecture, and to focus his examinations in the same area.

He spent the next summer on a long bicycle tour of France to study castles, covering more than 2,400 miles from the northeast down through Provence to the southwest, and back across the heart of France.[13] When he returned to Oxford he did not take rooms at the college again, but came home. There were not enough rooms in the house to provide Lawrence with a quiet room of his own, and he was serious enough about his studies and eccentric enough in his habits that they decided to build him a two-room bungalow at the bottom of the garden, complete with electricity, water, a coal grate, and a telephone to the house. Lawrence hung the walls with green cloth for quiet and immersed himself in his books. He was happiest alone, reading late into the night, not only in his subject area but also historical romances set in the Middle Ages. He discussed French medieval castles with C. F. Bell of the Ashmolean Museum, who suggested that Lawrence follow up his summer survey of French castles by traveling to the Holy Land to look at crusader castles. He would then be in a position to settle the question of whether the pointed arches and vaults of the crusader castles were copied from eastern sources or brought to the Arabs by the crusaders.

It was an inspired suggestion—a solid scholarly question that built on Lawrence's studies of the Middle Ages; an invitation to travel to Syria and the Holy Land; and the possibility of exploring the heroics and culture clashes of the Crusades, a subject that had fascinated Lawrence from childhood. He began reading the works of C. M. Doughty, the distinguished traveler and explorer of Arabia. It didn't take long before he had read enough to speak with modest authority on the Middle East and to turn Bell's idea into plans. Late in 1908 the Ashmolean Museum appointed D. G. Hogarth, an archaeologist with extensive experience and knowledge of Syria and the Holy Land, as Keeper. Lawrence met Hogarth early in 1909, and told him about his plans to visit Syria that summer.

It would be the wrong season to visit Syria, Hogarth told Lawrence. "It is too hot there now."

"I'm going," Lawrence said.

"Well, have you got the money? You'll want a guide and servants to carry your tent and baggage."

"I'm going to walk."

"Europeans don't walk in Syria. It isn't safe or pleasant."

"Well," Lawrence said, "I do."[14]

Hogarth urged Lawrence to write to Doughty for his opinion. Doughty wrote back that in July and August, when Lawrence planned to travel, the heat would be severe even in Damascus, and worse at lower elevations; that given the distances, the potential hostility of the local populations, and the lack of appropriate refreshments for a European, long daily marches on foot were "out of the question"; that a mule or horse, with its owner, and some Arabic, was essential; and that he would "dissuade a friend from such a voyage, which is too likely to be most wearisome, hazardous to health and even disappointing."[15]

Undeterred, Lawrence took Arabic lessons from a Protestant clergyman and drawing lessons from an architectural illustrator, read travel guides on the Middle East, and got the principal of Jesus College to ask Lord Curzon to arrange letters of safe conduct with the Turkish authorities. In June 1909, he took a steamer to Beirut, studied Arabic at the American Mission School in Jebail, then set off, initially with a guide and horse, then on foot, to visit the crusader castles of northern Palestine.

After so much anticipation, he found the Holy Land disappointing. He had imagined glorious public buildings, well-engineered Roman roads, and the lush landscapes of Renaissance paintings. Instead he found arid and strikingly poor land, scattered broken remnants of Roman columns, and the fading outlines of Roman roads lying helter-skelter amid "dirty, dilapidated Bedouin tents." "Miserable curs" rushed out to bark at a stranger. "Palestine was a decent country then," he wrote after his first, disillusioning impressions. "And could so easily be made so again. The sooner the Jews farm it all the better: their colonies are bright spots in a desert."[16]

In Syria Lawrence adapted to the cuisine of *labneh* (sour milk) and greasy bulgur (boiled wheat) and found the stark lives and generous hospitality of the Arabs he met a striking contrast to the world he had known in Oxford. "When I go into a native house," he wrote home,

> the owner salutes me, and I return it and then he says something to one of his women, and they bring out a thick quilt, which, doubled, is laid on the rush mat over the floor as a chair: on that I squat down, and then the host asks me four or five times how my health is; and each time I tell him it is good. Then comes sometimes coffee and after that a variety of questions, as to whether my tripod is a

> revolver, and what I am, and where I come from, and where I'm going, and why I'm on foot, and am I alone, and every other thing conceivable. . . . I am asked about my wife and children, how many I have etc. I really feel a little ashamed of my youth out here. . . . They mostly put my age as fifteen, and are amazed at my traveling on foot and alone. Riding is the only honourable way of going, and everyone is dreadfully afraid of thieves: they travel very little.[17]

He walked from one crusader castle to the next, from the huge and beautifully preserved hilltop Crac des Chevaliers to the ruined castle at Athlit on the Mediterranean coast. Once he was shot at by an attacker, "an ass with an old gun," and fired back with the Mauser pistol he carried.[18] When he ran short of time he hired a carriage to take him from Aleppo to Urfa, in northeast Syria, an area Hogarth had explored in search of Hittite seal stones. On the way back Lawrence's camera was stolen. A few days later he was attacked by a beggar, who beat him with a stone and bit his hand. Finally, out of money and with his boots walked to pieces, he set off for home, confident that he had the material for his thesis, and delighted with his newfound rapport with the Arabs. On the way back he briefly worked in Port Said, coaling ships.

The worlds of castles and medieval romances and the Arabs of Syria had become more attractive to Lawrence than the solitary undergraduate world at Oxford and the cultures of the military, business, and government to which so many of his contemporaries were headed. He did not question the core political values of late Victorian culture, the mantle of empire, or the hubris of the colonial mission of civilizing the world, but he had begun to shape his world as a kind of Puritan dream, antinomian in its morality, divided between the nobility of native Arab dignity and the shallowness and corruption of the Kultur and civilization of Europe.

At one point during his visit to Syria in 1909 Lawrence traveled from Nazareth to the crusader castle at Athlit on the coast of Galilee, before walking fifteen miles north to Haifa, and then on to Acre. The kaiser had passed through Athlit on his triumphant way to Jerusalem a decade earlier. The castle was in ruins, lacking the imposing grandeur of the great crusader castle at Crac des Chevaliers and not very useful for Lawrence's studies, but it was on a spectacular site, jutting out into the Mediterranean—a perfect spot from which to conjure up images of crusader fleets, knights in combat, and the noble struggles of the Crusades era. Although Lawrence admired the landscape in Galilee, especially the improved farmland developed by the Jewish settlements, he was probably not impressed by the arid lowland behind the castle at Athlit, interspersed with malarial swamps and on soils so unproductive that the native Arabs considered the land hardly worth cultivating. Part of the land was thickly overgrown with tamarisks, and much of the rest was pocked with pickleweed and other halophytes; some bare patches were too brackish even for pickleweed. If Lawrence had asked, the local Arabs would have told him that there had been cases of yellow fever in the area, and that the area had "bad water."[19]

Lawrence had no reason to suspect he was walking on another man's dream.

Fame

The righteous bloom like a date-palm;
they thrive like a cedar in Lebanon;
planted in the house of the Lord,
they flourish in the courts of our God.
In old age they still produce fruit;
they are full of sap and freshness.

—Psalms 92:13–15

The castle at Athlit was just visible from Zichron, a speck on the horizon in the direction of Haifa. Aaron Aaronsohn had ridden there, even walked up the coast, since childhood, sometimes with his sister Sarah. Athlit was peaceful and quiet, a good place to contemplate. The ruins jutted out into the Mediterranean, with beaches to the north and south and the foothills of the Carmel to the east. Aaron was especially interested in the land immediately behind the castle. It was covered with thistles and pocked with vernal ponds, breeding sites for mosquitoes, but it was flat and mostly dry, unlike the swampy land along much of the coast, including the land along the sea below Zichron. At Athlit Aaron would walk from the sea to the foothills, surveying elevations and drainage, testing the soil, recording details of the plants and soil types. He could picture the wet areas drained, the marsh converted into a pond for irrigation, the thistle-covered land cleared for fields and orchards, stones from the fields used to build a road leading to the station, and in a central clearing, a laboratory and research library, with sheds for equipment and a windmill to pump water for irrigation. As early as 1902 he had wanted to build an agricultural research station, and had sketched out his plans in a memo to the Zichron physician, Hillel Yaffe.[1] On land even the Arabs chose not to farm, he wanted to build an experimental farm where he could prove that science would pave the way for the future of Jewish Palestine.

Aaronsohn had become a celebrity after the publication of his discovery of wild wheat. Both sides of the long-running debate on the origins of civilization cited his work, one side arguing that Aaronsohn's discovery of what some were calling the mother of all wheats proved that civilization originated in the Fertile Crescent of southwest Asia, the other faction claiming that the primitive emmer would not crossbreed and was not productive enough to sustain a developed civilization. Aaronsohn stayed out of the debates: he believed that "grains created civilization, civilization did not create grains,"[2] and after more research he suggested that the wild emmer may have been cultivated together with barley, a practice that continued in native Arab agriculture and initially had been adopted by the Jewish settlers. He was less interested in the debate over the origins of civilization, or even whether wild emmer would invigorate world wheat harvests, than in the possibility that his discovery might draw support for more research on agriculture in Palestine.

Visitors to Zichron were introduced to the "clever, young botanist," and he was sought after as a speaker. "These colonists are a new type of Jew to me," an American ophthalmologist wrote after meeting Aaronsohn, "and yet different from farmers who are not Jews—a new generation."[3] Aaronsohn gave talks and seminars in France, Germany, Belgium, Austria, Tunisia, and Egypt, with each talk leading to more invitations, personal and institutional connections, and opportunities for research in areas like the Sahara Desert and the Arabian Peninsula. It was a heady time, the enthusiastic international reception to his discovery a sharp contrast to his isolation and unemployment only a few years earlier. But he couldn't support continued research with applause.

And the research mattered. Typically, scholars and authorities in agronomy were "hedgehogs" who worked a lifetime on a single theme or research area. Aaronsohn was a "fox," knowing many things and pursuing multiple parallel research efforts. He researched cereal crops, orchards, vineyards, and truck farming. He explored drip irrigation, which would maximize the utilization of limited water supplies, and lithic mulching, leaving or placing stones on cultivated land. Aaronsohn had seen his father and mother stooped over in the hot sun, painfully picking stones from the fields. Through experiments and library research he found that in a climate like Palestine's, leaving the stones on cultivated land not only did no harm for some crops, but could have benefits—shading the soil, limiting diurnal temperature fluctuations, and slowing the crusting of the soil, runoff, erosion, and the leaching of minerals and nutrients. He learned that his research on plant selection, cultivation, and irrigation techniques was ahead of what had been tried in California. He knew there were growers and investors in California and in Palestine who would welcome research to squeeze maximum profit from an acre or hectare of land, but he had another goal.

The Ottoman restrictions on Jewish ownership of land were so onerous, and the challenge of eking out a living from the soils of Palestine so difficult, especially with the crude techniques and equipment the first settlers had inherited from the local Arabs, that the familiar biblical passages about a land of milk and honey seemed a fantasy. Visiting newlyweds from a wealthy Anglo-Jewish family, charmed by Zichron, were told that the parcels of land available to the Jewish settlements "cannot be much intensified & therefore in the colony itself there is only room for one son—the others have either to go abroad or go to other colonies."[4] Many agronomists, economics experts, and politicians abroad subscribed to the belief that the agricultural land of Palestine was too unproductive and limited to support a large population. Even after influxes of cash and expertise from abroad, the laborious draining of the swamps, the introduction of irrigation, and the modernization of cultivation techniques finally produced successful crops for export, there was a widespread belief that there simply wasn't enough good land in Palestine to support a massive influx of Jewish immigrants. Aaronsohn disagreed. But to make his case he needed a research station.

He also had to contend with the official Zionist movement, which had its own agenda for Palestine. By the turn of the twentieth century widespread publicity about the Dreyfus case in France, the continued "Jewish problem"—the euphemism much of the world used for the consequences of anti-Semitism in Eastern Europe—and the inspired writings of Theodor Herzl had turned the once vague dream of Zionism into a thriving movement in Europe. Within years of the appearance of Herzl's novel *Altneuland,* the Hungarian feuilletonist had become a near-mythical figure in Jewish communities in much of Europe, with his photograph displayed in Jewish homes as a Catholic home might display a crucifix. Even devout Jews who believed that Israel could only be resurrected with the coming of the Messiah would hang a Hebrew micrograph portrait of Herzl, the entire lithograph made up of tiny Hebrew letters.[5]

Herzl's utopian writings and fame made the Zionist venture seem not only possible but almost inevitable. The first Zionist congress, held in Basel in 1897, issued a deceptively simple and straightforward manifesto: "Zionism seeks to establish a home for the Jewish people in Palestine secured under public law." The ambiguity of terms like "a home" and "under public law" was deliberate. In Constantinople the terms could be interpreted in the least threatening context, as "a residence" and "under public Ottoman law." The ultra-Orthodox could read from the same passage a reassuring echo of the biblical verse "Zion shall be redeemed by law." And among the Jewish masses the phrases could be read as "the first step toward statehood" and "under international law."[6]

Herzl attributed his idea of political Zionism and a massive migration to Palestine to his reactions to the Dreyfus trial, but his plans and vision may have owed even more to his readings about the seventeenth-century false messiah Shabbetai Ẓevi, who inspired massive migrations of Sephardic Jews across Europe. Like Shabbetai Ẓevi, Herzl could be intolerant, domineering, and narcissistic.[7] As Herzl's fame and authority grew, he began to see himself as a messiah king, condescendingly referring to the Jewish masses as "an army of *shnorers,*" and writing: "I stand in command of a mass of youth, beggars and jackasses."[8] He paid little attention to the Jewish settlements already in Palestine, and when he did it was dismissive: "Who among us would be capable of buying a railway ticket in Hebrew?" The traditional Jews of Jerusalem reciprocated: when Grand Duke Friedrich I of Baden arranged an audience for Herzl during the kaiser's triumphant visit to Jerusalem in 1898, the chief rabbi of Jerusalem demonstrated his adamant opposition to Zionism by refusing to meet Herzl.

The Jerusalem meeting with the kaiser was to be Herzl's triumph on the world stage. They met at the Jaffa Gate, Herzl on foot in his pith helmet, the kaiser on horseback with a keffiya draped over his *Pickelhaube*. (A later photograph showing them side by side had been doctored.) Herzl, inordinately impressed with monarchs, wrote in his diary about the kaiser's "truly imperial eyes—I have never seen such eyes. A remarkable bold, inquisitive soul shows in them." Herzl heard what he wanted to hear in the kaiser's words, and optimistically wrote that the kaiser was hoping the "unloved Jews" would leave Germany, and that he had declared himself "prepared to support the Jewish migration" if the sultan agreed to the colonization of Palestine. "That brief reception," Herzl triumphantly concluded, "will live on forever in Jewish history, and possibly may entail 'world consequences.'"

When Herzl carried his mission to Constantinople, hoping the sultan would provide the essential second piece of his plan, the sultan declared that he could not dispose of any part of the Ottoman Empire because it belonged not to him but to the Turkish people—a disingenuous announcement that was no doubt a surprise to many of his subjects. The sultan prophetically added: "When my empire is divided, perhaps they [the Jewish people] will get Palestine for nothing. But only our corpse can be divided. I will never consent to vivisection."[9] His declaration was all but an invitation to make long-term plans for a Jewish state, but Herzl wasn't interested in the distant future.

Herzl died in 1904, only a few years after Rothschild's withdrawal from actively funding the Jewish settlements in Palestine. The Zionist movement had thrived, and had created annual Zionist congresses, a directorate, officers, and publications, and had organized on every continent, which made the future of the Jewish experiment in Palestine seem inevitable. Yet the status of the settlements was terrifyingly insecure. The Jewish settlers were still reeling from the end of Rothschild's support. More than twenty years after the beginning of the new settlements, they were still barely tolerated by the Ottoman bureaucracy, and were denied full status as a community in the empire. Jews were allowed to reside in Palestine only within rings of legal restrictions, were ineligible for citizenship unless they renounced their faith, and were often resented by their Arab neighbors. The European powers remained standoffish toward Zionism, not always openly hostile—many of the European powers had internal agendas that were served by Jewish emigration to Palestine—but reluctant to openly support Jewish aspirations in the Holy Land. The Zionist movement debated proposals to settle Jews in Uganda, where some European regimes were willing to lend support they had withheld in Palestine. A major argument for some in the debate was that only the vast open lands of Africa could provide a viable Jewish homeland, that the available land in Palestine could not support the population needed to reach a critical mass, and that without enough productive land for both the native population and substantial Jewish settlement, the Jews would forever remain a minority, facing a future of acrimonious contention for the limited land with the native Arab population.

Even as the Zionists debated, the pogroms in the wake of the failed Russian revolution of 1905 and the socialist fervor that had fueled the revolution brought a new wave of Jewish immigrants from Poland and Russia to Palestine. Many of the new settlers had supported the ambitious agendas of the revolution, and had read Hayyim Nahman Bialik's moving Hebrew poem "In the City of Slaughter" about the brutal 1903 pogrom at Kishinev. Like an earlier generation that had emigrated from Eastern and Central Europe in the wake of the pogroms of the early 1880s, they were convinced that their hopes would never be realized in the old country. But for many of the new wave, the similarity with the first aliyah ended there. The earlier settlers, like Aaron Aaronsohn's parents, had been adherents of back-to-the-land movements, families eager for a simple life in the Promised Land, their motivations neither utopian nor even ideological: they were fed up with anti-Semitism and pogroms, and exhausted from the poverty and restricted economic opportunities of their shtetls in the Russian Pale of Settlement and Romania. They came to Palestine as families, and pursued the small private farms they had been denied in Russia and Romania.

Many in the vanguard of the second aliyah to Palestine, after 1904, were young, unmarried, and idealistic, often aggressively ideological, even fanatical, in their adherence to Tolstoyan or Marxist socialism. With the passion of youth, they were determined not only to build new lives for themselves in a new land, but also to reform the evils they saw in the world through their example. In place of the *moshavah,* the individual farms of the first aliyah, some of the new settlers wanted to build a revolutionary new life around a new institution, the kibbutz, a true collective where the land and tools of production would be held in common, private property would be reduced to a minimum, and physical labor would be glorified. They were secular rather than religious, eager to learn Hebrew as a new language that would bind people from many origins into a single nation, and intensely political. In late 1905, the Tolstoyans established the Hapoel Hatzair Labor Party at Chaim Bloch's pension in Jaffa, with A. D. Gordon as chief ideologist, declaring themselves opposed to violence, justifying self-defense only in extreme situations, and demanding that the Jewish pioneers plant every tree and bush in the Jewish homeland. Within a month the Marxists had established the Poale Zion Party at Spektor's pension a few blocks away, pledging to pursue a traditional Marxist approach to their socialist goals, and arguing that a Jewish state would never be achieved by appeals to the Great Powers, but only through the inexorable forces of the class struggle from the example of kibbutzim in the countryside and the growth of a Jewish proletariat in the cities.

This young vanguard of the second aliyah ran head-on into the anti-Zionist, ultra-Orthodox Jews of Jerusalem, Safed, and Tiberias, who adamantly opposed the secularization and modernization of Jewish life and the use of the sacred language of Hebrew for anything other than prayer and study, and who regarded calls for an ingathering of the Jews in Zion, a mission reserved by scripture for the Messiah, as nothing short of blasphemy. By 1905, relations between the two sides were so tense that ultra-Orthodox rabbis in Jerusalem ritually cursed Zionist educator David Yellin, who had established secular Hebrew-language schools, in an unprecedented ceremony called a *Pulsa Denura* ("whip of fire"), going beyond the snuffed candles and blowing of the shofar of a traditional *ḥerem,* or excommunication, to include calls for Yellin's death.

Many in the second aliyah also found themselves in conflict with the first aliyah settlers over the contentious issue of labor, especially the use of Arab labor. Aaron's parents and the other colonists who built Zichron Ya'aqov and the other early settlements had been no strangers to hard work. Agriculture in the late nineteenth century was scarcely mechanized, and even working with draft animals was exhausting work in the stony Palestine soils. Some tasks, like draining swamps and clearing thistles, had to be done by hand while the colonists were fighting malaria, yellow fever, trachoma, and other indigenous diseases for which they had no immunity. But for all their exhausting physical work, whether for twelve francs a month as indentured laborers under the Rothschild administration or on their own land, they rarely glorified labor. Work was only a means to a future of modest prosperity; when they could afford to, they didn't hesitate to hire Arab workers to do the backbreaking work in the fields.

~

The Arab village Faradis (Paradise) is a few miles north of Zichron, at the edge of the hills that rise up from the flat and swampy land on the Mediterranean coast. The Arabs of Faradis rarely traveled far, and they were unlikely to have seen religious urban Jews in Safad or Jerusalem, or any Jews, before the colonists from Romania, in Western clothing and speaking foreign languages, arrived to build a new settlement. As the newcomers began aggressively cultivating land the Arabs had long dreamed of owning, curiosity and fear mingled with jealousy, and sometimes turned to resentment and anger. The Jewish settlers, whose only knowledge of Arabs before their arrival in Palestine was *bobemayses* (grandmothers' tales) about Arab bogeymen and bandits, were sufficiently frightened to be standoffish or hostile toward their neighbors, an attitude that aggravated the tension between the brash newcomers and an Arab culture that valued hospitality.

Herzl had predicted that in Palestine religion would be relegated entirely to "the private realm," and that with no distinctions in religion "there would be absolutely no Arab opposition to Zionism, since the Arab inhabitants of Palestine would only benefit from the technological advance of their society and hence would unilaterally welcome massive Jewish immigration."[10] In *Altneuland,* one of the closest friends of the hero, Rashid Bey, asks, "Why should we have anything against the Jews? They have enriched us, they live with us like brothers." Like many of Herzl's pronouncements from Vienna and Paris, it was a compelling idealism that didn't always match the reality of Palestine.

Some of the early settlers in Zichron tried to initiate friendships with the Arabs of Faradis, but the gaps in culture and economics were not easy to span. The Arab farmers were sharecroppers, working small plots in the vast land holdings of absentee landlords who lived in Damascus, Jerusalem, or Aleppo. The fellaheen had strong attachments to the land they had long farmed,[11] but with no equity in the land and no guarantee that they would be able to continue farming the same parcel, they had little incentive to invest in agricultural techniques or inputs more advanced than plowing with a crude wooden plow and occasionally fallowing the land. Without irrigation, fertilizer, or improved seed they grew little more than subsistence harvests, while the fields and vineyards of Zichron, a few miles away and up the hill, were producing substantial crops, including export products. The Arabs soon learned that they could earn more, with less risk, as laborers on the Jewish farms.

When the Tolstoyans of the second aliyah arrived with wide belts over their peasant's blouses and tall boots modeled after the photographs of the aged Tolstoy in the fields at his estate, they were horrified to discover the neat individual homes and cobbled streets of Zichron, and that many of the farms, orchards, and vineyards of the settlement were effectively plantations, with hired laborers, usually Arabs, doing much of the physical labor. Each farmer in Zichron Ya'aqov provided for three to four families.[12] Those who did not farm worked as shopkeepers or managers, or by practicing trades, sometimes the very trades they had left behind in the shtetls of Russia and Romania. The socialists in their peasant's blouses were appalled by the petite bourgeois economy, calling the Zichron landowners "shtetl squires" and "armchair farmers." "We were happy enough working on the land," wrote Joseph Baratz, one of the founders of the first kibbutz, at Degania, in the Jordan valley, about working at Zichron Ya'aqov. "But we knew more and more certainly that the ways of the old settlements were not for us. This was not the way we hoped to settle the country—this old way with Jews on top and Arabs working for them; anyway, we thought that there shouldn't be employers and employed at all. There must be a better way."[13]

The socialists called themselves *chaver* (comrade) or *po'el* (worker). Aaronsohn and others from Zichron and the other early settlements called them Muscovites, or "the bare-footed ones." From sheer numbers, the freedom of movement they enjoyed without families, and the aggressive forcefulness of their ideological commitment the barefooted ones gradually gained the upper hand across entire swaths of Palestine, eagerly imposing their ideals. Near Mount Tabor in Galilee five Arabs were discovered among forty Jewish workers at a joint farm called Sejira; the owner was threatened with violence until he agreed to dismiss his native laborers. Later the owner was found murdered, probably by one of the Arabs he had fired. As the pressure against employing Arab labor increased, farmers in Zichron and other settlements circumvented the new bans by importing Jewish laborers from Yemen. In Zichron the Yemenite Jews became an agricultural proletariat, living town from the original Jewish settlers, their neighborhoods slums in the newly prosperous Jewish towns.[14]

Aaron Aaronsohn was rarely without an opinion on issues of politics or economics, and the question of hiring Arab labor was no exception. He found the entire issue "artificially bred," a phony problem introduced by the "anarchists, maximalists, etc.," who brought "bankrupt ideas and foolish dreams, without taking into account that, whether justified or not in Russia, where they originated, these dreams were entirely out of place, and, in fact, positively disastrous, as applied by them in Palestine." The Tolstoyans were trying to initiate "the wildest agrarian reforms . . . nationalization of the land, the grant to every individual of no more land than he could till with his own hands, the abolition of all capitalistic concerns and of the so-called exploitation of the Arabs; and to that end, however paradoxical it may sound, the interdiction of any other than Jewish labour on Jewish land, if we were to assert our national rights and national independence."[15]

Aaronsohn had studied labor economics, including Max Weber's magisterial *The Protestant Ethic,* which offers a convincing nineteenth-century version of a business-school case study of agricultural wages. Weber observed that raising piece rates at harvesttime in an effort to increase the productivity of workers had the opposite effect: in fact, the workers would not harvest more grain, but less, working only enough to make what had been their accustomed harvest pay. That inertia, especially among the Arab laborers, was one key to the profitability of the new Jewish agriculture.

Aaronsohn could list case after case where the Tolstoyan experiments had been tried and had failed, where the lack of Arab labor had crippled the production of cereal crops, and where potential investors had been discouraged by acts of sabotage at the hands of the zealous Tolstoyans. Asked to evaluate some farms by the famed Zionist economist Arthur Rupin, Aaronsohn reported that on one of the farms, run by Jewish workers as a collective, they had planted wheat in stony soil, so that modern mowers or reapers could not be used to harvest it. The workers proudly sang Jewish songs as they harvested with sickles, but if the wheat had been planted in well-prepared soil, a single Arab woman could have harvested the same amount of wheat in half the time and at a fifth of the cost.[16] Arab workers, he pointed out, often had skills that Jewish laborers lacked, and were sometimes resistant to mosquito-borne diseases that took a heavy toll on unadapted Jewish workers, especially in fields, vineyards, and orchards near the swampy coast. When the Arab laborers were replaced by untrained Jewish workers, production fell, Arabs could not find work, and the Jewish settlements found themselves dependent on "corrupt Turkish authorities to maintain law and order," or on their own institutions, which "these disturbing elements sometimes disregarded." Aaronsohn sarcastically pointed out that the opposition to Arab labor amounted to "a handful of fanatical talkers trying to 'protect' the poor Arabs from 'capitalistic exploitation' and, in order to do it, generously forbidding them to work at all."

The dispute went beyond the issue of Arab labor. Many of the Arabs in villages near the Jewish settlements fished, sharecropped, or raised sheep, goats, or cattle. The village of Faradis was close enough to Zichron that Arab shepherds were sometimes caught grazing their animals at night in the Zichron fields. The incidents could sometimes be defused with face-saving explanations ("The cows wandered when the boy watching them fell asleep!") and restitution, but there were also blatant cases of stolen crops, draft animals, and riding horses. As the farms and the village at Zichron developed, the incidents and accusations of thefts, vandalism, and robbery escalated. Some of the alleged incidents were real, others perhaps owed as much to fear or hysteria as to actual encounters. In time the climate of mutual distrust and reports of robberies and threats on the roads surrounding the village created a strong feeling of insecurity for many in Zichron.

In reaction to incidents like brigands robbing carriages and Arab youths attacking and beating the physician of the village unconscious when he tried to "defend the honor" of a girl of sixteen riding with him, a group of young people, grown children of the original settlers, formed "a strong society for the defense of the life and honor of our villagers and of our people at large."[17] They called themselves Gideonites, after the Gideon of the book of Judges who mobilized a defense force that put an end to raids on the Israelites by the Midianites and Amalkites. Elsewhere in Palestine Ha-Shomer groups organized for the same purpose—to protect second-aliyah kibbutzim—sometimes sharing a single horse and gun. The Gideonites of Zichron held meetings with the trappings of secrecy and conspiracy that made for strong bonds and accentuated their dedication and fervor. In a group portrait they posed with firm expressions, their dress ranging from keffiyas to scattered articles from military uniforms. Armed with revolvers, shotguns, and rifles their families owned for self-protection, they organized patrols of the roads and farms, and encouraged the formation of similar organizations at other settlements. At Zichron Aaron Aaronsohn's younger brother Alex was a leader of the group. The Gideonites reloaded cartridges for their guns on the Aaronsohns' kitchen table.

If some in Zichron praised the Gideonites and welcomed their efforts to organize social and cultural events, and to secure authority for the local Zichron Committee, the organization also drew strong opposition from some older members of the community. Some in the yishuv (settlement) called the Gideonites "Jewish anti-Semites." Others, perhaps no more friendly to the local Arabs than the Gideonites, were convinced that any confrontation with Arabs or with the authorities was counterproductive, and might threaten the privileges that had been won through negotiation and baksheesh. They campaigned against what they called the "private army" in Zichron. The emphasis on negotiation, partly inherited from Herzl's own efforts to negotiate with the kaiser and the sultan, was so ingrained that even aspiring second-aliyah Zionists like David Ben-Gurion prepared for leadership in the Jewish community by wearing a tarboosh and studying Turkish law at the University of Constantinople. "In order to get anywhere with Turkish authorities," he said, "we needed to know the Turkish language, Turkish law, and more about the Ottoman system of government."

Aaron was not a Gideonite—he was too old for their secret meetings and conspiratorial plotting—but he shared some of their views, and his fame and name made him the lightning rod for criticism of them and their positions. We "have strictly avoided Arab infiltration in our villages," he wrote, "and we are glad of it. From national, cultural, educational, technical and mere hygienic points of view this policy has had to be strictly adhered to; otherwise the whole Jewish Renaissance movement would fail."[18] In this dispute, as in the labor disputes with the second-aliyah Zionists, or his disputes with the Rothschild managers at the school in Metulla, or with his bosses at the estate he had managed in Anatolia, Aaron was unwilling to back down when he knew he was right. His agricultural research station remained a dream.

~

Early in the winter of 1909 the German paleontologist and botanist George August Schweinfurth sent a clipping from a Munich newspaper about Aaronsohn's discovery of wild wheat to David Fairchild, a research botanist at the USDA in Washington. Fairchild was so intrigued that he invited Aaronsohn to visit the United States to explore the subject with American researchers. Before Aaronsohn sailed from Italy to New York on June 1 he wrote his family that he hoped to meet influential and wealthy Jews in New York, but he knew that they would not accept the importance of his research until it was first acknowledged by gentile experts.[19]

When Aaronsohn arrived at Fairchild's office in Washington he explained that he had no formal scientific education except at Grignon, but that he had been an avid collector of botanical and geological books, and had conducted most of his research on his own, without the benefit of an institutional affiliation or funding. They spoke German—Aaronsohn didn't know English—but Fairchild was impressed: "I soon discovered that I was in the presence of an extraordinary man. Although Aaronsohn had never been there, his knowledge of California almost equaled his knowledge of Palestine. No foreigner had ever been in my office who had so keen an understanding of the soils, climates, and adaptability of plants to their environment."[20]

Within a week of his arrival, Aaronsohn was discussing the flora of Palestine and California with USDA scientists—in English—and after a few weeks he addressed a meeting of botanists. The researchers at the USDA were particularly interested in Aaronsohn's findings on crop varieties appropriate to the soils, climate, and geology of Palestine. California was then rapidly developing as the garden of America, and the climate and soil conditions were remarkably similar to those of Palestine. Aaronsohn seemed to know useful information on every detail of agriculture. "He was one of those rare pioneer minds which quickly leap to the essentials," Fairchild remembered. He was so impressed by Aaronsohn's breadth of knowledge and quick ability with language that he invited him to write an article on the cultivated plants of Palestine for the USDA's *Bulletin,* their most prestigious research publication. Aaronsohn's only previous writing had been in French or Hebrew, but he took on the project and promised to have seed samples of wild emmer and other plants collected in Palestine so that they could be sent and tested as crops in the United States. Fairchild also arranged a trip to put Aaronsohn in touch with agricultural researchers in the western states. "I have a special request to make of you," Aaronsohn said as he boarded the train for California, "but I will save it until I see you in the fall."

When Aaronsohn returned to Washington he brought Fairchild the page proofs of his article for the *Bulletin,* and reminded him that he had a request to make: "I want you to introduce me to some of the wealthy Jews in this country."[21] Fairchild said he only knew one prominent Jew, Cyrus Adler, the former librarian of the Smithsonian Institution who had recently accepted the presidency of Dropsie College, a noted institution of Jewish study in Philadelphia. Adler would later become the first lay chancellor of the Jewish Theological Seminary in New York. The next Sunday Fairchild and Aaronsohn traveled to Philadelphia to call on Adler, who introduced them to his houseguest, Oscar Strauss, the U.S. secretary of labor and commerce from 1906 to 1909 and the first Jewish member of the cabinet. Strauss's brother Nathan, the founder and owner of Macy's department store, was one of the best-known philanthropists in America.

Aaronsohn could be engaging and charming when he talked about his research, and in Adler and Strauss he had an ideal audience. Like many educated men of their day, they were proud of their wide-ranging interests and receptive to an energetic presentation like Aaronsohn's, with its dazzling combination of history, archaeology, agronomy, and science. Quoting Josephus and the Bible, and citing statistics of crop yields from experiments with his newly developed cultivation and irrigation techniques, Aaronsohn argued that with innovative agricultural techniques even the seemingly barren lands of Palestine could be fertile and productive. When Aaronsohn described his discovery of wild wheat, Adler and Strauss—as Aaronsohn had predicted—asked Fairchild whether the discovery would revolutionize wheat production. Fairchild hedged. Only the long-term results from wheat breeders would tell for sure, he said, but he enthusiastically vouched for the importance of Aaronsohn's research and the potential contributions of an experimental station in Palestine. By the end of the afternoon Aaronsohn had a letter of introduction to

Julius Mack, a judge on the appellate court of Illinois and an early supporter of Zionism, who was well connected and respected in the intellectual and financial communities of Chicago.[22]

On his way to give a series of presentations across the country, Aaronsohn stopped in Chicago and called on Judge Mack. He immediately impressed Mack, who as a committed Zionist was thrilled that the discovery of the earliest known wheat had taken place in Palestine. Mack took Aaronsohn to meet his friend Julius Rosenwald, the founder and chairman of Sears Roebuck & Co., and the two Chicagoans spent the day listening to Aaronsohn's stories of his research and its future possibilities. Rosenwald shared Judge Mack's enthusiasm for the articulate and energetic young Aaronsohn, but with reservations. If Zionism was a popular cause in the Russian and Polish Jewish neighborhoods on the west side of Chicago, the wealthy German Jews of the north side, like Rosenwald, were skeptical or downright hostile. At one of the Sunday morning services then typical for Reform Jews, Rosenwald's rabbi, Emil Hirsch, had thundered: "We are not Zionist. As long as I am in this pulpit Sinai Congregation will be unalterably opposed to Zionism. There is no cause for Zionism in America. Let those who favor a return to Jerusalem go there if they will."[23] As he listened to Aaronsohn, Julius Rosenwald made it clear that he was more interested in Springfield, Illinois, than in Jerusalem. But Rosenwald considered himself adept at identifying talent, commitment, and good ideas. Like his contemporaries Andrew Carnegie and John D. Rockefeller, he was a diligent philanthropist, fond of the Jeffersonian axiom that the "earth belongs to the living," and a firm believer that each generation should face its own problems.[24] And like Carnegie he favored lifetime rather than testamentary giving, applying the same critical due diligence to eleemosynary proposals that he would apply to a business proposition for Sears Roebuck & Co.

After a circuitous route that took him from Chicago to St. Paul, Lincoln (Nebraska), Fort Collins, Denver, and stops in Utah, Washington, and Oregon, Aaronsohn reached California, where he was fascinated to see up close the climate, soils, terrain, and plants he had studied for so long. In Berkeley the head of the agriculture school of the University of California, Professor Eugene Hilgrad, was particularly warm and welcoming. For days Aaronsohn met Hilgrad's colleagues and friends at parties, seminars, and on excursions. It was only when he was taken to the office of the president of the university that Aaronsohn realized that the warm invitations had all been an hors d'oeuvre. Hilgrad was retiring and Aaronsohn was offered Hilgrad's chair as professor and head of the agriculture department. It was an amazing opportunity: he was thirty-three years old, with no degree from any university. Agriculture was a huge industry in California, the University of California was in the midst of an effort to transform itself into a major research university in the sciences, and they were offering him incomparable laboratories and a virtually unlimited budget for research. Aaronsohn's reputation and friendships among the influential and wealthy men he had met in the eastern United States promised continued funding and a receptive audience for his work. His sisters, by mail, urged him to accept the offer.

Aaron wrote back to Sarah and Rivka that he had reservations about some aspects of American culture, especially the greed and lack of conscience he saw in American business, and about contradictions in American society. America seemed short of labor and employed Chinese and Japanese workers, even as they campaigned for strong immigration laws against the Chinese and Japanese; they grew grapes and had a wine industry even as a campaign was being waged in favor of prohibition. He admired the agricultural development of Colorado, which he attributed to investment capital, and contrasted it with the agricultural wasteland of capital-starved Utah and the destruction of the landscape in California by wealth-crazed gold miners. He was especially surprised and confused by many Jews he had met. Aaron was not observant, but he had grown up amid those, like his father, who attended traditional services in the Zichron synagogue. When he was taken to an American Reform service—Reform Judaism did not exist in Palestine—he found the rituals hypocritical and off-putting. A rabbi he met in New York told Aaron that he and his brother Alexander, who had come to Washington to work for the USDA, did not "look like Jews," and meant it as a compliment. Aaron decided that if he was going to have to battle—he seemed to accept that he would always be caught up in battles—he would rather fight the enemies in Palestine than the hypocrisy in American society. It was one way of saying that agronomy was only a stepping-stone on his agenda. He turned down the professorship.

On the way back to Washington he stopped at a Dryland Conference in Montana, where he addressed an audience of 1,500 and found himself the center of attention. He wrote to his sister that it took more than Jewish chutzpah to speak to an audience that large in a language he hadn't even known four months earlier.[25] But already Aaronsohn was tired of being lionized in America. Reporters followed him from city to city, writing that his research would double wheat production and might be the most important discovery ever made in the science of food production.[26] The University of California promised support for his research even after he turned down the professorship. Entrepreneurs approached him with schemes for developing the American West and offered to send him on lecture tours to promote the "new agriculture."

When he stopped again in Chicago Judge Mack and Julius Rosenwald took him out to dinner with a group of botanists from the University of Chicago, including Roscoe Pound, the former state botanist, who invited Aaronsohn to lecture before their society. A few days later David Fairchild was surprised to receive a phone call from Aaronsohn inviting him to come to New York to have lunch with Rosenwald at Delmonico's.[27] At the restaurant Rosenwald asked Fairchild whether Aaronsohn's discovery of wild wheat would "profoundly affect wheat-growing throughout the world." Fairchild hemmed and hawed, explaining that experiments on the wild wheat were still in progress. But even without the wild wheat, he assured Rosenwald, the research program at Aaronsohn's proposed experimental station would be vitally important for the future of agriculture worldwide. He mentioned

Aaronsohn's forthcoming *Bulletin* article on the plants of Palestine and how important the catalog would be for agricultural development in California. He probably quoted the expression *"ex Oriente lux"* from the opening paragraph of Aaronsohn's article.[28]

Fairchild's answers confirmed Rosenwald's own appraisal of Aaronsohn's talents, energy, and self-assurance. Rosenwald agreed to serve as president of the Jewish Agricultural Experiment Station (JAES), which would be incorporated in the United States and established at Athlit, on the coast of Palestine, under Aaron Aaronsohn's direction. Rosenwald assembled a distinguished board of trustees for the organization, people who had been impressed by Aaronsohn's dynamism and knowledge and were wealthy enough to contribute to the project: Judge Mack, Cyrus Adler, Nathan Strauss, Rabbi Judah Magnes of Temple Emanu-El in New York, labor lawyer and president of Temple Emanu-El Louis Marshall, soap magnate Samuel Fels, businessman and philanthropist Adolph Lewisohn, New York University chemist Morris Loeb, bankers Jacob Schiff and Paul M. Warburg, and Henrietta Szold, who would later found Hadassah. Their individual pledges to the project ranged from $300 (Louis Marshall, Adolph Lewisohn, Morris Loeb) to $12,000 (Jacob Schiff). The total was almost $20,000.[29] A few of the trustees, like Henrietta Szold, were ardent Zionists, and they supported the experimental station to put Jewish Palestine on the world scientific map, and for the potential of developing increased crop production in Palestine. Judge Mack saw Aaronsohn as the symbol of a new kind of Jew, contrasting him with the image of the "ordinary Jewish immigrant in America," and suggesting that men like Aaronsohn were a "vital answer to the doubters and critics of Zionism."[30] Others on the board, including Rosenwald, questioned the economic viability of a Jewish homeland but saw the research station as a promising investment to develop agricultural techniques and seed stocks for California and the world. Rosenwald may also have had a business motive for supporting Aaronsohn's research. The rural population of the United States shopped from the ubiquitous Sears Roebuck catalogs: an investment in agricultural research was an investment in the potential market for his company.

As delighted as he was with the commitment to his research station, Aaronsohn found the American obsession with money distressing. He wrote to his sisters about an American doctor he had met who was worth more than $100,000 but who seemed utterly without culture or any enjoyment of life, living and working only for money. When the trustees of the research station offered him an annual salary of $2,500 Aaronsohn only accepted $2,000, saying that a higher salary could cause demoralization among the workers at the station.[31]

His American trip had been successful beyond his dreams, but when Aaron Aaronsohn returned to Palestine with a certificate of incorporation and promises of funding for his experimental station, he still had to face the Turkish bureaucracy and the fractious splits in the Zionist movement. Obtaining the needed permits from the Ottoman officials was the easy part. From long years of experience Aaronsohn had learned the skill of finding loopholes in the Ottoman regulations and the art of paying the baksheesh that smoothed application procedures and forestalled last-minute glitches. The land in Athlit was owned by the JCA (Jewish Colonization Association), originally funded by the eccentric German Jewish millionaire Baron Maurice de Hirsch to promote the emigration of Russian Jews to Argentina. Later the JCA was involved in farming ventures in Palestine as Baron de Hirsch and Baron Edmund Rothschild competed in their efforts, much as Rockefeller and Carnegie competed in their eleemosynary ventures in the United States. When Jacob Schiff heard that a Zionist organization would donate the land for the experimental station, he was sufficiently concerned to offer to buy the land himself and donate it.[32] Ottoman regulations made it impossible for an American to own the land, and Schiff ultimately softened his qualms about working with an openly Zionist organization.

By 1910 the trust had the needed permits, and Aaronsohn could begin construction on a laboratory and an American Midwest–style windmill for the experimental station. He planted rows of stately palm trees on either side of the road leading into the farm. The Judean palm, praised for its beauty, shade, and medicinal qualities, and a stand-in for the tree of life in the Bible and the Qur'an,[33] had all but been destroyed by the crusaders in Palestine. The trees Aaronsohn planted were small, but from his soil tests and plant surveys he was confident that they would flourish.

~

The Ottoman government of Sultan Abdul Hamid was an anachronism, marvelous in the multinational adaptability of its archaic institutions, but so unyielding and inefficient that it had become a target for reformers bent on wholesale modernization. In Salonika in 1908 Mehmed Talaat, the founder of a secret society that had quietly opposed Ottoman rule, began to recruit members to a new political party, the Committee of Union and Progress, or CUP. His first recruit was Djemal Bey, a staff officer in the Turkish Third Army. Initiates to the party swore an oath on the Qur'an and on a gun. When a party member named Enver was ordered to Constantinople, he hid in the hills behind Salonika, and the troops the sultan sent to ferret him out promptly joined the rebels. Other party members emerged from their honeycombed positions in the army and the Ottoman bureaucracy, and the party suddenly became a visible and a powerful force. A year later the sultan abdicated in favor of his brother, a figurehead who yielded substantial power to the new party.

The British and some other foreign observers of the rise of the new party concluded—because of its radical agenda and its roots in Salonika, a city with a large Jewish population—that the CUP was dominated by foreigners, Jews, and Freemasons, and was following in the footsteps of the French Revolution.[34] In reality the CUP was fiercely Turkish and chauvinistic. Its members were called Young Turks, an expression that came into general use to describe brash young rebels against hidebound institutions and outmoded leadership. On paper the ideals of the CUP were appealing, promising long-needed modernization and change, and the Young Turks initially were greeted with wide enthusiasm, as a hope for reform after centuries of Ottoman stagnation. But after the deposition of the sultan, those who could follow the news—not a large number in a sprawling empire with poor communications, widespread illiteracy, and few newspapers with substantial circulation—realized that the reformist party and its Young Turk government were also centralizing their authority in Constantinople, which many Turkish nationalists had begun to call Istanbul, and were pushing for the aggressive Turkification of the multinational Ottoman Empire. Calling themselves the Unionists, they accused anyone who opposed the government of being members of the party of decentralization.[35]

The xenophobia of the new government emerged in increasingly vituperative speeches against foreigners and the Armenian minority. Broadsides blamed the Armenians for alleged economic exploitation, greed, connections to foreign powers, discrimination against Muslims and Turks, and disloyalty. As the broadsides were distributed and the speeches echoed in cruder formats in the provinces of the empire, the accusations against the Armenians became broader and uglier—the outside edge of a widespread campaign to deliberately erode the multicultural tolerance and political guarantees to the minorities that had evolved over almost four centuries of Ottoman rule. The immediate effects were minor. The official minorities of the empire—Jews, Armenians, Greeks, Kurds, Shia Muslims, Circassians—had long refined their bureaucratic skills, and had enjoyed the relative tolerance and lax bureaucracy of the last half of the nineteenth and early twentieth centuries. The Jews outside of Palestine especially had long enjoyed a privileged minority status, rewarded with bureaucratic positions in finance and tax collecting in exchange for their loyalty to the government and their quiet acquiescence to Islamic cultural and political domination. The rhetoric of the Young Turks and the increasingly harsh tone of newspaper editorials, public speeches, demonstrations, and shouts on the streets suggested that the future might be very different for the minorities, prompting some groups to articulate new political identities. In Palestine the native Arabs, who until then had been content to consider themselves Syrians, began for the first time to call themselves Palestinians.[36]

It was in that climate of political reform and clamors for change that Aaron Aaronsohn began to recruit a staff for the experimental station. The only experienced agronomists in Palestine were the Rothschild-trained graduates of the local agronomy programs, but Aaronsohn had spent enough time at Metulla to know that they were rigid in their curricula and programs, obsessed with French production techniques and varietals, and reluctant to experiment with new techniques and crops. Remembering their haughty orders in French, which many of the older settlers did not understand, Aaronsohn planned for the research station to issue regular reports in Hebrew, making the practical lessons of their research available directly and without delay. Instead of hiring experienced agronomists, he turned to men and women with little or no farming experience but who were fired up with the same enthusiastic, energetic, idealistic, and practical Zionism that had motivated his own research. He began his recruiting with members of his own family and the Gideonites.

He also hired Avshalom Feinberg, who already had a reputation as a poet in Palestine. Feinberg's parents were Russian intellectuals, members of BILU,[37] a return-to-the-land society, who had come to Rishon le Zion, an early Rothschild settlement between Jerusalem and Jaffa, around the same time Aaron's parents had come to Zichron. Avshalom's father was expelled from Rishon le Zion for openly opposing the Rothschild management, and with a small group of families he established an independent colony on the southern coast of Palestine at Gadera. Avshalom was born there in 1889, before the family moved to Hadera, on the Plain of Sharon south of Caesarea, where a dozen families heroically drained malarial swamps to recover farmland. Avshalom's strongest childhood memory was watching his father bent over in the swamps, planting the hundreds of eucalyptus trees that were needed to drain the land.

Avshalom was schooled by a local Arab scholar, and was soon fluent in Arabic as well as Hebrew and French. He wrote poetry even as a boy, and at fifteen was sent to France for more schooling. In four years in Paris he admired and eventually began to imitate the nationalist literature from newly emancipated countries like Bulgaria, Greece, and Romania. His letters to his family read like liberation manifestos:

> Do we stand at the opening of a joyous era in which law will prevail over power, in which the small and weary, the sick and hungry will be allowed to live, to breathe, to be sated and content and perhaps even to taste the taste of happiness? The time has come in which the small, oppressed peoples can take their place at the table, in the dining room of the nations, to nourish their physical body, and perhaps even enter the hall where all of the satiated may consider matters of faith, intellect and spirit! . . . The strength of armies is great these days but perhaps there is greater strength in a people which declares: we want a life of freedom and dignity, a life without shame, fear or enslavement, and we would rather die as heroes than live like this; we would rather drown in the blood of our enemies and die full of strength and dignity.[38]

When the young rebel returned from Paris he found himself arguing with his father constantly. Israel Feinberg believed that hard work—like the labor that had drained the Hadera swamps—diligent payments of baksheesh to the Turkish authorities, and a steady, gradual program of buying up Arab lands was enough to guarantee the future of Jewish Palestine. Avshalom Feinberg, with the revolutionary convictions and exuberance of youth, and fresh from reading George Eliot's *Daniel Deronda* and Laurence Oliphant's *The Land of Gilead, with Excursions in the Lebanon,* was impatient with gradualism, unwilling to countenance the bribes to corrupt authorities, the snail's pace of land acquisitions, and the second-class status of the Jews of Palestine. He became a Gideonite, leading a movement in Hadera like the one in Zichron. The Jewish settlements, he wrote, were bastions in "a struggle between culture and savagery. The reclamation of the desolate land of Palestine had been made possible by Jewish fortitude and firmness toward the Arabs. Jewish achievements in the country would be secure only if protected by barbed-wire fences." His contempt for Arabs was deep: "I have lived among them all my life and it would be difficult to sway me from my opinion that there is no more cowardly, hypocritical, and false race than this one."[39]

Aaron Aaronsohn befriended the Feinberg family when he was in his own rebellion against the rigid Rothschild administration of the settlements; Avshalom Feinberg was ten years old at the time. When Feinberg and Aaronsohn met again in 1911, they discovered an immediate rapport despite the thirteen-year difference in their ages. Feinberg had little experience in agricultural research, but he was bright, articulate, and fiercely committed to Zionism, and he and Aaronsohn shared many convictions, especially an aversion to what they both saw as the naïveté of the bare-foot ones. They differed in their views of the Ottoman government, for which Feinberg had no use and which Aaronsohn thought might provide opportunities for the development of the yishuv. Despite their political differences Aaronsohn seems to have recognized that Feinberg's passionate ideals and poetic talents were an ideal complement to his own scientific skills. If Aaronsohn's experiments in agronomy could develop the means to feed a Jewish nation, Feinberg's passion and poetry could fuel the revolutionary ideals that would be needed to overcome the frightened, reactionary opposition to change. They formed an immediate and deep friendship, and Aaronsohn appointed Feinberg director of a branch of the research station in Hadera.

None of the new staff had formal agricultural training. Some had worked on farms, and Alex, Sarah, and Rivka Aaronsohn had gathered around the dining table to sort and classify the specimens for Aaron's geological and botanical collections. What bound the group together was disillusionment with the status quo in the Jewish settlements and a shared enthusiasm for the agricultural research program and its long-term political application. At the research station they watched, read, and discussed politics endlessly. Enough of them had spent time in Europe and followed politics in foreign countries to be familiar with the upsurge of nationalist movements in territories like Greece, Romania, and Bulgaria that had once been part of the Ottoman Empire. They tracked the political and economic interests of the European powers and the United States in the Middle East, and the opportunities that chinks between the Great Powers and the precarious position of the Ottoman Empire could offer to aspiring peoples. From Egypt to Persia, from southeast Europe and the Caucasus to the tip of the Arabian Peninsula, the Ottoman Empire was stretched thin, vulnerable to implosion from within and predations from the stronger powers outside. The group at Athlit was determined not to miss out on those opportunities.

As they cleared and planted the first fields and orchards at the experimental station, Aaronsohn stayed in touch with David Fairchild at the USDA, and was appointed an unpaid associate; then in 1911, he was promoted to a $300-per-year consultant.[40] He continued to receive invitations to speak on dry-land farming and wheat production from Europe and America, and took advantage of the travel subsidies to pursue research on odd crops and climates. In 1911 he spent two months in Egypt studying dates, leaving Avshalom Feinberg in charge of the experimental station. Feinberg, despite a lack of formal training in agronomy, had a good eye for detail, and he became expert at observing flora and land use—the same skills that had led to Aaronsohn's fame.[41] Coincidentally, they were also good skills for a spy.

When the laboratory was expanded, a research library added, and more fields and orchards brought under cultivation, the experimental station took on the appearance and status of a full-fledged scientific research facility. The palm-lined road leading up to the station was improved and paved—a visitor wrote that it was "the one well-metalled piece of road in the country"[42]—and a sign in English and Hebrew identified it as the JEWISH AGRICULTURAL EXPERIMENT STATION. Before long the experimental plots at the research station were producing more wheat, barley, and oats per *dunam*[43] than long-established farms on much better soils. The production Aaronsohn and his colleagues achieved suited his agenda exactly, and the umbrella of research allowed them to travel widely within Palestine, ostensibly to collect seed samples, observe cultivation and irrigation techniques, and to measure crop yields and quality. For the young researchers, who often had grown up on a single settlement or in Jaffa or Haifa, it was an opportunity to explore Palestine.

As the station program matured enough to function without him, Aaronsohn took time in 1913 to return to the United States to lecture and meet with friends like Judge Mack in Chicago and Felix Frankfurter, including a lunch where he was seated next to former president Theodore Roosevelt. Aaronsohn recounted his discovery of wild wheat, and to the astonishment of Mack and Frankfurter, who knew Roosevelt's reputation as a nonstop talker, the former president did not interrupt except to ask whom Aaronsohn meant by his frequent references to *we*. "From now on," Aaronsohn wrote in his diary, "my reputation will be the man who had made the Colonel shut up for 101 minutes."[44]

At the Parker House in Boston, Mack and Aaronsohn had supper with labor theorist Harold Laski and the *New Republic* critic Francis Hackett. Hackett and Mack watched while, "like a little angry cock, Harold Laski walked round and round Aaronsohn, who watched him through his light eyelashes with benevolent but apprehensive eyes." The anticipated cockfight ended before it began. When the waiter appeared with caviar, Aaronsohn said, "That is Beluga caviar. I did not ask for Beluga caviar. I asked for Astrakhan caviar." The waiter crumbled. "If the Parker House could have blushed," Hackett remembered, "it blushed." The waiter somehow found Astrakhan caviar, and even Laski, who by proletarian preference lived on fish and chips, dove in.[45]

On the same trip Judge Mack introduced Aaronsohn to Louis Brandeis, then perhaps the most famous and most successful attorney in America. Brandeis was soon speaking about "one of the most interesting, brilliant and remarkable men I have ever met." Brandeis liked to repeat a story he attributed to Aaronsohn, that "in Palestine, in the little communities that have grown up in the last thirty-two years and now number 10,000 Jewish souls, not a single crime was known to have been committed by one of our people during all that time" because "every member of those communities is brought up to realize his obligations to his people," and that the children exhibited "none of the weakness, none of the servility, which they or their parents had when they came to Palestine." Brandeis later told others, including Mrs. Rosenwald, that meeting Aaronsohn and realizing that Palestine could produce individuals like him was what finally converted him to Zionism.[46]

After Aaronsohn returned to Palestine Julius Rosenwald and his wife visited Athlit. Rosenwald was impressed by the progress of the orchards on the once-barren land, but mostly remembered the summer flies and was skeptical about the long-term future of the Jewish settlements. He offered Aaronsohn half a million dollars if he would leave Palestine and resettle in the United States to carry on his research. Aaronsohn declined.[47] Instead, he built a house for himself in Zichron, next to his family's house on Founders Street. The house was compact but relatively luxurious, with dark wood paneling, bookshelves in every room to hold his ever-expanding library, and beautiful inlaid furniture from Damascus. In the bathroom he put a scale, unusual in a private home then and a token of his continuing battle with his weight. The Aaronsohns had always been close as a family, and with his brother and his sisters working at the research station, Aaron's home became an extension of the station.

Avshalom Feinberg frequently rode up to Zichron from Hadera, especially after he met Aaron's sisters, Sarah and Rivka, at a Purim ball. His horse was famed as the best jumper and one of the fastest racehorses in Palestine, and Feinberg was a dashing rider. Sarah, the older of the two sisters, was a beautiful and sensuous woman, tall like her brother, with wide-set blue eyes and the full-bosomed figure that was considered fashionable and alluring in the prewar years. She had been educated at the village school in Zichron; traveled in Switzerland, Italy, and Germany; read voraciously in Hebrew, French, Yiddish, and German; and was a fearless and adventurous horsewoman who had explored the Carmel valleys on her horse, Tayar. Sarah's younger sister, Rivka, was a tiny woman, strikingly fair, with open features that were sometimes compared to Rembrandt's often painted first wife, Saskia. Rivka was shy and retiring, not surprising for the youngest and smallest in a family of big and outspoken people. She became the custodian of Aaron's botanical collections in the research station in Athlit and at his home in Zichron, but never thought of herself as a full-fledged member of the experimental station.

Sarah and Rivka had grown up in the strait-laced settlement of Zichron Ya'aqov, in a household that had long been focused on the hardships and joys of farming, the petty politics of dealings with the Rothschild agents, and Aaron's science. Feinberg, with his liberation poetry and fiery critiques of the Turkish government, his soft green-brown eyes, his dash and reputation as a horseman and marksman, and his Byronic intensity, arrived at the Aaronsohn household like a *sharav,* the hot easterly wind that blew off the desert, so disturbing in its effect that courts would consider it a mitigating factor in criminal trials. Sarah and Rivka both fell in love with him.

Even Aaron did not realize how much their love for Avshalom Feinberg would become intertwined with the future of Jewish Palestine.

The Archaeologist

The perfectly hopeless vulgarity of the half-Europeanized Arab is appalling. Better a thousand times the Arab untouched. The foreigners come out here always to teach, whereas they had much better learn, for in everything but wits and knowledge the Arab is generally the better man of the two.

—T. E. Lawrence[1]

After his summer of adventure in Syria and Palestine, Lawrence moved into the detached bungalow at his parents' home. A side gate allowed him to come and go as he pleased, a rare freedom for an undergraduate, and to indulge his passion for solitude and fantasy, including reading all night long without the social or practical constraints of college regulations. "You know, I think," he wrote to his mother, "the joy of getting into a strange country in a book at home when I have shut my door and the town is in bed—and I know that nothing, not even the dawn—can disturb me in my curtains. . . . Why does one not like things if there are other people about? Why cannot one make one's books live except in the night, after hours of straining? . . . If you can get the right book at the right time you taste joys—not only bodily, physical, but spiritual also, which pass one out above and beyond one's miserable self."[2]

One of his fantasies was to establish a serious press for fine books, a pursuit fueled by his enthusiasm for William Morris. Vyvyan Richards, an Oxford friend two years older, was to be Lawrence's partner in the venture. Lawrence's parents were not enthusiastic about funding a project with little commercial promise, and seem to have recognized that if Lawrence was enamored with the ideals of William Morris, Vyvyan Richards was mostly enamored with Lawrence. "Quite frankly for me it was love at first sight," Richards later admitted. "He [Lawrence] had neither flesh nor carnality of any kind; he just did not understand. . . . He never gave the slightest sign that he understood my motives or fathomed my desires."[3]

Richards's love was unrequited. Lawrence's own love interest was a woman named Janet Laurie. They had met as children: her father was an estate agent in New Forest when the Lawrences lived there from 1894 to 1896. In 1899 Janet was sent to Oxford for boarding school, and after she graduated she continued to visit the Lawrences. Ned saw her often. "I always spent Sunday afternoon at tea with him," Janet Laurie recalled, "and sort of watched him grow up." She occasionally visited him in the detached bungalow, but mostly he kept his distance, quietly observing her from afar. Lawrence was shy and reticent around women, and when he and Janet were together their relationship was mostly teasing: Janet had been a tomboy, and Ned teased her about not being a boy. They did not discuss their feelings for each other, he told only a few confidants that he loved Janet, and she was only vaguely aware of his feelings. When Lawrence was around nineteen, Janet once said to him, "Ned, you never look me in the eye." He answered, "It gives me a painful sensation to look into your eyes." He was two years younger than Janet, very boyish-looking, overly shy, and the same height or shorter than she. She never seriously considered him as a suitor.

One night, when Ned was twenty-one and still an undergraduate, Janet Laurie came to the Lawrence home for dinner and stayed at the table after dinner to talk. Lawrence bolted the door so the parlor maid would not disturb them. They were joking about his brothers when Lawrence suddenly proposed marriage. Janet believed the proposal was serious, but she was so taken aback—there had been no warning, no lead-in to the delicate subject, not even a kiss—that she laughed at him. Lawrence said something like "Oh, I see," or "All right," but he seemed hurt, and the subject was quickly dropped.[4] Her laughter was undoubtedly painful for a young man who had been self-conscious about his short stature, lack of conventional graces, and shy awkwardness around women. It may have been traumatic: Lawrence never again had a serious relationship with a woman. Robert Graves later wrote that Lawrence

> could never squarely face the fact of the existence of women; he placed them in general on a romantic plane remote from reality, in which their actual presence made him rather uncomfortable. He seems to have felt at home only with practical not-very-young women of the good-wife-and-mother type; and had a peculiar sympathy for childless married women: He was afraid of women who thought for themselves. . . . He also told me once at Oxford that women were, historically, incapable of writing or painting anything first-class.[5]

~

To pursue an academic career Lawrence needed to do well on his finals, the six days of written testing that determined graduation and standing at Oxford. He had opted to supplement his finals with a thesis, and during the winter of 1909–10 he finished "The Influence of the Crusades on European Military Architecture—to the End of the XIIth Century," which together with his examination results earned him a first-class honors degree in modern history. His record was not spectacular—one of his examiners called it a "safe first"—and he must have known that academics were notoriously underpaid in Britain and that there was little opportunity for fame, glory, or exalted success in the narrow world of the universities. But for a young man who had always been more comfortable alone than around his contemporaries, the academic life was a chance to read, research, and write. Lawrence thought he might be able to pursue a B.Litt. that would combine his interests in medieval poetry, history, architecture, and archaeology. Jesus College gave him a grant of £50 for the project.

Even as he put together a plan of study, his fantasies of exploration and the Middle East persisted. He found a man who could get him the camera he wanted for his next trip to Syria at "half price," and searched out copies of Doughty's *Travels in Arabia Deserta* and David George Hogarth's *Wandering Scholar in the Levant,* calling the latter "one of the best travel books ever written."[6] Lawrence was inspired by Doughty's explanation that he had gone to Arabia "to redeem the English language from the slough into which it had fallen since the time of Spenser,"[7] and imagined books he would someday write—a "monumental work on the Crusades," an account of the intellectual and social background of Christ in the Galilee and Syria, and a travel book of adventures in "seven type-cities of the East"—not the precisely framed monographs of an academic career, but sweeping works, each broad in scope and clearly intended for a wide audience. Like many wannabe authors, he composed titles before he had written a single word of the proposed books: the volume on the Crusades would be called *Richard,* after his favorite hero of the period, and the travel book would take its title from Proverbs 1:9: "Wisdom has built her house, she has hewn her seven pillars."[8] Lawrence's rephrasing—*Seven Pillars of Wisdom*—may have been inspired by John Ruskin's *Seven Lamps of Architecture*.

While Lawrence was tentatively planning research on medieval pottery, David Hogarth, the keeper of the Ashmolean Museum in Oxford, began recruiting for a dig at Carchemish, a Hittite site on the Euphrates River in southern Turkey. The British Museum had sent expeditions to Carchemish in the late 1870s, but much of the fieldwork had been unsupervised and the excavations were poorly documented. In addition to continuing and expanding the general exploration of the site, one goal of the new expedition was to search for a Rosetta stone for the Hittite language. The Jerablus region on the Euphrates, a boundary between the Hittite and Assyrian empires, seemed a likely place to find a tablet with writing in both Hittite, which had not yet been deciphered, and Assyrian cuneiform, which could be read.

Lawrence had never studied the Hittites, knew little about the Carchemish site, hardly knew Hogarth, had no professional archaeological experience, and his only experience in the Middle East had been in the relatively urbanized areas of Palestine and Syria. But when he heard about Hogarth's plans for the dig, he knew the project—serious archaeological research in northern Syria—was exactly what he wanted to do. He asked E. T. Leeds at the Ashmolean Museum, for whom he had worked occasionally on pottery projects, to help. Leeds thought the plans for Carchemish were already in place, but he passed along word of Lawrence's interest, and Hogarth, impressed by Lawrence's Arabic and his intrepid tour on foot in Syria, agreed to take Lawrence on the dig, arranging for Magdalen College to award Lawrence the equivalent of a junior research fellowship of £100 pounds annually through the summer of 1914, enough to cover his expenses except for on-site food and lodging.

In preparation Lawrence studied Assyrian cuneiform on his own, and in December 1910 he sailed to Beirut, then traveled via Aleppo to the American Mission School in Jebail, which he had visited during his 1909 walking tour, and enrolled to study rudimentary written Arabic and the north Syrian Arabic dialect spoken in the Jerablus region. It was mid-March when he and Hogarth finally reached Jerablus and the excavation site on the opposite side of the Euphrates River. The ruins of Carchemish, a ten-acre oval site, had been undisturbed for thirty years.

Lawrence's duties, based on his experience in Arabic and his work on medieval pottery at Oxford, were to write up a journal of the project, draw sculptures and inscriptions, catalog the fragments recovered by the workmen, and to use his Arabic to direct the workmen. When Hogarth returned to the Ashmolean he left the site under the direction of his second-in-command, Campbell Thompson, with Lawrence as Thompson's helper. After only a few weeks together Hogarth had already formed an opinion of Lawrence's talents: "Thompson ought really to have a second helper besides Lawrence. The latter will second him admirably in observing and recording—

in fact he is a far better archaeologist properly speaking than Thompson—but not in driving."[9]

The living arrangements at Carchemish were crude, a cramped and leaky stone house that belonged to a licorice company. Lawrence had experienced rougher living in his travels in Syria, and delighted in the discomfort of his companions:

> . . . from the roof little bits drop all day and all night: and it is full of birds that baptize the bald-heads at their leisure. . . . Then there are the cats: Father (who is only suffered, not encouraged) . . . comes in at the holes in the roof and walls by night, and offends lewdly in our beds. . . . Of late Mother has been in the family way, with Thompson a very gallant midwife. Her four kittens . . . make a ghastly noise in the Expeditionary bedroom half the night: I am a tolerable sleeper, but the others get up two or three times each, and draw beads on each other with revolvers.[10]

His letters to his family and friends, like this one, were not casual scribbles. He saw himself as a writer, and poured out a stream of observations and reactions, both a chronicle of his adventures—the closest we have to a journal or diary—and an effort at artful prose. On the journey to Beirut, his ship had called at Athens, giving him his first look at the Acropolis. "Only this about Athens," he wrote, "that there is an intoxication, a power of possession in its ruins, and the memories that inhabit them, which entirely prevents anyone attempting to describe or estimate them." Despite the intoxication, he attempted a description: "[I] walked through the doorway of the Parthenon, and on into the inner part of it, without really remembering who or where I was. A heaviness in the air made my eyes swim, and wrapped up my senses: I only knew that I, a stranger, was walking on the floor of the place I had most desired to see, the greatest temple of Athene, the palace of art."[11] The awestruck tone was the reaction expected of an educated European visitor to the holy of holies of Greek art, but as in most of Lawrence's letters from this period, intimacy and candor took a backseat to artfulness, cant, and an arch tone, keeping the people he had seen and occasionally met at a comfortable arm's length.

During his journey on foot through Syria and Palestine, Lawrence had also sent home a stream of anecdotal letters about the houses, foods, hospitality, dress, and manners of the people he encountered, sometimes interspersed with comments on the climate, geology, flora, and fauna. Contrived humor was the frequent wrapper for his observations. "The Arabs say that the king of the fleas lives in Tiberias," he wrote, "but I can guarantee he has summer residences elsewhere as well."[12] The same distancing emerges in the photographs Lawrence brought home. In Syria most of his photographs were of the castles he was studying. He had better equipment in Carchemish, and took many photographs, ostensibly to document the archaeological site and excavations. Local natives appear in some of the Carchemish photographs, but as in the descriptions in his letters, there is a deliberate distance between the photographer and his subjects, the standoffishness of a British traveler wary of involvement with the locals.[13]

He was soon engaged with the novelty of his administrative responsibilities, the on-site living arrangements, the scale of the expedition, the challenge of drawing and cataloging the finds at the site, growing curiosity about both Hittite civilization and the native culture in Jerablus and the nearby villages, and the novel experience of living in a virtually all-male society—the women of the villages stayed indoors or at a distance from the intruders. There was also a hint of intrigue, as the planned route of the Berlin–Baghdad Railway, a major transportation link and significant propaganda project of the German empire, passed close to the Carchemish site. The German engineers planned a railway bridge over the Euphrates that would take several years to build, which kept the German-directed construction teams close to the British excavations, and made them a fierce competitor for the local labor needed at the dig. Meissner Pasha, the director of the German railway project, was known to be a collector of antiquities and art objects, and was suspected of having designs on loot from Carchemish.

Carchemish was "tremendous fun, and most exciting and interesting," but it was only a way station toward the life Lawrence had fantasized. After reading Doughty's *Arabia Deserta,* which he found "a book not like other books . . . a bible of its kind,"[14] Lawrence was enamored with the vast open spaces of Arabia Doughty described, a harsh but strikingly beautiful landscape of sand and stone and sky, and the Bedouin, a nomadic people living a lonely, pure life, as lean and stark as the desert stone, sand, and sky. The vivid images of Arabia were a striking contrast to the complexity of Edwardian society, and even to the Syrian villages Lawrence had seen. In place of the waistcoat, britches, jacket, garters, collar, tie, hat, and timepiece of the Edwardian gentleman, symbols of the links to time, place, clubs, and status that confined his life, the Bedouin wore only a simple robe, maybe sandals, a keffiya, and a dagger—each obvious in its purpose, perhaps beautiful in the richness of the material or workmanship, but elegantly simple. The Bedouin roamed as he pleased, not tied down by possessions or those obligations of place, time, and status that defined the civilized Englishman. The Bedouin were noble in their elegant simplicity, living by a rigid code of honor and pride, bound by the unspoken ties of clan and family. Women were all but invisible. Lawrence hadn't met men like those yet.

He was speaking Arabic and learning about Arab culture in Carchemish, and still saw himself as an author, though he hadn't yet written a word of the grand works he had planned. His experiences in Syria and the exercises of his imagination had convinced him that Oxford and book learning and the academic life he had pursued by default were no longer enough, that his books would be better—or perhaps only possible—if he spent time in open country, in the vast spaces of the Arabian deserts, living with the Bedouin, reading their stark lives as poetry. "I am not going to put all my energies into rubbish like writing history, or becoming an archeologist," he wrote home. "I would much rather write a novel even, or become a newspaper correspondent." Hoping to entice him back to Oxford, his parents sent him notices of vacant academic posts, but he was no longer interested. "I am afraid no 'open fellowship' for me," he answered. "I don't think anyone who had tasted the East as I have would give it up half-way, for a seat at high table and a chair in the Bodleian. At any rate I won't."[15]

~

The first year of excavations at Carchemish proved less fruitful and more complicated and expensive than anyone on the expedition had anticipated. By high summer they had not found any indication of a tablet with inscriptions in both Hittite and Assyrian cuneiform, and although their probing digs left the site looking "as though it has small-pox with complications, pits and eruptions everywhere,"[16] they uncovered only some Hittite houses, a courtyard, some limestone-lined graves with bronze ax heads, and some interesting pottery, like terra-cotta model horses, before they had to shut down operations for the year. They did not uncover any major architecture or especially important material, and Hogarth had a challenging task negotiating future funding for the project.

In May 1911 Gertrude Bell visited the Carchemish site. With her striking red hair, green eyes, slender figure, and intrepidity as a traveler and archaeologist in the Middle East, Bell had a reputation as the "queen of the desert." She told Thompson his ideas of digging were prehistoric, and Lawrence and Thompson decided to "squash her" with a display of erudition. In a bravado five-minute lecture they managed to mention Byzantine, crusader, Roman, Hittite, and French architecture, Greek folklore, Assyrian architecture, Mesopotamian ethnology, prehistoric pottery, telephoto lenses, Bronze Age metal technique, George Meredith, Anatole France, the Russian Octobrists, the Young Turk movement, the "construct state in Arabia," the price of riding camels, Assyrian burial customs, and German methods of excavation for the Baghdad railway. And this, Lawrence wrote, "was kind of hors d'oeuvre," which they followed up by each interrogating her on seven or eight subjects before they all had tea. Lawrence admitted in a letter home that he had been afraid she would question their methods in print. He needn't have worried. During the visit

Lawrence wore the shorts and red-tasseled belt of a local bachelor, which convinced the local villagers that he and Gertrude Bell would be married. When she left that evening the villagers would have stoned her had Lawrence not told an "ungallant but expedient lie."[17]

Gertrude Bell would later call Lawrence "an imp" because of his short stature, his elongated head, which she thought belonged on a bigger body, and his habit of wearing trousers that stopped at his ankles, as if he had outgrown them. After this initial meeting she was more forgiving and wrote only that she had spent a "pleasant day" at Carchemish with Mr. Thompson "and a young man called Lawrence (he is going to make a traveler)."[18]

~

Traveler, indeed. Free of responsibilities when the dig shut down for the summer, Lawrence tramped for two weeks among the crusader castles of northern Syria, caught a bad case of dysentery, and went home to Oxford to recuperate. In Oxford he negotiated with a publisher about a revised version of his thesis on crusader castles, but the project fell through, probably because Lawrence—who had strong ideas about printing—made too many demands for the inclusion of photographs. He also sent off a sarcastic letter to the *Times* about the Young Turk government's destruction of historic fortifications in Aleppo, Urfa (Edessa), Biredjik, and Carchemish, with the spoils of the desecrations going to build jails and the approaches for an iron-girder bridge over the Euphrates. When his anonymous letter to the *Times* was printed on August 9, 1911, it was the first publication of the aspiring author. The epics of his imagination would have to wait.

The second season of digging at Carchemish was in doubt when Thompson got married and demanded that his wife be allowed to accompany him at the site. While the negotiations were up in the air, Hogarth encouraged Lawrence's career by suggesting that he spend some of his downtime on a dig in Egypt under the renowned Sir Flinders Petrie. This was the high period of Egyptology, with teams from Germany, France, the United States, and Britain exploring sites along the Nile while major newspapers competed for scoops of new discoveries—an opportunity for an ambitious young man to make a career as an archaeologist. In January 1912 Lawrence took a steamer to Petrie's site at Kafr Ammar, fifty miles up the Nile from Cairo, showing up in his usual Carchemish attire, a blazer and football shorts, and prompting Petrie to say, "We don't play cricket here."[19] The Kafr Ammar site was a graveyard, which made for easy excavations compared to Carchemish, but Lawrence found the excavation of mummified corpses repulsive and the Egyptians "horribly ugly, very dirty, dull, low-spirited, without any of the vigour or the self-confident independence of our men . . . frenetic, and querulous, foul-mouthed, and fawning."[20] He stayed at the Nile site less than a month.

When Lawrence returned to Carchemish for the second year of digging, Leonard Woolley, eight years Lawrence's senior and that much more experienced in archaeology, had replaced Thompson as the on-site administrator. The local kaimakam demanded a bribe to allow Woolley to work, calling it a salary for an unofficial commissaire. Woolley boldly announced that he intended to work and that anyone who attempted to obstruct him would be shot. The bluff succeeded, and Lawrence's initial resentment of a new boss turned to admiration for Woolley's aplomb. Lawrence called him a "most excellent person."[21]

They worked together for a year, until Woolley sailed back to England in June 1912. Lawrence opted to stay behind and travel, taking as his companion a native boy named Dahoum. Dahoum was around sixteen, handsome and ambitious, and he spoke beautiful Arabic. He nursed Lawrence when he was ill with dysentery and became a photography apprentice, friend, student, companion, and trusted assistant. For Lawrence, Dahoum was the perfect noble savage, exotically handsome, untainted by the vices and weaknesses of the Europeanized Arabs, a surrogate for the noble, pure Bedouin Lawrence had read and fantasized about. There were later rumors about Lawrence and Dahoum, based in part on what Woolley described as "improper gargoyles" Lawrence had carved that were "faintly reminiscent of Dahoum . . . so it is in every sense of the word monstrous."[22] The scandalous allegations that Dahoum had modeled for the crouching naked figures, and any implications of a homosexual relationship, were most likely not true. Lawrence seemed to fear physical intimacy in any form, an apparent inheritance from his mother's harsh attitudes about sin, and Woolley, who shared close quarters with him, wrote that Lawrence's relationship with Dahoum was not sexual.[23] The gargoyles were probably another instance of Lawrence acting out, a deliberate effort to shock his colleagues as he had done at Oxford. Woolley got it right when he wrote that Lawrence "courted misunderstanding rather than tried to avoid it; it appealed to his sense of humour, which was broad and school-boyish. He liked to shock."[24]

The letters of introduction Lawrence obtained for his travels described him as a professor of the University of Oxford, "an inestimable person, whose worth archaeologically and intellectually they (the Government) were quite unable to express in words," and asked all kaimakams, mutessarifs, mirdirs, and government officials to see that he was well lodged and fed, and provided with transport, guides, interpreters, and escorts.[25] The letters proved superfluous when Lawrence once again chose to travel on foot with only Dahoum and a donkey for company. For Lawrence, the ability to travel in a style closer to the natives than to the traditional equipage of visiting Europeans, and especially his ability to speak Arabic, were matters of fierce pride. "I have had the pleasant experience since a week of being the best Arabic scholar in all the villages I entered," he wrote to his mother. "In every single one, except Rum Kalaat, someone knew a little Arabic but I knew more than all: the people were all Turks and Kurds; a few Armenians and Yezidis."[26]

When the dig was formally closed down the next summer, Lawrence brought Dahoum and Hamoudi, the local foreman from Carchemish, home to Oxford, housing them in his bungalow on Polstead Street. Hamoudi was impressed by the tap in the bathroom, which could produce hot water without building a fire, and by the hoops that marked off the grass in the public parks; it amazed him that anyone could step over the hoops and onto the grass, but that no one did.[27] But the visit was not a success. Lawrence's mother was frustrated that the visitors did not speak or understand English. She spoke French to them, of which they understood not a word, and she remained a resentful outsider to the conversations and jokes Lawrence shared with his guests. One day when his mother and Janet Laurie were both present, Lawrence asked Hamoudi how much Janet was worth.

"No good, no good, no worth," came the answer. Janet Laurie, by her own recollection, was a "scrawny and miserable-looking thing."

Lawrence then asked how much his mother was worth.

"Oh, a cow," answered Hamoudi.[28]

If Lawrence was amused, his mother almost certainly was not. Indeed, Lawrence's parents were increasingly apprehensive that he had gone native. Lawrence remained very much the Englishman in Carchemish, but he delighted in pressing the limits. On his earlier travels on foot in Syria he had worn European clothes. In Carchemish he sometimes adopted a costume of shorts and a buttonless shirt held together with a gaudy Kurdish belt, "fastened on the left hip with a huge bunch of many-coloured tassels, [a] symbol plain to all Arabs that he was seeking a wife." Lawrence's tassels were larger than anyone else's, although in his case it was not a signal of special eagerness in the search for a wife, but only a proclamation of his determined bachelorhood. In the evenings he would carefully brush his hair and wear a "white and gold embroidered waistcoat and a magnificent cloak of gold and silver thread, a sixty-pound garment he had picked up cheaply from a thief in the Aleppo market." On his travels with Dahoum Lawrence sometimes adopted native Arab dress, aware that he could not pass as an Arab, but hoping he could at least pass "as some other native speaking Arabic."[29]

Much has been written about Lawrence's alleged affectation or obsession with native clothes, including allegations that he was somehow a cross-dresser, wearing Arab robes as a substitute for a woman's dress. In fact, his actions, even in Carchemish, were entirely in keeping with the advice and cautions he later gave to others:

> Disguise is not advisable. Except in special areas, let it be clearly known that you are a British officer and a Christian. At the same time, if you can wear Arab kit when with the tribes, you will acquire their trust and intimacy to a degree impossible in uniform. It is, however, dangerous and difficult. They make no special allowances for you when you dress like them. Breaches of etiquette not charged against a foreigner are not condoned to you in Arab clothes. You will be like an actor in a foreign theatre, playing a part day and night for months, without rest, and for an anxious stake.[30]

Carchemish had been remote enough to be a refuge from Oxford and the world, a self-sufficient closed society. Even the turbulent news from Constantinople rarely intervened until surrounding countries circled the seemingly vulnerable Young Turk government like vultures. In September 1911 war broke out between Turkey and Italy over Italian ambitions on the coastal islands and in Tripoli. The day that Turkey signed a peace agreement with Italy (October 18, 1912), Bulgaria, Serbia, and Greece declared war against Turkey, hoping they too could capitalize on Turkish weakness. The Turkish army was woefully unprepared, and conscriptors roamed the countryside pressing men and donkeys into military service. At Carchemish the levies of able-bodied men put pressure on the recruitment of native labor for the dig.

Lawrence was fascinated by the reactions of the villagers to the Turkish conscription. He had gotten to know many of the "dark-eyed, richly coloured Arabs" and their children by name when they came to beg quinine for their malaria-fevered children or to show him their finds on the dig—the archaeologists paid a bounty for each discovery. He also befriended the Milli-Kurds who lived close by the Euphrates, and discovered that they followed the war news diligently. They told Lawrence that secret meetings had been held in Aleppo and Damascus, showed him their ammunition stores in the vaults of an old crusader castle, and said they were biding their time before they mounted their own attack on Aleppo with the ultimate aspiration of setting up an Arab sultan at Baghdad. "I am gathering a store of Arab news and notions which some day will help me in giving vividness to what I write," Lawrence wrote home.[31]

In reality, his Kurdish friends had greatly exaggerated the scale and coherence of anti-Turkish and pan-Arab organization: the opposition against the Young Turks was mostly ineffectual talk. The khedive in Egypt, and the sheikhs and sherifs throughout Arabia, had enough deep-seated conflicts among themselves to prevent any real cooperation, and the rumored conspirators who held secret meetings in Damascus, Aleppo, and Cairo were few in number and minuscule in impact. But if the stories Lawrence heard were the exaggerations that word-of-mouth rumors breed and feed, the excitement he witnessed among the subject peoples of the empire as they exchanged and recounted these tales were a good introduction to the potential scale and fervor of Arab aspirations and anti-Turkish feelings.

When he returned to Carchemish for the 1912–13 season, progress on the dig had advanced considerably, with a light railway now in place to move heavy material, and workers using dynamite to break up the Roman foundations that had been built over Hittite ruins. Well-placed and well-designed explosive charges were effective at demolishing even the massive Roman fortifications, a lesson Lawrence would not forget. He quickly picked up on his old friendships and connections with the Kurds. "The Kurds here are quiet," he wrote to Woolley, "with no intention of doing anything unless matters get bad in Stamboul. They are then going all out, and the Arabs have promised to move with them (our men as well!)."[32] The Balkan War was in the news, and there were enough rumors to cause Lawrence to practice marksmanship with a Mannlicher-Schönauer carbine.

As his parents feared, Lawrence had picked up decidedly un-British and un-Christian manners. "Today is Friday," he wrote home, "which is our Sunday." When his parents protested that he was observing the Moslem rather than the Christian Sabbath, he answered,

"You complain of our keeping Friday—but would it be quite considerate to make two hundred workmen miss their day for the sake of the two of us." He also praised what he saw as Bedouin asceticism: "To escape the humiliation of loading in food, would bring one very near the angels. Why not let him copy that very sensible Arab habit, of putting off the chewing of bread till the moment that instinct makes it desirable. If we had no fixed meal-hours, and unprepared food, we would not fall into middle-age." Yet his appreciation of Arab culture was still from a distance, and if he occasionally affected native dress, when his younger brother Will stopped in Aleppo and visited Jerablus on his way to a teaching post in India, Ned saw him off at the station wearing white flannels, socks, red slippers, and a white Magdalen College blazer.[33]

The information Lawrence gathered on the Kurdish tribes and their aspirations during the Balkan wars might have been useful to British intelligence agencies and others in the government, and some authors have claimed that Lawrence and Woolley were spying for the British, taking advantage of the cover provided by the archaeological expedition to report on the Baghdad–Berlin Railway and the status, organization, and plans of various populations in the Ottoman Empire. Archaeologists are often favored as spies because of their language skills, extended residence in inaccessible areas, the equipment they legitimately carry (Lawrence had a telephoto lens among his photographic equipment at Carchemish), and because their egghead mien provides an effective cover.[34] The Indiana Jones of recent films, who borrows some traits and history from Lawrence, is a good example. But Lawrence and Woolley had no training or prior experience as intelligence agents, and most of their contacts with the Germans working on the Baghdad–Berlin Railway, such as the periodic negotiations over labor or the use of spoil from the Carchemish site by the railroad project, would have provided little useful information. The railway was as much propaganda as potential logistics support: the Germans *wanted* to be seen, and for the scale of their construction to be known. On his return from Carchemish to England at the end of the digging season Lawrence did provide a casual report on the Kurdish tribes to the American vice consul in Beirut, whom he had met earlier at the American school in Jebail, but no trace of comparable information has shown up in British archives, and there is no real evidence that he did any official spying for British agencies at or around Carchemish.

Lawrence was effectively without future plans. He had visited the seven cities of his proposed travel book (Constantinople, Cairo, Smyrna, Aleppo, Jerusalem, Urfa, Damascus), and may have dabbled at the writing, but nothing survives. He kept busy at Carchemish cataloging and describing recovered sculpture from the site, but it was tedious and unrewarding work: the materials were fragments, and there seemed little chance of a major discovery or breakthrough. By fall of 1913 the weather had turned, Carchemish was cold and damp, outdoor photography was uncomfortable or impossible, and with his fellowship expiring the next summer, Lawrence was as gloomy as the weather. His once ambitious plans were approaching a dead end. "I have felt that (at least for the near future) to talk of settling down to live in a small way anywhere else was berating the air: and so gradually I slipped down," Lawrence wrote to Vyvyan Richards, "until a few months ago when I found myself an ordinary archaeologist. I have got to like this place very much: and the people here—five or six of them—and the whole manner of living pleases me. We have 200 men to play with, anyhow we like so long as the excavations go on, and they are splendid fellows many of them. . . . It is a place where one eats *lotos* nearly every day, and you know that feeling is bad for one's desires to do something worth looking at, oneself."[35] The growing sense of self-identity in this letter would reappear in Lawrence's later writings, especially notions like "an ordinary archaeologist," "men to play with, anyhow we like," and versions of the self-consciousness about "one's desires to do something worth looking at."

~

An unexpected new opportunity came in December 1913 when Lawrence and Woolley received a telegram inviting them to join a survey party making maps of the Sinai Desert south of Beersheba. The Ashmolean and British museums encouraged them to join the Sinai expedition, which would support the two archaeologists until new funds might be secured to continue work at Carchemish for the next season.

The Sinai was Turkish territory, the land gateway between British-controlled Egypt and the Suez Canal and Turkish-controlled Palestine and Gaza, which in turn opened the way to Syria and Arabia. Knowledge of the terrain, resources, and assets of the eastern flank of the canal was crucial to Britain's defense plans, and the only maps the British command had of the area were incomplete and ancient; wide swaths of the Sinai had never been mapped. With the Turks aware of the strategic importance of the approaches to the Suez Canal, any British survey mapping had to be done under a subterfuge, so the application for the expedition was filed by the private Palestine Exploration Fund, emphasizing the pursuit of archaeological research "in search of Moses' footsteps" that would be of interest to "the Bible student." Lawrence and Woolley had useful skills and experience in Arab country, and were qualified for the expedition on paper; although Lawrence looked only eighteen, he was thought to be very good with the Arabs, though very shy, with "the instincts of an explorer."[36]

The expedition planners allocated only two months to produce an accurate map of the Sinai on the scale of a half inch to the mile, make special plans of important localities and archaeological remains, take photographs of buildings and other points of interest and squeezes of important inscriptions, collect geological specimens and ancient stone and flint implements, and record all names in use in the area. Two months was nowhere near enough time for the digging, cataloging, and study that the supposed archaeological goals of the expedition would require. It didn't take long for Lawrence to guess that with Captain Stewart Newcombe of the Royal Engineers in charge of the project, "we are obviously only meant as red herrings, to give an archaeological colour to a political job."[37]

Lawrence and Woolley also discovered the night-and-day contrast between the procedures, timetable, and working conditions of a quasi-military expedition and their accustomed leisurely pace of archaeological research. When they reached Beersheba, on the edge of the Negev Desert, the setting-off point for their initial assignments, they learned that no equipment or stores had been provided for them. Fortunately, Lawrence had brought a camera and some squeeze paper to make impressions of inscriptions. The first town they were assigned to map was "the most desert place we have seen: there was no water and no soil for miles round: only a ruined town of white limestone in a gently rolling upland of red flints." "It speaks wonders for the Children of Israel that they left Moses alive after he brought them to a place like that," Woolley wrote of another town.[38] The familiar biblical references made the research exciting, and Lawrence could not shake the feeling that they were walking in the footsteps of Moses, but they found nothing from the biblical period of the Exodus, and the demanding schedule left little time to explore the few Byzantine-era ruins they stumbled upon. Lawrence visited the Nabatean city of Petra with its imposing siting and monumental structures carved out of the multicolored sandstone, and was intrigued with Captain Newcombe's leadership of the expedition, his first exposure to military discipline and the dynamics of small quasi-military units in the field. Newcombe worked as hard as anyone under him, an example as well as an incentive to his men; once the assignment or mission of each group under his command was clear, he let them work without interference. These were useful lessons. On their explorations south to Aqaba Lawrence noted that the Wadi Aqaba had never been a route from north to south, and that the Turkish guardhouses on the approaches to Aqaba covered ancient remains. He would not forget those details.

The digging permit at Carchemish was not renewed in 1914, but the site had become a regular stop for travelers. In late May Captain Newcombe and his assistant, the Royal Engineers officers who had been in charge of the Sinai survey, visited on their way back to England, eager to follow up on Woolley's suggestion that Newcombe tell Lord Kitchener that "our camp is within a stone's throw of the bridge of the Euphrates which is being built by the German Baghdad Railway Company, and that you can pick up a whole lot of useful military information in our district." Newcombe learned little that was new in Carchemish, but he arranged to travel 150 miles westward into the Taurus Mountains, hoping to find the exact route of the railway through that difficult and unfamiliar terrain. When he reached Constantinople he wrote to Lawrence and Woolley that he had found the railway route—which he had to do with compass and dead reckoning—but had been unable to gather much information about the railroad. He asked if they could take the same route home when they left in June. The two intrepid archaeologists were delighted to oblige. Lawrence took his camera, and on the construction road built to support work on the Berlin–Baghdad Railway they stumbled upon a disgruntled senior Italian engineer who had been fired by the Germans. Woolley spoke Italian fluently, made friends with the engineer, and they got all the information Newcombe needed. "It was the only piece of spying I ever did before the war," Woolley later recalled.[39]

Lawrence didn't write much about his dabbling in intelligence work. In July 1914 he returned to England, utterly without plans, and encountered Gertrude Bell, just back from her pioneering exploration and adventures in Arabia. She was full of information on the tribes of Arabia, especially the Howaitat and the tribes along the Hejaz Railway. Her dramatic stories were fascinating for Lawrence, who had not forgotten his own dreams of Arabia and the Bedouin. In a morning together at Hogarth's house, "she and Lawrence traversed most of Arabia."[40]

One month later, Britain was at war.

6

War

For if you refuse to let my people go, tomorrow I will bring locusts on your territory. They shall cover the surface of the land, so that no one will be able to see the land. They shall devour the surviving remnant that was left to you after the hail; and they shall eat away all your trees that grow in the field. Moreover, they shall fill your palaces and the houses of all your courtiers and of all the Egyptians—something that neither your fathers nor fathers' fathers have seen from the day they appeared on earth to this day.

—Exodus 10:4–6

And Pharaoh said to Joseph, "Since God has made all this known to you, there is none so discerning and wise as you. You shall be in charge of my court, and by your command shall all my people be directed." . . . And when all the land of Egypt felt the hunger, the people cried out to Pharaoh for bread; and Pharaoh said to all the Egyptians, "Go to Joseph; whatever he tells you, you shall do."

—Genesis 41:39–40, 55

On July 27, 1914, four days after the Austro-Hungarian ultimatum to Serbia that set off the Great War, Rear Admiral Sir Arthur Limpus of the British naval mission to the Ottoman Empire sailed home from Constantinople to meet up with the *Reshadieh* and the *Sultan Osman I,* two huge dreadnoughts that had been built for the Ottoman navy in British naval yards. His mission was to escort them back to

Constantinople, where a "navy week" and lavish ceremonies had been scheduled. Turkish women had sold their jewelry and children had contributed their pocket money to a patriotic public subscription to make the purchase of the ships possible. The mighty ships—the *Osman* mounted more heavy guns than any warship in the British or German fleets—were Turkey's hope to maintain neutrality in the war that was rapidly enveloping Europe.

By autumn 1914 it was hard to argue what Turkey would gain from taking sides in a European war, or which side Turkey should take. The German presence in Turkey was already unmistakable: the kaiser had visited not once but twice, demonstrating his vaunted majesty and might with parades and spectacular gifts and leaving behind advisers, investments, and German training, weapons, and officers for the slowly modernizing Turkish army. The long rivalry with Russia in the Caucasus and the Black Sea, and Turkish resentment over Russian claims to Constantinople, had long inspired coarse cartoons and commentary about the Russians and their potential allies inside the Ottoman Empire. But ties to Russia's allies England and France were substantial and deep. Anglophone and Francophone businesses, signs, merchandise, and culture were familiar in the shops and cafés, and in the homes of the wealthy and powerful in Constantinople and other cities of the empire. In the initial days of the war, with optimistic reports arriving from both sides, the safest course of action was wary neutrality. In the cafés, over cups of thick, dark coffee (even as much of Europe already found coffee in short supply), the pundits read the battlefield reports as if they were tea leaves.

For minorities in the empire like the Jews of Palestine, the prospect of war was terrifying. The older generations of Jews in Jerusalem, Safed, and Tiberias had felt the stings of a threatened Turkish administration in previous wars. For the newer settlers, only first or second generation on Turkish territory, and often with relatives and friends in the old country, residual allegiances meant that Zionists from Russia could find themselves at odds with neighboring settlers from Austria or Romania. In the past the Ottoman conscriptors had rejected Jews, afraid that they would prove disloyal, but that was no assurance for the future, and many of the settlers had left countries like Russia where conscription had taken a heavy toll on young men. It was easy for most of the Jews of Palestine to conclude that their best hope was for Turkey to stay out of the war.

Winston Churchill, the young first lord of the Admiralty, watched the events unfolding in Turkey closely. In the years before the war he had overseen the transformation of the British fleet from coal to fuel oil, and he had encouraged dreadnought construction to outpace the upstart Germans, but he worried that the British margins of superiority over the German fleet were too slim, that brilliant tactics or fortuitous luck on the part of the Germans could lead to the unthinkable. He knew the two huge dreadnoughts that British yards had built for the Ottoman navy could change those odds. While the Turks anxiously awaited delivery of their ships, Churchill relied on a 1912 ruling of questionable legality to post British security forces around the ships in their British yards, preventing the Turkish crews from boarding or raising the Ottoman flag. On July 31, 1914, with the agreement of the Cabinet, Churchill ordered British sailors to board the *Sultan Osman I*. The Foreign Office took several days to send a formal notice to the Ottoman government of their desire to have the contracts for the construction of the vessels transferred to His Majesty's government. By then the Turks had realized that they would never get their ships, and they had already turned to Germany for help.

It wasn't an obvious alliance on either side. Some prominent members of the Young Turk government, like Djemal Pasha, the military governor of Constantinople and minister of the navy, were openly Francophile, and the Germans knew that the Turkish mobilization would be too slow to tie down the Russians and help the German plans for a swift war in Europe. Some documents suggest that the Germans did not know that the British had seized the *Sultan Osman I* and may have expected the Turks to give them the dreadnought.[1] Whatever the reasons, which we may never know, Germany and Turkey signed a hasty alliance, and the Germans committed to bring two powerful German warships, the battle cruiser *Goeben* and the light crusier *Breslau,* to Constantinople to bolster the Ottoman fleet in the Black Sea. In the first of many demands, the Turks insisted that they be allowed to preserve their public neutrality by pretending they were purchasing the ships. The Turks lacked trained crews, so the German admirals had to order the crews of their warships to dress in tarbooshes and Ottoman uniforms to sail up the Dardanelles.

When Churchill heard from his naval attaché that Constantinople was "almost completely in German hands," he ordered the Admiralty and the War Office to prepare contingency plans for an attack on Turkey and proposed to the Cabinet that a flotilla be sent up the Dardanelles to sink the *Goeben* and the *Breslau*. In reaction to the British threats, the Ottomans mined the Dardanelles strait, confronting Churchill with a risky contingency: the Bosporus and the Dardanelles were Russia's only ice-free passage for wheat exports, her principal source of income. If the straits remained closed for even a few months, Russia would not be able to pay for arms and might be susceptible to revolution from within. If revolutionaries took power in Russia and forced a Russian withdrawal from the war, England and France would face the full might of the German army.

Despite the visible mining operation in the Dardanelles, Turkey clung to the shaky public charade of neutrality. Enver Pasha, the head of the Young Turk government, was playing a crafty game. He requested gold payments from the Germans to support the Turkish army, and even after the gold arrived did not declare war against Germany's enemies. He also took advantage of the declared neutrality to address old grudges. On September 8, 1914, the Sublime Porte announced the unilateral abrogation of the capitulation privileges of all foreign powers, which had for centuries allowed citizens of European states resident in the Ottoman Empire recourse to the protection of their own governments and legal systems. In one of the more bizarre scenes of the opening months of the Great War, the German and Austrian ambassadors joined the ambassadors of Britain, France, and Russia to present a joint protest to the Sublime Porte, even as British, French, and Russian troops were engaged in bloody trench warfare against German and Austrian troops on the Marne and the frontiers of Russia.

The joint protest of the Great Powers may have seemed evidence of Turkish neutrality, or at least proof that the Turks were capable of equal-opportunity provocations, but the day after the Young Turk government signed their treaty with Germany they ordered a general mobilization, and Enver Pasha issued orders allowing German rear admiral Wilhelm Souchon to sail the *Goeben* and the *Breslau* through the Bosporus into the Black Sea. One of the German ships ignored orders and shelled the Russian coast, and by early November 1914, Turkey was at war with Britain, France, and Russia.

Palestine felt the impact of the war declarations almost immediately. To avoid the Turkish conscriptors who roamed the countryside, some Arabs mutilated themselves or became so weak from purges and herbal medications that they died within days of being drafted. Public transportation was curtailed as carts, wagons, and horses were requisitioned by the military. Foreign publications from France and England, hard to get even in peacetime, disappeared. Mail, infamously pokey in the Ottoman Empire, all but ceased, as the censors and the military took over the post offices. Shipments of fruit and other agricultural products from the Jewish farms to France, Britain, and Russia were suspended. Ripe oranges sat in crates or on the trees; if they couldn't be harvested and shipped soon, there was nothing to do but let them rot or feed them to the cattle. And there was no market for orange-flavored milk.

The Jewish farms were dependent on irrigation, and the British and French blockade of the Mediterranean coast would soon cut off the import of the gasoline and diesel fuel needed to run irrigation pumps, with devastating effects on future harvests. An even bigger threat came from the Turkish army. The productivity of the Jewish farms was renowned, and the Turkish troops promptly requisitioned crops, draft animals, livestock, and tools. Some of the levies were legal under regulations that placed the needs of the army above the property rights of citizens and noncitizens alike. But the soldiers and officers went beyond the authorized requisitions with systematic looting of the Jewish colonists. "The word 'pay' officially does not exist today in the dictionary recognized by the Ottoman government," wrote a bitter Avshalom Feinberg after he watched Turkish officers lead away the best horses and mules and leave behind a worthless receipt, "a scrap of paper, signed by Mr. So-and-So Mohammed, Moustapha or Ali," a pure "abstraction . . . a cock-and-bull story to make honest men laugh."[2] At Zichron, Aaron Aaronsohn watched Turkish soldiers systematically take clothing (including women's lingerie and baby clothes), carts, wagons, water buffaloes, agricultural implements, tools, firearms, medical instruments (including those for obstetrics), microscopes, and the fence posts and barbed wire needed to protect the fields.

The scale of levies from the Jewish farms outstripped the logistics capabilities of the Turkish army. The Turks stored the wheat they had seized uncovered, and the upper layers germinated in the rain, providing a banquet for pigeons and doves. Fence posts, desperately needed at the settlements to protect crops and animals, were stacked in army depots and never used. Sugar confiscated from Jewish farms was stored outside in Nablus, exposed to drenching rain and unguarded, "much to the delight of street boys." Four hundred barrels of cement confiscated to build bridges was poorly stored, so the contents were ruined by rain. Draft animals that had been kept healthy by the Jewish farmers were so neglected by the Turks that they ended up being sold for 5 percent to 10 percent of what they were worth.[3] With those losses the Jewish settlements were transformed almost overnight from productive enterprises with surpluses that could be exported into subsistence farms with no income, barely enough food to feed their residents, and without the tools and animals they needed to grow more crops.

In August 1915, Herr Dieckmann, the general manager of the Hejaz Railway, demanded forty thousand tons of wood from the Jewish colony at Hadera for railway ties, a levy the Jewish settlers could meet only by chopping down the eucalyptus trees they had laboriously planted to drain the local malarial swamps. Avshalom's strongest memory from childhood was of his father stooped over in the swamps, planting those trees, the key to controlling mosquitoes and developing agriculture on the coastal soils. Aaronsohn urged the railway to accept jujube trees or bituminous asphalt instead, which would have spared the eucalyptus trees and the fields they were draining. "I need to keep the trains running," Dieckmann said. "The eucalyptus are good, so I take them. If there aren't enough I'll take the olive trees, the orange trees, *all the trees*."[4]

The Jewish communities had long been adept at dealing with the Turkish authorities, but protests of the levies were futile. The Turkish troops in Palestine were under the command of Djemal Pasha, who after the declaration of war had been promoted from minister of the navy to supreme commander of the Turkish Fourth Army and de facto ruler of Syria and Palestine. Before the war Djemal had been known in the Jewish settlements only by reputation and from photographs—a short and stocky man with a terrifying full black beard and elaborate uniforms with ornate epaulettes and medals. He was said to pride himself on his worldly knowledge and his ability to speak French. It did not take long for Djemal to earn a new reputation and nickname in Palestine: behind his back he was called "the hangman" because those who defied him usually ended up on the gallows. Djemal's memoirs show no qualms or shame in recording his unbridled self-confidence and exaggerated notions of discipline. He once showed up for a formal review in his full dress uniform to find the fleet unprepared. The commander in chief of the fleet explained: "I thought, Effendim, that in view of the wet weather, you would certainly not come, and so I have not brought the men to save them from getting wet unnecessarily." Djemal had the commander arrested and held for three days before cashiering him. When Djemal found graffiti on the doors of the officers' cabins of a warship, he had the captain of the ship dismissed from the navy, and had the second in command imprisoned for two weeks. When a court-martial went against Djemal's views, he put the members of the court on half pay, "on the ground that they had revealed a lack of judgment and discrimination in questions of military honour."[5]

Djemal's harshest punishments were reserved for the minorities in Syria and Palestine, especially the Jews. The Turkish government was paranoid about Russian spies, and focused their suspicions on the Jewish settlers, many of whom still had Russian accents and spoke Yiddish or Hebrew instead of Arabic or Turkish. Most of the Jewish colonists from Russia had declined to apply for Ottoman citizenship, which was routinely denied to Jewish applicants in any case. After the declaration of war Jewish settlers with enemy (Russian) citizenship were rounded up and put aboard neutral ships bound for Alexandria. The deportations were halted only after pleas from leaders of the Jewish community in Palestine and from concerned Jews in America had persuaded the U.S. ambassador to intervene. The Turks then offered a compromise: subjects with enemy citizenship who were willing to accept Ottoman citizenship and pay a special tax could stay in Palestine, and they would be exempt from military service for one year. The compromise was hardly a welcome offer for either the ultra-pious Jews, who had long forsworn any state citizenship and considered themselves citizens only of a kingdom of God, or for Zionists, who had been routinely treated as second-class subjects by the Turkish bureaucracy, and who understandably questioned the sincerity of the offer of citizenship. Many Jews also realized that if they accepted Ottoman citizenship they might find themselves on the opposite side of the battle lines from family and friends who had not emigrated.

Djemal demanded that all Hebrew signs be taken down, ordered post offices not to accept mail with Hebrew addresses, and forbid the display of Jewish flags and the use of Jewish stamps (which were not legal postage but were sold to raise money for causes). In mid-December 1914, he ordered five hundred Jews to leave Jaffa, giving no reason. A month later he moved his headquarters to Jerusalem and clarified his position in newspapers: the Jews would be allowed to remain in Ottoman territory, but there would be zero tolerance for Zionism or secret organizations.[6] That same month he summoned thirty-two leaders of the Jewish communities to meet with him, made them wait for a tense hour—a reminder that the Young Turks had not abandoned the power gestures of the Ottoman bureaucracy—then announced that they were being exiled for the winter to a remote area in Anatolia. It was a virtual death sentence given the harsh weather and endemic diseases of the area. When the Jewish leaders protested their loyalty and support of the Turkish government, Djemal magnanimously agreed that only fifteen of the leaders would be sent away, to Tiberias, and for only two weeks. A few of the Jewish leaders, who had long relied on compromises and negotiations with the Turks, came away from the meeting convinced that Djemal's antipathy toward the Jews had been tempered.

Djemal's first military offensive was in the spring of 1915, when he ordered his forces to launch an attack on the Suez Canal. The Turkish troops were surprisingly successful in crossing the Sinai and reaching the canal, then were quickly repulsed by British artillery units that rushed to the defense. There were no Jewish farms in the area for the Turkish troops to plunder, and each Turkish soldier had been issued one liter of water for thirty-six hours in the desert, tantamount to a sentence of death by thirst. They also had no provisions to cross the canal. Aubrey Herbert, a British intelligence officer, wrote sarcastically that the Turkish plan had been "to bring thousands of camels down to the Canal and then set a light to their hair. The camel, using its well-known reasoning powers, will dash to the Canal to put the fire out. When they have done this in sufficient quantities the Turks will march over them."[7]

But Djemal was a brilliant propagandist, and when it became clear that the attack on the canal had failed, he issued an order of the day proclaiming, "All the troops had done their duty worthily and patriotically. The object of our enterprise had been to carry out an offensive reconnaissance against the Canal with a view to finding out the resources at the enemy's disposal, and also the resources we ourselves should require to effect a crossing of the Canal. As our purpose had been completely attained, it was now advisable to retire."[8] Publicly, he had turned defeat into a victory. Privately he made the Jews scapegoats for the failed attack, ordering massive expulsions of Jews from Jaffa into the countryside. When he heard later that there was talk in Egypt of forming a Jewish Legion, he ordered another round of deportations of Jews from Palestine cities. The implication of both orders was that the Jews in Palestine were somehow responsible for the setbacks of the Turkish forces.

With exports embargoed and fuel for irrigation pumps expensive or unavailable, moneylenders ended up with whatever crops the military levies left behind. The newly homeless Jewish exiles from the cities were dependent on the rural settlements for food and shelter, more mouths to feed just when the shortage of seed stock, drought conditions, and a lack of skilled labor restricted the area that could be sown for 1915.[9] Many of the Jewish settlements were close to starvation.

Aaron Aaronsohn watched the expanding impact of the war with the eyes of a trained observer. As an experienced agronomist he could look at a field or orchard and estimate how much of a crop it would produce. He could quickly calculate the impact of the lack of fuel and the Turkish seizure of the irrigation pumps. He knew the transportation routes for harvests—as he had known the transportation routes for foodstuffs in the Roman era in Palestine—and could calculate the impact of the requisitions of wagons and draft animals on the distribution of food to a hungry population. He also could recognize the signs of hunger and desperation. He managed to sequester enough production from the agricultural research station to feed its workers and their families, both Jewish and Arab. To circumvent Turkish regulations he had the kitchen at the station expanded into a commissary so entire families could be fed. He used some of the American subsidies to buy quinine tablets for everyone at the research station—there had been outbreaks of malaria—and to pay baksheesh that kept staff members of the research station out of the hands of the Turkish conscriptors. He knew that whatever he did was a token gesture.

All men, noncitizens and citizens alike, were required to report to the authorities for determination of their military status. Jews and other noncitizens were not allowed to serve in the army, but were drafted for labor battalions. The experience of Aaron Aaronsohn's younger brother Alexander was typical. Late in the fall of 1914 he was ordered to report with twenty other young men from Zichron Ya'aqov, many of them also Gideonites. They sang and danced all night in Zichron before they were picked up by Turkish transports in the morning and taken to Acre to register with the Turkish authorities. Instead of being released as noncitizens, they were confined overnight in a caravansary, given greasy boiled rice for breakfast, and marched to Safed in northern Galilee, a four-day journey on foot, then billeted in a crowded mosque and issued filthy green Turkish uniforms—boots, spiral puttees, and an *enverieh,* the Turkish army headgear named for Enver Pasha, who had designed it to combine the appearances of a turban and a German helmet. Alex Aaronsohn bribed his way into being allowed to stay in a hotel kept by a Jewish widow with the promise of a new blanket to an officer.

As non-Muslims, Alex and his group were assigned to a labor corps. There were no lubricants for their wheelbarrows, and when the laborers protested the friction and hideous squeaking they were told to grease the wheels with the spoonful of olive oil they were issued each day with their bread rations. Most days the bread ration was Turkish army biscuits thrown to the workers off the backs of carts. The soldiers jokingly called the dry, flat biscuits "armor" when they put them in their pockets. Those who didn't know better would break off and swallow bits of the biscuit and then wake up in the night screaming in agony, frothing black at the mouth until they died a painful death from enteritis. The biscuits were only edible if soaked in water and cooked on a fire, but the labor brigades didn't always have fires. They were expected to labor thirteen hours a day. Baksheesh to the guards could shorten the hours, or even purchase exemption from military service. Because he had already been signed up, Alex had to bribe a half dozen officers before he was finally given a discharge with the declaration by a physician that he had "too much blood."[10]

When he returned to Zichron Alex discovered that the military authorities had stripped the settlement of everything they could carry away, even the barbed wire from the fences. They had taken elderly men to drive the seized mules and horses. He spotted his own Smith & Wesson revolver in the hands of an Arab boy of fifteen.

The campaign to disarm the Jews was deliberate, prompted as much by Djemal's fear of Jewish conspiracies as by a requisitions policy that seized even the ancient shotguns and rifles the settlers used for protection against wild animals and local thieves. In Zichron, the last village to be disarmed, the Jews were threatened with guns if they did not surrender all their firearms and reveal the location of any arms caches. When the young men of the village resisted, the Turkish officer in charge calmly announced that he would round up the young women of the village and bring them to the Turkish officers if the hidden weapons were not produced.[11]

As the impact of the army requisitions, the embargo, and the deportations from the cities deepened, the Jews in Palestine turned their pleas for help to the United States. The United States was a declared neutral in the war, had a large Jewish community with a tradition of financial support for the community in Palestine, and despite an aggressive effort by Washington to stay out of the war, many individuals and newspaper editorials openly expressed sympathy for humanitarian issues arising from it. Henry Morgenthau, Woodrow Wilson's ambassador to the Sublime Porte and a trustee of Aaronsohn's research station, was particularly concerned about the treatment of the Jews in Palestine, and had the support of Louis Brandeis and others who were active in the Zionist movement. Through Morgenthau's efforts, funds were delivered to Jewish communities in Palestine; he also appointed a representative to meet with experts on the Jewish economy in Palestine, including Aaronsohn and Arthur Rupin. Morgenthau was sufficiently persuaded by the reports he received to arrange for a shipload of food to be delivered to Palestine, but by the time the ship arrived on May 20, 1915, the foodstuffs had to be shared with the native Arab population and hardly made a dent in the shortages.[12] Still, the tentative links between the United States and the Jewish community of Palestine were invaluable, if only to keep Djemal Pasha from unleashing his most extreme measures against the Jews.

~

Many Jews in Palestine had already been cursing their fates by February 1915 when news arrived of the first sightings of locusts. The "pilgrim" or "wandering" locusts from Egypt hadn't been seen in Palestine for forty years. Within days of the first sighting the swarms coming out of the south and west were thick enough to block the sun. The locusts devoured the new sprouts of winter wheat, the leaves and buds in vineyards and orchards, garden vegetables, flowers—everything green in sight, leaving behind lifeless trees and fields stripped bare. When the foliage was gone the locusts swarmed animals, driving them mad. They covered animal carcasses like carpets. They attacked the uncovered faces of children. The Arabs called the locusts *djesh Allah* (Allah's army) and threw up their hands in resignation. Any measure to deter the locusts, they said, would only drive them to attack the lands of a neighbor. Some Arabs captured female locusts by hand to roast them over an open fire as a delicacy.

At the Jewish settlements tocsins were sounded at the first appearance of locust swarms, in some places using bells that hadn't been rung since the departure of the Rothschild agents. Men, women, and children waved sheets and shirts at the swarms, threw soil with shovels, pounded on pots and pans, lit fires, even used the precious gasoline and diesel fuel that had been husbanded for the irrigation pumps. The locusts swarmed until they had devoured every leaf and blade of grass, ending all hope of a harvest that year.[13]

Every other wartime misfortune that had befallen the Jews of

Palestine—the end of trade, requisitions and the resulting starvation, the embargo of fuel, expulsions from the cities, conscription into labor battalions—could be blamed on evil men or the horrors of war. The locusts seemed a curse from God. Life for the Zionists had never been rosy. They had conquered the rude land, drained swamps, learned to make the desert bloom, held off the predations of Turkish bureaucrats, defended themselves against the raids of neighboring Arabs. They had answered the naysayers who said the land was too hot and dry, that crops would never grow in a desert, that Jews didn't belong in such a wasteland. They had countered the opposition of the ultra-Orthodox who condemned their Zionist ideals as blasphemy, and overcome their polyglot origins and differences by adopting Hebrew as a living language. They had built schools, research institutes, concert halls, theaters, and libraries. And they had withstood Djemal Pasha's requisitions and humiliations—only to find themselves victims of a biblical plague. Some cursed and questioned their future: were our struggles and labor only so we could succumb to starvation and locusts, the woes of Job and the plague on Pharaoh? Pious Jews read the book of Joel with its descriptions of locust plagues and mourned—*"Lament, like a maiden girt with sackcloth / For the husband of her youth!"*—an age-old response to pending catastrophe.[14]

Aaronsohn angrily watched the disaster unfold. He knew the life cycle and swarming patterns of the locusts, and techniques to fight them. With trained personnel, organization, and resources the eggs could be plowed deep or buried in trenches, which would at least avert the next round of devastation after the hatch. But that would require a massive collective effort, trained leadership, and above all access to the railroads, roads, tools, and fuel that were available only to the Turkish army. All around him the farmers, Arabs and Jews alike, seemed resigned to the loss of the spring crop and the inevitable widespread starvation that would follow. He feared that the locusts could be the final straw that would spare Djemal Pasha the effort to destroy the Jewish community.

Djemal had a different worry. If crop loss from the locusts reduced the next harvest, how would he feed his army? The Arab natives and the Turkish bureaucrats reacted as they always had, with resignation: if Allah sent locusts, perhaps he would send storks to devour the locusts, and the storks would leave behind manure to make the fields fertile. Whatever happened, it was the will of Allah. Arab agriculture in Palestine was primitive; they had invested less in their crops than the more productive Jewish farms, and they had less to lose. There were no native research institutes or agronomy schools, no native experts on swarming insects or the procedures that might effectively eradicate them. The success of Djemal's Fourth Army, and his own future, depended on a solution to the locust problem. When he asked for expert advice the American and Italian consuls told him there was only one man who could help him.

In March 1915, when the locust infestations were at a peak, Djemal invited Aaronsohn to his office in Jerusalem. Aaronsohn had learned Turkish in his years in Anatolia, but Djemal was eager to show off his French. It was destined to be an interesting encounter. The pasha rarely made any effort to conceal his disdain for Jews, and Aaronsohn was not one to put diplomacy ahead of frankness, even when dealing with the commander of the Fourth Army and de facto ruler of Palestine. Aaronsohn told Djemal that the military requisitions from the Jewish communities were an economic and social disaster. He explained that the Jewish farms, the most productive in Palestine, could not produce bountiful crops without fuel for the irrigation pumps and a return of the equipment that had been confiscated to supply water to the Turkish troops in their attacks across Sinai. He said that for the Jewish farms to produce they needed their workers released from the forced labor brigades, and a return of the tools and draft animals that had been requisitioned by the army. Even those measures would not help unless proper measures were taken to combat the locusts.[15]

Djemal was not known to suffer arrogance or challenges gracefully, and he liked to toy with his audiences. He asked Aaronsohn: "What if I were to have you hanged?"

Aaronsohn, self-deprecating about his considerable heft, calmly answered: "Your Excellency, the weight of my body would break the gallows with a noise loud enough to be heard in America!"[16] Later Aaronsohn wrote that when Djemal threatened him, he "repeated the Themistocles to Eurybiades: 'Strike, but hear me'" and that Djemal "listened and seeing the inadvisability of killing me changed his policy."

Djemal no doubt did not enjoy being bested in repartee by a Jew. He also did not welcome the reminder that Aaronsohn enjoyed strong support in still-neutral America. He was wise enough, though, to realize that Aaronsohn's expertise and knowledge of the terrain and conditions in Palestine were his only hope to contain the locust damage and provide a new harvest that the Fourth Army could requisition to feed itself. On March 27, 1915, Djemal Pasha appointed Aaronsohn to be in charge of fighting the locusts throughout Palestine, granting him the freedom to move around the countryside, and access to the resources of the Turkish army, the post, railroad, and road transportation. Aaronsohn wrote that he had become "a disliked but often listened to advisor of our Satrap."[17]

Aaronsohn and Feinberg recruited additional staff at the agricultural research station in Athlit. They soon had fifty willing men and women who were taught the techniques of digging trenches to bury the locust eggs and the use of controlled fires and chemicals to stop the spread of the infestation. Aaronsohn led a team from the research station to southern Palestine, where he lectured army and civil officials on the needed measures. Feinberg went with another team to the Galilee, and then to the Jordan valley, teaching the eradication methods to farmers, officials, and soldiers. Workers from the experimental station traveled around the countryside, utilizing many of the passable roads and rail lines as they visited army bases, railroad stations, and supply depots. All nonmilitary travel had been severely restricted after the declaration of war, so the campaign against the locusts was the first opportunity anyone in the Jewish community had to see the extent of the wartime deprivations and devastations across Palestine.

Some in the Jewish community sarcastically described Aaronsohn's relationship with Djemal Pasha as "friendship," but Aaronsohn took an almost perverse delight in ignoring criticism, and had precious little patience for extremists who would rather the Jewish community starve to death than cooperate with the Turks to relieve the locust plague. He also had scant tolerance for the inefficiency and corruption of the Turkish bureaucrats and army officers who were supposed to assist his efforts. Many Turkish soldiers refused to work on the locust campaign, and took advantage of the situation to exact private extortion from those who desperately awaited extermination procedures.

Aaronsohn saw enough of the swarms in different regions, and examined enough locusts under his magnifier, to conclude that the locusts would not reach sexual maturity in Palestine and that there would be no new hatch. He also spent enough time with Djemal Pasha to realize that no matter what services he provided it would not result in improved treatment of the Jews. In late April 1915, Aaronsohn learned that in Jaffa Jews were being fined or beaten if they did not present quotas of locusts to Turkish officers, who then sold them to Arabs as delicacies for the grill, all under the neglectful eyes of Hassam Bey, the local governor. Aaronsohn angrily resigned his role in the locust campaign, protesting that it was futile to continue the work when the bey was doing everything possible to interfere with their efforts. Djemal accepted his resignation, but did nothing to investigate or censure the bey.

In the weeks before Aaronsohn resigned he and his assistants had seen and recorded notes on the Turkish military installations, the state of rail and road transportation available to the troops, and the disposition, state of training, and preparation of Turkish military units throughout Palestine.

~

Early in January 1915, Sheikh Abdul Latif, from an Arab village near Avshalom Feinberg's hometown of Hadera, began spreading rumors that the Jewish settlers there were secretly loading wheat onto British ships at night. The allegations apparently originated with Arabs who claimed that they had seen Jewish men on the beach on a moonlit night. It was a bizarre charge: the local wheat crop scarcely met the needs of the settlers and those who had been expelled from the cities. There was nothing left to export, and smugglers would be unlikely to pick a moonlit night to load an enemy ship. But on January 16, the sheikh and a group of Arabs from Jenin went to the police in Hadera with the story. A platoon of soldiers was called in, and thirteen Jews, six of them married and heads of families, were arrested, charged with "open armed rebellion against the authorities in exercise of their functions during a state of war," and ordered to Jerusalem for a military trial. Feinberg and a friend of his named Liova Schneersohn were among those arrested. To justify the arrests, over fifty people from Hadera were beaten or subjected to the bastinado to try to persuade them to testify that they had made deliveries of wheat for the British.[18]

The arrests were made during a driving rainstorm, and Feinberg escaped and galloped on horseback through the storm to inform Aaron in Zichron. Alex Aaronsohn was also there, and the three men agreed that unless they could think of a way to intervene, the thirteen arrested men would be hanged. Feinberg railed against the cautious policies of the Jewish settlers, who were terrified to defy the Turkish authorities: "We can't let idiots dictate our policy. Our worst enemy is the Turk. Now that the hour of his downfall has struck, can we stand by and do nothing? The Turks are right to suspect us. They know the ruin they are planning for us. Anyone who didn't have a rabbit's heart would be proud to spy against them, if it would help to bring the English."

Aaron sent Feinberg back to Hadera to encourage the arrested men while he set off for Beirut. Hadera was in the *vilayet* of Beirut, and Aaron hoped to find sympathetic allies at the local governor's palace, or perhaps at the American consulate.

In the morning the arrested men in Hadera were marched off amid the weeping of the villagers. Feinberg remained defiant: "To the devil with all this sentiment. You have to be ready for the worst. If the time has come for us to die, we'll die. A lot of people are being killed in Europe. Why should we be better than they?"

A voice protested: "But if we do die, we must die for justice, not because someone has told a lie about us."

Feinberg turned in disgust, pointing to one of the Turkish soldiers: "From this you expect justice? For thinking it, you deserve to be hanged."

When the group stopped for lunch on their forced march, they were in high spirits, drinking wine and brandy their families had provided for the journey. Feinberg sat quietly by himself, imagining Aaronsohn in Beirut trying to persuade the governor to intervene. Feinberg, who knew the roads, tried to calculate whether he and the other prisoners would reach Jerusalem before or after a telegram arrived from the governor. By evening, the prisoners were in Jaffa, where they were confined for the night. Feinberg suffered an attack of malaria with a raging fever; his friend Liova Schneersohn stayed up all night, putting cold compresses on Feinberg's head. Schneersohn's family lived in Hadera, although he had spent many years in Russia studying anarchism, Russian thought, and mysticism.

"Put a lot of ice on my head," Feinberg told him. "Put a sea of ice on my head. My blood is boiling. All the East is boiling in me. . . . You are cold people, people who make calculations. You like mathematics. You cannot understand the beauty of the East. My father was from the north, like you. But I am different from him. I am a Jew of the East. I can understand the mystery, the beauty, the gaiety of the East. The hot nights in summer, the windy nights in winter. I hear the song of the Bedui, the song he sings on the night watch, and it says much more to me that the music of your Wagner and your Beethoven. Wait, we'll show the world."

"Avshalom, my friend, don't get so excited," Schneersohn said. "The compress is falling off your head."

Feinberg would have none of it. "Get away from me, you cold

man of the north. We'll show the whole world what our people can do. I don't mean the 'Jews' from the Galuth, the miserable ones from Berdichev and Mohilev, but we, from the land of Israel, the new ones, the unknown until now. The proud Jews, the brave ones, whose hearts are not eaten by the germs of the Galuth. Don't you feel that a new generation is born? Don't you hear it coming with slow steps, angry, vengeful? Don't you hear, poor thing?"

Then he told Schneersohn his plan.

> Listen, there is something I want to tell you. I've wanted to tell you for a long time. Don't think I'm talking from fever. . . . We can't defend ourselves against the Arabs. We haven't any arms. What are we going to do? Sit with folded hands? Are we preparing ourselves to give help to the redeeming army? It's impossible to remain idle now. We must make contact with the English, somehow or other. Surely we can find brave men amongst us, who will answer the call. I know we can. . . .
>
> We will go and make contact with the enemy. With their help we will get arms. We will reveal to them the secrets of the country. We will organize the freeing of Palestine. We'll do this in secret, without any committee meetings or discussions.
>
> If they catch us on the borders, or here in Palestine, they'll sentence us as spies, and hang us. Good. They'll hang us. They'll shoot us. Even if the whole Yishuv suffers for this, we must do it. We must do it, so that we will have the right to tell the world, not only about our agricultural settlements, but that our blood as been spilled for our country. Whoever doesn't want to join us in this can stay at home!

Schneersohn tried again to calm his feverish companion. "It's not hard to guess what will be happening here in the country," he said. "But what if someone finds out what we're doing and informs on us?"

Feinberg's smile was wry and mocking. "They're already preparing to condemn us to death. And for what? If we must die, better to die for something we've done."[19]

Cairo

I am sending you out this week . . . a youngster, 2nd Lt. Lawrence who has wandered about in the Sinai Peninsula, and who came in here to help in the Map branch.

—Major General Callwell, Director of Military Operations in London, to Sir John Maxwell, General Officer Commanding in Egypt[1]

After the years of colonial and naval rivalry with Germany, and the embarrassingly close relationship of the two monarchies, the declarations of war against Germany and Austria were greeted with wild enthusiasm in England. A few cautious souls like Foreign Secretary Sir Edward Grey pronounced gravely, "The lights are going out all over Europe," but for most the long dread of war was over. Cartoonists savaged the Hun, jingoists defended the glories and responsibilities of empire, and the young men of Britain rushed to join the war effort. So many men turned out to enlist that by the time T. E. Lawrence made his own queries, the War Office had announced a temporary rule raising the minimum height for enlistment. Lawrence was short of the new mark.[2]

As for so many other young men, for Lawrence the war seemed to offer the promise of adventure and a course for a rudderless career. He had been engaged in the archaeology work at Carchemish, but it was still schoolboy stuff, research on a fellowship with little promise of an academic career that he had already rejected as soulless. He had gotten nowhere in his literary efforts. He and Leonard Woolley wrote to Captain Newcombe, who had commanded their quasi-military research assignment in Sinai, asking whether they might be able to work in intelligence in Cairo. Newcombe suggested that they wait until the situation with Turkey was sorted out. Woolley, impatient to be part of the war effort, joined an artillery company bound for France. Lawrence kept himself busy with illustrations and maps for their report on Sinai, *The Wilderness of Zin*.

In late October 1914 Lawrence found himself a civilian position in the geographical section of the General Staff. Hogarth, who had gotten Lawrence his appointment in Carchemish, knew the head of the geographical section and may have gotten Lawrence this job as well. Most of the experienced map officers had been called to the front, and Lawrence soon found himself alone in the bureau with huge responsibilities. When the head of the section concluded that Lawrence's civilian dress was a distraction in dealings with War Office staff, Lawrence was commissioned a temporary second lieutenant interpreter.[3] For someone with ambitions toward intelligence work it was a plum of an assignment, but the map section in London was far from the British GHQ and intelligence operations for the Turkish theater. Lawrence knew that the intelligence that mattered was in Cairo.

~

In 1882, when the weakness and profligacy of the khedive and the financial collapse of the Suez Canal provided a ripe opportunity, the British had occupied Egypt, declaring that their goal was to restore order. They left the khedive in place as the figurehead ruler, but British and Egyptians alike recognized that the British governor-general had become the virtual ruler of Egypt. In 1914 the position was held by Field Marshal Horatio Herbert Kitchener, hero of the Sudan, avenger of the murder of General C. G. (Chinese) Gordon, vanquisher of the French at Fashoda, and victor of the Boer War. Kitchener's explanations of his views were often incomprehensible (David Lloyd George said Kitchener "talked twaddle"), but his striking military bearing—tall, broad-shouldered, and square-jawed, with bushy eyebrows, a bristling mustache, icy blue eyes, and an intimidating glower—was ubiquitously recognizable. British troops under his command had always been victorious. His secretive nature and taciturn shyness only enhanced the British public's trust in him as a methodical, dedicated, and unerring commander. "Kitchener is there," the expression went. "It is all right."[4]

From his headquarters in Cairo Kitchener looked out over an Arab-speaking world that stretched from the deserts of Africa to the border of Persia, roughly the area of the Arab caliphate of one thousand years earlier. The caliphs had once exercised spiritual authority comparable to the Holy Roman emperors: they alone could legitimize and delegate temporal and feudal power to the sultans, kings, and emirs who ruled provinces within the vast territory. The authority of the caliphate by then was long dormant, especially after the Ottoman Turks conquered the entire region in the sixteenth and seventeenth centuries and the sultan in Constantinople gradually assumed the title of caliph. But the shadow of the institution had survived. The British commissioned studies to see if the caliphate could be revived in Britain's favor.[5]

Kitchener could imagine himself comparable in rank, authority, and standing to the viceroy of India, ruling over an empire even more vast, if less populous. But whatever his imagination, in 1914 the British were still only a garrison force in Egypt. British officers and agents played polo and hunted fox on the cultivated grounds of the Nile basin, belonged to the Sporting Club and the Turf Club, and enjoyed a social whirl of balls, teas, and luncheons at the select Cairo hotels and cafés of the expatriate enclave. They rarely mixed with the locals, and few British officers or civilians outside the intelligence offices had any knowledge of Arabic, experience in Arab-speaking lands, or education in Arab history and culture.

With the declaration of war against the Ottoman Empire, the Cabinet in London announced their eagerness to annex Egypt, which nominally was enemy territory (officially, the khedive was the sultan's viceroy). Kitchener, already in London advising the War Office, had long thought that some sort of self-rule under British guidance might replace Turkish rule in the Arab provinces, but he was opposed to the outright annexation of Egypt. He had his oriental secretary, Ronald Storrs, protest the Cabinet recommendation on the grounds that the British had always assured the Egyptians that their occupation was temporary; annexation would send the wrong message to the Arab-speaking world. Kitchener's prestige was too great to challenge, especially in the opening days of a war, and the Cabinet quickly yielded, allowing the office of the British agent in Cairo to establish a protectorate over Egypt. With Kitchener in London, Sir Henry McMahon, formerly foreign secretary to the government of India, was named high commissioner in Egypt.

The protectorate was a novel arrangement. The hereditary khedive, cabinet ministers, and governors of Egypt were permitted to promulgate decisions over their own names, thus maintaining the appearance that they were ruling Egypt, but British advisers attached to their various offices recommended their policies to them. In the delicate words of Ronald Storrs: "We deprecated the Imperative, preferring the Subjunctive, even the wistful, Optative mood."[6] The idea of the protectorate and the initial plans for an active campaign against the Turks were Kitchener's. Even from London he dominated decision making about the Middle East. Foreign Secretary Sir Edward Grey wrote on one telegram from Cairo: "Does Lord Kitchener agree? If so, I will approve."[7] Grey could have written the same note on every Middle East policy memo.

It wasn't only Kitchener's prestige that prompted the deference. London was woefully ignorant of the Arab world. Sir Mark Sykes, one of the few MPs who had traveled in the East, complained that there was no English-language history of the Ottoman Empire available, and none in any European language based on original research, and that the only available histories were all derived from a German work that stopped at 1744. Despite the importance of Syria to British plans, there wasn't a single recent book in any European language on the region.[8] Indeed, Kitchener seemed to have gathered every career officer or diplomat with a command of Arabic and experience in Cairo or Khartoum; his staff were the de facto British experts on the Arab-speaking world, and they preemptively took over the intelligence and policy offices in Cairo. Ronald Storrs, the son of an Anglican clergyman and educated at Cambridge, had more than ten years of experience as oriental secretary in Cairo. Sir Francis Reginald Wingate, a veteran of Kitchener's Khartoum campaign and governor of the Sudan, was an expert on intelligence and had spent his entire military career in the Middle East. Wingate's own agent in Cairo, Gilbert Clayton, was the director of intelligence for the Egyptian army. A personable man and adept at bureaucratic wrangling, at the end of October 1914 he was made head of all intelligence services in Cairo. He rapidly rose in rank from captain to general.

When Turkey entered the war in November 1914, mapmaking responsibility for enemy-held territory in Sinai, Syria, and western Arabia—Lawrence's job—was transferred to Cairo. With Carchemish now behind enemy lines, Lawrence tried to clean up the loose ends of his archaeological work before he traveled overland to Marseilles and caught a steamer to Port Said. In Cairo, he found himself joined by his friends Leonard Woolley and Captain Newcombe, and two young MPs who had served as attachés at the British embassy in Constantinople. They were all young—Newcombe, the senior in rank, was thirty-four—and cocky. "There wasn't an Intelligence department it seemed," Lawrence wrote to Hogarth, "and they thought all was well without it:—till it dawned on them that nobody in Egypt knew about Syria. This was the day we got there, so they changed their minds about sending us flying as good riddance—and set us to collect intelligence instead."[9]

As he had done when he first got to Carchemish, Lawrence wrote glib letters about the group that would be his colleagues and companions in Cairo: "Today we got the Office, and we all have the Intelligence: it is only a simple process of combining the two. . . . One Lloyd who is an M.P. of sorts and otherwise not bad looks after Mesopotamia . . . and Aubrey Herbert who is a quaint person looks after Turkish politics: between them in their spare time they locate the Turkish army, which is a job calling for magnifiers. . . . I am bottle-washer and office boy pencil-sharpener and pen wiper . . . and I think I have more to do than others of the faculty."[10] The sarcastic tone and forced humor were his style whenever he was an outsider or newcomer. He had known Newcombe and Woolley previously, but the others in the group were new, and had Etonian and Foreign Office credentials that Lawrence found both challenging and off-putting. In the settled expatriate military culture of Cairo, Lawrence was very much on the outside.

He found Cairo unpleasant: "Anything fouler than the town buildings, or its beastly people, can't be." When the city was gussied up for the opening of the Suez Canal, Baron Georges-Eugène Haussman had redesigned the downtown area with broad boulevards and grand, circus-style intersections. The British turned the Savoy, a celebrated turn-of-the-century hotel on the Midan Suleyman Pasha, one of Haussman's new boulevards, into their GHQ, which meant the officers worked in the midst of the better shops and cafés, and only a short block from the Nile. The British officers' club on Sharia Alfi Bey and the Continental Hotel across from Esquebia Park (where many junior officers were billeted) were a short stroll away. In between, on Sharia Mahgrabi—near the Turf Club, which Lawrence shunned, though it was popular with other officers—was a charming café called Groppi's. Lawrence liked to stop there for an iced coffee, and sometimes for chocolate when the weather wasn't too warm.[11] Directly across the street from Groppi's the dominant structure was an imposing neo-Pharonic synagogue built in 1899. Storrs called it "self-respecting but architecturally painful." The Egyptian Jews who built the synagogue were prominent in Egypt's banks, department stores, transport companies, and urban and suburban developments, and were major supporters of the Islamic Museum and the Museum of Modern Art. For Lawrence, who still dreamed of the Bedouin, Cairo was altogether too cosmopolitan.

He and his colleagues were soon working from morning to night. Lawrence's first assignments were to interpret data and write "little geographical essays," not as exciting as explorations in the Sinai or the years near the Berlin–Baghdad Railway construction outside Carchemish, but, Lawrence wrote, "it has been far and away the best job going in Egypt these few weeks. The people at the Pyramids or on the Canal have had a very dull time." Later, he and Philip Graves compiled the *Handbook of the Turkish Army,* mostly from talking to Turkish prisoners; the handbook was GHQ's primary source on the Turkish order of battle.[12]

The offices in the Savoy Hotel were new; the issues facing the new intelligence officers were not. The quintet of Newcombe, Woolley, Lawrence, Lloyd, and Herbert were responsible for interpreting information on the Turkish army, and on the potential battlefields and resources of the wide-flung Ottoman provinces; for making maps of remote areas; and for general strategic research. In addition to background research for tactical planning—the Turkish army was expected to attack in the Sinai—they had to inform a mid- and long-term British strategy for Mesopotamia, Syria, Palestine, Sinai, and Arabia, and as the local experts on the Arab world they were expected to pick up the pieces of the diplomatic initiatives Kitchener's staff would launch. Many of the provinces of the Ottoman Empire with non-Turkish, especially Arabic-speaking, majorities were potentially valuable to Britain, and even more valuable when Britain's competitors in the Middle East, including her allies France and Russia, also pursued them.

British and Indian experts thought that Mesopotamia, with its famously lush river valleys, was fertile enough to feed the hungry and growing populations of India; it was also close enough to Russia to bring back memories of the Great Game of diplomatic and military bluffs and feints Britain and Russia had played in Central Asia throughout the nineteenth century. Petroleum had been discovered in Mosul province, between Syria and Mesopotamia, and promising oily tars had been discovered in Basra province. In 1914 the British easily met their oil needs with purchases from the United States—even Persia, where the British had a toehold, supplied only 1/140 of the oil Britain got from the United States in 1913—but with the fleet already converted to oil, no one could venture a guess at future petroleum needs.

Palestine, or as the British preferred, the Holy Land, had been a British dream long before the nineteenth-century evangelical movement brought pilgrims, archaeologists, and conversion societies to Jerusalem. British memories and claims on the Holy Land went back to the Crusades and Richard the Lion-Hearted. The dream wasn't unique to the British. Russia sent so many pilgrims to Jerusalem that huge hostels had been erected in the Russian quarter to house the pious visitors. French histories of the Crusades awarded the credits and glories to French rather than British heroes, and France had rescued the popes often enough to consider themselves godfathers to the Church. The late nineteenth century had also brought a new contestant into the fray when the triumphant and much-photographed turn-of-the-century visits of Kaiser Wilhelm to Jerusalem and Constantinople established a German imperial presence in the Middle East. German schools and charitable organizations in Palestine rivaled the British and French institutions. The Jews had their own claims to the Holy Land, dating to the Bible; they had established a continuous presence predating the Romans, and could point to the economic and cultural achievements of the burgeoning Zionist settlements.

No one had paid much attention to the Arab aspirations for the same land. The British were vaguely aware of obscure secret societies in Damascus and Cairo that talked of an Arab nation, and Négib Azoury in Paris had tried to articulate a concept of Arab nationalism in his writings, but the secret societies, with their handful of members, and Azoury's readers together were a minuscule audience. When the Arabs held a congress in Paris in June 1913, it was attended by twenty-five people, apart from two Iraqi students who happened to be in Paris. To the British diplomats and generals who stared at the maps in London, Cairo and Simla (the Indian summer capital, which became a shorthand for the Indian government), the words "Arab" and "nation" seemed a strange juxtaposition: there were no institutions of statehood in the Arabic-speaking world, no parliaments, no national economies, and scarcely any cultural or educational institutions, except a few madrassas that deliberately distanced themselves from anything as worldly as politics and diplomacy.

Sherif Hussein of Mecca had hinted at relegitimizing the caliphate, and even of moving it to the Hejaz. The khedive in Egypt also seemed to see himself as a potential rival to the sultan; there had been talk that he planned to seize the Muslim holy places in the Hejaz and declare himself caliph. Fear of the Turkish authorities kept these schemes undercover and secretive until the declarations of war between the Entente and the Ottoman Empire. Then, suddenly, shadowy figures appeared in Cairo, requesting urgent meetings with British officials. It remained for British intelligence to determine whether the clandestine groups and hidden armies they purported to represent were well-kept secrets that had been concealed from the Turks, deliberate deceptions to decoy or mislead the British, or figments of the imaginations of those mysterious figures who found ways to sneak their stories, plots, and schemes through the social and geographical barriers that kept native Egyptians out of the British circles in Cairo.

One of the first proposals was from Abdul Aziz al Masri, an Arab who quietly approached the British in Cairo in August 1914. Al Masri had served with distinction in the Turkish army, and had founded a secret society in Damascus called al Ahd, its members Arab officers in the Ottoman army dedicated to the establishment of a "united Arabian state, independent of Turkey and every other Power except England," extending from Alexandretta, on the Mediterranean, to Mosul, in the Kurdish lands between Mesopotamia and Syria, and on to the Persian frontier. He claimed that the strength of his movement was in Baghdad, Nejd, and Syria, that a majority of Syrian Christians and Druze were on his side, and that in return for British support in the form of "money and armaments . . . handed over secretly in Mesopotamia or elsewhere" he was willing to promise Britain "preferential mercantile treatment throughout a rapidly developing Arabia (including Syria)" and assurance "for ever against a movement through Persia on India."[13]

Months later, when it was clear that Turkey would end up allied with Germany and against Britain, al Masri sought an interview with Captain G. F. Clayton, the head of British intelligence. Clayton asked him whether the Arabs would back the Turks in the war. Al Masri said that the Arabs were not yet organized, and that without a definite lead they would almost certainly side with the Turks, who had been diligently soliciting Arab support with presents and "every kind of promise" to the Arab chieftains. Despite the Turkish efforts, al Masri told Clayton, seeds of disloyalty had been sown in the Mesopotamian army, and if they got sufficient funds, artillery, rifles, and ammunition from the British he could equip a nucleus force that would form a rallying point for the Arab chieftains and their forces. Al Masri called it a natural partnership: "Great Britain would supply the sinews of war and the Arabs would supply the fighting element. In this way a close alliance would be cemented between Great Britain and the newly formed Mohammedan Power, to the mutual advantage of both."[14]

On its face, it was an appealing proposal. The British command in London, including Kitchener, were eager to concentrate their efforts in Europe and reluctant to commit substantial forces to the Turkish theater. Using Arab troops against the Turks would not only relieve the demand for British and Commonwealth troops, but would face the Turks with the challenge of native rebellions. Still, Clayton was skeptical. An Indian army expeditionary force had already sailed from Bombay and launched a thrust into Mesopotamia to secure the British oil terminals at the head of the Persian Gulf. The operation was controlled from Simla, the headquarters of the government of India. The Indian government had expansive ambitions in Mesopotamia, with designs on the vast plains between the Tigris and Euphrates rivers as a breadbasket for India. Simla was wary of independence movements, which in India had led to outbursts of nationalist fervor and episodes of bomb throwing. When the Anglo-Indian expeditionary force subdued the Shatt al Arab, the lower reaches of the confluence of the Tigris and Euphrates, they proclaimed victory and issued promises of a new British administration: "We have nothing to fear from the populace of Baghdad and there is good reason to hope that once we are in control over Baghdad and the river and telegraph to Basra, the tribes in the Euphrates valley . . . will accept our regime automatically."[15] The Indian commanders gave no credence to al Masri's warnings that the Anglo-Indian forces would face major difficulties without local support from Arab leaders.

Al Masri wasn't the only one with a proposal for the British. Early in 1914, Sherif Hussein, the emir of Mecca and guardian of the holy places, sent his son Emir Abdullah to Cairo for private meetings with Kitchener and Storrs. Abdullah was eager to know what the attitude of the British would be if the Turks were to try to depose his father. In early 1914, when it wasn't at all clear that Turkey would be Britain's enemy in the war, Kitchener was noncommittal. By September, when war against Turkey seemed possible if not inevitable, Storrs suggested that they open a correspondence with Abdullah to reassess the situation. London authorized the probe, and Kitchener sent a message asking whether in the event of war with Turkey, Abdullah "and his father and the Arabs of the Hedjaz would be with us or against us." The reply was noncommittal, but Sherif Hussein's request for "a written promise that Great Britain will abstain from internal intervention in Arabia and guarantee the Emir against foreign and Ottoman aggression" was encouraging. The messenger who brought the reply said he had been told that if Britain agreed to this condition, Sherif Hussein would not support the Turkish war effort. The British did not question that the nominal ruler of the Hejaz had taken it upon himself to speak for all of Arabia.

By the time Hussein's reply arrived in Cairo, Turkey had entered the war, and Kitchener, with the approval of the prime minister and Foreign Minister Sir Edward Grey, agreed that Britain would provide the assurance Hussein sought should "the Arab nation assist England in this war."[16] This exchange of messages has been controversial for almost a century. There was no entity in 1914 that could reliably be identified as "the Arab nation," indeed no group that manifested any of the institutions of a nation. Some historians have suggested that the British staff in Cairo distorted Kitchener's intent by rephrasing and embellishing his message before it was sent to Abdullah, and that what sounded like a grand call to an "Arab nation" in his message was really meant only as an appeal to Sherif Hussein's nominal subjects in the Hejaz. On the other hand, Kitchener did not protest when the full text of the message was forwarded to London.[17]

Emir Hussein was no doubt encouraged by another sentence in the message the Cairo staff had sent him over Kitchener's name: "It may be that an Arab of the true race will assume the Caliphate at Mecca or Medina, and so good may come by the help of God out of all the evil which is now occurring." Hussein's ambitions toward a revived caliphate were no secret, and Hussein openly claimed that he, as a direct descendant of the Prophet, was "of the true race." The messenger who delivered the letter was received secretly by Hussein and brought back notes of their conversation, reporting that Hussein said that he had every intention of breaking with Turkey, but that with the hajj pilgrimages to Mecca disrupted by the war, his principal sources of income—tariffs and transportation of pilgrims to the holy places—was so diminished that he was in financial straits and dependent on Turkish aid. In the meantime, he said he would try to avoid taking any action against British interests.

On this last point Hussein was true to his word. In mid-November the sultan, in his authority as caliph, issued an Islamic jihad against the Entente. The powers of the caliphate had not been tested for a long time, and Britain, France, and Russia were afraid that Muslim soldiers in their own armies might heed the call for a holy war against all infidels and mutiny. Sherif Hussein, who as guardian of the holy places was widely respected in the Muslim world, found a host of excuses not to lend his support to the call for jihad. His main reason was probably to deny any recognition of the sultan as caliph, but British officials in Cairo and London were grateful for his skillful inaction, which they saw as another pointer to a potential alliance.

The negotiations with al Masri and Emir Abdullah, and the hints toward a potential alliance and recognition of Sherif Hussein's ambitions, were a fait accompli in December 1914 when Lawrence and his colleagues were installed as intelligence officers in Cairo. They soon found themselves in the thick of fundamental policy issues. The war planning for the Turkish theater was still fluid, and bureaucratic lines had not yet hardened in Cairo and London, although the authorities in Simla had preempted some areas as falling exclusively under their interest. The young intelligence agents in Cairo, and even their boss, Clayton—who had been there long enough to recognize the complexities of negotiations with sheikhs, emirs, chieftains, and those shadowy figures who claimed to represent secret groups plotting against the Turkish authorities—were still open to new ideas. The notion of an independent Arab state was batted around freely, although for the most part the British viewed the idea more as a potential thorn in the side of the Turks than as an actual component in the future of the Middle East. Clayton also explored an alliance with Sayid Mohammed ibn Ali (called the "Idrisi"), the ruler of Asir province, north of Yemen, who was known to oppose the Turks. The Idrisi welcomed the attention, but the government of India, claiming a special role in dealings with him and with the Wahhabi chieftain ibn Saud, titular ruler of vast areas in the center of the Arabian Peninsula, remained sufficiently wary of separatist and nationalist movements to downplay any talk of an Arab Revolt.

Despite all the talk of Arabia, the initial focus of strategic planning for Lawrence and his colleagues was Syria, the province of the Ottoman Empire that extended from the southern border of Anatolia to Gaza and Sinai, encompassing contemporary Syria, Lebanon, Israel,

Sinai, and parts of northern Iraq and Jordan. Lawrence had been fascinated by Syria from the time he studied the great crusader castles, and was comfortable enough in his knowledge to write up a handbook, "Syria: The Raw Material," for British intelligence. In the usage of the time, his comments are about the Ottoman province of Syria, which included Palestine. Much that he wrote was harsh, judgments reflecting his own sense of what constituted a "true" Arab. The people of Jerusalem and Beirut, he wrote, were too cosmopolitan to be considered Arab: the residents of Jerusalem, "with the rarest exceptions, are characterless as hotel servants, living on the crowd of visitors passing through. Questions of Arabs and their nationality are as far from them as bimetallism from the life of Texas." Beirut, he wrote, "is as representative of Syria as Soho of the Home Counties." He described the Syrian politicians as superficial and lawless, with a passion for petty politics but little ability to master the subtleties of the political situation: "They are all discontented with the government they have, but few of them honestly combine their ideas of what they want. Some (mostly Mohammedans) cry for an Arab kingdom, some (mostly Christians) for a foreign protection of an altruistic thelemic order, conferring privileges without obligation." A few demanded "autonomy for Syria," but there was no developed Syrian nationalism; even the words "Syria" and "Syrian" were foreign terms: "By accident and time the Arabic language has gradually permeated the country, until it is now almost the only one in use; but this does not mean that Syria—any more than Egypt—is an Arabian country." To Lawrence the "verbal poverty indicates a political condition. There is no national feeling. Between town and town, village and village, family and family, creed and creed, exist intimate jealousies, sedulously fostered by the Turks to render a spontaneous union impossible."

Lawrence's harshest comments were reserved for the Jews in Palestine, especially "the foreign (German inspired) colonies of agricultural Jews, who introduce strange manners of cultivation and crops, and European houses (erected out of pious subscriptions), to a country like Palestine, at once too small and too poor to repay efforts on such as a scale." He allowed that the Jewish settlements of North Palestine (Galilee) were at least "honest in their attempts and colonization . . . in comparison with the larger settlements of sentimental remittance-men in South Palestine. Locally, they are more than tolerated; one does not find round Galilee the deep seated antipathy to Jewish colonists and aims that is such an unlovely feature of the Jerusalem area." One group he placed "a degree lower," the "German Zionist Jews, speaking a bastard Hebrew and German Yiddish, more intractable than the Jews of the Roman era, unable to endure near them anyone not of their race, some of them agriculturists, most of them shop-keepers, the most foreign, most uncharitable part of its whole population." Like most of the Jewish settlers from Romania and Russia, Aaron Aaronsohn came from a family that often spoke Yiddish at home.

Lawrence's contempt for the Jewish settlers was not coupled with any sympathy for the native population of Palestine: "Behind these Jews is their enemy, the Palestinian peasant, more stupid than the peasant of North Syria, materialist and bankrupt." The only hope for Syria, he concluded, the only "imposed government that will find, in Moslem Syria, any really prepared groundwork or large body of adherents is a Sunni one, speaking Arabic, and pretending to revive the Abbassides or Ayubides."[18] The obscure historical references shielded his analysis even from much of the staff at the intelligence office. Lawrence was arguing that inland Syria, the Syria of the four great cities of Damascus, Homs, Hama, and Aleppo, should belong in a new Arab caliphate. Given Kitchener's hints of support for a new caliphate, and Sherif Hussein's ambitions, Lawrence's suggestion was a scheme for a vast new Arab nation, stretching from the Hejaz to incorporate much of the Ottoman province of Syria, including Palestine.

The harsh language and judgments, and obscure references, were typical Lawrence. In Cairo, as at Oxford, Lawrence affected an eccentricity and penchant for mischief and humor that many, especially outside his small circle of trusted colleagues, found off-putting. Aubrey Herbert, as an upper-class Etonian, may have been snobbish in his reaction to Lawrence's antics, but he wasn't the only one to find the second lieutenant "an odd gnome, half cad—with a touch of genius." "It was not only the pompous, the inefficient and the pretentious whose co-operation Lawrence's ways tended to alienate," wrote Ernest Dowson, the director of the Survey of Egypt. "Many men of sense and ability were repelled by the impudence, freakishness and frivolity he trailed so provocatively." Lawrence's cultivated unmilitary appearance—a solitary pip on his sleeve, trousers that stopped at his ankles worn without a belt, his peaked hat askew, a Sam Browne belt as often as not buckled loose over his unbuttoned shoulder strap or forgotten altogether—along with his shockingly youthful face and toussled hair—added to the impression of frivolity and rebellion.[19]

Lawrence, Woolley, and Newcombe lived at the Continental Hotel, across from the opera house and the Ezebekiya Gardens. The hotel was a huge shambles of a place, famed for the plaza in front where every manner of unusual merchandise, from boa constrictors and caged leopards to old issues of the New York *Tribune* and the *Daily Mail,* had once been for sale, and acrobatic baboons had performed on the backs of donkeys. With the coming of war the plaza had become a casual parade ground of suede boots, fly whisks, and swagger sticks. The three intelligence officers took their breakfasts, lunches, and dinners together, rode together on bicycles from the hotel to their temporary offices in the Egyptian army office, and shared the reports that arrived.[20] Aubrey Herbert and George Lloyd, upper-class Etonians with good connections in London, condescended to Newcombe and Lawrence. They no doubt got snubbed in return, and ultimately left. But even with long-term friends like Woolley and Newcombe, Lawrence's antics and manner left him a loner. Behind the apparent frivolity, verbal one-upsmanship, and sometimes forced humor his colleagues saw, Lawrence was immersed in his own grand strategic and tactical ideas for the future of the Middle East.

~

Five days after he arrived in Cairo, Lawrence wrote, "The interest may shift violently to the north almost any day:—so far as we are concerned it has shifted already."[21] He was referring to a plan the intelligence staff had worked on for an amphibious assault by British troops at the extreme northern border of Syria, designed to cut Syria, Egypt, and Arabia off from the Turkish homeland in Anatolia, and to provide Britain a foothold from which they could easily reach Aleppo, Hama, Homs, Damascus, and Palestine. More important for Lawrence: "A landing at Alexandretta in February 1915 would have handed over Syria and Mesopotamia to their native (Arab) troops . . . and automatically established local governments there." He expanded the rationale for the plan in two intelligence memos, pointing out that Turkish supply lines to Syria, Sinai, and Mesopotamia had to pass through Alexandretta because the Berlin–Baghdad Railway tunnel through the Amanus Mountains had not been built. He cited a Turkish officer's opinion that "the Power that held Alexandretta would control Cyprus . . . and be virtual master of the Eastern Mediterranean and of the Suez Canal." And he claimed that the Germans feared nothing as much as a landing by the British in the north of Syria, because "a general Arab revolt, directed by the pan-Arab military league, would be the immediate result of our occupation of Alexandretta following on a defeat of the Turkish forces in the south."[22]

The War Office and Kitchener initially supported the plan, although both the War Office and the Admiralty revised the optimistic intelligence office estimate of 1,000 to 2,000 men needed for an invasion force upward to 21,000 men. What the Cairo intelligence officers had not included in their enthusiastic memos was an assessment of the reaction of the French, Britain's ally in the overall war effort and a nation with independent aspirations in the Middle East. The French had long considered Syria to be in their sphere of influence, had plans for the area after the war, and had mobilized Syrian exiles and the French community in Cairo to lobby for their position. To reinforce the propaganda efforts of their diplomatic staff and the Maronite and Roman Catholic clergy in Cairo, the Quai d'Orsay sent François Georges-Picot, a career diplomat who had served as consul-general in Beirut and as secretary at the French Agency. Lawrence and his colleagues argued that Arab interests in Syria, including the non-Maronite Christians, would be eager for a British protectorate on the Egyptian model to prevent future French colonization of Syria. But Picot and the pro-French lobby in Cairo made enough of a stir about French interests in Syria to forestall the proposed British invasion. "So far as Syria is concerned," Lawrence wrote home, "it is France and not Turkey that is the enemy."[23]

The final decision about the Alexandretta plan was up to London. On February 17, Sir Edward Grey telegraphed McMahon in Egypt that, on the issue of British annexation of Syria, "French opinion is most sensitive and you should do all you can to discourage any movement of the kind even as regards Alexandretta or places near Syria. . . . We have promised to associate the French with us if we undertake serious military operations in that region."[24] There were in fact logistical problems with the tentative plan, and conflicting demands for British naval power: the Russians wanted a direct British attack on Constantinople, or at least on the straits, to distract the Turkish military while the Russians launched an attack in the Caucasus. But from the perspective of the intelligence office in Cairo, it was the French aspirations for Syria that had waylaid the attack on Alexandretta.

Lawrence saw the aborted plan as a bitter defeat. He wrote to Hogarth, urging him to try to pull strings to revive the plan, and arguing that conditions were almost ripe for a general Arab uprising. In another letter, Lawrence pinned his hopes for an Arab uprising on the Idrisi, Sayid Mohammed ibn Ali, the leader of Asir province. Lawrence hoped that he and Captain Newcombe might be sent to advise the Idrisi, but the opposition of the Indian government ended Lawrence's hopes of working for an Arab uprising from that corner of the Arabian Peninsula. "Everything has been left undone, that we ought to have done," he wrote to his friend Leeds. "And we have done nothing at all. So I'm as sick as might be, and yet not so sick as the rest of us. . . . So you see I'm bored, and Woolley's bored and Woolley wants to go home, and I want to go somewhere where there are no politics." A month later he again vented his frustration: "The only branch I want, Arabian politics, they won't give us, but leave in the hands of a status quo."[25]

Despite the policy frustrations, Lawrence's job had become intense and absorbing. He still didn't like Cairo, but he had found a sympathetic friend in Ronald Storrs, who was a fluent Arabist and shared Lawrence's love of books. "I would come upon him in my flat," Storrs recalled. "Reading always Latin or Greek, with corresponding gaps in my shelves."[26]

In early May 1915 T. E. Lawrence's brother Frank, the favorite of the family, was killed on the western front. "To die for one's country is a sort of privilege," Lawrence wrote his father. "Mother and you will find it more painful and harder to live for it, than he did to die: but I think that at this time it is one's duty to show no signs that would distress others: and to appear bereaved is surely this condemnation." His mother wrote back with something that upset him, and Lawrence answered: "You *will* never understand any of us after we are grown up a little. *Don't* you ever feel that we love you without our telling you so?"[27] As much as he had grown used to disappointing his mother, he seemed never to escape his vulnerability to her criticism.

He kept busy, exploring the use of aerial photography, then in its infancy, for mapmaking, using data taken with handheld cameras under the supervision of the Survey of Egypt. When the intelligence department started issuing daily intelligence bulletins in April 1915, it was Lawrence who assembled the military and political information from agents, travelers, reconnaissance flights, prisoners, captured documents, and the intelligence reports of other commands. He described the enterprise with his usual sarcasm: "We edit a daily newspaper, absolutely uncensored, for the edification of twenty-eight generals: the circulation increases automatically as they invent new generals." The daily reports were his "only joy: one can give the Turkish point of view (in imaginary conversations with prisoners) of the proceedings of admirals and generals one dislikes: and I rub it in, in my capacity as editor-in-chief."[28]

Tweaking the mustaches of the generals was a distraction, but Lawrence still dreamed of Arabia. He wasn't alone in his interest. Sir Reginald Wingate, governor general of the Sudan (he was called "Sirdar," a borrowed Persian-Indian term) encouraged talk of a new caliphate that would undercut the role of the sultan. Sir Edward Grey authorized publication of a statement saying "that His Majesty's Government will make it an essential condition in any terms of peace that the Arabian Peninsula and its Moslem Holy Places should remain in the hands of an independent Sovereign State," and that while the size and boundaries of any future state were "not possible to define at this stage," the idea of a new caliphate was left as an issue that "must be decided by Moslems without interference from non-Moslem powers" and with the assurance that their decision would be "respected by His Majesty's Government." Others, like McMahon in Cairo, had their doubts, cautioning that "the idea of an Arabian unity under one ruler recognized as supreme by other Arab chiefs is as yet inconceivable to the Arab mind."[29] But even with McMahon's doubts, the British acceptance of the idea of an independent Arab state was meant to reach Sherif Hussein, who enjoyed respect and a following as the guardian of the Muslim holy places. To make sure, in mid-June airplanes dropped versions of Grey's message over selected areas of the Hejaz.

But only a few of the generals and politicians shared Lawrence's interest in Arabia in the spring of 1915. The attentions of most of the generals, the Admiralty, and the War Office were focused on a small town on the peninsula that parallels the Dardanelles strait. For many of them it was the first time they had heard of a place called Gallipoli.

8

Sarah

The famine became more intense and devoured whole houses and families. The roofs were covered with women and babies too weak to stand, the streets full of old men already dead. Young men and boys, swollen with hunger, haunted the squares like ghosts and fell whenever faintness overcame them. To bury their kinsfolk was beyond the strength of the sick, and those who were fit shirked the task because of the number of the dead and uncertainty about their own fate; for many while burying others fell dead themselves, and many set out for their graves before their hour struck. In their misery no weeping or lamentation was heard; hunger stifled emotion; with dry eyes and grinning mouths those who were slow to die watched those whose end came sooner.

—Josephus, *The Jewish War*[1]

And the Jews who were sold as slaves, their masters had to let them go because Jews were bad slaves. Where are the days that Jews did not know how to be slaves?

—Avshalom Feinberg[2]

Sarah Aaronsohn grew up between two worlds.

In the pioneering world of the Zionist settlers she was a free spirit, adventurous, working alongside men, ready to ride off into the countryside on her horse at a moment's notice, spending long hours with her brother and Avshalom Feinberg in earnest discussions of politics and the future. Although she was an experienced seamstress and known for her ability to re-create the latest Parisian fashions, she dressed in the simple and uninhibiting clothes of the agricultural pioneers. Outside the home she spoke French and Hebrew, a newly revived spoken language for a new land. Eretz Israel saw itself as a new community, a society free of the myriad taboos and rules that had constrained life in the shtetls of the Old World. Sarah had a reputation for being the first woman in Palestine to refuse to wear a corset.[3]

But Sarah lived in a household that still spoke the Yiddish of the shtetl. She was educated in the Zichron school and was well-read, and she could be passionate and obstinate about Palestine, but she had grown up in a world where women were not encouraged to think of themselves as intellectuals. "What do I need learning for?" her mother, Malka, would say. "Give me character."[4] Ephraim and Malka were not overtly observant in their Judaism, but the stories of the Hebrew Bible were as familiar in their household as tales of George Washington to an American schoolchild. The patriarchs and matriarchs, and biblical heroines like Deborah and Esther, became models of social conduct for the family and a shorthand for describing proper or prescribed behavior—in the same way that the characters of Greek mythology have lent their names to psychology and myth. Sarah and her sister, Rivka, were both named after matriarchs, as were many children in the settlements. The young socialists of the second aliyah debated what they called "free love" and questioned the institution of marriage, but families like the Aaronsohns clung to Old World ideas of the roles of men and women. Women worked in the Jewish settlements, often alongside men, but among the first generation of settlers it was assumed that whatever her talents, a woman would ultimately be a homemaker and helpmate to her husband. The early Zionist movement hadn't paid much attention to women either: at the first congress in 1897, when Dr. Moritz Kornblüh asked Herzl where women attending could vote, Herzl answered "The ladies are of course very honored guests, but will not take part in the vote."[5] After Malka died at the age of fifty-three, it fell to Sarah to take on the burdens of the Aaronsohn household. The family called her Sarati, my Sarah.

When Avshalom Feinberg, with his brooding gaze and poetic pyrotechnics, arrived in Zichron, he was like a hero out of the romances Sarah and Rivka had read. Sarah was a sensual woman, close to Avshalom's age; she was also a proud and independent spirit, not about to be swept off her feet, especially when Avshalom's intensity and poetry sometimes seemed to mock her fierce independence. By contrast, Rivka was reserved, the quietest of the Aaronsohns. For years Avshalom seemed to be in love with both of them, sometimes using one to carry messages to the other. "Yes," he wrote to Rivka. "Take Sarah, kiss her like you know. Give her marks on her neck. Hug her with all your strength. When we meet, I will pay you back."[6]

But gradually, after the death of his father, to whom he had been very close despite their arguments about the future of the yishuv, Avshalom began to choose. From Paris, and even when he was away for a few days in Hadera, he wrote long letters to both sisters, but most were to Rivka. Even then, his letters to Sarah were passionate and held little back. "Sarati—," he wrote. "In spite of everything, here we are, still friends, and I love you with all the strength of my heart. But you make me furiously angry, and for that you are a naughty girl, Saraleh, my darling. I would like to enjoy a quieter happiness, so I ask you to send me quickly, in a registered parcel, your little sister. We will talk about you here, I promise you, and think of you when the sun goes down. In the moonbeams we will see something of your dreaming eyes, and in the flame of the setting sun, your ardent heart."[7] When Avshalom and Rivka began to talk of marriage, he wrote Sarah: "It seems that the situation of being a bride can drive a person crazy. If in addition there are women who will drive a person crazy every day then everything is perfect. . . . Well, a blue veil I do not have to bring to you. Too bad, this way I would look for Leah and see her."[8]

Proud and fiercely independent, Sarah had no desire to be the Leah of the Bible, the unbetrothed older sister who foists herself on Jacob when he thinks he is marrying his beloved Rachel. She resigned herself to Avshalom marrying her sister. And because she had grown up with a strong sense of the Old World tradition that an older sister must marry first, before Rivka could marry Avshalom, Sarah had to find herself a husband.

In the early spring of 1914, a Bulgarian businessman from Constantinople named Chaim Abraham was in Palestine on a business trip, and was introduced to Ephraim Aaronsohn as a potential husband for his oldest daughter. Chaim was well dressed and well mannered, and spoke effusively about his home in Constantinople and the rich social and cultural life there. Sarah agreed to the betrothal before she met Chaim, and invited her younger sister to join them in a double wedding. Rivka declined, and in March 1914, Sarah was married to Chaim Abraham. In the wedding photographs Sarah has put on weight and looks glum and uncomfortable. The bride and groom left for Constantinople with a trousseau Sarah had made herself.

The gracious home and rich social life of Constantinople Chaim Abraham had described so enthusiastically turned out to be a dark, damp house and a gossipy *kaffeeklatsch* of Chaim's mother and aunts. Before Sarah could unpack, her new mother-in-law told her she could not go out alone in Constantinople, that her life would be with the women of the household, perhaps at an occasional tea with other ladies of the Jewish community, while the men, including her husband, would spend their days in business. When Sarah announced that she wanted to explore the city she was told that it was much too dangerous for a young woman to be out on the streets alone. Sarah, who had fearlessly ridden alone in the desert and the foothills of the Carmel, carrying a revolver for protection, who had grown up in the camaraderie of Zichron and Athlit, sharing work and talk with her brothers and other men of the community, was appalled at the isolation imposed upon her. She protested, and her rebellious attitude became gossip fodder for the tight-knit Sephardic community in Constantinople.

As the Ottoman Empire slid into war, Sarah found herself cut off from news of Palestine. The postal resources of the empire were allocated to military use, which let the paranoid Young Turk government censor rumors and news they deemed unpatriotic. Sarah could report little of what she saw and heard in the capital to family and friends in Palestine, and only learned of the woes that had come to Palestine, and especially the Jewish settlements, through occasional visitors to Constantinople and rare hand-carried letters. She would occasionally write of her unhappiness, and sometimes sneak a message in microscopic writing under the stamps on postal envelopes. The infrequent reports from Palestine compounded her loneliness, and she fell into helpless despair. "Only God knows how much I hate the life I lead here," she wrote to Avshalom's sister Tzila, who was in Berlin. "Famine reigns in Palestine, and I sit here without even lifting my little finger."[9] Chaim, absorbed in his male world of business, was as oblivious to the wartime news of starvation in Palestine as he was to Sarah's unhappiness.

And while she was married, Avshalom was still part of her life. Not long after she moved to Constantinople, Avshalom wrote:

> You do not know, beloved and longed-for child, and you cannot imagine, as we could not before, how great a part of my heart you took. The lion's share you took for yourself, you left almost nothing for us. Sometimes, at home, I forget that you are gone. . . . In the room, your empty bed is standing. And it is chasing the thought without giving it a rest. And every corner, every thread, every breath is speaking of you. And we are close, the two that were left behind, and we want to forget. . . . More than blood connections and bonds are tying us and our love, the habits, and the common torments. . . . We two who remain are drawn together and try to forget, but someone is missing, missing. But these words are selfish. If we who are left amongst our own, and in our own homes, are so full of complaints, how difficult and bitter it must be for you. For you, poor child, are alone, from morning until evening, alone and unhappy. And our hearts come out to you Sarah, all our hearts and love. Remember the tale we used to be quiet for? The daughter after her wedding day, getting ready to leave, crying with tears streaming down her face. The mother comforting: do not cry, my girl, after all, you are going

with your husband. I went also; I left my parents' house. And the daughter answers: easy for you to say, you left with a father, I am leaving with a stranger.[10]

~

Feinberg wrote of politics with the same passion as his letters to Sarah. When Djemal Pasha ordered the Jews expelled from Jaffa in March 1915, he wrote that the Turkish expulsion policy had been ordered by the Germans, that the Turks were under the thumb of the Germans, and with the Germans backing the Turkish policies against the minorities, "the Yishuv stands on the brink of annihilation."[11] If he was right, the only hope for the Jews of Palestine was to take their destiny into their own hands by organizing a revolt against the Turks.

Aaronsohn shared Feinberg's feelings about Germany and the German influence on the Turks. Although he had worked with Warburg and other prominent German scientists, and admired their scholarship, he found the same authoritarianism and condescension both in German science and in the attitudes of the German officers and officials who had come to advise the Turkish army and authorities. In 1912, Nathan Strauss, a trustee of the research station and advocate of the pasteurization (or as it was then called, "sterilization") of milk, had urged Aaronsohn to pursue public health research alongside his agronomy programs; with funds from Strauss, the Hadera branch of the research station, close to coastal swamps, had begun medical and public health research that would lead to the eradication of mosquito-borne diseases. Aaronsohn talked to Dr. Zeev Brin about directing the medical research, a decision that angered Dr. Hillel Yaffe, the Zichron physician, who assumed the job would be his. Brin and Aaronsohn ultimately had a falling-out when Brin proved too beholden to German science and German advisers.[12] But unlike Feinberg, Aaronsohn did not yet put the Turks in the same category with the Germans. Aaronsohn still had many positive memories of the years he had spent in Anatolia, and the Turkish efforts against the Jews, even the requisitions and the arbitrary expulsions of Jews from the cities, seemed amateurish alongside the cold efficiency of the Germans.

At almost the exact moment that Feinberg began to consider a Jewish uprising against the Turks in Palestine, in Alexandria a different Jewish revolt against the Turks was already under way. The idea began with Vladimir Jabotinsky, a journalist and essayist from Odessa who had become a celebrity in the Jewish communities of Europe after the publication of his Russian translation of Bialik's powerful Hebrew poem about the Kishinev pogrom of 1903, "In the City of Slaughter." The quote from Hillel that Jabotinsky chose as the epigraph for his translation—"If I am not for myself, who will be for me?"—became the touchstone of his fervent advocacy of Jewish self-defense.[13] Jabotinsky's notoriety grew after his passionate speeches at the Zionist congresses, where he criticized the incremental tactics of the leaders of the movement in Berlin and London. He compared Herzl's meetings with the kaiser and the sultan to a Jew who boasts of a conversation with the governor:

> "How come the Governor spoke to you?" someone asks. "And what was the conversation about?"
> "Oh, it was very simple," the braggart answers. "I came to see the Governor during reception hours. As soon as I uttered the first few words, he shouted, 'Get out!' "[14]

Jabotinsky was in France when he learned that Turkey had allied herself with Germany. He came to Alexandria with credentials as a war correspondent and immediately began to organize the eighteen thousand Jewish refugees who had been deported to Alexandria from Palestine in the early days of the war. They became the Jabotinsky Regime, with their own police force, and by March 1915 Jabotinsky was demanding that the British permit the formation of a Jewish legion to fight in Palestine. The British resisted, distrustful of Jabotinsky and afraid that the organization of a Jewish military unit would set off civil strife between the Arab and Jewish populations in Palestine. As an alternative they allowed Captain Joseph Trumpeldor, a celebrated Jewish veteran of the Russo-Japanese War, to recruit Jewish men into a military unit under British officers. Trumpeldor was popular and charismatic; he had lost an arm at the battle of Port Arthur and had been personally decorated by the tsar. He recruited 650 Jewish volunteers, including a professor at the lycée in Alexandria, students of law and divinity, a physician, a rabbi, a tinsmith, tailors, and men who listed no occupation. The volunteers sewed Star of David insignia on their uniforms and drilled in Hebrew and English with five British and eight Jewish officers, under the command of Captain Trumpeldor and British lieutenant colonel J. H. Patterson, an Irishman. Many spoke little English, but they knew the Bible well enough to appreciate it when Colonel Patterson called their mules "sons of Belial." In April 1915 the unit paraded in Alexandria to great cheers from the local Jewish community. Their honorary chaplain, the grand rabbi of Alexandria, blessed the troops, exhorting them to bear themselves as good soldiers and to call on the name of the Lord in times of adversity. They then gave up the old weapons they carried for their parade, and 562 men with 20 riding horses for the officers and 750 mules boarded two small ships. They were not told their destination.[15]

~

Early in 1915 the Russians had urgently requested that the British mount a diversionary attack on the Dardanelles strait, pleading that without a relief operation to draw Turkish troops from the Caucasus front, Russia might be driven out of the war. With the western front strategy stalemated in the French trenches, the War Cabinet in London also sought a diversion, and Winston Churchill, eager to see the navy engaged, volunteered to attack the Dardanelles as a preemptive blow against Constantinople. The initial attempt to force the strait by aging British and French warships encountered mines: three battleships were sunk and another French warship was beached. Churchill's admirals did not realize that they had encountered a single line of mines that had hastily been laid parallel to the European shore, and that a second attempt with their warships could easily force the strait.

Instead, the British and French withdrew their ships and prepared an amphibious assault on the Gallipoli peninsula. The Jewish brigade that sailed from Alexandria became part of a vast amphibious assault force, ships bringing men from the far corners of the British and French empires—troops from India and Ireland, Gurkhas from Nepal, New Zealanders and Australians from Egypt (the Egyptians were glad to see them leave after their boisterous antics in Cairo),[16] Senegalese troops that fought alongside the French—all destined to assault the beaches and steep cliffs of Gallipoli.

Gallipoli was a needless battle. By the time assault troops were at strength and preparedness to launch their attack, the Russians had already overpowered the Turkish troops in the Caucasus, and the diversion in the Dardanelles was no longer necessary. The Turks, realizing that they would have to defend against an amphibious assault, moved troops to the strait and turned the command of the Ottoman forces at the Dardanelles over to the German general Liman von Sanders, who in turn assigned key responsibility to a formerly passed-over officer named Mustapha Kemal, an enthusiast for European ways who scorned Ottoman backwardness and proved a brilliant tactician in seizing the high ground at Gallipoli. The gears of decision-making in London turned too slowly to save the brave Australian, New Zealander, British, French, and Jewish soldiers who would disembark on the beaches under the withering fire of Kemal's guns.

The Jewish soldiers from Alexandria were known as the Zion Mule Corps. They were issued no weapons. Each of their mules carried a wooden pack frame with four four-gallon kerosene tins for water for the troops. Leading the mules ashore, up the steep slopes, and on the unprotected paths between the Allied trenches left the unarmed Jewish soldiers exposed to murderous Turkish artillery, machine-gun, and small-arms fire. Trumpeldor was shot in his good shoulder, but refused care so he could continue to command his men. More than half of the soldiers of the Zion Mule Corps were wounded, and many died at Gallipoli, but the unit came away with no glory and no credentials as fighting men. For the ANZAC troops who died on the rugged hills or climbing the steep cliffs, and who are buried in well-tended plots that are the site of annual pilgrimages from Australia and New Zealand, Gallipoli was a chance to prove themselves and their young nations in battle. The Jewish soldiers of the Zion Mule Corps, with neither arms nor a nation, could prove nothing.

But news of the Zionist Mule Corps spread. Some in Palestine, Europe, and America saluted the bravery and achievements of the men who had volunteered and served. Others argued that whether under the Turks or the British, the Jews of Palestine would always be mule drivers.

~

The day before the British started landing troops at Gallipoli, Aaronsohn met with Djemal Pasha to report on the state of the locust infestation. He had already realized that cooperating with the Turks offered no possibility of aiding the Jewish settlers or of preparing for their future. The meetings with Djemal were only one more frustration, a reminder that he was powerless to help the Jewish settlers.

For weeks that spring Alex Aaronsohn heard his older brother's heavy footsteps wearing holes in the carpets at Athlit and in Zichron.[17] Aaron paced when he was trying to think his way through a difficult problem. He and Avshalom knew that if an unarmed mule corps was the closest Jewish soldiers would get to fighting the Turks, ideas like Avshalom's call for an uprising against Turkish oppression were futile. Turkish rule was the only government most Jews in Palestine had ever known, negotiation and accommodation with the Turks the only political experience they had. Even if the Jews had been eager to revolt, few had military training or experience. Those who had not bribed their way out of the Ottoman draft had served only in labor brigades. They had no weapons beyond the rifles and revolvers they owned for personal protection, and the Turkish army had seized most of those in the early days of the war. With barely enough food and supplies to fend off starvation, and with their carts, wagons, and draft animals already requisitioned, the Jewish communities lacked both the food supplies and logistics that an organized uprising would require. A revolt was destined to be stillborn.

The Zionists held a profound disdain for the despairing tales of Jewish history, but memories in Palestine were long, and after almost two thousand years the story of the great Jewish revolt against the Romans was still vivid. "Once, Rome had all the world," Feinberg wrote to an uncle.

> All the nations did what you think we should do now with Turkey. And all those nations stopped being who they were and became Rome's. Only one nation did not give in, did not cooperate with Rome. A nation that did not send an army for an army, a nation for a nation, every person went against the enemy. All that was on the land was protected with iron and saturated with blood. And when everyone fell on the battlefield, Rome could say: We have conquered a land but not a nation. That nation was the Jews.[18]

Many Jews in the yishuv drew very different conclusions from the same history. Before the first-century revolt against the Romans, the Jews of Palestine had for the most part coexisted peacefully with the Romans, speaking the same language (Greek), borrowing architecture and customs from each other, tolerating each other's practices. It was only after repeated provocations—Caligula declaring himself a deity in 39 C.E. and ordering his statue displayed in every temple; Roman soldiers burning Torah scrolls and exposing themselves in the Temple in Jerusalem; the last Roman procurator, Florus, stealing huge quantities of silver from the Temple; and the Jews finding themselves subjected to confiscatory special taxes—did moderate Jews join ranks with the zealots in revolt. Feinberg would have enjoyed telling how when riots broke out in Jerusalem in 66 C.E., the Jewish masses easily defeated the small Roman garrison and then as the revolt spread to the Jewish towns in the Galilee, they defeated Cestius Gaius and his much larger force from Syria. Two millennia later most Jews still knew the end of the story: the Romans returned to Palestine with 60,000 heavily armed troops, crushing the revolt in the Galilee and killing 100,000 Jews before the legions marched south to Jerusalem. Inside the city zealots burned the food that had been stockpiled in preparation for a siege, hoping to compel universal participation in the revolt. Moderates fought back against the zealots, and the internecine war and famine magnified the suffering and casualties as the Romans breached the walls of the city in 70 C.E. The Roman orgy of destruction culminated with the looting and destruction of the Second Temple—a disaster that changed the direction of Judaism forever.

The horrendous price of the failed revolt was known to every Jew, marked by the annual fast day of Tisha B'av, by three daily prayers observant Jews said for the restoration of the Temple, and by a ruling of the sages that, in permanent mourning for the lost temple, "a man may stucco his house, but he should leave a little bare. . . . A man can prepare a full-course banquet, but he should leave out an item or two. . . . A woman can put on all her ornaments, but leave off one or two."[19] In 1915, a full-course banquet was already a distant memory in the yishuv, and any woman with jewels had sold or pawned them to buy food. The Jews of Palestine hardly needed reminders of how much worse their fate could be.

What other options were there for the Jews? The Gideonite self-defense groups and the Ha-Shomer watchmen were perhaps a precedent, maybe even a framework for a larger paramilitary organization. Disciplined military units under the blue-and-white Jewish flag could spark the consciousness of the Jewish community, define Palestine as both a Jewish homeland and a nation, and prepare for a future of self-government. But both groups lacked the training, numbers, weaponry, and supplies to fight against an organized army. They even lacked the mules and uniforms of the Zion Mule Corps, who at least had the backing of the British fleet and armies.

The British made the difference. Aaronsohn and Feinberg concluded that the only hope for the Jews to rid themselves of the Turks and Germans was a British victory in Palestine. But by late spring 1915 the British army in Egypt was still manning static positions guarding the Suez Canal. The canal was the highest priority in the region for the British, but it was of little strategic interest to the Zionists, and while the British army focused their efforts on protecting the canal, the Turks had free rein in Palestine. The most effective move into Palestine would be a direct invasion on the coast, cutting off supply lines from the north, but even the Turks no longer feared a landing; their defensive positions were concentrated in Sinai, opposite the British forces on the canal.

Aaronsohn was sure the British lacked detailed mapping of Palestine. They could spy on the coast from the sea or take crude aerial photographs of areas within range of their single-engine, single-seat planes, but without native agents in the field the British could not know the details of the terrain, the Turkish order of battle, or the status of their training and preparedness—the very information that Aaronsohn, Feinberg, and the group they had gathered at the research station in Athlit knew better than anyone. Aaronsohn's expeditions for botanical and geological research had accumulated unparalleled knowledge of the terrain and water supplies. The researchers who had been sent out to work on locust eradication had visited Turkish military facilities in every part of Palestine. They had traveled over the roads and railroads the Turks would use to move troops and equipment; they had seen the supply depots and knew what equipment had been stockpiled, and the level of ammunition, uniforms, arms, and food available to the Turkish army; they had seen military units in training and knew the level of preparedness of various elements of the Turkish forces. The researchers had listened to the grumbles of German and Turkish officers and enlisted men about poor equipment, shortages of ammunition, and logistics logjams. They had well-placed friends who could monitor railway junctions and key roads for traffic. Aaronsohn had met several times with Djemal Pasha, the commander of the Turkish Fourth Army, and had a close-up sense of the man.

Aaronsohn had no training in military strategy and tactics. "It is humiliating for an observing man of science to be . . . ignorant of war questions which he has always scorned and which, nevertheless, are today of such overwhelming influence in everybody's life," he confessed in his diary.[20] He also had no experience in the complexities of wartime diplomacy and the vagaries of coordinating operations with allies. He saw the strategic issues of a Palestine campaign in simple terms: if the British had the up-to-date intelligence that he, Feinberg, and their group could provide, they could attack Palestine in force, preferably by a direct invasion on the Mediterranean coast—a plan similar to what Lawrence had urged on the British command, except that Aaronsohn wanted the attack close to the main concentration of population in Palestine, and was in a position to supply detailed intelligence on the defenses the British would meet. Early in the war, Aaronsohn knew, the Turks had feared an invasion on the coast because a landing would cut off the Arabs in the south, who might then revolt. The Ottoman commanders had posted sentries and concentrated defensive forces along the Mediterranean from Haifa south. As the war progressed and the British seemed content in their static positions protecting the canal, the rumors and defensive preparations against a landing on the coast all but disappeared, which by itself was a compelling argument in favor of Aaronsohn's strategy.[21]

In late spring 1915 Aaron and Avshalom decided to approach the British command. Aaron's younger brother Alex, then twenty-six years old, would be the contact person. Alex had gone to the United States at Aaron's urging in 1910—in part because his activities with the Gideonites had gotten him in trouble with the Turkish authorities—and had stayed there, working for the USDA, until 1913. His English was excellent, in appearance he could almost pass for a British junior officer, and there were compelling reasons to get him out of Palestine. When Alex finished his labor brigade service he had told Djemal Pasha in an interview that one of the pasha's trusted senior officers had organized a gang of men who were stealing official supplies for their own use, and otherwise abusing their power. The pasha investigated and discovered that the officer Alex had named was too well connected to censure. When the officer learned of Alexander's testimony, he began a vindictive campaign against him. Aaron thought Alex was in danger if he stayed in Palestine.[22]

Rivka, Aaron's youngest sister, would accompany her brother. Aaron may have feared for Rivka; she was tiny and shy, unlike her brothers and older sister, and probably seemed especially vulnerable. Avshalom's engagement to Rivka was quietly set aside—he was too determined to actively oppose the Turkish military, or perhaps he realized that Sarah, off with her new husband in Constantinople, was his true soulmate. At the end of the school year Rivka and Alex set off for Beirut by donkey, Alex wearing his old Turkish uniform to avoid questions from the Turkish patrols. On the road they lived off bread, dried figs, and chocolate they had brought with them, drinking water from ponds and streams. Alex talked his way through a military checkpoint at the outskirts of Beirut, and he and Rivka abandoned the donkey, changed into civilian clothes, and bought forged Spanish passports as a married couple. They dressed to match the photographs in the passports, bribed a dragoman to get access to the bureaucracy, passed a cursory examination by a Turkish official, and boarded HMS *Chester,* bound for Alexandria. Before the ship departed British officials announced that they would not allow refugees from the Ottoman Empire to disembark in Egypt, so Alex and Rivka disembarked and talked their way onto the American cruiser *Des Moines,* sailing on July 15, 1915, for Rhodes with Greek and Italian refugees, then on to Egypt. They were searched when they boarded—the Ottoman authorities allowed no one to leave with more than $25—and Rivka's Bible was discovered. Alex told the officials that they needed the map of ancient Canaan in the Bible to know which way to turn for prayers.

The *Des Moines* took a roundabout route, reaching Alexandria in early August. Alex was not allowed to disembark, but sent notes to friends in the city who intervened with the local officials. Once they landed, he and Rivka found their way to the Continental Hotel, where Lawrence and the other British intelligence officers were billeted, and he presented himself at the British GHQ in the Savoy Hotel, only to discover that no one would meet with him: British intelligence routinely turned away walk-in offers. To legitimize himself Alex published articles in the *Egyptian Gazette,* a local English-language newspaper, about the economic situation in Palestine and Syria, the impact of the locust plague, and the weakness of the Turkish defenses on the Palestine coast—knowing British intelligence would read them. On August 18, he was interviewed by Colonel Newcombe, Lawrence's colleague and the commander of Lawrence's prewar expedition to Sinai.

Alex Aaronsohn spoke excellent English. He explained Aaron's plan to Newcombe, how his brother had used the research station in Athlit and their role in the locust campaign to gather intelligence on the Turkish army in Palestine, and that he was prepared to supply that information to the British command. He listed the incredible range of intelligence they could provide and explained that they could use Aaron's relationship with Djemal Pasha to obtain a continuing stream of new information. Newcombe asked what the Zichron group wanted in return. When Alex said they wanted nothing, Newcombe lost interest.[23] He made no further appointments to meet with Alex and made it clear that he wasn't interested in the offer.

Even years later neither Alex nor Aaron could understand why Alex's mission had failed, but the explanation may not be difficult. At the time Alex met Newcombe, British intelligence in Cairo was in the midst of delicate negotiations with Sherif Hussein in the Hejaz. The potential Arab alliance was a top priority for British intelligence, and the possibility of an Arab Revolt was considered so important that motions were under way to set up a separate Arab Bureau within British intelligence. The negotiations with Hussein followed months of offers and proposals from Arabs and Turks, from former Ottoman military officers to freelance agents to sitting emirs. Every proposal that came to British intelligence, whether from an adventurer with no address and fantastic promises or an emir offering his troops to the British war effort, had come with a quid pro quo—an expectation of sterling, gold, arms, equipment, services, or promises of future recognition and support from the British. Newcombe and his colleagues were not surprised by the demands: they knew from experience that everything in the Middle East came with a price, and that every price could be bargained. Alex Aaronsohn, an Ottoman subject, a Jew from Palestine, speaking English with an American accent, no doubt seemed suspicious on his arrival at Alexandria. When he offered a fantastic array of intelligence on Turkish deployment, preparedness, and plans in Palestine *and wanted nothing in return,* Colonel Newcombe must have concluded that he was either an enemy agent sent to ferret out British plans, a counterspy sent to plant false information, or a self-deceived crackpot.[24]

Instead of asking for more information the British ordered Alex Aaronsohn to leave Egypt.

~

At the research station in Athlit months went by with no word from Alex. After a last payment of $5,000 in November 1914, Turkish censorship and the British-French blockade of the coast had cut off the American funds on which the station was dependent. The spring harvest had been poor, and more signs of starvation were showing up in the Jewish communities. The intelligence on the Turkish military that Aaron, Avshalom, and their colleagues had gathered was perishable, as were their military and administrative contacts throughout Palestine; if they didn't make an arrangement with the British soon, the information and contacts would go stale. With no messages from Alexandria, by early summer Aaron and Avshalom concluded that Alex's mission must have failed, and that they needed a new effort to make contact with the British.

One possibility was to send a messenger across the Sinai to Cairo. The Sinai was terrifyingly harsh in summer, but an experienced camel or horse rider might be able to evade the Turkish patrols by dressing as a Bedouin and traveling at night—if he was somehow able to find friendly wells. Only the desert buzzards would know the fate of a rider who did not find water. Avshalom and Aaron wondered how British troops, wary of another attack on the canal, would greet a rider coming out of the desert from Turkish-held territory.

An alternative was to quietly launch a boat off a Palestine beach at night, sail for the open Mediterranean, and hope to be picked up by one of the Allied ships enforcing the blockade of the Syrian and Palestinian coasts. Feinberg knew a willing boatman with a capable boat, and had a sympathetic companion eager to reach Egypt for his own reasons who was willing to accompany him on the journey. In early August 1915, before he could complete the arrangements for a boat, the French command announced that they were tightening their blockade. Under the new policy French warships would sink on sight all suspicious boats in the territorial waters of the Ottoman Empire.

All spring and into the summer the American cruiser *Des Moines,* the same ship Alex and Rivka had taken from Beirut, had been calling at Haifa and Beirut to take on refugees and to deliver relief supplies. Those missions were scheduled to end with one final call in Haifa to rescue eligible refugees. Feinberg urged Aaronsohn to leave before the blockade sealed their last route of escape; at least Aaronsohn would be able to communicate with their supporters in the United States and raise funds for the station and the local population on the Galilee coast. Aaronsohn refused. "I have the responsibility of a captain on board ship," he wrote in explanation. "A faithful captain abandons his ship when the waves sweep him off the bridge. I will abandon my responsibilities when I have a rope around my neck."[25]

Instead, they agreed that Feinberg should try to get to Egypt on the *Des Moines*. On the morning of August 2, Feinberg set off for the harbor in Haifa, carrying a falsified Russian passport. He had experimented with disguises, and had asked Alex Aaronsohn to get him a keffiya and jalabiya months before. At the port Feinberg saw four Turkish officers who could have recognized him, but their laziness or his disguise worked, and he was allowed to board the *Des Moines*. On August 30, the ship weighed anchor and lowered the Ottoman courtesy flag they had displayed in port, leaving only the American flag flying. "When the flag was taken down," Feinberg wrote, "I think the beautiful stars of the flag were never saluted with so light and grateful a heart, and with such artistic antics, for I got rid of all the accessories which I had provided myself—a baroque hat, incredible eye-glasses, and a momentary seriousness of mien."[26] The ship arrived at Alexandria on September 6, three days after Alex and Rivka left for Gibraltar. Feinberg had no money and nothing to eat, but he had the address of an interpreter with British naval intelligence at Port Said, a Christian Arab refugee named Charles Boutagy, the son of the former assistant British consul in Haifa. Boutagy's father was to have been Feinberg's companion on the aborted mission to cross from Palestine in a small sailboat.

The young Boutagy put Feinberg in touch with Lieutenant Leonard Woolley, Lawrence's colleague in Carchemish and on the Sinai expedition. Woolley had been seconded from the British intelligence office in Cairo to naval intelligence at Port Said. He thought of himself as an archaeologist on temporary assignment with the intelligence services, and lacked Newcombe's many years of experience and cynicism about offers of information from undercover sources. Woolley also shared Lawrence's enthusiasm for literature, and may have been drawn to Feinberg, with his intense, brooding gaze and poet's facility with language.

Woolley was wary of Feinberg's talk of an armed rebellion in Palestine, but was intrigued by his detailed information about the Turkish military and their preparations in Palestine, and by his description of the group at the research station and their proposal to provide a steady stream of updated intelligence reports. The British had occasionally sent a ship up the coast to make contact with Arab agents on the coast of Lebanon, and Woolley suggested that the ship could stop at Athlit if the right signals were given from shore. He introduced Feinberg to Captain Lewen Weldon of naval intelligence, a gruff Yorkshireman and a regular passenger on the runs of the spy ship; Weldon would give Feinberg the codes that could be used from Athlit to signal the ship.

While they awaited the first dark night for a run of the ship, Feinberg exchanged letters with Alex Aaronsohn, who was in Gibraltar with Rivka waiting to get passage to America. Alex urged Feinberg to join them in the United States, where they could campaign together for American support and contributions for the communities in Palestine. Feinberg could write manifestos and appeals while Alex lobbied. Feinberg refused. "If I have things to say," he wrote, "then I have to say them in the room of the leader, in the office of those of influence, and not in the columns of the newspaper. I know that the objective we have set ourselves is difficult, and the way will be long. But that doesn't bother me. My aim is to succeed: either to be victorious or to die."[27] As a Francophone with a penchant for drama, he may have had a sense of himself as a Rimbaud.

Feinberg waited months for the British ship to be ready to make a run up the shore of Palestine, using the time to compose a long letter, over three hundred pages, to Henrietta Szold, the secretary of the research station board of trustees and one of their most enthusiastic American supporters. In precise and expressive French he described the conditions in Palestine in wartime, the ravages of Djemal Pasha and his administration, the loss of crops, production tools, draft animals, and weapons for self-defense, and the need for their cooperation with the British. He knew he was speaking to a still-neutral American audience, and that a majority of the board members of the research station were not Zionists. He also knew enough about the popular opinion of the war and Palestine in the United States to write Alex and Rivka urging that they not focus their efforts in America only on fundraising but also appeal to the hearts and minds of young American Jews.[28] He smuggled the long letter to Henrietta Szold in the luggage of a Jewish refugee who had gotten passage to the United States.

The British schedule for spying runs up the coast was dependent on moonless nights, fair weather, calm seas, and the needs of the intelligence bureaus. It was November 8, 1915, before the small ship was finally ready for a trip from the base at Port Said along the coast of Lebanon. At one-thirty in the afternoon they passed offshore at

Athlit, and Feinberg was able to signal to the group ashore that he would be back later that night. At eleven that night, under a moonless sky, the ship anchored below the great crusader castle, and Feinberg was rowed ashore. He showed one of the sailors from the ship where to meet them on the next rendezvous, then walked up to the research station, where he surprised Aaronsohn, who was working late. They went together to Zichron, and Feinberg distributed gifts he had bought in Alexandria and announced that in ten days another ship would come by and signal. If the ship got a signal from shore that the coast was clear, it would return in darkness to send a man ashore for the newest intelligence on the Turkish military. Feinberg sent a message back to Woolley, marking the day their operation began: "Friday, November 5, when I had the honor to receive a farewell blessing from you and return to Palestine."[29] The group celebrated that night in Zichron: the plan had worked!

With communications to British intelligence established, Aaronsohn set off on a long ride through the north of Palestine to gather fresh information. Despite his heft, he was a strong rider, able to ride and observe from 4:30 A.M. until after dark, day after day. He was also a phenomenal observer: once, when he was in Berlin with Sonia Suskin, he pointed out a woman at another table of a café and said that he knew from the way she was eating a plum that she was Ukrainian.[30]

In a few days of riding across the Galilee Aaronsohn filled three pocket notebooks with detailed information about the placement of artillery, routes and schedules of troop and equipment trains, the training level of units, and the conditions of roads and railroads. A scientist at heart, his military notes ("I was seized with emotion as I thought that this little camp—situated at hardly 10 kilometers from the coast could be reached in less than ten minutes by an hydroplane and strewn with those deathly flechettes of which Captain Abdul Hamid spoke with so much fear on his return from the Canal Expedition") were juxtaposed with the observations of a passionate botanist and agronomist ("I wonder if it was my love for trees that grieved me so much at sight of such wanton destruction of our forests—or rather the hurt pride of an inventor whose system has not been applied. Still I believe that they would have obtained better results had they followed my plan"). He noticed the progress of construction on new roads, the price of grain, the varieties of oxen the Turks were using ("If these Balia oxen could become acclimatized to our country, they would be excellent draught-oxen"). He saw what looked like telegraph posts, analyzed the wood, and determined where the poplar trees had come from. That the long and heavy trunks could be transported told him the quality and condition of specific roads. He saw signs of locusts and studied them with his magnifier to predict whether they would breed. He speculated on where radio signals could be picked up and whether radios would be useful to him and his colleagues for contact with the British. Some of his notes were written in a code so they would be unintelligible if police or military authorities stopped him. He took a gleeful delight in concealing his purpose with irony: describing the plans for a large Turkish celebration, he listed the officers who would be there, and added that Djemal was so brave, so unafraid of enemy aircraft, that he would attend the celebration even in an area that lacked antiaircraft defenses![31]

Aaronsohn's curiosity turned spying into science. In Beirut he was "struck by black and white wooden boards at the bottoms of the masts of hospitals, schools, and similar institutions, both Turkish and German," and speculated that the French had requested the markers so that they could avoid shelling those buildings. He later noticed that the marker boards were turned away from the sea, which meant either that the Turks did not understand the French request or that his earlier explanation of the marker boards was wrong. With his blond hair and fluent German he could pass well enough to solicit comments from German officers. A young doctor told him: "This German Army must reach Constantinople not as much to relieve the Turks who should take care of themselves—but to relieve us." In three days Aaronsohn rode from Haifa across the Galilee to Rosh Pinah (close to where he discovered the wild emmer on the slopes of Mount

Hermon), then back across northern Galilee to Sidon, in Lebanon, and on to Beirut—a remarkable distance for a rider and a single horse, and considering the copious and detailed notes he compiled, a remarkable achievement of information-gathering.

Feinberg made a comparable information-gathering sortie to the south. Others at the research station upped the pace of their own spying, covering the countryside on horseback, camel, or on foot to visit railroad junctions, military bases, supply depots, schools that had been transformed into hospitals, road and telegraph construction, and other potentially useful military sites. If they were stopped, they would explain that they were conducting geological or botanical research for the research station. The intelligence reports piled up, hidden in haystacks or buried in a leather box at the research station. When the ten days expired Feinberg and a colleague, Menashe Brunstein, waited at the designated spot for a signal from the British ship they were expecting. They made sure someone was always on duty at the research station, night after night, watching for a signal. Some nights were stormy, or the moon was too bright for a ship to approach. On December 2, they spotted a ship and signaled, but the ship never returned. On December 14, men waiting on the shore saw a ship sail up and down the coast in front of the crusader castle; they thought the ship had signaled them and frantically waved back. Aaronsohn, aware that soldiers in the area had been told to watch the locals whenever a ship approached, had to warn the men that their frantic signals risked the safety of the research station.[32]

Weeks went by, with many calm, moonless nights that would have been perfect to pick up the reports. But no ship came.

~

Sarah Aaronsohn was in Constantinople while the city prepared for the British and French attack at the Dardanelles. Until she was married she had known the Ottoman Empire only from the hilltop village of Zichron Ya'aqov, a world so distant from the capital that she had never had the opportunity to realize the truth of Gertrude Bell's observation: "No country which turned to the eye of the world an appearance of established rule and centralized Government was, to a greater extent than the Ottoman Empire, a land of make-believe."[33] Sarah was in Constantinople in 1915 when the make-believe facade began to crumble, after Turkish forces were handed a resounding defeat by the Russians in the Caucasus, and the battle cruiser *Goeben,* the prize wrung from the Germans at the beginning of the war, made ready to flee to the Black Sea to take her chances against the Russian fleet. The cafés buzzed with rumors that the British and French fleets were massed at the mouth of the Dardanelles. Cynics whispered that Djemal Pasha's "reconnaissance in force" had actually been a failed attack, and that the feared British forces were still in place across the Sinai preparing an attack of their own. Crowds in the streets watched the state archives and gold reserves being taken out of the city to safety, and saw special trains prepared to evacuate the sultan and foreign diplomats. Highly placed members of the government readied private cars with long-range fuel tanks for their own escapes. The victory at Gallipoli raised spirits from the spring nadir, but the Turkish casualties there were high, and the long battle had drained reserves of ammunition and trained men. Even with German officers urging them on, all the sultan's camels and all the sultan's men could not restore the make-believe that had sustained the empire for centuries.

While morale slowly collapsed in Constantinople, Sarah was confined to the dark and damp house, isolated, bitterly unhappy, and lonely. Her marriage was loveless, and her mother-in-law and the other women in the tight-knit Constantinople Sephardic community regarded her as a rebellious outsider. After Alex and Rivka left for Beirut, Sarah stopped receiving reports or mail from Palestine. "I want to tell you something interesting," she wrote to Feinberg's sister Tzila, who had stayed a close friend, "but I am still disconnected from everything. I can't wait until I will be able to go home and live with those I love. I am not in touch with my family, they don't write to me, my father is alone and my heart goes out to him. I can't keep writing because of my tears."[34]

In August 1915, Chaim Abraham left Constantinople for a business trip to Vienna and Berlin. Sarah quietly contacted Yitzhak Haus, a member of the Ha-Shomer self-defense organization who had been sent to Constantinople to negotiate the release of Ha-Shomer leaders who had been arrested and held in Bursa. She persuaded Haus to allow her to accompany him on his return to Palestine, and on November 25 they set off. They were able to board trains for part of the journey, but as nonmilitary passengers they were bumped repeatedly by troops or had their engine commandeered for military trains. When trains weren't available they rode for stretches in peasant carts. The journey took three weeks. Nothing had prepared Sarah for what she saw.

Across Anatolia she saw abandoned villages left behind when Turkish troops had driven the Armenians out of their homes. Some villages were still smoldering. Women and children walked or even crawled along the roads, clothed in rags, their bodies emaciated, begging for scraps of bread. She saw troops evicting entire populations with whips and rifle butts, kicking, beating, or shooting the stragglers. Soldiers, deserters, and bandits roamed through the abandoned shops and houses, looting whatever they could find. Packs of dogs drove off the vultures to gnaw on unburied corpses. When they stopped in small towns she met women who had been raped, who had seen the men of their villages lined up and shot, who had helplessly watched their children starve or die of exposure. Women were dazed, wandering aimlessly, on the verge of madness. Typhus and dysentery raged. She saw a Turkish train deliberately drive over typhus-stricken Armenians waiting on the tracks of a station.[35]

On December 13, Aaron received a telegram sent from Aleppo four days earlier, telling him that Sarah was coming to Zichron for the winter. She arrived in Afula in mid-December. Aaron went to get her in a rented carriage. "Today, just as before," he wrote in his diary, "she is the same splendid girl we have always known. Her trip lasted three weeks exactly, and what sights her eyes have seen! She has known exhaustion, suffered from want, and in front of her very eyes has seen the Armenians tortured by the Turks." A month after she got home Sarah could still talk of nothing but the Armenian massacres. "If we do not succeed in liberating ourselves from them [the Turks] in time," she told Feinberg's friend Liova Schneersohn, "they may yet do to us what they have done to the Armenians."[36]

During Aaronsohn's marathon spying ride across Palestine and back he had taken advantage of his blond hair and fluency to talk to German officers. They had repeated rumors that the Armenians had poisoned flour so that three thousand Turkish soldiers had died after eating Armenian bread. Another rumor said that Armenian women had seduced entire platoons of Turkish soldiers in the mountain passes of the Caucasus, giving them diseases and weakening their will to fight. He heard that Armenian girls were being sold for two or three gold pieces each. A Turkish officer bragged: "There were two and a half millions Armenians before the war. After the war there will not be half a million left. A beautiful prospect!"[37]

Aaron had recorded the remark in his diary, as he had recorded the species of plants he saw. There were always rumors in wartime. A scientist by training, he was skeptical of rumors and hearsay until he had seen the evidence himself or had read an eyewitness report from someone he trusted. And there was no one he trusted more than his sister Sarah. She had always been the levelheaded one, the one who could pick up the responsibilities of a large and busy household after their mother died.

Once Aaron and Avshalom heard Sarah's descriptions of what she had seen across Anatolia, they could no longer discount the stories of Turkish persecution and outright massacres of the Armenians as rumors. Cut off from information by distance and censorship, and with the ready comparison of the escalating measures against the Jews in Palestine, they concluded that they could only expect the same fate as the Armenians. Just weeks before, new regulations had been announced in Haifa drafting all Jewish men from twenty to forty-five. The new recruits would be issued no bread rations, and had no stores of food at home for their families, which made the levy "nothing less than a death sentence—through starvation—not only for the enlisted men but for the women and children they shall leave behind."[38] At the end of 1915 the Turks would still let men buy their way out of breaking rocks on the roads, but after years of starvation few could afford the baksheesh. It was "only a pretext," Aaron wrote in his diary, "the truth being that they would meet a shameful, cruel, and certain death." The Jews of Palestine, he and Avshalom concluded, would soon have no escape from the fate that Sarah had already seen inflicted on the Armenians.

"My teeth are ground down from worry about whose turn is next," Feinberg wrote in a note to Woolley that could not be delivered. In another note he wrote that Djemal Pasha wanted to hang the Jews after he had hanged Christians and Muslims: "Our turn will come one fine morning, when a moment of ill-will, or a fluttering butterfly, or a sunbeam, or any other poetic reason pushes the great commander to implement his cherished plan. And so I mostly ask myself upon whom fate will descend, on that day when the pasha says he wants to have his wish 'for breakfast.'"[39]

Their only hope was a British victory in the war. And the victory had to come soon. But weeks had gone by with no British ship. Feinberg had been so trusting of the scheme he and Woolley had put together that they had failed to establish an alternate connection. After weeks without a signal from a British ship, there was no way to ask why the ships had not come.

9

The Arab Bureau

So you see I'm bored, and Woolley's bored and Woolley wants to go home, and I want to go somewhere where there are no politics.

—T. E. Lawrence[1]

By August 1915 Lawrence—who still had his boyish looks and still dressed with conspicuously disheveled nonchalance—was a senior member of the intelligence staff in Cairo. Newcombe had been posted to the Dardanelles to work on the Gallipoli campaign, and Woolley had been seconded to naval intelligence in Port Said to coordinate with the French navy and with agents on the Lebanon and Palestine coasts. Lawrence's job was

> finding out where the Turkish army is: that is, to know at any moment where each of the 136 regiments is:—how many men are in each, who commands it, and what artillery is round about it. Then we have to tell anybody who wants to know what any place in Turkey is like: what the landing places are, what the roads are like, if the people are friendly or not, and how long it would take to get reinforcements there. Then we have to try and find out what is happening politically in the interior of the country, and how the harvests are, and who are the local governors, and things like that.

One of his main duties was mapmaking: "not the actual drawing of course, but the style of it, the colours to be used, and what is to be put in or left out. That is the most interesting part of the work, though I am very fond of my army. Following it about is like making a map of the movements of a fly before breakfast."[2] What Lawrence needed, but did not know about, was the information that Aaron Aaronsohn and his group at the research station in Athlit were eager to provide. Without their firsthand intelligence, collecting information on the Turkish order of battle and preparations was mostly guesswork.

In August 1915 Lawrence was sent to Athens for a week to coordinate with the Levant branch of British intelligence. He found Athens "very hot, the glare of the sun very bad. Otherwise not dull." He bought nothing, and saw "nothing except the Acropolis from the window."[3] When he returned to Cairo he learned that a messenger had arrived from Sherif Hussein with the long-awaited answer to the British offers of support for Arab independence in exchange for Arab military action against Turkey. The British proposals had been deliberately vague, carefully couched to avoid alienating the French, the government of India, and the tribal chieftains in Arabia. Hussein's reply was jarringly precise. He expected recognition of a new Arab caliphate that would include not only the Hejaz and the Arabian peninsula (which the British had hinted they could support), but also Mesopotamia and all of Syria, including the great cities of Damascus, Homs, Hama, and Aleppo, and Palestine—an area comprising the entire Arabic-speaking world in Asia. He insisted on a yes-or-no reply within thirty days.

Ronald Storrs, who read the message first, thought it was a bargaining position, like the first offer a seller makes in a souk. He and everyone else in British intelligence in Cairo knew that Hussein's proposal would receive little support among the many chieftains whose territories would be swallowed up by the proposed new caliphate, that France would oppose any giveaway of Syria, and that India would adamantly oppose losing their influence in southern Arabia. After considerable debate Cairo sent Hussein's messenger back with a polite reply that effectively ignored Hussein's demands. "We could not conceal from ourselves," Storrs recalled, "(and with difficulty from him) that his pretensions bordered upon the tragi-comic."[4]

While Cairo waited for Hussein's next response, a young Arab officer in the Turkish army named Sherif Mohammed al Faroki crossed the British lines at Gallipoli under a white flag, supposedly to arrange burials for the Turkish dead, and announced that he would provide information on Arab nationalist movements if the British guaranteed that he would not be treated as a prisoner. Al Faroki's initial story seemed plausible, he was sent to Cairo for debriefing, and Lawrence, as a senior intelligence officer with a good knowledge of the French and Arabic al Faroki spoke, was assigned to interview him. Al Faroki offered information on the Turkish military, but Lawrence and British intelligence were more interested in his avowed membership in al Ahd, the secret Arab nationalist society headed by Abdul Aziz al Masri, with whom the British had already held talks. Al Faroki explained that he and other officers had joined al Ahd even before Anglo-Indian troops attacked Mesopotamia. When he was later posted to Syria he learned about Fatat, a secret civilian organization with goals similar to al Ahd's, and he had been instrumental in building bridges between the two organizations through a secret coordinating committee that had been given details of the British negotiations with Sherif Hussein. Al Faroki claimed that a central office of secret Arab nationalist societies in Damascus was "in continual communications with the Headquarter Office," that they had branches "in every important town or station," a cipher, and a treasury of £100,000 from members' subscriptions. They were so powerful, he said, that neither the Turks nor the Germans had dared to attempt to suppress their activities though they were fully aware that the organization's "attitude has been, at least passively hostile, and in the cases of many of its members actively sympathetic toward the Allies, more especially Great Britain." He also said that their members agreed with the boundaries Hussein had demanded for a new Arab caliphate, that an Arab rebellion had been planned on the north Syrian coast in expectation of a British landing in Alexandretta, that anti-Turkish feeling among Arab troops in the area bordered on mutiny, and that they had a plot to have a sympathetic Arab officer in the Turkish army design useless defenses for the city.[5]

Al Faroki's information was a shock for British intelligence. If what he reported was true, Sherif Hussein represented not only his own interests and his ambitions for his sons, but had broad-scale backing among Arab nationalist leaders in both Syria and Mesopotamia, which made the expansive boundaries he sought for his caliphate no longer seem ridiculous, and suggested that the negotiators in Cairo had been cavalier in brushing off his offer. Hussein had partially proved himself by not supporting the sultan's call for a jihad. If he had the support to do more, if he could marshal broad Arab support over an enormous area of Ottoman territory, Britain stood to gain enormously in the negotiations with Hussein: it would not take much unrest in areas like Syria, Mesopotamia, or Arabia to divert substantial Turkish resources from defense to domestic peacekeeping. Indeed, intelligence reports had already come in about Djemal Pasha's determination to deal with potential Arab traitors: he had dispatched Arab units in the Turkish army from Syria to Gallipoli, publicly hanged eleven alleged Arab traitors in Beirut, sentenced forty-five others to death in absentia, and exiled or imprisoned others.

For Lawrence, al Faroki's testimony was a revelation. If his report about the preparation of an uprising in north Syria was trustworthy, it validated Lawrence's long advocacy of an invasion of Alexandretta. Lawrence knew that France was as much a problem for a British landing in northern Syria as Djemal Pasha. Still, he had not given up his hopes, and had continued to lobby for the plan, reporting that there was an "off chance of it. Only the big show [Gallipoli] must go wrong or go right first."[6] Even if the Alexandretta operation never happened, al Faroki's reports that Sherif Hussein enjoyed broad support among Arabic-speaking officers in the Turkish army and in sectors of the civilian society were fuel for Lawrence's imagination and strategic thinking. Some in Cairo had regarded Hussein as a clownish, overambitious pretender, a peripheral figure trying to take advantage of the war for self-aggrandizement. It was no secret that Hussein pictured his sons on the thrones of Arabic-speaking nations that could be carved out of the Ottoman Empire, and saw himself taking the sultan's place as caliph with the seat of Islamic spiritual and temporal authority moved from Constantinople to Mecca or Medina so that he and his sons would rule the Arabic-speaking world in Asia. With al Faroki's report Hussein suddenly seemed the potential leader of a large-scale revolt. Words like rebellion and revolution, and the images of Bedouins that had haunted Lawrence's imagination since he first read Doughty, were now a striking new possibility.

Al Faroki's information also carried a potential threat. The Turks had already successfully wooed some Arab chieftains, and the Arabs also had enough experience with the Turks to imagine the reprisals against allies of the British if Turkey and Germany prevailed in the war. When Clayton, as head of intelligence, asked al Faroki whether the Arabs might switch their preferred allegiance to the Turks, he was told, "We would sooner have a promise from England of half what we want than a promise from Germany and Turkey of the whole, but if England refuses us we must turn to Germany and Turkey."[7]

Clayton and his colleagues were still mulling the situation when another telegraphed message arrived from Sherif Hussein, announcing the "paramount importance the Sherif attaches to an immediate understanding on the boundaries question in a manner satisfactory to Pan Arabic aspirations." Cairo put pressure on London for a decision that could be communicated to Hussein, citing the threat of a successful jihad, the importance of the new information from al Faroki, and the time pressure to resolve the matter satisfactorily before the war news turned or the Arabs lost patience with British delays and apparent indifference. In his memo "Syria: The Raw Materials" Lawrence had already set out his ideas for dividing Syria between a religiously diverse coastal region and the predominantly

Arab interior, including the great cities of Damascus, Homs, Hama, and Aleppo. His idea gathered momentum in Cairo, and talk of Hussein's proposed boundaries began to concede the Syrian interior and the great cities to Hejaz rule.

Clayton then wrote a memorandum intended for the War Office, presenting the case that the negotiations with Hussein had reached the point where "action is imperative" because "a feeling of doubt and uneasiness is spreading," and "that the attitude of the Sherif is that of the majority of the Arab peoples there can be little doubt." He suggested that a favorable reply to the Arab proposals, even if it did not satisfy all of Hussein's aspirations, would "probably put the seal on their friendship," while a rejection of their proposals would "throw the Young Arab party into the arms of the enemy." He summed up the Arab demands in al Faroki's words: "Our scheme embraces all the Arab countries including Syria and Mesopotamia, but if we cannot have all, we want as much as we can get."[8]

Clayton's memo reached the War Office in October 1915, at a critical moment in the war, when Kitchener was worried enough about the Gallipoli campaign to ask the commander there to estimate the British losses in the event of an evacuation. If the British withdrew from Gallipoli, the freed-up Turkish troops might put Egypt at risk. The War Office was also concerned about the Turkish railroad construction from Palestine toward Egypt, and the progress of the unfinished tunnels in the Taurus and Amanus mountains on the Berlin–Baghdad Railway. If the Turks could finish those expansions of their railroad network, they would be able to move troops and equipment rapidly toward Egypt, and bring heavy guns and troops across Sinai to threaten the defenses of the Suez Canal.

Lawrence, who had helped Newcombe gather information on the Berlin–Baghdad Railway before the war, worked on estimates of the railway construction.[9] He had little information on the railbed work in Palestine; Aaron Aaronsohn and his group in Athlit knew the status of the railroads there but no one had picked up their information. From the scattered data and reports Lawrence could gather he estimated that it would take twenty to thirty days to move a battalion from Constantinople to Beersheba, and that if the railways were better organized the capacity of 1,000 to 1,500 men daily could be doubled.

When Sherif Hussein wrote again, responding to the earlier, unenthusiastic reply to his proposal, his message was in courtly, obscure Arabic, the flattering greetings intermixed with impatience ("the coolness and hesitation which you have displayed in the question of the limits and boundaries . . . might be taken to infer an estrangement"), bellicose declarations ("it is not I personally who am demanding of these limits which include only our race, but that they are all proposals of the people, who, in short, believe that they are necessary for economic life") and scarcely veiled threats ("the whole country, together with those who you say are submitting themselves to Turko-German orders, are all waiting the result of these negotiations, which are dependent only on your refusal or acceptance of the question of the limits").[10]

Lawrence was optimistic about the negotiations. "I am pleased on the whole with things," he wrote to his family. "They have gone against us so far that our Government has become more reasonable, and the final settlement out here, though it will take long, will I think, be very satisfactory." At least part of his pleasure was pride. Hogarth wrote that Lawrence "was still a second lieutenant in the Cairo military intelligence, but with a purpose more clearly foreseen than perhaps that of anyone else, he was already pulling the wires."[11] For Lawrence, an agreement with Hussein and the possibility of a full-scale Arab revolt was more than another problem to be solved; it was the promise of a new era in the Arab world, the beginning of a new history, perhaps of a grand saga like the Crusades tales he had loved since childhood.

McMahon's answer to Sherif Hussein was composed quickly, given the complexity of the issues, and sent on October 25. It was drafted with intentionally ambiguous loopholes, so it could be read as granting all of Hussein's demands for the boundaries of his proposed caliphate with the exception of the areas around Alexandretta and Mersina on the northern coast of Syria and Lebanon, to the west of Damascus, Homs, Hama, and Aleppo. The calculated vagueness allowed the British to simultaneously pretend to their French allies that French interests had been protected, while also implying to Sherif Hussein that with the exception of a few minor exclusions the British had agreed to support his demands. Important territories within the proposed area, such as Palestine, are not specifically mentioned in the letter, although McMahon and his Arab-aware colleagues no doubt knew that Sherif Hussein would assume that Palestine and Jerusalem, a city ranking next to Mecca and Medina in holiness and importance to Muslims, were recognized as part of his caliphate. Even the language excluding the area west of the great cities of Syria (modern-day Lebanon) on the grounds that it was predominantly Christian does not actually state that the four cities and the rest of the interior of Syria would be recognized as part of the new caliphate. Another ambiguous clause reserving "special administrative arrangements" to protect British interests in Basra and Baghdad has been interpreted variously to exclude British privileges in the rest of Mesopotamia, to reserve British and Indian claims in Basra and Baghdad, and even to preclude the Indian government's claims on the two cities.

The intentional ambiguities in the letter have subsequently led to the McMahon letter becoming one of the most controversial diplomatic documents of the twentieth century, and the subject of cycles of revisionist historical analyses. The correspondence has been cited from the time it was drafted as both the basis for expansive claims by Arab groups and nations, and simultaneously as supporting the denial of those claims by British, French, and other interests. Some have argued that the letter, as drafted in Cairo, did not represent the real views of His Majesty's government in London; that Zionists, oil interests, and others have sought to obfuscate or misrepresent the British intention of recognizing an Arab nation; or that the British were deliberately cynical and deceptive in making promises they had no intention of keeping.

The one point that is not challenged is that the letter to Sherif Hussein represented the prevailing viewpoint in Cairo in late 1915, at least at the intelligence service offices where Second Lieutenant Lawrence worked on maps and Arabic documents.

~

In the winter and early spring of 1916, during and after the evacuation from Gallipoli, the British were so concerned about the possibility of a renewed attack on the Suez Canal from the Turkish forces freed up in the Dardanelles that they overlooked the potential threat to other fronts. In London, war decision making was dominated by those who considered the western front in France not just the highest priority but the only priority; no one was willing to commit 100,000 troops to the Turkish theater who could instead be sent to the slaughterhouse of the western trenches. There was a brief mention of perhaps landing a small force of Arab POWs captured from Turkish units via the port at Aqaba, and letting them move inland to cut the Hejaz Railway at Maan before they joined up with Sherif Hussein's forces. Given the fluid state of the negotiations with Hussein, the plan was deemed too chancy to pursue.

The one active war effort against the Turks was in Mesopotamia, where British-led Indian forces had taken Basra early in the war. In 1915 the expeditionary force expanded their foothold in the delta of the Tigris and Euphrates rivers to occupy much of southern Mesopotamia. General Townshend was then sent with a division-sized force to take the town of Kut al Amara, a strategically important target inside Turkish-held territory. Using the Tigris River for supplies and communications, Townshend occupied Kut in September 1915. By late November he had advanced to within twenty miles of Baghdad. Townshend was unaware that the defending Turkish forces had been reinforced with experienced troops, and after encountering resistance he had to retreat back to Kut, where his 17,000-man force was surrounded. The rest of the British-Indian forces, some two hundred miles to the south, tried unsuccessfully to relieve him. By the end of 1915, as the siege tightened, river steamers on the Tigris could no longer reach Kut. Townshend's situation was so grave by February 1916 that the War Office ordered him to negotiate a surrender.

Kitchener, aware how disastrous news of a surrender would be on the heels of the bad news from Gallipoli, asked Wyndham Deedes, an agent fluent in Turkish, to offer the Turks as much as £1 million to secure favorable terms in the surrender. Deedes had spent time with the Turkish gendarmerie in North Africa, and had been attached to the Turkish Ministry of the Interior in Constantinople before working in military intelligence in London at the beginning of the war, and then transferring to Cairo in 1915. He was not enthusiastic about the proposed mission; as an alternative Cairo suggested reviving talks with Abdul Aziz al Masri, in the hope that appropriate concessions and promises to the Arab party might inspire an uprising that would draw pressure off of the besieged Anglo-Indian division at Kut.

Kitchener decided to combine the two ideas in a single mission. Lawrence, who was familiar with the various Arab proposals, was selected to go. He also had been the liaison with the Royal Flying Corps photographers in Egypt, and his experience interpreting aerial photographs was thought useful by Gertrude Bell, who was advising the British on Mesopotamia and had suggested using aerial reconnaissance there. "I have always thought an exchange of people in the various Intelligence Departments would be an immense advantage," she wrote to Lawrence in Cairo. "And I should think yet more favorably of the scheme if it involved your coming out here."[12] Her letter crossed paths with Lawrence, already on his way to Basra.

Lawrence, who had begun to believe the accounts of informants like al Faroqi and al Mazri, thought the Shiite holy cities of Mesopotamia ripe for revolt:

> The conditions were ideal for an Arab movement. The people of Nejef and Kerbela, far in the rear of Halil Pasha's army, were in actual revolt against him. The surviving Arabs in Halil's army were, on his own confession, openly disloyal to Turkey. . . . If we had published the promises we had made to the Sherif . . . enough local fighting men would have joined us to cut the Turkish line of communication between Baghdad and Kut. A few weeks of that and the enemy would either have been forced to raise the siege and retire, or have suffered investment outside Kut, nearly as stringent as the investment of Townshend within it.

Despite Lawrence's enthusiasm, the British were not ready to publish the promises they had made to Hussein, and Deedes's instructions for Lawrence included a caution from Clayton that even if some measure of Arab independence should emerge, "we do not intend to tie ourselves down to any details as to our future relations with such Arab government. . . . We refuse to discuss with this [Arab] party today any other consideration but a simple promise to do all we can to help Arab independence."[13]

Lawrence spent three days in Basra. We "made vast schemes for the government of the universe," Gertrude Bell remembered, but she seems not to have known the details of Lawrence's mission. He searched out the local pan-Arab party, discovered that they were "about twelve strong,"[14] and concluded that there was no hope for an Arab Revolt in Mesopotamia before the besieged Anglo-Indian division in Kut neared starvation. He joined the negotiations to get the siege lifted, including melodramatic blindfolded treks across the enemy lines, but Kitchener's hope that a bribe of £1 million, or even the £2 million that was later authorized, would buy a face-saving exit from the siege was a gross misestimation of the Turks. The Turks insisted on an unconditional surrender, and made the most of the propaganda value soon after the British defeat and evacuation from Gallipoli. The British censors did their best to keep reports about Kut from reaching Britain.

Lawrence's subsequent report to Clayton was highly critical of the lack of preparedness and languages among the intelligence officers in the Mesopotamian campaign, the inadequate procedures used to berth and unload supply barges, the lack of preparedness of the medical authorities and logicians, the assumptions and conduct of the higher command, and the overall conduct of the campaign. When the commander in chief in Cairo, General Sir Archibald Murray, asked to see the report, the intelligence staff quickly bowdlerized it, fearing Murray would die of apoplexy if he read Lawrence's original.[15] For Lawrence, the real lesson from his first adventure into a battlefield situation was a profound disdain for the entire scheme of imperial military organization and command, especially the haughtiness and contempt of the Indian army officers toward their native troops. He would later strongly oppose sending British officers into the Hejaz.

~

In November 1915, the MP Sir Mark Sykes arrived in Egypt after a trip to India and Mesopotamia. He had been an observer on the de Bunsen Committee, which had been set up to review British policy in the Middle East, had long been interested in the region, and was concerned that decisions affecting the area were being made in London, Cairo, Simla, Aden, and Basra without coordination—and sometimes with contradictory policies—wasting manpower, fragmenting the front presented to the Allies and the Turks, and guaranteeing inefficiency in the preparation of a propaganda campaign, war plans, and for the postwar future.

Sykes was socially well placed, personable, and well connected in Whitehall. He was no scholar—he had attended a long list of schools but had never completed a degree at Cambridge—and he had neither held a Cabinet post nor served in the bureaucracy. Through a friendship with Kitchener's private secretary he had access to the War Office, and he impressed many in Parliament with his eagerness for hard work, familiarity with issues concerning the Arab world, tempered ambition, and reputation as an honorable and sincerely religious man. He had been the first in Britain to use the term "Middle East," which he had gotten from Alfred Thayer Mahon at the American Naval War College, and he became a strong advocate of creating a separate Arab Bureau, detached from the regular intelligence office. Although the proposed Arab Bureau would recognize their separate expertise and the importance of the Arab question, Lawrence and his colleagues were guarded or even hostile in their attitudes toward Sykes. To the intelligence agents Sykes seemed an enthusiastic amateur, appreciated for his interest in their issues but still a politician with an appetite for grand, impetuous, understudied, and potentially dangerous actions. Lawrence called him "the imaginative prophet of unconvincing world-movements, and also a bundle of prejudices, intuitions, half-sciences."[16]

When Sykes appeared in Cairo the intelligence staff was dealing with the fallout from their negotiations with Sherif Hussein. The French had discovered the contents of the latest reply to Hussein within a few days of its dispatch, and they were sufficiently concerned to send François Georges-Picot, then at their London embassy, to negotiate with the British about the future of the Middle East. The Indian government was also concerned, fearing that an agreement with Hussein would deprive them of their goal of annexing the Basra and Baghdad provinces and would threaten their position in Yemen. They were particularly concerned that the terms of McMahon's tentative agreement with Hussein might become generally known in Mesopotamia, which could complicate their ambitions there, and perhaps even inspire Muslim revolts in India. Hussein's own reaction also complicated the situation. Although the last letter to him could be read as ceding almost everything he had demanded, his reply, again written in ornate, heavily embellished, and hard-to-translate court Arabic, refused to yield Lebanon and the north Syrian coast, and demanded assurances that if Turkey were defeated in the war, the British would not abandon their commitments to the Arabs.

Lawrence also faced a personal crisis in the midst of the negotiations: the news that his younger brother Will was missing in action.

Will had spent two years in India, and had returned to England via the Suez Canal; Lawrence had gone to Port Said to meet up with him but missed his delayed ship. Before going to India Will had been in love with Janet Laurie, the young woman to whom Lawrence had proposed marriage. After returning Will enlisted and had been in France as a Royal Flying Corps observer for only a week when he was reported missing. His death was later confirmed. "First one and now another of my brothers has been killed," Lawrence wrote. "Of course, I've been away a lot from them, and so it doesn't come on one like a shock at all . . . but I rather dreaded Oxford and what it may be like if one comes back."[17]

Another distraction was Gertrude Bell, who arrived in Cairo in late November to provide her expertise on Arab tribes and sheikhs to the intelligence operation. Hogarth, Lawrence, and Clayton added her considerable knowledge to their information on the Arabs, hoping it would strengthen their case for the tentative agreements with Hussein and for British support of an Arab revolt. But even as they met, Georges-Picot had begun a series of secret meetings in London with Sykes to plan a long-range future for Syria, Mesopotamia, and the entire Middle East. Only fragmentary reports of those meetings reached Cairo, leaving the intelligence office to read tea leaves, trying to guess what was being discussed and agreed to in London from what they knew about Sykes and Picot. The operation was like much of the research they did as intelligence agents, except that they were trying to guess the moves of their own side in the war.

In December Sykes wrote to Clayton: "I have been given the Picot negotiations. I have proposed to concede Mosul and the land north of the Lesser Zab if Haifa and Acre are conceded to us—Picot seems to waver on this and I have good hopes of getting the essential."[18] Sykes's terse message only hinted at the far-reaching agreement that he and Georges-Picot were hammering out. They were actually carving up the entire postwar Arab Middle East, from the Suez Canal to the borders of Persia, including vast areas of Anatolia and the Arabian Peninsula, much as one would slice a pie into portions to suit various appetites. Eastern Anatolia and the Caucasus provinces of the Ottoman Empire were sliced off for Russia. France and Britain would split the rest. Central and southern Anatolia, all of Syria, and the Kurdish lands around the upper valleys of the Tigris and Euphrates, including Mosul, were assigned to France; the rest of Mesopotamia and Transjordan were assigned to Britain. Palestine up to the Jordan River, including Jerusalem, was to be an internationally administered territory. Within the British sector the area encompassing Basra and Baghdad was reserved for direct British administration, with the rest reserved as a British sphere of influence. The French sector was similarly divided, with southern Anatolia and the entire Syrian coast under direct French administration, and the balance of Syria, including the area around Mosul, as a French sphere of influence. With some of the most valuable regions of the vast area that had been offered to Sherif Hussein for a future Arab caliphate earmarked for direct French, British, or international administration, and the rest of the area allotted as spheres of influence for Britain and France, the Sykes-Picot agreement would virtually gut the promises Britain had made to Hussein.

In January 1916, a joint Sykes-Picot memorandum and an accompanying map were distributed widely in Whitehall but not sent to Cairo for comment. Sykes may have urged that the memo not be circulated in Cairo for fear that the implications of his agreement with Georges-Picot would be criticized by both the military planners—who would lose the flexibility to attack Palestine and Syria directly—and the intelligence experts, including Lawrence, who had been advising the sensitive negotiations with Hussein in the hope that an Arab Revolt would become an important element of British strategy against the Turks. Sykes also had ambitions that he would head the proposed Arab Bureau, and may have been reluctant to acknowledge that there were other Arab experts with more experience and knowledge. Withholding information about the Sykes-Picot agreement from Cairo and from Sherif Hussein guaranteed that if or when Hussein and the other Arab leaders found out about the agreement,

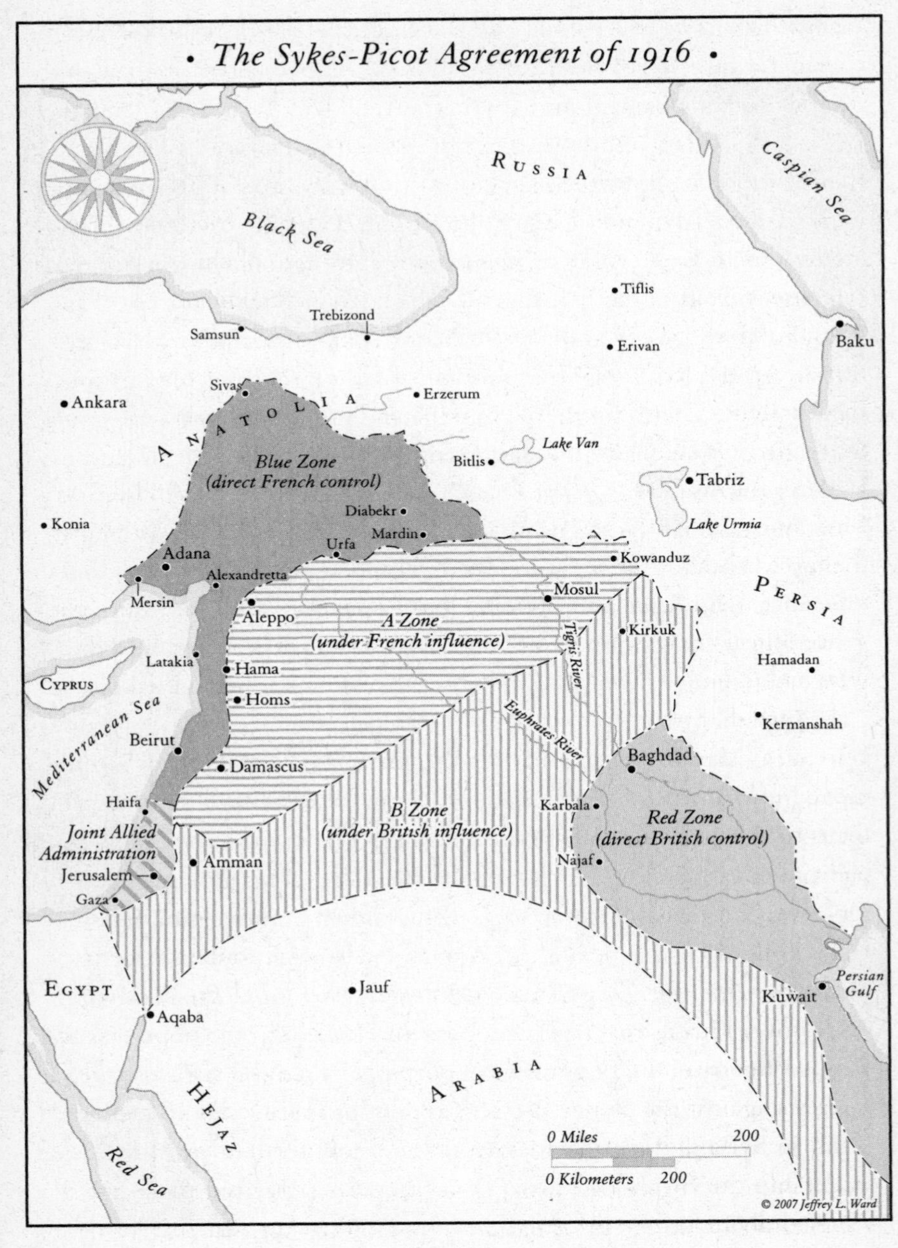
• The Sykes-Picot Agreement of 1916 •
RUSSIA
Caspian Sea
Black Sea
Tiflis
Trebizond
Samsun
Erivan
Baku
Sivas
Ankara
ANATOLIA
Erzerum
Lake Van
Bitlis
Blue Zone
(direct French control)
Tabriz
Diabekr
Konia
Mardin
Lake Urmia
Urfa
Adana
Kowanduz
Alexandretta
Mersin
Mosul
PERSIA
Aleppo
A Zone
(under French influence)
Kirkuk
Tigris River
Latakia
Hama
Hamadan
CYPRUS
Homs
Mediterranean Sea
Euphrates River
Kermanshah
Beirut
Baghdad
Damascus
Haifa
Karbala
B Zone
(under British influence)
Red Zone
(direct British control)
Joint Allied
Administration
Amman
Najaf
Jerusalem
Gaza
EGYPT
Jauf
Persian
Gulf
Kuwait
Aqaba
ARABIA
HEJAZ
0 Miles
200
0 Kilometers
200
Red Sea
© 2007 Jeffrey L. Ward

it would already be a fait accompli—to the Arabs, a perfidious betrayal and a slap in the face.

~

In January 1916 Hussein wrote again to Cairo, this time with no further territorial demands other than a request that any concession regarding "what we now leave to France in Beirut and its coasts" be reconsidered at the end of the war. His message concluded with a reference to "that action, the time of which has now come near, which destiny drives toward us with great haste and clearness,"[19] implying that an Arab Revolt, and the possibility of opening a new front against the Turks, was imminent. For Cairo this was welcome good news after the British defeats at Gallipoli and Kut.

After the evacuation of British units from Gallipoli, Sir Archibald Murray consolidated the Mediterranean Expeditionary Force with the forces under his command in Egypt, and transferred military intelligence to his headquarters in Ismailia. That left only seven intelligence officers in Cairo under Clayton, including Wyndham Deedes, who had joined the group as an expert on Turkish affairs.

In early February the Arab experts were separated into an Arab Bureau, as Mark Sykes had urged, but with Clayton as its head. They moved into a suite of three rooms in the Savoy Hotel, letting them focus their energies without the distraction of the wider issues they had previously pursued. As one of their earliest assignments, Lawrence was urged to draft a confidential, unsigned memorandum on "The Politics of Mecca" for the Foreign Office, no doubt to placate the Anglo-Indian interests who had supported ibn Saud, the Wahhabi leader, over Hussein of the Hejaz. Lawrence argued that the narrow-minded bigotry of the Wahhabis could never be a basis of uniting Arab interests against the Turks, and that in the more civilized centers of Islam in Syria and western Arabia only Hussein could provide the leadership the British needed. His memo also reassured those who worried about long-term commitments by pointing out that while Hussein was an important leader in the Arab world, he lacked the resources and experience to create a state or states that would threaten

British interests. Lawrence wrote with a tone of authority, although he had never met Hussein or his sons.

Lawrence's daily responsibilities ranged from designing stamps for Sherif Hussein to editing the first issue of the *Arab Bulletin,* a closed-circulation journal with a press run of less than twenty intended for a high-level audience in the Foreign Office, the War Office, the Admiralty, the government of India, selected diplomatic stations, a small circle of intelligence officers in Cairo and London, and interested policy makers like Mark Sykes. He presented his version of the Arab Revolt in the first issue: "At the beginning of the war all available Arab Sheikhs were enrolled in a society and an envoy was sent to the Sherif [Hussein] asking him to take the lead. . . . The Khalifate, if it passes from the sultan, must fall to a member of the Sherif's family who would command the adhesion of Islam. The Sherif is deeply venerated . . . and could at once raise a jehad among Arabs and Kurds. All Moslem Syrians are anti-French."[20]

Lawrence's gloss did not mention Sherif Hussein's insatiable demands on the British, especially for specie—gold sovereigns. As Hussein and his sons readied their plans to detach Arab units from the Turkish forces and prepared for an attack on Medina, Hussein asked for supplies to be stockpiled at Port Sudan and announced that his secret representative would be coming to collect fifty thousand gold sovereigns. Hussein also requested that British troops land in Syria to seize the railway lines to Anatolia—the plan Lawrence had argued for without success—on the grounds that without British intervention to cut off supplies to the Turkish troops, an Arab rising in Syria would be stillborn. After secretly ceding a sphere of influence over Syria to the French in the Sykes-Picot agreement, the British could not agree to Hussein's request, and McMahon had to answer the request with platitudes: "It is always wise to concentrate rather than divide one's forces; and for this reason we strongly advise Your Highness to recall your son from Syria and to take the action which you propose in Hejaz and the south alone for the present."[21]

Hussein responded with more demands. He wanted sixty thousand gold sovereigns to be delivered secretly by Ronald Storrs to Emir Abdullah. When the British sent ten thousand, reserving the balance until there was some proof that the Arab Revolt had begun, Emir Zeid, another of Hussein's sons, announced that the revolt had begun the day before and brought a letter from Sherif Hussein asking for the remaining fifty thousand sovereigns, along with machine guns, mountain guns, ten thousand rifles, ammunition, and an additional twenty thousand sovereigns. Lawrence monitored the traffic to Hussein and to London, and realized that Hussein's escalating demands were only a minor problem compared to the ruffled feathers in Cairo: "Sir Archibald Murray, the General in Egypt, wanted, naturally enough, no competitor and no competing campaigns in his area. . . . He could not be entrusted with the Arabian affair, for neither he nor his Staff had the necessary competence to deal with so curious a problem. On the other hand he could make the spectacle of the High Commission running a private war sufficiently ridiculous. When he found the opportunity he bent his considerable powers to crab what he called the rival show."[22]

With little trust in the Arab Revolt, General Murray had approved tentative plans for attacks on both El Arish, in the north of the Sinai Peninsula, and on the port of Aqaba, at the head of the Gulf of Aqaba, within seventy miles of the Hejaz Railway. Lawrence was asked to research a landing at Aqaba and recommended against it: the actual landing would not be difficult, but the beaches were exposed to artillery bombardment from the surrounding hills. Any attempt to advance beyond Aqaba would subject the British forces to flank attacks from fortified Turkish positions on the narrow and deep wadis that led to the Hejaz Railway. "In fact," Lawrence concluded, "a British landing there was out of the question."[23]

~

News of the Arab Revolt appeared in a Reuters telegram, and Lawrence wrote to his family: "The Reuter telegram on the revolt of the Sherif of Mecca I hope interested you. It has taken a year and a half to do so, but now is going very well. It is so good to have helped a bit in making a new nation—and I hate the Turks so much that to see their own people turning on them is very grateful."[24] As involved as he was with the Arab Revolt, Lawrence was still only an observer in Cairo, reading dispatches, making maps, designing stamps, and analyzing strategic proposals. He had not been in the field as part of the Arab Revolt. Indeed, he had not yet been in Arabia. His break came when Storrs was planning a visit to Arabia to meet with Emir Abdullah, and perhaps with Sherif Hussein. Clayton urged him to take Lawrence with him, both for the quality of Lawrence's reports from Mesopotamia and his skills in Arabic, and because he was the only agent who was free. To avoid difficulties with the GHQ, which might oppose his going along on an intelligence mission, Lawrence applied for a leave, his first since being posted to Egypt, writing that "I would like a holiday and joy-ride in the Red Sea" with Storrs.[25]

On October 12, 1916, he and Storrs traveled by train to Suez, where they boarded the *Lama*. The midday sun on their three-day sail down the Red Sea to Jidda was so hot that Lawrence's uniform stuck to the red leather of the gun-room armchairs, leaving scarlet streaks down the back of his uniform jacket.

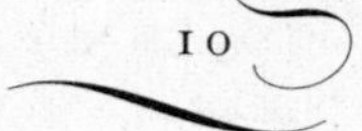

10

Aaron Alone

The country is ravaged,
The ground must mourn;
For the new grain is ravaged,
The new wine is dried up,
The new oil has failed.
Farmers are dismayed
And vine dressers wail
Over wheat and barley;
For the crops of the field are lost.
The vine has dried up,
The fig tree withers,
Pomegranate, plum, and apple—
All the trees of the field are scar.
And joy has dried up
Among men.

—Joel 1:10–12

How hard it is to be a Jew, in the year of 1914. It would have been enough to have one thing different—not being a Jew, not having a heart, being born 200 years later. . . . But I look around and my fist rises.

—Avshalom Feinberg[1]

On New Year's Day 1916 Aaron Aaronsohn watched from a hotel in Herzilya as French ships bombarded the coast. Ever the scientist, he timed the interval between the flash of the guns on the battleship

Jeanne d'Arc and the explosions when the shells detonated to calculate the distance of the ship offshore. In his diary he recorded the comment of a Turkish officer: "The great harm caused by such shelling is that the public grows accustomed to look upon military operations disrespectfully." In other words, Aaronsohn added, the shelling "means real demoralization."[2]

The Jewish communities in Palestine that winter were close to the breaking point. In the countryside Aaronsohn saw misery at "a stage nearing famine." Families rummaged for edible wild berries in the woods or went into the fields, "grazing like cattle." Three- and four-year-old children picked through garbage in the streets looking for chewable refuse like spiny cactus peels, relishing citrus rinds as high "delicatesse."[3] Aaronsohn had been able to pay enough baksheesh to keep the staff of the research station out of the forced labor brigades, and found funds to buy exemptions for the members of the teacher's association in Haifa, but he worried how long the Jewish communities could hold out. As the first sprouts of the winter wheat and barley crops began to appear, he wondered whether the Turkish army would again levy the crops or "if, by any chance, we shall be spared from feeding the troops this winter and from disastrous commandeering?"

As the evenings wore on without contact from a British ship, he worried about the safety of the lookouts who waited on the beach at Athlit, watching for a signal. One night they discovered a Turkish officer in the area; Feinberg had to drop the poem or manifesto he was working on and get the officer drunk before he became too suspicious. Early one morning three Turkish soldiers shot at a lookout on his way back to Zichron after he'd been watching all night. The lookout ran, but the soldiers caught him and began beating him and the farmers who tried to hide him, shouting that they knew that the man was trying to make contact with the enemy and demanding baksheesh for their silence. When the story got back to Aaronsohn he knew the episode would not end with the payment of a bribe, and boldly wrote to the district commander of the area, demanding that the commander discipline his soldiers for attacking and beating an innocent man. The bluff worked: the commander made the soldiers return the baksheesh and issued an order that in the future the soldiers could take whatever measures were necessary to keep the enemy from approaching the shore, but were not to track or ambush those on shore.[4] But the situation remained perilous.

One afternoon Aaronsohn saw a camel chewing on a castor oil plant. He had studied the diets of domesticated animals and knew that camels instinctively avoided the poisonous castor oil plant. If the camel was too hungry to follow instinct, hungry enough to eat a poisonous plant, how long would it be before the entire Jewish community of Palestine was too hungry to act in their own best interests?

~

Aaronsohn had been juggling those worries in early December 1915 when he looked out toward the southwest from the hilltop of Zichron Ya'aqov and saw a red cloud on the horizon. It looked like smoke, perhaps from a forest fire. Aaronsohn knew which forests to the south were dry enough to burn, but as the red cloud came nearer he could see that it was not smoke. It was a swarm of locusts, at least six miles long and almost a mile wide, larger than any swarm he had seen the previous spring.[5]

When the locusts were at a peak the year before he had reread the book of Joel. "The man who has witnessed such an invasion can only admire and shudder at the reading," he wrote in his diary.[6] In the spring, farmers, even whole settlements, had trusted his advice on whether they should even sow seeds, whether crops of wheat or barley would have a chance against the locusts. Aaronsohn had urged them to plant: he had concluded that the locusts of the first infestation were sexually immature and would not produce viable eggs. And it had been too early to surrender to starvation.[7] His prediction had been right: there had been no local hatch from the first infestation. But now the locusts from Egypt were upon them again.

He knew how to minimize the damage of the new infestation. They could erect portable laboratories in the Sinai and inoculate the swarms with a bacterium (Herelle's *Coccobacillus acridiorum*) that would render them sterile. But the Sinai had become a war zone after the failure of the second Turkish attack on the Suez Canal. And even if they were allowed into the Sinai, the Turkish authorities would refuse to believe that inoculation stations in a nearly empty area like the Sinai were the best defense against locust infestation in the cultivated areas hundreds of miles to the north. Another option was arsenic salts. "I am rather loathe to place this remedy in the hands of ignorant and malevolent Arabs," Aaronsohn wrote, "when it could be as dangerous for them as for their neighbors." The solutions were in any case only theoretical: the research station did not have enough funds even to buy the wood and tin they had used to protect their own plantings.

As the new year approached Aaronsohn and Feinberg realized that the plan Feinberg and Woolley had put together in Port Said had failed. There was no way to get a message across enemy lines to Woolley, no way to know whether the British had sent a ship or not or if the signals had somehow gotten mixed up. Whatever the explanation, the British were not getting the intelligence reports from the research station and would not be able to launch an amphibious assault on the shore of Palestine, the one strategy Aaronsohn and Feinberg believed would save the Jewish communities from the ravages of conscription, starvation, locusts, and the whimsy of Djemal Pasha.

Feinberg decided to attempt another trip to Egypt, this time by crossing the Sinai. Aaronsohn tried to dissuade him, but Feinberg stubbornly argued for his plan: he was fluent in Arabic, an experienced camel rider, had been practicing with disguises for years, and was sure he could pass as a Bedouin. He called it a mission of honor, saying he would not want Woolley or the British to think that they should not have trusted him. With his Byronic flair, Feinberg said that if it was to be his last mission he wanted it to be in the service of His Majesty King George V.

He wrote out a message for Woolley in case contact with the ships miraculously resumed, said good-bye to Aaronsohn in Hadera, and left in the research station cart for Petah Tikvah, where a friend named Efriam Cohen joined him. At the home of Feinberg's cousin Na'aman Belkind in Rishon le Zion, they disguised themselves as Bedouins, and on December 18, 1915, they set off on camels for the Sinai. Cohen could not keep up with Feinberg's pace and turned back, only to find himself arrested by Turkish soldiers—a single rider coming out of the desert from the direction of the battle lines no doubt looked suspicious. Cohen managed to escape and get to Athlit, where Aaronsohn hid him.

Riding fast and with little rest, Feinberg crossed the northern Sinai, passing El Arish, El Mazar, and Bir el-'Abd in two days and nights of hard riding. He was most of the way to the Suez Canal when he suddenly found himself surrounded by Turkish soldiers. He swallowed the officer's buttons on his jacket and the secret information he had written down, but he had no *wassika,* the special permit required for travelers in predominantly Arab areas, and the soldiers caught him with a German book, a letter from a woman to someone in Egypt, binoculars, a gun, and a Qur'an. He told the soldiers that he was conducting research on the migration patterns of locusts, and that he had the Qur'an because he was interested in Arabic, but he had no documents identifying him as a scientific researcher, and the Sinai was a military zone, closed to all civilian travel. The soldiers took him to El Arish for questioning, then to a jail in Beersheba, where the officer in charge accused him of being a spy, had him beaten to force him to confess and identify other spies, and told him he would be hanged.

When Turkish officers appeared in Zichron to investigate Feinberg's story, Aaronsohn first thought they were trying to identify a body. Once he straightened out the misunderstanding, Aaronsohn verified Feinberg's alibi and said it was unusual that he hadn't heard from him for a while.[8] Aaronsohn then sent Josef Lishinsky, a staffer at the research station who spoke fluent Arabic, was an excellent horseman, and was experienced with disguises, to visit Feinberg in Beersheba. Lishinsky was able to smuggle some of Feinberg's writings out of the jail, including a song he had written, but the Turkish authorities refused to release him, and continued torturing him to persuade him to confess.

In January 1916, Eliahu Mizrahi, with whom Feinberg had stayed on his way to Beersheba, told the Turkish authorities that Feinberg wanted to be a hero and had previously been in contact with the British in Egypt. On the basis of that testimony the Turks escalated the torture. Josef Lishinsky offered to help him escape, but Feinberg refused, saying his escape would endanger Aaronsohn, the research station, and their entire operation. Aaronsohn went to Rishon le Zion to talk to Feinberg's cousin Na'aman Belkind, and through his efforts, and bribes to Turkish officers and officials (Josef Lishinsky was expert at identifying who should receive baksheesh), Feinberg was moved from Beersheba to Jerusalem. He was still held in jail, accused of spying, and faced hanging.

There was only one option left for Aaronsohn. It was not easy for a proud and stubborn man, but only eight months after he had quit in a huff, on January 9, 1916, he met with Djemal Pasha in Haifa and agreed to resume work as the director of the locust control program. In return Djemal agreed that Aaronsohn and his colleagues would again have full access to military bases and facilities for the war on locusts, and that their messages would be assigned the same priority as military communications on the telegraph system. With his new authority, Aaronsohn and Lishinsky arranged for wine and gifts to bribe the Turkish officers in Jerusalem. Feinberg was released the day after Aaronsohn's meeting with Djemal Pasha.

When Feinberg came back to Zichron and Athlit, his once passionate friendship with Sarah resumed, and they traveled to Damascus to meet with Aaron. The three of them agreed on a new plan to reestablish communication with the British: instead of trying to reach Egypt, Feinberg would travel via Constantinople to neutral Romania, with the goal of going on to England. If he was stopped on his journey, his excuse would be that he was going to visit his sister in Berlin. Aaron gave Feinberg a letter addressed to the American ambassador in Constantinople, Henry Morgenthau, a trustee of the research station, introducing Feinberg, explaining that he was on a mission for the station, and requesting that Morgenthau please give him money. Feinberg made it to Constantinople, where he joined the many who waited there, searching for trustworthy news of the war amid the constant rumors. He wasn't alone: thousands were queued for travel permits, waiting for a Turkish bureaucrat to take their bribes.

~

For a lawyer like David Ben-Gurion, then working with the Labor Party, or a poet like Avshalom Feinberg, there was little conflict between the struggle for a Jewish Palestine and their professions: Byronic had already become an adjective to describe a passionate life committed to both poetry and revolutionary politics, and a lawyer's adversarial and rhetorical skills required no adaptation to serve a political cause. In England, Chaim Weizmann had shifted from his Manchester chemistry lab, where he had synthesized acetone, a crucial war material for the British, to active leadership in the Zionist movement. Weizmann the brilliant scientist had become an effective lobbyist and politician. But it was a one-way journey. He could not easily return to his laboratory.

Aaronsohn saw himself as a scientist. His observational and analytic skills might be useful for intelligence work, but his science was a mission. He was convinced that science was essential for the development of Jewish life in Palestine, for the realization of the Zionist dream. He had only begun to develop the agricultural techniques and crop varieties that would take advantage of the climate, soils, and terrain of Palestine. Who else could lead the agronomy and public health research? Who else could get the funding that continued research required? Who else would push aside naive idealistic schemes and press for the scientific developments that would enable Palestine to become a Jewish homeland?

Aaron understood himself well enough to entrust the active roles in the secret spying program to Avshalom Feinberg, and before that to his younger brother Alexander. They had been sent to Cairo to negotiate with the British, and both had failed. Alex had offered the research station's information to Captain Newcombe of British intelligence and had been turned away as if he were a charlatan or a

Turkish double agent. Feinberg had succeeded in negotiating an arrangement with Captain Woolley and British naval intelligence, but that too had inexplicably failed. Aaron did not know the British—he had spent more time on the Continent than in Britain, and English had been the last of his many languages—but he wondered if Feinberg and Alex had failed because they were not well enough known to the British. Perhaps only someone with a reputation, with a name that could be "vouched for," would persuade the British how much the group at the research station could offer.

In mid-March word arrived from Feinberg in Constantinople that he had finally gotten papers allowing him to continue his journey. The same week, on March 13, two workers at the research station in Athlit found a message in an envelope. No one had been waiting for a ship the night before—after so many months they had given up hope—and no one heard the dogs bark when a swimmer came ashore, left the note, and went back to the ship.[9] The message was from Captain Woolley in Port Said. The messenger who left it was a friend of Abulafia's, a mutual friend of Feinberg and Woolley's. There was no way to answer the message. The messenger had expected someone to be waiting for him. The connection would remain broken.

With spring approaching, Aaronsohn realized that the locusts were disappearing without laying masses of eggs. The failure of the hatch again vindicated his predictions. At the end of March Aaronsohn quietly announced that the locust danger had passed. The farmers had still only planted 60 percent of the usual acreage, and in May a heat wave "the like of which we have fortunately not seen within 35 years" struck Palestine, "and like a widespread fire, burned our crops and killed our hopes." The temperature at the research station reached 109 degrees Fahrenheit. The outside thermometer (Aaron was a stickler for careful climate records) hit 126 degrees Fahrenheit. Aaronsohn estimated that the food supplies in Palestine would carry the Jewish communities only to October, "surely not beyond."[10]

Aaronsohn recalled Feinberg to Palestine. He had come up with a new plan.

~

On one of his horseback spying trips Aaronsohn had noticed Turkish experimental plantings of castor oil plants near the Arab village of Bet-Lahm. He knew enough about the poisonous castor-oil plant to conclude that the plantings were an effort to produce lubricating oil, which was in desperately short supply because of the Anglo-French blockade. He knew men on the labor brigades were given no lubricants for the wheels on their wheelbarrows, and were told to use the minuscule allotments of olive oil they were given with their bread rations. If there was no oil for wheelbarrows, Aaronsohn reasoned, more sophisticated war machinery, like wagons, gun carriages, and machine guns, would be severely hampered. At one point he saw huge locomotives moved in pieces on oxcarts. "Poor buffaloes!" he wrote. "Poor roads! Poor Taurus."[11] The observations were the key to his new plan.

In one of their meetings Aaronsohn told Djemal Pasha that he might be able to develop a usable lubricant from a new variety of the sesame plant he had bred. The pasha trusted his skills as a scientist; Djemal also knew that before too long the British would attack Palestine, and that without lubricants the mobility of his forces, and even the operation of machine guns and artillery, would be severely compromised. When Aaronsohn explained that he would need to do more research and consult with agronomists and botanists elsewhere, including in Germany, Djemal issued approvals that would get him travel documents from the Turkish authorities. Aaronsohn was not eligible for a passport, but he got a declaration authorizing him to travel to Constantinople and Vienna.[12]

Aaronsohn's plan was to travel to Germany, and from there to neutral Sweden or Denmark. His explanation at each stage of the journey would be that he needed to consult with additional scientists on the sesame oil question. Once in Sweden or Denmark, he would establish connections to the British embassy and make arrangements to travel secretly to England. There, he hoped, he was known well enough from his scientific reputation to expect an attentive audience in British intelligence and strategic circles. The trick was to somehow get to England without looking like he had gone over to the enemy. If he was exposed as a spy, the staff of the research station, Aaronsohn's family, the village of Zichron Ya'aqov, perhaps even the entire yishuv would be implicated by association. Djemal Pasha could be counted on to go on a hanging spree if he learned he had been betrayed by a Jew.

Although he was not married, had no children, and had spent more of the last twenty years outside Palestine than at the only place he called home, Aaron Aaronsohn was tied to Palestine by a thousand threads of family, friends, and responsibilities. What would happen to the support of the trustees if he left? Who would take his place in dealing with the authorities? Who would direct the agricultural research program? Who would take care of his father and Sarah? Aaron wrote to the trustees of the research station in New York that he was traveling to Germany and perhaps Switzerland; he knew the Turkish censors would read his mail and the messages to the trustees would confirm his public story to the Ottoman authorities. He arranged codes with Feinberg: the message that he was going to America would mean that he was on his way to London. A foot problem, variously diagnosed as lymphitis or an edematous tumor, held up his departure; with wartime rationing, even common remedies and dressings like boric acid were proscribed or unavailable.[13]

In mid-July 1916 Aaronsohn's foot was well enough for him to travel. He put Feinberg in charge of the research station and set off for Constantinople. Liova Schneersohn, Feinberg's friend from Hadera, got a Spanish passport under the name Haim Cohen and accompanied Aaronsohn as his secretary. As always, Aaronsohn recorded voluminous observations in his pocket journals, beginning with the temperature (90 degrees Fahrenheit) and humidity ("very high") when he started off. On the roads from Beirut to Damascus, he saw "babies in the streets, crying for food and dying in the arms of their starving mothers," hundreds of aimlessly wandering starving people, dozens of dead bodies. Djemal Pasha, he later learned, was driven over the same road on the same day, apparently oblivious to the starvation and devastation. In Damascus, Aaron mentioned the famine conditions he had seen to Lieutenant Colonel Ali Fuad Bey, chief of staff of the Fourth Army. "You are a healthy, strong fellow," Fuad Bey answered. "You are not going to be mollified by the 'crocodile tears' of half a dozen hysterical, mendicating women." Aaronsohn realized that the Turks could not admit to the widespread starvation: it would have been a confession that they did not have the resources to fight a long war. In any case, he noted, they had made sure that no Turks were starving: "Only Christian dogs, Jewish dogs, and unfaithful Arabs."[14]

In a tiny café he was served an unexpected bottle of Schlitz beer. "The beer that made Milwaukee famous," he remembered, recalling how long it had been since he had drank Schlitz beer in the United States. He noted how much of the forests had been cut down for train fuel and railroad ties, noticed military preparations, such as explosive charges wired on bridges, and wondered what sort of attack the officials expected. He saw a plant that had been built to extract gas and oil from bituminous limestone, and was able to calculate from the dimensions of the facility the quality, quantity, and cost of the extracted fuels and lubricants. He got a special permit allowing him to travel on autobuses and the Baghdad–Berlin Railroad, and he dined with an actress, Schwester Wachtener, "who plays ingenue parts. . . . She is said to be wonderful under fire. I thought her rather nice even when not under fire."[15]

The journey to Constantinople was challenging. German officers on the trains were provided with fawning service; the civilian passengers had to scrounge for water and food in the stations and during the frequent breakdowns. The roadbed and running stock were in terrible condition: on some stretches the passengers had to take rude carts from station to station, or walk. On the mountain passes horses struggled to pull the carts up the mountain slopes; passengers huddled in fear when they began the descents without brakes.

Aaronsohn arrived in Constantinople on July 22, and checked into the Pera Palas Hotel in the Galata district. The Pera Palas, with its ornate wrought-iron-and-brass elevator, grand dining room, popular bar, and marble-tabled café, had become famous since the completion of the Orient Express route from Paris, attracting a cosmopolitan clientele and providing a pleasant oasis from the hubbub of the city and the perils of the infamous Ottoman bureaucracy. Aaronsohn needed almost a month to secure the permits to go on to Germany. He changed his plans (or at least, that's what he told the authorities) repeatedly, explaining at the German consulate that he was going to Germany, and later to Switzerland via Germany, and naming distinguished scientists in Germany that he planned to meet. The officials seemed to have no idea that Aaronsohn's journey was anything other than a noted scientist off to consult on a problem that could help the war effort. When he applied for a special *wassika* from the Ministry of Agriculture, the minister thanked him for his work on the locust problem. Aaronsohn protested that he "had merely done my duty."

Constantinople was full of surprises. He visited the neighborhood where Sarah had lived, and discovered that it was not grand, as he had been led to expect, but poor. He met the few friends she had known there and talked with her husband, who showed Aaron the affectionate letters he had received from Sarah—which Aaron knew had been written to avoid problems with the authorities after she decided to stay in Zichron. The rooms in what had been her house were locked, and Chaim Abraham did not have the keys.[16]

Aaronsohn heard Henry Morgenthau, the American ambassador and a trustee of the research station, give a speech highly critical of the Turkish government before he returned to the United States. Aaronsohn obtained a copy of an article by Jabotinsky calling for the formation of a Jewish legion in London, not as an unarmed auxiliary unit like the Zion Mule Corps but as an armed regiment of the British army that would train and fight as a Jewish legion. He also learned that in the United States his brother Alex had published a memoir of the first years of the war in the *Atlantic Monthly*.[17] Alex's article was critical of the Turks, and described Aaron's efforts at the research station and in relieving the famine and fighting the locust plague. Young, impetuous, and focused on his own future, Alex hadn't thought about the possible impact of his article on the trustees and other supporters in America, or in Zichron and the rest of Palestine if the Turks ever got hold of a copy. Aaron was outraged that Alex had acted on his own, without clearing what he was doing beforehand. It was no way to run an operation as risky as theirs, especially while Aaron was himself on a mission that potentially put the research station and its entire staff, and the whole Zichron community, at risk.

Before he left Constantinople for Germany Aaronsohn called at the American embassy. The United States was still neutral in the war but had not been able to provide relief funds to Palestine for over a year. He arranged for the American embassies to aid him in his travels, and discussed visiting the United States, carefully laying tracks to distract the curious, especially the Turkish authorities, from his real plans. When he left Constantinople on August 21, Liova Schneersohn stayed behind to route messages. Aaron's first message to Zichron, sent in an innocent letter from Sarah's husband, Chaim Abraham, did not reach Feinberg until October 5.[18]

In Germany Aaronsohn discovered that his reputation with Djemal Pasha and the travel documents from Ottoman authorities held little sway. He was in Berlin for four weeks, trying to put together the last pieces of his plan. He used the name of his friend Otto Warburg as a reference, but carefully avoided any mention of Warburg's or his own connections to Zionism. He told the authorities that he needed to consult with experts in Denmark and Sweden, and spent more time at the American embassy, where he became friendly enough with the ambassador to be invited several times for dinner, and learned that the United States might join the war in the next few months. Aaronsohn also spent time with Judah Magnes, the former rabbi at Temple Emanu-el in New York City, an active Zionist, a trustee of the research station, and an early supporter of the planned Hebrew University in Jerusalem. As his final plans took shape, he wrote letters to Sarah, reporting—for the eyes of the censors—that Warburg had endorsed the importance of his research and the need for him to continue the work in Sweden, but that he was still waiting for the police to certify the value of his research for the German war effort.

He finally got permission to travel to Copenhagen in mid-September, borrowed money to pay his hotel and restaurant bills, asked Henrietta Szold in New York to forward money for the rest of his journey, and spent a few days in Hamburg visiting Sonia and Zalig Suskin. When he crossed into Denmark on September 16 he went through an exacting search at the border, then found a telegram from his brother Alex waiting for him at the American legation in Copenhagen, urging Aaron to come to America. He realized that he was still under surveillance by German agents, and asked other friends to write him about how important it was for him to visit America, hoping the German agents would note the letters. He had had no experience as a spy, but he knew he needed a red herring to throw them off his real plans.

Aaron had confided his plans to Tzila, Feinberg's sister in Berlin, and they had set up a code. She would be his link by mail to Avshalom and Sarah in Palestine, and to Liova Schneersohn in Constantinople. Aaron also laced his diary with the guarded comments of a man who was beginning to act and feel like a spy: "I met an odd sort of chap at the American Legation—John Barning—who pretends he is an American. He did not claim the latter nationality, to my knowledge, when he was a Turkish official in Constantinople." He met the actress Sigrid Enghardt at his hotel, and invited her to dine with him. The "champagne, etc. lasted until one am."[19] Even that diary entry may have been for the censors.

His diary is also interesting for what he did not record. Aaronsohn met with the local Zionist leaders in Copenhagen, where the international Zionist organization maintained an office as part of their pretense of neutrality in the war. And while he continued to visit the American legation publicly to establish his cover, he negotiated secretly with the British consulate. The British, particularly the general consul, Sir Ralph Paget, were not as cooperative as Aaronsohn had hoped.[20] Sir Ralph initially suggested that Aaron travel to the United

States, and from there back to Britain. Aaronsohn refused. He had already spent a month in Constantinople, a month in Berlin, and almost a month in Copenhagen. There wasn't time for more delays. He told Sir Ralph about Feinberg's contact with Leonard Woolley, and how important it was to reestablish those connections.

The British also refused him a written safe-conduct—hardly surprising since he was a Turkish subject and a confidant and assistant to their chief enemy in the Turkish theater—and suggested he go to Bergen, Norway, and travel on from there with "doctored papers." Again Aaronsohn refused. He wrote to Tzila in Berlin that Levi's sister-in-law was giving him a hard time. "Levi" was his code name for Woolley, the only British contact with whom they had ever established a connection; "sister-in-law" was the British embassy.[21]

Aaronsohn learned that Judah Magnes, who had come to Copenhagen, was planning to sail to New York with Alexander Dushkin, his colleague in the New York Kehillah and a leader of Jewish education in America. Magnes and Dushkin had a three-berth cabin, and offered to share it with him. Ships to America from Copenhagen stopped at Kirkwall in the Orkney Islands, for refueling—where Aaronsohn could conveniently be discovered as a Turkish agent by the British authorities. It was a perfect cover for his defection, but the shipping company was wary of allowing an enemy alien aboard without a laissez-passer. When the British offered only a verbal assurance that he would not be interfered with at Kirkwell, Aaronsohn stormed over to the British legation to demand a written statement from Paget confirming that he would not be interfered with when the ship stopped in the Orkney Islands. It was all playacting, especially the careful chronicle in his diary. If Djemal Pasha or Turkish or German agents investigated Aaron's disappearance, there would be plentiful documentation that he fully intended to go on to the United States.

On Yom Kippur Eve, the beginning of the holiest day of the Jewish calendar, while the Jews in Copenhagen, including the local Zionist leaders, attended solemn Kol Nidre services in the Copenhagen synagogue, Aaronsohn stayed in his hotel room writing a long letter to Judge Mack in Chicago. He would later call the letter his confession. Precisely and artfully (he was writing not in familiar French or Hebrew, but in English), Aaronsohn chronicled the impact of the war on Palestine, the steady deterioration of the situation for the Jews and other minority populations, his efforts to distance himself from the don't-rock-the-boat attitude of official Zionism, the efforts to send first his brother Alexander and then Feinberg to secure the cooperation of the British, and the moment when he realized that by staying in Palestine "I personally was of no great use." Without specifics about his journey or his secret negotiations with the British, he wrote, "I succeeded in getting out of the Turkish, and what was still more important, the German clutches. . . . Now I can begin and shall begin all over again. Here you have my confession."

His description of how and why he decided to put aside his science research to work for a British victory in Palestine is self-conscious and histrionic, the tone verging from Zola's *"J'Accuse!"* to melodrama: "Would I have left the country and openly taken service on the English side, it would already have been bad enough. My character, my standing would be impaired. But I did worse. I stood where I was, I organized a whole movement, I became connected with the Intelligence Office, as people who are afraid of words call it. I do not like mincing words. Put it clearly and I became a Spy, *horresco referens*. I am told that General Baden-Powell has written a book in apology of the spy, I do not feel the need of any man's apology."

The letter reads as if he were still arguing with himself about whether leaving Palestine and science was the right decision, and persuading himself that he had become the leader of a movement:

> Every man realized that when Djemal would have good reasons to hang me he would not stop at that; hundreds if not thousands of others would share the same fate. Still no one complained, no reproach was uttered, no blame pronounced. . . . All believed I was the best judge of what there was to be done and everybody was ready to take his share if I failed.

I never believed in Jewish solidarity before, I am a strong believer in it now, *et pour cause.* And I learned to believe in something else, in Jewish discipline. Not a man moved a finger unless I authorized him to do so, but then you should have seen with what devotion and self-sacrifice they did their task. Men who not very long before were opposing me, in mere political trifles, but still, were talking or drawing their revolvers at me, those same men, when they realized that I was not playing at trifles, were risking their lives in order to bring me any slight information which might be of value to the cause. . . .

Neither myself nor anyone of my collaborators touched a penny for his services. I have put in the enterprise every cent I possessed and so did my collaborators. Nobody can say we were doing it for the sake of vile money, leave that for Arab spies. We are not doing it for honours either, for nobody is more conservative, in this respect, than the Britisher, and we do not see the showering of honours on spies, no matter how great the services. We are not even sure of their confidence; they may think us capable of betraying them just as we were of betraying the Turks. We do not do it for vengeance; we do it because we hope we are serving our Jewish cause. We did not even ask for promises. We considered it our duty to do our share and we are still foolish enough to believe in right and justice, and recognition of the Cause we are serving.[22]

The letter was written for an audience beyond Judge Mack, and Aaronsohn accompanied it with a private note, analyzing who among their mutual acquaintances should see the letter. He knew that many of the trustees of the research station were skeptical about Zionism: the trustees had committed their funds and support because they were impressed with him as a scientist, not to support the goal of a Jewish homeland. Aaronsohn was eager for the exceptions to see the letter. "Felix [Frankfurter] is open minded, free and prudent and has such a wonderfully subtle mind," Aaronsohn wrote in the private note. "I have been too well treated at the 'House of Truth'; I owe him the truth." (The "House of Truth" was Frankfurter's name for his house on Nineteenth Street in Washington, where Aaronsohn had stayed in 1914)[23]. Of Justice Brandeis: "Speaking of converts . . . from Mrs. Rosenwald's report I gather that Brandeis publicly declared me somewhat responsible for his conversion [to Zionism]. . . . I see no necessity of informing him, unless you judge otherwise." On "Miss [Henrietta] Szold . . . I think of her not only as a very sweet soul but as the greatest Jewess it was my lot to know. But I am afraid it will be such a shock to her. . . . May be give her the news in homeopathic doses and as she is so nicely womanly and *'raisonne avec le coeur'* she may after sometime recover her balance."

"The hardest case for me," Aaronsohn wrote, "is with Mr. and Mrs. Rosenwald. They ought to know but here I hesitate. . . . With the R's, to whom I owe much it is much harder; they are so 'bourgeois' in their thinking that may be it is better to keep them in the dark till it ends." Because "J[acob]. H. S[chiff]. would drop dead," Aaronsohn urged not telling him: "He will certainly despise a spy! And will find a *post factum* justification in the dislike he always felt for me." Lewis Marshall is a "good lawyer but too much a lawyer. Will see the legal side only." Aaronsohn's comments on his American friends, the most powerful and influential Jews in America, were candid and accurate assessments of their likely reactions. "Curious, it is not," he summed up, "when it comes to such a serious situation, when it may be turning your back on all you loved and respected during a lifetime; there are, of the hundreds of people you like and approached, about a half a dozen you really but deeply care about."[24]

The next day he wrote to Feinberg's sister in Berlin that Alfred was planning to visit the Levi family. "Alfred" was his code name for himself; "the Levi family" was Woolley's country, Britain. Because the code was prearranged he continued to refer to Levi/Woolley, but Aaronsohn had already begun to speculate that Woolley might be dead. What other explanation was there for the failure of the ships to show up off Athlit? When Aaronsohn told Paget about their earlier contacts with Woolley, Paget had not responded, even after he had had time to confirm the story with London or Cairo. Only later did

Aaronsohn learn that after Feinberg returned to Athlit, the naval signaling codes had been changed, and Woolley, despairing of reestablishing contact with the group at Athlit, had switched to other naval intelligence projects. On August 17, 1916, Woolley was dispatched on a secret mission to Alexandretta Bay. The Turks had mined the bay heavily, twelve men on the mission were killed, and Woolley and several others were captured and incarcerated by the Turks.[25]

As meticulous in his travel as in his science, Aaronsohn obsessed to have every "i" dotted and "t" crossed in advance, but when he showed up to board the *Oscar II,* the manager of the steamship company refused to allow him to board without a laissez-passer from the British legation. There wasn't enough time to go to the consulate before the ship sailed, so he telephoned, only to be told that both the minister and his secretary were absent. Aaronsohn angrily called them liars. Finally "some sort of secretary" introduced himself and promised to arrange everything by telephone. The steamship company received the assurances they needed, and Aaronsohn was allowed to board.[26] Plenty of people saw the argument and his angry demands for the document—more "proof" that he intended to travel to the United States. Privately, he asked Dushkin, his cabin mate, to hide and deliver the long confession and covering letter to Judge Mack. Before he boarded the ship Aaronsohn got off a last message to Tzila in Berlin, who promised to pass it along to Aaronsohn's colleagues in Palestine. The message reported that he was sailing to America to visit friends.[27]

In less than a week Aaron Aaronsohn would be at Scotland Yard. He could only hope that in Palestine they would know what his message really meant.

11

At the Savoy Hotel

In my view, if they did not reach the main battlefield against Turkey, they would have to confess failure, to remain a side-show of a side-show.

—T. E. Lawrence[1]

Had I been alone, striving towards a personal goal, I should have long ago sent them to the devil. But we are not concerned—neither are our nerves our shims. The cause is concerned and we must lay aside pessimism and begin anew. So be it. . . . Perhaps it is better thus. If we fail, we alone shall suffer. But if we succeed, at least we shall not be indebted to anyone, and we shall have the right to say that our own efforts and merit have overcome all obstacles.

—Aaron Aaronsohn[2]

The generals were not prepared for either Lawrence or Aaronsohn.

On June 5, 1916, Lord Kitchener, the one general who appreciated the complexity and importance of the Middle East campaign, died when HMS *Hampshire,* en route to Russia, struck a German mine during a gale in the North Sea. The news shook Britain. Decades later people still remembered where they were and what they were doing when they heard that Kitchener had been killed. The Arab Revolt had begun the day before.

General Archibald Murray, commander in chief of the British forces in Egypt, was a traditional army man, contemptuous of newfangled plans and untrustworthy allies. In late 1916 he was busy planning a new offensive against the Turks, cleaning up the remnants of the messy situations at Gallipoli and in Mesopotamia, and guarding the crucial British asset of the Suez Canal. Despite his large military intelligence staff at Ismailia, compartmentalization kept him unaware of Aaron Aaronsohn. Murray was informed about but skeptical of Lieutenant Lawrence's mission. He thought the Arab Revolt at best a ragtag band of untrained Bedouins of little or no military value. Like the Jews of Palestine, the Arabs were a peripheral issue for Murray, distractions from the job of fighting the Turks. Along with much of the General Staff in London, Murray considered the entire Turkish campaign a distraction from the main task of the war, the battle against the Germans in France. He had grudgingly approved Lawrence's extended leave to allow an appraisal of Hussein's sons, especially Faisal and the Arab army, but the mission was supposed to be only long enough for the lieutenant to gather information and return to Cairo and his desk job in military intelligence. When Deedes asked his opinion after he had met with Lawrence, Murray said: "I was disappointed he did not come in dancing pumps."[3]

~

In London, Sir Basil Thomsom found Aaron Aaronsohn's information too promising to ignore. After their interviews at Scotland Yard, Sir Basil passed the imposing blond man along to a Lieutenant Colonel French in the War Office, who sent him over to the General Staff. Aaronsohn met a Major Walter Gribbon, who was sympathetic, and discovered a good "little French-Italian restaurant on Oxford Street" and a neighborhood where he could get French newspapers.[4] He wrote to his brother and sister in New York: "For the first time in two years I can write freely without feeling the insidious watching of Turco-German censorship. For the past few nights I have slept in peace, untroubled by nightmares, and without the fear of being awakened—for the last time—by the Turkish dagger or the degrading Prussian boot. Here—I had the good fortune to meet eager ears and open minds. I have reason to believe that had our friends been better informed sooner, they would have acted in consequence. Had I come earlier I should have probably served our cause better, spared our country some suffering, and rendered more efficient service to our friends."[5]

That euphoria ended when he found himself bounced from official to official in the War Office, which did not share Sir Basil's enthusiasm for Aaronsohn and his story. He was accustomed to the Ottoman bureaucracy, where making a petitioner wait and deferring decisions had been honed to an art. The British, he learned, could be just as sticky and inefficient. He would sit for long waits in outer offices, cooling his heels with only a clerk or a guard for company, before an officer or official would hear him out. They would listen politely. Some asked a few questions, or jotted notes. No one would give him a definitive answer, or even a promise that his proposals would be acted upon. With the Ottoman bureaucrats a petitioner could smooth the rough edges with a discreet offer of baksheesh. Aaronsohn knew the British didn't do business that way. There was nothing to do but wait and somehow control his impatience and temper.

He had lived a life of science, of species and samples that could be identified and cataloged with certainty; certainty about his discovery of the wild emmer had earned him recognition and fame on four continents. And he had never been more certain of anything than he was of the importance of his group and their mission. He had risked his life traveling to England. The colleagues he had left behind in Athlit and Zichron were in even greater danger. They knew the consequences if they were caught by the Turkish police or army, and that hanging would be a welcome surcease after the beatings and torture that awaited an arrested spy. But the facts and the situation that were so obvious to Aaronsohn didn't seem to matter to the British.

Bitter and frustrated, he filled the empty hours between appointments with long walks around London, twelve miles or more a day, for physical exercise "as well as diversion for the mind, as if I brooded continually over the situation, it would be enough to drive me mad.

What slowness in decisions! It will soon be two months since I have left Berlin, and after all nothing of consequence has been done to discover the Athlit people."[6] The walks were also a chance to get a feel for the British. He went to the Parade of Guards and thought the men awkward and lacking the "automatic stiffness" of German troops. He watched as an old Englishwoman, "obviously of the lower middle class, in mourning (who had no doubt lost a son at the Somme) . . . made a shaky and awkward salute to the boys passing."[7] At the Lord Mayor's show near the Guildhall, on November 9, he watched Dominion troops parade for the first time in khaki, the uniform they would need for a desert campaign. Aaronsohn, who had observed the Turkish and German troops in Palestine, thought the Dominion troops had properly "martial faces," but no "militarism in their blood. A Prussian would have criticized every movement of these fine fellows. Not enough ensemble and no stiffness whatever. Drilling did not make automatons of them."[8]

For their part, the British, unsure exactly who this man was or whether they could trust him, were understandably cautious. British intelligence resources in Cairo had been focused on the Arabs. To the extent that the War Office and Foreign Office had thought about or planned for the Middle East, at least since the disaster at Gallipoli, they had concentrated on diplomacy with the French and Sherif Hussein. Palestine was only one component of the Middle East campaign, and the British had no capability of independently researching or confirming what Aaronsohn told them. Even those who were initially sympathetic to him, like Major Gribbon and Mark Sykes, probably considered his insistence on haste incomprehensible.

Aaronsohn drafted a series of memoranda, laying out information he thought the British should act upon. In one he wrote that although he was a Zionist he did not agree with the official Zionist position. He did not need to add that Chaim Weizmann, Nahum Sokolov, and the official Zionist movement, convinced that any breach of their neutrality in the war might ultimately come back to haunt them, would not agree with what Aaronsohn and his group were doing.

The disputes were hardly news to the British: in September 1917 a Foreign Office official wrote that "the internal feuds in Jewry are too complicated for the mere Gentile to follow."[9]

Aaronsohn wrote in one memo that Britain should have control of Palestine to protect the Suez Canal, and should take control over Mesopotamia; that Britain and Palestine should establish cooperative financial arrangements; and that the support he expected for the Jewish communities of Palestine from powerful American Jews should be included in the arrangements. He wrote a memo entitled "Pro Armenia" about the treatment of the Armenians in the Ottoman Empire, recommending that they have their own country, which would enjoy friendly relations with Palestine. His memoranda were concise, well informed, and well written—astonishing achievements considering how recently he had learned English. But he still had no audience to read them.

He met in Gribbon's office with Mark Sykes and G. M. FitzMaurice, the former dragoman in the British embassy at Constantinople. Aaronsohn was impressed with their awareness of the massacres of Armenians and their apparent support for Zionism. Sykes was especially friendly, asking about Aaronsohn's "nuances" on Judaism, and inviting Aaronsohn to visit him at his house at Buckingham Gate. Sykes's knowledge was broad but shallow, his views often refreshingly different from the official positions in the War Office and the Foreign Office. But even Sykes could give Aaronsohn no assurances that his information, or the pipeline of information available from the group at Athlit, would be used.

Major Gribbon was the most supportive. He pointed out to Aaronsohn that when Woolley had made arrangements with Feinberg he had done it on his own responsibility, without coordinating with his colleagues or the various intelligence agencies, and with Woolley now a prisoner of the Turks at Kastamouni, there was no one to verify the arrangements he had made earlier.[10] Gribbon suggested that perhaps contacts with Athlit could resume before Aaronsohn went to Egypt. Aaronsohn refused, arguing that after their previous experience he did not trust the sailors and agents to make the arrangements and guarantee the safety of his people in Palestine. He insisted that he be transferred to Egypt first, where he could then coordinate and supervise the connections to his colleagues in Palestine.

It was mid-November when Aaronsohn heard that he needed only one more visit to the War Office to complete arrangements for him to be sent on to Egypt to talk to the British staff officers there. There were more delays to arrange transport and the necessary papers, but on November 24, Aaronsohn sent a coded letter to Tzila Feinberg in Berlin, written as if it were from a woman, and signed Oubi, the nickname they all used for Aaron's sister Rivka. The letter reported that he had finally received his degree and diploma (that he could go to Egypt) and to tell Salma (Avshalom) not to try to visit Levi (Woolley) because he was in the hospital (prison).[11] Aaronsohn could only hope that the message would get to Zichron intact, and that the code would be understood.

He had hoped to travel via Paris and to meet with Baron Rothschild, but the British routed him via Marseilles. He protested: "I explained to Gribbon that if they wanted our work to yield good results they must consider it as a contribution—modest perhaps—but nevertheless a contribution. If we continue to have—on one side—people who risk everything and work with all their heart—and on the other—people who accept everything but promise nothing and remain distrustful—then the whole thing must be dropped." Gribbon's explanation that Woolley's work with Feinberg had either been unknown to his superiors in intelligence or that they did not share Woolley's enthusiasm validated Aaronsohn's conclusion before he had started his own journey—that the British would only listen to someone with a name they recognized. "That is why they waited for my military report in Egypt," he wrote in his diary. "As it was considered a good report, they are willing to put me to trial. It is certain that I shall again be subject to cross-questioning &c. in Egypt. . . . Instead of having to make my way from a junior officer to the higher spheres, I have already reached that point. It is therefore an established fact. I shall be put to trial with all possible chances." The Foreign Office, he concluded, cannot "bind themselves in any way. Their silence is proof that they are disposed . . . as the English say:—'A wink or a nod are the same for a blind mule.'"[12]

Aaronsohn read the newspapers, and followed the war news closely. He knew that the British were reeling from the Somme campaign, the desperate attempt to gain ground against the Germans after the horrors of the battle of Verdun. The British had lost more than 19,000 men on the opening day of the Somme campaign, and 60,000 men on a single day later in the campaign; after months of desperate fighting, and a loss of over 400,000 men, they had advanced less than seven miles against the Germans. But reading about other campaigns of the war did not make him a strategist of the big picture. If he was a fox in his agronomy, seeing many problems at once, on the war he was a hedgehog, focused on a single problem, unwilling to accept that it was only one of many concerns for the British. When he left for France he confessed to his diary that

> so far as wasting time is concerned—without being able to remedy it in any way—I have certainly wasted enough for the past 4 months . . . for what I have obtained, three days would have been more than sufficient. What did I obtain after all? Nothing—I must say.
>
> I have probably been too frank with them, or else they have taken it all for cunningness, but the fact remains that I have obtained nothing. They do not give us any "credit" for this whole year of suffering and danger. . . . They want us to show what we can do. Happy Absa! An enthusiast himself—he found in Woolley another enthusiast. They excited each other and started off wildly without any foundation between them. But at least they had their illusions! Now—Egypt takes no account of the past and wants to put us to the test.[13]

On board the *Karmala* he found himself surrounded by passengers dressed in tuxedos for dinner, many of them en route to vacations in Gibraltar and Algeciras. It was a jarring sight only weeks after he had seen the paucity of foodstuffs available in Berlin, and months away from the near-starvation conditions in Palestine. A woman on the ship protested that she had been given lime instead of lemon for her tea. "The idea of leaving London with no lemons!" Aaronsohn wrote in his diary. "There was no end to what she said."[14]

He was barely allowed ashore in Marseilles, even after identifying himself as a scientist studying cotton yields in Egypt, and they crossed the Mediterranean under warnings of German submarines in the area, with life jacket drills, blackouts, a watch posted for mines, and passengers asked to serve as lookouts for enemy submarines. They were still at sea when the news arrived of Asquith's resignation and Lloyd George's appointment as prime minister. Aaronsohn was aware of Asquith's views of Zionism: Asquith had once written "an almost dithyrambic memorandum urging that . . . we should take Palestine, into which the scattered Jews c[oul]d in time swarm back from all the quarters of the globe, and in due course obtain Home Rule. (What an attractive community!)"[15]

Aaronsohn had his own prejudices. That night "Hindoos" at his table at dinner were openly critical of Lloyd George. "There is no doubt," he wrote in his diary, "but that 3 or 4 years ago these Hindoos would not have permitted themselves such strong criticisms of British politics and politicians. A sign of the times, I suppose, but were I in the place of the British, I should beware of it."[16]

As he so often did when he was thinking, he paced on deck—nine, fifteen, once nineteen miles in a day—while he planned a strategy for dealing with the British. His roundabout route to Cairo, less than three hundred miles from where he started, was taking far longer than he or anyone else imagined. And in Palestine, where the future of a people depended on his plan, no one knew his whereabouts.

~

He arrived in Port Said in mid-December 1916, desperate for news after so many days of travel, and eager to get on with the long delayed connections to Athlit and Zichron. When he asked for news about the United States, then at the conclusion of an election campaign, he was told, "Yes, Smith, the new President is one of my friends. . . .

Smith was elected in June." Aaronsohn, never one to welcome sloppy research, was appalled by the ignorance.

He settled into the Regina Palace Hotel in Alexandria. The first intelligence agent he met, Captain William Stanley Edmonds, initially seemed "not only very intelligent but shrewd as well," but when Aaronsohn asked how soon they would be setting up contacts with Athlit, he was told that they did not want him going on any voyages to the coast of Palestine. Aaronsohn announced that if they did not have full confidence in him, perhaps it would be better "to give up everything" then and there. The intelligence officers reassured him that they wanted him there. "It was not because they distrusted me," he wrote in his diary. "If such were the case, they would not have sent for me. The true reason was that I was too precious for them. If an accident should befall me then everything would collapse."[17]

The British, still uncertain what to do with Aaronsohn, sent Norman Bentwich to interview him and report back on whether he could be trusted. Bentwich, a British lawyer, knew Clayton well, and had met other intelligence agents, including Lawrence; he was the brother of Nita Lange, a wealthy English Jewess who had come with her husband to settle in Zichron and had been impressed by Aaron Aaronsohn in 1910. Bentwich and Aaronsohn spent a day walking along the banks of the Nile, long enough for Bentwich to be convinced "that his [Aaron's] one and only purpose was to aid Great Britain in redeeming Palestine from the Turkish yoke."[18]

Despite Bentwich's voucher, Aaronsohn's disputes with the intelligence office escalated. He asked for £1,500 to reimburse the expenses of his journeys to England and Egypt, and the considerable funds they had spent on Feinberg's earlier efforts to reach the British. Captain Edmonds said the figure made their "services rather expensive," and offered him a stipend of £1 per day, less than the cost of his hotel room in Alexandria. Edmonds also repeated that Woolley had left no documentation of his alleged arrangements with Avshalom Feinberg, and that the British could only make payments on the submission of actual receipts of expenditures.

Aaronsohn cabled Henrietta Szold for an advance of $500. "If they cannot cover all my expenses I would rather receive nothing from my friends," he wrote in his diary. "On the whole, I have encountered nothing but distrust and reticence, smallness and pettiness. I must try and control my nerves so that I can establish another connection with Absa. So far as I am concerned, I have had enough of it. I am not going to continue working under such conditions."[19]

But even as he harangued his diary, his mission was too important to abandon in a fit of pique. He kept reminding the British staff officers why he was there, demanding that they listen to his information and establish secret contact with his colleagues in Palestine. When Edmonds said that he had found a messenger that he would use to establish contact with the group in Palestine, and asked if Aaronsohn had a message he wanted to send—ignoring everything Aaronsohn had explained about the need for someone who knew the terrain of Athlit and the workings of the group—Aaronsohn blew up: "That, indeed, was too much. My fears were thus realized. These people did not trust us and, with the help of my information, wished to send some 'blunderer' who might cause the loss of our people's lives, and ruin our work.

"I did not mince my words . . . telling him what I thought of this lack of confidence, also that in future I would refuse any co-cooperation or association. I reminded him of the fact that it would not only be an abuse, but a veritable crime to use any information against my will."

Edmonds said, "If we do not trust you—you don't trust us either."

Aaronsohn was appalled. How could the British not understand the difference? "We have reasons to doubt their ability, but we do not distrust them. They—on the contrary—do not doubt our ability but they distrust us. It is an insult that neither I nor those who help me can bear."[20]

Again and again Aaronsohn tried to explain that his colleagues at the research station in Athlit were incomparably familiar with the terrain and the positions of Turkish units. They were experienced at traveling throughout Palestine and Syria to gather information, had contacts at strategic points, and a cover as agricultural researchers. And they were in great danger, not only from the Turkish army and police but also from their fellow Jewish settlers, who were afraid that any sign of resistance or rebellion would bring on repressive measures from the Ottoman authorities. The group desperately needed confirmation that Aaronsohn's mission had been successful, and a regular communications channel for the information they were secretly gathering on the Turkish defenses. His contacts in the United States were willing to send funds for relief of the beleaguered Jewish communities in Palestine, which could be delivered on the same ships that picked up the intelligence reports from Athlit. The advantages to both sides were obvious: the British would get needed intelligence, and Aaronsohn's colleagues would get relief funds for the local population and the assurance that their spying efforts were not for naught. Surely the British would understand that they wanted a British victory in the war as much as the General Staff.

On Christmas Eve 1916 the British finally allowed a small trawler, the *Goeland,* under the command of a Captain Baul, to motor up to the coast of Palestine to reconnoiter in the area of the research station at Athlit. As preparations were under way, Aaronsohn bought sugar, condensed milk, chocolate, cocoa, semolina, Quaker oats, coffee, tea, and coal oil to take with him to Athlit. A Captain Smith, the naval liaison in charge of the ships used for spying missions, insisted that he leave the food behind. Aaronsohn pointed out that they would only unload the boat if they met their own people at Athlit, and that those people were suffering from hunger. "Let them starve," Smith answered. "What do we care?"

"Needless to say that the blood rushed to my head," Aaronsohn remembered, "and that Smith received the only reply that he deserved, but I no longer thought of convincing him." The foodstuffs were left behind. On board the *Goeland* he complained that there were no proper marine glasses, which they would need to watch for activity or signals from shore. The captain answered that better glasses would be of no use. "This exasperated me," Aaronsohn wrote. "But there was nothing I could do about it."

The voyage was slow: the ship was underpowered and had been fueled with low-grade, cast-off coal that limited their speed. When they reached the coast at Athlit the captain admitted that perhaps they could have used better binoculars, but they got close enough to shore to see two men on the balcony at the research station with a black cloth, a signal that the ship had been recognized. A storm was coming up as they motored offshore waiting for dark. When they returned to the coast under the cover of the moonless night, the seas were rough, and the captain announced that they could send only a single experienced swimmer and a guide ashore. Aaronsohn and Captain Smith argued about whether Aaronsohn would be allowed to go ashore, whether it was too late to land men and get them back before daybreak, and whether the flashes of light and the bivouac fire they saw on shore were danger signals. A swimmer and another man (younger and slimmer than Aaron) were finally rowed toward shore with money, instructions, and Aaronsohn's Hastings magnifying glass and penknife, either of which anyone at the station would recognize. The launch put the men into the water and returned to the ship, reporting that it was too rough to wait for the swimmers. Captain Smith then announced that it was also too dangerous for the ship to wait offshore, that they would leave the men at Athlit.

Aaronsohn argued for at least setting up a system of signals so the group in Athlit could notify the British about threatening dangers, such as Turkish massacres in the area, a forced evacuation of the base, or the capture of one of the spies. How else would they maintain regular communication?

"This does not interest us very much," the captain answered, "as it has no influence on the military situation. Military information alone is what matters."[21]

The trawler headed back to Port Said, leaving the two men who had been put into the water to make their way to the research station.

When he got back to Alexandria, Aaronsohn, who had expected to be transferred to Cairo where intelligence decisions were being made, was told it was best for him to stay in Alexandria to await further instructions. "It was bad enough in London to have to wait days and weeks pending an order or a mere word," he wrote in his diary. "But here in Alexandria, it is a thousand times worse. I do not cease from cursing the day we made the unfortunate decision of co-operating with our friends. One must have neither nerves nor warm blood to be able to work with them. . . . Regarding administrative activities, the British—to me—almost seem beneath the Turks."[22]

Angry and frustrated, he passed time at the Alexandria museum, where papyrus scrolls from the Ptolemaic period recorded the complaints of farmers that an aggressor had tried to take their fields and prevent their sowing. "Is this not the same as what is happening at home nowadays?" Aaronsohn asked his diary. At a New Year's Eve party with officers and agents, servants brought in that most British of delicacies, a plum pudding, and at midnight the guests threw balls of bread at one another. "This mere fact proves that the war is not yet felt by the Allies as it is in the Central Countries," he wrote. "Balls of white bread wasted here, while people die of hunger a few hundred kilometers north—in Palestine."[23]

He expected a better reception in Cairo. He arrived on January 4, 1917, and found a room in the Continental Hotel, where Lawrence and his colleagues stayed. Aaronsohn knew Cairo—he had been there as recently as January 1914 for a scientific meeting—and was familiar enough with the local spots to hold an early meeting with Gertrude Bell at Groppi's, the same pleasant café between the Continental Hotel and British GHQ where Lawrence liked to stop for an iced coffee. Aaronsohn knew how valuable he could be to the British headquarters staff in Cairo as they planned their campaign in Palestine, but his skills, training, and experience earned him an icy reception at GHQ. To the staff and intelligence officers Aaronsohn was a stranger with a Jewish name in a rumpled suit, speaking English with an accent. Over six feet tall and powerfully built, with a huge head and neck, he stood out like a carnival giant alongside the English officers and men. Themselves strangers in a strange land, the officers were wary of Turkish spies and suspicious of Jews, especially "Oriental" Jews, who in British minds combined the worse character traits of what they openly called Wogs and Hebrews.

"Empire" wasn't a dirty word in 1916. The British officer corps and the intelligence services at GHQ shared a belief in the idea of empire and a code of authority, superiority, mission, and especially class. They accepted a British duty, what some would have called a divinely granted responsibility, to civilize and rule, and that noblesse oblige came with a strict code of values. As a colonial power the British favored what they considered *good* locals, subject peoples who were passive, appreciative, and respectful toward Britain. Despite occasional misunderstandings in their negotiations, the Arabs were *good* locals. By contrast, the British officers and intelligence agents had little patience for *bad* locals, those who were rebellious, or who seemed to consider themselves more qualified or more deserving of authority than the British. The Jews in Palestine, in the British view, were bad locals—too intellectual, ambitious, and cocky. The typical terms used for Jews at GHQ were "pushy" and "grasping." Aaron Aaronsohn, self-assured, brimming over with knowledge, confident of his skills and experience, blunt and direct in his manner, fit the British stereotype perfectly.

Aaronsohn took the brush-offs as a sign of British disrespect. Used to the authority of knowledge, he was forced to be a diplomat, to wait to be summoned so he could plead his case. The British style was controlled. Anyone he talked to would tell him the bare minimum he was deemed to need to know, and hold back everything else. Orders and decisions were filtered through layers of bureaucracy. Compartmentalizing knowledge might have been proper intelligence procedure, but to Aaronsohn the terseness, secrecy, and condescension he saw in British reticence was an inefficient and ineffective alternative to the openness he had known in Palestine and in the world of science. He found the lack of straightforward communication unbearable. "People are desperately slow," he wrote. "Stupid bureaucrats (red-tapists) unable to compete against the Boches who show in all instances much initiative coupled with a bright, determined mentality. The French and English are equally guilty. It is heart-rending to think that the German successes are only due to the nauseating incompetence of the Allies."[24]

His frustration mounted as he waited an entire week for a meeting with the captain, Edmonds, he had worked with in Alexandria. "Our conversation was positively maddening," Aaronsohn wrote. "More than twenty times I felt like throwing up to their face what I thought of their complete and irremediable inability to understand the situation. A hundred times daily I curse the moment when we decided to work with them. Better for us to stagnate with the Turks and keep our illusions about the Allies than to approach them and see this hopeless incompetence. If the Boches are finally beaten by these '*kakers*' [Yiddish for "worthless people"] they will have reason to doubt God and Justice. The Allies' unskillfulness in small as in important questions is sickening. In the meantime we are the ones to suffer."[25]

Aaronsohn had never learned or valued the prized British trait of false modesty. As a scientist he was unaccustomed to having to persuade when the facts were so obvious, and he had little experience with the compromises, juggled demands and priorities, and cautious delays that marked decision making in an operation as large and complex as the British headquarters. As his frustrations mounted he fell into a funk, wondering if he would ever find a way to cut through what he saw as the cockiness and inertia of GHQ. After the weeks in London and Alexandria, his frustrations at what he saw as incompetence turned to anger. He considered leaving. "Better commit suicide than to continue under such conditions with people whom we thought were our friends and who are incompetent and selfish—although individually—most of them are charming."

He had spent his working life alone, or as the head of his own research institute, setting his own agendas. He had no experience of a huge enterprise with a complex agenda in which his own project—no matter how important—was only one of many priorities. The British were fighting on three continents and on the seas, on many fronts against multiple enemies, while coördinating intelligence from a huge range of sources, diplomatic negotiations with friends and foes, and an incomparable logistics challenge. Yet Aaronsohn could not understand why he was not immediately given the materials he needed to work on a map of southern Palestine, or why the missions to Athlit were not given the highest priority. If only the British would recognize him and his colleagues in Zichron and Athlit as the incomparable resource they were, he kept telling his diary, if only they would pay attention to the information he and his colleagues could supply—they could become masters of the whole coast of Palestine. He had seen the conditions, seen the poor training and equipment of the Turks. The British didn't seem to want to know. "Are they laughing at me here?" he asked his diary. "Or don't they care about the work?"[26]

Isolated, out of contact with Palestine and out of the loop of British intelligence, Aaronsohn was brimming with ideas and plans but no one asked him his views. He wasn't asked about the Zionists until he met William Ormsby-Gore, the son of Lord Harlech. Ormsby-Gore complimented Aaronsohn on a report he had written in London, was curious about various Jewish personalities and others in Palestine, and was fascinated by Aaronsohn's agricultural research and its implications for the future of Palestine. Aaronsohn found him sympathetic, but Ormsby-Gore told him that the British government "does not seem to be in a position to favor the Zionists. They are afraid of rivalry and therefore want to remain entirely neutral, giving everyone 'fair play.'"[27] Ormsby-Gore was either dissembling or no more aware than Aaronsohn that the British were already devoting considerable effort and funds to advancing the Arab cause.

From Philip Graves, Aaronsohn learned that there was "some sort of an agreement between the English and the French regarding

Palestine; the British go up to Acre and the Plain of Israel, in which Jerusalem would remain English and Protestant, while the French would have Upper Galilee so that Nazareth would be French and Catholic." He knew an agreement like that would be a misfortune for the Zionists, and that until solid contacts were established they were too weak to have anything to say in the matter. That even Aaronsohn, an outsider to British intelligence, found out about the Sykes-Picot agreement suggests how easily the terms of the secret agreement were batted around in Cairo. Late in January, he met Deedes, who had been assigned to the intelligence office at the time of the Kut surrender negotiations. He thought Deedes "more American-like in his methods of work," assumed he was in charge of the intelligence service, and that with Deedes in command his own position would improve. In fact Deedes was only a staffer who had been seconded to the Arab Bureau as a Turkish expert. Aaronsohn, who knew the Turkish order of battle in Palestine, was sufficiently out of the loop in British intelligence not to know who was in charge.

He was in an optimistic mood the day after he met Deedes, when Captain Edmonds found him and said, "You are the very man I am looking for. I have been looking for you all morning. You must go immediately to Port Said. One of your men came across the desert." Aaronsohn learned that the man was Josef Lishinsky. He wondered if Lishinsky was wounded, why they were sending him to Port Said instead of bringing Lishinsky to Cairo, and why Lishinsky had crossed the Sinai. In his diary he wrote: "These gentlemen are so uselessly and so unfortunately mysterious!"[28]

Aaronsohn reached Port Said at midnight. Lishinsky told him to send their go-between away, and then told Aaronsohn that after months of not hearing from him he and Feinberg had decided that they could wait no longer and set off across the desert to make contact with the British. Sarah had opposed Feinberg going, saying it was too dangerous, but he insisted. They had dressed as Bedouins, taken a guide with them, and ridden across the Sinai. At a rest stop they were attacked by a band of Bedouins. The guide fled, and

Feinberg and Lishinsky had no choice but to fight. Feinberg was shot through the back and killed. Lishinsky, though wounded, made it across the desert and was picked up by Australian troops.

Aaronsohn was so shocked by the news he could hardly sleep. At five in the morning he woke up and confided to his diary: "So Absa, the Brave, was shot by vile, rapacious Bedouins—he fell dying into the hands of those whom he despised most. And to think that the best we could wish for him and for us all was that he has been disfigured and buried without the least trace being left. How many hundreds of innocent people would die if his body should ever be identified! The thought is maddening!"[29]

The next day he rode the train "alone with his sorrow" back to Cairo. Deedes saw him and invited him to his office. Aaronsohn wept openly. When he saw Captain Edmonds, Aaronsohn angrily accused him of being "morally responsible for our misfortunes."

Perhaps out of guilt and the fact that there was a dark, moonless night, two days later the British attempted another boat run up to Athlit, this time on the torpedo boat *L'Arbalete*. Their initial signals got a response from the balcony of the research station building, they returned at midnight, and a strong swimmer was put ashore from the launch, despite strong seas and rising wind. When the launch returned to *L'Arbalete* they heard screams from shore. A second run of the launch failed to pick up the swimmer, even when crewmen on the launch jumped into the water. Aaronsohn's instinct was to "go back with a rope," but he was overruled, and they turned around "155 to 165 times" and finally returned to Port Said.

Days later the British brought Josef Lishinsky to Cairo, and Aaronsohn visited him in the hospital. Hogarth, Lawrence's patron and boss from the Arab Bureau, was there, and Deedes reported that a Bedouin sent to search for more news of Feinberg had returned and said there was no sign of a grave. "So our brave knight is dead!" Aaronsohn wrote. "Without even confessing it to myself, I had entertained a wild hope that he had survived. But now, we can do nothing except to complete the work for which he gave his life."[30]

But after four missions—his brother Alexander's attempt, Feinberg's meeting with Woolley, Aaronsohn's seven-month journey, and Feinberg's tragic final mission—none of the vital information Aaronsohn and his colleagues had gathered in Athlit had reached British intelligence.

Instead of returning directly to Cairo from his meeting with Emir Faisal, Lawrence detoured by ship across the Red Sea to the Sudan, where he met with Reginald Wingate, who was in charge of military liaison with Sherif Hussein while McMahon remained in charge of political negotiations. Wingate was slated to become high commissioner in Egypt. Lawrence assumed he would be sympathetic and boldly suggested that if the Bedouin troops of the Arab army were deployed as guerrilla forces they could tie down Turkish troops in the Hejaz. The Turks would need to maintain a string of garrisons to suppress the Bedouin raids, and the effort to maintain long supply lines for those garrisons would weaken the Turkish defense of Palestine considerably. British-organized efforts by the Arabs might also preclude French intervention in Arabia and Palestine. Given the striking lack of British successes on the Turkish fronts, and the building rivalry between Britain and her French ally over the future of the Middle East, Lawrence's idea was a timely proposal.

Wingate agreed, and when Lawrence returned to Cairo GHQ agreed to transfer his proposed operation to the Arab Bureau, despite the reservations of some who had worked with him. Colonel Wilson, who had been present at some of the meetings in Jidda, called Lawrence a "bumptious young ass who spoils his undoubted knowledge of Syrian Arabs etc. by making himself out to be the only authority on war, engineering, running H.M.'s ships and everything else. He put every single person's back up I've met, from the Admiral down to the most junior fellow on the Red Sea."[31] When Lawrence's report on his mission indicated the support the Arab army might be able to provide, and did not ask for British troops, heavy guns, or for the British fleet to support the Arab operations, he was not only seconded to the Arab Bureau but was sent back to Yenbo, on the coast of the Hejaz—despite his pro forma protests of "complete unfitness for the job"—to establish an intelligence liaison with Faisal.

By early December Lawrence had taken up a position with Faisal, the first British officer to spend time with the Arab army inland from the coast. Sherif Hussein had been unwelcoming to infidels anywhere but on the coast, and Faisal asked Lawrence to wear Arab dress, so "the tribesmen would then understand how to take me. . . . If I wore Meccan clothes like him . . . they would behave to me as though I were really one of the leaders, and I would be able to slip in and out of his tent without making a sensation which he had to explain away each time to strangers."[32] Lawrence had already worn Arab dress on occasion in Syria, and had found the headcloth comfortable and practical in the desert. He had no trouble adapting to the flowing robes, and found them comfortable for the highly mobile operations in the Hejaz.

Lawrence's initial enthusiasm and optimism faded when he realized that the Arab troops were terrified by artillery and aircraft, dispirited, disorganized, and unable to achieve successes against the Turkish defenses. "I rode all Saturday night," he wrote in his first message to the Arab Bureau, "had alarms and excursions all Sunday night, and rode again all last night, so my total of sleep is only three hours in the last three nights and I feel rather pessimistic. All the same, things are bad."[33] The hill tribes, which Lawrence had earlier assessed as the most valuable Arab troops, quickly evaporated as a fighting force, and Faisal lacked local knowledge and the ability to weld the disparate tribes into a single fighting force. Only British sea patrols with their guns prevented the Turks from overrunning more of the coast of the Hejaz. The Arab Revolt seemed near collapse.

In Yenbo Lawrence encountered Major Hubert Garland of the Egyptian army, an expert on explosives, who had invented his own devices for mining trains and felling telegraph poles. Lawrence was impressed. The British sappers handled explosives like a "sacrament," but Garland would shove a fistful of detonators into his pocket, grab a string of primers and jump on his camel for a week's ride to the Hejaz.[34] He taught Lawrence about explosives, and helped overcome Sherif Hussein's intractable insistence on sending valuable supplies, like the explosives, back to the British on the grounds that the Arabs did not know how to use them.

Lawrence's colleague Captain Newcombe was also advising a branch of the Arab army, and in late January the combined Arab forces, including five hundred Arab troops brought aboard a British supply ship, the *Hardinge,* scored a victory over the Turks at Wejh, on the coast. The attack was sloppy and undisciplined, but the success over Turkish troops built confidence for the Arab army. The population of Wejh was predominantly Egyptian, and the battle was followed by wholesale looting as the Arab troops "robbed them, and sacked the town: they broke every box and cupboard, tore down all fittings, cut open every mattress and cushion for gold." Faisal had warned the town before the attack that if they remained and let the Turks stay, "the resulting damage would be on their heads. So he made no effort to recover their goods." Lawrence defended the Bedouin looting as traditional in Arab warfare. Unlike the Turks, he was quick to point out, the Arabs never attacked women and children.[35] Other British observers were shocked.

Faisal was impressed by Lawrence's advice in the two months he had been in Arabia, and especially by his apparent sympathy for the Arab Revolt. In battle report after battle report, Lawrence would highlight the positive aspects of the Arabs' conduct, praising soldiers for not firing wildly and wasting ammunition. Other British officers were skeptical, pointing out the total lack of organization and discipline of the Arab troops, and their questionable motivation. One Royal Flying Corps observer who saw much of the early action wrote a cynical assessment: "So far as I have been able to judge we have not here a budding Arab nation struggling to be free of Turkish dominance. If the Turk is disliked it is only because all authority is disliked, even the most rudimentary law and order. The rebellion is an attempt on the part of the Shereefian family to secure for themselves a greater position and power in Hejaz."[36]

Clayton planned for Lawrence to return to Cairo and the Arab Bureau after two months of intelligence liaison with Faisal. Two days before Lawrence was to leave Arabia, Faisal wrote to his father, Sherif Hussein, asking him to cable British intelligence that he was "most anxious that Lawrence should not return to Cairo as he has given such very great assistance." Lawrence went back to Cairo on January 27, 1917, and Clayton and British intelligence had no choice but to accede to Lawrence's return to Arabia, with an indefinite posting as liaison to the Arab Revolt. Lawrence gleefully wrote home: "The position I have is such a queer one—I do not suppose that any Englishman before ever had such a place. . . . I cannot enter into details. I act as a sort of adviser to Sherif Feisul, and as we are on the best of terms, the job is a wide and pleasant one. I live with him in his tent, so our food and things (if you will continue to be keen on such rubbish!) are as good as the Hejaz can afford."[37]

When Lawrence returned to the Arab Bureau at the Savoy Hotel to report on the progress of the Arab Revolt, Medina was still in Turkish hands, but the Arab army, despite tactics and logistics that had British commanders shaking their heads, had blunted and even stalled the Turkish advances in the Hejaz. After the stunning British defeats earlier in the war and the stagnation of the British forces at the Suez Canal, Lawrence's reports of even modest successes against the Turkish army were welcome news.

At the Savoy Hotel Lawrence wore his uniform with the studied insouciance and sloppiness that had become his headquarters persona and annoyed colleagues up to General Murray, but a memo he had sent from the field argued that the Arabs could defend Rabegh if they were provided with advice and guns, and that they would scatter to their tents if foreigners landed. Opposition to landing British troops had also been General Murray's position: he was in favor of any recommendation that did not put extra demands on his troops.

Sycophancy got some of the staff at GHQ to describe Lawrence as "observant, with a pungent style, and character." They also praised themselves for sparing him to help the Arab cause.[38]

The short, slight, untested second lieutenant who only a few months before had made maps and translated obscure newspapers was suddenly riding the whirlwind of his imagination and Arab aspirations. He began to strut around GHQ like a conquering hero.

Aaron Aaronsohn had also been assigned temporary office space at the Savoy Hotel. On February 1 he was sent up to the Arab Bureau to meet their expert on Palestine, who had recently returned from the field. His diary recollection of the meeting is terse: "At the 'Arab Bureau' there was a young 2nd Lieutenant (Laurens)—an archaeologist." The French spelling of Lawrence's name may have been from Aaronsohn's ear for French, or perhaps an affectation.

We can only imagine their encounter: Lawrence, his uniform awry, full of stories of his adventures with the Arabs, ready with anecdotes to demonstrate his knowledge of the region. Compared to his colleagues at GHQ, his knowledge of Palestine was wide-ranging. He also had strong opinions about the Jews of Palestine, including the "German Jews, speaking German or German-Yiddish, more intractable even than the Jews of the Roman era, unable to endure contact with others not of their race . . . in the main the most foreign and uncharitable part of the whole population."[39] He was just back from a combat mission with Emir Faisal's troops, the commander of British forces in the theater supported his position, at least on the use of British forces with the Arabs, and he was about to head off for an indefinite posting with the Arab army. It was enough to make a man cocky. For the slight lieutenant, short even among his colleagues, it was enough to make his already large head even larger.

Aaronsohn towered almost a foot taller than Lawrence. He was an imposing figure, weighed over two hundred pounds, and with his blond hair and blue eyes fit no stereotype conveniently. Lawrence may have spent a summer or two tramping between crusader castles in Palestine; Aaronsohn had ridden and walked the hills and deserts of Palestine since he was a child; had conducted exhaustive and definitive surveys of the geology, flora, and water resources; advised on agriculture and economic development; developed plant varieties and agricultural techniques uniquely suited to the Palestinian soils and climates; and tracked the water supplies. Probably no one in the world knew the terrain of Palestine more intimately than he did. For over a year he had had incomparable access to the Turkish military installations and to Djemal Pasha. By temperament he was not one to hide his knowledge or to let a wrongheaded comment pass unchallenged.

He also had strong feelings about what many in Cairo were calling the Arab Revolt. Although the Palestinian Jews had good reason to hate the Turks and to try to rid the country of them, he had seen enough of conditions and attitudes in Palestine to realize that the Jews were in no position to take up arms against the Turks, and that even if they were able to do so, they would hesitate to join the Arabs. Like many Jewish settlers of his generation he had strong views of the Palestinian Arabs. "So far as we know the Arabs," he had written, "the man among them who will withstand a bribe is still to be born." He often quoted what he called the Arabs' own proverb: "Fifty prophets would turn liars, before a Bedouin would speak the truth."[40] It wasn't language Lawrence would welcome.

Aaronsohn didn't find the meeting important enough to record in detail. In his diary he wrote only that he found Lawrence "very well informed on Palestine questions—but rather conceited."[41]

It would not be their last meeting.

12

Aqaba

I've decided to go off alone to Damascus, hoping to get killed on the way: for all sakes try and clear this show up before it goes further. We are calling them to fight for us on a lie, and I can't stand it.

—T. E. Lawrence[1]

Lawrence returned to Arabia serving two masters.

As a serving British officer he had a sworn duty to pursue British war interests. And as a veteran of the intelligence service, he knew the current state of Britain's evolving war goals in the Middle East. Despite the long negotiations with Sherif Hussein and apparent recognition of his vision of the creation of a vast new Arab caliphate from the ruins of the Ottoman Empire, the British already had other priorities in their long-range diplomatic and military thinking. They had cautiously maintained a tight screen of secrecy around the Sykes-Picot agreement, and while Lawrence had not been involved with the negotiations and was not officially informed of the terms, he and his colleagues in the intelligence service were aware of the contradictions between the agreement and their earlier promises to Sherif Hussein. When Lawrence rode back to his assignment as liaison with Faisal and the Arab army, he carried heavy secrets with him.

Lawrence was also an admirer and friend of Emir Faisal, and the historical possibilities of the Arab Revolt matched up compellingly with Lawrence's imagination and the secret ambitions he had harbored from childhood. In the Arab Revolt, and the glorious spectacle and pageantry of the Arab armies, so reminiscent of the Crusades he had loved since childhood, he could become not only a witness but a participant in that history. "The order of march was rather splendid and barbaric," Lawrence wrote, describing the Arab army on the eve of a march.

> Faisal in front in white. Sharaf on his right, in red headcloth and henna-dyed tunic and cloak, myself on his left in white and red. Behind us three banners of purple silk, with gold spikes, behind them three drummers playing a march, and behind them a wild bouncing mass of 1,200 camels of the bodyguard, all packed as closely as they could move, the men in every variety of coloured clothes, and the camels nearly as brilliant in their trappings—and the whole crowd singing at the tops of their voices a war song in honour of Faisal and his family! It looked like a river of camels.[2]

Lawrence was aware of the potential and real tension between his masters. When his colleague Newcombe was scheduled to visit Arabia to advise the Arab forces in January 1917, he crossed paths with Lawrence, who had been rotated back to Cairo. Lawrence left him a note: "I prepared Feisul (who is an absolute ripper) carefully for you. . . . This show is splendid: you cannot imagine greater fun for us, greater vexation and fury for the Turks. We win hands down if we keep the Arabs simple . . . to add to them heavy luxuries will only wreck their show, and guerrilla does it. . . . After all, it's an Arab war, and we are only contributing materials—and the Arabs have the right to go their own way and run things as they please. We are only guests."[3]

It was a position Emir Faisal and his father would appreciate.

~

There were two ways to move men and matériel up and down the length of the Hejaz. Turkish logistics depended on the Hejaz Railway, originally built to carry hajj pilgrims on the long trek from Damascus to the holy sites in Mecca and Medina. The single-track line ran unprotected across open desert, and the Turkish garrisons were spaced far enough apart that long stretches of the railway were unguarded. The trains were slow, averaging ten miles per hour, and the telegraph line, the only communication over the vast distances, ran along the roadbed, making the railway an ideal target for guerrilla operations.

The other way was by sea. The British navy controlled the Red Sea, and British ships could deliver men and equipment anywhere on the Arabian coast if the ports were not in Turkish hands. Sherif Hussein and Emir Faisal had ambitious plans to transport the Arab army in British ships, and their first major victories in the Arab Revolt were in the battles for the ports of Wejh and Rabegh. But those battles also revealed the weakness of the Arab forces, especially in November and December 1916, when the Arabs found themselves driven back from their inland position to Yenbo, which they could only hold with support from British naval guns. In those early days of the Arab Revolt, there was even talk of sending British forces ashore.

Every negotiation with the Arabs was subject to Sherif Hussein's whimsy. He had little grasp of military strategy, no familiarity with modern weapons, and seemed determined to defy diplomatic conventions. If the British understood the caliphate that Hussein craved for himself as representing spiritual authority over the Arab Muslim world, Hussein saw the caliphate in terms closer to the Baghdad rulers in the centuries after the Muslim conquest, who held both temporal and spiritual power over their followers. At the end of October 1916, without consulting his putative allies, Hussein proclaimed himself king of the Arab nation, a title of dubious impact since there was no Arab nation, but one that was likely to provoke outrage among both rival Arab sheikhs and Britain's allies. Hussein blamed the military difficulties of the Arab armies on Britain's failure to cut the Hejaz Railway, despite the fact that Britain had never offered to cut the Hejaz Railway. When Hussein realized that the Arab Revolt was near collapse, he was torn between the need to protect his beleaguered forces, which despite deliveries of British weaponry, ammunition, equipment, and funds had been overwhelmed by the Turks, and his instinctive opposition to the landing of Christian troops in Arabia.

In 1917, Brémond suggested that Allied forces could be landed at Aqaba, at the head of the Red Sea, the last major port on the Hejaz still in Turkish hands. Brémond stressed the military objectives—by seizing the port the Allied forces would be able to supply and support a major attack that would cut the Hejaz Railway—but he had ulterior motives: he no doubt hoped that French and British troops at the head of the Red Sea would prevent the Arab Revolt from expanding out of the Arabian Peninsula into Syria, where the Sykes-Picot agreement had secured British and Russian recognition of a French sphere of influence. Brémond argued that foreign troops in Aqaba, far from the holy cities of Mecca and Medina, would not offend Islamic sensibilities, and that he was willing to commit to the effort two Senegalese battalions from Djibouti as well as the French forces camped at Suez. The War Office in London and General Murray in Cairo promptly rejected the plan. In Cairo, Lawrence told Brémond that he knew Aqaba from before the war, and that although an invading force could take the beach, they would be under the guns on the hills behind the town, and "as unfavorably placed as on the Gallipoli beach." A landing at Aqaba, Lawrence argued, would require thousands of the best Indian troops, and they would encounter stiff resistance from the local Arabs, who would "certainly resist a British invasion. In my opinion Akaba, whose importance was all and more than what he said, would be best taken by an irregular force of Arabs, descending from the east without naval help."

Lawrence recognized that Brémond's real goal was to head off the Arab Revolt. When Brémond traveled to Egypt via Wejh, on the Arabian coast, to lobby for his plan among the Arabs, Lawrence remembered that he had not warned Faisal that Brémond was "a crook." Lawrence left immediately for Wejh and Faisal's headquarters.[4] There, on February 6, 1917, less than a week after his meeting with Aaron Aaronsohn, Lawrence learned that Faisal already had no intention of supporting Brémond's proposal to land an Anglo-French force at Aqaba. But Faisal did not understand the reason the Frenchman had been so eager for the landing until Lawrence explained.

Lawrence considered Faisal a friend, and had spent long enough in Syria and Arabia to know what friendship and trust meant in the Arab world. If he lied to Faisal—and hiding the truth would be a form of lying—their friendship would someday shatter into broken trust. And with the friendship any cooperation between the British and the Arab Revolt would also end, along with Lawrence's role in making history in the Middle East. So instead of stopping at the "need to know" point that was the basis of any tight intelligence operation, Lawrence went on to explain that the French wanted the Arab Revolt confined to the Hejaz because they feared that an Arab movement might inspire a nationalist uprising in Syria, where through a secret agreement Britain had acquiesced to a French sphere of influence, and the same agreement had given Britain a comparable sphere of influence in Mesopotamia and made provisions for control of Palestine. He told Faisal that the secret Sykes-Picot agreement had effectively trumped the language of the McMahon correspondence, that Lebanon was certainly lost, and the four great cities of Syria (Damascus, Homs, Hama, and Aleppo) along with the interior of Syria would also be under French control unless the Arabs captured the territory first. The consequences of the secret agreement, Lawrence said, were "only to be set aside if the Arabs redoubled their efforts against the Turks, not with them in revenge; for we were sure to win the war, and would then have to enforce it. His [Faisal's] only escape was to do so much to help the British that, after peace, they would not be able, for very shame, to shoot such allies down in fulfillment of a secret treaty."[5]

Telling Faisal about the Sykes-Picot agreement was a fateful decision. For Lawrence, it was a decisive step away from his duties and oath as a commissioned officer in the British intelligence services. He had often been cavalier about his rank and duties, flaunting his casualness with his uniform and disrespect for regulations, procedures, and the bureaucratic jargon of his colleagues and superiors. But that had all been on the order of his pranks at Oxford. Telling Faisal about a secret diplomatic agreement was defying British policy at the highest levels, taking strategy and tactics into his own hands. The news, which Faisal quickly understood, also changed the strategic priorities of the Arabs. Attacks on the Hejaz Railway, which suited the British because they tied down Turkish troops that might otherwise be sent to defend Palestine and the Sinai, were no longer as important to the Arabs as a northern campaign, a thrust from Arabia up into the valley of the Jordan and into Syria. Lawrence could not have been surprised by the changed Arab strategy, and surely knew that it was not only directed squarely against Britain's ally France, but was also undermining, or at least failing to support, the broad British strategy in the Middle East.

Lawrence went a step further by suggesting that the Arabs might be able to mitigate the harsh boundaries laid out in the Sykes-Picot agreement, including the denial of a port to Syria, if the Arab armies could seize a strip of the Mediterranean coast before the conclusion of hostilities. It could only be north of Lebanon, where French claims were weak; an attempt to seize Christian Lebanon, he told Faisal, would almost certainly jeopardize Allied support for legitimate Arab claims, and the Bedouin troops were ill equipped and ill prepared for operations on the Mediterranean coastline within range of Allied naval guns. Lawrence also counseled Faisal on the limits of the strategies the Arabs could pursue. The Arabs would need Allied support in the form of guns, ammunition, and supplies, which made it essential to maintain close ties to Britain and to support British strategy by advancing on the right flank of a British move into Palestine. If the British had their way, he assured Faisal, the French would not be involved in an attack on Palestine, so Syria would not fall to French troops, and the Sykes-Picot clauses that assigned only French advisers to any Arab government in Syria could not be invoked. "There at least would be a modification, in which he would secure something," Lawrence wrote of his advice to Faisal, "while if the Arabs did as well as I intended there would be no one-sided talk of shooting, for they would be in place to return shot for shot, and as armed men in their own houses to get their won freedom recognized by their victorious allies. I begged him not, like his father, to trust our promises. . . . Faisal, a reasonable and clear-eyed statesman, accepted my point of view as the normal between nations, and his conviction of the hollowness of promises and gratitude did not sap his energy."[6]

Their once unspoken Faustian agreement had taken a new turn.

~

There was still Aqaba. Lawrence and Faisal agreed that the port was an important objective for the Arab armies, for roughly the same reasons that Brémond thought it a crucial objective for an Anglo-French force. Whoever held Aqaba controlled the last Turkish-held port on the coast, access to the Hejaz Railway (bringing supplies from Damascus and beyond), and the gateway to the great valleys that led north through Transjordan and Palestine into Syria. Faisal's plan for the capture of Aqaba was an incremental march up the coast, capturing interim bases before a final assault with Arab troops landed from Royal Navy ships. A similar tactic had worked at Wejh, and Newcombe, who had been coordinating Arab raids on the Hejaz Railway, supported Faisal's plan as another effort to tie up Turkish troops that would otherwise be assigned to the defense of Sinai and Palestine.

Lawrence disagreed. He had gotten as far as Aqaba during his Sinai expedition before the war and knew the terrain of Wadi Itm, the steep, high-walled valley that led northeast from Aqaba to the Maan plateau. He had also studied aerial reconnaissance photographs taken by British pilots that showed how easily the Turks could establish defensive positions in the wadi, or move forces there from their major railroad and supply hub at Maan. A relatively small amphibious landing might take the port of Aqaba, but the generals in Cairo estimated that it would take at least three well-equipped divisions to seize the wadi, and that the Turks could reinforce for a counterattack faster than the British could land the needed troops. So at best a landing in Aqaba would be a hollow victory, taking the port but leaving the inland logistics route to the Hejaz in Turkish hands. Control of that route was important to the British, because it would cut off the movement of Turkish troops and matériel from the Hejaz to Palestine, Transjordan, and Syria. Control of the routes into Arabia was even more important to the Arabs: "I wanted to hurry the Arabs northward, disregarding the Turkish garrisons in Arabia," Lawrence wrote. "I wanted them to join up with the British, to act as the right wing of the Allies in the conquest of Palestine and Syria, to assert the Arabic-speaking peoples' desire and desert of freedom and self-government."[7]

Other than his studies of medieval castles, Lawrence had no formal military education or tactical experience, but he knew that for desert battle the lessons of ancient and crusader tactics were valuable even in the twentieth century. He proposed the dramatic alternative of taking Aqaba not from the sea, but from the east—by a surprise attack through Wadi Itm. With the element of surprise the Arabs could seize the inland end of the wadi, cutting it off from Turkish reinforcements in Maan, and could then sweep down the valley to take Aqaba. The city, with its guns and garrison pointed at the sea, would be defenseless. Moving an entire Arab army to the inland end of the wadi, on forbidding and unfamiliar terrain, would be impossible, so Lawrence's plan depended on recruiting local forces. It also required total surprise so the Turks would not have time to garrison Wadi Itm. And since the Turks might counterattack with forces from Maan, the plan would require the prompt arrival of reinforcements by sea after the port was taken. Lawrence knew the plan would raise eyebrows at GHQ, not only because it was tricky and controversial but also because its young author did not enjoy a reputation as a tactician. His response was to not consult Cairo. He also knew that news moved quickly in the desert, and through unpredictable channels, and decided to hold his plans back from Faisal's extensive entourage of bodyguards, sheikhs, lieutenants, and camp followers. Brémond had not given up on his own idea of an Anglo-French invasion, and tried to press French advisers on Faisal, but the emir wasn't interested. Emir Faisal already had an adviser he trusted.

In a brief return to Cairo Lawrence learned that after General Murray's advance across Sinai in December 1916, which positioned his forces for an offensive against the Turks between Gaza and Beersheba, the responsibility for coordination with the Arab forces had been divided: Wingate remained in charge of operations in the Hejaz, but Murray would be in charge of coordination and supplies to the Arabs in the areas to the north. Lawrence considered this bad news: Wingate had been consistently supportive of efforts with the Arabs, but Murray's lack of interest would greatly complicate Lawrence's semisecret plans for the capture of Aqaba and for an Arab campaign in Palestine and Syria.

In the Hejaz, Garland, the explosives expert, working with a party of Arabs, succeeded in derailing a train during a night raid on the Hejaz line. The Arab Bureau had calculated how much rolling stock the Turks would need to supply their troops in the Hejaz, and concluded that every locomotive that could be put out of action would take a substantial toll on the Turkish ability to move men and matériel. Garland was not as enthusiastic about their operations. He found wearing Arab attire annoying and encumbering, and thought little of the Arabs as soldiers. Along with looting a defeated enemy, which the Arabs treated as a right, they plundered strangers, and nothing would persuade them from singing and shouting within earshot of the enemy or approaching enemy positions by riding up the middle of broad wadis in plain view from the tops of the small mountains along the rail lines.[8] Garland's tactics and the guerrilla war effort needed a different leader in the field.

In early March captured telegraphed instructions from Djemal Pasha revealed that his commander in Medina had been ordered to evacuate his besieged Turkish troops from there to Maan, the main depot and support base north of Aqaba. Lawrence knew the Turkish move would be pleasing to the Arabs, who had not been successful in their long siege of Medina and had continued because of the spiritual and symbolic importance of the holy city. But the arrival of 25,000 well-equipped Turkish troops on the Beersheba front, where Murray was poised to attack, was a serious concern for the British, and it fell to Lawrence to persuade Faisal that Allied interests in this case required the sacrifice or at least the postponement of the Arab plans to attack Aqaba.[9] Faisal rose to what Lawrence called "a proposition of honour," and on March 10, 1917, Lawrence set off to explain the changed circumstances to Emir Abdullah, to reconnoiter, and to possibly mine the railway or capture one of the stations on the line to disrupt the movement of Turkish forces and matériel north.[10] His plans were a bold ambition for a man who had no experience as an officer in the field, had never commanded men in battle, and was planning to rely on Garland's experimental and only partially tested explosive mines.

With a small escort, Lawrence crossed the desert to Abdullah's headquarters in Wadi Ais. On the journey Lawrence suffered from dysentery, fever, and horrendous boils that left him so sick he had to be helped into his saddle. In the midst of the journey Lawrence learned that a member of his escort had killed another man in the group, from a different tribe. It was too late to mediate the dispute, which threatened to escalate into a blood feud between tribes unless the guilty man was executed. Lawrence, belonging to no tribe, volunteered to carry out the sentence but was so inexperienced with a pistol that he needed three shots at close range to kill the unarmed man. It was the first time he had killed a man.

Day after day he had to ride on the painful boils. When he wasn't riding Lawrence lay sick in a tent, trying to put together a strategy for the desert fighting. "Battles in Arabia were a mistake since our contest was not physical but material," he wrote. "Our successes were [measured in] square miles of country occupied. . . . Our best line was to defend nothing and to shoot nothing. Our cards were speed and time, not hitting power. . . . As to strategy, range was more than force." The strategy suggested a tactic: by attacking the Hejaz Railway they could frighten the Turks off their plan to evacuate Medina, "a conclusion serviceable both to the Arabs and to the English."[11] It only remained to persuade the Arabs, especially Emir Abdullah, whose troops and camp were positioned to harass the Hejaz Railway.

"Abdulla," Lawrence observed, "would sometimes ride a little, and sometimes shoot a little, and would then return exhausted to his tent for massage, and afterward reciters from the camp would be introduced to sooth his aching head. . . . Abdulla made very little of the tactical situation, pretending pettishly that it was Faisal's business. He had come to Wadi Ais to please Faisal, his younger brother, and there he would stay. He would not go on raids himself, and hardly encouraged those of his men who did. I detected jealousy of Faisal's successes in this."[12] With Abdullah clearly unenthusiastic about leading raids against the railway, Lawrence relied on two of his lieutenants who were eager for more actions against the Turks. By the end of March Lawrence was leading raiding parties on their first attacks against the railway.

The trials were not entirely successful: they did not succeed in destroying a locomotive, and on one raid Lawrence buried the detonation trigger so deep in the ballast it did not go off when the train passed. The detonator had to be recovered later in a nerve-racking operation. But he set a pattern for using dynamite and swift-moving mounted raiders against the railway, and convinced Abdullah's lieutenants to stagger attacks on different sections of the railway. Turkish repair crews could quickly replace the rails and repair the roadbed, but Lawrence hoped the frequency and unpredictability of the attacks would deter the Turks. Troops tied down in Medina could not move to Maan to threaten a British attack on Palestine or an Arab thrust toward Aqaba.

At Emir Faisal's urging Lawrence returned to Wejh, where Faisal was cementing the allegiance of the sheikhs of tribes in the northern areas of the Hejaz. Many of the sheikhs had heard of Faisal's Englishman, but they were not drawn to Faisal's tent by the emir's friendship with Lawrence, by Lawrence's support of the Arab Revolt, by his opposition to bringing British troops inland into the Hejaz, or by his support of guerrilla warfare by camel-mounted Bedouin soldiers. Nor did they join the movement from feelings of nationalism or rebellion against the Turks. The sheikhs came to Faisal's camp at Wejh because the emir had been victorious in battle. He promised that his army would be moving north in a few months' time, presenting an opportunity for more victories and the spoils and booty that

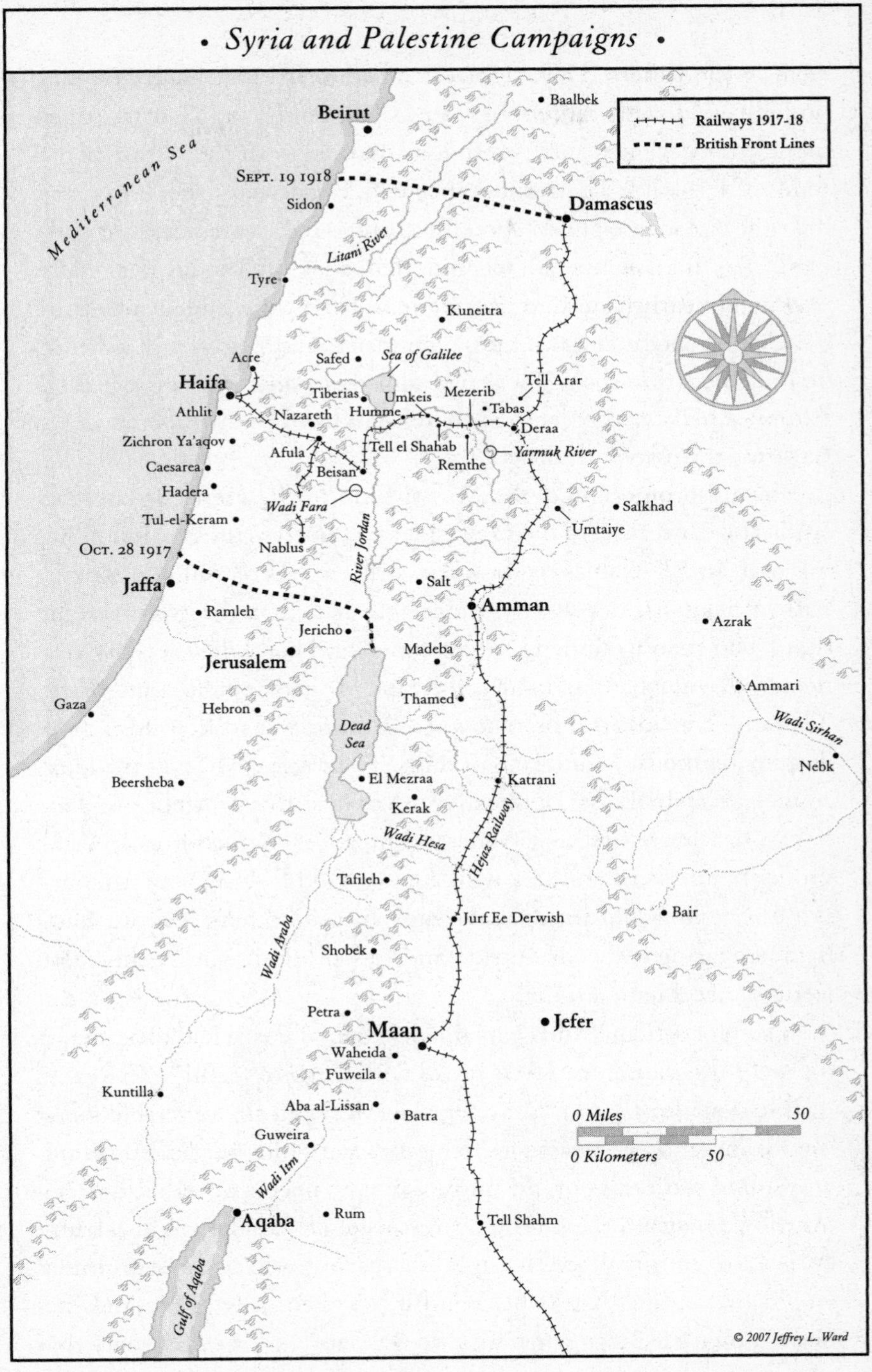

• Syria and Palestine Campaigns •

went to the victors. The sheikhs also had heard that Lawrence had brought gold with him from Cairo. The Arabs didn't trust paper money; they wanted gold sovereigns marked with the stamp of the Bank of England. The rumors they had heard were true. Lawrence brought the sovereigns in specially constructed canvas bags. Wyndham Deedes remembered spending Saturday afternoons personally packing the sovereigns into cartridge cases that were loaded onto camels. Colonel Brémond, thinking it an insult, once said that Lawrence "represented" £200,000. The actual sum was many times his estimate. Almost a half century later Bedouin sheikhs still remembered Lawrence as "the man with the gold."[13]

The most important of the Arab sheikhs for Lawrence's plans was Auda abu Tayi, chief of the Howeitat and famed as the greatest fighting man in all Arabia. Auda was a striking figure, tall and strong, with a haggard, deeply lined face. He had married twenty-eight times, had been wounded thirteen times, and had killed seventy-five men by his own hand in battle, all Arabs. He had kept no count of the Turks he had killed. His renowned generosity had kept him poor despite the spoils of hundreds of raids. To Lawrence he was the ideal counterpoint to Faisal, a warrior to balance the princely prophet. When Lawrence first met Auda and they were served bread, Auda suddenly jumped to his feet with a loud "God forbid!" and ran outside the tent. From inside Lawrence and the others heard a loud hammering. They went outside and saw Auda pounding his false teeth to pieces with a stone.

"I had forgotten," Auda explained. "Djemal Pasha had these made for me. I was eating my lord's bread with Turkish teeth!"

"He saw life as a saga," Lawrence wrote, "and all events in it were significant, and all personages in contact with him heroic. His mind was stored with tales of old raids, and epic poems of fights, and he overflowed with them on the nearest listener." Auda was also stubborn. Lawrence realized that if Auda disapproved nothing on earth would make him change his mind or obey an order: "He took no heed of men's feelings when his face was set."[14]

Lawrence had spent enough time in the intelligence service to anticipate the British opposition to his plan for Aqaba: "The occupation of Akaba by Arab troops might well result in the Arabs claiming that place thereafter, and it is by no means improbable that after the war Akaba may be of some considerable importance to the future defense scheme of Egypt. It is thus essential that Akaba should remain in British hands after the war."[15] As a precaution, Lawrence gave only the sketchiest hints of his plans to his colleagues in the field, and mentioned nothing at all in his reports to Cairo, thus avoiding the possibility of receiving a direct order to abandon the plan. Timely intelligence from a British naval raid on Aqaba in late April confirmed that the port was held by only 330 men, many of them Arabs, and that the guard posts on the track toward Maan were lightly manned.[16] Quietly, Lawrence refined his plans, now focused on a march with Auda abu Tayi to the Howeitat spring pastures behind Aqaba. The desert track, across hundreds of miles of harsh terrain, was too rugged for heavy weapons or stores. They would travel with only a small party, raise a camel force of Bedouin irregulars from local tribes in the area, and rush Aqaba in a surprise attack "without guns or machine-guns." Faisal made up a purse for the expedition of 22,000 gold sovereigns—supplied by Lawrence—"all that he could afford, and more than we asked for, to pay the wages of our party, and of the new men we enrolled, and to make such advances as should stimulate the Howeitat to swiftness." On May 9, Lawrence, Auda abu Tayi, and a party of forty-five Arabs set off toward the northeast, each man carrying a share of the sovereigns and a half bag of flour.

"I decided to go my own way, with or without orders," Lawrence wrote. "I wrote a letter full of apologies to General Clayton, telling him that it was with the best intentions: and went."[17] For the second time in only a few months Lawrence was defying official British policy to pursue the Arab cause.

~

The desert trek was harsh and demanding. After four days Lawrence suffered a relapse of the debilitating boils and fever, but they pushed on, dynamited a section of track when they crossed the Hejaz Railway near Deraa, and after eleven days started across El Houl, a bleak, desolate plain without a sign of life, not even a blade of grass. Lawrence felt tiny, dwarfed by the vast emptiness, the progress of his small party all but imperceptible on the vast, barren plain. "The only sounds," he wrote,

> were the hollow echoes, like the shutting down of pavements over vaulted places, of rotten stone slab on stone slab when they tilted under our camels' feet, and the slow but piercing rustle of the sand, as it crept slowly westward, before the hot wind of the open desert. . . .
>
> It was a breathless wind, with the furnace taste sometimes known in Egypt when a khamsin blew, and as the day went on and the sun rose in the sky it became stronger, and more filled with the dust of the Nefudh, the great sand-desert of Northern Arabia, close by us over there, but invisible behind the haze. By noon it was a half-gale, and so dry that our shriveled lips cracked open, and the skin of our faces chapped, while our eyelids, gone granular, seemed to creep back and lay bare our shrinking eyes. The Arabs drew their head-cloths tightly across their noses, and pulled the brow-folds forward, so that they became visors for them, with only a narrow loose-flapping slit of vision.[18]

A few days later, as they crossed the hard-surfaced Biseita, closer to the coast, Lawrence saw that one of his men, Gasim, "a fanged and yellow-faced outlaw" from Maan, was missing. Gasim's camel, loaded with his gear, was following along, riderless. Lawrence realized that Gasim must have dozed off in his saddle and fallen from the camel. The others, exhausted from the heat, wind, and relentless pace, hadn't noticed him. There were no footprints to follow on the hard shingle, and they all knew a man on foot would not last long. Unless someone rescued him, he would die. Gasim was Lawrence's man, and "by desert law there could be no desertion between us [so] it was clearly marked that on me lay the responsibility for him."

Lawrence looked at his other men, wondering if any of them would go back for Gasim. As a foreigner he knew he could shirk the duty, "but that was precisely the plea I did not dare set up while I presumed to lead these Arabs in their own revolt. It was hard anyway for a stranger to influence another people's national movement, and doubly hard for a Christian and a sedentary person to lead Moslem nomads. I would make it impossible for myself if I claimed the privileges of both societies." Lawrence turned his camel around—she protested loudly—and relying on a reciprocal compass course, rode back for an hour and a half until he found Gasim, nearly blinded, his mouth gaping open, half mad from thirst. Lawrence had to hit Gasim with a stick and shout at him to keep him still on the camel for the ride back. Auda intercepted Lawrence as he rode back, and said he would never have let him go. He gestured at Gasim and said, "For that thing, not worth a camel's price."

"Not worth a florin, Auda," Lawrence said.[19] Even with an illiterate sheikh, Lawrence enjoyed verbal one-upsmanship.

Just by surviving the difficult journey Lawrence proved, at least in gesture, that he was a worthy ally. When they reached Wadi Sirhan, a long shallow valley with vegetation and wells, they camped and went to a series of feasts with local tribal chiefs and their followers. Over huge platters piled high with mutton and rice, dripping with fat and butter, they recruited troops for their mission. "These people were achieving for our sake the height of nomadic ambition a continued orgy of seethed mutton," Lawrence wrote, "and it was our duty to live up to it. . . . I had been for twenty-eight years well-fed, and if Arab imagination ran on food-bowls, so much the better for them. They had been provident expressly on our account."[20] The indigestion and satiety of sodden meat and greasy rice troubled Lawrence less than the difficult question the local sheikhs asked him. They wanted to know whether they were truly fighting for their own independence, not only from the Turks, but also from the British and French.

"The abyss opened before me suddenly one night upon this ride," Lawrence wrote, "when in his tent old Nuri Shaalan [emir of the Rualla] bringing out his documents asked me bluntly which of the British promises were to be believed. I saw that with my answer I would gain or lose him: and in him the outcome of the Arab Movement." Lawrence told him that he should trust the most recent of the contradictory pledges. "I passed definitely into the class of principal," Lawrence wrote. "Indeed, a year later I was almost the chief crook of our gang."[21]

Two days before the expedition departed Lawrence had encountered Mark Sykes at Faisal's camp. Sykes had come to secure the emir's agreement to the appointment of a French political officer to Murray's command in Palestine.[22] Lawrence did not trust Sykes; none of the Arab Bureau officers did. They were sympathetic to the Arabs and knew that the secret agreement that bore Sykes's name overrode the central aims of the Arab movement and the promises Britain had made in support of those aims. Lawrence may have enjoyed the fact that he had already told his friend Emir Faisal about the Sykes-Picot agreement, which probably gave Faisal the upper hand in his talks with Sykes. He also knew he could not reveal the terms or potential consequences of the agreement to Auda and the other Arab leaders who were being asked to fight in Aqaba. If he told them about Sykes-Picot and the Anglo-French map of the Middle East that had already been drawn up, the Arabs of the northern Hejaz, and even Auda, would not have joined the attack. But by not telling them Lawrence was trapping himself in a web of half-truths that bordered on outright lies.

It weighed on his sense of personal honor. He had always emphasized, perhaps exaggerated, his image and sense of personal independence. It may have been a consequence of his childhood awareness of his illegitimacy, or of his mother's harsh moral regime at home. At Oxford and in the army he held himself apart by flamboyant stunts, outrageous manners, and the defiance of norms of behavior, decorum, and uniform. That deliberate independence left him scant social or institutional membership to fall back upon: he would not allow himself to be judged as a British soldier, or justify his behavior or decisions with the excuse that he was following orders. The burden of his half-truths and lies to Auda and the other sheikhs, and the contrast with the codes of honor and chivalry that had permeated his imagination as far back as childhood, fell on his own slim shoulders. "I was in a reckless mood," he wrote, "not caring very much what I did, for in the journey up from Wejh I had convinced myself that I was the only person engaged in the field of the Arab adventure who could dispose it to be at once a handmaid to the British Army of Egypt, and also at the same time the author of its own success."[23]

~

When the recruiting operation was complete a main force of camel-mounted Bedouin gathered some thirty miles east of Maan. In preparation for the attack a small group of tribesmen took Fuweila, the Turkish post at the head of the pass leading down to the Wadi Itm and Aqaba. Small units were then sent out in diversionary actions to distract and confuse the Turks. The Turkish command in Maan got word that the Aqaba road had been taken, and sent out a fresh battalion of reinforcements to retake the post at the head of Wadi Itm and the Aba al-Lissan springs nearby. Lawrence and Auda knew they had to take action. They brought a force to Aba al-Lissan, surrounded the Turkish camp, harassed the Turks with sniper fire for most of a day, and attacked at dusk, killing 300 Turks and taking 160 prisoners. Lawrence tried to join the decisive charge, but ended up shooting his own camel in the head and was thrown to the ground.

From there the Arab force rode down into the Wadi Itm and on to Aqaba. As their intelligence had predicted, the guard posts on the road were lightly held, and the swift-moving Bedouin camel cavalry faced virtually no resistance. On July 6, two months after they had left Wejh, they captured Aqaba without firing a shot, taking 650 prisoners. There was no food to feed the prisoners, or supplies for the assembled Arab army, and Lawrence left immediately with a small party along an old pilgrimage road that led to Suez. They traveled fast, hardly stopping, and reached Suez, 160 miles away, in forty-nine hours. It was a remarkable feat, and one Lawrence would later brag about, exaggerating the speed of his journey by a day.[24]

From Suez Lawrence traveled by rail to Cairo. He bathed in a hotel in Sinai, and on the train wore his white silk robes, gold headrope, and dagger. The officers in Cairo who first saw Lawrence in his robes were shocked, though perhaps not as much as Lawrence when he learned that while he and Faisal's army were taking Aqaba, General Murray had been replaced as commander in chief.

13

Allenby

You will no doubt remember the great campaign of Lord Allenby in Palestine and perhaps you are surprised at the daring of his actions. Someone who is looking from the sidelines, lacking knowledge about the situation, is likely to think that Allenby took unwarranted risks. That is not true. For Allenby knew with certainty from his intelligence (in Palestine) of all the preparations and all the movements of his enemy. All the cards of his enemy were revealed to him, and so he could play his hand with complete confidence. Under these conditions, victory was certain before he began.

—Major General George MacDonough, director of military intelligence[1]

Aaronsohn kept Feinberg's death a secret. A British mission into the Sinai confirmed Josef Lishinsky's story of the Bedouin attack but found no trace of Feinberg's body or grave. Aaronsohn was not observant, but under Jewish religious law only a body can confirm a death, and he could not shake a sense that maybe Feinberg had not died. He also felt a suspicion and resentment that Lishinsky had survived while Feinberg had not, and that Feinberg, with his fiery rhetoric and intrepid passion, was irreplaceable in their effort. He mourned the loss for months, fearing that the news would disillusion and demoralize his colleagues at Athlit. While Lishinsky was recuperating in Cairo and Port Said from his own wounds, he and Aaronsohn made up a story that Feinberg had reached the British and had gone to England to train as a combat pilot. After his many daring encounters with the Turkish authorities, one more tale of Feinberg's invincibility was credible, and for those who knew him or the legends that followed him, it was easy to imagine the handsome, dashing, and intrepid Avshalom Feinberg in the white silk scarf of an aviator.

The fiction did not assuage Aaronsohn's sense of loss or his frustrations with the British intelligence bureaucracy. Because he didn't fit any of the pigeonholes of the British intelligence services, he was left to deal separately with naval intelligence in Port Said, with Deedes and Ormsby-Gore at the political and national intelligence services, and occasionally with the Arab Bureau. He was a priority for none of them, and the constant runaround compounded his anger and frustrations.

In the spring of 1917 the British created yet another intelligence branch in Egypt, the Eastern Mediterranean Special Intelligence Branch (EMSIB), with responsibility for liaison with secret sources on the Palestine and Syrian coasts. Captain Edmonds, Aaronsohn's contact at EMSIB, could on occasion seem sympathetic, but more often was bureaucratically opaque, and when asked for more attention to the people in Athlit, he answered with excuses. "You must now realize," Edmonds told him, "that we are [as] anxious to contribute to your work as you are yourself, but we are not in Turkey, and no one can have his own way with the English. Nevertheless we are progressing—and we must get used to it. Besides we did not know you at all—and your offer is 'so unusual.' "[2]

They needed to recruit a reliable and capable swimmer to go ashore from the launches at Athlit, and Aaronsohn asked Raphael Abulafia, a friend of Feinberg's, to recommend someone. Abulafia lived in Alexandria and had served as a sergeant in the Zion Mule Corps; he found Leibel Bornstein, who had been in his regiment at Gallipoli. Tall and rangy, Bornstein was from Petah Tikva, north of Jaffa, and knew the coast near Athlit from the many years when he had driven a diligence (a rubber-tired carriage) between Acre and Jaffa on a route close to Athlit and Zichron Ya'aqov. He had sometimes driven Aaronsohn, was honored to be associated with the famed agronomist's project, and was a strong swimmer who thought he could swim the quarter mile from the launch to shore and back, even in strong currents, high winds, cold water, and the blackness of moonless nights. He was also a man they could trust to say nothing about the secret operation.

As with almost every question that came up, Aaronsohn found himself in a battle with EMSIB over Bornstein's compensation. Bornstein was a laborer, and to remain available on short notice for the missions he needed to be paid enough to support his wife and children in Egypt. Edmonds had decided that their branch of the intelligence service needed to economize, and refused to pay the £10 monthly allowance Bornstein said he needed.

"The Arab Revolt is being kept alive by a stream of gold," Aaronsohn told Edmonds. "But we will give maximum value without affecting your cash reserves. We know very well how to appreciate national independence. We don't have to be paid to accept it."[3] He offered to pay the £10 himself until Edmonds finally relented.

Aaron gave Deedes a telegram to send to Alex Aaronsohn in New York, telling him to notify the trustees of the research station officially that Aaron was in Cairo "engaged in hopeful work." Aaron did not tell the trustees about Feinberg's death; few trustees had met him, though some had read Feinberg's detailed and eloquent report on Palestine under the wartime Turkish administration. Aaronsohn anticipated a harsh reaction to his telegram—the trustees had donated funds and their names in support of an agricultural research station, not a spying operation, and many of them were openly anti-Zionist. His hope was that before long the United States would sever diplomatic relations with Germany and enter the war, and that the trustees would then understand how important it was for him and the research station staff to work for a British victory over Turkey instead of trying to develop new plant cultivars and agricultural techniques in the midst of the wartime deprivations.

Mostly, Aaronsohn waited. To work off his frustrations, he explored Cairo and the environs, walking or on a bike. He rode enough to get his weight down to 213 pounds and to reduce his waistline from forty-four inches to forty-one inches. Some days he would ride from the Savoy Hotel out to Mena House, the British headquarters close to the pyramids, a thirty-three-mile ride.[4] He took pride in his fitness. He heard talk of plans for cavalry raids near Beersheba, and recommended to Philip Graves that the British wait until March or April, when the barley would be near maturity. Impressed by Aaronsohn's local knowledge, Graves asked if he was interested in being part of the attack.

"I should deem it a great favor," he answered. "If necessary, I could sit saddle as well as any Australian."[5]

The British did not take him up on his offer.

In mid-February 1917, on another moonless night, the *Managem,* a small steamer with an Arab crew under Captain Weldon, sailed up the coast past Athlit. The ship signaled in daylight, got a signal back—this time the captain had taken good binoculars along—and returned in calm seas at ten o'clock that evening to land Josef Lishinsky on the beach next to the ruins of the Athlit castle. Sarah was not there that night, but Liova Schneersohn and Reuven Schwartz were waiting on the beach with the latest intelligence reports when the launch came back for them after midnight. Aaronsohn was allowed to go along in the launch for the pickup. Reuven Schwartz threw his arms around Aaronsohn and kissed him. "We left at once—happy!" he wrote.[6]

Schneersohn returned with them to Egypt, swapping places with Lishinsky. A Russian, diligent, almost scholarly in his mien, he was a quiet counterpoise to Lishinsky's rough-and-tumble eagerness for battle. On the *Managem,* steaming back to Port Said, Aaronsohn told him that they needed a password for future operations. Schneersohn, who knew his Bible well, opened it to 1 Samuel and suggested a passage: "The glory of Israel does not deceive."[7] The first letters of the words in Hebrew (*Nezah Israel Lo Ieshaker*) spelled NILI, a succinct and easily remembered password. As the response password, they used the name of Lishinsky's son, Tuvin, which was also the name he had used in his false passport. NILI soon became a shorthand name for the organization. The British refused to use the codename, referring to it as the A Operation (for Aaronsohn).

The name also remained a secret in Palestine, but the contacts with the *Managem* on that and later journeys were soon known in coastal Galilee. Before long Jewish settlers were spreading quiet rumors, asking whether the stories about the disappearance of Aaron Aaronsohn and Avshalom Feinberg were true, asking what was *really* going on at the research station, and whether the secret activities were putting the Jewish community at peril. To many Aaronsohn and his group had long been outsiders—in their attitudes toward Arab labor, their participation in the Gideonite movement, and especially in what some saw as the arrogance of the first-aliyah settlers and their American-funded research station. Fears and wartime paranoia compounded the gossip and occasional observations of nighttime activity into rumors of a secret organization that was endangering the entire Jewish community.

After the first successful run the *Managem* began sailing up the coast regularly—at least on moonless nights. The ship would stay offshore in the daytime. If they saw a white sheet hung out of the upstairs window at the research station the ship would return that night, and a launch would bring Leibel Bornstein close enough to shore for him to swim to the beach at Athlit. Sometimes he would be met at the beach, sometimes he would follow the trail to the research station to pick up the latest intelligence reports and return to the beach. When the information got back to Egypt, Aaronsohn would translate the documents and distribute them, mostly to his handlers at EMSIB, but sometimes to military intelligence, naval intelligence, or even the Arab Bureau. With information flowing from Athlit he began bargaining with the British, asking for political information and communication links in return for the information his group was supplying. He asked about events in Turkey and Germany, and for help communicating with Jewish centers in the United States, Britain, and Russia. When he heard that Graves was leaving for a "very important mission of reconnoitering near the Howeitat and other Bedouins whom they would like to win over for the Akaba-Tebbouk region,"[8] he wanted to know more about the plans there. The British penchant for compartmentalization made sure he knew next to nothing about Lawrence's operations.

Aaronsohn also found himself called on for information. A Lieutenant Seymour Jones wanted to know what mechanical and animal resources were available in southern Palestine that the British army could use; Aaronsohn told him they would need spare parts for "Tangyes, Hornsby engines and McCormick and Deering reaping machines," typical water-pumping and harvesting equipment that had been seized from the Jewish settlements by the Turks. Though not asked, he also told the lieutenant that the British would need "intelligent propaganda—superior to the bribing of a few rascally Arab chiefs." He corrected Hogarth's research on the Jordan valley, identified transportation lines that were potentially vulnerable to aerial bombardment, and argued the importance of bombing the Jordan Bridge. When Lieutenant Jones brought out an aerial photograph of Gaza, Aaronsohn identified individual plantations and offered the unsolicited tactical advice that an attack through Gaza would require crossing difficult wadis that would give a tactical advantage to Turkish snipers. He recommended that instead of another attack through Gaza the British turn the flank of the Turks in Gaza, send Bedouin raiders to worry the Turkish outposts, and focus the main attack from the south at Beersheba. He told them to take drilling machines and pipe with them so they could move quickly over the Plain of Sharon, because supplying water to Jerusalem would be important both for the health of the soldiers and as a "moral benefit" to the population. He described the black-and-white target boards he had seen on public institutions in Beirut, and gave General Clayton, the head of British intelligence in Cairo, strategies for an attack on Jerusalem based on his analysis of the wars of Vespasian, Titus, Bonaparte, and Ibrahim Pasha, four military leaders who had succeeded in conquering Jerusalem. "You have sound logics and thorough local knowledge," Clayton said of Aaronsohn's information. "You interested me immensely."[9]

After so long as an outsider, Aaronsohn reveled in the occasional audiences and compliments. Captain Edmond and Norman Bentwich joked that "Aaron runs the GHQ."[10] They no doubt meant it sarcastically: the idea that a Jew from Palestine would run *anything* at British headquarters was preposterous to the British officer corps in 1917. But even as the officers snickered, the flow of information from Athlit and Aaronsohn's encyclopedic knowledge of Palestine proved useful enough that he was granted an interview with General Murray, then the commander in chief of the expeditionary force in Egypt.

Murray had seen Aaronsohn's requests for information and communications channels to Zionist organizations, including to Vladimir Jabotinsky in London, who was trying to organize a Jewish brigade. "I want to tell you personally and privately how deeply I am moved by incidents in Palestine," Murray said to Aaronsohn. "I shudder when I think of the Jews meeting with the same fate as the Armenians, and I greatly regret that we are powerless." On the subject of a Jewish brigade, he was adamant: "A Jewish division would do no good. We need well-trained troops. You know better than I do that I have against me the Turkish defenses and infantry, German machine guns and Austrian artillery, and faithless Russians in their back. Moreover I must—with my single railway line—feed every mouth, and every man and horse that are with me shall be put to the test. Jewish divisions could only be used on the Palestinian front within a year at the earliest, and I want you to live under no misrepresentation, as we want to be straight and fair. America has understood the situation and will send only trained troops to France."

Never one to conceal his own knowledge, Aaronsohn pointed out that in France Joffre was actually in a "hurry to have American soldiers and cannot wait for them to be perfectly trained." Murray answered that the feeding problem in France was not like Palestine.[11]

Murray had yielded nothing to Aaronsohn, and was not interested in his information or his tactical advice. His refusal to accept a Jewish legion on the Palestine front meant that NILI was the only Jewish organization actively fighting for the future of the Jewish community in Palestine.

~

In April, when the trips of the *Managem* up the coast became regular enough that each arrival didn't have to be met with special preparations in Athlit and Zichron Ya'aqov, Sarah agreed to come to Egypt on one of the return voyages. Aaron boarded the *Managem* when the ship docked at Port Said, found Sarah "extremely anemic," and was surprised that Josef Lishinsky had come with her, an arrangement that had not been discussed with him, and which left NILI temporarily without leadership in Palestine.

Aaron and Sarah went directly to Cairo, where she checked into the Continental Hotel and he took her for tea to Groppi's. Others who had heard of Sarah, local Jews and the few active Zionists in the city, came by the tearoom to see them. "People always like to see a heroine," he wrote.[12] They went to the theater, called on people, and took walks in the city. Sarah was suffering from a fever, but she was still a handsome and sensuous woman, and wore stylish gowns she had copied from Paris fashion. Both Lishinsky and Schneersohn had long ago fallen hard for her, and tagged along, competing for her attention and affections like schoolboys with crushes. The threesome posed together for a Cairo photographer.

Sarah told Aaron about events in Jaffa, where two Yemenites had been hanged from trees, the Jewish population had been forcibly expelled from the city, and "under the fatherly eyes of the Turkish Police" everything Jewish in the city had been plundered. It would be weeks before the Jews of Jaffa would succeed in getting a wire via Wingate to the British Foreign Office: "During Passover the entire Jewish population of Jaffa expelled towards North," their wire reported. "Homes, property sacked, population in flight, robbed in connivance with Turkish authorities. Jews, resisting, pillaged, hanged. Thousands wandering helplessly on roads, starving. Overcrowding of

Colony increasing misery, disease. Masses of young Jerusalem Jews deported, northward, destination unknown."[13]

Cairo was flooded with news in April 1917. Schneersohn, as a Russian, was the local expert on the Russian revolution and on the question of whether the new Menshevik regime would continue the war. The British were afraid that the Mensheviks would make a separate peace with Germany and Austria, leaving Britain and France to bear the full brunt of the German military machine in Europe. Aaronsohn's own analysis was that the United States would be more likely to enter the war after the fall of the tsar, since they would not have a Russian autocracy as an ally. He considered himself an expert on American policy, and when the news arrived that President Wilson had asked Congress to ratify a declaration of war against Germany, Aaronsohn told Deedes that "if I were authorized to benefit off the enthusiastic movement which now exists there [in the United States], I could call volunteers together and gather friends. Perhaps I should enlist and obtain a commission among Teddy's 'Rough Riders'—or else solicit a military rank here."[14] Deedes agreed that he might be valuable in soliciting support for the war in America, but said that they would have to wait to hear what London had to say about the proposal.

Mark Sykes also showed up in Cairo in April. "Since you left London your Zionistic affairs have made tremendous progress," Sykes told Aaronsohn in a warm greeting in Deedes's office. Aaronsohn's efforts to have a private meeting with Sykes at Shepheards Hotel were postponed repeatedly. "There is no doubt but that Sir Mark must be very busy," he wrote in his diary, "but I suspect that these postponements are due to other causes. He must be preparing something which is not yet ripe."[15] He wondered if Sykes was lined up to become the future governor of Palestine.

When they finally met privately, Aaronsohn gave Sykes his views on Djemal Pasha and the Gaza campaign, where a second attack by General Murray's forces was failing. When Aaronsohn asked about the rumors that France was to have "Syria from El Arish [in Sinai] to Adana [in Turkey]," Sykes said that he had been working "in harmony" with Georges-Picot, and that he had warned "the Arab Chiefs that if they should stir up Jewish antagonism, neither France, nor England nor Germany put together would be able to overcome it—and that this might tend to make a failure of Arab independence. But if they—the Arabs—have for them England and the Jews, they can defy France. It is therefore up to the Arab Chiefs to make a choice. They have done so—and they believe it is better for them not to have the Jews against them."[16] That news, and Sykes's assurances that the question of a Jewish brigade would be decided "very soon," were exactly what Aaronsohn wanted to hear. He did not realize that Sykes spoke mostly for himself, and was trusted by neither the Arabs nor by British intelligence, at least not in the Arab Bureau.

In late April the news arrived that Djemal Pasha had finished the sack of Tel Aviv. Nine thousand Jews had been expelled. With every horse requisitioned by the Ottoman army, the refugees fled on foot, without shelter or food. They were allowed to appoint a dozen watchmen to guard the property they were forced to leave behind. Aaronsohn, using a British cipher, informed the Zionist bureau in London and other Jewish agencies of the disaster, reporting from sources available in Egypt, "considered to be reliable," that ten thousand were now homeless: "Djemal Pasha had decided that Armenian policy would be applied to the Jews."[17]

The mixed success of his mission kept Aaronsohn at a crossroads. He had not succeeded in persuading the British to land in force on the coast, which he believed would have ended the war quickly, relieved the starvation and privation in the Jewish communities, and left the Jews in a strong position. The *Managem* was finally making regular trips up the coast to pick up the latest intelligence from Athlit, but none of the spying activity had resulted in any changes in British plans or benefits to the Jews of Palestine. And the continued NILI activity had put their own members and neighbors in Athlit and Zichron in increased peril. Aaronsohn knew that many in Palestine did not agree with NILI's goals. They either did not believe the stories about the massacres of the Armenians, did not consider attacks on the Armenians a precursor of what might happen to the Jews, or simply could not imagine more widespread attacks on the Jews and the destruction of their villages and towns. Whatever their reasons, they were not willing to risk the predictable life they had known under the Turks for an unknown future under Britain or France. Perhaps they had seen enough of British anti-Semitism in the restrictions put on the formation of a Jewish brigade, or had followed the Dreyfus case closely enough to fear a future under the French.

Aaronsohn knew that if he and NILI were to have a voice and influence in the future of Palestine and Zionism, they needed to have their role and contribution widely known. "I had become the spokesman of our people with Djemal Pasha," he wrote, "—and therefore their hope. When I left the country I destroyed my influence. It was natural that now—considering the danger on one side and the few tangible results on the other—they should oppose that our organization continue its work. It was therefore necessary to restore prestige, and for that purpose I should send a circular to the chiefs in Palestine, so that they would know how matters stand, and at the same time send them substantial sums."[18]

Aaronsohn asked the British, via Deedes, for £2,000 as an initial relief fund to be brought to the Jewish communities of Palestine on the *Managem,* and 4,000 francs for the next shipment. He formed a committee with Jewish businessmen from Palestine, including Gluskin, a founder and exporter from the Carmel Mizrahi vineyards in Rishon le Zion and Zichron who was in touch with Weizmann in London, to raise funds for distribution in Palestine. The *Managem*'s departure on a mission to Athlit had to be held up because Gluskin announced that he could not release funds without additional paperwork. Aaronsohn accused Gluskin of only being interested in people knowing about his contributions. The dispute escalated until Aaronsohn found himself in long-distance negotiations with London, demanding that Weizmann and Zionist International secretary Nahum Sokolov (in his diary, Aaronsohn called him "that idiot Sokolov")[19] take a public stand. Gluskin ultimately apologized for his behavior, and the funds were transferred to Athlit, but to the official Zionist organization in London it was Aaronsohn who was seen as the intransigent and disruptive outsider. At one point in the negotiations it was pointed out to Aaronsohn that he often wrote "I want" or "I do not want" instead of "we want."[20]

Aaron tried to persuade Sarah to stay in Cairo, telling her that a return to Palestine would put her in danger. She answered that "her duty called her to where danger existed," and that he should not try to prevent her from going back. The night before Sarah and Lishinsky were due to sail back to Athlit, they had a long and painful argument with Aaron, pointing out that she was still needed at Athlit and Zichron. Aaron finally yielded, writing in his diary that he accepted her "sacrifice. . . . How bravely and calmly she offered herself." The next morning at the pier at Port Said Aaron found Lishinsky "wild and obstinate." Lishinsky knew Aaron was suspicious about his report of how Feinberg had been shot during their journey across Sinai, and probably believed that Aaron wished that it had been Feinberg who had survived. He also knew that he was considered a firebrand, without Feinberg's eloquence and élan, and that Aaron disapproved both of his own goal of raising and training a fighting unit, and of his relationship with Sarah. He and Aaron argued until it was time for Lishinsky and Sarah to board the *Managem*.[21]

~

Alone again, in May 1917 Aaronsohn heard the "sensational news" that Weizmann had announced in a meeting of the Zionist Federation in London that "Palestine would be Jewish."[22] The news was premature but so exciting that Aaronsohn put aside his reservations about Weizmann and the official Zionists in London to celebrate the news in his diary.

Two days later Major Richard Meinertzhagen arrived in Cairo from London. A former staff officer for General Jan Smuts and head of intelligence for the British campaign in East Africa, Meinertzha-

Aaron Aaronsohn.
This image was later used on a 1979 Israeli postage stamp.

T. E. Lawrence, looking uneasy in his Arab robes.

Sarah Aaronsohn, taken in Hamburg before the war.

A brooding Avshalom Feinberg, taken in Paris before the war.

Aaron Aaronsohn as a young farm supervisor, 1897.

Avshalom Feinberg as a young man, dressed in Arab clothes, 1903.

The Gideonites at Zichron Ya'aqov.

Aaron Aaronsohn before the war.

Janet Laurie, 1914.

Lawrence and Leonard Woolley at Carchemish, 1913.

Avshalom Feinberg and Rivka Aaronsohn, before the war.

16 Pittsburg à Chicago
1.7.09
En dépassant Crestline on trouve champs immenses parsemés de vieux troncs non déracinés entre lesquels on cultive maïs.
Le maïs semé à la machine est disposé si régulièrement (dans terrains défrichés) qu'on peut [illegible] bien croisés à la houe à plusieurs rangs.

Fairchild m'a demandé si je pensais m'arrêter à Washington à mon retour. Je lui dis qu'ayant jugé nécessaire de consulter les spécialistes avant de

17 me mettre en route je considérais indispensable de faire contrôler par les spécialistes les opinions que je me suis faites.
F. estime que c'est la seule façon de voyager profitablement. Tchermack est resté 2 jours à Washington et a filé vers l'intérieur avant d'avoir rien vu. F. croit que Tchermak ne sait pas voyager profita[illegible] Erreur: Il y a 2 manières de voyager.
a) Voyager pour apprendre
b) Voyager pour enseigner.

Pages from Aaronsohn's diary; he was traveling from Pittsburgh to Chicago on July 1, 1909, and planning to return to Washington for discussions with Fairchild at the USDA.

Sarah Aaronsohn at her wedding in March 1914. Her sister Rivka and her brothers Aaron and Alex are on the right, next to the groom, Chaim Abraham. Her father is next to Sarah.

Sherif Hussein,
close to the time of Lawrence's
first visit to Arabia.

Lawrence and Auda abu Tayi.

The sign at the JAES research station in Athlit, at the beginning of the rows of palm trees leading into the farm.

Aaronsohn's research station at Athlit (JAES).

The Savoy Hotel, site of the British GHQ in Cairo, where both Lawrence and Aaronsohn had offices.

Djemal Pasha, here with only a few of his decorations.

T. E. Lawrence posed as the iconic "Lawrence of Arabia."
Taken by Lowell Thomas's photographer, Harry Chase.

Captain Newcombe, Lawrence's commander in the Sinai and his colleague at British intelligence, who refused Alex Aaronsohn's offer of information.

Alex Aaronsohn, in British uniform after the war.

Sarah on her horse Tayar. Even intrepid young Palestinian women rode sidesaddle.

The *Managem,* the steamer that made most of the secret runs to Athlit.

Sarah Aaronsohn, Liova Schneersohn, and Josef Lishinsky in Cairo, 1917.

Lawrence in front of the personal bodyguard he assembled after the incident at Deraa.

General Allenby entering Jerusalem on foot, December 1917.

An exhausted Lawrence entering Damascus in a Rolls-Royce tender, October 1918.

Lawrence on the balcony of the Victoria Hotel in Damascus, just before he left the city and the Arab Revolt.

General Allenby at the peak of his authority, 1918.

Mark Sykes, cartooned in *Vanity Fair*.

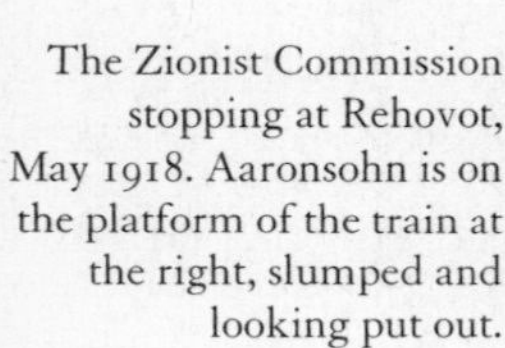

The Zionist Commission stopping at Rehovot, May 1918. Aaronsohn is on the platform of the train at the right, slumped and looking put out.

Faisal and his entourage in Paris. Lawrence is over his left shoulder; Faisal's slave is in the top row.

Ephraim Aaronsohn in front of his house in Zichron, now part of the Aaronsohn Museum, 1928.

Sarah Aaronsohn's grave at Zichron Ya'aqov. The marker with the single name is hers.

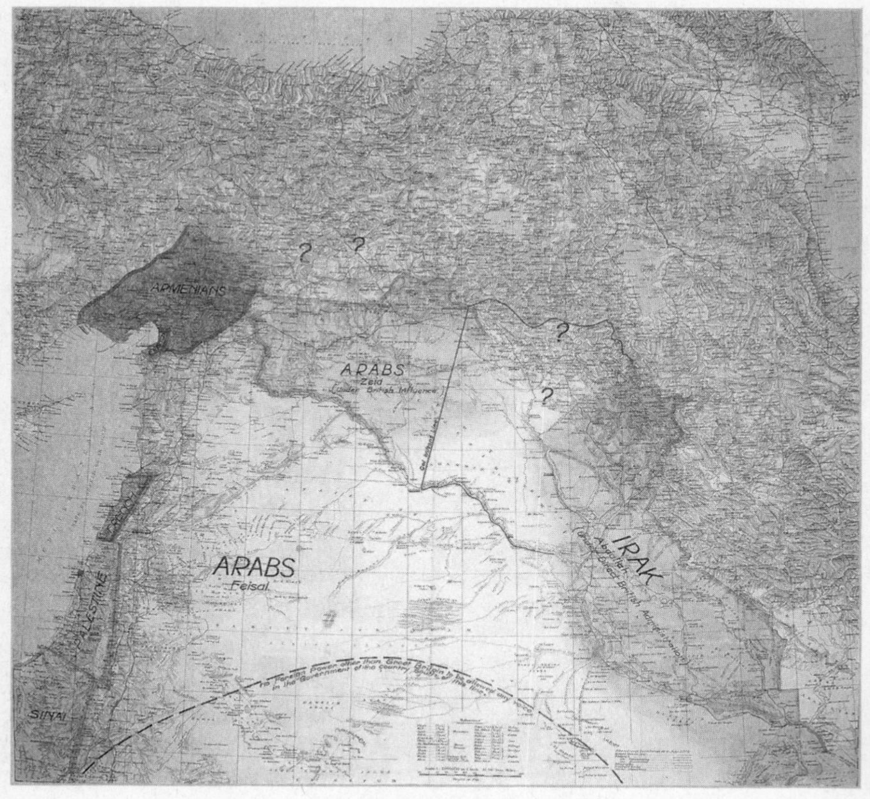

Lawrence's Plans for the Middle East, November 1918

The map Lawrence presented to the War Cabinet in November 1918 included a huge Arab state (the large light area in the center) to be ruled by Faisal; a new Iraq to be ruled by Faisal's brother Abdullah under direct British administration; a northern Arab kingdom to be ruled by Faisal's brother Zeid under British influence; areas set aside for the Kurds (noted with question marks); and an Armenian state around the Gulf of Alexandretta (Iskenderun) and its hinterlands. The coastal area of Lebanon and a tiny section of the Gulf of Alexandretta are earmarked for the French. The dashed semicircular arc beginning at Aqaba marks off an area to the south where no foreign power except Great Britain would be allowed any voice.

gen had been sent to Egypt to work with the intelligence services, where it was hoped that his fresh (some would have said "wild") ideas would turn around the stagnant operations against the Turks. He told endless stories about his exploits. He claimed that his ship from Marseilles had been torpedoed, and that he had spent five hours in the water with only a bottle of brandy before being picked up by a Japanese destroyer. The many amazing tales added to his legend. Like Aaronsohn, Meinertzhagen had "an immensely powerful body, and a savage brain not hampered by doubts or prejudices, habits or rules of game."[23] He also was renowned as an ornithologist, and as fellow scientists he and Aaronsohn quickly hit it off. As two bright and inventive men with encyclopedic knowledge, and as outsiders to the regular intelligence staff, they got along well.

Meinertzhagen defined his job as proposing ideas to weaken the Turkish forces, including dropping opium-laced cigarettes from aircraft to the Turkish troops and planting false British attack plans for the Gaza-Beersheba front in a haversack to be found by the Turks. Aaronsohn was recruited to help with some of the schemes, such as the cigarette drop, which required intimate knowledge of wind conditions. Meinertzhagen called Aaronsohn "my best agent in the 1914–18 war . . . a man who feared nothing and had tremendous intellect."[24] They formed a friendship because they took each other seriously, a unique experience for both of them at British GHQ. Meinertzhagen invited Aaronsohn to come to the front with him for one of his schemes, but nothing came of the invitation or of Meinertzhagen's fanciful schemes—which did not stop him from later claiming that they had all been successful and had enabled the British victories on the Palestine front.

It was not so easy to find quick agreements when Aaronsohn had to deal with the regular British intelligence officers. After Deedes reported that the £2,000 of relief funds would be delivered on the next ship that was sent to pick up intelligence reports from Athlit, Aaronsohn asked to also use the sequestered £4,000 to £5,000 of the American relief funds in Palestine. He demanded permission to publicize the sacking of Jaffa among the Jews of Egypt to "make them understand that I had obtained the right to follow the British Armies and bring help." He repeated his request to send telegrams throughout the world with information on "the true situation in Palestine."[25]

~

Volumes of useful information had come from the pickups in Athlit, and they were being passed on to British intelligence, but both in Cairo and Athlit there was a growing sense that the British could not rely too much longer on getting information to Cairo via the ships. There had already been incidents of Turkish sentries shooting at swimmers and launches. Couriers sometimes swam to shore and found themselves forced to hide from sentries or Turkish patrols; some had to return to the ship without reaching the research station, or had been forced to hide for so long that they could not be picked up later that same night. As Turkish intelligence noticed signs of attack preparations in the Sinai and along the canal, the Turks had become even more suspicious of potential spies. Sightings of French and British patrol boats offshore, the omnipresent wartime rumors of spy rings, and Djemal Pasha's paranoia about the Jews fueled their suspicions.

Aaronsohn, the British, and the Athlit group toyed with alternate techniques to pick up the NILI information. As an experiment the British sent a wireless unit to Athlit, but the batteries had to be charged every five to six weeks; everyone feared that the signals could be intercepted and the codes broken; and the unit proved too large, delicate, and difficult to maintain. Mendel Schneersohn, Liova's brother, suggested that the British send aircraft to pick up the messages, and identified a field near Zichron where the pilots could land. Aaronsohn proposed that the British lay a cable on the seabed, ending twenty yards from the coast. Another cable could then be buried in the riverbed that ran to the sea at Athlit, terminating close to the shore. The gap between the ends of the two cables, at the shoreline where waves might expose a buried cable, would be bridged by transmission through the ground, a scheme sometimes used for electric bells. The British technology officer in Cairo opened his eyes wide when Aaronsohn proposed the idea—he had never heard of anything quite like that—and promised to study it, but the British never pursued the suggestion or any of the other ideas from Aaronsohn and NILI. Instead, they proposed carrier pigeons, and brought cooped birds into Palestine. The birds flew correctly in tests without messages, but the initial pigeons had not been trained for the long flights to Egypt. Aaronsohn was skeptical.[26]

On one of the trips of the *Managem,* sentinels on shore fired at Liova Schneersohn and Leibel Bornstein as they disembarked from the ship, and they had to return without delivering the gold for relief funds, and without picking up the latest intelligence reports. Aaronsohn blamed the mishap on Captain Smith, whom he had never trusted after their first voyage together. "I pointed out to him [Edmonds]," Aaronsohn wrote, ". . . that in dealing with independent people with broad views and high aspirations who are making great sacrifices in doing work—low in itself—, their task must not be made harder—even unbearable—through certain stiffness and haughtiness which might seem natural to an Englishman—but are exceedingly offensive to our people who are at once more democratic and 'orientalized.' "[27]

The argument escalated as Captain Smith answered that Aaronsohn's people were no good, and that the work could be done better by others; he cited one eight-day period when the group at Athlit had not been able to bring fresh reports from Afula, only twenty-five miles from Athlit. Aaronsohn steeled himself in his diary: "Capt. Smith evidently does not know me and does not know that when he takes such a tone with me—he gives me back all my self-control and warns me against my usual sincerity and exuberance." He tried passive aggression: "I told these gentlemen plainly that if they believe others could do better, I should be happy to retire. My ambition was to give them such assistance, as others were not in a position to render. . . . They are wrong to believe that it is a question of competition. . . . Let others 'go to it' if they want to. I shall simply retire from the game." Once again, his pique threatened the entire project. "Smith's insinuations have made it a matter of principle. Now I cannot do anything save discuss the principle, the foundations of it.

"Either the situation shall be clear and shall not depend on the caprices of a Captain X. or other hazards . . . or we shall part."

In the privacy of his diary he turned to the one person he could depend upon for reassurance and consolation: "Two years of hard work, and Absa lost! A heavy price, indeed! But Absa would have been the first to say to me: 'Master, you did well,' and he would have loved me still more, if possible. Some might call it Don Quixotism? Perhaps."[28]

~

After two failed advances toward Gaza, and with British and Egyptian forces still bogged down at the Suez Canal, General Murray was fired in July 1917. His replacement was General Edmund Allenby, a cavalry officer in the British Expeditionary Force in France. Allenby had been promoted commander of the Third Army after the first battle of Ypres, then made the mistake of arguing tactics with Field Marshal Douglas Haig, which got him the demotion of appointment as commander in chief of the British forces in Egypt. Allenby was fifty-six, a big man—he was called "the Bull"—with a proper officer's mustache, a swagger stick, a chest full of decorations, unconcealed self-confidence, and a reputation for ferocity when angered. Many in the officer corps in Cairo, beaten down by the indignity of the disasters at Gallipoli and Kut, two failed attacks against the Turks in Gaza, and a persistent sense of waiting forever in the wings, found Allenby's self-confidence and moral authority a refreshing change. Allenby sat straight in his chair and looked directly at a visitor, asked focused questions, and paid careful attention to maps. Some found his intensity disconcerting, especially those who had become accustomed to the diffident General Murray.

Aaron Aaronsohn had been waiting for a man like Allenby since the moment he'd left Palestine. When Allenby brought him in for an interview in mid-August 1917, Aaronsohn laid out a sweeping presentation, like those he had given to Julius Rosenwald, Henry Morgenthau, Louis Brandeis, and Theodore Roosevelt. With his confident and encompassing style, Aaronsohn sketched the deteriorating economic situation in Palestine, its effect on civilian and military morale, and the mentality of the population. There was "nothing to fear," he told Allenby. "Those who have been deceived will not 'acclaim' the invader, but they will 'surely' not resist." He analyzed the state of the Turkish army, calling it an inferior force, but "infinitely superior to what we had expected" because they were so much better equipped than in the past. He dismissed Djemal Pasha as "absolutely null from a military standpoint," though vain, superficial, inclined to plot, and "clever at it." He called Colonel Franz Kress von Kressenstein, the German chief of staff and effectively the commander of the Turkish forces, an "officer of value, adventurous, almost imprudent, and determined. A dangerous opponent—all the more so because he is likely to do the unexpected."[29]

Allenby was under pressure from London to take Jerusalem by Christmas, a task he believed impossible with limited water supplies and the incompatibility of British rolling stock with the Turkish railroad tracks. He listened intently, asking intelligent questions, and learned that Aaronsohn had up-to-date information on the Turkish railroads and a solution for the problem of providing water to the troops that did not require special piping from the United States. When Aaronsohn then offered to explain the agricultural problems in Palestine, a subject on which he had kept even Teddy Roosevelt engrossed, Allenby listened. Allenby may also have been impressed by Aaronsohn's style of reasoning, including his skill in identifying water resources from the remains of ancient cities. British intelligence agents later borrowed Aaronsohn's technique, identifying additional potential water resources from the proximity of the remains of Nabataean cities.[30]

On July 3, Na'aman Belkind, a NILI agent in Rishon le Zion, in the south of Palestine, reported to Athlit that the Turkish army was fully prepared for another British attack in Gaza, but that they feared a flanking attack through Beersheba. Sarah, pulling together information from other spies in the NILI network, confirmed the information when she sent it via one of the shipborne information pouches to Cairo. Aaronsohn had tried to argue the same strategy to British intelligence for months. It had always fallen on deaf ears. General Murray had favored a direct attack via Gaza, even after the British forces had been driven back twice on the difficult Gaza terrain, and had refused to change his tactics. With the new information and a new commander in chief, Aaronsohn tried again to explain the tactic of attacking Palestine not via Gaza, but from the south, through Beersheba.

Allenby listened.[31] And after that interview, Aaronsohn, who had suffered uncomfortably and sometimes gracelessly through almost a year of bureaucratic delays and runarounds, who had repeatedly been close to storming off in a pique of anger, suddenly found himself respected and sought after. He advised Clayton about the members of an American mission that was arriving to gather information: "Morgenthau—a soap bubble; Lewin-Epstein, a vulgar demagogue. The former, however, may lead financial circles along, and the latter Jewish masses. Felix [Frankfurter] is the only man with a level head."[32]

Within days he found himself almost too much in demand; the jealousy among the intelligence services was "nerve-racking . . . particularly in view of the fact that they feel that both I[ntelligence] B[ureau] and A[rab] B[ureau] are gathering firsthand political information from me."[33] He was asked for meteorological reports and predictions of wind direction for possible gas attacks and to help aviators plan their routes. The sudden appreciation went to his head. "Our Palestinian public is already anxious to send me delegates," he wrote in his diary. "It is extremely important. Today I may say that the mission which I have undertaken has succeeded."[34]

He acted as though he believed what Norman Bentwich had said sarcastically: "Aaron runs the GHQ."

Lawrence returned triumphantly from Aqaba just as Aaronsohn was hitting his stride around GHQ, and was not shy about his accomplishments: "Akaba had been taken on my plan by my own effort.

The cost of it had fallen on my brains and nerves. There was much more I felt inclined to do, and capable of doing. . . . I had earned the right to be my own master. The Arabs said that each man believed his ticks to be gazelles: and I did, strenuously."[35]

He made a dramatic reappearance at GHQ. Claiming that moths had eaten his uniform while he was in Arabia, Lawrence showed up for an interview with General Allenby wearing a flowing white silk Arab shirt and headcloth, a golden headrope, and a gold-trimmed dagger. The cagey general turned sideways in his chair, but did not ask Lawrence many questions. He studied the maps Lawrence showed him and listened to Lawrence's explanation of "the nature of eastern Syria and the inhabitants."

Allenby was less interested in the surprise victory at Aqaba than in the reconnoitering Lawrence had been able to do in the north, along the eastern flank of Palestine and Syria. Lawrence had sketched a map showing his ideas of points where Arab units could cut off railroad traffic in Syria and Palestine—north of Maan, south of Deraa, on the main track leading to Damascus, and between the major cities of Homs and Hama in northern Syria. His sketch also showed Arab forces attacking across the Jordan River north of the Dead Sea and on the coast north of Acre. "These various operations," he explained, "fortunately need not be accurately concerted. If they come off, the line of communication of the Turkish force in the Jerusalem area would appear threatened—but I do not think the Arabs can be advised to take action unless the Egyptian Expeditionary Force can retain the Turks in front of them by a holding attack."[36] It was an expansive plan, nothing less than an orchestrated Arab conquest of Syria under British protection—exactly the plan he had told Faisal was the only hope for the Arabs to undermine the still-secret Sykes-Picot agreement.

Clayton had expanded Lawrence's plans into a formal memorandum. All that was needed, Lawrence could assure Allenby, were guarantees of the necessary matériel and financial support for the Arab troops, and an acceptance that the "operations are entirely contingent on a decision to undertake major operations in Palestine with which the movement of the Arabs must synchronise. If minor operations only are intended in Palestine, the Arab operations as suggested above would probably lead to the destruction of many of the Arabs' elements, and most certainly to that of the Druses were they to take action. Unless operations of such magnitude as to occupy the whole of the Turkish Army in Palestine were undertaken the proposed Arab operations must be abandoned."[37]

"Well," Allenby said, "I will do for you what I can."[38]

After that interview the Savoy Hotel wasn't big enough for Lawrence and Aaronsohn.

14

Athlit

A sacred obligation remains to us. We can honor his memory and his undertaking only by devoting all our energies and all our abilities to fulfilling the great things that will stand in his name. Oh that we may soon seek the redemption of our people and our land.

—Aaron Aaronsohn, on Avshalom Feinberg

This remarkable man was the most daring and unassuming agent. . . . I am not at liberty to divulge many of his exploits as it would publicize methods better kept secret.

—Richard Meinertzhagen, on Aaron Aaronsohn[1]

Sarah tried to run NILI the way her mother had managed the Aaronsohn household. They had always been an intensely close family, with Aaron at the center. His brothers and sisters had sorted his childhood collections of stones and botanical specimens, found space for his growing library, worked at his research station. Dinner-table conversations were family lovefests, famed for their civility and erudition, often given over to Aaron's wide-ranging knowledge.[2] From the desperate early years of Zichron to the years when Aaron's success and fame made the family a target for criticism, Malka had juggled the competing demands of her family and the harsh criticism from outside with moral force and folk wisdom. When Malka died the challenge of resisting the centrifugal forces of a family spinning out of control fell to Sarah. It was her preparation for the task of holding the disparate men and women of NILI together and focused on the goal of supplying intelligence to the British and gold to the relief effort within Palestine.

Some of the workers at the research station in Athlit were strictly agriculture laborers, following Aaronsohn's experimental protocols as they tended the experimental plots, orchards, and vineyards. Even in the midst of the war, with fuel and fertilizer shortages, they proudly maintained the most productive fields in Palestine. Others on the staff were friends and relatives of Feinberg and Aaronsohn's who had originally joined up to work in the locust-control programs, often with little prior agricultural experience: men like Reuven Schwartz and David Sokolovitsch, who had grown up with the Aaronsohns in Zichron, Feinberg's cousins Eitan and Na'aman Belkind, and Raphael Abulafia in Egypt. They were more comfortable gathering information on the Turkish military installations and order of battle than working in the fields. Friends of friends joined, like Liova and Mendel Schneersohn, Avshalom Fine, Nissan Rutman, and Dr. Moshe Neumann in Afula. Frida Lulu, the housekeeper at the research station, knew about the spying and joined the effort. Former Gideonites and members of Ha-Shomer joined NILI; some were so young that there were concerns about sending them on missions on the *Managem* because their parents might object. The NILI group also had broad contacts across Palestine and Syria—a water supply manager in Damascus, a city engineer in Jerusalem, a railway inspector in Afula—who could only vaguely identify who was receiving the intelligence they passed along, but who had been assured by a trusted friend that good use would be made of the information. By 1917 it fell to Sarah to hold the disparate group together, to temper the potential disputes, to keep the lid on hotheads like Lishinsky, and to keep the rivals for her attention and affection at peace and loyal to the cause.

The task was complicated because two of the men she most depended upon were in love with her. Liova Schneersohn had joined the effort because he admired Aaron, and he had been his loyal secretary, waiting patiently as a contact person first in Constantinople, and later in Alexandria and Cairo, trusted with the most secret messages when Aaron traveled to England, and then Egypt. He fell in love with Sarah in his own shy way, titling his private diary "To Sarah" as he recorded details of the NILI missions in rapturous prose, with Sarah the constant heroine: "Most important to Sarah is the smoke, because the smoke is one of our signs. This black smoke pours out of the funnel of the ship. Hurrah, Sarah! . . . The ship, when it comes opposite the houses of Athlit, makes a sharp turn, with its prow straight for the open sea. This is the second sign. Tonight, Sarah!"[3]

Josef Lishinsky, Schneersohn's rival for Sarah's attentions, had joined NILI because it was the closest he could come, as a Palestinian Jew, to open warfare against the Turks. An orphan of the pogrom in Kishinev in 1903, he had been among the founders of the tiny settlement at Beit Gan, in the Galilee, until he rejected farming to join Ha-Shomer, the watchman's association of the second aliyah. Impetuous and impatient, he rebelled against the controlled discipline and moderation of Ha-Shomer in favor of aggressively pursuing marauding and pilfering Arabs. When he was accused of killing an Arab in an unauthorized action he fled Beit Gan to escape both tribal retribution from the Arabs and Ha-Shomer censure. He started his own self-defense organization called Magen, which guarded settlements in communities where Ha-Shomer did not have a presence. He joined up with the group at Athlit after meeting Avshalom Feinberg. Young, impulsive, more comfortable on a horse than in an office, Lishinsky actively cultivated an image and a style that owed more to Wild West stories than to Aaron's own model of careful study and research.

Lishinsky and Schneersohn were not the only ones to fall in love with Sarah. Avshalom Fine, another NILI recruit, wrote that he got the chills when he met this tall, beautiful, blond, delicate woman at Na'aman Belkind's house in Rishon le Zion. Aaron wrote to Rivka that all the men in NILI were like children beside Sarah, and that they all said that without her they would be leaderless. Yet, for all the men infatuated with her or fantasizing about her, Sarah remained lonely. She wrote to Schneersohn in Cairo, telling him that everything for him, including her, was a fantasy and an illusion, and that he would soon tire of her because she was too real. Her heart, she wrote, was like a stone, and if he imagined her embracing and kissing him, he should not conclude that they were lovers.[4]

There may have been only one love in Sarah's life. With his dark, brooding poet's eyes, his dash on a horse, his daring in the face of the Turks and Bedouin marauders, and his passionate poetry and political writing, Avshalom Feinberg was the personification of Sarah's Zionist and personal dreams. They had been close—perhaps in love—from the time he first came to the Aaronsohn house in Zichron.[5] Even when he had become engaged to her sister, Rivka, Sarah and Avshalom had maintained an intense and intimate correspondence. She had grown up in an old-fashioned household, and was not a subscriber to the free-love ideals that were sometimes identified with the second aliyah. But in the midst of a war the traditional proprieties of courtship and marriage were unaffordable luxuries for members and leaders of a secret organization caught up in the excitement, danger, and purposeful dedication of their cause.

When Sarah returned to Zichron from Constantinople and her failed marriage to Chaim Abraham, NILI was inseparable from Avshalom Feinberg. Especially after Aaron left for England in the summer of 1916, Sarah and Avshalom held the spying organization together. They spent days and evenings together gathering information and waiting for messages from Aaron and Tzila, Avshalom's sister in Berlin. Those months were an idyll of hope and freedom for Sarah Aaronsohn, a caesura between the dreariness of life in Constantinople and the grinding horrors of war in Palestine.

Sarah learned about Avshalom's death when Lishinsky returned to Zichron from Egypt. Those who knew her said she changed overnight. From the time she returned from Constantinople she had been gay and lively, joyous to be relieved of the dead weight of her marriage and the prisonlike life in Constantinople. With Avshalom dead her dreams for herself and for Palestine seemed to die too. "To continue what my dear one began—" she wrote Aaron. "That is all I wish. And vengeance, great vengeance, on the wild ones of the desert and on the cruel Turk. May God only give us life to continue."[6]

Once he told Sarah the truth about Avshalom, Lishinsky stepped boldly into the vacuum his death had left, acting as though he were Sarah's confidant and partner in the leadership of NILI. He was married and had a child, but he spent all of his time in Zichron and Athlit. Sarah—from some combination of a rebound from the devastating news of Avshalom's death, a conviction that NILI needed another intrepid mounted knight in its leadership to rally the troops, or a variation of the Stockholm syndrome that drew her to the man who had been with Avshalom at his death—stood by him. He was not a poet like Avshalom, lacked his wonderful command of language, and was impetuous, intemperate, and often foolhardy; but he was there when Sarah needed someone, and they immediately became close, in a relationship that angered and annoyed many in Zichron and Athlit.

The story they told publicly was that Avshalom was not dead but had made it to British lines and was training as a pilot. That, and Josef's marriage and child, made Sarah's relationship with Lishinsky a double betrayal in the eyes and stories of the village gossips. He, unlike Avshalom, commanded little respect in Zichron and Athlit. The gossip about Avshalom and Sarah had often been tinged with jealousy of the happy couple who seemed kindred spirits. But Lishinsky was married, militant, abrasive, and defiant. He seemed determined to accentuate his distance from the villagers of Zichron. In a town of farmers he bragged that he had turned his back on farming; among those who had been diplomatic in their relations with the Arabs of nearby villages, he bragged of his raids against Arab villages; among those who were cautious in their relationships with the Turkish authorities, he talked of open rebellion that threatened to bring the full might of Turkish repression to Zichron. Even those who had defended Sarah and Avshalom against earlier rumors were offended when she did nothing to dispel or deny the rumors that she and Lishinsky were lovers.

Many in Zichron and Avshalom's home town of Hadera also began to question the story Sarah and Lishinsky had given about Avshalom's whereabouts. When Avshalom's mother asked why she never heard from him, Lishinsky suggested to Aaron that he write a letter in English to Avshalom's mother and Sarah to quiet the doubts and rumors. For her part Sarah ignored the askance looks and whispered gossip. She seemed content that Lishinsky was unwavering in his dedication to NILI and the struggle against the Turks.

~

From Cairo, the dark-night missions of the *Managem* up the coast to Athlit seemed a milk run of retrieved intelligence and delivered satchels of gold. As the ship approached under a moonless sky, Leibel Bornstein would slip into the launch with a package of dry clothes, a flashlight, the watertight package with any papers that were being delivered, and a bottle of whiskey to warm himself with when he got ashore. On his earliest trips the captain of the *Managem* gave him a loaded revolver to carry in his leather pack, and they inflated the pack with air to provide some flotation. As the launch approached the shore Bornstein would jump into the water, swim ashore, warm himself with few slugs of the whiskey, change into the dry clothes, and find his way along the path to the research station, arriving dripping wet, his breath reeking of whiskey.

In reality, the trips were rarely that easy. Sometimes rain or fog would reduce daytime visibility so the smoke of the approaching ship could not be seen from shore, or the ship would not see the white-sheet signal in the open window on the watchtower at the Aaronsohn vineyard or on the clothesline or the window of the second floor of the research station at Athlit. Even when the signals worked the surf was sometimes so rough that the launch could not approach close to the shore, and the swimmer would have difficulty reaching the beach with the heavy pack. Bornstein's vision was poor—the crew on the *Managem* called him "the Owl" because of his large, round-framed glasses[7]—and sometimes Arab swimmers would have to accompany him so he could find the beach. Sometimes he would hear or see Turkish soldiers lounging or patrolling, and would have to hide for hours in a cave on the path up to the research station. Once the *Managem,* which normally waited two and a half miles offshore, drifted close to the beach while waiting for the return passengers; if the ship had run aground, the Turks could have brought in a field gun, destroyed the steamer, and tortured the crew for information before hanging them.

The day Sarah and Lishinsky boarded the *Managem* at Port Said to return to Athlit from their stay in Cairo, the ship had been fueled with low-grade coal, which slowed it down so they arrived at Athlit too late to land anyone and had to return to Port Said. Lishinsky was furious, complaining that there was "no organization at home, that the public was not with us, that the people ought to receive information." Aaron urged him and Schneersohn "to try to hold their tongues," but Lishinsky aired "all the usual demagogic theories."[8] Aaron got so angry at the undisciplined outbursts that he slammed his fist down on a table, breaking his wristwatch.

When they sailed again, the *Managem* was caught in a sudden, violent storm. To avoid the German submarines that were rumored to patrol the eastern Mediterranean, the steamer was rerouted to Famagusta, on Cyprus, where Sarah and Lishinsky were confined in hot and close quarters. They came down with the violent chills, fever, headaches, convulsions, and delirium of malaria. Unable to communicate with Aaron in Cairo, or with anyone in Palestine, they had to stay in Cyprus until they were well enough to get passage back to Egypt on another ship. The only good news they could report was that when the *Managem* had approached the coast off Zichron before being rerouted, they could see the white sheet signal in the window at Aaron's house: the NILI organization was still ready for them. But for weeks no information passed between Athlit and British GHQ.

Aaron decided that it would be cruel to send Sarah back to Palestine again. "I do not see the necessity of it," he wrote in his diary, "now that the most precious time is past."[9] He took her out shopping in Cairo to take her mind off the horrors of the weeks on ship and in Cyprus. While they shopped Lishinsky met with experienced sappers in what the British called the Red Barracks, learning how to detonate explosives and to conceal the preparations. Even as he trained for offensive action he was fanatically suspicious, watching and sometimes shadowing Bedouins he suspected of spying on him. Aaron found him "exasperating" and "extremely difficult to deal with. . . . He has no breeding and has an exaggerated opinion of his personal value."[10]

But Sarah was determined. She, Lishinsky, and Schneersohn left again for Athlit on the *Managem* in mid-May, bringing gold francs for the relief effort and explosives for a planned attack on the strategic bridges at Tul Karem and Dalharmia. The gold coins had all been carefully checked to make sure they bore dates of 1914 or earlier; a later date would have revealed that the gold had been smuggled in during the war. Lishinsky, Sarah, and Schneersohn carried the gold ashore in twenty-two-pound canvas sacks and hid it in a cave until relations with the relief committee could be sorted out. Lishinsky was so afraid the gold would be discovered or appropriated by the authorities that he insisted on staying with the hidden sacks. The seas were too rough to unload the explosives, and Aaron, who did not trust Lishinsky's ambitions after his brief sapper training, was "glad of it." He and Lishinsky only came to a peace after Lishinsky wrote that despite their arguments he missed Aaron; he asked whether Aaron thought him crazy. Aaron answered that he had never had a friend with whom he did not fight, and that arguments were inevitable when two strong-minded people were together. They agreed that the strategy of blowing up bridges was too risky; even having the British bomb the bridges would result in the Jews being blamed at a time when the Jewish community in Palestine was already in peril.

But even as Aaron grudgingly accepted Lishinsky alongside Sarah in the leadership of NILI, he was increasingly frustrated with the organization. He wanted strict accounting of the funds they received so that there would be no questions afterward from the British or from the trustees of the research station. He even used the word "embezzlement" in one letter. His concerns were an unnecessary delicacy: the funds dispersed to NILI—probably not more than £24,500 overall[11]—were pocket change in the British intelligence budget. The organization was too fluid for the kinds of records Aaron wanted, with clear distinctions between funds paid to workers at the research station who needed to be fed and housed, NILI volunteers like Lishinsky who spied full time and needed support, and funds that had been dispersed as relief. Aaron also had borrowed money to support the research station; in the midst of war, the funds were all commingled. "Our brothers are too annoying," Aaron wrote. "But what a brave, wonderful girl is Sarati!"[12] He had to trust her to run NILI; there was little more he could do from Cairo.

Aaronsohn had given the British a steady stream of tactical suggestions, and plunged into the daily operations of NILI from Cairo, but he was uncomfortable with the vagaries of tactics. His model for political action owed more to the careful plans of science than to the immediacy of tactical decisions, and he had already begun to analyze the new factors that were changing the overall situation for the British, and for the Jews of Palestine. America was now in the war against Germany and Austria, with fresh U.S. troops expected on the western front in France. Who would get Jewish interests and funds in America lined up in support of the Zionist dream? Russia had been in turmoil since the deposition of the tsar, their army was rapidly fading away on the eastern front, and rumors about a Bolshevik revolution and a separate Russian peace with Germany and Austria were rampant. Who would rally the Jews of Russia in support of the war? Aaronsohn knew that Weizmann and the Zionists in England were consolidating their power and influence with the Foreign Office in London, but his relationship with the official Zionists was rocky: his abrasive relationships with the relief committee and with Gluskin had left bruised feelings, and Weizmann and Sokolov ignored or actively resisted aggressive schemes to oppose the Turks, like NILI or Jabotinsky's efforts to organize a Jewish brigade, on the grounds that any departure from neutrality by the Zionists risked alienating one side in the war. Compared to Aaronsohn's mostly passive role in Cairo, the problems in London seemed immediate and real.

Aaronsohn had spent enough time in GHQ to learn about the British cooperation with Sherif Hussein, and their plans to make him a ruler, or at least a surrogate governor for Arab areas in a British sphere of influence after the war. Lawrence, who enjoyed bragging and tweaking those with whom he argued, may have told Aaronsohn about his ambitions for the Arabs. By summer 1917 neither the British recognition of Hussein's authority nor the limits of the area he and his sons would rule were clear, but Aaronsohn had begun to question the legitimacy of Arab ambitions, especially the inclusion of Syria and parts of Palestine into an Arab entity. "A Syrian nation does not exist," he argued, "and never did. It is a French invention, a clever one, but not more than a political invention."[13] Lawrence had also argued against an independent Syria, though for very different reasons: he feared that France would use Syria as a rhetorical and geographical lever to pry off chunks of a grand, unified Arab state.

Aaronsohn was riding his bicycle in the moonlight one night at the end of July, thinking of the problems that needed his attention, when he had a sudden idea: *why should I not go to London?*[14] One month later he met with Sir Reginald Wingate, the British high commissioner in Egypt. They agreed that the futures of the British and the Jews of Palestine were linked, and Wingate urged Aaronsohn to go to London to see the "great ones, and to explain to them what we know and what they don't know."

"From today onwards we have the right to look on our activities with confidence," Aaron wrote to Sarah. "Up till now we were just a few, isolated dreamers who endangered ourselves, and even dragged others after us, against their will. Now at last, when the highest authorities have given their official approval of our work, no one can doubt the rightness of our vision and of our action."[15]

As Allenby prepared for a massive advance into Gaza and Palestine, British intelligence escalated their demands for current information about the Turkish defenses. The EMSIB queries Leibel Bornstein brought ashore from the *Managem* asked for specific information on troop concentrations, logistics, and the preparedness of various units of the Turkish Fourth Army. Unlike Aaron, who had been a familiar figure anywhere in Palestine and had the cover of his scientific surveys or his status in the locust-control program, Sarah had to be both clever and bold in gathering information. Sometimes she would ride off in the research station carriage, dressed in a stylish blue suit she had copied from a Paris design, with a high-necked white blouse and proper shoes, Lishinsky sitting beside her in a proper jacket, like a German. The research station had owned an automobile since 1912, one of the first in Palestine—Aaron had always been on the forefront of technology—but even if scarce fuel could have been spared from the few irrigation pumps that had not been seized by the Turks, driving an automobile would draw unwelcome attention and critical comments. Instead, Abu Farid, the station employee who had driven Aaron, drove them out of town, looking like a young bourgeois couple off on a visit to the city. That alone was enough to inspire more gossip and rumors from the second-aliyah Russians in Zichron, who had little tolerance for chauffer-driven carriages and Paris couture.

Before the carriage left Zichron Sarah would be taking notes. She manned the weather station Aaron had set up at his father's house, recording wind and sky conditions, barometric pressure, and humidity data to pass along to the British meteorologists and attack planners.[16] When the carriage reached the outskirts of Zichron, Sarah would record the state of the crops in the surrounding fields, the impact of recent rainfall and the delayed sowing of crops, and the positions of the Turkish military guards, whether they were stationed up on the highway or close enough to the shore to see arriving ships. She and Lishinsky would follow the highway north to Haifa, where the officials would routinely announce that no permits were available for travel to Jerusalem. Sarah knew the Turkish bureaucracy well enough to anticipate the demands for baksheesh, and would bring gold with them. A few days and many bribes later they would be back on the road again with the papers they needed.

To the gossipmongers in Zichron, their tour in the carriage looked like a honeymoon. But everywhere they traveled Lishinsky was rooting out information and Sarah was taking notes. In Nazareth, a Turkish garrison town, they heard about an arms cache hidden in the courtyard of the Carmelite Sisters convent, and learned that Turkish soldiers were driven to pilfering the forage for the pack animals because their officers had taken their rations. In Lishinsky's home village of Beit Gan they tried to enlist spies for NILI, and learned that the farmers of the northern Galilee were doing relatively well and were unwilling to work against the Turkish authorities.

In Afula, the railway junction for supply and troop trains from Constantinople, Aleppo, and Damascus, an old friend of Aaron's, Dr. Moshe Neumann, a bachelor who brought his mother with him to each new position, was stationed as a physician with the Turkish army. Neumann spoke English, Yiddish, French, German, Turkish, and Arabic in addition to Hebrew, was adept at engaging Turkish and German officers in conversations when the trains stopped, and was willing to detain soldiers "for medical reasons" so he could talk to them privately, asking where they were being posted and details of their orders. The Turks conveniently provided him with a schedule of troop trains. When Sarah brought him a letter from Aaron, asking for his continued help, he told her, "I'll be playing with my head if I do this."

Sarah pointed at her own head. "You see," she said, "my head also sits firmly on my shoulders, but I am endangering it all the time. If you call yourself a man, you should be prepared to do the same."

Neumann took on the responsibility of counting the trainloads of Turkish soldiers that passed through Afula. He measured the gauge of the tracks and carriages of the rolling stock, information that would let the British bring matching rolling stock with their invasion forces so that they could use the existing tracks all the way to Damascus. NILI also had an agent in Damascus, so they were able to compare information on trains that left Damascus with Neumann's reports on those that arrived in Afula. Neumann's information was so important that when he had to leave Afula in June 1917, Sarah persuaded her cousin David Sokolovitsch, a farmer, to open a refreshment stand at the Afula station as a cover for spying on the trains.[17] Neumann and later Sokolovitsch would also report when Enver Pasha, Djemal Pasha, or the German generals came through Afula on their special trains.[18]

When Sarah and Lishinsky reached Jerusalem they contacted an informant in the Turkish headquarters who reported that "from Shellale and Sharia, and southeast from Beersheba the Turks are planning to hold only a temporary defensive line, and afterwards to retire to the mountains of Jerusalem and Hebron, which they are already fortifying."[19] This was key information for General Allenby, who had been undecided whether to follow the pattern of General Murray's previous attacks on the direct route through Gaza. Sarah and Lishinsky stayed in the expensive Hotel Fast, the residence and headquarters of German commander Kress von Kressenstein and his staff. There, Lishinsky mixed with the German officers and learned the size of the German presence in Palestine (50,000 soldiers) and where they were stationed. Sarah sat demurely in the hotel lounge, pretending to write a letter while she eavesdropped on the German officers' conversations about their estimates of British strength in the south. Another informant in Jerusalem, an engineer in the Turkish army named Nahum Wilbosovich, gave them a map of the city with the fortifications marked. They had already gotten a map of Damascus from an informant there, with marks on buildings used for military purposes: Djemal Pasha's residence, transportation bases, factories, garages—all useful targets for the planners who advised the British air forces in Palestine.[20]

At Rishon le Zion, in the south, they met with Na'aman Belkind, Feinberg's cousin, who worked in the Carmel winery and provided information about the Turkish army. Na'aman's brother Eitan had been drafted into the army and posted in the south, where he provided information on German codes and targets that could be bombed from the air. Na'aman constantly asked about Feinberg and seemed disapproving of Sarah's traveling with Lishinsky. When they told him the story about Feinberg training with the British to be a pilot, he gave them a letter for Avshalom to be sent via the British.

They returned to Zichron after twelve days on the road, still dressed in their city clothes, stepping down from the carriage as if they had had been off on a holiday. Tongues wagged openly at the two young people who seemed to have been off having a high time, riding about and staying in fancy hotels when so many Jews in Palestine were desperate for food and fuel. Sarah returned to the house where she had grown up and wrote Aaron: "The house is always sad and lonely, and all kinds of terrible thoughts come into my mind, for after all, our work is very black, and always in danger. Thank goodness, that until now everything has been all right."[21]

But everything was not all right. Aaron claimed that the leaders in Palestine were eager to send him deputies, but he was only extrapolating from the respect that Allenby and the intelligence services had begun to accord him. In reality, the leaders of factions and organizations in Palestine were turning against NILI. The relief committee, which Aaron had quit before he left for England, had been virtually defunct, without funds or crops to distribute. When the first shipments of gold arrived on the *Managem,* Lishinsky had opposed giving it to the relief committee on the grounds that they, like most of the Jewish settlers, were opposed to NILI's activities. His attitude became known, and the gossip against him escalated. People questioned Feinberg's supposed training as a pilot. Rumors circulated that Feinberg was not in England, that he had never made it to the British lines, that he had been killed in the desert. Some said it hadn't been an accident or a Bedouin attack, that Lishinsky had killed Feinberg to take his place with Sarah. Even those who had previously defended Sarah joined these rumormongers. Sarah's brother Zvi, who had worked enthusiastically with Aaron and Sarah from childhood, said that her relationship with Josef Lishinsky was driving people away from the Aaronsohns; Zvi finally told her that as long as she was with Lishinsky, she was not welcome in his home. Even Sarah's father questioned the gossip directed at their family, and had to mediate between her and her brother.

In August 1917 Sarah angrily announced that she would move to Athlit and live at the research station, where she and Lishinsky could work undisturbed by the gossip. She argued as if her only goal was to preserve the independence of NILI, but it was undoubtedly also her own independence that she was protecting. Around this time she received an unexpected letter from her husband, who was in Holland. He enclosed £20, telling her that she could use £5 for the refugees in Zichron. "The poor man doesn't know how many thousands of pounds are passing through my hands," she wrote to Aaron, "and how many thousands of francs I hand out!"[22] More than the insult to her skills running a complex spying organization, Abraham's letter was a reminder of the years she had spent in Constantinople as a virtual prisoner in a ghetto of Sephardic women who spent their days in gossipy kaffeeklatches. Her husband had never imagined that she was not only a free spirit, but that she could have the responsibility for the future of a nation in her hands.

Even with Sarah and Lishinsky at Athlit, the gossip about a Jewish spy ring aroused the strong opposition of the Ha-Shomer watchmen, who saw any militant organization as a threat to their own self-defined role. They particularly opposed Josef Lishinsky, a former Ha-Shomer member who had broken away and accused them of cowardice. Ha-Shomer contacted the political committee of the worker's movement in Jaffa, demanding that NILI be broken up, and delegates of the Zichron Committee traveled to Athlit, demanding that Sarah and Lishinsky cease all NILI activities and threatening to close down the research station until Sarah pointed out that the station was American-owned, that even the Turks had left it alone during the war, and that the relief committee didn't seem to have problems with the French francs and British sovereigns NILI had brought from their contacts in Egypt. Sarah's only concession to the committee was to agree that Lishinsky would stay out of Zichron.

As he prepared to leave for London, Aaron tried to get Sarah to visit Cairo again. She wrote back that she might come to say good-bye to Aaron, but only if she could return immediately to Palestine. "I want to be together with the others in the place of danger at the time of danger," she wrote. "I can't leave the work and the workers just at the time when the greatest difficulties are ahead of us. . . . Do you remember Fontaine's fable of the dog who begged to have his collar put on again when they freed him? That's how I am."[23]

On August 30, during a full moon, Sarah sent off two pigeons with coded messages requesting that the *Managem* be sent to Athlit on September 10. She had doubts about the pigeons; they were trained to fly directly to Allenby's advanced headquarters in Wadi Gaza, but in a trial only one of six pigeons had made it to Egypt. Sarah was also well-enough read and had spent enough hours at the Aaronsohn dining table to know of an ominous precedent. In 1111, during the Crusades, the governor of Tyre (forty-five miles up the coast from Athlit), fearing a Frankish siege, sought help from the Seljuk governor in Damascus, who sent a carrier pigeon to the Egyptian court with a message saying that he was sending ambassadors to aid in their defense. An Arab intercepted the bird—the Arabs considered pigeon a delicacy—and took the message to Baldwin, the Frankish king of Jerusalem, who had men in disguise intercept the ambassadors from Damascus and put them to death.[24]

She had no option but the pigeons. For weeks the weather had been good, and only token Turkish sentries were posted on the shore, but no British steamer had appeared to pick up the information they had gathered. Sarah did not know that in Port Said the British were refusing to pay the £30 per month Leibel Bornstein's wife had demanded for her husband to continue swimming ashore. Despite Aaron's pleas the British refused to send a ship. Sarah and Lishinsky knew the British were planning an advance into Palestine, and the information buried in the courtyard was too valuable to wait. The next day she sent two more pigeons with the same request for the *Managem*. One pigeon flew erratically, and later that day when she went to swim in the sea near the Athlit castle she saw the pigeon perched on a water tank. She threw a pebble to startle it into flying off.

Two days later Zichron was buzzing with rumors that the chief of police in Caesarea, Ahmed Bek, who kept pigeons of his own, had spotted a strange pigeon at his feeder with a cylinder attached to its leg. The message in the cylinder was in code, with English letters swapped in position (A=K, B=P, C=U) and numbers that represented cities (1=Aleppo, 2=Damascus, 4=Jerusalem). The Turks had little expertise in cryptography, but they took the Roman letters as evidence that there was an active spy ring dealing with the British. They had also recently apprehended Arab agents carrying propaganda leaflets and British sovereigns minted after the start of the war. Under interrogation the Arab agents revealed that they had heard about British spies in Athlit.[25]

Following Djemal Pasha's precedents, the Turkish police and military focused their suspicions on the Jews, and started their investigation of the spying activity in Hadera, Avshalom Feinberg's hometown and the Jewish settlement closest to Caesarea. The farmers they questioned said nothing, but the news of the investigation inspired new complaints in Zichron.

At Athlit Lishinsky killed the remaining pigeons, except for a few they saved for emergency messages, buried the carcasses in a field, and plowed over any trace of the grave. At an agricultural research station there was nothing suspicious about a newly plowed field. He also reburied the documents they were holding for pickup by the *Managem*. Sarah went to Aaron's house in Zichron, where he kept his priceless library and much of his botanical collection, to make sure that there was no incriminating evidence there, and to try to save at least part of the library and collections. If Turkish investigators came to Zichron—and eventually they almost certainly would—the collections would be a target. The Turks would rip apart books and destroy the precious botanical specimens. NILI's purpose might soon end, but Aaron's goals for the library and his botanical and geological research were forever: they both believed that science and knowledge were the key to the future of Zionism, and his collections and library—the largest scientific library in Palestine—were tools in that future.

Aaron's house had been built with double walls between the rooms and ornate doorways that concealed their thickness. A natural cave under the foundation had been excavated into a storeroom, reached via a steep ladder from a trap in the floor outside the bathroom and through a second, concealed entrance on the hillside behind the house. During the worst of the Turkish requisitions the Aaronsohns had used the storeroom for caches of weapons and food. When it was clear that the Turks would soon be in Zichron, Sarah pressed plant specimens from Aaron's collections between sheets of paper and hid them in crevices and nooks in the storeroom. She hid books and documents inside the walls of the house. The pistol Aaron had once given her for self-protection was hidden inside a wall next to the front entrance.

"They are saying all sorts of things about the pigeon they caught," Sarah wrote to Aaron, sending the message on one of the pigeons they had kept for emergency messages. "That it knows languages, Yiddish, English and French. At the end they add 'Arabic,' not to let on how much they suspect the Jews. They certainly know that the pigeon was sent by Jews. They say he was sent from London." With Sarah all but banished from Zichron, her father had to be her eyes and ears there. He sat in the marketplace, listening and watching. Ephraim had been skeptical about NILI, but when he heard news in town, he would send a messenger to Sarah. "He isn't very pleased with our work," Sarah wrote of her father. "He wants the world to be quiet so that he can have a little rest too. After all, he is of the old generation, an honest man, but simple."[26]

By then Aaronsohn's request to travel to London had been approved. On September 5 he wrote to Henrietta Szold that he had not been in touch with Athlit and sensed something might be wrong there.[27] He did not want to leave Cairo, but his feuds with Chaim Weizmann and Nahum Sokolov in London continued, and he concluded that only a meeting could settle their differences. He had rarely stopped complaining about the laziness and pokey pace of the British, the inefficiency of their bureaucracy, and their reluctance to commit to a plan, and was astonished by the speed of the British paperwork when he decided to go to London. There were some last-minute delays until they could find him a place on a ship, but once the gears were in motion, everything was ready for his departure in two hours![28] As much as GHQ had depended on his suggestions and NILI intelligence in planning the Palestine campaign, there was little love lost when he left Egypt on September 13.

~

The day Aaronsohn sailed a messenger arrived in Zichron from the south to report that the Turkish authorities had arrested Na'aman Belkind.

Belkind had joined NILI out of loyalty to his cousin Avshalom Feinberg. He had been distrustful when Josef Lishinsky seemed to be taking Feinberg's position in the organization, and was frustrated that he never got an answer to the many letters he sent to Feinberg via Athlit. He had never liked Lishinsky, and had been suspicious of the story Lishinsky and Sarah had told about Feinberg, convinced that if his cousin was in Egypt or had been sent on to Britain to be trained as a pilot, he would have answered letters. Belkind concluded that Lishinsky had either killed Feinberg or was concealing information about him. He had asked Sarah and Lishinsky to send him to Egypt on the *Managem,* and became so persistent in his demands that they got Aaron to write that no one from Palestine could travel on the steamer, including Belkind.

Finally, frustrated by the continued silence from Feinberg, Belkind set off across the Sinai with a Bedouin guide, hoping to reach Egypt, where he expected to find Feinberg, or at least the truth about him. In the heart of the Sinai Belkind became sick and was taken to a Bedouin tent for water, where he and his guide were beaten, robbed, and turned over to the local sheikh. The guide escaped, but Belkind was handed over to the Turkish authorities, taken to Beersheba, and arrested as a Jewish spy. The German commander in Beersheba wanted to hang him as a warning to other spies in Palestine, but the Turkish officials assumed anyone crossing the desert toward Egypt had useful information. They prided themselves on their ability to get information from suspects.

For Sarah and Lishinsky the news of Belkind's arrest was more worrisome than the wayward pigeon. The *Managem* had not come for weeks, they had turned most of the funds that had arrived on the last shipment over to the relief effort, and they had little money for baksheesh to try to get him released. Lishinsky took the little money they still had and went south with six men, planning to dress as Turkish gendarmes and free Belkind on the pretext of moving him to another prison. Before Lishinsky could unleash his far-fetched scheme he came down with another bout of malaria and had to abort the plan.

Sarah was desperate for a British ship. She and Lishinsky had recent information on Turkish troop movements, and there were people they had to get to Egypt. They had been hiding a Turkish officer from Albania named Baha al-Din, who was eager to lead a movement against the Turkish government and had valuable information for the British. He had been in Hadera for weeks, staying in a small house where he had to go outside to use the outhouse; they were terrified that he would be discovered. The wife of Sarah's brother Samuel was also with them and eager to leave Palestine. Samuel had been in New York for the previous two years, along with his sister Rivka and his brother Alex, though unlike them he had opposed NILI's spying activities and refused to help. But his wife was still family. Sarah also desperately needed gold for the relief committee, to pay and feed the workers at the research station, and for baksheesh. Their only hope to get Na'aman Belkind out of the Turkish jail in Beersheba was with bribes.

With the stories and rumors about the Turkish investigation of a spy ring strengthening daily, the Zichron Committee summoned her to a meeting. "In the name of our Committee, and the committees of Judea and Galilee," they told her,

> we have to inform you that you are working at unclean [*traife*] work, and that you are the head of all this work. You are a daughter of this village. Your family stands to bear the brunt of the whole danger. . . . Today we don't want to hear any more explanations from you. Only one word, the right answer: Your promise to stop this work, which has gone beyond all bounds. . . . If you want to work at espionage, leave the territory and the lands of the Jews and go and work in some distant land. Otherwise, there will simply break out a war between Jews and Jews![29]

The most Sarah would agree to was to quiet down NILI's activities for a while. A few days afterward, during the Rosh Hashanah new moon, a British steamer was spotted from the watchtower. The *Managem* landed Liova Schneersohn that night, with the news that Aaron had left Egypt for England, and that Alex had arrived from the United States to take Aaron's place at British GHQ. Schneersohn's reports of the imminent British advance were optimistic, but when Lishinsky, still sick with malaria, returned from the south with no good news about Na'aman Belkind, Sarah and Lishinsky discussed evacuating some of the NILI volunteers. It was a difficult choice: evacuating anyone would put those who stayed behind in even greater peril. Could they take those who had spied and leave their families behind? Zichron had been such a tight community that half the town was related to someone who had worked in the NILI operation.

They agreed that the British should send ships with room aboard for sixty people on the night of September 25, Yom Kippur Eve, when many in the village would be in the synagogue. Those to be evacuated would be waiting on shore. Sarah hoped that by then they would know what had come of Belkind's interrogation.

There would be a quarter moon at Yom Kippur, enough light for a steamer to be seen easily from shore, but British headquarters approved the request anyway, and on September 25, while most of Zichron was gathered in the synagogue for the solemn Kol Nidre service, the *Managem* arrived at Athlit with another steamer, the *Varesis*. Schneersohn came ashore and reported that British intelligence still had no information about Na'aman Belkind. With Lishinsky bedridden with malaria, Sarah stayed at the research station. Only Samuel Aaronsohn's wife and her young son elected to leave. The captain of the *Managem* was on the launch, and amazed that the child said not a single word during the evacuation from the beach and the long row out to the ship. The captain asked what was wrong, and the mother explained that when they left the house she had told the boy not to make a sound. The boy had dutifully crept in silence to the beach and through the surf, and sat quietly while they were rowed out to the ship before he finally asked, "Mommy, may I cry now?"[30]

~

In Beersheba, Na'aman Belkind was held for days in chains, alternately tortured with the bastinado and plied with wine and hashish. A strong young man can hold out for a long time against torture, especially if his will is bolstered by fervent faith in a cause. But Belkind's faith was shaky. When the Turkish interrogators promised that the tortures would stop and he would be released if he answered their questions, he finally broke down and admitted he was a spy. When he finished testifying he was sent to Damascus, where he told a judge: "I've kept my word to you. I've told you all I know. Now you must keep your word and release me."

"Yes, yes, my son," the Turkish judge assured him. "You will be released. But I'm sure there is just a little bit more you can tell us first."[31]

~

The *Managem* was supposed to return to Athlit again on September 27, but British intelligence refused to risk the steamer on a trip under an almost-full moon. The EMSIB scheduled no mission to the coast until the moon was dark again, on October 12, leaving Sarah and Lishinsky to their own resources.

"Their personal life is of no account to them," wrote Schneersohn. "They have ceased to exist as people. They are carrying out a historic task. They are only clay in the hands of the potter."[32]

15

Deraa

I would embark on little problems, observing the impact of this or that approach, treating fellow men as so many targets of my ingenuity. I would roughly annoy an individual, and then still myself to smooth him, by some whimsical perversity, or intrigue him by some misplaced firey earnestness: and run away, hoping he wished to know whom that odd creature was.

—T. E. Lawrence[1]

In late August 1917, before he left Egypt for London, Aaronsohn wrote in his diary: "I had a chat with Capt. Lawrence this morning."[2]

Lawrence and Aaronsohn were both flush with self-confidence. The British were finally listening to Aaronsohn and accepting the intelligence from his group at Athlit. Lawrence, fresh from the victory at Aqaba with Emir Faisal's army, had become a hero at GHQ. Their first encounter, months before, had been hostile. Their sudden ascents within GHQ only accentuated their competitiveness.

The meeting was again at the Savoy Hotel, where both men had offices. From a letter Lawrence drafted after the meeting, it seems that Aaronsohn had told him that "the Jews intended to acquire the land-rights to all Palestine from Gaza to Haifa, and have practical autonomy therein."[3]

Lawrence answered by lecturing Aaronsohn on Palestine, telling him about "the *mentalités* of the people—the feelings of the Arabs." "Nothing can be done in Judea and Samaria where Faisal will never gain access," he told Aaronsohn, but "there might be something to do in Galilee." Lawrence promised to conduct an "investigation by his own methods in order to learn of the *mentalité* of the Jews in Galilean colonies."

The discussion was heated. Aaronsohn had studied Palestine more than anyone alive, he had discovered wild wheat in the exact area of the Galilee on which Lawrence was pretending to be an expert, and he had seldom been a gracious listener to those he considered ignorant. "As I was listening to him," Aaronsohn wrote, "I could almost imagine that I was attending a conference by a scientific anti-Semitic Prussian speaking English. I am afraid that the German spirit has taken deeper root in the minds of pastors and archeologists."

Eight years before, when Lawrence had tramped through northern Palestine as a student, he had written home: "The sooner the Jews farm it all the better: their colonies are bright spots in a desert."[4] He had spent almost no time in the Galilee since; had never done serious research on the people or terrain; did not speak Hebrew, Turkish, or Yiddish. Indeed, he had paid scant attention to Palestine since writing his report, "Syria: The Raw Material" in 1915.[5] But lecturing an expert on his own subject, and ending conversations with provocative, even outrageous, utterances, was vintage Lawrence—usually when he felt himself an outsider. Probably with a pause for dramatic emphasis, Lawrence told Aaronsohn that the Jews of the Galilee would have no choice but to accept their fate: "If they are in favor of the Arabs, they shall be spared, otherwise they shall have their throats cut."

Aaronsohn saved his contempt for his diary. "Our interview was devoid of amenity," he wrote. "He [Lawrence] has been too successful at an early age—and is infatuated with himself. . . . He is still at the age where people do not doubt themselves—happy young man! He is plainly hostile to us. He must be of missionary breed."[6] After almost a year in London and Cairo, living alongside and dealing daily with the scarcely concealed anti-Semitism of much of the British officer corps, Aaronsohn was not surprised or shocked by

Lawrence's remark. Once he blew off his rage and contempt in his diary, he seemed to forget the encounter.

Not Lawrence. He drafted a long letter to Mark Sykes reporting Aaronsohn's claim that the Jews would acquire the land rights and have "practical," if not political, autonomy over Palestine. "Is this acquisition to be by fair purchase or by forced sale and expropriation?" Lawrence asked in his letter. "The present half-crop peasantry were the old freeholders and under Moslem landlords may be ground down but have fixity of tenure. Arabs are usually not employed by Jewish colonies. Do the Jews propose the complete expulsion of the Arab peasantry, or their reduction to a day-labourer class? . . . I can see a situation arising in which the Jewish influence in European finance might not be sufficient to deter the Arab peasants from refusing to quit—or worse!"[7]

Sykes, who had been anti-Semitic and anti-Zionist before he met Aaronsohn and got himself involved in the question of Palestine, would surely understand the reference to "Jewish influence in European finance," implying that the Jews could simply buy up all of the land. The comments were typical for a British officer of the time. The "Jewish issue" was suddenly important for Lawrence because he was speaking for Faisal, representing Faisal's aspirations and plans through Mark Sykes to the British Foreign and War offices.

"About the Jews in Palestine," Lawrence explained, "Faisal has agreed not to operate or agitate west of the [Wadi] Araba–Dead Sea–Jordan line, or south of the Haifa-Beisan line." The demarcation may have seemed generous to Lawrence and Faisal, but the latter line would cut through Afula, and would include in the area Faisal claimed the northern Galilee settlements and the cities of Tiberias and Safad, where Jews had lived from Roman times. Speaking in the name of Faisal, Lawrence drew a distinction between "the Palestinian Jew" and "the colonist Jew." The former, he claimed, spoke Arabic, and the latter, "German Yiddish." Lawrence and Faisal seemed not to realize that most of the Jews of Palestine, including those who had arrived only a decade before in the second aliyah, spoke Hebrew by 1917.

Lawrence claimed that Faisal was

> in touch with the Arab Jews (their H.Q. at Safed and Tiberias is in his sphere), and they are ready to help him, on conditions. They show a strong antipathy to the colonist Jews, and have even suggested repressive measures against them. Faisal has ignored this point hitherto, and will continue to do so. His attempts to get into touch with the colonial Jews have not been very fortunate. They say they have made their arrangements with the Great powers, and wish no contact with the Arab Party. They will not help the Turks or the Arabs.
>
> Now, Faisal wants to know (information had better come to me for him since I usually like to make up my mind before he does) what is the arrangement standing between the colonist Jews (called Zionists sometimes) and the Allies. . . . What have you promised the Zionists, and what is their programme?[8]

Lawrence's concern was understandable. But the victory at Aqaba and Allenby's assurances of support for the Arab campaign had gone to his head. No Jews in Palestine owned up to the meetings Faisal claimed to have held, and except in Lawrence's secret plans for him, Faisal did not have a "sphere," at least not in Palestine.

~

The Jewish question was only one of Lawrence's concerns. He also probed Sykes on the Sykes-Picot agreement, asking "what we have to give the Jews, and what we have to give the French."[9] Lawrence had always opposed the concessions to the French, knew the promises of the agreement stood in the way of his strategies for Faisal, and from early in the war had proposed schemes that would effectively exclude or limit the French presence in Syria.

Clayton, still Lawrence's boss, decided not to send the letter on to Sykes, telling Lawrence that Sykes had "dropped the Near East just now and the whole question is, for the moment, somewhat derelict. . . . The Sykes-Picot agreement was made nearly two years ago. The world has moved at so vastly increased a pace since then that it is now as old and out of date as the battle of Waterloo or the death of Queen Anne. It is in fact dead and, if we wait quietly, this fact will soon be realized: it was never a very workable instrument and it is now almost a lifeless monument."[10] For Clayton, for the British intelligence establishment—and to some degree for the Foreign and War offices—wartime commitments, whether to the Arabs in the McMahon correspondence, or to the French and the Russians in the Sykes-Picot agreement, were not treaty obligations but flexible and interim arrangements, reactions to the changing conditions of the war. If Clayton and Lawrence realized this and schemed to work around conflicting British promises, Faisal and others who depended on the British could only with difficulty understand their "flexibility" toward their commitments. And if he could not trust the assurances in the McMahon correspondence, Faisal must have asked, how could he trust the later assurances that the unfavorable Sykes-Picot agreement would not be imposed?

Lawrence also worried that Britain might make a separate peace with the Turks before the Arab armies had advanced to positions that would give them bargaining power. He worried about the entry of the United States into the war, and especially President Wilson's ideas about self-determination. If those concepts were to be imposed on the Middle East, how would Arab populations that had never exercised political power be recognized? Bedouin society, based on tribal and clan organization, recognizing a quasi-feudal loyalty to a king, did not easily adapt itself to Wilson's standards.

Mostly, Lawrence worried about how to keep up the momentum of the Arab advances. What he and Faisal called the Arab army was still a ramshackle band of irregular troops, skilled as camel riders, able to traverse great distances with little logistics support, but untrained in unit operations and ill equipped for more than guerrilla operations. The victory at Aqaba had enhanced Faisal's reputation and drawn new recruits, but like Auda abu Tayi's Howeitat whom

Lawrence had recruited for the attack on Aqaba, the new recruits saw their military service in terms of a few attacks, or perhaps a season of campaigning, and they expected looting after the anticipated victories as their just compensation for service. They still saw their campaigns in tribal or clan terms. On a trip from Salt to Jerusalem in 1916, William Yale, an American, watched an Arab from Transjordan point out snarling hungry dogs tearing the putrefying body of a dead camel to bits and say to his companions (who were not Turks): "Look at the Committee of Union and Progress at work."[11] The Bedouin troops in Faisal's irregular army would not have understood the remark. They were not focused on nationalist goals or xenophobic hatred of the Young Turk government in Constantinople. To hold the army and Faisal's ambitious plans together, Lawrence needed a new campaign goal, a decisive step on the road to Damascus and the creation of an Arab state.

Aqaba had been transformed into a military base. British warships stood watch while cargo ships ferried in supplies and Arab troops from other ports. But the British were not prepared for the influx of troops, supplies were not ferried over fast enough from Egypt, and there were no antiaircraft defenses. When German and Turkish aircraft attacked the disorganized Bedouin units at Aqaba, morale collapsed. The Bedouin soldiers, accustomed to fighting with sword and rifle, were terrified of artillery, and especially of aircraft. As the raids persisted, rumors circulated that the Turks might mount a massive attack from Maan to retake Aqaba.

To preempt a Turkish offensive, and especially to quiet the disruptive rumors, Lawrence decided to mount an attack against the Hejaz Railway south of the juncture and supply depot at Maan, hoping the attack would distract the Turks, break up their lines of communications to Medina, and revive Arab morale. The point he picked was the Mudawara station, the only substantial watering point for locomotives in the one hundred miles of rail line south of Maan. Without water supplies from the Mudawara station, Turkish trains, including repair trains needed to respond to attacks on the line, would have to carry so much water that they would have almost no capacity for troops, supplies, or repair materials for the sections of track that were destroyed in Bedouin raids.

Despite his efforts at rallying the demoralized Bedouin troops, Lawrence was unable to recruit enough men and camels for a full raid on the station at Mudawara. He settled instead for an attack on a train, using—for the first time—an electrically detonated mine instead of an automatic detonator. Two English machine-gun instructors from Aqaba accompanied the raiding party. The mine destroyed one of the two locomotives on the train, and when the Turkish soldiers tried to escape, murderous fire from the machine guns mowed them down, killing seventy Turks and wounding thirty. Only one Arab was killed, and four wounded. Lawrence was appalled by the slaughter. "I hope this nightmare ends," he wrote, "that I will wake up and become alive again. This killing and killing of Turks is horrible. . . . You charge in at the finish and find them all over the place in bits, and still alive many of them, and how that you have done hundreds in the same way before and must do hundreds more if you can."[12]

There had been good looting on the raid, and the Bedouins considered the mission a great victory. Volunteers showed up in numbers for more attacks on the railroad. On occasion the troops would identify themselves as members of the Arab army, but they bickered constantly. Between tribes, and even within tribes, the followers of one sheikh or another would get into arguments about divisions of plunder, allegations of thefts and assaults, ancient feuds over marriage settlements, and accusations of bewitchments and the casting of evil eyes. The constant disputes threatened further joint military action, and Lawrence, who would have preferred to plan major operations to advance Faisal's strategic goals, was forced to accompany the attacks on the rail line—only someone respected but from no tribe could lead a unit composed of men from feuding tribes, and only an outsider with a knowledge of tribal customs and rivalries could mediate the disputes. Lawrence spent weeks on long camel rides instead of planning strategy and tactics.

In October an airplane was sent to pick him up in Suez to meet with Clayton and Hogarth at the Egyptian Expeditionary Force's temporary headquarters north of El Arish. There they told him that orders had come from London for a fall offensive to take Jaffa and Jerusalem. The attack plans should have been welcome news; Lawrence had hoped that with a month of good weather Allenby would take not only Beersheba and Jerusalem, but even Haifa, driving the Turkish army "in one shapeless ruin through the hills."[13] But he was no longer confident of what he had offered Allenby in the heady days of July—a general Arab uprising in Syria that would sap the strength of the Turkish forces. Faisal's forces were bogged down in Aqaba, untrained, ill supplied, in no position to inspire or support a general uprising. "Faisal does not get any bigger—even T.E.L. admits that," Hogarth wrote. "[Lawrence] . . . talks rather hopelessly about the Arab future he once believed in."[14]

The news left Lawrence torn between his duty to support Allenby's plans and his commitments to Faisal's ultimate success. He was one of Allenby's officers, in his commander's confidence, and was expected to do his best for the British effort. He was also Faisal's adviser and knew that Faisal relied without question or argument on the competence and honesty of his advice. Yet he could not explain the whole Arab situation to Allenby, and was not empowered to disclose the full British plan to Faisal. "It was not the first or last time that service to two masters irked me," he wrote. ". . . It was strange and often difficult to choose between the two voices that were trusting me. . . . Of course we were fighting for an Allied victory, and if in the end the sake of the English, the leading partner, was to be forwarded only by sacrificing the Arabs on the field of battle, then it would have to be done unhesitatingly: but it was hard to know just when it was the end and necessary: and in this case to cast the die and lose meant to have ruined Faisal's cause."[15]

If Allenby would not reach Haifa, Lawrence reasoned that instead of the major Arab attack that would trigger an uprising—an attack he knew Faisal's forces were not prepared to make—he could suggest a more modest plan, a guerrilla attack mounted by a swift-moving band of Bedouins that would not depend on recruiting and training an army like the one necessary for the attack on Aqaba. If the action were coordinated with Allenby it would increase the prestige of the Arab forces in the eyes of the British, and if the attack were successful, it would also impress the Turks. The latter's respect or fear of an Arab army would greatly aid in organizing an eventual uprising, and in recruiting for the Arab army.

But the most Lawrence could offer by October was an attack on the main Turkish communications and supply hub at Deraa, at the junction of the rail route from Haifa with the Hejaz Railway running south from Damascus. Seizing Deraa would disrupt Turkish communications and logistics, leaving the Turkish forces defending Palestine without supplies and reinforcements. By hastening Allenby's victory in the south, it would perhaps let Allenby's forces advance to Haifa. And once coastal Palestine and Jerusalem were in British hands, the supply routes to Syria would be secure. Faisal's army, on the right flank of the British forces, could then sweep into Syria in time to meet an orchestrated Arab uprising against the Turks.

Allenby would not confirm how far his attack would go or when his forces would move into Palestine. As the Arabs waited, Lawrence cautiously watched the approach of the cold rains of winter, which would make the roads muddy and impassable. "The rain had now set in steadily," he wrote in late October, "and the whole country was sodden wet. It confirmed us that Allenby had failed in his weather and that there could be no great advance to Haifa this year."[16]

The weather was an excuse; he also knew that Faisal's forces were not capable of an attack on Deraa. The core of irregular camel-mounted troops would need to be augmented by recruits from the local tribes, as they had done for the attack on Aqaba, but there was no great warrior leader like Auda abu Tayi in this, the Hauran country, the local tribes that far north were not as sympathetic to Hussein of Mecca and his sons, and while proud of their prowess as warriors, they weren't willing to join an attack unless they could be sure of the spoils. Lawrence abandoned the idea of an attack on Deraa and instead chose as his target the Yarmuk Bridge, where the railway from Haifa crossed the Jordan depression on its route toward Deraa and on to Damascus. At Yarmuk the railway ran over a series of large steel spans. The remote bridges had been difficult to build, and destroying even a single span would isolate the Turkish forces in Palestine, leaving them without supplies, reinforcements, and communication—and vulnerable to Allenby's planned attack. Faisal and the Arab army would reap their reward later, when they could rely on British supply routes through Palestine.

The Yarmuk Bridge was a good strategic target, but the tactics were complex. Lawrence's forces would have to ride 320 miles from Aqaba, a distance that lulled the Turks into leaving the bridges lightly guarded. His plan was to attack the bridges from the north through uninhabited country, a tactic modeled after the successful attack on Aqaba. Allenby welcomed the plan and asked that the bridges be blown up on November 5, or within a few days after that date, to coordinate with his own plans for the advance to Jaffa and Jerusalem.

On October 24, Lawrence and his small expedition of camel-mounted troops left Aqaba with Sherif Ali ibn al-Hussein of the Harith as their nominal Arab leader. They were also joined by experienced Indian machine-gunners, an Aqaba-based sapper officer, George Lloyd from British intelligence in Cairo, and Emir Abd al-Kader, an Algerian who controlled villages of Algerian exiles on the north side of the Yarmuk valley. Al-Kader had a reputation as a fanatic, and the Frenchman Brémond warned that he was in the pay of the Turks, but Lawrence was eager for local intelligence and the possibility of recruiting local support for the mission. He was also skeptical enough of French ambitions to instinctively ignore advice from Brémond.

On the long ride from Aqaba, Lawrence told George Lloyd about his ambitious plans. If the raid on the bridges was successful, if the British advanced quickly enough into Palestine, and if a rebellion could be unleashed in Syria from Damascus to the north and west, Lawrence told Lloyd, he hoped to "ride north [to] Tadmor [Palmyra,] stay and plan taking Aleppo—if successful send party out to Jerablus [Carchemish], march to Kalma, raise Antioch and have a go at Marmourique—if successful go on to Chak al Dere (bridge between Adana and Topra Kali) then come to Alexandretta."[17] The goal of these far-flung travels was to rally an expanded Arab rebellion that would wrest all of Syria, including disputed areas of southern Anatolia and the Mediterranean coast, into Faisal's dream of a new Arab nation. Lawrence's proposal was in flagrant defiance of the Sykes-Picot agreement and the promises Britain had made to France.

His immediate plan was to recruit a Howeitat escort in the open country east of the Hejaz Railway, but the Howeitat were not eager to join a mission that promised no looting. Lawrence rode on, expecting to meet up with volunteers from Abd al-Kader's villages near the Yarmuk valley, but as they approached the valley, Abd al-Kader disappeared. Lawrence feared that he had gone over to the Turks with the plans for the attack on the bridges. There was no way to know for sure, and attacking with limited forces if the Turks knew their plans would be a suicide mission.

The only promising alternative was to attack a lone span at Ell al-Shehab, far enough from the original target to avoid the consequences of Abd al-Kader's treason. Ell al-Shehab was a difficult ride, and Lawrence's raiding party did not reach the span until November 7, two days after Allenby's target date. As the demolition party crept toward the bridges in the darkness, someone dropped a rifle. Turkish guards on the bridges heard the noise and started firing. Fearing that a bullet would set off the explosives, the tribesmen with Lawrence and his sapper threw the package into the ravine below. Lawrence ordered his troops to beat a hasty retreat.

Only enough explosives survived for an attack on a train. Lawrence chose a spot on the line between Deraa and Amman. A disruption on that line would not affect supplies to Palestine, but it might at least salvage Arab morale and provide some looting to satisfy the troops. They managed to derail a train, and to damage two locomotives beyond repair, but the Turks successfully attacked the raiding party, and the Arab troops scattered on their camels. Lawrence rode back to the Arab camp at Azrek, two hundred miles northeast of Aqaba and far from Palestine, knowing that the Turks would easily repair the damaged track. He and the Arab army had not been part of the great advance into Palestine.

~

Thanks in large measure to the intelligence that the NILI group had provided, Allenby's long-delayed advance reached the Gaza-Beersheba line quickly. The British were surprised at the ease of their initial advance, but despite extensive propaganda efforts by the British, including leaflets dropped from aircraft, months of planted rumors about the scale of the massed British forces, and growing Turkish skepticism about Djemal Pasha's repeated claims of the invincibility of his own army, the Turks surprised the civilian population, the British, and their own ranks by mounting an orderly retreat and formed new defensive positions protecting Jerusalem. Instead of pursuing the Turks, the British forces paused at Beersheba and regrouped while they brought up reserves, additional supplies, pipes, and pumping equipment, and began drilling wells in the areas where Aaron Aaronsohn had told them to expect water.

While the British and Turkish forces prepared for the battle for Jerusalem, Faisal's forces regrouped at Azrak, two hundred miles northeast of Aqaba and due east of Amman. It was a relatively comfortable winter camp, but far from Palestine, and without the challenge of raiding missions and the promise of loot, the troops grew lazy. Faisal and Sherif Ali ibn al-Hussein received visitors, cementing their relationships with the local tribes, but Lawrence was bored. "I drew myself again into the present," he wrote, "and forced my mind to say that it must profit by this wintry weather in which no man could fight, to explore the country lying about the junction at

Deraa of the three railways." He got Sheikh Talal, from a village near Damascus, to take him on a tour of the Hauran country. Talal had been declared an outlaw by the Turks, and the price on his head increased his appeal to Lawrence: "He rode up to us with six followers, all splendidly mounted, himself the most dashing figure of a man in the height of Hauran fashion. His sheepskin coat was of the finest Angora obtainable, covered in green broadcloth, ornamented with silk patches, and designs in brown braid. His other clothes were silk, and his high boots, his silver saddle, his sword, his dagger, and his rifle, matched his reputation."[18]

As he and Talal rode, Lawrence contemplated a raid on Deraa, imagining plans and operations for "the next time when we would bring men and money and guns with us, and start the general rising which must end in inevitable victory."[19] Talal was cautious enough not to venture into Deraa, but Lawrence could not resist a quick survey of the fortifications and military installations. Arranging to meet up with Talal later, Lawrence walked into the city. He was so accustomed to his Arab attire and had spent so much time among the local peasantry that he was confident he wouldn't be noticed. He and "an insignificant peasant, old enough to be my father, and respectable" walked through the muddy streets to the railway station and the airport. German Albatross aircraft were parked in the sheds, and a man in one shed struck up a conversation, asking Lawrence about his village and whether there was much "government" there. Lawrence assumed that the man was about to desert and looking for an offer of refuge.

Lawrence shook off the man and started to walk away when he heard shouts in Turkish. He continued to walk, ignoring the shouts, until a Turkish sergeant took him roughly by the arm and said, "The Bey wants you." Lawrence didn't fight or flee, but went with the sergeant into a military compound, where he was questioned by a Turkish officer. Lawrence gave his name as Ahmed ibn Bagr, and said he was a Circassian from Kuneitra.

"A deserter?" the officer asked.

"But we Circassian have no military service."

The officer, who hadn't even looked at Lawrence until then, stared at him. "You are a liar," he said. He told the sergeant to keep Lawrence until the bey sent for him.

Lawrence was locked up in a guardroom for the rest of the day, fed, told to wash himself carefully, and that he might be released the next day if he "fulfilled all the Bey's pleasure" that evening. After dark he was taken to a two-storied detached house, and led upstairs to the bey's bedroom.

Lawrence wrote several versions of what happened afterward, and critics over the years have questioned the authenticity of each version. Some have argued that nothing at all happened, that the stories in different versions of *Seven Pillars of Wisdom* and the mentions of the incident in letters were all dramatic inventions, even that Lawrence never went to Deraa at all.[20] What seems likely—at least from Lawrence's subsequent attitudes and actions—is that Lawrence was fondled and ultimately raped by the bey, beaten with a whip with many men watching, and finally kicked and shoved into a guardhouse, where he suffered further indignities and brutalities.

He seems also to have been recognized by the bey, which may have been the impetus for the beatings, and perhaps for the sexual humiliations. In *Seven Pillars of Wisdom* Lawrence does not admit that he was recognized, but in a private letter to a fellow officer he wrote that he was "identified by Hajim Bey, the governor, by virtue of Abd el Kadir's description of me. . . . Hajim was an ardent paederast and took a fancy to me. So he kept me under guard till night, and then tried to have me."[21] Lawrence's reluctance to admit that he was recognized may stem from his sense of responsibility for the failure of the Yarmuk Bridge attack, which was in large measure due to his misplaced trust in Abd al-Kader.

For a man who had lived as a sexual ascetic, rigorously avoiding intimate physical contact with men or women, the night in Deraa was a devastating experience. Lawrence was aware of the homosexual encounters between some Arab soldiers, and excused them as necessary relief. He had long derived satisfaction from his own lack of needs; in college he would go without food or water or sleep, and on the long camel treks he would prove his own physical strength and willpower by a comparable asceticism. The willpower to resist, and the self-image he had built upon that sense of personal control, was shattered that night. "I was feeling very ill," he wrote, "as though some part of me had gone dead that night in Deraa, leaving me maimed, imperfect, only half-myself. It could not have been the defilement, for no one ever held the body in less honour than I did myself: probably it had been the breaking of the spirit by that frenzied nerve-shattering pain which had degraded me to beast-level when it made me grovel to it; and which had journeyed with me since, a fascination and terror and morbid desire, lascivious and vicious perhaps, but like the striving of a moth towards its flame."[22]

After the rape and beatings he woke up in an empty wood-and-mud lean-to room, piled with quilts. An Armenian dresser washed and bandaged him. When the soldiers left, one whispered in a Druze accent that the door to the adjoining room was open. Lawrence explored, found a suit of shoddy clothes, and managed to escape before dawn. On the way out of town, before he found his way back to Azrak and the camp of the Arab army, he discovered a "hidden approach to Deraa for our future raiding party." He stayed in Azrak only a few days before riding on to Aqaba. Lawrence did not talk about the incident at Deraa, but as soon as he returned to Aqaba he recruited a personal bodyguard who accompanied him for the rest of the war.

Another airplane was sent to bring Lawrence from Aqaba to the advanced British headquarters at Wadi Gaza. There he learned of the British victories at Beersheba and Gaza, and the later battles on the Philistine plain and the Judean hills that had brought the British forces within sight of Jerusalem. He expected criticism of his failure at the Yarmuk Bridge, but Allenby "was so full of victories that my short statement that I had failed to carry a Yarmuk bridge was accepted as sufficient, and the rest of my failure could remain concealed." He was still with Allenby when the unexpected news arrived that the Turks had pulled out of Jerusalem during the night, and that civilian officials had approached the British lines searching for someone to accept the surrender of the city.

One week later, on December 11, 1917, Allenby made his ceremonial entry into the old city of Jerusalem through the Jaffa Gate. In poignant contrast to centuries of conquerors, including the German kaiser, Allenby entered the city on foot. There was no formal parade, but airplanes circled overhead, and Allenby's solemn entrance was accompanied by machine-gun and antiaircraft fire. Lawrence got there just in time, dressed in the borrowed uniform of a British major with red collar tabs and a brass hat insignia.[23] As he watched Allenby enter the city, Lawrence reflected that only a few days before he had stood before Hajim Bey, listening to his hateful words and anticipating his terrifying actions.

"Seldom did we pay so sharply and so soon for our fears," Lawrence wrote. "We would have been by now, not in Jerusalem, but in Haifa, or Damascus, or Aleppo, had I not shrunk in October from the danger of a general rising against the Turks. By my failure I had fettered the unknowing English, and dishonoured the unknowing Arabs, in a way only to be repaired by our triumphal entry into a liberated Damascus. The ceremony of the Jaffa Gate gave me a new determination."[24]

16

Sarah Alone

To S.A.
I loved you, so I drew these tides of men into my hands
and wrote my will across the sky in stars
To gain you freedom, the seven-pillared worthy house,
that your eyes might be shining for me
When I came.
—T. E. Lawrence[1]

Aaron Aaronsohn arrived in Paris on September 21 and immediately sought out his old friend and mentor Baron Rothschild to ask him for open, public support of NILI and its efforts. The baron, as always, was cautious and circumspect, wary of any Jewish alliances with non-Jewish entities and reluctant to make any statement that would bring his loyalties to France under question. He told Aaronsohn that he generally sided with the Zionist leadership, but that he would not make a public statement. Aaronsohn, usually infuriated by those who hid behind caution, was tolerant of what he saw as his mentor's idiosyncrasies. "He feels as we do," Aaronsohn wrote, "that if Great Britain would rule over our land, we could obtain great things."

He also met William Yale in Paris. Yale, an American petroleum engineer, had worked for Standard Oil in the Middle East as an explorer and then as their resident agent in Jerusalem from 1915 to 1917. The U.S. State Department was impressed by a report Yale had written, no doubt finding his power-politics language a relief from President Wilson's vague idealism, and sent him to Cairo as a special duty representative with free reign to investigate the situation in the Middle East. Yale was an anti-Zionist—his interest in oil led him to support the Arabs, who he assumed would inherit the petroleum-producing areas of Mesopotamia and northeast Syria. He was also adept at soliciting and collecting gossip. In Cairo Yale had heard from Miss Annie Landau, the former head of the Evalina de Rothschild School in Palestine and an outspoken anti-Zionist, that Aaron Aaronsohn was an ignorant, uncultured upstart, a selfish and unscrupulous opportunist who under the cloak of Zionism was working to "feather his own nest." She claimed that even the discovery of wild wheat was "stolen" from "a poor Alsatian Christian woman."[2]

Mark Sykes was also in Paris. He knew Weizmann had a good working relationship with the Foreign Office, and that Aaronsohn had connections and experience with the War Office; he was eager to get them to work together. Aaronsohn and Weizmann had already tangled on issues, and Sykes told Aaronsohn that one of his letters to Weizmann, about the dispute with Gluskin, had been "like a thorn in the latter's eye." He begged Aaronsohn to make peace with the London Zionists. Aaronsohn answered that he was not going to London to quarrel, "only to tell them their mistakes and to show them the way to do things properly."[3] Aaronsohn, who considered political relationships as absolute and as dependent on total candor as science, no doubt did not consider his comment provocative.

From Paris he traveled on to London, arriving on October 1. He met with Chaim Weizmann that night, reporting on all that NILI had accomplished in supplying intelligence for the British advance into Palestine. They had a friendly talk, and Weizmann promised to send a telegram congratulating the members of NILI on their successful operations. Neither man was observant, and they seemed to have paid no attention to the fact that it was the first day of the holiday of Sukkoth, when Jews eat outdoors in booths in memory of the wandering of the Israelites in the desert after the exodus from Egypt.

~

Sarah Aaronsohn and Josef Lishinsky had come into Zichron that day to be with Sarah's father for the holiday. Sarah had known that it would not be long before the Turks closed in on Zichron, but it was still a surprise when Turkish police and soldiers, under the personal command of Hassan Bey, the kaimakam of Haifa, surrounded the village. The bey, notorious for his ferocity toward the Jews, ordered his troops to search from door to door to find Josef Lishinsky or Joseph Tuvin, the name he had used in his false passport. Na'aman Belkind had identified him as the head of the spy ring in his confession to the Turkish interrogators.

Sarah had already sent the young men who worked with NILI off to hide in the vineyards outside the village. She gave Lishinsky a gun, and waited at the gate of the Aaronsohn house with her father and her brother Zvi. The Turkish soldiers arrested the three of them, took them to an empty house, and began to beat Sarah's father, tying his hands and feet to a rifle so they could beat the soles of his feet in an impromptu bastinado, and demanding that he tell them the whereabouts of Josef Lishinsky. Ephraim cried out with the blows, and Sarah berated the soldiers for attacking an old man of seventy. As the bastinado went on, Ephraim began to recite the Sh'ma, the central prayer of his faith: "Hear O'Israel, the Lord our God, the Lord is One." As an observant Jew he knew that it was a blessing to die with the words of the Sh'ma on his lips.

Sarah urged her father to be strong, to hold out. She reminded him that he had always been an honest man, that their ancestors had also been tortured by the Romans and had never given in.

"You warn me?" he said, angrily. Ephraim told the Turks nothing.

The next day the soldiers returned and tied Sarah's hands to the gatepost in front of the house. The soldiers, unaccustomed to beating a woman, held back, but Hassan Bey goaded them on, insisting that they beat her until she revealed where Lishinsky and the other spies were hiding, what information she had told the enemy, and the whereabouts of Avshalom Feinberg. As the blows fell on her Sarah cursed the soldiers and the bey. "You are murderers!" she shouted. "Bloodthirsty wild beasts, cowards! And me, alone, a weak woman who stood up to protect my people so that you will not do to us what you have done to the Armenians. . . . Me, alone, with my own hands I dug your grave. . . . You are too late! You will not succeed. . . . For nothing you torture me. For nothing you torment me. For nothing will you torment innocents. . . . You are lost! The saviors are coming. . . . I have saved my people, I have revenged the blood of the Armenians, curses will hunt you to the end of time."[4] The soldiers beat her until she collapsed. When they untied her hands, she fell to the ground, unconscious.

Hillel Yaffe, the village physician, called at the Aaronsohns' that evening and saw Ephraim, who had been badly beaten, and the whip marks on Sarah's limbs and body. When Yaffe protested Sarah's torture to the kaimakam, he was told that the officer responsible had already been punished. Hassan Bey then transferred those he had arrested to another house and told Dr. Yaffe that he would have his soldiers use the bastinado on Ephraim Aaronsohn and the other prisoners until they revealed where Lishinsky and the other members of the spying ring were hiding.

True to his word, the next day the kaimakam had his soldiers beat the arrested men in public. Their screams could be heard throughout the village. Some of the older men called out the names of their sons or nephews, begging that they come out of hiding and end the excruciating tortures. Reuven Schwartz, Sarah's lifelong friend who worked at the research station, heard his father's screams from the vineyard where he had been hiding, came into the village, and surrendered. The Turks promptly beat him, demanding that he name his colleagues and reveal their hiding place.

Zichron was a small village: neighbors knew every victim of the tortures, could recognize every voice in the agonized screams for mercy. Many houses closed their doors and blinds, fearing that being on the street or having an open shutter was an invitation to the Turkish police and soldiers. For those who had long opposed NILI's activities, it was a time to prove their loyalty to the Turks and to settle old debts. As the Turks rounded up more men for the bastinado, four hysterical viragos ran through the streets, loudly rejoicing as each new victim was put under the Turkish whips, even falling upon the arrested men with blows and shouted abuse. They ripped the coat off Nisan Rutman, a NILI collaborator from Hadera, as he was dragged through the streets,[5] perhaps convinced that their actions would persuade the local governor of their own husbands' loyalty. In Zichron, people recognized the deep social chasms at the base of the viragos' motives: Rutman's girlfriend had also worked with the NILI group and had a tainted reputation. The viragos would leave nothing unsettled.

On Thursday, October 4—still Sukkoth, when families should have been dining peacefully in their booths outside—the kaimakam called a meeting of the Zichron Committee to announce that he knew the spy ring was in Zichron, that he had information that Sarah Aaronsohn had traveled around the countryside with Josef Lishinsky, and that the interrogations would not stop until he was told where Lishinsky was hiding. He swore that he would punish a hundred innocent people if he had to: if the town did not produce Lishinsky he would level the houses of the settlement and leave no trace of the village. A few villagers who had been arrested had avoided the bastinado by discretely offering gold jewelry or coins to the Turkish guards. Sarah had given the Zichron Committee £500 from the last shipment of gold that arrived on the *Managem,* but no one on the committee suggested using the emergency funds as baksheesh to secure a modicum of mercy for Sarah and the others under interrogation.

On Friday and again on Saturday Sarah was tortured. The interrogators were methodical and experienced. They knew which parts of the body were sensitive to pain and when to pause the beatings and begin anew to multiply the subject's anxiety. When they were not whipping her or pulling her fingernails with pincers or burning her palms, they beat her father and her younger brother Zvi, letting her hear their screams of pain. Through it all she taunted the soldiers, shouting that she would never tell them anything, that if they thought she was weak because she was a woman, they were wrong. She told them that only she had anything to do with the spying, that everyone else was innocent. She swore she would never tell them anything. A Turkish general, brought to assist in the questioning, was impressed by her defiance. "She is worth a hundred men!" he said.[6]

After three days of systematic tortures even the Turks seemed to accept that their methods had failed, at least temporarily. Sarah heard carts brought up to take those who had been tortured to Nazareth, where the chief medical officer of the Turkish Fourth Army, Hassan Bek, was famed for the effectiveness of his interrogation procedures. By then Sarah's body was a mass of welts and lacerations; the palms of her hands were burned; her hair and some of her fingernails had been pulled out. Through the shuttered windows and closed doors the villagers had heard Sarah's semidelirious cries of pain. She had called out for her mother. But she had told the interrogators nothing about Lishinsky, about NILI, or about the information they had provided to British intelligence.

When Sarah realized that she would be taken to Nazareth for more interrogation, she asked if she could go home to change her blood-soaked clothing for the journey. A Turkish officer agreed. Most of the windows of the town were still shuttered, but as the screams of the tortures ceased, people opened their windows to see what had happened. They watched as Sarah, beaten and bloody, was led down Founder's Street with a rope around her neck like a dog on a leash. Outside Aaron's house she glared at the guard, who had assumed he would follow her into the house. He undid the rope and let her into the house alone.

She had held out for three days from sheer defiance. She knew they would use even more persuasive tortures in Nazareth or Damascus.

How much longer could she resist the beatings? Alone in the house, she wrote out detailed instructions for the care of the families who were dependent on NILI and the research station. Some had worked as spies, others had been loyal agricultural laborers, most had been dependent on the research station for years. In the midst of the war there was nowhere else they could go. She named none of them, for their own protection, but wrote that they were to be given 30 francs per month if the Turks allowed them to continue working at the station where they could live off the wheat and barley crops, 50 francs per month if they were not allowed to work. She added a final instruction for Lishinsky: "Tell him from Sarah: Never give yourself up. Kill yourself, but don't give yourself up. They are coming. I cannot write any more."[7] She hid the note in the pocket of her skirt.

The pistol that Aaron had sent her from Egypt for protection was hidden in a compartment in the double wall next to the front door of the house. She took the pistol with her into the bathroom near the rear of the house. A few moments later the guard waiting outside the front door heard a shot.

Dr. Yaffe found Sarah unconscious on the floor of the bathroom. Her pulse was slow, and blood was gushing from her mouth. After an injection of caffeine, she regained consciousness, recognized him, and pleaded: "I beg you to kill me. I cannot live and suffer. I cannot." Yaffe lifted her to the bed in the room next door to examine her. She had shot herself in the mouth. The bullet had passed through her tongue and lodged in her spine. Her arms and legs were paralyzed. She was in excruciating pain.[8]

As Sarah lay there Yaffe heard the Turkish carts rumbling off toward Nazareth with the men who had been arrested. Outside, a crier announced that the kaimakam had put a price of £100 in gold on Lishinsky's head, that fourteen elders of Zichron would be held as hostages until Lishinsky surrendered, and that the village had forty-eight hours to produce him. That night the men of Zichron gathered in the synagogue. Before the open ark with its Torah scrolls—a symbol of the seriousness of their oath—they swore to hand over Lishinsky to spare the village. There was no one left to argue the other side of the issue.

Dr. Yaffe told the kaimakam that he would not treat Sarah unless the Turks promised that they would not torture her anymore, and said that she should be taken to Jerusalem for an operation. The kaimakam promised that she would not be harmed if she recovered, and said that there were Turkish surgeons available so there was no need to move her. As they spoke, men in the village—not Turks, but Jews—went from door to door searching for Lishinsky.

Sarah's brother Zvi's wife and daughter stayed with her. The young girl wept when she saw her aunt's condition and obvious pain. "Don't cry," Sarah told her. "There is nothing to cry about. It will be all right." She quietly told her niece about the letter in the pocket of her skirt.

It seemed impossible that Sarah could survive. Her temperature raged from infections of her wounds. She pleaded to die, begged for poison. On Sunday evening Yaffe gave her an injection of morphine. Outside the house, the village was in a panic. The forty-eight hours to hand over Lishinsky was ticking down. No one knew what the kaimakam would do.

On Monday and Tuesday, while the villagers awaited their fate, Sarah drifted in and out of consciousness. She cried out that she feared going mad. On Tuesday evening her relatives gathered to say good-bye. She asked them to look after her father, one of the hostages held by the Turks. He had never committed any crime, she said. She begged them to get him freed.

Sarah Aaronsohn died the next morning, on Simhat Torah, the day when the old men of the congregation would dance with the Torahs to celebrate reaching the end of the cycle of reading the law and beginning anew. She had told the Turks nothing.

Following Jewish tradition, she was buried without delay, her shroud a mosquito net from the house. The entire village joined the procession to the Zichron cemetery, and stood under the overcast sky while the grave was dug. Sarah was buried beside her mother. A light rain began to fall after the brief ceremony at the grave. For a day the splits and tensions in Zichron had abated.

Sarah Aaronsohn was twenty-seven years old.

~

In the commotion when the Turks first arrived in Zichron, Josef Lishinsky escaped from the storage room under Aaron Aaronsohn's house by the secret entrance on the hillside behind the house and disappeared into the countryside. He first hid at Bet Shlomo, a tiny Jewish settlement just north of Zichron. When the search widened he dressed in a keffiya and jalabiya, and hid in caves in the mountains above the Arab village of Faradis for three days, until hunger drove him back to the roads. He took an Arab cart to Karkur, a kibbutz behind the Haifa highway near Hadera. The fiancée of Liova Schneersohn's brother Mendel lived there, and Lishinsky begged her and her father for food and a cart or horse, alternately offering gold and threatening them with the pistol Sarah had given him. The farmers explained that they had nothing; everything at the kibbutz was owned communally, and only the kibbutz could give anything away. When others in the kibbutz learned Lishinsky's identity, they turned him away.

He hid in the fields until a horse-drawn diligence appeared on the road. He recognized two of the passengers as members of Ha-Shomer from the Galilee. They stopped, and despite Lishinsky's long-standing disputes with Ha-Shomer, gave him a ride to Tel Adashim, at the foot of the Nazareth Mountains, where the diligence was unloaded. He did not realize that it was carrying the gold that had been brought to Athlit on the *Managem*. The gold had found its way from the relief committee to Petah Tikva, the administrative center for the Jewish community after the expulsions of the Jews from Haifa and Jaffa. The Turkish dragnet for spies and the chaos of the retreating Turkish armies from Gaza and Beersheba had made even Petah Tikva unsafe, so the gold was being smuggled north.

While Lishinsky was in Tel Adashim, a few miles away in Nazareth the hostages from Zichron were being held in a former French convent. Hassan Bek, the physician notorious for his interrogations, alternated torturing and questioning the hostages from midnight to dawn, letting those in the adjacent common cell hear their screams.

He had seventy-year-old Ephraim Aaronsohn beaten. When Hassan Bek asked him Lishinsky's whereabouts, Ephraim recited the Sh'ma. So soon after the holiday of Yom Kippur, he probably thought of the story of Rabbi Akiva in that day's service, who was so secure in his faith that as the Romans tortured him he rejoiced because he could die reciting the Sh'ma. Ephraim's defiance seemed to inspire the other hostages. Sarah's friend Reuven Schwartz was tortured seven nights in a row, until he could no longer walk unassisted. When he was found hanged in the cell early one morning, the guards said it was a suicide. They kicked the body when Reuven's father tried to say kaddish for his son.

At Tel Adashim the Ha-Shomer guards debated what to do with Lishinsky. He had a price on his head, both Turks and Jews were hunting for him, and Ha-Shomer had long thought him a loose cannon and a dangerous rebel against their organization. Guarding him so close to the hidden gold cache was risky. Rumors spread that Lishinsky was hidden there, and a delegation from Zichron arrived to demand that he be surrendered to the Turks. The Ha-Shomer guards refused. They were afraid to be caught with him, but also afraid to surrender him to the Turks, who were already suspicious that Ha-Shomer was smuggling guns and gold and might follow up by arresting the guards or searching for the hidden gold. Someone suggested killing Lishinsky and turning his body over to the Turks, but no one was willing to murder the exhausted, emaciated fugitive. Despite his record of rebellion against Ha-Shomer discipline, the guards admired his bravery and defiance of the Turks. They decided to help hide him in the extreme north of Palestine, close to his hometown, where he had friends among the Druze.

Lishinsky and a guard rode north on horses. When the news of his escape reached Zichron a delegation from the village rode north to try to capture or kill him. They made an arrangement with his guard, but a firefight broke out. Lishinsky was wounded in the shoulder and escaped into the mountains. In Metulla, his shoulder bandaged in a handkerchief Sarah had given him, he went to the house of relatives, only to discover that the Ha-Shomer were waiting for him. He fled south, hiding in stables and outhouses, sleeping during the daytime, traveling at night, disguising himself as an old lady and later as a Bedouin. He was too late to meet up with the British steamer scheduled to arrive at Athlit on October 12, but he walked, rode, and hitched cart rides on to Petah Tikva, and then south to Rishon le Zion. On October 20 an Arab boy spotted him with a camel. The Arabs captured him, took his money, and turned him over to the Turkish authorities in Ramallah. The pasha of Jerusalem and the kaimakam of Jaffa came south to identify him, and had him taken to Jerusalem for questioning.

He readily admitted that he was Josef Lishinsky, but would confess nothing else, even when confronted with information from Na'aman Belkind's confession. He was finally taken to Damascus by train, and then by heavily guarded cart from the railway station to the Han al-Basha, a caravansaray that had been converted to a prison. There he and Na'aman Belkind were incarcerated in private cells. The other men in the prison, including Sarah's brother Zvi and a dozen others who had worked for NILI, were held in a common cell with deserters and criminals.

Lishinsky was interrogated repeatedly, and each time gave misinformation or mocked his interrogators. When they asked how he had brought money into the country, he asked how it was possible that Britain, trying to win a war of starvation against Palestine, would bring in money. Djemal Pasha promised amnesty to any prisoner who would provide information about Lishinsky. No one did. The unheated prison was bitterly cold, and the prisoners were without beds or blankets and on minimal food rations. Lishinsky and Na'aman Belkind soon looked like caged animals.

~

On October 7, only days after Aaron arrived in London, Alex Aaronsohn in Cairo got a message from Aaron saying that the spying operations should stop and the NILI people should be taken out of Palestine, but that if possible they should not cut the connection until the last minute. Alex campaigned aggressively at British GHQ for a rescue mission to Athlit, but the intelligence officers at EMSIB pointed out that with the British forces advancing on the Gaza-Beersheba line, the Turks were on alert everywhere in Palestine, and a mission before the dark of the moon would endanger the ship and the entire intelligence network in Palestine. After a year of Aaron's demands, Edmonds and Captain Smith at EMSIB were probably less than enthusiastic to be confronted with renewed demands from a younger Aaronsohn. When the ship finally sailed, Alex persuaded the EMSIB staffers to provide £5,000 for baksheesh in Palestine and extra personnel and weapons on the *Managem* in addition to the Lewis gun on the stern and Captain Weldon's rifle and revolver.

They had had no direct communications from Zichron for weeks when the *Managem* steamed past Athlit on October 12. A lookout saw what appeared to be a signal from the watchtower on Ephraim Aaronsohn's vineyard, and later that night a launch brought Liova Schneersohn and Alex Aaronsohn ashore. They found no one waiting for them at the beach next to the ruins of the crusader castle, or on the path leading to the research station, and when they heard a shot from the direction of the highway they decided not to risk going to the research station. For an hour they hid in a field until Schneersohn signaled the ship to pick them up again. Alex had brought with him a telegram for NILI from Chaim Weizmann:

> WE ARE DOING OUR BEST TO MAKE SURE THAT PALESTINE [WILL BE] JEWISH UNDER BRITISH PROTECTION. YOUR HEROIC STAND ENCOURAGES OUR STRENUOUS EFFORTS. OUR HOPES ARE GREAT. BE STRONG AND OF GOOD COURAGE UNTIL THE REDEMPTION OF ISRAEL.[9]

It wasn't until the fall of Beersheba, at the end of the month, that Alexander Aaronsohn and Liova Schneersohn learned from independent reports gathered by British intelligence that no one from NILI was left in Zichron to receive the message.

~

The final court date for Josef Lishinsky and the other prisoners in Damascus was December 1, 1917. The judges had been bribed by people outside NILI to spare some of the prisoners, including Zvi Aaronsohn, but those Lishinsky had protected, including local Zionist leaders who had access to the relief funds, did nothing to secure his release. In the courtroom Na'aman Belkind said he had already confessed everything he knew and deserved to be released. Lishinsky was defiant, telling the judges that he was guilty of no crime. Both were sentenced to be hanged. The others were sentenced to jail terms of six months to two years.

On Friday, December 14, while the prisoners were lighting makeshift Hanukkah candles, they heard that Belkind and Lishinsky would be hanged that Sunday. They deliberately avoided telling the condemned men that the date had been set, but early Sunday morning the prisoners were awakened by the voice of Lishinsky shouting, "Goodbye Jews, I am going to die!" A large crowd had gathered outside for the execution, and as the two men were led up the steps of the gibbet, dressed in suits and ties, Lishinsky told Belkind that they must be strong, die as heroes, and not give the enemy the pleasure of their deaths.

On the gallows a sign listed Lishinsky's crimes, and a crier announced, "This will be done to a person who is a traitor to his country!" Lishinsky was allowed a last word. "We are not traitors," he said in Arabic. "To betray there must be love. . . . We NILI members dig a grave for the Ottoman Empire. We helped the British army, which is here to relieve Palestine and give it to us. While you are busy hanging people, the British are moving ahead, taking Jerusalem with no battle. And your army runs away, like cowards. Despicable Turkey was never our homeland. The day I am being hanged, I curse you forever!" An officer ordered a bugler to blow his trumpet to drown out the translation of Lishinsky's speech into Turkish.

After they were hanged, the crowd was so agitated that the soldiers had to use clubs to extricate the truck carrying their bodies. The rest of the prisoners were taken by train to Constantinople, with no food or blankets; forty out of one hundred died on the journey.[10]

It had been a week since General Allenby and the British forces entered Jerusalem.

~

Before Aaron Aaronsohn arrived in London, General Clayton, the head of British intelligence in Egypt and a strong supporter of the Arabs, wrote that it would be unwise for the Cabinet to make any statement about the Zionist plans or claims in Palestine, because the Arabs were already confused about British plans. Clayton, who tended to see Jews behind every conspiracy, including the rise of the Young Turks in the Ottoman Empire, also wrote directly to Mark Sykes that it would be best to keep Aaronsohn and the Jews in play without any direct declaration of British intentions.[11] Clayton wasn't the only one in Britain with fears of the Jews that ranged from conspiracy theories to claims that the "Jewish money interests" were behind the war. Even in 1917 there were some in Britain who thought the Jews were secretly negotiating support for Germany.

Clayton's memo was in part a response to a strong memo Sykes had written to the War Cabinet about agricultural development in Palestine, citing the research station at Athlit and the agricultural development at Zichron and Petah Tikva as examples of the productivity possible with the agricultural techniques Aaronsohn had developed in Palestine. The agricultural successes of the Jewish communities, Sykes argued, were the key to a substantial expansion of Jewish immigration and proved the viability of a Jewish homeland in Palestine. For Sykes, Zionism was part of a broader dream of liberating the "downtrodden people of the world." Although the Arab Bureau thought of Sykes as an amateur and a bungler, his connections in Whitehall, his travels in the Middle East, his familiarity with the many issues he presented at the War and Foreign offices, and the sense that he was a counterweight to the military and foreign affairs bureaucracies meant that his memoranda sometimes got attention at the highest levels of the Cabinet.

The Zionist Federation was officially neutral during the war, but Zionism as an idea had a long history in Britain. The nineteenth-century evangelical Christian movement believed that the Second Coming was only possible after the gathering of the Jews in Zion, and even many non-evangelicals in Britain reacted to the "Jewish question," the late-nineteenth- and early-twentieth-century anti-Semitism and pogroms in Russia and Romania, by supporting the idea of a restoration of the Jews to their own land. Two years after Chaim Weizmann came to Britain in 1906 he met Arthur James Balfour, the future foreign secretary. Balfour was working on the idea of settling Jews in Africa and asked Weizmann why the Zionists wanted Jerusalem instead of the wide-open spaces of Uganda.

"Mr. Balfour," Weizmann said, "supposing I were to offer you Paris instead of London, would you take it?"

Balfour answered, "But Dr. Weizmann we have London."

"That is true," Weizmann said. "But we had Jerusalem when London was a marsh."

"Are there many Jews who think like you?" Balfour asked.

Weizmann answered, "I believe I speak the mind of millions of Jews whom you will never see and who cannot speak for themselves."

"If that is so," Balfour said, "you will one day be a force."[12]

Balfour's prediction proved true. By 1917 Weizmann had been sufficiently relentless in his campaigning for Zionism that many in the British government had long considered any debt for his gift of the process of synthesizing acetone repaid. Weizmann and his colleagues were skilled propagandists, and had many in Britain believing that the Jews of Russia wielded enormous influence with both the Kerensky government and the Bolsheviks, and that a British gesture of appeasement to them might keep Russia in the war, forcing Germany to continue fighting on two fronts. The United States had declared war on Germany and Austria in April and had broken off diplomatic relations with Turkey, and American doughboys were on their way to France. The London Zionists suggested that the wealth and influence of the American Jews might be marshaled to provide or encourage a significant war loan or gift if there were some British gesture of appeasement to the Jews.

There were also some who backed a declaration of support for the Jews as a counterweight to the commitments that had been made to the French and the Arabs in wartime agreements. In their secret promises to Sherif Hussein in the McMahon correspondence and in the later Sykes-Picot agreement with France, Britain had effectively sold the same horse twice. Adding a third contradictory commitment, to the Jews in Palestine, could have the effect of so confusing Britain's wartime agreements that it would provide a basis for Britain to renege or at least water down the earlier commitments.

Wingate had briefed Aaronsohn about the discussions of a commitment to the Jews before he left Cairo. Negotiations were well under way when he reached London on October 1.[13] Weizmann and Balfour, with input from Sykes and Edwin Samuel Montagu, the secretary of state for India and an anti-Zionist Jew, hammered out the simple declaration:

> His Majesty's Government view with favour the establishment in Palestine of a national home for the Jewish people, and will use their best endeavours to facilitate the achievement of this object, it being clearly understood that nothing shall be done which may prejudice the civil and religious rights of existing non-Jewish communities in Palestine, or the rights and political status enjoyed by Jews in any other country.

Little record remains of their deliberations,[14] but the final text incorporated some careful and deliberate choice of language. Favoring a "national home" instead of a "state" reflected Britain's own ambitions in Palestine and concerns about the ambitions of the Zionists. The prepositional phrase "in Palestine" was an effort to preclude reading the document as a commitment for the whole of Palestine at a time when the term "Palestine" was ill defined but was assumed by most to include Transjordan. And the promise not to "prejudice the civil and religious rights of existing non-Jewish communities in Palestine, or the rights and political status enjoyed by Jews in any other country" was incorporated into the document at Montagu's insistence lest the declaration unleash waves of anti-Semitism in Palestine and abroad. The final change before the document was signed was to substitute "Jewish people" for "Jewish race."

On October 31, after Balfour presented the declaration to the War Cabinet, Sykes ran out of the Cabinet Room waving a piece of paper. "Dr. Weizmann," he shouted, "it's a boy!" After lunch Weizmann and Aaronsohn were invited into the Cabinet Room to meet with the Cabinet and express their gratitude. Leo Amery, a member of the Cabinet Secretariat, wrote afterward: "Aaronsohn is a real Palestinian. . . . If all the Jews in their own country turn out as sturdy, frank-looking fellows as he, Zionism will certainly be justified."[15]

On November 2, the typed letter from Foreign Secretary Balfour was delivered to Lord Rothschild (Baron Walter Rothschild), in his capacity as a leader of the Jewish community in Britain. "I should be grateful if you would bring this declaration to the knowledge of the Zionist Federation" was the closest Balfour came to publicly acknowledging Weizmann. The Balfour Declaration, as it came to be known, was soon publicized among the allies, in Germany and Austria, and throughout Europe and America. Lloyd George recalled, "The actual timing of the declaration was determined by consideration of war policy. . . . The launching was due to propagandist reasons. . . . Public opinion in Russia and America played a great part, and we had every reason at that time to believe that in both countries the friendliness or hostility of the Jewish race might make a considerable difference."[16]

While the final formulation of the Balfour Declaration was being hammered out, Weizmann and Aaronsohn ate together at Cohen's Restaurant (jokingly called the Kosher Ritz) in Houndstooth. They argued: Weizmann respected Aaronsohn's knowledge of Palestine and his connections in the United States but had qualms about his ability to work with others in the Zionist movement. Aaronsohn thought Weizmann was trying to boycott him. Weizmann had sent the principal clauses of the declaration to Justice Brandeis well before it was issued, considered Brandeis's support crucial, and the Foreign Office recommended that Aaronsohn be sent as a liaison officer to the United States to publicize the declaration and rouse Zionist enthusiasm. Aaron was the obvious choice, because of his close friendship with Brandeis and his connections to influential American Jews, but Weizmann was reluctant, especially when Aaronsohn insisted that he was to have a free hand. Aaronsohn and Weizmann discussed a letter of instruction for the trip, based on a draft by Sykes. With characteristic Sykes enthusiasm, the draft specified that along with publicizing the Balfour Declaration and coordinating between American Zionism and the Zionist Federation in London, Aaronsohn was to work to consolidate an alliance of Zionist forces with the representatives of the Arabs and the Armenians. Weizmann, who could be charming when it suited his purposes, assured Aaronsohn that he had been wrong to think there was a plan to boycott him. "The old man is not a fool," Aaronsohn wrote in his diary, "—but I am not so naive either."

When Aaronsohn subsequently opened the final version of the letter of instruction, it included a clause specifying that in the United States he was to make no public speeches, give no interviews, and take no action of any kind except through Brandeis.[17] He exploded: "I became very angry—especially because of Weizmann's lack of frankness." Weizmann said that other leaders of the Zionist Federation had insisted on the limits. "Why did you not say so at the office?" Aaronsohn asked.

"Verily, every day brings me another proof of Weizmann's hypocrisy," he wrote. Sykes tried to soft-pedal the restrictions, saying that if he were going in Aaronsohn's place he would like the restrictions as a shield against reporters. Aaronsohn concluded that Weizmann wanted him to refuse to go. "I feel that he has an idea at the back of his head. He would like the trip to be postponed until next week. They will discuss the matter—they may send someone with me etc." He decided to foil their schemes by leaving the next day. "Weizmann did not seem to like this sudden decision," he wrote. "I am sure it interferes with his plans." As he left, he told Weizmann: "What I wanted above all was frankness—brutal frankness—no mysteries."[18]

When he boarded the *St. Paul* in Liverpool, bound for New York, Aaron Aaronsohn had still heard nothing about the fate of his sister Sarah, his father, his younger brother Zvi, Josef Lishinsky, and the rest of the members of NILI.

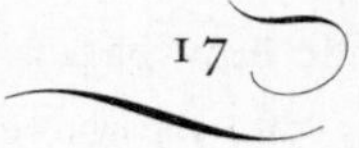

17

The Desert Meeting

There are no gods but God, and Jesus is his prophet.
—T. E. Lawrence[1]

Christ: *"What is the way, O Muhammad, to set our two nations, Syria and Lebanon, in unison?"*
Muhammad: *"Ask Moses to send them a party of his men."*
—*Al-Maarad* (Damascus newspaper)[2]

The North Atlantic was rough in late November, and the *St. Paul* was an old ship. The reading room was uncomfortable, the cramped cabins were closed "hermetically," there were no pretty women aboard as a distraction, and waves swept over the deck so Aaronsohn couldn't pace. "One really does not know where to stay or how to kill time," he complained to his diary. "The only thing left is to eat—but the food is so poor."[3] His one consolation was that the ship arrived in New York ahead of schedule, on December 2, 1917, letting him keep the appointments he had made for his first morning in New York.

America had changed. After years of resolute neutrality, the country had switched overnight to war footing. In short order Congress had enacted a Selective Service Act, an Espionage Act, a Trading with the Enemy Act, a War Revenue Act, the Smith-Lever Act—establishing control over food and fuel with Herbert Hoover in charge—a War Industries Board, a grain corporation that fixed the price of grains, and an act prohibiting the use of food products to make distilled beverages. The newspapers whipped up enough war fever to get German measles renamed Liberty measles, and the identification of German owners of many distilleries and breweries added to the congressional fervor for a constitutional amendment prohibiting the manufacture, sale, or transportation of intoxicating liquors. Even the Jewish leaders Aaronsohn had come to see were focused on the war and paid scant attention to the wild celebrations in Trotsky Square (the corner of Fifth Avenue and East One Hundredth Street) after the Jewish working class in New York elected a list of Socialist Party officials.

As soon as he disembarked he met his friend Judge Mack for lunch at the Harvard Club, then met with Jacob Schiff, another trustee of the research station. Later that day he went to the office of the Zionist Federation, where people were excited by the news of the Balfour Declaration. Someone there handed Aaronsohn a cable from Egypt. His brother Sam had arrived in Cairo, and relayed news from a prisoner who had been captured in Palestine—the first news Aaron had heard from his home in weeks. The cable reported that NILI members had been arrested in Palestine, including his father, Sarah, and Lishinsky: "After torture Sarah died bravely by her own hand," the shock of her death "killed father," and "Na'aman [Belkind] has been executed."

It would be months before Aaron would learn the details of Sarah's death, the extent of the roundup and prosecution of the NILI members and volunteers, or that his father had miraculously survived the Turkish purge. In his diary he wrote: "The sacrifice is accomplished. I knew that we still had to face the greatest misfortune. But it is one thing to fear it and another to know that all hope is lost. Poor father, poor Sarati. . . . Her loss is the most cruel."[4]

He had no time to mourn. He had been sent to the United States to meet with Brandeis and other influential American Jews because U.S. support of the Zionist efforts was crucial for the future of Palestine. Later on the day he got the telegram, he met with the distinguished labor lawyer and president of Temple Emanu-El in New York, Louis Marshall, another trustee of the research station. When Marshall talked about his son, Aaronsohn told him about Sarah and his father. Marshall said he could not understand the heroism of those who "had preferred certain death by remaining where they were—rather than to desert the cause—as they had the opportunity of doing."

Marshall was sympathetic to Zionism. He and Henrietta Szold may have viewed the dedication of the NILI volunteers and the personal sacrifice in Aaronsohn's own family as persuasive arguments for the course Aaronsohn had taken at the research station, and Aaronsohn was perhaps comforted by their recognition of Sarah's, Feinberg's, and his father's sacrifices. Henrietta Szold warned him that it might be a bad time to talk to some of the trustees, and that his relationship with Julius Rosenwald especially might be near the breaking point. He could anticipate that the trustees were all decent enough men to express sympathy on a personal level for his losses, but some would still see the spying activity and active support for the British victory as a betrayal of the charter of the research station and a misuse of the funds they had contributed.

Aaronsohn's meetings with most of the trustees went well. Even those who were equivocal about Zionism seemed to admire his tenacity, dedication, and long-term commitments to both Zionism and his agricultural research. The exception was Rosenwald, who was critical and harsh, calling Aaronsohn's long confessional letter his "Scroll of Fire"[5] and his activities a personal betrayal by a man in whom he had put extraordinary trust. Aaronsohn defiantly accused Rosenwald of assuming that everyone who talked to him only wanted his money, and told him that he would have to understand that Aaronsohn really did not want his money, only to save his soul. Strikingly, at the beginning of the first aliyah which had brought Aaron's parents to Palestine, the Mohilever rabbi gave almost the identical speech to Edmond Rothschild when he sought help and support to settle Jews in Palestine.[6] The rabbi had been successful in persuading

Rothschild to begin his beneficence to the Zionist settlements. Aaronsohn was not as successful with Rosenwald, who turned his back on Aaronsohn and the research station.

The restriction Weizmann and the London Zionists had imposed on Aaronsohn against giving speeches in America proved meaningless. He was received as an old friend in the Department of Agriculture and asked to give a talk. He told his audience that he would speak about agriculture and not politics, then proceeded to talk about the link between the agricultural and political development of Palestine. He spoke at the Hebrew Union College, a seminary for Reform rabbis, where the head of the seminary had announced that the word "Zionism" would never be heard at his institution. Aaronsohn carefully avoided the word, but after his talk one of the students came up to him to say that he had the strong feeling that Aaronsohn had been talking about Zionism for two hours.[7]

Aaronsohn's formal credentials certified the importance of his mission to both the British and American governments. His close relationship with Justice Brandeis, who was a trusted adviser of President Wilson, was intact. He spoke frequently with both Brandeis and with Felix Frankfurter, who stood in for Brandeis in political and diplomatic situations that would be inappropriate for a sitting justice of the Supreme Court. But Zionism under the British administration of Palestine—the program Aaronsohn was advocating—was a tough sell in America, and when he tried to persuade Americans to join the Zionist Commission that was being assembled in England to investigate the future of the Jewish presence in Palestine, he ran into strong reservations: the U.S. government had not declared war on the Ottoman Empire, they had only broken off diplomatic relations, and the State Department was not eager for Americans to be members of a commission that would have formal connections with the British conquerors of the Ottoman Empire. Aaronsohn also tried to seek out Arab spokesmen in America, with little success. Weizmann, who had met with Arab representatives in London, wrote that the gulf between the Christian and Muslim Arabs was so great and the organization of the Arabs abroad so weak that cooperative efforts were impossible. Aaronsohn and Weizmann separately decided that Sykes's dream of joint Jewish-Arab-Armenian action was impossible or impractical, and that they should place their hopes for future cooperation with the Arabs on a direct meeting with Emir Faisal as the public leader of the Arab Revolt, and as the Arab leader who seemed most attuned to British administration of Palestine.

At the end of January Felix Frankfurter joined Aaronsohn on the trip back to London on the *Adriatic,* and told Weizmann and others about Aaronsohn's influence in the United States and his unique grasp of the American mentality. Frankfurter understood the difference in temperaments between Brandeis and Weizmann, and the degree to which Aaronsohn alone had the experience and insights to bridge the enormous difference between "the rigorous, economically oriented outlook of Justice Brandeis and the entire consequence of the disciplined, even if inspired, mind that he was, and the kind of passionate, romantic, quasi-messianic temperament of Weizmann." Frankfurter recognized that while Weizmann was shrewd, hardheaded, cunning, and crafty, when it came to the promotion of Zionist interests he was less a scientist than "a man filled with a great dream which because of its adventuresomeness, daring to his mind and anyone's mind, required something more and beyond the careful calculation of an enterprise influenced by economic considerations, or the kind of hard-headed regard for details that was so characteristic of Mr. Justice Brandeis."[8] Only Aaronsohn knew how to speak to both Brandeis's love of detail and Weizmann's expansive dreams; his life and work could appeal to both Weizmann's respect for science and Brandeis's admiration for men of knowledge *and* action. Frankfurter's enthusiasm and praise did much to elevate Aaronsohn's standing in the London Zionist circles.

Indeed, Weizmann had accepted one of Aaronsohn's memos, recommending that Palestine should be governed by Britain, and that the holy places should be accorded religious autonomy, as a framework for the Zionist future. The implications were expansive: the immediate goal of Zionism would not be a new state, but to develop industry and commerce in Palestine on the pattern of Aaronsohn's agricultural research program as a precursor to extensive agricultural development. The memo was fuel in an ongoing debate about the future of Palestine in Zionist circles. Aaronsohn, backed by Brandeis, supported a policy of investment and development as the basis for increased settlement; faith in the efficiency of market processes in developing industry, agriculture, and commerce; and taxation to provide public services. Aaronsohn had become the strongest advocate of an American view of the future of Zionism. The alternative view, much favored by European Zionists, saw philanthropic funds—rather than capitalist investment—as the engine of increased development in Palestine, and recognized the political parties as the legitimate agents to nationalize and distribute land and public assets.[9]

In mid-February Aaronsohn met Foreign Secretary Balfour, a sign that he was finally accepted in official London Zionist circles. For the first time Aaronsohn's views on not only technical issues but the major political issues facing Zionism were discussed, and in some instances endorsed by the organization. When the Zionist Commission that would visit Palestine and make recommendations to the British government about the future of the Jews in Palestine was assembled, Weizmann endorsed Aaronsohn as a member. Sokolov and the Zionist leaders in Palestine adamantly opposed having him on the commission. Aaronsohn wrote to Brandeis, pointing out, among other complaints, that Sokolov's allegiance to France threatened to divide Palestine between Britain and France. Aaronsohn was ultimately named to the commission, but only as a liaison to Brandeis and the American Zionists, because the commission included no influential American representative. Others on the commission continued to object to his membership, and after a few months his status was downgraded to "technical expert." When the commission was on its way to Palestine via Paris and Rome, he had to press Weizmann to ask whether he was a member or not.

~

The fall of Jerusalem, on the heels of the Balfour Declaration, signaled the beginning of the end of the war in the Middle East, and the beginning of a rush for political position by every nation, political party, prince, tribal chief, and sheikh with ambitions anywhere in Palestine, Syria, Arabia, and Mesopotamia. Georges-Picot had wrangled a place beside Clayton during General Allenby's triumphal entry through the Jaffa Gate in Jerusalem. At the picnic lunch celebration later that day he revealed the French intentions: "And tomorrow, my dear General, I will take the necessary steps to set up civil government in this town."

Lawrence watched as "a silence fell on us, as when they opened the seventh seal in heaven. Salad and chicken mayonnaise and *foie gras* sandwiches hung in our mouths unmunched while we turned our round eyes on Allenby and waited." General Allenby took a moment to compose himself, dropping his chin in a gesture those who know him recognized and loved, before he said, "In the military zone the only authority is that of the Commander-in-Chief, *myself*."[10]

The French diplomats would have more to say on the question, but at least for Allenby, Clayton, the Arab Bureau, and Lawrence, the French situation seemed to be on hold. The rest of the diplomatic situation was not as sanguine. After the Bolshevik revolution in early November the new government in Petrograd, as they had promised, immediately pursued peace with the Central Powers. That, the British knew, would mean Russian withdrawals from the eastern front and the Caucasus, leaving Britain and France to oppose the full might of the German armies in France, and leaving the Turks free to shift troops from the Russian front in the Caucasus to the Palestine and Mesopotamian theaters. Then, in the spirit of the Petrograd Soviet's famous appeal "To all the Peoples of the World," the Bolsheviks published the secret treaties Russia had made with the Allies, including the Sykes-Picot agreement. Djemal Pasha read out portions of the agreement at a banquet in Beirut, and the text appeared in newspapers, providing a field day for Turkish propaganda and forcing British bureaus and agents who had dealt with the Arabs to produce some quick explanations. Even Arab leaders like Faisal, who unofficially knew about the treaty, were sufficiently embarrassed by the publication to demand public answers from the British. Rumors of the Balfour Declaration, which hadn't been formally published in the Middle East, further complicated the situation.

Clayton, from his position as head of British intelligence in the Middle East, had been opposed to the Sykes-Picot agreement, claiming the Turks would use it and the Balfour Declaration to generate propaganda allegations of British perfidy as the basis for an offer of independence to the Arabs under Turkish suzerainty. A secret letter from Djemal Pasha to Faisal, which Wingate obtained and passed on to the Foreign Office, bolstered Clayton's point. "There is only one standpoint from which your revolt can be justified in the interest of the Arabs," Djemal had written to Faisal.

> And that is the possibility of establishing an independent Arab Government, which would secure the independence, dignity and splendour of Islam under its influence. But what sort of an independence can you conceive in an Arab Government to be established, after Palestine has become an international country, as the Allied Governments have openly and officially declared, with Syria completely under French domination and with Irak and the whole of Mesopotamia forming part and parcel of British possessions?

Djemal suggested the possibility of a general amnesty for the Arab Revolt, urged Faisal to "reopen negotiations with a view to solving the problem in favour of Islam," and claimed that by writing his letter he was "discharging a religious duty."[11]

Picking up on Djemal's appeal to Islam, some Arab voices encouraged Faisal to negotiate with him, or even to let fate decide which side the Arabs would choose. Lawrence, aware that the British had also opened secret negotiations with conservatives in the Turkish government, counseled Faisal to send "tendentious answers to Djemal, argumentative enough to cause to continue the exchange." The strategy worked, and as Lawrence had hoped, Djemal's offers to

Faisal became more and more generous, first offering independence for the Hejaz, then Syria, then Mesopotamia, then "a Royal Crown to the offered share of Hussein of Mecca." Djemal finally allowed that the Turks "saw deep and reasonable logic in the claim of the Prophet's family to the spiritual leadership of Islam."[12] In other words, the Turks would recognize Hussein as caliph.

Lawrence did not report the details of these negotiations to British intelligence, and no doubt Djemal Pasha did not report the substance of his end of the negotiations to the sultan. If it seemed like a phony negotiation, Lawrence and Faisal came out on top: they had bought time for Faisal and the Arab Revolt by fending off the Turkish enticements; they had forced the Turks to negotiate with Faisal not as the temporary leader of a collection of tribes that drew together for battle and spoils, but as if he were the head of a sovereign nation; and Lawrence had been able to counsel Faisal directly on both the immediate negotiations and the future of the Arab Revolt. The role as a kingmaker went to Lawrence's head. "As soon as the war ends I'm going to build a railway in South America, or dig up a South African goldfield, to emancipate myself," he wrote to his friend Leeds. "Carchemish will either be hostile (Turks will never let me in again) or friendly (Arab), and after being a sort of king-maker one will not be allowed to go digging quietly again. Nuisance."[13]

The second lieutenant and archaeologist had come a long way from the days of designing postage stamps.

~

After he took Jerusalem Allenby decided that the British forces would need months to regroup and reequip themselves before moving north. During the lull, he decided, the Arab forces could be employed usefully in the area around the southern end of the Dead Sea, where they could protect Allenby's forces from Turkish attacks, deprive the Turks of the major source of wood for fuel on the Hejaz Railway, halt the Turkish lighter traffic across the Dead Sea that brought food to Jericho, and be in position to further harass the railway between the important junctions of Deraa and Maan. Lawrence suggested one more objective: if the Arab forces could occupy the entire area between the Dead Sea and the Hejaz Railway, they could be supplied by the British directly from Palestine instead of by sea through Aqaba, and the Arab army would then be able to move to the northern end of the Dead Sea in preparation for the final assault on northern Galilee and Syria. Syria, of course, had been his and Faisal's objective from the beginning of the war, especially after they knew about the Sykes-Picot agreement.

To support the proposed Arab operations, GHQ granted permission to publicize the Arab Revolt as part of a broad publicity program focused on the Palestine campaign. In memos Mark Sykes suggested the sorts of material he would like to see: "Articles should give striking actualities, and descriptions of scenes; picturesque details. Rivet the British onto Holy Land, Bible and New Testament. . . . Perorate all races (not religions), acclaim justice, humility, and nobility of conquerors." He even suggested targeted propaganda. For the Catholics: "Holy Places, Sepulcher, Via Dolorosa, and Bethlehem; dim religious light, chant." For the Orthodox: "Ditto, laying stress on peace in Holy Places now the Turk has gone." The Jews were to get "full details of colonies and institutes and wailing places. *Vox humana* this part." Muslims were to be rallied "on Moslem control of Mosque of Omar; quote Sherif's words." Sykes wrote in one article that "the grotto of Notre Dame de Lourdes" had been turned into a latrine by the German commander at Bethlehem, which was valuable information for propaganda, and that he wanted any similar cases reported to him. He also suggested that "we ought to use pogroms in Palestine as propaganda. A few spicy tales of atrocity would be eagerly welcomed by the propaganda people here—and Aaron Aaronsohn could send some lurid stories to the Jewish papers."[14]

~

The Turks had a price on Lawrence's head: £20,000 alive or £10,000 dead. There was little certainty that the Turks would ever pay, but Lawrence often found himself in remote and hostile country after Aqaba. The personal bodyguard he had recruited to protect himself after his experience in Deraa grew from a few men to a troop of as many as ninety, "lawless men, fellows whose dash and vigour had got them into trouble elsewhere . . . hard riders and hard livers, men proud of themselves, without ties or families to drag upon them." The men he chose were proud of the distinction, and developed a professionalism "almost flamboyant," dressing "like a bed of tulips, in every imaginable colour, leaving unused only white, since that was my constant wear, and they did not wish to seem to presume." They were camel mounted, proud of their ability to ride long and hard, risking camels that "an ordinary Arab" could not afford to see founder.[15] Close to sixty men died serving in Lawrence's personal bodyguard.

Lawrence had made some long, hard rides of his own, but after Deraa he relied increasingly on two Rolls-Royce armored cars. As the once-isolated port of Aqaba grew into a base and supply depot, a roadway was built through Wadi Itm up to the Guweira plain, and the armored cars the British had supplied to the Arab forces were shifted from Wejh to Aqaba to be used in probes against the Hejaz Railway. Lawrence and his drivers delighted in speeding across the desert, sometimes hitting sixty-five miles per hour as they traversed stretches of sand, corduroy roads, and stony terrain that would test any vehicle. The cars held up marvelously, and with Lieutenant Colonel Pierce Joyce in command of what came to be known as the Hejaz Armoured Car Company, Lawrence could write that "for the first time I was at a fight as a spectator. The novelty was most enjoyable; armoured-car work seemed fighting de luxe, for all our own troops were steel-covered and could come to no hurt. This relieved us of every anxiety and we made a field day of it like the best regular generals, sitting on our hilltop, and watching the battle intently through binoculars."[16] It was another heady time, but as Lawrence had said when he first met Faisal, far from Damascus.

Lawrence had promised Faisal Damascus as a symbolic capital of a great Arab state. As 1917 faded into 1918, it was increasingly clear that the Arab armies could not move except on the flank of a British advance into northern Galilee. Faisal's army waited across the Jordan River, conducting occasional raids on the Hejaz Railway, losing momentum and prestige as it became apparent that they were dependent on the British for supplies, logistic support, leadership, and direction. Other Arab voices spoke out against Faisal and his father, Sherif Hussein. Some opponents were Christian, most were Muslim; voices appeared in Syria and on committees in Cairo, Paris, London, Beirut, New York, Berlin, and Berne. Some were in favor of negotiation with Djemal Pasha; others favored open revolt against the Turks, unhindered by obligations to or coordination with the British. The dissident groups opposed the imposition of a ruler from the Hejaz, considering Sherif Hussein and his son Faisal outsiders to Syria and Palestine.

Lawrence took on the dissidents in an essay entitled "Syrian Cross-Currents." He wrote in English: his audience was not the actual dissidents but the British military command and Foreign Office, lest they be tempted to compromise Faisal and the Arab Revolt. The circulation of the essay was sharply limited to an audience even smaller than the tightly controlled *Arab Bulletin*. Lawrence dismissed the opposition of native Syrians to the prospect of Hashemite rule as "obscurantist," calling the Syrian claims of nationalism nothing more than "a pretty name for a European control, loose enough to give their coreligionists excessive place in the administration." He labeled the opponents of Hussein and Faisal survivors of the prewar Muslim intelligentsia who culled their political ideas from books, "spoke foreign languages as often as they could, wore European clothes, were often wealthy, used to entertain and be entertained by foreigners." His prose was scathing, calling the opponents "jejune" and pointing to their "pathetic belief in the idiot altruism of Britain and France. . . . For their sake (or rather for their words' sake) we are to pull down the new (and to us rather comfortable) Moslem Power we have so carefully set up, to launch armed expeditions into Syria, expel the Turks, and police the country at their direction. . . . The only difference between the Sherif's conquest of Syria and theirs (and they call it such a little difference!) is that the Sherif achieves it by the hands of the Syrians themselves, and they wish it achieved by our blood."[17]

Lawrence's vehemence and accusations made for a forceful essay, but his indirect paean to the Bedouins and staunch defense of Hussein and Faisal elided over some realities of wartime Syria, where an effendi class was often pro-Turk or pro-Britain with little or no Arab feeling, and where many Syrians looked down on Bedouins. Lawrence himself had written, "The Syrian, from the height of his education and 'refinement' looks down on the Bedouin in his 'dirt and sand' as being beyond real consideration, while the Bedouin in turn despises the effeminacy of the Syrian."[18] And for all Lawrence's claims of the purity of Hashemite motives and the dedication of Faisal's troops, even long after Aqaba the Bedouin soldiers were motivated more by the expectation of booty than by ideological commitment. After a raid in October 1917, Lawrence wrote in the *Arab Bulletin:* "The plundering occupied all the energies of our Bedouins, and Turkish counter-attacks came up unopposed from N. and S."[19]

The real question for Lawrence in the spring of 1918 was momentum. After the successful attack on Aqaba, the operations of the Arab Revolt had been limited to a series of guerrilla attacks on the Hejaz Railway, a deliberate strategy of hampering but not destroying the railroad, so that Turkish troops would be tied up repairing the roadbed, replacing damaged or destroyed rolling stock, and defending against further attacks. The first conventional battle for Arab forces was at Tafileh, a village the Arabs captured with little resistance in the early days of January 1918. On January 23 the Turks launched a surprise attack to recapture the village. "The Turks should never, by the rules of sane generalship, have ventured back to Tafileh at all," Lawrence wrote. "It was pure greed, a dog-in-the-manger attitude unworthy of a serious enemy, just the sort of hopeless thing a Turk would do. . . . We had every advantage, and could checkmate them easily: but to my wrath that was not enough. We would play their kind of game, deliver them a pitched battle such as they wanted, on the pygmy scale of our Arab war, and kill them all." The Arab counterattack the next day turned into a merciless slaughter, killing close to one thousand Turks and capturing hundreds more, along with valuable field artillery.

Lawrence was not pleased. He was appalled by the losses the Arabs had suffered: "I was frightened that, by my decision to fight, I had killed twenty or thirty of our six-hundred men, and the wounded would be perhaps three times as many. It was one-sixth of our force gone on a verbal triumph, for the destruction of the thousand poor Turks would not affect the issue of the war."[20]

A week later an Arab attack destroyed the Turkish lighters on the Dead Sea, fulfilling one of Allenby's requests. But that attack and the battles at Tefilah had provided no strategic advantage to the Arabs. Damascus was no closer, and the actions had only delayed an advance to the north. Lawrence calculated that he would need £30,000 to continue the advance. With winter snows making any further action unlikely, he went to Guweira to collect the funds in person. There he met Lieutenant Colonel Alan Dawnay, who had been given responsibility for liaison between Allenby's Egyptian Expeditionary Force and the Arab Revolt. An experienced professional soldier, Dawnay would serve as head of a small Arab operations unit at Allenby's headquarters called the Hedgehog staff, in charge of translating Lawrence's suggestions into formal plans and coordinating the streaming of supplies, air reconnaissance, and bombing with Lawrence's requests. Freed up from tactical concerns, Lawrence could focus on intelligence and broad strategy, traveling back and forth freely between Faisal's and Allenby's headquarters. Lawrence and Allenby agreed that the railway junction at Maan should be the Arab objective; Dawnay, supporting Lawrence's sense of the limitations of the Arab army, suggested that a direct attack on the railway junction would be impractical, and that the Arabs instead should try to cut the railway north of the city—essentially a continuation of the guerrilla tactics Lawrence had been pursuing with small units since the beginning of the Arab Revolt.

When Lawrence returned to Tafileh he found that no preparations had been made for an advance: Emir Zeid, the titular head of a northern Arab force, seemed incapable of organizing his own forces or successfully recruiting others. "These Arabs are the most ghastly material to build into a design," Lawrence wrote to Clayton.[21] Even so, with £30,000 Lawrence was confident that he could finance his own plans as well as support Zeid's needs. He set off on a long reconnaissance and concluded that camel-mounted troops could take advantage of the terrain to the east of the Dead Sea and meet up with the British forces north of there. He returned to Tafileh and found Emir Zeid cold to his plan. "But that will take a lot of money," Zeid said. Lawrence assured him that the funds they had in hand would cover his plan and more. Zeid then admitted that nothing was left of the funds. Lawrence gaped at him, and Zeid "muttered rather shamefacedly" that he had spent the £30,000. Lawrence thought Zeid was joking until Zeid began to rattle off the names of sheikhs to whom he had already given money, all men so sedentary or tied up in blood feuds that they could never be part of an attack force.[22] Lawrence realized then that his plans for an advance were stillborn, and that for a second time he had failed in a promise to General Allenby.

Losing face twice was too much. He decided to quit the Arab operations. "I was a very sick man," he recalled years later. "Almost at the breaking point."[23]

Allenby was making his own plans. With the Russians now out of the war, the Cabinet in London concluded that the war against Turkey should be given temporary priority, even if it meant postponing an offensive on the western front in France. At Allenby's headquarters the decision was made to place operations in Mesopotamia on hold and to concentrate forces on a further advance in Palestine. Units from Mesopotamia and Indian units from the western front were to augment Allenby's forces.

Allenby was too clever to allow Lawrence to quit. Explaining his new plans for a massive advance in Palestine, Allenby told Lawrence that he needed the Arab forces to neutralize the Hejaz Railway, which would otherwise be a threat to the security of the British forces. To enable Lawrence and Faisal to close down their present operations and advance toward Maan, Allenby agreed to provide seven hundred baggage camels from the Egyptian Camel Transport Company, with drivers, equipment, and British officers. He planned to first take Salt, just beyond the Jordan River, and hold it with an Indian brigade to protect his flank. Lawrence and the Arab core units would then raise "all the people between Madeba and Kierak, and support the British retention of Salt. . . . As soon as Maan fell, the Arab Regulars would move to Madeba, and base themselves there, drawing supplies from Jericho."[24]

Allenby would then launch a grand attack "along the whole line from the Mediterranean to the Dead Sea" that would lead to the capture of Damascus. The Arab role would be to cut the railway in the rear of the Turks in Palestine, probably near Deraa, cutting their forces off from any retreat. Lawrence, who had strong memories of Deraa, asked Allenby for the Imperial Camel Brigade as shock troops for an assault on the railroad junction. The well-trained unit of big Yeomen and Australians on their grain-fed Sudanese camels lacked the nimble, desert-crossing capabilities of the Bedouin troops, but Lawrence planned an operation that would require no more than forty miles of riding per day and, like his assault on Aqaba, would attack unexpected from the desert. The camel brigade officers were skeptical, but Lawrence persuaded them to retrain the men and camels and be ready for battle by mid-May.

From Allenby's headquarters Lawrence traveled to Jerusalem, where he met up with Ronald Storrs, his companion when he first traveled to Arabia and now a special liaison in Jerusalem. Storrs had daily battles with Georges-Picot, the French commissioner for Palestine and Syria, who made petty but symbolic claims for French authority in the city, like protesting the posting of an Italian guard outside the Church of the Holy Sepulcher or negotiating the celebration of a Te Deum in the Latin sector of the church at which Georges-Picot would be seated on a special throne.

While Lawrence was in Jerusalem Storrs introduced him to an American journalist and public speaker named Lowell Thomas, who was gathering material for slide lectures about the war. Thomas had been trying to find a subject that would build American support for the war effort and had concluded that the grim trench warfare of the western front would not suit his purpose. He got permission to visit Palestine, where he and his photographer, Harry Chase, hoped the desert terrain and exotic costumes might prove more photogenic. Lawrence, eager for publicity for the Arab Revolt and aware of the value of American support, talked to Thomas about the politics of the Arab movement, and posed for Harry Chase on the balcony of the British residency.

Thomas was intrigued by Lawrence's photogenic robes and his stories of the Bedouin, and persuaded Allenby to allow him to visit Aqaba, the scene of Lawrence's earliest triumph. Lawrence and Thomas met in Aqaba in March, during a lull in the Palestine and Arab campaigns. There had been heavy snows in the hilly region across the Jordan—one of Lawrence's two servants, Ali (called Daud in *Seven Pillars of Wisdom* and in the movie *Lawrence of Arabia*), died of the cold—and the Arab troops were inactive in their winter camps. Lawrence agreed to Chase's request that he sit for more portraits in various poses, and urged him to take photographs of the Arab troops and leaders. After ten days in Aqaba Thomas left for Petra, before returning to Egypt by sea. He later claimed that he had witnessed a fierce battle between Arabs and Turks at Petra, with Lawrence commanding the Arab troops. But the only battle in Petra had taken place earlier in the war, and Lawrence had not been there. Indeed, Thomas was never in battle with Lawrence. He only saw Lawrence in Jerusalem and at the rear staging area at Aqaba, and later admitted that in Arabia, "I found it impossible to extract much information from Lawrence himself regarding his own achievements. He insisted on giving entire credit to Emir Faisal and other Arab leaders, and to his fellow adventurers. . . . So I went to them for much of my material."[25]

But those facts hardly mattered. Like William ("Buffalo Bill") Cody, who at twenty-three was a scarcely known adventurer only to become the mythical embodiment of the American West after he met the writer Ned Buntline in 1869, Lawrence's meeting with Thomas in Jerusalem was the beginning of the transformation of the plucky Major Lawrence in his quaint Arab robes into the iconic Lawrence of Arabia.

~

In the month or so that Lawrence was in Jerusalem and Aqaba with Lowell Thomas, at Allenby's headquarters, and conducting reconnaissance in the country north Faisal's camp, the war situation changed dramatically. Allenby's campaign in Palestine, which had seemed invincible before reaching Jerusalem, now seemed bogged down. The planned offensive against Amman and Salt had not gone as planned, the offer of the Imperial Camel Corps to Lawrence and the Arabs had been withdrawn, and the extra troops promised to the Palestine campaign had been reassigned to the western front in France. More than six months after the conquest of Jerusalem, the British forces, supposedly resupplying and preparing for the conquest of northern Palestine and Syria, were still not ready to attack. Without the firsthand intelligence information from NILI that had given the British such an advantage in the initial assault on Gaza and Beersheba, Allenby seemed to change his plans and timetable daily.

Emir Faisal was also aware of the changed situation. The apparent British stalemate in Palestine, and the news from Europe hinting that Britain and France were desperate now that they had to fight Germany alone, on top of what he already knew about the Sykes-Picot agreement, left an opening to reconsider the commitments he and the Arabs had made to Britain. Secretly Faisal continued his correspondence with Djemal Pasha. By June 1918 Faisal had set conditions for an alliance with the Turks, including areas from which Turkish troops should be withdrawn, the return of Arab officers and men from Turkish units outside of Syria to an Arab army in Syria, separate commanders for an Arab army if it were to fight on the side of the Turks, the surrender of all supplies and foodstuffs in Syria to the Arab army, and a future relationship of Syria to Turkey modeled after the relationship between Prussia, Austria, and Hungary.[26] Lawrence discovered the correspondence by accident. He knew that the British command would be outraged to discover that their ally was negotiating with the enemy, but he had been involved in Middle East diplomacy long enough to not be surprised. "Faisal and Jemal were carrying on quite serious peace negotiations all 1918," he wrote. "I saw both side's letters unbeknownst: I should have been morally indignant with Faisal, only England was secretly negotiating with the Talaat [the first among equals at the head of the Turkish government], also to my unofficial knowledge, all 1918 too. All is fair in love, war and alliances."[27]

The Balfour Declaration was not published in Palestine, because the British were cautious about its potential impact on both the Muslim and Christian populations, but word spread about it through both official channels and rumors. Lawrence probably found out about the declaration from Clayton at the Arab Bureau, who warned: "The recent announcement of His Majesty's Government on the Jewish question has made a profound impression on both Christians and Moslems who view with little short of dismay the prospect of seeing Palestine and even eventually Syria in the hands of the Jews, whose superior intelligence and commercial abilities are feared."[28] The other reasons that may have prompted the issuance of the declaration, such as the Foreign Office's interest in diluting British obligations to the Arabs and the French; recognition of the contributions of Chaim Weizmann, Aaron Aaronsohn, and NILI; or long-term British ambitions in Palestine—were accorded little weight at the Arab Bureau.

Lawrence called the declaration payment for the support of the American Jews and the Russian Jewish revolutionaries.[29] He had already spent enough time with Faisal and the Arabs to be cynical in his views of Britain's wartime diplomacy: "The British Government in its joyous fashion gave with the left hand also . . . to show us that its as many hands as an ape's were ignorant of what one another did, and that it could give as many promises as there were parties, the British at once countered documents A to the Sherif, B to their allies, C to the Arab Committee, with document D to Lord Rothschild, a new power, who was promised something equivocal in Palestine."[30]

As cynical and opposed as they might be, British intelligence could not ignore the development. In February 1918 Clayton urged Lawrence to impress on Emir Faisal the necessity of an entente with the Jews in Palestine as "his only chance of doing really big things and bringing the Arab movement to fruition." Lawrence told Clayton, "As for the Jews, when I see Feisul next I'll talk to him, and the Arab attitude shall be sympathetic, for the duration of the war at least. Only please remember that he is under the old man [Sherif Hussein], and cannot involve the Arab kingdom by himself."[31] Lawrence's goal was simple: his eyes were still on Damascus and the conquest of Syria by the Arabs. His only concern with Weizmann and the Jews was whether they could somehow help Faisal and the Arabs achieve that goal.

From the other side, Aaron Aaronsohn believed that Sherif Hussein would never give up his claims to all the Arab-speaking lands of the Ottoman Empire. He urged Weizmann to meet with Faisal, who because of his strategic concerns about Syria might be more flexible. Arguing that with Brandeis's support the Zionist movement was stronger than it had been, that the promise of good prices for their land in Palestine would draw support from the wealthy absentee Arab landowners in Syria, and that there were good reasons based on terrain and natural geography for a separation of Palestine from Syria, he persuaded Weizmann to meet with Faisal.

~

The Zionist Commission traveled to Egypt via Paris and Rome. Aaronsohn had never been in Rome before, and stood awestruck at the Arch of Titus, with its depiction of the sacking of the Temple in Jerusalem. An airplane flew overhead while he walked around the Coliseum. "I cannot express my feelings then!" he wrote in his diary. "Titus passed—Nero passed—and now members of the race which they believed annihilated are treading upon this same soil as a springboard to dart towards Jerusalem. Nero—in your wildest dreams—you did not foresee the advent of aeroplanes—nor the return of the Jews."[32] Ormsby-Gore was along as British liaison to the Zionist Commission, and he and Aaronsohn resumed the friendship they had begun in Cairo, joking at dinner that a university should provide "a chair not only for the production of fortunes—but to educate wealthy people how to use their fortunes." Aaronsohn no doubt found it easier to express those ideas to Ormsby-Gore than he had a few months before to Julius Rosenwald.

When they reached Cairo, Aaronsohn met with Sir Reginald Wingate at the British residence, near the pyramids and the sphinx. He saw a dirigible, and with his usual fascination for technology jotted down notes on its flight duration and fuel. Cairo and its ways were familiar to him. Weizmann, he wrote, had not yet "acquired the suppleness and the complimentary and flattering tone to which High Officials of the Orient are accustomed—but he is too clever not to adapt himself rapidly and easily."[33]

Aaron's sister-in-law Marie told him the details of Sarah's death and the welcome news that his father was still alive. Ormsby-Gore had sent the same details on to the Foreign Office in London, adding that the Aaronsohns "were admittedly the most valuable nucleus of our intelligence in Palestine during the war . . . nothing we can do for the Aaronsohn family will repay the work they have done and what they have suffered for us." Aaron was so affected by the story of his sister's martyrdom that every experience reminded him of Sarah and Avshalom. When Ormsby-Gore spoke over the telephone to Storrs in Jerusalem, Aaronsohn wrote: "He told us about it as if it were the most simple matter without suspecting how it affected me! To telephone from Cairo to Jerusalem! If only Sarati and Absa could have lived to see that!"

It was almost two years since he had left on his journey to England. "My heart sank as the familiar sights of the past greeted my eyes—ragged Bedouins walking behind their thin horses, etc. So it is that these blackguards may enjoy a little sooner the advantages of British Dominion—which they will betray at the first opportunity—that the Absas and Saratis have fallen!" Still the inveterate scientist, he noted the progress of crops and the Arab agriculture, with plows still pulled by camels, oxen, or donkeys: "There does not seem to be any change in the country. Still . . . we travel by train—and are with the English! Absa, Absa, where are you? Sarati!"[34]

From his brother Alexander he learned about the intensity of the feelings against NILI and their spying activity in Palestine. Alex said that he and Schneersohn were the loneliest people in Palestine. When they walked down the street people who saw them would stop talking or whisper that they were spies, as if it were a curse. The father of Na'aman Belkind and other survivors and relatives of those who had been in NILI had become pariahs. Some of the local leaders in Palestine were saying that what Aaron and the others had done was unforgivable. There were calls for their expulsion from Palestine. After Aaronsohn visited Athlit he wrote to Felix Frankfurter that his life work was gone. The research station had been looted and destroyed by Turkish troops. Pages from his books were being used to wrap butter in the markets.[35]

While the Zionist Commission tried to pull the centrifugal arguments of its members into a coherent position to present to the British, Aaronsohn quietly started work on an agricultural plan. He would request a concession on much of the land the British had conquered, which would be used for advanced agricultural development, to provide crops to feed the occupation army, and also to reinforce Zionist claims on the land. His old friend and supporter Deedes endorsed the idea, and by May a special committee was formed, with Aaronsohn one of the members. He foresaw discussions of the plan in London, followed by another trip to the United States to raise funds to buy the latest agricultural implements; he would charter a ship in San Francisco to bring the equipment and his sister Rivka back to Palestine.

Working alone, out of the mainstream of the Zionist Commission's agenda, he thrived. He watched, a bystander and observer, as civic institutions started up in Palestine. In Jaffa a city council was installed, with five Arab and two Jewish members. Aaronsohn remembered the British attitude toward what they saw as "pushy" or demanding Jews from his stay in Cairo, objected to the apparent favoritism extended to the Arabs, and told Weizmann that perhaps they needed a new spying organization.

Aaronsohn was also caught up in the debate about a Jewish legion. In London Jabotinsky had been campaigning for a Jewish legion since the Zion Mule Corps returned from Gallipoli. On February 4, 1918, the Jewish Battalion, composed primarily of Jewish volunteers from the East End of London, marched with shining bayonets through the City of London and Whitechapel. The lord mayor in his robes of office took their salute, standing next to Major Lionel Rothschild, who had opposed the formation of the unit and watched with a dreary expression. Aaronsohn had long supported the idea of a Jewish legion as a focus for nationalistic sentiments and a symbol of recognition and support of Zionist aims, but Lishinsky's convictions had frightened many in the Jewish community in Palestine, and there was talk that Aaronsohn's association or support could taint the Jewish legion effort. When his old friend and colleague Rachael Yanait asked for his support on behalf of the socialist parties, he told her that his endorsement would contaminate the purity of the group she represented. General Allenby ultimately mooted the controversy when he told London that he favored the assignment of a Jewish battalion to the Palestine theater.

Along with his encyclopedic technical knowledge of Palestine, Aaronsohn was the only one on the Zionist Commission who was friends with Clayton, Woolley, and others in British intelligence. The Arab Bureau had already received information that might have blunted their instinctive opposition to the Zionist Commission, including a report that the commission was "opposed both to expropriation or exploitation of existing land owners, and also to any Jewish political control of Palestine." The same report argued that for the "very moderate number of Jews, expected to desire to settle there the almost derelict crown lands and unappropriated marshy and sandy areas will provide ample scope," and that the goals of the commission were "to inspect the possibilities of such lands, to look into the economic condition of the existing colonies, to resolve difficulties which have arisen about Jewish Relief funds, and to give practical expression to the idea of a Jewish University at Jerusalem."[36] Aaronsohn could have been helpful in persuading his acquaintances in the Arab Bureau, who had several times granted him the rare privilege of publishing extended notes in their *Arab Bulletin,* that the commission had no greater ambitions.

But the local opposition to Aaronsohn would not abandon their relentless complaints. He lost his temper at one meeting, and Weizmann ruled that he could no longer be an official member of the commission. When Allenby held a gala dinner for the commission in late May, Aaronsohn was not on the guest list. Official photographs do not show him with Weizmann, Allenby, and the other senior officials, or even in the second-row positions reserved for staff and advisers, but at the edge of the picture. He angrily refused to meet with Clayton—who was important in setting up the crucial meeting with Faisal—until Weizmann pulled him aside and persuaded him that the future of Jewish Palestine depended on the meeting.

The meeting with Faisal was finally arranged, and Weizmann traveled to Aqaba on June 4 and donned an Arab headcloth for the occasion. Weizmann was guardedly diplomatic, not telling Faisal what he had previously told Wingate and others—that only the Jews could organize and develop Palestine, and that because they knew the country and the Arabs, and had the financial and organizational resources, only they could offer Faisal the help he would need to secure Damascus and other territories to the north. Faisal, who had learned diplomatic craftiness from the British and French, politely listened to Weizmann but refused to commit himself or the Arabs, saying that in questions of politics he was acting only as his father's agent.[37]

Weizmann said that the Jews did not propose setting up a Jewish government in Palestine but planned only to work with the British authorities. They came, he said, with a view to colonizing and developing the country without in any way encroaching on the legitimate interests of others—effectively inviting talk about some sort of an agreement between the Arabs and the Jews. Faisal answered that "as an Arab he could not discuss the future of Palestine, either as a Jewish colony or a country under British Protection. These questions were already the subject of much German and Turkish propaganda, and would undoubtedly be misinterpreted by the Bedouin if openly discussed," and that while he "personally accepted the possibility of future Jewish claims to territory in Palestine . . . he could not discuss them publicly."[38] The whole meeting, including the small talk and gestures of hospitality essential at any meeting hosted by an Arab, lasted forty-five minutes.

Weizmann later wrote to his wife about Faisal: "He is the first real Arab nationalist I have met. He is a leader! He's quite intelligent and a very honest man, handsome as a picture! He is not interested in Palestine . . . [and is] contemptuous of the Palestinian Arabs whom he doesn't even regard as Arabs." Weizmann, who had complained to the British that the governing system in Palestine did "not take into account the fact that there is a fundamental qualitative difference between Jew and Arab," welcomed Faisal's attitude. Ormsby-Gore shared the same sentiment: "The true Arab Movement really existed outside Palestine. The movement led by Prince Faisal was not unlike the Zionist movement. It contained real Arabs who were real men. The Arabs in Trans-Jordania were fine people. The west of the Jordan the people were not Arabs, but only Arab-speaking."[39]

Before the date of the meeting was announced Lawrence had traveled north to see Sherif Nasir and observe the Arab operations between Maan and Amman. He was pleased by what he saw in the north—"As for the effect of the bombing, the war showed me that a combination of armoured cars and aircraft could rule the desert"[40]—but missed the meeting with Weizmann. When he returned to Allenby's headquarters Lawrence met privately with Weizmann, and afterward reported his read of the situation: "The real imminence of the Palestine problem is patent only to Faisal of the Sherifians. He believes that we intend to keep it ourselves, under the excuse of holding the balance between conflicting religions, and regards it as a cheap price to pay for the British help he has had and hopes still to have." Lawrence concluded that Weizmann hoped "for a completely Jewish Palestine in fifty years, and a Jewish Palestine, under a British façade, for the moment," and that Weizmann was battling for his own role among the British and American Jews and hoped by offering "the spectacle of British help, and Arab willingness to allow Jewish enterprise free scope in all their provinces in Syria, he will then secure the financial backing which will make the new Judea a reality." Lawrence warned that Weizmann was not in a position to make good on any promises yet: "In negotiating with him the Arabs would have to bear in mind that they are worth nothing to him till they have beaten the Turks, and that he is worth nothing to them unless he can make good amongst the Jews. . . . Until the military adventure of the Arabs under Faisal has succeeded or failed, he does not require Jewish help, and it would be unwise on our part to permit it to be offered."[41]

Aaronsohn also had not been at the meeting with Faisal. After helping arrange the meeting, Aaronsohn told Weizmann that the new Palestinian Office of the Zionist Commission in Ben Shemen was hopelessly inefficient, with muddled responsibilities for financial and managerial responsibility and a disastrous mix of public figures with the few individuals who had the necessary technical expertise to develop agriculture and other industries. His criticism of the fledgling venture was not welcome. He wrote to a friend that he would quit politics and return to science.

As they neared the moment of triumph, Aaronsohn was once again on the outside.

18

Damascus

So here ends my connection with the Arab revolt . . . but at least we have made a nation, and a few little groups of staff-officers have done so much. The rest is for the gods.

—T. E. Lawrence[1]

Lawrence reached his thirtieth birthday in August 1918. He was ill with a fever—the frenetic pace, irregular food and sleep, constant exhaustion, and his fanatic indifference to pain took a toll during the desert campaign—but even wracked with fever and worn down by almost two years in the desert, he looked younger than his age. His rank as a lieutenant colonel, his accomplishments in the complex statecraft and warfare of the Middle East, and his influence on Faisal and the Arabs and Allenby and the British command were remarkable achievements at such a young age, but Lawrence made no special note of the birthday. Whether because the temporary lull in the campaign gave him too much time to think, or because he and the Arab army were nearing their goal of Damascus, he had been caught up in weeks of introspection, occasionally perceptive, often morose. "A difficulty for me was the lack of instinct in my own performance," he wrote. "I could not for long deceive myself, and my eyes would open. . . . To man-rational, wars of nationality were as much a cheat as religious wars, and nothing was worth fighting for: while life was so deliberately private that no circumstances could justify one laying violent hands upon another's."[2]

Beyond his doubts about Arab nationalism, Lawrence ruminated on his own role in the war and the Arab Revolt, and his future. In a long letter to Vyvyan Richards, with whom he had once planned to open a printing press, Lawrence poured out self-doubts:

> I have been so violently uprooted and plunged so deeply into a job too big for me, that everything feels unreal. I have dropped everything I ever did, and live only as a thief of opportunity, snatching chances of the moment when and where I see them. My people have probably told you that the job is to forment an Arab rebellion against Turkey, and for that I have to try and hide my Frankish exterior, and be as little out of the Arab picture as I can. So it's a kind of foreign stage, on which one plays day and night, in fancy dress, in a strange language, with the price of failure on one's head if the part is not well filled.[3]

The malaise persisted. After a day in the spectacular scenery of Wadi Rum, visiting the British camel corps who were preparing for an attack on the Mudawara watering station he had failed to take or destroy with Arab troops, he looked at the

> healthy-looking tommies, like stiff-bodied schoolboys in their shirts and shorts, seeing them wander about the cliffs of Rum (which had been my private resort), anonymous and irresponsible. . . . Three years of Egypt and Sinai had burned all the colour out of their faces to a deep brown—in which their blue eyes flickered weakly like sky-gaps, against the dark possessed gaze of my men. For the rest they were a broad-faced, low-browed people, blunt featured beside the decadent Arabs, whose fine-curved shapes had been sharpened by generations of breeding to a radiance ages older than these primitive blotched honest Englishmen. Continental soldiers looked lumpish beside our lean-bred fellows: but against my supple Nejdis [Arabs from the interior of the Arabian Peninsula] the British in their turn looked lumpish.

When he left to ride back to Aqaba, passing through the high-walled canyons of Wadi Itm with his Arab bodyguard, an "extravagantly brilliant" sunset became a metaphor for the ambiguities of his own effort to straddle cultures, and for the future he would find after Damascus. "I was dead-tired of life," he wrote, "longing as seldom before for the peaceful moody sky in England. . . . We English, who lived years abroad among strangers, went always dressed in the pride of our remembered country. . . . When away, we were worth more than other men by our conviction that she was the greatest, straightest and best of all the countries of the world, and we would die before knowing that a page of her history had been blotted by defeat. Here, in Arabia, in the war's need, I was selling my honesty for her sustenance, unquestioningly."[4]

It was one of those moments when Lawrence's sometimes evasive ruminations touched the rawness of his emotions and exhaustion. The great saga of the Arab Revolt he had encouraged, watched, protected, chronicled, and sometimes led was nearing a critical moment.

In June 1918, with the plans for a British offensive to take the rest of Palestine and Syria still stalled, and the Arab army caught up in negotiations between Faisal and the tribal sheikhs, Lawrence left Aqaba for Cairo and Allenby's headquarters. He discovered that the mood at GHQ had changed dramatically. Indian troops had arrived to reinforce Allenby's units, training and preparations for a new offensive were ahead of pace, and the advance into northern Palestine and Syria was now scheduled for September. Lawrence no longer had to worry about the seemingly impossible challenge of putting together an independent Arab attack.

In the meantime, Sherif Hussein, in whose name the Arab Revolt was fighting the Turks but who had not previously involved himself in the details of the war, began to speak up on the future of the Arab world. As a direct descendant of the Prophet and keeper of the holy places, Hussein considered himself above the quotidian give-and-take of the war. He saw himself as a caliph-in-waiting, a spiritual and even temporal leader of all Arabs, including those, like the subjects of ibn Saud in the interior of the Arabian Peninsula, who did not recognize the Hashemite dynasty and its expansive claims. To protect his reputation as a man of profound Islamic faith, Hussein refused to meet with the Christian infidel Lawrence. As King of the Arabs—a self-proclaimed title—he would communicate only with Sir Reginald Wingate, who as British agent in Egypt was at least almost a coequal in rank. In June 1918 Hussein had his agent question Wingate about the Sykes-Picot agreement. Wingate, sensitive to the politics of the British working alliance with Hussein, wanted to answer that "we regard the Agreement as dead for all practical purposes," but the Foreign Office refused to approve that wording, so Wingate replied to Hussein that Djemal Pasha's posting of the agreement had omitted important clauses "regarding the consent of native populations and the safeguarding of their interests."[5]

For Hussein, who had been aware of the agreement years before, the whole discussion was a sham. It only mattered because Hussein was in an open conflict on the inland border of the Hejaz with ibn Saud, the Wahhabi ruler of much of the interior of the Arabian Peninsula.[6] Ibn Saud had also broken with the Turks, but with the fighting against the Turks concentrated along the Hejaz Railway in Hussein's territory, ibn Saud was free to devote his wartime efforts to strengthening his own position among the interior tribes. Hussein saw ibn Saud as a rival for power in Arabia, and wanted both to clarify his independence from the recent revelations about the Sykes-Picot agreement, and to keep his Arab troops in the Hejaz to defend against incursions by ibn Saud, rather than see them sent north on Faisal's campaign with Lawrence.

Sherif Hussein also began to question Faisal's authority to command the army. When Faisal protested, his father invented excuses to prevent Faisal from visiting him. Lawrence sailed to Jidda in late June 1918 with letters for Sherif Hussein from Wingate and Faisal, and Hussein refused to see him, with the excuse that he could not leave Mecca during Ramadan. Lawrence reached Hussein by telephone and tried to raise the issue of moving troops from the Hejaz to the northern campaign in support of Allenby's advance; Hussein pretended he could not hear Lawrence over the phone.[7] Lawrence then wrote a letter to Hussein in Arabic, listing the Turkish defenses at strong points like Maan and the need for additional Arab troops to bolster the planned attacks. "I beg you, Sir," he concluded, "to burn this letter after reading it, because I am writing to you about matters which I should have disclosed orally."[8] Lawrence got no reply and took the next transport back to Cairo, carrying the still-unopened letters from Wingate and Faisal.

In Cairo, Lawrence and Dawnay planned an attack by Arab forces riding on Allenby's flank that would rely on the speed of camel-mounted Arab troops to convince the Turks that geographically separated raids were being carried out by multiple Arab units. The planning was complicated by Allenby's precise timetable. "Three men and a boy with pistols in front of Deraa on September sixteenth . . . ," Allenby told Lawrence, "would be better than thousands a week before or a week after."[9] Dawnay and his colleagues in Cairo turned Lawrence's outline for a sweeping attack into a precisely scheduled plan, with detailed protocols for transport and stockpiling of forage, ammunition, and food for the troops. The demanding timetables of the new plans did not take into account that Arab troops were unaccustomed to watches or even calendars, and Lawrence reacted to the overcomplicated schedules by retreating to a corner of the mess tent in Aqaba with his copy of *Morte d'Arthur* and an impish smile, until Hubert Young, the officer sent as liaison to Lawrence, agreed to simplify the plans.[10] Lawrence later praised Young for his abilities at crabbing together supplies for the camel-borne troops.

Lawrence was in Aba al-Lissan in late August, reviewing preparations for an attack on Deraa, when they learned that Sherif Hussein had published a note in his Mecca newspaper challenging the rank and appointment of Jaafar Pasha, a Turkish officer from Baghdad who had defected early in the war and had become the commander of Faisal's forces in the north, one of many Syrian and Iraqi officers upon whom Faisal had become increasingly dependent. Hussein claimed that Jaafar could not be the general officer commanding the northern army because he had not been officially appointed to the position, and because there was no such rank in the Arab army. Strictly speaking, Hussein was correct: Hussein had not approved Faisal's appointment of Jaafar, and the Arab army had been casual about the official rank structure. But Lawrence was convinced that Hussein's challenge to the appointment, a "gross insult to all of us," was published only because Hussein had read that Allenby had personally decorated Jaafar, and out of pique at "his son's [Faisal's] too-great-success."[11]

Jaafar promptly resigned, followed by his divisional, regimental, and battalion officers and their staffs. Allenby's timetable loomed, with the deadline to send off the supply trains and the 400 camel-mounted assault troops only days away. Faisal protested to his father by telegram; a return telegram from Mecca called Faisal a "traitor and outlaw." As word of the dispute spread among the irregular forces who had agreed to join the advance, many of the tribal elements became uneasy, especially when the Syrian and Iraqi officers, fearing Hussein's intentions, demanded a formal retraction of his proclamation. As more caustic telegrams from Hussein arrived, escalating his threats, some of the troops came close to mutiny. Lawrence told them about the "silly coffee-cup storm which was raging among the high heads, and they laughed merrily," but the Syrian and Iraqi officers still demanded a formal apology from Hussein.

The telegrams from Hussein were sent in cipher via British radio operators in Egypt to Aqaba, then delivered by car to Lawrence after the cipher was decoded. To break the stalemate, Lawrence decided to "mutilate undesirable passages by rearranging their figures into nonsense, before handing them in code to Faisal." When Hussein came close to an apology in one message, only to follow the near apology with a restatement of his objectionable proclamation in "a new and glaring form," Lawrence turned the second half of the message into indecipherable nonsense, marked the apology in the first part of the message "very urgent," and took the revamped message to Faisal's tent. Faisal read the edited message aloud to his circle of advisers and officers, and proclaimed: "The telegraph has saved all our honour."[12]

~

The Arab armies gathered in readiness for battle: 450 camel-mounted troops of the Arab army, Lawrence's personal bodyguard, two airplanes from Aqaba, Vickers and Hotchkiss guns, quick-firing .65 caliber French mountain guns, three British armored cars with tenders, a demolition company of the Egyptian Camel Corps, and a section of camel-mounted ghurkas. Emir Faisal arrived to review the army, and tribal sheikhs, hearing about the preparations for the final advance toward Damascus, galloped up with armed peasants to join the effort, swelling the attack force to more than a thousand.

At dawn on September 14, as the main column of the Arab army moved north, Lawrence learned that raids on the railroad south of Deraa that were to precede the Arab advance had miscarried. There was no time to dispatch a full raiding party, so Lawrence set off with the armored cars, surprising a small garrison of Turks and destroying a four-arched bridge with 150 pounds of gun cotton. The next day the main column advanced to the Turkish post at Tell Arar, north of Deraa, defeated the garrison there, and spent a day demolishing the southernmost ten miles of the only rail line connecting Deraa to Damascus. The Arab troops burned rolling stock, destroyed rails and switches, planted mines, and cut the telegraph lines to Palestine. A demolition party blew up a bridge on the rail line from Deraa to the Hejaz, completing the destruction of the route connecting Palestine to Damascus and the Syrian cities, and to the south. The units were finished and back at their temporary base in Umtaiye by September 19, the date scheduled for Allenby's surprise advance to the north. "It was the only railway, not merely of Palestine, but of Hejaz also," Lawrence wrote, "and I could hardly believe that our fortune was real, and our word to Allenby fulfilled so simply and so soon."[13] After Lawrence's previous unfulfilled promises to Allenby, this was a sweet victory.

The British had arranged to send an airplane from Palestine to the

Arab base on September 21 with news of Allenby's advance, and Lawrence hoped to fly back to Allenby's headquarters to arrange air cover for the Arab army, which was vulnerable to attacks from German and Turkish airplanes. The news that arrived on the plane was extraordinary: Allenby's surprise attack in the west of Palestine had met little resistance, and he had quickly taken Beisan, Afula, and the enemy headquarters in Nazareth. His cavalry had broken through, closing off the possibility of an orderly Turkish retreat, and the British forces were poised to destroy or capture the Turkish Seventh and Eighth armies. The only possible escape route for the Turkish armies was across the Jordan River valley, and Allenby was depending on the Arabs to close that off.

Allenby detailed the positions where he expected the Arab forces to block the retreat of the Turkish armies, including cutting off Djemal Pasha's Fourth Army by completing the destruction of the railway south of Deraa. The unofficial orders included a warning: "Above all he [Allenby] does NOT wish Faisal to dash off, on his own, to Damascus or elsewhere—we shall soon be able to put him there as part of our own operations, and if he darts off prematurely without General Allenby's knowledge and consent, to guarantee his action, there will be the very devil to pay later on, which might upset the whole apple cart." Allenby's formal orders were equally specific and underlined: "The Commander-in-Chief wishes you to ensure that Emir Faisal . . . does not embark on any enterprise to the north, such as an advance on Damascus, without first obtaining the consent of the Commander-in-Chief. (In this connection you can, if necessary, quote King Hussein's definite statement that Emir Faisal and his Army are directly under the orders of the Commander-in-Chief.) . . . There must not be any independent or premature action by Emir Faisal." As Lawrence put it in his own words, two of Allenby's three thrusts were to "converge on Damascus. We were to assist them: but I was not to carry out my saucy threat to take Damascus, till we did it all together."[14]

At Allenby's headquarters Lawrence learned that on the night of September 20 the Turkish Seventh and Eighth armies had attempted to escape to the east by road. British aircraft caught the column between cliffs and precipices on the narrow road from Nablus to the Jordan valley, and with a hailstorm of grenades, bombs, and small-arms fire decimated a Turkish corps, losing only four RAF men in the battle. Allenby's victory in Palestine was so overwhelming that he had decided to move ahead without delay, driving toward Deraa in the east and Damascus in the north. Allenby's decisive victory was celebrated in the War Cabinet and in the press, and Lawrence was personally commended in the War Cabinet minutes. Four days later a Parisian newspaper, the *Echo de Paris,* printed a story about him, which was picked up by the British press: "The name of Colonel Lawrence . . . will become historic in Great Britain. At the head of the cavalry force which he had formed with Bedouins and Druses, he cut the railway at Deraa, thus severing the enemy communications between Damascus and Haifa and the eastern side of the Jordan."[15] The articles prompted the Censorship and Press Committee to warn editors not to publish photographs of Lawrence because the Turks, who had put a price on his head, did not know him by sight.

Allenby had been unambiguous in his orders for the Arab army, and as the remnants of the Turkish Fourth Army streamed toward Deraa in total disarray, Lawrence saw his own plan for the Arabs in shambles. Lawrence could argue that by destroying the railroads leading into Deraa and thrusting around Deraa the Arabs had put "unrivalled pressure on the Turks and did them more harm than any British unit was in place to do," and that by that action "we as good as took Damascus, which meant the end of this war in the East, and I believed the end of the general war." But in reality, his plan had always been that only if an Arab army took Damascus, inspired an Arab uprising in Syria, and established a presence and the elements of a government could it preempt the French claims and designs on Syria. If the Arabs arrived in Damascus only in the van of the British forces, there would be little opportunity for an Arab uprising, and Faisal would be seen not as a conquering leader but as a pawn of the British or even of the French. "To my mind we owed no duty to anyone," Lawrence wrote,

> though we served Allenby to our best ability, because there lay our interest to win the war. Yet I was very jealous for the Arab honour, and for them I would go forward at all costs. They had joined the war to win their freedom, and while winning it was easy, the abiding resolve to keep it could be sealed only by their blood and effort. Scientifically speaking we had perhaps done enough for this: at least we had earned the right to it: but we were dealing with masses in their ignorance, and the recovery of their old capital by the force of their own arms was the sign they would most fully understand.[16]

Lawrence's position was complicated by recent British clarifications of their interpretation of the Sykes-Picot agreement. Allenby's rapid advance had prompted a visit to Foreign Secretary Balfour by the French ambassador, who reminded him that according to the Sykes-Picot agreement Syria was within the French sphere of influence, and that "this fact should not be lost sight of in any arrangements that General Allenby, as Commander-in-Chief, might make for the administration of the country he was presumably about to occupy." Lord Balfour replied that Britain would adhere to their declared policy, and that if Syria "should fall into the sphere of interest of any European Power, that Power should be France," and that "whenever officers are required to carry out civilian duties, these officers should (unless the French Government express an opinion to the contrary) be French and not English; without prejudice of course to the supreme authority of the Commander-in-Chief while the country is in military occupation."[17]

The qualified diplomatic language reflected the pincer Britain found herself in, caught between the conflicting promises they had made to their French allies and to the Arab forces that were assisting the British advance. With Allenby's forces on the verge of their final advance into Syria proper, tactical considerations would temporarily win out. Allenby was aware that the Arab army had completed its assigned task of dealing with the retreating Turkish forces around Deraa, and that Lawrence would be moving the Arab army north. He issued new instructions to Faisal on September 25: "There is no objection to Your Highness entering Damascus as soon as you consider that you can do so with safety." Allenby also ordered his own officers to avoid entering Damascus if possible, and that "Damascus will be left under the . . . civil administration and no national flags will be flown."[18] The message for Faisal was delivered by air to his camp. Lawrence and the Arab army had already turned north in high spirits, eager for the long-awaited final victory.

British airplanes dropped messages for Lawrence, including a report that Bulgaria had surrendered to the Allies—Lawrence had been so wrapped up in his own campaign that he had all but forgotten that the war was also being fought in the Balkans—and a second reporting that two columns of Turkish troops were evacuating from Deraa by road, one 6,000 strong, another of about 2,000, both close to his position. Lawrence dispatched a small raiding party to harass the larger column, concluding that with 500 men he could scatter the smaller column. With half his mounted infantry and their machine guns, he turned south on a route that would pass close to Tafas, the home village of Sheikh Talal, who had ridden with Lawrence for more than a year.

As they approached the village they saw pyres of smoke, and met up with remnants of the inhabitants, old men, women, and children with terrible tales of what the Turks had done. As they rode closer they saw young children with horrible wounds and unburied corpses, including the body of a pregnant woman folded across a low wall, "bottom upwards, nailed there by a saw bayonet whose haft stuck hideously into the air from between her naked legs. . . . About her lay others, perhaps twenty in all, variously killed, but set out in accord with an obscene taste."

Sheikh Talal, viewing the rape and destruction of his own village, rode to the high ground overlooking the retreating Turkish column. Lawrence rode after him until Auda abu Tayi caught Lawrence's rein and pulled him back. Talal drew his headcloth across his face, dug his stirrups into his horse's flanks, and charged alone down the hill toward the retreating Turks, shouting his war cry, "Talal! Talal!" A hail of Turkish rifle and machine-gun fire cut him down.

Auda, cold and grim, a warrior who had seen too many battles, said, "God give him mercy: we will take his price." He reined in his horse, and led a charge that divided the Turkish column into three. Lawrence said to his men, "The best of you brings me the most Turkish dead."

With that order, "there lay on us a madness," Lawrence wrote, "born of the horror of Tafas or of its story, so that we killed and killed, even blowing in the heads of the fallen and of the animals, as though their death and running blood could slake the agony in our brains." Peasants followed the cavalry, picking up rifles, horses, donkeys, and spoils from the slaughtered Turks. One group of peasants, unaware of the no-prisoners policy, captured 200 Turks. When Lawrence went to see the prisoners he was led to where a wounded Arab trooper was pinned to the ground like a collected insect, with bayonets driven through his shoulder and legs. Asked who did it, the wounded trooper nodded at the Turkish prisoners. The Arab troops then machine-gunned the prisoners, leaving no one alive. Lawrence did not object. "The common delusion that the Turk is a clean and merciful fighter led some of the British troops to criticize Arab methods a little later," he wrote, "—but they had not entered Turaa or Tafas, or watched the Turks swing their wounded by the hands and feet into a burning railway truck, as had been the lot of the Arab army at Jerdun. As for the villagers, they and their ancestors had been for five hundred years ground down by the tyranny of these Turks."[19]

Perhaps without realizing it, Lawrence had crossed a line.

~

On September 29, 1918, Lawrence waited in Deraa to meet with Emir Faisal while seventy miles away Major General George Barrow set off with his Indian cavalry for Damascus. The Arab regulars were to advance along the railway to cover Barrow's right flank while the Arab irregulars harassed the Turkish forces retreating from Palestine. The next morning Lawrence set off for Damascus in a Rolls-Royce tender, accompanied by a British officer, Colonel Walter Stirling. Along the road they saw the detritus of the retreating Turkish columns—broken-down vehicles, scattered equipment and arms, the rotting corpses of horses and men. The escape routes from Damascus had been sealed off by General Henry Chauvel's Australian troops to the north and west of the city, General Barrow's Indian troops to the south and west, and the Arab troops south of the city.

Allenby hoped "we would go in first," Lawrence wrote, "partly because he was generous, and knew how much more than a mere trophy of victory Damascus would be to the Arabs: and partly for prudential reasons. . . . Allenby valued and used the Arabs not for their fighting, but for their preaching." Lawrence also claimed that "Faisal had in Damascus a powerful committee, who for months had been prepared to take over the reins of administration when the Turks crashed. We had only to get in touch with them, to tell them the movements of the Allies, and what was required of them." Strictly speaking, neither claim was true. Allenby did order General Chauvel and his Australians to "let the Arabs go in first, if possible," but that was a symbolic protocol and an effort to avoid ugly reactions to Christian troops in Damascus. There had been some unpleasant episodes in Cairo earlier in the war when Australian soldiers had enjoyed bawdy hijinks in the streets, and Allenby was not eager to see a repeat performance in Damascus. And while Faisal may have had a committee in Damascus, many Syrians, especially urbanized Damascenes, felt little identification with the Sherifian leadership or Faisal's army of Bedouin irregulars. As Lawrence conceded: "It was our burden to make each new yard of country ours in sentiment before we took it."[20]

Lawrence was in his full Arab robes in the open Rolls-Royce. Stirling wore an Arab headdress and camel's-hair abaya over his uniform. They stopped by a small stream outside Damascus to wash and shave—it would not do to enter Damascus unshaven—and were getting ready to move on when a patrol of Bengal Lancers galloped up and took them prisoner. Neither Lawrence nor Stirling spoke Urdu, and when Stirling tried to show the soldiers the red gorget patches on his collar to prove he was a British regular, he was answered with the point of a lance in his back. They were driven cross-country as prisoners until a British officer believed their explanations of who they were and had them set free.

They got to Damascus at 9 A.M., and found the city filled with shouting and dancing crowds, men yelling themselves hoarse, flashing daggers and swords, and firing volleys of rifle and pistol fire into the air. Lawrence and the Arab sheikhs, including Auda abu Tayi, were cheered by name, covered with flowers, and splashed with attar of roses from housetops. At the town hall they learned that an Arab government had already been proclaimed, the Sherifian flag had been hoisted, and the new administration had proclaimed its loyalty to Hussein as king of all the Arabs. A rival group led by two Algerians—Abd al-Kader, who had betrayed Lawrence in his unsuccessful assault on the Yarmuk bridges, and his brother Mohammed Said, who had been appointed governor by the retreating Djemal Pasha—also claimed power. Lawrence ordered the Algerians to leave the town hall. They refused and started a ruckus, making threats with a knife until Auda abu Tayi and Sheikh Nuri Shalaan of the Rualla personally expelled them, though not before the brothers vowed vengeance on Lawrence as a Christian.[21] Within weeks one brother was shot down and the other arrested.

The celebrations were short-lived. An observer arriving after Lawrence noticed only Damascene indifference: "There were no cheers or other signs of joy, which one might have expected from a population supposed to be in the process of liberation. . . . I was rather pained at the lack of popular enthusiasm."[22] When General Chauvel, commander of the Australian forces, drove into the city, he was appalled by the looting and breakdown of order, and told Lawrence that he "could not recognize the King of the Hedjaz in the matter without further instructions," but that he was agreeable to "Lt. Col.

Lawrence, with the Military Governor, carrying out the civil administration as a temporary measure pending instructions to the contrary being received from General Headquarters."[23] Chauvel then told Lawrence that his own troops, specifically the Third Light Horse Brigade, had passed through the city earlier that morning, and that the senior officer present had dismounted at the town hall and took what he understood to be the surrender of the city from Mohammed Said, who was then governor.

Lawrence was furious: "These sporting Australians saw the campaign as a point-to-point, with Damascus the post which the best horse would pass first. We saw it as a serious military operation, in which any unordered priority would be a meaningless or discreditable distinction."[24] What he really meant was that arriving first in Damascus and accepting the Turkish surrender was essential for the Arab claims that he had hoped (or pretended) would preempt the agreements England had made with France. From his first meeting with Faisal two years earlier, Lawrence had held out Damascus as their goal. For the British, in the form of an Australian cavalry unit, to have been the liberators of Damascus reduced the Arab army and Faisal to the level of helpmates.

For the next three days Lawrence worked to restore a semblance of order in the city. He did not want the Arabs to accept technical or police help from the British except on their own terms, but the city was chaotic. Abd al-Kader campaigned openly against Lawrence and Faisal as "English creatures" and tried to incite a rebellion. The electric lighting and the trams had been out of service since 1917 and could only be partially restored. The lack of draft animals and fuel, and the long neglect of street maintenance, sanitation, water supplies, and the public and military hospitals left services fragmentary at best. The chaos in the streets did not calm until Chauvel's forces, with a symbolic Arab contingent leading, marched through the city on October 3 as part of the preparations for General Allenby's arrival in his gray Rolls-Royce. Emir Faisal arrived the same day by train from Deraa.

The two leaders met at the Victoria Hotel. Lawrence was asked to translate the orders Allenby had received from the War Office for Faisal. "None of us knew what it meant in English, let alone in Arabic," Lawrence wrote, but the orders were in fact clear: Faisal would be allowed to establish Arab self-government in Syria, except that "if . . . the Arab authorities request the assistance or advice of European functionaries, we [the British] are bound under the Anglo-French [Sykes-Picot] Agreement to let these be French in Area 'A' [Syria]."[25] With Lawrence interpreting, Allenby explained to Faisal that France was the protecting power over Syria, and that as the representative of his father Faisal would have the administration of Syria (less Palestine and Lebanon) under French guidance and financial backing, but that the Arab sphere would include only the hinterland of Syria, with no claims on Lebanon, and that Faisal was to have a French liaison officer at once, who would work with Lawrence and expect Lawrence's assistance.

Faisal angrily claimed he knew nothing of France in the matter, that he was only prepared to have British assistance, that he had understood from Lawrence that the Arabs were to have all of Syria including Lebanon, and that he had no need for and would not recognize a French liaison officer.

Allenby turned to Lawrence and asked: "Did you not tell him that the French were to have the Protectorate over Syria?"

Lawrence said, "No Sir, I know nothing about it."

"But you knew definitely that he, Faisal, was to have nothing to do with the Lebanon?" said Allenby.

"No Sir, I did not," Lawrence insisted.

Lawrence and Faisal were both dissembling: they had known about the Sykes-Picot agreement for almost two years. They could pretend to be surprised by the immediate administrative arrangements, but they had both known that Lawrence's plan to sweep into Damascus, and for Faisal to declare an Arab state, was only a dream. Their protests of ignorance about the spheres of influence and authority that had been ceded to the French were duplicitous—

face-saving gestures for the benefit of the Arabs present, the crowds in the streets, and history.

Faisal's fingers moved continuously, as if he were nervous, and Faisal and Allenby talked in circles for a moment. Allenby would later write of Faisal that "he has beautiful hands, like a woman's."[26] Finally Allenby reminded Faisal that he, Sir Edmund Allenby, was commander in chief, that Faisal was a lieutenant general under his command, and that Faisal would have to obey orders.

Faisal left, and Lawrence told Allenby that he would not work with a French liaison officer, that he was due for leave, and that he had better take it now and return to England.

"Yes!" Allenby said. "I think you had."[27]

Mapmakers

A common sight at the Peace Conference in Paris was one or other of the world's statesmen, standing before a map and muttering to himself: "Where is that damn'd . . . ?" while he sought with extended forefinger for some town or river that he had never heard of before. . . . But however vague they may be about geography, politicians are invariably cocksure on abstractions such as a moral issue. They are always ready to talk about Right and Wrong.

—Italian diplomat at Versailles[1]

As wheat cut down too soon,
He is cut down;
But we, his people reap forevermore
the harvest of his planting.

—Jessie E. Sempter, on Aaron Aaronsohn[2]

The issues would not be settled on the battlefields.

Even before the Armistice, eyes had turned to the Peace Conference in Paris, and American president Woodrow Wilson, with his condemnations of the Old Europe of secret agreements and his promises of a new order of open agreements and self-determination. At the Peace Conference, he told the world, they would settle disagreements over territory and resources, colonies and conquests; they would rule on the aspirations of peoples, the legitimacies of nations, and the validity of prewar and wartime agreements; and they would draw the postwar borders. Those who had fought in long military campaigns, in the wartime bureaucracies, and in patient quiet diplomacy were to discover that the miles and sometimes yards of land they had fought for, the goals and objectives they had held out to inspire their forces and the home fronts, the agreements they had hammered out in battlefield tents, the corridors of foreign ministries, and over the tables of well-laid state dinners would all be be tossed aside. The claims of old nations and new, European conquerors and native peoples, idealists, cynics, schemers, and frauds would all be heard and weighed by Woodrow Wilson's Council of Ten, and later the Council of Four. They, the European and American victors, would award the territories and mandates that would define the future, partitioning and assigning huge chunks of the defeated empires, including much of the Arab-speaking areas that Lawrence and Faisal had sought for an Arab state, and the Palestine that Aaronsohn had worked to free from the Turkish yoke.

To realize their passionate visions Lawrence and Aaronsohn would have to join the parade of politicians, generals, princes, diplomats, and intelligence agents who came to Paris to plead and argue their cases. There they would have to fight as forcefully in the marbled and mirrored hallways and around the baize-covered tables spread with maps as they had on the battlefields of Palestine and Arabia, and in the hallways of Cairo and London.

~

As soon as British forces were on the ground in Palestine it became apparent that in daily interactions they were more sympathetic to, or at least more comfortable with, the Arab population than with the Jews of Palestine. The appointment of the first city council in Jaffa, composed of five Arabs and only two Jews, was the most blatant example, but there were frequent other instances, from street disputes to the appointment of minor officials. Ormsby-Gore, in London, argued that British officers in Palestine had served in Arab countries but were not familiar with Zionism, and that while many officers had picked up a smattering of Arabic in Egypt or the Sudan, almost no British officers or soldiers knew Hebrew. Aaron Aaronsohn, indeed any Jew who had worked in close quarters with British officers, would have said that the problem was not a question of familiarity or language but a deep-seated attitude based in British social values, a lingering anti-Semitism that might never be expressed openly in proper British society but was scarcely concealed in colonial situations. British colonial officers were comfortable with docile local populations like the Arabs, while the Jews of Palestine found themselves ignored, deprecated, even vilified as too intellectual, litigious, or "big for their britches."

Sokolov and the French Zionist leaders pointed to the British favoritism toward the Arabs as an argument against linking the future of Zionism to a British protectorate or mandate in Palestine, leaving Weizmann and Aaronsohn to defend the British. After a March 1918 conference Weizmann said that British favoritism toward the Arabs was understandable: until the end of the war the Arabs offered a military advantage to the British; after the war, he predicted, the Arabs would prove a burden and the tables would be turned. Aaronsohn's explanation was simpler. He said the British were not dealing with true representatives of the Arabs, and when they did they would recognize the Jews as their natural partners in Palestine. In late April 1918 he wrote to Justice Brandeis, explaining that it was not the British government that was to blame for the apparent pro-Arab British policy in Palestine, but the local British clerks and officers. In the end, he assured Brandeis, mutual understanding and respect would develop, and the relationship between the British and the Zionists would prosper and grow. The tone of the letter was unusually moderate for Aaronsohn: he may have been suspicious that the British or the Zionists were reading his mail.[3] He could rarely escape his suspicions.

Despite their agreement on many issues, Aaronsohn and Weizmann did not repair their relationship in the summer of 1918. In the fall Weizmann announced that he would himself travel to the United States to meet with Brandeis, Frankfurter, and perhaps with President Wilson to clarify and seek approval for the Zionist aims. Ormsby-

Gore objected: the war situation was too critical for Weizmann to leave England, and Aaronsohn, with his strong following in the United States, was the obvious ambassador to send. Weizmann, unwilling to ruffle feathers at the Foreign Office on the eve of the Peace Conference, got Foreign Secretary Balfour's approval before agreeing to send Aaronsohn back to the United States. Aaronsohn chafed that he would again not have the authority to speak for the Zionist International, but at least in the United States he would be among friends, and privately would be able to talk to audiences eager to hear his predictions and prescriptions for the future of Palestine.

In London, on his way to the United States for the second time in a year, Aaronsohn met old friends like Walter Lippmann, who were in Europe anticipating the end of the war. In the lobby of the Savoy Hotel he encountered Julius Rosenwald.[4] The meeting was an accident, and they had little to say to each other: both men were good at holding a grudge. In Paris Aaronsohn called once more on his onetime mentor and patron Baron Rothschild, who still opposed the British plans for Palestine and was distrustful of Weizmann and Aaronsohn for their support of the British. Aaronsohn again excused the baron's attitude, calling it the temporary triumph of his French citizenship over his loyalty to the Zionist cause.[5] Aaronsohn also learned that he would have a shipmate on the crossing to New York. The French government, equally eager to lobby Brandeis and President Wilson, was sending Silvain Levi, the distinguished Sanskrit scholar, Dreyfusard, and founding member of the Human Rights League to express the French viewpoint. Aaronsohn had met Levi, and they shared many interests as scholars, even if Levi didn't call himself a Zionist.

With doughboys coming home, and Wilson getting ready to leave for Paris, Aaronsohn landed in an America that was fascinated by France. Vaudeville was singing "Mademoiselle from Armentières," and there was a sudden fascination with lacy lingerie and French food. Zionism had little support in the United States outside select Jewish circles, and Wilson had not approved of the Balfour Declaration.[6] American sentiments on Palestine followed the French propaganda portraying themselves as a force for *liberté,* and in support of indigenous populations—and the British as a colonial power imposing its will. Aaronsohn found himself reminding audiences that it was Britain that had stood up against the Germans and Turks in Syria and Palestine.

His advantage in the impromptu debates was that he had Brandeis's ear. The day he arrived the two men spoke for fourteen hours; the next day, for six more. With the war close to an end, Brandeis, both as head of the American Zionist movement and as an adviser to President Wilson, was eager for insider reports and news. Aaron Aaronsohn was the voice from Palestine Brandeis most trusted. For Aaronsohn, who had for months struggled to gain an audience among the Zionist leaders, Brandeis's trust was a calm and welcome port in the gathering storm of Zionist and wartime politics. But he could only stay in the United States for a few short weeks. In early November, as news from Damascus and the western front foretold the nearing end of the war, Weizmann called Aaronsohn back to Europe to help with preparations for the Peace Conference.

He boarded a ship for England on November 6, and was still at sea when street demonstrations celebrated the Armistice on November 11. He did not reach London until November 19, and was only there for a week before leaving for Paris. One week was long enough for him to learn that King Hussein and Emir Faisal had begun a barrage of propaganda demanding that Palestine be added to the territory of their new Arab state.

~

While Aaronsohn was in America, Lawrence left Damascus for Cairo. He stayed in Egypt until October 15, cleaning up his affairs, giving away mementos he had collected, and arranging a promotion to the temporary rank of full colonel before he boarded a steamer from Port Said to Taranto, on the boot of Italy. "Sleeping berths were given only to full colonels and upward," he later told a biographer, adding ". . . I like comfort!"[7] The new rank entitled him to a private cabin on the ship and a three-day express to Le Havre instead of the ten-day journey by troop train.

Back in England for the first time in almost four years, he visited his family in Oxford briefly before meeting privately at the War Office with General Sir George MacDonough, the wartime director of military intelligence. Lord Robert Cecil, the assistant secretary of state for foreign affairs, arranged for Lawrence to address the Eastern Committee of the War Cabinet, where Lord Curzon, chairman of the committee and former viceroy of India, welcomed him, praising "the great work which Colonel Lawrence had been doing in Arabia." When Lawrence cut off the introduction, saying, "Let's get to business. You people don't understand yet the hole you have put us all into," Curzon burst into tears.[8] Lawrence's assessment of the situation in the Middle East was grim, as he pointed out the geopolitical needs of the Arabs, their distrust of the French, and Faisal's willingness to work with British or American Zionist Jews. Curzon asked Lawrence to write a memorandum to the War Cabinet with his views and suggestions. The next day Lawrence called at Buckingham Palace for a private audience with King George V. He turned down the honors when the king tried to decorate him.

Lawrence knew that Britain and France would soon be refining their wartime agreements as a prelude to the upcoming peace negotiations. He dreaded the consequences of a revised Sykes-Picot agreement, and spent the weekend drafting his memo to the War Cabinet and preparing an accompanying map, setting out his own proposal for the future of the Middle East, based in large measure on the dreams of the Arab campaign.[9] His memo was succinct but sweeping: "When war broke out an urgent need to divide Islam was added [to the British interest in preserving the quadrangle of land between Egypt, Alexandretta, Persia, and the Indian Ocean,] and we became reconciled to seek for allies rather than subjects." It was sometimes frank: "The Sherif had no idea that we wanted him only as a figurehead; throughout the [McMahon] correspondence he spoke as the mandatory of the Arabs—meaning everyone under Turkish rule who spoke Arabic." It was daringly candid: "The loyalty to their word and allies of the old King and his sons, who have refused from the Turks successive offers of autonomy in Syria, and of the Khalifate, with independence in Arabia and autonomy in all the Arabic provinces, may be recommended as an example to the Power which persuaded him to revolt, but which was ready, without his knowledge, to hand him over, with the people for whom he stood guardian, to the Turks on much worse terms." And it was prescient: "The Kurdish question is likely to be much larger and more difficult than the Armenian one."

His reference to "allies rather than subjects" was technically correct, but certainly did not reflect British colonial attitudes. And, as Lawrence knew, Faisal, his brothers, and Hussein had continued to negotiate with the Turks during the war, craftily balancing the offers they received from both sides against their changing estimates of the course of the war. The Arabs chose to stick with the British, despite the betrayals of the Sykes-Picot agreement, because they were convinced the British would win the war.

The memo then laid out Lawrence's summary of Arab expectations. Sherif Hussein expected to be the "unquestioned head" of the Arabian Peninsula, including Kuwait and the interior of Arabia. To that end, Lawrence urged that Cairo, Baghdad, Damascus, and Simla all stay out of the affairs of Arabia proper. His claim that "ibn Saud is friendly to us" optimistically elided over ibn Saud's building struggle with Sherif Hussein, and the open split between the Indian government, which supported ibn Saud, and the British War Cabinet and Foreign Office, which had supported Hussein.

In Syria, Lawrence wrote, the Arabs required "equal rights with any other power" in the Gulf of Alexandretta, the coast to Tripoli and the port there, the railways to Haifa and to the major industrial cities of Syria, "and all the country East of this line and the Jordan." That last phrase, and the huge area of the coast and interior that Lawrence blocked off on his map for the Arabs under Faisal, effectively would have given Faisal all of present-day Jordan and Saudi Arabia, along with most of Syria, with no recognition of the French sphere of influence in the Sykes-Picot agreement. Lawrence added that "Faisal requires to be sovereign in his own dominions, with complete liberty to choose any foreign advisers he wants of any nationality he pleases. These advisers will be part of the Arab Government and will draw their executive authority from it and not from their own Government" and that "Faisal . . . will not consider himself bound by any agreement to which he is not a party." Lawrence's map and memo effectively granted to France only a thin strip of Lebanon, running from the northern border of Palestine to the outskirts of Tripoli, and another tiny strip on the Gulf of Alexandretta.

Lawrence's proposed borders for Palestine were generous compared to the limited area allocated in the Sykes-Picot agreement. His boundaries do not follow terrain features but are straight lines: from Quneitra south, incorporating the Golan Heights, the eastern side of the Jordan River, and all of the Dead Sea; from east of the southern tip of the Dead Sea through Beersheba to the Mediterranean coast north of Gaza; and due west from Quneitra to the Mediterranean. With its straight borders, ignoring terrain, resources, cultivation patterns, economic development issues, and history, it was not the Palestine Aaron Aaronsohn would have mapped.

The Arab position on Palestine, Lawrence wrote, was that they hoped Britain would keep what they had conquered, that they would not approve "Jewish Independence for Palestine" but would support "as far as they can Jewish infiltration, if it is behind a British as opposed to an international façade." The threat behind this assurance was, "If any attempt is made to set up the international control proposed in the Sykes-Picot agreement, Faisal will press for self-determination in Palestine, and give the moral support of the Arab Government to the peasantry of Palestine, to resist expropriation." In other words, Faisal would allow Jewish development in Palestine as long as the Jews did not press for independent statehood, and as long as the governing power was Britain; if those demands were not met, he threatened to call for a Wilsonian plebiscite, confident that it would be won by the Arab majority.

Lawrence's map also provides for an Armenian region surrounding the Gulf of Alexandretta and incorporating the large coastal Armenian population there, with the exception of a narrow strip on the

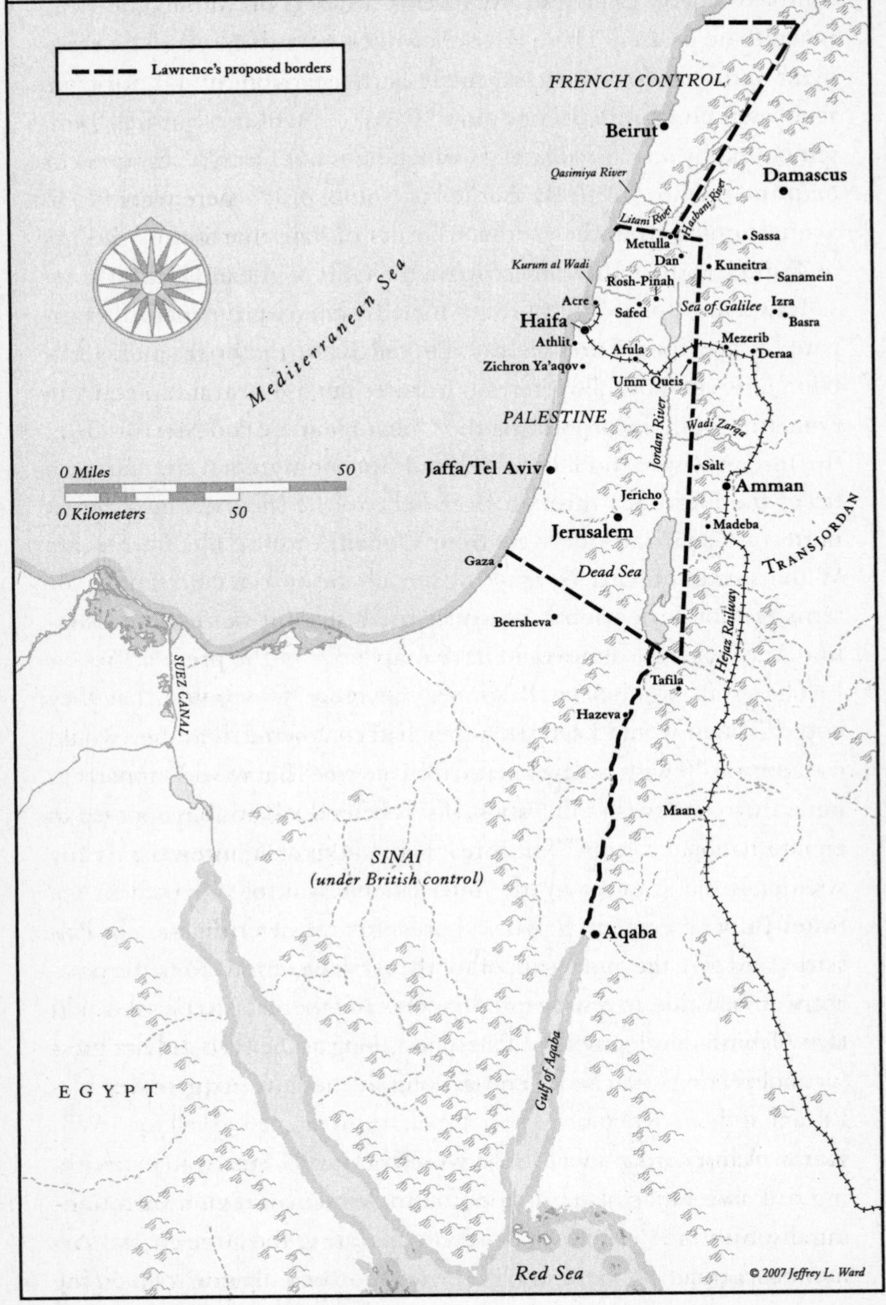
• T. E. Lawrence's Proposed Boundaries for Palestine •
Lawrence's proposed borders
FRENCH CONTROL
Beirut
Qasimiya River
Damascus
Litani River
Hasbani River
Metulla
Sassa
Dan
Kuneitra
Kurum al Wadi
Sanamein
Rosh-Pinah
Mediterranean Sea
Acre
Safed
Sea of Galilee
Izra
Haifa
Basra
Athlit
Mezerib
Afula
Deraa
Zichron Ya'aqov
Umm Queis
PALESTINE
Wadi Zarqa
Jordan River
0 Miles
50
Jaffa/Tel Aviv
Salt
Amman
0 Kilometers
50
Jericho
Madeba
Jerusalem
TRANSJORDAN
Gaza
Dead Sea
Hejaz Railway
Beersheva
SUEZ CANAL
Tafila
Hazeva
Maan
SINAI
(under British control)
Aqaba
Gulf of Aqaba
EGYPT
Red Sea
© 2007 Jeffrey L. Ward

southeast coast of the gulf assigned to France, presumably a token recognition of France's long-term demands in that area. Lawrence marked off for the Kurds a triangular area around Jesirah, the region where he had spent three years in archaeological research at Carchemish. The area is marked with two large question marks on the map, and his memo admits that the "Arab Nationalists" there were in "an unsatisfactory geographical position, until a proportion of the nomadic and settled Kurds can be persuaded to join hands with the local government required there." Finally, his map provides both an Iraq, where "the Arabs expect the British to keep control" and where Sherif Hussein "hopes for a nominal Arab administration," and an Arab kingdom in eastern Syria and the region around Mosul, which was to be granted to Sherif Hussein's son Zeid under British influence. The memo concludes with a scarcely veiled threat: "If representations of small nations are admitted to the Peace Conference the cry of self-determination is likely to be raised, and agreements made semi-secretly between the Powers previously may be regarded with some suspicion. The geographical absurdities of the present [Sykes-Picot] Agreement will laugh it out of Court, and it would be perhaps as well if we spared ourselves a second effort on the same lines."[10]

Lawrence knew his map and memo would be met with resistance not only from the French, but from the British War Cabinet and Foreign Office. The day he submitted it he called on Winston Churchill, who had been discredited and forced to resign as first lord of the Admiralty at the time of the disastrous campaign at Gallipoli, and had settled for the lowly position of minister of munitions for the rest of the war. It was widely assumed that Churchill would accept an important Cabinet post after the general election in December. Lawrence was cultivating what he assumed would be a useful acquaintance.

~

Aaron Aaronsohn, newly back from the United States, knew nothing of Lawrence's memo and map, but he had his own ideas on the same subject. He was eager to stay in London, and wrote a pseudonymous article for a popular magazine about Britain's changing positions on the Middle East, opening with a telltale quote from Jabotinsky: "The root of the present plague is in Asia Minor and the first and last aim of the War is the solution of the Eastern question." Aaronsohn took a harsh view of British attitudes since the end of the war: "Of all the allies, Great Britain was seemingly in the best position to watch and to read Germany's machinations in Western Asia. Of all the Allies, Great Britain has seemed to be the last and the slowest one to grasp the dangers of the situation and to take effective measures in order to avert them."[11] He would have liked to stay and campaign for British support on Palestine, but by the end of November delegates and journalists for the Peace Conference were already arriving in Paris, including an American delegation. Sokolov, the official Zionist representative in Paris, did not know any of the Americans, so Weizmann arranged for Aaronsohn to travel to Paris on a British diplomatic passport as a member of the British delegation to the peace talks, in the hope that he could lobby the Americans.

Aaronsohn arrived in Paris on November 26. Walter Lippmann, William Bullitt, and Louis Strauss were there with the American delegation—he knew all three of them from New York. He also knew the military and intelligence attachés in the British delegation, including Walter Gribbon, Clayton, Sir Basil Thomson, General MacDonough, and Mark Sykes. Gribbon, Sir Basil, and Sykes had been sympathetic to Aaronsohn's ideas and plans, and even Clayton had shared enough meetings with him to make their relationship easy.

Paris was in love with President Wilson and the Americans. The talk in the cafés was about Wilson's Fourteen Points, Four Principles, and Five Particulars—none of which mentioned the Jews or the Arabs. The scholars Colonel House, the president's factotum, had assembled at the New York Public Library as a Middle Eastern group in preparation for the Peace Conference included an expert on the Crusades, a specialist in Latin American studies, an expert on Native Americans, and two professors who specialized in Persian languages and literature. They did their research in encyclopedias; their working papers did not mention potential petroleum reserves.

For Aaronsohn, who could talk with authority and ease about the political future of Albania, the future regime in Constantinople (which was increasingly being called Istanbul), and obscure former subject peoples most of the diplomats could not identify, the endless rounds of café analyses were an ideal forum, and the querulous reporters an ideal audience. Ignoring the general euphoria in Paris, he told those who would listen that it was not Germany that had lost the war, but France: the war had been fought on French soil, not in Germany; the French had suffered an incomparable loss of manpower and leadership; postwar Germany remained a larger state than France, with more resources and people; there was little to stop the Austrian Germans from joining Germany; and the German economy had more potential vitality than that of the French. Although his official roles were liaison with the Americans and technical adviser on Palestine, he used the café conversations to float ideas such as granting portions of Spanish Morocco to France in return for the French abandoning their claims to Syria. In an atmosphere where the Canadian diplomats were proposing that the United States give up the Alaska panhandle in exchange for islands in the West Indies or British Honduras,[12] his proposals did not seem out of the question.

Aaronsohn had written on the Armenian situation for the British, and had often discussed the parallel situations of the Armenians and the Jews with Sykes.[13] They shared an old-fashioned view of the Armenians as the primary Christian population in the Middle East, ignoring the substantial Maronite population of Lebanon; the many non-Armenian Orthodox and Catholic Christians of Syria, Palestine, and Iraq; and the evangelical missionaries and their followers. Most of Paris ignored the Armenians: President Wilson did not encourage an Armenian delegation, the Bolsheviks were not eager to see the population of the small Armenian state on the Russian side of the border united with the Armenians on the Turkish side, and the French saw the Armenians as territorial rivals in the area around the Gulf of Alexandretta and challengers for the role of championing the Christian populations of the former Ottoman Empire. The French scheme for Turkey, Aaronsohn wrote, gave the Armenians a real "self-extermination" instead of "self-determination."[14]

But Aaronsohn was stubborn. In December 1918 he shuttled between London and Paris eight times, meeting with Armenian leaders in both cities, counseling them to organize and declare independence before the peacemakers in Paris yielded to Turkey's demands for territorial integrity or excluded them from the distribution of those portions of Turkey with predominantly Armenian populations, and urging the Armenian leaders to settle for less aggressive land claims, and that they consider the option of a partnership with Britain like the one the Zionists were proposing.[15] His convictions about the Armenians were no doubt sincere, and a tribute to his sister's memory, but he had an ulterior motive: just as he had long feared that the fate of the Jews of Palestine during the war might parallel the fate of the Armenians, he worried that the lack of attention to the Armenian question in Paris signaled the difficulties the Zionists could face in recruiting support for their own future.

In January 1919 Weizmann and his staff arrived in Paris. Like the other minority delegations the Zionists had been asked to submit a memo with their demands. They decided to leave any feuding with France to the British, but on the most fundamental questions the delegation was divided: one faction wanted to demand a Jewish administration for Palestine, with only a few limits falling under British jurisdiction. The rest of the delegation, including Weizmann and Aaronsohn, favored a joint British-Jewish administration. The joint proposal won out, but campaigning for the Zionist position required that they convince the British and the Americans, including President Wilson. And as Aaronsohn had anticipated, they had competition in Paris.

~

Lawrence's interest in the Peace Conference was in getting Faisal's claims to Syria heard. He was delighted in late November when the Eastern Committee of the War Cabinet agreed that it would be in Britain's best interest if Faisal attended the Peace Conference to back up Britain's aspirations for protectorates in Mesopotamia and Palestine. The day the War Cabinet committee met, Faisal boarded HMS *Gloucester* in Beirut for the journey to France.

The emir's journey turned into an unanticipated adventure. His mission was not formally announced to the French until his ship was almost at Marseilles, but they had learned of his pending arrival through private sources and were not pleased at the prospect of an Arabian prince, known to oppose their ambitions in Syria, arriving on a British warship and pleading his cause before the American president, who would no doubt be impressed by Faisal's rank, entourage, and exotic attire. The French much preferred to settle their differences with the British quietly before the Peace Conference officially opened, away from the glare of publicity and the Americans, whom they considered hopelessly naive and idealistic. Lawrence arrived in Marseilles after the *Gloucester* docked and was told he was not welcome. French officials also prevented the British representatives in Marseilles from putting the emir on a train for London. The French plenipotentiaries then announced that they would receive Faisal as a military leader and the son of a friendly sovereign, but not as an official diplomatic representative. A retired Foreign Office official named Emmanuel Bertrand was given the assignment of keeping Faisal and his entourage busy with a relentless schedule of visits to silk workshops, gun foundries, tank exercises, refineries, and refrigeration plants—none of which Faisal wanted to see—while French officials told him how inconsiderate his British advisers had been to encourage him to journey to France without making a prior agreement with the French authorities.[16]

When the exhausted and annoyed emir finally got to England, he was decorated by King George V. Lawrence wore full Arab dress for the occasion as a member of Faisal's staff, providing sensational copy and photographs for the newspapers. The newspapers so preferred the robes that they seemed determined to ignore that on all other occasions with Faisal, in England and in France, Lawrence wore at most an Arab headdress with his British khaki uniform. When Faisal took an official tour to Glasgow and Edinburgh, he was asked to give an address at a civic function. He had not prepared a talk and nonchalantly recited passages from the Qur'an while Lawrence, pretending to interpret, made an impromptu speech.[17] The tour was good press copy, but before Faisal got to London the Eastern Committee of the War Cabinet had already decided that Britain would comply to the letter with the Sykes-Picot agreement. With that decision Britain effectively could offer Faisal nothing but sympathy and help getting a hearing at the Peace Conference. They offered him Lawrence as an adviser and translator, and added Lawrence to the British delegation.

Emir Faisal agreed to one more meeting before he left London. He and Chaim Weizmann had been wary and sparring at Aqaba, unsure of each other and of the positions of the Great Powers. By the eve of the Peace Conference each had a firm agenda and something to offer the other. The Zionists needed Arab acquiescence to their plans in Palestine. Some might argue that Faisal, as a Hashemite prince from the Hejaz, was in no position to represent the Arabs of Palestine, but as the only Arab leader at the Peace Conference, and with his impressive robes and entourage (including an African slave and the celebrated Lawrence as his translator and adviser), Faisal came across with a weighty authenticity. With no support from the British, and with the French adamantly opposed to his presence and plans in Syria, Faisal needed any support he could get. After the Aqaba meeting with Weizmann Lawrence had already pointed out that Jewish capital and technical skills could be useful to an Arab state, and that support from the Zionists might swing American opinion to Faisal's side.

Faisal and Weizmann met at the Carlton Hotel, with Lawrence acting as interpreter. Weizmann, eager to avoid an Arab challenge to the Zionist aspirations in Palestine, assured Faisal that the Zionists should be able to carry out public works of a "far-reaching character," and that the country would be "so improved that it would have room for four or five million Jews, without encroaching on the ownership rights of Arab peasantry." Faisal graciously answered that "it was curious that there should be friction between Jews and Arabs in Palestine. There was no friction in any other country where Jews lived together with Arabs," and added that he did not think there was any scarcity of land in Palestine: "The population would always have enough, especially if the country were developed."[18] Like their earlier talk in Aqaba, the meeting was long on civility, but this time they signed an understanding, agreeing to establish boundaries between Palestine and the Arab state Faisal hoped to create in Syria and Palestine, recognize the Balfour Declaration, and accept "all necessary measures" to "stimulate immigration of Jews into Palestine on a large scale, and as quickly as possible to settle Jewish immigrants upon the land through closer settlement and intensive cultivation of the soil" while recognizing and protecting Arab peasant and tenant farmers. The understanding was typed in English. Before signing the document Faisal added a proviso in Arabic: "Provided the Arabs obtain their independence as demanded in my [forthcoming] Memorandum dated the 4th of January, 1919, to the Foreign office of the Government of Great Britain, I shall concur in the above articles. But if the slightest modification or departure were to be made, I shall not then be bound by a single word of the present Agreement which shall be deemed void and of no account or validity, and I shall not be answerable in any way whatsoever."[19]

Before Faisal left for Paris in early January 1919 Lawrence wrote a statement out in longhand for him to submit at the Peace Conference, stressing Sherif Hussein's role in the war and his status as a leader, Faisal's claims on Syria and his insistence that no foreign power be imposed there, and his concession that Jezireh and Iraq would require the support of a Great Power. On Palestine, the statement declared that "the enormous majority of the people are Arabs. The Jews are very close to the Arabs in blood, and there is no conflict of character between the two races. In principles we are absolutely at one," but that the "clash of races and religions that have, in this one province, so often involved the world in difficulties" justified "the super-position of a great trustee as long as a representative local administration commended itself by actively promoting the material prosperity of the country."[20]

The demand for "the super-position of a great trustee," which could only be Great Britain, sounded much like something Aaron Aaronsohn could have written.

~

President Wilson's messianic idealism was a problem for the Peace Conference, especially his calls for self-determination and his insistence that secret treaties and covenants not be the basis for the peace settlements. The seasoned diplomats, accustomed to tit-for-tat negotiations, and with the long peace after the 1815 Congress of Vienna as a model, were wary of the constraints that Wilson's naive idealism imposed on their own agendas. The French feared a plebiscite in Syria and a disregard of the boundaries and spheres of influence agreed to in the secret Sykes-Picot agreement. The Zionists feared a plebiscite in Palestine, where the Jewish population was a minority among the vastly more numerous Arabs, although Brandeis came up with the argument that it would be wrong to use "numerical self-determination" because so many potential inhabitants of Palestine lived outside its borders. The French and the British would have preferred a different way of getting things done. In December 1918, amid the post-Armistice celebrations, French premier Georges Clemenceau had made a ceremonial journey to London, where he and British prime minister Lloyd George had a few minutes alone at the French embassy. Clemenceau asked what they might talk about.

Lloyd George answered, "Mesopotamia and Palestine."

"Tell me what you want?" said Clemenceau.

"I want Mosul," said Lloyd George.

"You shall have it," said Clemenceau. "Anything else?"

"Yes, I want Jerusalem too," said Lloyd George.

"You shall have it," said Clemenceau. "But [French foreign minister Stéphen Pichon] will make difficulties about Mosul."[21]

It was typical of the gentlemen's agreements they could make without interference. Even contentious issues like Zionism they would have preferred to settle the old way. Balfour's argument for

Zionism was that the Great Powers were behind it. The French delegation cringed, but did not object.

But Wilson and his idealistic protocols were inescapable in Paris, and with the agenda of the formal sessions focused almost exclusively on Germany and Austria, the Middle East and especially Palestine became what Lawrence had once labeled "a side-show of a side-show."[22] For Emir Faisal, seeking an opportunity to address the representatives of the powers meant negotiating with the French, who were legendary in their skills at bureaucratic intractability and obfuscation, and were determined to offer him no podium. Jean Gout, the assistant director of the Asian section of the French Foreign Ministry, told the emir that he was recognized "only as a visitor and honored guest, not as having any connection with the Peace Conference."

Faisal insisted: "I cannot understand why I am omitted from the list of representatives to the Congress."

"It is easy to understand," Gout answered. "You are being laughed at: the British have let you down. If you make yourself on our side, we can arrange things for you."

When Faisal pointed out that he was there on his father's orders, and that he had been informed by General Allenby that the French and British governments had recognized him and his troops as belligerents, Gout answered: "That is a lie. We know nothing of an Arab army in Syria." The most Gout would yield was that while France would not abandon any of her interests, they were "ready to discuss things with you privately."[23]

The British had discussed matters privately first. They needed Faisal in Paris to bolster their claims that their border demands and aspirations for mandates over Palestine and Iraq accorded with Arab interests. "Through Mark Sykes and Colonel Lawrence," Lloyd George wrote, "we informed the Arab leaders, King Hussein and his son Faisal, of our proposals. We could not get in touch with the Palestinian Arabs as they were fighting against us."[24] The British argued successfully for two delegates from the Hejaz and got Faisal credentials as a delegate. With that step Lawrence's sole duties in Paris were to translate for Faisal, and occasionally to introduce him.

Lawrence was already staying at a different hotel from most of the British delegation, and with time on his hands he turned to the project that had been at the back of his mind even before the war. He had long before named the epic he would write: *Seven Pillars of Wisdom*. As sources he drew "from notes (mostly impressions) jotted daily on the march, strengthened by some reports to my chiefs in Cairo" and his fresh memories of the Arab campaign. Between mid-January and June 1919 he wrote a draft of books 2 through 7 and 10, approximately 160,000 words. He did not mention the manuscript in letters, but Richard Meinertzhagen, in Paris as a member of the British delegation, claimed that Lawrence lowered the manuscript to him on a string from his hotel room directly overhead so Meinertzhagen could read it.[25] Like most of Meinertzhagen's tales—and some of Lawrence's—the details of that arrangement probably should be taken with a grain of salt.

~

Shortly after Emir Faisal arrived in Paris a newspaper published an article reporting that Faisal was opposed to separating Palestine from Syria, and instead was demanding that Syria be held together as part of a new Arab state. When Faisal did not respond to the article, Aaron Aaronsohn suspected immediately that Lawrence was behind it. It is not hard to understand his reaction: his last meeting with Lawrence had been openly hostile, with Lawrence declaring that if the Jews of Palestine did not follow the will of the Arab majority they would find their throats slit. Aaronsohn traveled to London to confront Lawrence, did not find him—Lawrence was in Paris, working on *Seven Pillars of Wisdom*—but found friends and former colleagues who convinced him that what he had read was not Lawrence's position. They said that Lawrence had declared his position on Palestine independently to the War Cabinet, and that it provided for a Palestine separate from the portion of Syria claimed by Faisal and the Arabs for their proposed new state.[26] When Aaronsohn got back to Paris he told his colleagues in the Zionist delegation that Lawrence no longer had control over Faisal.

He was right. Faisal was under pressure. The French adamantly opposed him in Syria, the India Office opposed him in Arabia, he feared the Zionists, and with his father still aspiring to establish a caliphate over the entire Arab-speaking world, Faisal had to promote, or at least acknowledge, the demands of some of the more radical pan-Arabists. The Balfour Declaration was no longer a secret, and the grand imam of the Al-Aqsa Mosque in Jerusalem was already complaining of pro-Zionist rallies and Zionist aspirations to establish a Jewish state in a Palestine that would have no place for Christians and Muslims. Faisal had been close to an open split with his father over strategy during the Arab Revolt, and he hoped "to put off the breach between his father and himself as long as possible."[27] To present himself as the spokesman of the broad range of Arabs he had to take positions toward the Jews far harsher than those Lawrence had recommended and articulated for him. Appearing in Paris with the now famous Lawrence of Arabia would give Faisal some legitimacy before the Council of Ten. His legitimacy before the Arabs of the former Ottoman Empire depended on his willingness and ability to stand up to the French, the Anglo-Indians, and the Zionists.

Aaronsohn's close friend Felix Frankfurter was in Paris, holding what he called a watching brief as the personal representative of Justice Brandeis. Frankfurter was known to be close to Brandeis, and it was widely rumored that his views would find their way to President Wilson. Faisal was aware that Wilson's support for self-determination was potentially a useful argument for the Arabs, and he agreed to meet with Frankfurter, with Lawrence as translator. Meinertzhagen was also at the meeting at Faisal's villa in the Bois de Boulogne. Frankfurter told Faisal and Lawrence that as "American Jews with a tradition against colonialism, with strong affirmative traditions in favor of the dignity of man," the last thing in the world the American Zionists would support was "restoring Jewish civilization at the expense of Arab peoples and Arab civilization, that one involved the other."

Faisal agreed that Lawrence and Frankfurter should write up letters with their understanding on the issue, and the letters they exchanged at the Hotel Meurice have become iconic documents, frequently cited to prove that the Zionists and Arabs could get along well in Palestine. "With the chief of your movement, Dr. Weizmann, we have had and continue to have the closest relations," Lawrence had written for Faisal. "He has been a great helper of our cause, and I hope the Arabs may soon be in a position to make the Jews some return for their kindness. We are working together for a reformed and revived Near East, and our two movements complete one another. The Jewish movement is national and not Imperialist, and there is room in Syria for both of us." "This remarkable letter," Weizmann wrote, "should be of interest to the critics who have accused us of beginning our Zionist work in Palestine without ever consulting the wishes or welfare of the Arab world. It must be borne in mind that the views here expressed by the then acknowledged leader of the Arabs, the bearer of their hopes, were the culmination of several discussions."[28]

Faisal was only one of the worries that kept the Zionist delegates arguing and refining the position they would present to the Supreme Council. They also had to deal with the missionaries, idealistic educators, and representatives of oil companies, who had ambitions in Palestine, and who saw Wilsonian self-determination as a possible easy route to potential converts and an opportunity to buy up oil rights cheaply. Aaronsohn knew many members of the U.S. delegation, but the only American opinions that really mattered on issues that fundamental and close to Wilson's idealism were those of Colonel House and the president. At Weizmann's urging Aaronsohn got appointments to meet with Colonel House on January 6, 1919, and with Wilson a week later.[29]

But even as he proved essential for his connections to the Americans, his friendships with so many of the staff members in the British delegation, and his technical and political expertise, Aaronsohn's relationship to the Zionist delegation remained contentious. The European Zionists still resented his pro-British positions, his insistence on scientific and development priorities, his record as a spy and organizer of NILI, and his sometimes abrasive manner in meetings. The differences were less geography—Europeans versus British and Americans—than political and economic culture. Aaronsohn admired, supported, and was identified with the Americans, with capitalist development, and with what many Europeans saw as the petite bourgeois culture of the first aliyah. In the era of socialist revolutions in Russia, Germany, Hungary, and Austria, and huge socialist movements in most of the continental countries, the Europeans saw themselves as a bulwark against the American model.

There were also personal issues. Menachem Ussikin, who had opposed Aaronsohn in Palestine, and was said to live "in Odessa at the corner of Iron Street and Stubborn Avenue," still opposed him. "We can use spies," Ussikin said, "but we should not reach out to them." Aaronsohn angrily answered that by kicking him, Ussikin and his allies hoped to justify their cowardice during the war, and mitigate the horrors the victims of their cowardice suffered.[30] Sokolov, who had long been an advocate for the French against the British, opposed Aaronsohn's long-term alliance with the British both during the war and in the peace talks. The only European Zionist leader who trusted and respected Aaronsohn was Vladimir Jabotinsky. Jabotinsky's revisionist Zionism was far too militant for most of the delegation; both he and the delegation agreed that Jabotinsky should stay in Palestine.

From the other side, members of the American delegation insisted that Aaronsohn be made a full member of the Zionist delegation. It fell to Chaim Weizmann to decide, and he kept postponing a decision, leaving Aaronsohn in limbo. On December 11, 1918, Aaronsohn wrote to a friend complaining that he had no one to consult with, no access to meetings, and no power. Weeks later he wrote to Weizmann, reminding him that in June, when he had threatened to leave the Zionist Commission, Weizmann had promised that he would have a future role. Now, Aaronsohn wrote, it was time to decide. If he did not have a role to play in Paris as an official member of the delegation, he would go back to America, where his opinions and advice at least mattered.

Aaronsohn also wrote Brandeis for support, telling the justice that if he refused to come to Paris he would have to face the consequences of history.[31] In his anger, Aaronsohn had misread cues. Brandeis, though a good friend and a staunch admirer of Aaronsohn's, had always strictly separated his obligations to the Supreme Court from his role as the leader of the Zionist Organization of America. After the Balfour Declaration, Brandeis's position was that the political fights within the Zionist movement were over, and that it was time for everyone to work together. It was a position Aaronsohn would never accept. He believed and relentlessly argued that the battle for an active Zionism that NILI had begun had to be continued.[32]

By mid-January 1919 Aaronsohn realized that Weizmann and Sokolov would share the leadership of the Zionist delegation, and that he would not be an official delegate, but would only be allowed to stay on as a technical consultant. Bernard Flexner, a member of the American delegation, told him that he would never be forgiven if he quit—an argument strangely like the one Aaronsohn had tried to use on Brandeis—but Aaronsohn, who for long intervals would confine his bitterness to his diaries, unleashed a virulent storm, accusing the Zionists of forgetting those who had risked their lives for the Jews of Palestine, and Weizmann of growing up with the "machine," using it and getting used by it. He said he was through with the fighting, and would either go back to Palestine and his science, or go to Brandeis, the only true leader of Zionism. He made plans to leave Paris.

He was meeting on Monday, January 27, with Flexner and Jacob De Haas, another member of the American Zionist delegation, when he got an unexpected phone call telling him that the Zionist delegation now had to submit their final proposal to the Supreme Council, including proposed borders for Palestine, by Friday. "They need me to write a memo about the borders including justification," Aaronsohn wrote in his diary. "I hate the way they work. Give important missions to people and at the last minute realize nothing was done because they didn't let experts do it. I didn't even have a map."[33]

The British military attachés in Paris, especially Gribbon, urged

Aaronsohn to take on the border project, especially the complexity of the northern borders of Palestine, including the delicate frontier with Lebanon and the areas where the French had claims. He did not need urging. Defining the borders of Palestine was the project Aaron Aaronsohn had prepared for his whole life. His lonely search for early cultivars of wheat, the experimental work at Athlit, his wartime journey to England and Egypt, the battle to get the British to recognize and use the information NILI supplied—all were an effort to define a secure place for the Jews in Palestine. There might be room for compromise on the political issues he had argued with British intelligence and with Zionist leaders, but on the question of borders, he was sure of himself.

Aaronsohn understood the complications of the question: the territorial demands of the French and of Faisal, the reluctance of the British to provoke or defy their wartime allies, the leverage of absentee landowners in Jerusalem and Syria with their huge holdings in Palestine, the relatively small numbers of Jews in Palestine, and especially the short attention span of the Supreme Council, the decision-making body at the Peace Conference. The council was comprised not of scientists and economists, but of diplomats and politicians, who were sufficiently focused on what they considered the larger issues of the European war to give at most one day to the Zionist presentation.

Aaronsohn would have to persuade the peacemakers that scientific criteria—watersheds, hydrology, terrain, transportation routes, and cultivation patterns—were important enough to overrule politics. There had already been some quiet compromises: he had heard that Lloyd George had privately agreed to give up Palestinian rights to the water basin of the Yarmuk River, which began near the present Syrian-Jordanian border and flowed into the Sea of Galilee, in exchange for oil concessions in Iraq[34]—exactly the kind of backdoor dealing Aaronsohn feared. But he was confident of his ability to bring men like Woodrow Wilson and the other members of the Supreme Council around to his scientific view of the proper borders for Palestine. He had enthralled men like Julius Rosenwald, Justice Brandeis, Judge Mack, Felix Frankfurter, Henry Morgenthau, and Jacob Schiff, men of similar backgrounds and perspectives to the diplomats in Paris, with his dazzling combinations of history, scientific expertise, and intimate knowledge of the Holy Land. William C. Bullitt remembered how "diplomats [in Washington] sat open mouthed, astonished" by Aaronsohn's insights, and how they were "warmed by his picture of Zion." At the Hotel Crillon in Paris Aaronsohn told Bullitt that he expected "to appear before the Council of Four to plead for Zion," and asked Bullitt whether he thought "Clemenceau, Orlando, Lloyd George and Wilson would understand if he [were to explain] that a particular five-acre field should be included in the Zionist state . . . because it contained a unique specimen of a wild plant, which should be preserved for the service of science and would be tended by the Jews, but might be neglected by the Arabs."[35]

He was suddenly under an impossible deadline, but with a lifetime of study and conviction at his fingertips, it took him only a day to articulate boundaries and a closely argued rationale based on his extrapolation of the future water, transport, and security needs of Palestine: "In Palestine, like in any other country of arid and semi-arid character, animal and plant life and, therefore, the whole economic life directly depends on the available water supply. It is therefore, of vital importance not only to secure all water resources already feeding the country, but also to insure the possession of whatever can conserve and increase these water—and eventually power—resources."[36] "The only scientific and economically correct lines of delineation," he explained, "are the watersheds."

There had been no open conflict between the Zionists and their Arab neighbors, but long-term strategic considerations were the subscript for his arguments for an expansive Palestine. He called the Hermon range—where he had discovered wild emmer—the genuine "Father of Waters," which could not be severed from Palestine "without striking at the very root of its economic life," so that it must be "wholly under the control of those who will most willingly as well as most adequately restore it to its maximum utility." The Litani River was "of vital importance to northern Palestine both as a supply of water and of power. Unfortunately its springs lie in the Lebanon. Some kind of international agreement is essential in order that the Litani may be fully utilized for the development of North Palestine and the Lebanon."

His arguments, and the style and force of the rationale he laid out, were familiar to those who had heard him describe the history and future of Palestine:

> The fertile plains east of the Jordan, since the earliest Biblical times, have been linked economically and politically with the land west of the Jordan. The country which is now very sparsely populated, in Roman times supported a great population. It could now serve admirably for colonization on a large scale. A just regard for the economic needs of Palestine and Arabia demands that free access to the Hedjaz Railway throughout its length be accorded both Governments. . . . An intensive development of the agriculture and other opportunities of Trans-Jordania make it imperative that Palestine shall have access to the Red Sea and an opportunity of developing good harbours on the Gulf of Akaba. Akaba, it will be recalled, was the terminus of an important trade route of Palestine from the days of Solomon onwards. The ports developed in the Gulf of Akaba should be free ports through which the commerce of the Hinterland may pass on the same principle which guides us in suggesting that free access be given to the Hedjaz Railway.[37]

He had used the same ideas—the critical area for population growth in Palestine, the discovery of the large population in Roman times, the need for controlled water supplies and transportation routes, and the emphasis on intensive agriculture—to recruit support for the JAES in Athlit, and to dazzle Theodore Roosevelt and General Allenby. Those arguments had now become the justifications for the borders of a new postwar Palestine.

For the contentious northern border Aaronsohn drew a line from the Mediterranean, beginning south of Sidon and dividing the basins of the Wadi al-Korn and the Wadi al-Teim, the eastern and western slopes of Mount Hermon, and finally, from Beit Jenn following the watersheds of Nahr Mughaniye to the Hejaz Railway. Every twist and turn of his proposed line follows watersheds, allocating the all-important sources of irrigation water and the future hydroelectric resources either to the proposed Palestine, to Lebanon, or to the still-undefined Syrian successor state to the north. In the east, his proposed border was "a line close to and west of the Hedjaz Railway terminating in the Gulf of Akaba." Aaronsohn believed that the Negev and much of the Sinai were essential to the future of Palestine, but with all of the territory under occupation by British and Egyptian forces, he agreed that the proposal to the Peace Conference would have to leave the southern border undefined, "a frontier to be agreed upon with the Egyptian Government" and appropriate Arab authorities. His proposal also requested a land commission with the power to survey and propose measures for the "close settlement, intensive cultivations, and public use" of lands "unoccupied or inadequately cultivated" or "without legal owners." This was a continuation of the agricultural development ideas he had proposed and developed under the Zionist Commission since April 1918.

The proposal was well received by the Zionist delegation: even those who had been most critical of Aaronsohn considered the completion of the proposal on such a short deadline something of a miracle. At a party with close to twenty members and friends of the delegation, Major Gribbon—who had worked closely with Aaronsohn from the days when he first showed up at British GHQ in Cairo—stood up to say that the people of Palestine should never forget that the man who was most of all responsible for the wonder that happened that day was Aaron Aaronsohn. Weizmann wrote Brandeis to say that little events and personal views had sometimes led to people forgetting that Aaron Aaronsohn was necessary.[38]

The next day another meeting was scheduled to discuss the actual

• *Aaron Aaronsohn's Proposed Boundaries for Palestine* •

Maximum border according to Aaron Aaronsohn.
Compromise border proposed by the Political Section of the Borders Commission in the British Delegation to the 1919 Peace Conference.

FRENCH CONTROL
Beirut
LEBANON
Qasimiya River
Damascus
Hasbani River
Litani River
Metulla
Sassa
Dan
Kurum al Wadi
Kuneitra
Rosh-Pinah
Sanamein
Mediterranean Sea
Acre
Safed
Sea of Galilee
Izra
Basra
Haifa
Athlit
Afula
Mezerib
Deraa
Zichron Ya'aqov
Umm Queis
PALESTINE
Jordan River
Wadi Zarqa
0 Miles 50
0 Kilometers 50
Jaffa/Tel Aviv
Salt
Amman
Jericho
TRANSJORDAN
Jerusalem
Madeba
Gaza
Dead Sea
Beersheba
Hejaz Railway
SUEZ CANAL
Tafila
Hazeva
Maan
Aqaba
SINAI
(under British control)
EGYPT
Gulf of Aqaba
Red Sea

presentation to the Supreme Council of the Peace Conference. "Naturally," Aaronsohn wrote in his diary, "they were very careful not to invite me. . . . Matters have reached a point that is absolutely unbearable. It is impossible to keep up one's self respect under such condi-tions." When Weizmann asked him if he was coming to London for meetings there, Aaronsohn answered, "For what? To receive further insults? Many thanks. . . . [I am] sick and tired of remaining in the false position of a mistress who is loved in the privacy of one's room—but not recognized before the world."[39]

That same day brought the heartbreaking news that Mark Sykes had died. Sykes had come to Paris after a disappointing mission to Syria, where he had tried to bring Arab leaders and Georges-Picot together. He discovered that few in Paris were willing to listen to him. His aggressive efforts to create a joint solution for the Arabs, Jews, and Armenians had long been discredited, and most British officials facing the consequences of their contradictory wartime promises felt that Georges-Picot and the French had gotten the best of Sykes. Only old friends like Aaronsohn had remained loyal. Ill and exhausted, Sykes had contracted influenza—during the Spanish flu pandemic—and died of pneumonia.

Weizmann and Aaronsohn went to the wake at the Hotel Lotti. Lady Sykes was there, crying. "It was dreadful for that poor woman to be alone in a hotel room," Aaronsohn wrote in his diary, "without relatives or friends."

Faisal presented his proposal to the Council of Four on February 6, a few weeks before the Zionists. He had hardened his positions, especially toward the Zionists, with Lawrence's help. An aide in the American delegation was embarrassed when Lawrence showed him a memorandum he had prepared for Faisal. "If the views of the radical Zionists . . . should prevail," Lawrence had written,

> the result will be a ferment, chronic unrest, and sooner or later civil war in Palestine. But I hope I will not be misunderstood. I assert that

> we Arabs have none of the racial or religious animosity against the Jews which unfortunately prevail in many other regions of the world. I assert that with the Jews who have been seated for some generations in Palestine our relations are excellent. But the new arrivals exhibit very different qualities from those "old settlers" as we call them, with whom we have been able to live and even co-operate on friendly terms. For want of a better word I must say that the new colonists almost without exception have come in an imperialistic spirit. They say that too long we have been in control of their homeland taken from them by brute force in the dark ages, but that now under the new world order we must clear out; and if we are wise we should do so peaceably without making any resistance to what is the *fiat* of the civilized world.[40]

The distinction between "old settlers" and new was vintage Lawrence, while the "if we are wise we should do so peacefully" neatly reversed the ultimatum he had once given Aaronsohn in an antagonistic meeting at the Savoy Hotel in Cairo.

Perhaps because he recognized that Faisal's new position would not be welcome among the all-important American delegation, Lawrence took time off from his work on *Seven Pillars of Wisdom* to charm the Americans. He didn't need much effort. The American delegation was instinctively sympathetic to the Arabs for their revolt against their Turkish oppressors, they found Faisal exotic and elegant, and they were especially enchanted by Lawrence, "the twenty-eight year old conqueror of Damascus, with his boyish face and almost constant smile—the most winning figure, so everyone says, at the whole Peace Conference." Lawrence was actually thirty, and Harold Nicolson observed that "he would glide along the corridors of the Majestic [Hotel], lines of resentment hardening around his boyish lips: 'an undergraduate with a chin.' "

Faisal's new demands eschewed scientific and historical arguments for an emotional appeal on behalf of the Arabs and their contributions to the war effort. Lawrence's appearance at the formal presentation, in

British khaki with an Arab headdress, and his adept translations of Faisal's Arabic into English, and then into French, left a memorable impression. "I have seldom seen such mutual affection between grown men as in this instance," an observer wrote. "Lawrence would catch the drift of Faisal's humor and pass the joke along to us while Faisal was exploding with his idea; but all the same it was funny to see how Faisal spoke with the oratorical feeling of the south and Lawrence translated in the lowest and quietest of English voices, in very simple and direct phrases, with only here and there a touch of oriental poetry breaking through."[41] There were a few rumbles from those who knew Arabic that Lawrence's translations of Faisal's remarks were more creative than precise—some even compared them to the occasion in Scotland when Faisal recited from the Qur'an and Lawrence pretended his own impromptu speech was a translation of Faisal's remarks—but Faisal's presentation was, on the whole, received well.

The Zionists presented their proposals to the Supreme Council on February 27, three weeks later. President Wilson had taken a quick trip to the United States in between. The speakers for the Zionists were Nahum Sokolov, Menachem Ussikin (who spoke in Hebrew), and two Frenchmen, the poet André Spire and Sylvain Lévi, who had crossed the Atlantic with Aaronsohn on his last trip.[42] None of them was an expert on Palestine. Most of the language in the proposal they presented on the future borders, including the scientific and economic rationales, had been drawn verbatim from Aaronsohn's draft, with only a few minor changes to placate anticipated objections. Aaronsohn, intolerant of even a moved comma and bitter that he had not been invited to present the proposal, called the redraft *"a disgrace and a calamity."* In an angry letter to Weizmann he complained that for some of the Zionist delegation, "a 'watershed' is the same as a 'thalweg' [the hydrologists' term for a line tracing the lowest points of a stream or valley]. Incredible but true . . ."[43]

The Zionist and Arab presentations to the Supreme Council were a draw: neither Aaronsohn's precise science nor Faisal and Lawrence's righteous passion deterred Wilson from his idealistic dreams of self-determination. To Woodrow Wilson the decisions about new borders and new nations came down not to the diplomats' questions of what was possible or how conflicting demands could be reconciled, but to plebiscites and local preferences. The challenge of identifying a consensus of self-determination in a land where the Jews were a politically sophisticated minority and the Arabs a politically naive and inexperienced majority, in addition to the prior agreements of the British and French, the wartime alliances of Arabs and Jews with the British, and even the private talks of the Jews and Arabs, did not deter Wilson. He browbeat the council into appointing an Inter-Allied Commission to visit Palestine and investigate the views of the Palestinians. The French promptly refused to participate in the commission unless the British forces in Syria were first replaced by French troops; Lloyd George determined that if no French participated Britain would also boycott. Felix Frankfurter also refused to join. That left a commission headed by Dr. H. C. King and C. R. Crane, Americans with good intentions but little experience. Aaronsohn was invited to join but he had been spurned once too often. He wrote that he appreciated the feelings of the others on the committee and would spare them the unpleasantness of his company.[44]

While the King-Crane commission was at work in Palestine, the British delegation in Paris, confident that they would ultimately receive the mandate for Palestine, continued technical work to refine their economic development plans and the border proposal. The French, on behalf of Lebanon and a future Syria, had protested the northern and eastern borders in the Zionist proposal, demanding that both the source of the Jordan River and the Litani River were needed for future economic development in Lebanon, and that the snowmelt from Mount Hermon provided water to Damascus. Aaronsohn, with his strong supporters and fans among the British delegation and intelligence officers, was asked to address those and other objections. For weeks he traveled back and forth from Paris to London for consultations, and to utilize intelligence and library sources in England. Ever fascinated by new technology, he often traveled by air instead of the overnight journey by ship and train, relishing the three-hour flights to Boulogne on converted Handley-Page bombers, and occasionally as the sole passenger on a mail plane.

He met his sister Rivka in England in mid-February, before she left for Palestine to see their father, and pondered his own future. He had been a diplomat in a suit for too long, caught up in the vagaries of politics and politicians. He had done what he had to do, including the border proposals that perhaps only he could have drafted, but he had never been comfortable in that world of diplomatic compromises and imprecision, so different from the world of science, where knowledge and facts rather than politics governed. On a trip to London in April he bought khaki clothing and leather boots in anticipation of a summer of geological and botanical research in the Negev and Sinai, a beginning to rebuilding the collections the Turks had destroyed.[45] Science, he still believed, was the key to the future of Palestine. And in the Sinai there was the chance that he could find Avshalom Feinberg's grave: Absa deserved a proper burial as a hero.

On May 11, Aaronsohn flew to London for a conference with Weizmann and others in preparation for the final Peace Conference decision on the borders of Palestine. He had reservations for a return flight on May 15. Weizmann did not need to get back to Paris early, so he took the train and ship and agreed to carry Aaronsohn's baggage and clothes, letting Aaronsohn travel only with a document case for his precious final map of the borders of Palestine and his diary. On the morning of May 15 he showed up at the Kenley RAF airfield in Surrey to find the skies fogged in and his flight canceled. He quickly arranged to fly as the solo passenger in the closed cockpit of an Airco DH-4a mail plane, and he and the pilot took off for the three-hour flight to Boulogne in France, but the pilot decided that the visibility was too low and returned to the airfield. Aaronsohn placed a call to Paris to say that "the weather reports were such that he probably wouldn't fly."

At 11:40 A.M. the pilot offered to try again. The conditions were still foggy, but they took off against heavy headwinds and headed out over the coast and into the foggy skies over the Channel.[46]

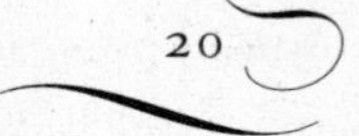

20

Endings

Our schemes for the betterment of the Middle East race are going nicely: thanks. I wish I hadn't gone out there: the Arabs are like a page I have turned over: and sequels are rotten things: do you want to make a happy ending to a tragedy? On paper it isn't virtuous, but in flesh and blood? I wish I knew.

—T. E. Lawrence[1]

We don't desire to turn out Mohammed in order to put in Mr. Cohen as a large landowner.

—Chaim Weizmann[2]

Two days after Aaron Aaronsohn took off from Surrey with his final maps of Palestine for the Peace Conference, T. E. Lawrence was on a Handley-Page bomber en route to Egypt. With few duties in Paris after Prince Faisal's appearance before the Supreme Council, Lawrence had been busily writing *Seven Pillars of Wisdom*. He was eager to check notes and papers at the Arab Bureau for his manuscript, and when he heard that the British were moving bomber squadrons from France to Egypt, he talked his way onto the flight with the excuse that he needed to fetch the belongings he had left in Cairo.

His plane arrived for a stop at the Centrocelle airstrip in Rome after nightfall on May 17. The pilot made a good touchdown, but decided he did not have enough runway to stop. When he attempted a go-around for another try, the right wing of the plane struck a tree and the plane crashed, killing the pilot on impact. Two mechanics escaped with shock. The copilot and Lawrence were rushed to the hospital. A few hours later, the copilot died from a skull fracture. Lawrence suffered a cracked shoulder blade and strained muscles, and was kept in the hospital for five days.[3]

~

Chaim Weizmann arrived safely in Paris via boat and train on the morning of May 16, bringing Aaronsohn's luggage. He learned that Aaronsohn's plane had not landed in Boulogne. British and French officials reported that calls had gone out to airfields in the south of England to see if the plane had returned for an emergency landing, and that ships were dispatched to search the Channel for the missing aircraft. The loss of the plane at sea was soon confirmed. The captain of a small fishing boat reported that he heard a loud noise as an airplane flew low over his boat and crashed into the water fifty yards away. He found mail floating on the water, but no sign of anyone.[4]

Almost immediately there was whispered speculation that the flight might have been sabotaged. Aaronsohn had political enemies, some ideological, some viciously personal. In Palestine he had long been resented for what many saw as his arrogance and overbearing manner, his strong and often controversial views on issues like the use of Arab labor, his advocacy of Britain as a protectorate power for Palestine, and especially his wartime spying. In Paris, tempers had been hot over the Palestine border question—the Arab nationalists and the French claimants to Syria both stood to lose their own land claims if Aaronsohn's map were accepted by the Peace Conference—and the once cooperative tone of Faisal's agreements with Weizmann and later with Frankfurter had long been lost in the aggressive propaganda from both sides.

Terrorist attacks against individuals were nothing new in Europe. The world war started with a political assassination in Sarajevo, and many could remember the bomb-throwing attacks of the anarchists, noisily targeting heads of state, aristocrats, capitalist enemies, even innocent bystanders. Those too young to remember the newspaper stories and cartoons could read Henry James's *Princess Casamassima* or Joseph Conrad's *The Secret Agent*. But Paris in 1919 was a long way from the days of the anarchists. Even the charged and sometimes acrimonious atmosphere of the Peace Conference, where tempers flared and speeches took flights of sarcasm and vituperation, was still a world of striped trousers and cutaway coats. As many potential enemies as Aaron Aaronsohn had, there was no evidence of foul play in the disappearance of the mail plane. Indeed, the late change from his scheduled flight seemed to eliminate the possibility of premeditated sabotage.

By Jewish tradition there can be no funeral without a body, so there was no service for Aaronsohn in Paris, London, or Palestine. The French and British newspapers carried obituary notices, and friends like Gribbon, Ormsby-Gore, and Weizmann made brief remarks about Aaronsohn's contributions during the war and the peace. The comments were no doubt heartfelt: Aaronsohn and his maps were sorely missed as the British were drawing up their final proposals for the borders of Palestine. As news of his death spread, many who knew him or had worked with him issued statements. "The death of Aaron Aaronsohn," General Allenby wrote, "deprived me of a valued friend and of a staff officer impossible to replace. He was mainly responsible for the formation of my Field Intelligence organization behind the Turkish lines. . . . His death is a loss to the British Empire and to Zionism, but the work he has done can never die." William Bullitt, who had worked with Aaronsohn at the Peace Conference, wrote: "I believe he was greater than all the people I have ever known. He was like the giants from the old ages—like Prometheus. It is not easy to express his greatness in words. He was the quintessence of life, of life when it runs torrential, prodigal and joyous. . . . I have never known anyone like him." Frankfurter said: "I do not need the fingers of my two hands to include him among the most memorable persona I have encountered in life." "All who loved and admired him," Henrietta Szold wrote, "must pledge themselves anew to the service of the land that was his first and last thought. In addition to what we do for Zion because we love the Jewish land, we must do a bit more in order that Aaron Aaronsohn, who has no sepulcher, may have a monument."[5] Others were generous but cautious in their comments, and many who had known Aaronsohn well were conspicuous by their silence. Some in the Zionist battles took no prisoners.

Paris was too busy to pause. The German delegation had arrived at the end of April. They argued that the harsh terms of the peace treaty presented by the victorious Allies at Versailles did not match the conditions on which they had laid down their arms and were virtually impossible to fulfill, but even as they protested they knew they had no chance of winning their case. For those who looked beyond the treaty with the Germans, Turkey was suddenly back in the news. On May 15, the day of Aaronsohn's flight, Greek forces landed at Smyrna with the support of the Allies, hoping to take advantage of the political and economic chaos in Turkey to seize a foothold in Asia, and claiming that the Turks had already begun to displace and massacre the Greek population of Smyrna and the coast. The Turks counterclaimed that the Greeks had begun to massacre Turks in the same region. Italy, hoping to advance its own aspirations against a weakened Turkey, landed troops in southwestern Anatolia. Aaronsohn, who had seen the horrors of the Armenian situation and Djemal Pasha's expulsions of Jews from the Palestinian cities, would have recognized the parallels in what was happening on the Turkish coast.

In Palestine, there was even less of a memorial for Aaronsohn than in Paris. Zichron was still bitterly divided. Those who had cheered on the Turkish police and soldiers during the arrests still hadn't forgiven Aaronsohn, and those who supported or worked in NILI hadn't forgiven those who watched from behind closed shutters while brave men and women were tortured. Ephraim Aaronsohn, still lame from the beatings by the Turks, had said kaddish for his martyred daughter, Sarah, and now had to say kaddish for his oldest son. It wasn't supposed to be that way, he no doubt told himself. Aaron had been the hope and pride of the family, precociously bright, hardworking, destined for success. It was Aaron's collections of plants and stones they had cataloged on the dining table, Aaron's voluminous library that filled and overflowed the shelves of their homes. It was Aaron who was famous everywhere, Aaron that people had come to see, who had been called to advise presidents and pashas and generals. To Ephraim, he was a kaddish, the son to whom would fall the responsibility of reciting the prayer in memory of his parents. A father wasn't supposed to bury his children. What more could they take? Would they remember nothing of what Aaron had done?

~

After five days in Rome, Lawrence was well enough to resume work on *Seven Pillars*. He caught a military flight via Taranto and Athens to Crete, and after a delay long enough for him to visit Knossos, another flight to Cairo. A fellow passenger was Harry St. John Philby, an Arab specialist on his way to mediate the continuing border dispute between King Hussein and ibn Saud. Philby was a soldier and Orientalist, considered himself an expert on ibn Saud, and had long held forth at the Athenaeum in London, offering eccentric solutions to problems in the Middle East to whoever would listen. One day he would tell a fascinated Chaim Weizmann that the solution to the conflicts between Jews and Arabs in Palestine was to give ibn Saud £10 to 20 million in return for accepting a transfer of all of the Palestinian Arabs to Arabia. Weizmann liked the idea. He and Philby agreed that the United States could help fund the proposal.[6]

In 1919, the problem for the British was more immediate. Ibn Saud was a protégé of the Indian government, Hussein had been a key figure in Britain's war effort, and their continuing feud was embarrassing for the British. Lawrence, engaged in his writing and long identified with Hussein and Faisal, was passed over as mediator; the job was given to Philby. When their plane reached Cairo from Crete, Philby set off on his diplomatic mission. Lawrence spent his stay in Cairo rummaging the files of the Arab Bureau for notes and documents he could use for *Seven Pillars*.

There was nothing left for Lawrence to do in Paris. Faisal had left. Pro-Indian interests accused Lawrence of creating propaganda for an Arab federation that would encompass not only Syria but also Mesopotamia. The British were wary of Faisal's new claims on Palestine, and with reports arriving from Jaffa and other cities of pro-Faisal demonstrations, they had backed away from their former ally and his spokesman.

From Cairo, Lawrence returned to Oxford, where he had been granted a research fellowship at All Souls College, £200 per year for seven years, a modest but comfortable income, since he was also given rooms at the college. The warden of the college and Lawrence's mentor and friend D. G. Hogarth had drawn up the fellowship in deliberately vague terms: Lawrence was to "prosecute his researches into the antiquities and ethnology, and the history (ancient and modern) of the Near East."[7] Questions were raised about whether Lawrence was still an adviser to the government or to General Allenby, but the India Office had been so effective in its attacks against Faisal and Lawrence that the Foreign Office made it clear that it no longer welcomed Lawrence's services in Paris.

Syria and Palestine were still in limbo. The King-Crane commission had a small staff, little prior experience in the Middle East, a paucity of knowledge of the politics and social conditions in Palestine, lacked language skills in Arabic and Hebrew, and found Jabotinsky and others in Palestine actively opposed to the purpose of the commission and unwilling to cooperate. After two weeks in Palestine the commission reported that the population would prefer an American mandate to any of the alternatives. It's hard to imagine who even read their report. President Wilson's catastrophic stroke, though concealed from the public and even from the Cabinet, seemed to postpone indefinitely all American decisions, and Henry Cabot Lodge, the Republican leader in the Senate, confidently announced that he had the votes to make sure there would be no American mandate in Turkey or its former territories. Even if the United States had been willing to establish a mandate, British troops still occupied Palestine and Syria, letting the French press their claim that the King-Crane commission was at best a vehicle of English propaganda.

By September 1919, Lloyd George, determined to keep his word and Britain's wartime agreements with the French, had already decided that Syria would go to France. The British delegation urged Faisal to return to Europe to participate in the Anglo-French talks, knowing he had no chance of reaching Paris in time. Lawrence, who might have spoken up for Faisal's position, was not invited. He stayed in Oxford, sometimes sitting "the entire morning between breakfast and lunch in the same position, without moving, and with the same expression on his face." At All Souls he read and reread the same poem by Doughty, "Adam Cast Forth," about the expulsion from the Garden of Eden.[8]

Lawrence feared that the outcome of further talks between Britain and France would be even worse than the terms of the Sykes-Picot agreement, which at least allowed Arab rule—under French and British spheres of influence—in portions of Syria and Mesopotamia. With no official outlet for his views, he wrote a letter to the *Times,* arguing that the weight of the many agreements compelled giving the Arabs "Damascus, Homs, Hama, Aleppo and Mosul for their own, with such advisors as they themselves judge they need," and that "the necessary revision of this [Sykes-Picot] Agreement is a delicate matter, and can hardly be done satisfactorily by England and France, without giving weight and expression also to the opinion of the third interest—the Arabs—which it created."[9] The *Times* supported Lawrence's position, but Lawrence was now a private citizen, and his letter made little difference. The future of the Arab lands and the Arabs would be decided not by Arab arms or will but by the Great Powers. The best Lawrence could hope for was a good ending for his book.

Lloyd George and Clemenceau agreed that in the absence of a formal Peace Conference agreement about the future of Syria, "the [British] garrison in Syria west of the Sykes-Picot line and the Garrisons in

Cilicia will be replaced by a French force and the [British] garrisons at Damascus, Homs, Hama, and Aleppo will be replaced by an Arab force."[10] The latter clause sounded like an Arab victory, but it was granting the Arabs only the lands they had originally been promised in the hated Sykes-Picot agreement that Lawrence had determined to undo in the Arab Revolt. And as Lawrence, the British, the Arabs, and the French knew, without the protection of the British, Emir Faisal's declared Arab kingdom in Syria was defenseless, at the total mercy of the French.

Lawrence put a good face on it. "I must confess to you," he wrote in a draft letter to Lloyd George, "that in my heart I always believed that in the end you would let the Arabs down:—so that now I find it quite difficult to thank you. It concerns me personally, because I assured them during the campaigns that our promises held their face value, and backed them with my word, for what it was worth. Now in your agreement over Syria you have kept all our promises to them, and given them more than perhaps they ever deserved, and my relief at getting out of the affair with clean hands is very great. . . . My first sign of grace is that I will obey the F[oreign].O[ffice]. and the W[ar]. O[ffice]. and not see Faisal again."[11]

He kept his word. Faisal arrived in London the day Lawrence drafted his letter to Lloyd George. He did not see Lawrence, and after a month of unproductive protests that the British agreement with France would leave him cut off from the Mediterranean, he was told that his only hope was to negotiate directly with the French. He left for Paris, where his negotiations were equally unsuccessful.

~

Lawrence should have been free to return to the quiet of Oxford to finish his epic, but it wasn't to be. One month before he drafted his promise to Lloyd George, a British impresario named Percy Burton opened an illustrated lecture program at the Royal Opera House in Covent Garden, featuring bold, colorful posters of the Arab campaign and the stentorian voice of Lowell Thomas. "At this moment," the narration began, "somewhere in London, hiding from a host of feminine admirers, reporters, book publishers, autograph fiends and every species of hero-worshipper, is a young man whose name will go down in history beside those of Sir Francis Drake, Sir Walter Raleigh, Lord Clive, Charles Gordon, and all the other famous heroes of Great Britain's past. . . . The young man is at present flying from one part of London to another, dressed in mufti, with a hat three sizes too large pulled down over his eyes, trying to escape from the fairer sex. . . . His name is Thomas E. Lawrence."

Thomas went on to recount that he had met Lawrence in Jerusalem, "on one of the narrow streets near the Church of the Holy Sepulcher" and that "a little later Allenby consented to my joining Lawrence and the Arab Army."[12]

Lowell Thomas had a knack for stretching the truth. Lawrence wasn't flying around London in mufti, they hadn't met near the Church of the Holy Sepulcher, and Thomas never accompanied Lawrence and the Arab army. By the time Thomas returned to the United States after meeting Lawrence, the Armistice had rendered his search for war propaganda moot, so he transformed the material he had gathered into fanciful romanticized travelogues. New York audiences especially liked his program on Allenby and Lawrence, and as additional promotion Thomas wrote an article for *Asia* magazine in which he claimed to have accompanied Lawrence on raiding parties against the railroads. The article was filled with vivid details of the raids, which Thomas had gotten from copies of the *Arab Bulletin* he had seen in Palestine. When Lawrence objected to Thomas's "red-hot lying," Thomas agreed to eliminate the invented material before the articles were published in England, in exchange for Lawrence's providing material about his background. Thomas would later claim that Lawrence had helped him with the articles.[13]

One million people saw Thomas's spectacle in London, which ran for so long the show had to move from the Royal Opera House to Albert Hall to Philharmonic Hall and finally to Queen's Hall. The heroic figure of Lawrence proved such a draw that the original title, *With Allenby in Palestine, Including the Capture of Jerusalem and the*

Liberation of Holy Arabia, was shortened to *With Allenby in Palestine and Lawrence in Arabia*. Only a change of the preposition was needed for the final transformation to Lawrence's iconic public name, Lawrence of Arabia.

Lawrence was in a funk when the show opened in London, depressed about the apparent abandonment of Faiṣal and the Arab Revolt, and by his father's death. It was only after his father's death that he learned that his perception of his own illegitimacy—a secret he had never discussed with either parent—was wrong, that the man he had known as Mr. Lawrence was actually his father *and* Sir Thomas Chapman, who had given up his original family, fortune, social position, and title for love. Lawrence kept to himself in Oxford, turning down interviews and the invitations of eager hostesses who wanted the exotic hero of Lowell Thomas's show at their soirées. But even as he fiercely criticized the romantic inventions of the show and the invasion of his privacy, he could not resist attending the show several times. He went anonymously, apparently fascinated by the enthusiasm of the crowds and by the spectacle he had become.

He kept working on *Seven Pillars of Wisdom*. He met Robert Graves and through him other contemporary poets, and began to see himself as a serious author. By late November 1919 he had written all of *Seven Pillars* except the chapters covering the spring and summer of 1918. His former army colleague from the Arab Revolt, Alan Dawnay, was at Sandhurst and agreed to read the chapters for accuracy, and Lawrence went down for a visit to discuss Dawnay's comments. When Lawrence left, Dawnay offered him an official attaché case to carry the manuscript home. At Reading, Lawrence changed trains and forgot the case at the station. He anxiously phoned Reading from Oxford, but there was no sign of the case. He had lost the only copy of eight of eleven sections of the book, along with the photographs, negatives, and wartime notes he needed for the remaining chapters.

~

In May 1919, when friends and enemies were quietly marking Aaron Aaronsohn's death, and Lawrence was rummaging files in the Arab

Bureau, the local chapter of the Muslim-Christian Association in Jaffa held a public meeting at the Zohar Cinema. Printed invitations announcing the agenda for the meeting had been widely distributed, and by ten in the morning on a Sunday a crowd of more than five hundred residents of Jaffa and neighboring villages showed up. The keynote speaker was a Christian; three other speakers were Muslims, including a blind sheikh from Ramle, where General Allenby had his wartime headquarters. The backdrop on the stage for the meeting was made up of four cloth screens—red, green, black, and white, each with a poignant caption. The red represented blood: "In the name of Arabia we will live and in the name of Arabia we will die." The green was for liberty: "Arabia will not be divided." The white screen represented Prince Faisal as leader of the Arab Revolt, and the black screen represented Zionist immigration into Palestine. (When Mark Sykes designed a flag for Sherif Hussein during the war, he used the same four colors: black for the Abbassids of Baghdad, white for the Omayyads of Damascus, green for the Alids of Kerbela, and a red chevron for Mudhar heredity.)[14]

The speakers at the Zohar Cinema emphasized the cruel repression the residents of Palestine had suffered during the Turkish period, praised the British liberators, and proclaimed that their own hour of freedom had arrived. They described the great past of the Arab nation and the Arab gift of enlightenment to Europe, and declared that the Arabs deserved a great future of national independence. The crowd was enthusiastic: Christians and Muslims together proclaimed themselves united on an independent homeland granting equal rights to all, including the Jews. "We do not at all oppose the Jews," one speaker said. "We only oppose Zionism. That is not the same thing. Zionism has no roots at all in Moses' law. It is an invention of Herzl's."

The assembly passed a resolution that Palestine was part of Syria, that it should be given autonomy in the framework of greater Syria under the rule of Prince Faisal, and that there would be no Jewish homeland. When someone proposed that those who attended sign a declaration confirming the resolution, there was an uproar as people shouted that they were unwilling to sign their names, that they hadn't been warned in advance. The crowd turned to angry blows. One young man jumped onto the stage and shouted: "You have no national consciousness! You are a herd! You don't understand what this day is for our nation! At this moment its fate is being sealed for generations to come! We will not let ourselves be led like lambs to the slaughter!" Tempers only began to ebb when the military governor appeared and ordered the meeting dispersed.[15]

Although no one credited or blamed them at the time, the fray had its roots in Aaronsohn and Lawrence's ideas and wartime efforts. Aaronsohn, at his research station, had convinced the British and the Americans that agriculture and industry in Palestine could support large-scale Jewish immigration. The war was hardly over when a third aliyah began bringing a wave of new Jewish immigrants from Poland, Russia, and other areas that had felt the shocks of the war and the Bolshevik revolution. Vicious new pogroms in the Ukraine and the anti-Jewish attitudes of the new Polish government added to the impetus, and the Arab population of Palestine, already aware of the sophisticated political and cultural organization and economic development of the Zionists, watched as new immigrants stepped off ships at Haifa and Jaffa. Absentee Arab landlords in Jerusalem and Damascus were eager to accept what they saw as generous offers for their land from Zionist organizations and individuals: there was always more land available for sale than the Jews could afford to buy. Fellaheen who had once sharecropped those lands, and who thought of themselves as having rights to the land—not ownership, but at least the right to crop the land—watched as the land they had marginally sharecropped was developed for sophisticated export agriculture, while they found themselves unemployed with no land to farm. They blamed not the landlord who had sold the land but the Jews who bought it. To the Arabs, the Jews were no longer one more minority, as they had been to a large extent under the Ottoman Empire; they had become rivals for the control of Palestine.[16]

The Arab frustrations with Zionism and with increased Jewish immigration and land ownership might have remained inchoate and disorganized. There had been little political organization of the Arab population of Palestine under the Ottoman Empire. The Arab nationalists, themselves a tiny group, had met and conspired in the cafés of Cairo and Damascus, not in Haifa or Jaffa, and there had been little organized affiliation between the Arabs of Palestine and those of Syria proper or Egypt. The Arabs of Palestine had also played little role in the Arab Revolt. Faisal and Lawrence drew their irregular troops from Bedouins with strong tribal organization and fighting experience, especially on camels. Arabia and Transjordan were their recruiting grounds. Palestine had a weaker tribal organization: many of the Arabs were urban or semiurban and felt few cultural ties with the Bedouins of the Arab Revolt.

But even urbanized Arabs admired the images of the Arab Revolt, the heroic photographs and reports of victories in battle, the triumphs of Arab warriors over highly organized Turkish armies and their German advisers. That Arabs could master explosives and destroy modern bridges, guns, and railroads—that pious Arabs could triumph over German technology—was both inspiring and promising for the future. The Arabs of Palestine were well aware of the technical and organizational advantages the Zionists enjoyed; they had seen the mechanized farms, the advanced agronomy at the JAES, the productive export crops of the coastal and Galilee settlements. They had lived amid the technological display of the British occupying forces for almost two years. The successes of the Arab Revolt gave local Arabs confidence and hope that they could survive and thrive in the era of modern technology ahead.[17] The Palestinian Arabs were no fans of Lawrence, but his efforts had both found a role for the Arab Bedouin army and publicized the Arab Revolt in the West, lending the revolt credibility in England, on the Continent, in America, and even among the Arabs, especially in areas like Palestine where Western media were available. Lawrence had legitimized Arab nationalism to the world outside those conspiratorial cafés in Damascus and Cairo.

What he had not done was to secure a state for Faisal or a basis for Hussein's hopes for a new caliphate. In 1919, the kingdom Faisal claimed to rule was undefined. He had made promises to sheikhs in Arabia, Transjordan, and Syria, to urban Arabs in Syria and Palestine, even to Christian Arabs. But no country recognized his kingdom, and it had no functioning political institutions. From Damascus he ruled a fantasy kingdom, which had the one advantage that it could be whatever any potential subject imagined. The Arabs of Palestine were free to claim or demand that Palestine would be autonomous within Faisal's greater Syrian kingdom—even though the French had made it clear that Syria was theirs, and the British had made it clear that they expected a mandate over Palestine.

For Britain, Palestine still represented an age-old dream. Richard the Lion-Hearted and the Crusades were vivid to British schoolboys, Jerusalem almost as integral a part of British history as the long wars with France. The nineteenth-century British evangelical movement was still alive, the Anglicans had built cathedrals and churches in Palestine, and missionary groups were active. The British forces in Palestine were fascinated by the biblical scenes of shepherds with their flocks of sheep, olive groves, rock-strewn slopes of the Judean hills, and camel caravans; they had seen similar scenes in Sunday school, evoking familiar passages from Scripture. When Weizmann met with Lloyd George on the day of the Armistice, he found the prime minister "moved to the depths of his soul, near to tears, reading the Psalms."

A mandate in Palestine would also be a foundation for larger British aims in the Middle East. The India Office still talked about the need for an overland route between Britain and India, and while many British generals and admirals were ready to jettison that argument and admit that the essential Suez Canal could be protected from Egypt, Palestine remained strategically important. "Has not the whole history of the war shown us," Lloyd George wrote, "that Palestine is really the strategical buffer of Egypt, and that the Canal, which is the weak side of Egypt, if it has to be defended in the future, will have to be defended—as it has been in this war—from the Palestine side?"[18] With the British fleet already converted to oil, and oil companies expanding their Middle East exploration after finds in Mosul and Persia, there were vague hopes that Palestine might also have oil. A British mandate would protect a possible future interest in that oil. The Mediterranean coast of Palestine would also allow the British to straddle the Middle East. The British still talked of the responsibilities of empire: "There'd been a war, the Turks had been defeated, the Middle East was divided up between France and England and it was the white man's burden," said Edwin Samuel, a district officer and the son of the high commissioner in Palestine[19]—and the British had reasons to want this part of the empire.

The most important reason for British enthusiasm for a mandate over Palestine owed much of its force to Aaron Aaronsohn. If there were British officers and politicians who still harbored old reservations about the Jews, and perhaps let anti-Semitic remarks and jokes slip out in private gatherings at homes or clubs, the war had brought a widespread conviction that the Jews were a powerful force in the world, and one with which Britain should be allied. Weizmann's relentless lobbying of the Cabinet had succeeded in persuading the British leaders to equate his Zionist movement with "world Jewry," "the Jewish Race," and "the Zionists"—even while the Zionist office occupied four small rooms in Piccadilly Circus, and its archives were a single box under Nahum Sokolov's hotel room bed. Weizmann succeeded because in Britain, America, and on the Continent there were many who believed that the Bolshevik revolution was a Jewish revolution, just as they had believed that the prewar Young Turk revolution was engineered by the Jews.[20] A typical joke said that three Jews ran Russia: the tea by Wissotzky, the sugar by Brodsky, and the state by Trotsky.[21] Many in the Foreign Office had long subscribed to the myth; Mark Sykes, according to his professor at Cambridge, saw "Jews in everything." Winston Churchill spoke for many when he wrote: "Some people like Jews and some do not, but no thoughtful man can doubt the fact that they are beyond all doubt the most formidable and the most remarkable race which has ever appeared in the world." He credited the Jews for both a system of ethics, "incomparably the most precious possession of mankind, worth in fact the fruit of all other wisdom and learning put together," and also for bolshevism, a system of morals and philosophy "as malevolent as Christianity was benevolent." The future of Britain was with the Jews: "If, as may well happen, there should be created in our own lifetime by the banks of the Jordan a Jewish State under the protection of the British Crown which might comprise three or four millions of Jews, an event will have occurred in the history of the world which would from every point of view be beneficial, and would be especially in harmony with the truest interests of the British Empire."[22]

Many also began to believe in the power of Jewish science, especially when Albert Einstein and other distinguished Jewish scientists were much publicized in the postwar years. Weizmann's synthesis of acetone was a modest achievement in the history of science, but so timely for the British pursuit of the war that many came to believe that "Jewish science" was not only advanced but also presciently focused on exactly those areas of technology important for the future. Aaronsohn's agricultural research, and his demonstration that the climate and soils of Palestine could support an expanding population and highly productive export crops, was more convincing evidence of the power of "Jewish science."

Aaronsohn's and NILI's contributions to the British military effort in Palestine and Syria provided another argument for the power and efficacy of the Zionists. Britain had poured manpower and sterling into the wartime alliance with the Arabs, sending experts, arms, officers, equipment, and vast sums of specie to Faisal and the local sheikhs. In return they got the capture of Aqaba, a campaign of harassment of the Hejaz Railway, Faisal and Lawrence's support on Allenby's right flank during the advance from Jerusalem to Syria, and unfulfilled promises that an Arab uprising would distract or cripple the Turks in the Arab-speaking areas of the Ottoman Empire. In the same period, Aaronsohn and NILI had provided a steady stream of intelligence, detailed and invaluable information about Turkish defenses and defense plans that greatly facilitated Allenby's advances. Aaronsohn had asked for nothing in return except British help in bringing modest sums of gold into Palestine for the relief effort, and his demands for British efficiency and respect. The fighting contribution of the Zion Mule Corps and later the Jewish Legion had received praise from the generals, including Allenby, and in Paris Aaronsohn had proved invaluable, the one man who knew Palestine intimately from one end to the other, who could put together maps and arguments for borders based on scientific and economic arguments that the French and other Great Powers could not easily dismiss.

Within Palestine, although the officers and soldiers on the ground in the occupation forces often favored the Arabs over the sometimes testy and demanding Zionists, it was the Jewish settlers who had built a functioning infrastructure within Palestine, from schools, orchestras, and the Hebrew University to local self-defense organizations like Ha-Shomer and the vast administrative structure of the Zionist Executive, which had taken over from the temporary Zionist Commission. They raised money from outside, mostly from Jews in America, to support their enterprise, although when Jerusalem educator David Yellin went to Chicago to ask Julius Rosenwald for support for the Hebrew University, he learned a lesson that Aaronsohn could have explained. Rosenwald had generously supported schools for African Americans in the southern United States, but would not support schools in Palestine: Blacks in America shopped at Sears, Roebuck & Co., Jews in Palestine did not.[23]

The Zionists also became an enthusiastic ally of the British, which represented a huge change of attitudes in the Jewish community in Palestine. During the first two years of the war, most Jews in Palestine wanted nothing to do with Britain. David Ben-Gurion and other young leaders had cultivated relationships with the Turks, and had offered and even begged to organize Jewish fighting units for the

Turkish army. When the Turks proclaimed the war against Britain a jihad at a prayer meeting at the Al Aqsa Mosque, in Jerusalem, many in the Jewish community in Palestine advertised their loyalty to the Turks by donning tarbooshes and proclaiming themselves Turkish patriots. Even in June 1916, almost two years into the war, when the news arrived that Lord Kitchener had drowned at sea, Jews in Tel Aviv decked the streets and organized parades to celebrate the death of the man they considered their nemesis.

One man, above all, switched Jewish allegiance in Palestine from the Turks to the British. While the crowds in Tel Aviv were celebrating Kitchener's death, Aaron Aaronsohn and Avshalom Feinberg had already concluded that the only hope for the Jews of Palestine was a British victory in the war, and Aaronsohn had taken the first steps on his journey to England and Egypt. When his plan to spy for Britain was rumored in Palestine, he was widely attacked by much of the Jewish community. Old enemies and those who had cast their lot with the Turks claimed that Aaronsohn's spying activities had placed the entire Jewish community in peril, that his activism was a greater danger for the yishuv than the Turkish expulsions, levies, even conscriptions into labor brigades. As late as the end of 1917, when British troops were already advancing into Palestine, some Jewish leaders in Palestine saw the death of Sarah Aaronsohn and the pursuit, capture, and hanging of Josef Lishinsky as the price of Aaron Aaronsohn's advocacy of an alliance with Britain. Allenby's stunning victories and the British advance into Galilee and Syria—made possible by information from Aaronsohn and NILI—were the turning point for Jewish views.

The Zionists debated the future endlessly, and even though Aaronsohn was sometimes excluded from the debates many of his ideas triumphed. He had long advocated the development of Zionism under British sovereignty, arguing that Zionism needed the peace and order that the British government could provide to achieve a critical population and reach a critical development of agriculture and industry. Although Ben-Gurion and the Labor Party were ever eager to proclaim their socialist allegiance and had long opposed Aaronsohn, they too shifted their hopes for peaceful protection from the Ottoman Empire to the British, even as they deliberately downplayed Aaronsohn's sense of Zionist superiority and mastery. In effect, the Labor Zionists were betting that a period under a British mandate would allow growth of the Jewish economy and population so that down the road a ready-for-nationhood Jewish state would be a fait accompli.

~

The Peace Conference fell apart before it had finished its work. Ill, Woodrow Wilson went home; other delegations left in a huff or from fatigue, leaving many contentious issues unsettled. The prime ministers of the European Great Powers decided to resolve the remaining questions relating to the former possessions of Turkey at a conference in San Remo in April 1920. In return for France's mandate in Syria, Britain was given formal mandates over Palestine and Mesopotamia, although it had to accept a smaller Palestine than the one Aaronsohn had so carefully drawn: there was no one to argue with his bravado and expertise for the watersheds, transportation routes, and agronomy- and population-based borders he had articulated. Lloyd George, who knew his Bible better than the atlas, had demanded repeatedly during the Peace Conference that Britain rule from Dan to Beersheba. It was a full year after the Armistice that General Allenby located Dan for him; it was not where Lloyd George had wanted the border, so he shifted his demand farther north and east.[24]

Lawrence watched from England, helpless as the last shreds of his promises to the Arabs were ripped up. Faisal, realizing that his vast claims were hopeless, had begun to argue for the territory granted to the Arabs in the Sykes-Picot agreement, which at least granted inland Syria and the Mosul region to the Arabs. But the quiet postwar agreements between France and Britain had already divided the spoils of war, leaving Faisal with empty promises. When the British left Syria, the French wasted no time driving Faisal and his entourage out of Damascus.

In the early months of 1920, Lawrence rewrote the books of *Seven*

Pillars he had lost, working from memory, "many thousands of words at a time, in long sittings."[25] He lived alone in a rented room in London, eating sandwiches from nearby rail stations, washing at the public baths, keeping warm with a flying suit—a re-creation of the marathon sessions of his years at Oxford. "I thought that the mind I had," he wrote later, ". . . if joined to a revival of the war-passion, would sweep over the ordinary rocks of technique. So I got into my garret, and . . . excited myself with hunger and cold and sleeplessness more than did de Quincy with his opium."[26] He was in a hurry because he intended the book not only as an epic saga, but as a political polemic, creating a war record of the Arabs and justifying Faisal's claims. Lawrence's version of the war is decidedly one-sided, seeing glory in the Arab efforts even when they were marginally successful, and denying proper credit to Allenby, the Indian troops, the RAF, and other branches of the intelligence services, including the EMSIB and the information it got from NILI. He was already a celebrity when he wrote the versions we read, and the book is also strikingly autobiographical—sometimes pensive and introspective, and as often as not surprising in the juxtaposition of odd reactions and familiar situations, as if he could not escape the old impulse to shock.

Yet if he was eager to shock, Lawrence feared the inevitable notoriety his book would bring and refused to sell the British rights to the work. In the hope of realizing enough money for the scheme he had long entertained of building a press for fine books with his old friend Vyvyan Richards, Lawrence negotiated to have an abridged edition published in America by Doubleday; he canceled the plan when he realized that an American edition would not raise the funds he needed. He met with Eric Kennington about illustrations for *Seven Pillars*—he had sat for portraits with Augustus John and other well-known artists, which gave him easy access to artists and illustrators—but finally concluded that the manuscript he had hurriedly written in early 1920 was "hopelessly bad as a text."[27] His striking decisiveness in war was replaced by constant self-doubt and tergiversation when it came to dealing with his peacetime literary masterpiece.

Syria and Palestine were settled at San Remo, although Ataturk's (he had been Mustapha Kemal at Gallipoli) Turkey did not sign the agreements for two years. Much in the Middle East remained dangerously unsettled. Mesopotamia was in the midst of a revolt in the summer of 1920, Arabia was still contested between Hussein and ibn Saud, and the vast territory between Palestine on the west, Mesopotamia on the east, and the Arabian Peninsula was undefined. Lawrence wrote about the situation in letters to the newspapers, comparing British policy in Mesopotamia to French policy in Syria. In January 1921 Winston Churchill invited Lawrence to join him as an adviser on Arab affairs. One month later Churchill was named colonial minister with a mandate to sort out the mess in the Middle East.

Lawrence was reluctant and tried to make a condition of his working with Churchill that Britain's wartime promises to the Arabs would be honored. When that was refused, he accepted because "Winston . . . offered me direct access to himself on every point, and a free hand, subject to his discretion. This was better than any condition, because I wanted the best settlement of the Middle East possible, apart from all the promises and treaties."[28] Churchill established a separate Middle East department in the Colonial Office, and gave Lawrence a formal appointment for one year, despite the warnings from some senior Colonial Office officials that Lawrence was used to dealing only with ministers and was not a team player.

To settle the many open issues, Churchill scheduled a conference in Cairo. Lawrence, who had planned a trip with Eric Kennington to Petra, Maan, Azrak, and maybe Medina to collect Arab portraits for a future edition of *Seven Pillars,* abandoned his travel plans to work on the conference. He and Churchill were determined to leave no loose ends: their agenda would define the questions to be raised, with little room for decisions other than the ones they wanted. "Talk of leaving things to the man on the spot," Lawrence wrote, "—we left nothing."[29]

They gave the throne of Mesopotamia to Emir Faisal, fulfilling at least one of Lawrence's and Britain's wartime promises. Lawrence professed himself satisfied, and later wrote that by 1919 he had already concluded that the center of Arab independence would eventually be Baghdad and not Damascus: "I envisaged Damascus as the capital of an Arab state for perhaps twenty years. When the French took it after two years, we had to transfer the focus of Arab nationalism at once to Bagdad."[30]

Faisal, before he accepted the new throne, announced that he would only accept if his brother Abdullah had no interest. The conference solved that problem by making Abdullah the ruler of Transjordan, over the objections of Herbert Samuel, the first governor of Palestine, and the Zionists, who had plans for the region across the Jordan. Lawrence had never had a high opinion of Abdullah, but he undertook the task of traveling to his camp in Amman and going through the familiar rituals of Abdullah receiving the sheikhs and chieftains. "Our schemes for the betterment of the Middle East race are going nicely: thanks," he wrote afterward. "I wish I hadn't gone out there: the Arabs are like a page I have turned over: and sequels are rotten things." Later, looking back, he wrote: "I take most of the credit of Mr. Churchill's pacification of the Middle East upon myself. I had the knowledge and the plan. He had the imagination and the courage to adopt it and the knowledge of the political procedure to put it into operation." Lawrence ultimately called the settlement "the biggest achievement of my life: of which the war was a preparation."[31] It was his good-bye to the Arab world.

The war had taken a personal toll. Lawrence had lost two brothers and his father. As executor of his brother's estate he followed Will's verbal instructions to take care of Janet Laurie. Lawrence may have retained a fondness for her: although his proposal had been rejected in what may have been a humiliating experience, she seems to have been the only woman to whom he had ever felt close. The hysterical pursuit by women enamored with his fame after the Lowell Thomas lectures made him avoid women even more.[32]

Lawrence rewrote *Seven Pillars* once more during 1921–22, working in London, Jidda, and Amman. This time he revised with great care and published an edition of eight copies in Oxford in 1922. The Oxford edition is the one generally referenced in this book, although it was not available in an accessible form until 2004. A slightly abridged and much rewritten version of *Seven Pillars* was later published in a limited subscriber edition in 1926, and in an edition of ten in New York to secure an American copyright. The edition of 1935, which has come to be the standard published version, is derived from the 1926 edition.

The idea that Aaron Aaronsohn had bequeathed to the Zionists—peaceful economic and political growth toward statehood under a British mandate—was too optimistic. The Zionist Commission stayed for three and a half years, reorganizing itself as a shadow government, and was adept at taking over the functions of Allenby's expansive occupation staff, with its chief political officer, financial adviser, chief of staff, and, beneath the latter, a chief administrative officer directing separate departments for general administration, finance, trade, health, legal, police, and public works. Allenby had also appointed district governors and assistant district governors, preserving Ottoman district boundaries and municipal governments. Ronald Storrs, who was appointed military governor of Palestine, described his own staff as "a cashier from a bank in Rangoon, an actor-manager, two assistants from Thos. Cook, a picture dealer, an army coach, a clown, a land valuer, a bo'sun from the Niger, a Glasgow distiller, an organist, an Alexandria cotton-broker, an architect, a junior service London Postal official, a taxi driver from Egypt, two schoolmasters, and a missionary"[33]—none of them trained to run a country. Even allowing for Storrs's affection for hyperbole, the British bureaucracy was a motley crew, and little competition for the efficient Zionists.

But the Zionists had not reckoned with the skills with which some of the Arab leaders played the British, nor the continuing favoritism toward the Arabs among the British soldiers. Early in the Mandate years, Humphrey Bowan, the British Mandate's director of education, wrote in his diary: "It is indeed difficult to see how we can keep our promise to the Jews . . . without inflicting injury on nine-tenths of the population." Wyndham Deedes showed Chaim Weizmann reading material he had found in British officer quarters, including *The Protocols of the Elders of Zion*. One officer wrote of the Zionists: "Their belief in what they are doing is terrible and selfish in its intensity. . . . They ask bounty and protection from England, but never pause to consider how many troubles they have heaped upon us in the past few years." Some senior British officers called Palestine "Jewland," and many British officers saw the Jews as Bolsheviks, routinely referring to them as "damned Jews" or "bloody Jews." One police officer excused the language by saying that "we scarcely regarded these people as human," and that he had heard similar terms used for the Arabs. Another reported that the soldiers preferred dealing with Arabs to the "hordes of Jews from Eastern Europe" because "the Jews are the most intolerant and arrogant people in the world." Richard Meinertzhagen, who had become chief political officer in Syria and Palestine, called the British military's hostility toward the Jews "Hebraphobia."[34]

The Zionists also did not anticipate that the Arabs would learn organizational and political skills from them. Some Arab leaders openly pointed to the Zionist organization and history as a model for Arab action; one wrote in his diary, "The Arab nation needs a man like Rothschild, who will put up money for its revival."[35] The Arabs also learned the power of calls to Arab nationalism. The nationalists had not succeeded in building an Arab state anywhere from the ruins of the Ottoman Empire: Syria, meant to be the heart of a new Arab state, had become a French mandate; Transjordan and Iraq were creations of the British. But the once obscure Arab Revolt had by the 1920s become famous. Millions in Britain and America saw Lowell Thomas's spectacles with their stirring narratives about Lawrence and the brave Arabs, and by 1921, the movie *The Sheik,* starring Rudolph Valentino, focused attention on an imagined Arabia. The Arabs of Palestine were not afraid to borrow from the Hollywood and Lowell Thomas imagery of noble Bedouins for their own cause.

Open troubles between the Arabs and the Zionists began in March 1920, at an isolated Jewish farm in the upper Galilee. The borders of Palestine were still not defined, and the French, who thought the upper Galilee should fall into their sphere, had soldiers in the area. A group of Arabs gathered outside the courtyard of an isolated Jewish farm named Tel Hai, demanding to search the yard because they thought some French soldiers were hiding there. What happened next at Tel Hai is lost under decades of myths on both sides. There were no French soldiers at the farm and the Jews put up no resistance to the Arabs searching the courtyard, but one of the settlers fired a shot in the air, a signal for reinforcements from neighboring farms. At Kfar Giladi, nearby, Josef Trumpeldor set out with ten men to answer the alarm.

Trumpeldor, a highly decorated, one-armed veteran of the Russo-Japanese War, was famed throughout Palestine for his heroic leadership of the Zion Mule Corps at Gallipoli. He had returned to Petrograd after the war, then come back to Palestine to prepare for the arrival of socialist-Zionist pioneers of the third aliyah. When he and his men reached Tel Hai, shots were fired. It isn't clear who fired first, but in the melee five Arabs and five Jews were killed, and Trumpeldor was wounded in his hand and stomach. He died while being driven to Kfar Giladi for medical attention, and in the days that followed, his last words—variously quoted as "No matter, it is worth dying for the country" or "It is worth dying for the land of Israel"—were transformed by hagiographic eulogies into the foundation of a legend.[36] Tel Hai and Kfar Giladi were evacuated after the attacks, but that inconvenient detail was put aside as the battle was cast into a symbolic Zionist victory. The agricultural settlements—especially the kibbutzim—were already powerful symbols of Zionist economic development, the promise of a self-sustaining nation. The events at Tel Hai transformed their defense into a rallying cry, elevating duty to the nation and land over individual lives. Those who had opposed Aaron Aaronsohn and NILI's efforts during the war as too risky would find in the defense of settlements against Arab attacks a manageable and less terrifying goal and enemy.

But even as Tel Hai initiated new myths of Zionism, the Arabs read a parallel message from the deaths of Arab fighters at Tel Hai. At a memorial service in Damascus honoring Arab nationalists who had been executed by the Turks, the speakers claimed that the way to honor the dead was to continue the fight against the Zionists. "There is no death more beautiful than death for the sake of the homeland," said one speaker.[37]

One month after Tel Hai, the Nebi Musa celebration in Jerusalem, a Muslim procession to a shrine associated with Moses, drew large crowds in a city already crowded with Christian pilgrims who had come to celebrate Easter and Jews celebrating Passover. Suddenly gangs of thugs surged through the Jewish quarter, attacking individuals and breaking into Jewish shops. From the balcony of the Arab Club speakers shouted, "Independence!" and waved pictures of Faisal, who had just proclaimed himself king of Syria. They urged the crowd to shout, "Palestine is our land, the Jews are our dogs!"[38] a rhyming couplet in Arabic. The demonstrations turned into a riot, with mobs accosting Jews in the streets and breaking into apartments to steal candlesticks, jewelry, and other valuables. A mob broke into a yeshiva, ripping up the Torah scrolls and setting fire to the building. When the British declared a curfew and later martial law, their searches discovered Arab women concealing stolen goods from the Jewish quarter under their robes. Rachel Yanait, who had worked with Aaronsohn during the war, walked through the Jewish quarter and found herself in a snowstorm of feathers from pillows and comforters the Arabs had ripped open. To anyone who remembered or had heard stories from Russia and Poland, the feathers—part of every story of a pogrom—were a painful reminder.

More rioting in Jaffa in 1921 followed the pattern of the Nebi Musa riots. With clubs, knives, swords, and pistols, Arabs attacked Jewish pedestrians, destroyed Jewish shops and homes, and beat and killed Jews, including children, in their homes. Feathers from slashed pillows and quilts again rained down on the streets as Arab men broke into Jewish buildings and murdered the occupants; women looters followed them. An Arab mob attacked an immigrant hotel, claiming it was a Zionist stronghold and a den of iniquity where young Jews engaged in "mixed bathing in the nude." An orgy of rape and beatings followed. News of the rioting reached the Jewish Legion, demobilized but not yet officially disbanded at its billet twelve miles from Jaffa. Soldiers of the legion set out for Jaffa with rifles, and the next morning Jews took to the streets for revenge, breaking into Arab homes, beating and even killing occupants, looting Arab houses and shops. Despite their long tradition as efficient colonial rulers, the British lacked the will to stop the rioting. A sergeant later testified, "When it was a question between the Jews and the Arabs we did not think it was for us to interfere. . . . Which were we to stop?"[39]

For the Zionists, the collective memories of pogroms in Russia, Poland, and Romania, and the experiences and attitudes of the yishuv in the years of the Ottoman Empire set an emotional and political context for the riots. The Jews had little opportunity for military organization or experience in Russia and Romania, and aside from the Ha-Shomer watchmen at some of the settlements, there had been no Zionist military operation other than the few Jews who had enlisted in the Zion Mule Corps or the Jewish Legion, and the few who had joined NILI. The Zionist Agency quietly condoned occasional smuggling of weapons into Palestine, but Ben-Gurion's labor government, with its moderate socialist economic goals and emphasis on the kibbutz as an instrument of expanding settlements and as an experiment in social and economic organization, followed a careful and deliberate policy of self-restraint (*havlagah*) toward its Arab neighbors. Comparisons with the pogroms in the old country or the new wave of pogroms in the Ukraine—where estimates of the death toll ranged from 75,000 to 200,000—were discouraged as part of a broad campaign to replace the image of diaspora Jews as victims with a new image of strong Hebrews, able to defend themselves as well as create a new land.[40]

Instead of building strong defense organizations, the Zionists concentrated on cultural, educational, and economic objectives and institutions, as if to prove to themselves and the world that the Zionist enterprise was ready for nationhood. They weren't beyond faking. At a reception for Winston Churchill, municipal officials in Tel Aviv cut down trees and set them in the sand around Mayor Meir Dizengoff's house to make an impression on their distinguished guest. When the bustling crowd accidentally knocked over one of the trees, exposing the ruse, Churchill wryly said, "Mr. Dizengoff, without roots it won't work."[41]

With the pattern of violence established in the first outbreaks of violence, the later riots in 1929 and 1933 seemed almost choreographed, as if the participants had learned their roles and were following a script of action and reaction. The trigger in 1929 was the erection of a screen between men's and women's prayer areas in front of the Western Wall of the Temple in Jerusalem; the Arab authorities answered by limiting access to the wall, sparking a series of riots marked by increasingly sophisticated organization, momentum, and deadliness. Those riots were the harshest yet, until the wave of violence that began with the murder of two Jews in April 1936, followed by a swift retaliation that took two Arab lives. The 1936 riots rapidly expanded: instead of being focused in a single city, the rioting targeted both urban areas and the settlements and kibbutzim that had spread over large areas of Palestine. Arabs attacked Jews on the roads, set kibbutz fields on fire, uprooted orchards, and organized a boycott of Jewish products. The Arab executive issued expansive demands: the end of Jewish immigration to Palestine, the outlawing of land sales by Arabs to Jews, and the establishment of a representative governing body with an Arab majority—a program that would have ended Britain's commitment to the Zionists. As the rioting and boycott expanded, the Arabs called their collective actions the Great Arab Revolt in Palestine—associating themselves with the glory, though not the reality, of Faisal's and Lawrence's Arab Revolt two decades before. The new Arab revolt lasted until 1939.

Some Muslim Arabs justified the continued rioting by citing the Qur'an and other Islamic texts as evidence that the Jews were a superceded people, despised by Allah for their disdain of the Prophet and punished by being turned into a cowardly, humiliated, and servile race for eternity. That a people so damned by Allah could lay claim to Islam's third holiest city, buy up the land of Arabs in Palestine, create institutions that outshone the remnants of Islamic glory, and defeat Arabs in battles for public opinion and the support of the British, these voices claimed, was an assault on Islam. Some imams and Islamic authorities in their Friday sermons might have condemned this highly political interpretation of the Qur'an, but it supported a hatred based in faith. Some Christian Arabs took a similar position, condemning the ascendancy of Jews, who by church doctrine had been superceded by Christianity and were to be punished for denying, or, in some interpretations, killing, Jesus. That this cursed people should ascend to economic and political power in the Holy Land was an affront to some Christian Arabs in the same way that Muslim control of the Holy Land had been an affront to the crusaders.

The Zionists reacted with practical measures to resist the attacks, economic moves to counteract Arab boycotts, efforts to expand Jewish settlements in anticipation of British partitioning schemes, and attempts to maintain or even increase the level of Jewish immigration. Kibbutzim and other settlements had long been built with watchtowers and stockades for defense, and the signaling system that had come into play at Tel Hai became more sophisticated to protect isolated settlements. The forerunner of a Zionist defense force, the Haganah, had been quietly organized in the 1920s, drawing from the experiences of the Ha-Shomer, the Gideonites, the Zion Mule Corps, and the Jewish Legion, all the while maneuvering cautiously to stay within the British restrictions on weapons and organized military forces. Later the Irgun, a more radical fighting force, was secretly established with Vladimir Jabotinsky as its political leader.

The continued boycott of Jewish businesses, the relentless violent attacks, and the rise of faith-based anti-Semitism tested the mostly secular faith of the Zionists. At Kibbutz Haboneh, near Avshalom Feinberg's hometown of Hadera, the Haggadah for the secular Passover seder in 1937 recast the traditional four questions as woes of the new Arab Revolt:

> How is this year different from all other years?
>
> *For in all other years* we traveled securely on the roads of this land.
>
> *This year*—only crowded together in caravans, with policemen before us and behind us.
>
> *For in all other years* night was for rest and the evening for discussion and mutual clarification.
>
> *This year* night is for guarding at our posts, and the whole evening is wasted in training exercises.
>
> *For in all other years* the crops grew according to the blessing of the sky, either for good or for bad, but for sure! Trees grew in the orchard, flowered and gave forth their produce, but for sure—
>
> *This year* the crops in the fields in our settlements were set on fire, and the trees of Jewish orchards were uprooted and destroyed—so utterly destroyed—
>
> *For in all other years* we thought the English authorities ruled the land as they arrested every murderer or criminal and brought him to justice.
>
> *This year* the armed gangs took control of our land with murder and destruction, they murdered a hundred Jewish souls and hundreds of dunams of planting—the shed blood cries out to heaven with no redeemer! —For the authorities have become too weak to arrest the murderers and no murderer receives his due.[42]

At other kibbutzim that year, Passover haggadot quoted Hayyim Nahman Bialik's powerful poem on the Kishinev pogrom of 1903, "On the Slaughter," evoking a comparison to old country pogroms that had been discouraged by the Labor Zionists in their campaign to create an image of a strong Hebrew nation. Zionist attitudes hardened as the revolt persisted, and by 1939, when the Arab Revolt collapsed, even longtime supporters of the Labor Party had turned from the self-restraint policy of *havlagah,* which trusted the British to restore law and order, to a military activism, preparation for future armed struggle against the Arabs.[43]

The British became targets in the riots of 1933. By 1936 they found themselves unable to maintain order in Palestine. They had been accustomed to governing a population of 300 million with the 1,000 members of the Indian Civil Service, but the noblesse oblige, aloofness, and noninterference in local matters that had worked so successfully in India failed in the face of the hardening attitudes and competing claims of the Jews and Arabs of Palestine. The British appointed commissions and offered partition schemes, only to find them rejected by both sides as it became increasingly clear to all parties that the differences between the Zionists and the Arabs would only be settled by war.

T. E. Lawrence would have been horrified. Aaron Aaronsohn probably would have told the British—or perhaps his diary—that if they had only listened to him and stuck to the borders he had drawn it would not have happened.

21

Legacies

I'm a rather complicated person, and that's bad for a simple biography.

—T. E. Lawrence[1]

The name of Aaronsohn will through the ages be remembered as that of a family who, with the entire disregards of self, endured all—even to martyrdom—in the cause of Civilization and Humanity, and whose courage and devotion were largely instrumental in carrying that cause to final success.

—Field Marshal Edmund Allenby, 1923[2]

Lawrence and Aaronsohn were dreamers, with the passion and self-assurance of youth and the conviction and single-mindedness of men on the outside. They sought to change history by the brute force of their ideas and leadership—a formidable, perhaps impossible challenge, all the more difficult in the political maelstrom of the world war, amid collapsing empires, aspiring new states, and peoples finding and creating new political identities. Adamant and alone against the might of empires, generals, and diplomats, fighting the inertia of institutions and authority, they made political miscalculations and personal missteps, sometimes losing momentum and sinking into solipsism or petulance. They were celebrated for their achievements and triumphs, but never realized their dreams and never saw their ideas play out on the world stage. Yet they came closer than they realized, as their ideas long outlived them, ultimately succeeding in ways they could not have imagined.

Lawrence served his two masters well. As liaison to Faisal and the Arab Revolt he gave the British Foreign Office and the military command in Cairo the diversionary actions they sought from the Arab army, especially at Aqaba, on the Hejaz Railway, and in Allenby's advance north. Lawrence knew, almost from the days of his first ride to Faisal's camp, that the Arab Revolt was doomed, that the secret diplomatic agreements of France and Britain had preempted the great Syrian-centered Arab state Faisal believed he had been promised, that neither the Arabs nor the Great Powers were ready for the new states or the revived caliphate that Hussein and his sons claimed. He knew as well as anyone in British intelligence about the internal divisions within the Arab world, the long traditions of tribal and clan loyalties, and the lack of political institutions and experience among the Arabs of the Ottoman Empire. But Lawrence remained convinced that there was still much the revolt could achieve: if the Arab army had reached Damascus, if the tribes and clans and sheikhs could have overcome their squabbling and functioned as a fighting unit, they would have achieved a measure of Arab unity previously thought impossible. That alone would have impressed the diplomats of Europe, America, and the Middle East with the possibility of an Arab nation.

Many of the Bedouin soldiers had no political objectives; they had joined only for the glory of battle and the looting that was the traditional reward of victory. Even the city dwellers of the Arab-speaking world had known only Ottoman authority; though Muslim, they had been second-class citizens under the Turks, their quiet aspirations toward nationalism or independent political institutions ruthlessly suppressed, even their language unrecognized in official dealings. Through the experience of marching together in an Arab army the followers and supporters of the revolt experienced the thrill of victory and a sense that Arab independence was possible. That their revolt was recognized and supported by Britain, and that France actively manipulated opposition to the revolt, told them that they were legitimate players on the world stage, that the very idea of Arab nationalism could inspire fear and respect. That legitimation of Arab nationalism in the West and the recognition of the Arab army as a fighting force were Lawrence's achievement.

Lawrence also served himself well: the Arab Revolt and his part in the Arab campaign became the warp that would be woven with his fascination with the desert and the noble Bedouin, and the raw heroics and pageantry of the Crusades, to become the saga he had been intent on writing from his college days at Oxford. He had picked the title *Seven Pillars of Wisdom* long before he had a subject. The book chronicles, and perhaps exaggerates, the bravado, verbal sparring, and contentious baiting that characterized many of Lawrence's wartime dealings with the British command, his meetings with men like Aaron Aaronsohn and Mark Sykes, and his occasional representation of the more extreme positions into which politics forced his friend Emir Faisal. But Lawrence also recognized and occasionally acknowledged a nonpartisan understanding of the Middle East, and especially the politics of the Arabs and Jews of Palestine, which might have gone far toward avoiding the long conflict and even longer stalemate that characterizes modern Israeli-Arab relations. Unlike the more extreme elements of Arab nationalism today, Lawrence saw a potential for mutually beneficial progress in the Zionist development of agriculture, industry, and cultural and social institutions in Palestine. He openly admired the achievements of the Zionists on his first trip to the Holy Land, and acknowledged that admiration later—though too late to have any impact on the Peace Conference and the future of Palestine.

If Lawrence's campaign with Faisal, both on the battlefields and in Paris, did not realize an independent Arab state, his ideas on guerrilla warfare, desert operations, and the conduct of Westerners with Arab units were pathbreaking and in many cases have become canonical. Recently, Lawrence's "Twenty-Seven Articles," guidelines for appropriate conduct with the Arabs he wrote for the *Arab Bulletin* in August 1917, has been cited by American and British generals as justifications for their conduct of the war in Iraq and their efforts to train Iraqi security forces. Lawrence's name and fame give the citations gravitas, and the geography seems to make his observations relevant, but as so often has happened with Lawrence, the subsequent mix of history and myth loses track of the original reality. Lawrence's recommendations in 1917 were intended to deal only with Bedouins. "Townspeople," he wrote, ". . . require totally different treatment." He was writing about efforts to foment and encourage a revolt, not to suppress an insurgency, and he qualified his recommendations with the proviso that "handling Hejaz Arabs is an art, not a science, with exceptions and no obvious rules."[3]

~

Aaron Aaronsohn told the world that he understood Palestine better than anyone, and from his too-brief life as a scientist he may have been right. He concluded and demonstrated that the land of Palestine could support the increased population that would make the realization of the Zionist dreams possible, developed the agronomy techniques that would realize that prediction, and persuaded wealthy men and women in America to support continued research. When the war came, he ventured his scientific career, his family, his home, and all he had achieved in an effort to make certain the British won the war, never wavering from his convictions that the future of Palestine was with science, that a development of the agricultural and industrial infrastructure would enable the immigration and the expansion of the economy. Against the tide of second-aliyah socialism, he fought for agricultural and industrial expansion based on capitalist investment. Against the moderation and diplomatic acquiescence of others, he argued for borders that would guarantee the natural resources and security that would permit that development.

He insisted on the absolute solutions of a scientist at the very moment when the politics and diplomacy of war were at their most complex, when the contentiousness of the Great Powers, the nexus of secret treaties, the idealism of Woodrow Wilson, the aspirations of princes without thrones, and the conflicting demands of newly liberated peoples tied the politics of the Middle East into a great Gordian knot. In the simpler prewar world, Aaronsohn was a remarkably persuasive man; in the war-making of 1916 or the peacemaking of 1919 his words could not match Alexander the Great's sword.

We can only imagine the history of the Middle East if a Palestine had been created with the borders he urged on the peacemakers at Paris, borders drawn to allocate water resources, arable land, and transportation access by geographical criteria rather than by the diplomacy of give-and-take or the cease-fire lines of military conflicts; if the scientifically directed and investment-driven development he advocated had been pursued, unbridled by the socialist and agrarian ideologies of the Zionist labor government; if Jewish political attitudes toward the Arabs and the British had followed the precedent of NILI activism instead of the self-restraint of *havlagah;* and if a viable state, or two states, had been established in Palestine before the rise of Arab nationalism and the national identities of the new states created by the British and French as they divided the Ottoman Empire into the geographically arbitrary boundaries of Syria, Lebanon, Jordan, Iraq, and Saudi Arabia, leaving the contentious lands of the West Bank, the Golan Heights, the Lebanese border, Gaza, and Sinai to be buffeted back and forth between those states, Egypt and Israel.

~

Lawrence had taken off his Arab robes for good by the time the French swept away Faisal's kingdom in Syria and the British gave him a new kingdom in Iraq. He and Faisal met again in September 1925 when Faisal visited London. Lawrence wrote that his old friend was "lively, happy to see me, friendly, curious." But, Lawrence wrote later, "I've changed, and the Lawrence who used to go about and be friendly and familiar with that sort of people is dead. He's worse than dead. He is a stranger I once knew."[4]

Lawrence insisted on living in the present, *his* present. The Arabs lived in the future and the past. They remembered the great moments of Islamic triumph, including the Arab Revolt, and dreamed of a new caliphate and new kingdoms, but sometimes overlooked present realities. By 1924, Sherif Hussein was demanding from his throne in Mecca that all Arab states except his return to their prewar boundaries, that all newly acquired areas be ceded to him, and that he be recognized as supreme over Arab rulers everywhere. The outrageous demands bore no relation to his power and position in the postwar world, and when he refused to sign a new Anglo-Hashemite treaty that ignored his claims, the British withdrew their support. Hussein was forced to abdicate, leaving the way open for his longtime rival ibn Saud to take over Mecca and eventually absorb the Hejaz into a new kingdom of Saudi Arabia. The Saudis wanted nothing to do with Lawrence's legacy. That it was his fame, his writing, and his contributions to Faisal and Hussein's revolt that had given Arab nationalism wartime legitimacy in the capitals of Europe and America has never been acknowledged or celebrated in the Arab world. Lowell Thomas's shows transformed Lawrence into an iconic figure in the West, but he never became a hero to the Arabs or the Jews of Palestine. Even today, Arab presses produce mocking biographies of him. In Israel he is called Lorens ish Arav, a construction that to a Hebrew speaker recalls Judas Iscariot.

Lawrence's hasty departure from Damascus in 1918 was a mostly symbolic separation. He had realized that his grand adventure was quixotic: "It was a fantasy:—to believe that an illiterate spirit of nationality, without authority, without a city or a ship or a factory or a shop or a rifle or a leader of its own could meet Turkey in arms and wrest away its old capital."[5] After his service with Churchill and the Colonial Office, he turned to new lives. Broke and desperate for privacy, he tried unsuccessfully to get the Foreign Office to block publication of Lowell Thomas's book about him on the grounds that Thomas had illegally used a copy of the *Arab Bulletin* as a source.[6] He turned down academic offers, and instead decided to join one of the service branches as an enlisted man under an assumed name, hoping to find anonymity, a measure of privacy, the camaraderie of fighting men that he had admired among the Bedouin, and a place where he would not be encumbered by his short stature (he had too often heard himself referred to as little Lawrence),[7] the demands of concealing his illegitimacy, or the possessions and social demands of a conventional life. In 1922 Leo Amery, the first lord of the Admiralty, who as a member of the Cabinet Secretariat had written admiringly about Aaronsohn at the time of the Balfour Declaration, met Lawrence at a dinner and tried to get him a posting in the Royal Navy under an assumed name.[8] The navy was apparently afraid of the adverse publicity if the "uncrowned king of Arabia," as the press had dubbed him, were to be found masquerading as an ordinary Jack Tar, and Lawrence instead joined the RAF under an assumed name assigned by the air ministry: John Hume Ross. He bought a motorcycle, and took advantage of his relative anonymity to work on *Seven Pillars* and other projects. After a year, his identity was exposed and he mustered himself out of the RAF and joined the tank corps under a second assumed name, T. E. Shaw. He later transferred back to the RAF, and served for many years in India, then in England, where he developed rescue boat designs.

With his fierce powers of concentration, Lawrence took advantage of whatever free time was available to him to maintain a voluminous correspondence, to finish his seemingly endless revisions of *Seven Pillars of Wisdom,* and to shepherd publication of an abridged version, *Revolt in the Desert,* which became a best seller in America and England. He was determined not to profit from his service in the Arab Revolt, and assigned the royalties for *Revolt in the Desert* to a charitable trust. After he completed the proofs for the subscriber edition of *Seven Pillars of Wisdom* in 1926, he wrote *The Mint* about his experiences in the RAF, did translations, including an edition of the *Odyssey,* and worked with Robert Graves and B. H. Liddell Hart on their proposed biographies of him. He never overcame a self-consciousness about his writing, especially after some critics found *Revolt in the Desert* too Victorian in style and self-consciously close in language to Doughty's writings on Arabia. "I agree that the *Seven Pillars* is too big for me," Lawrence wrote, "too big for most writers, I think.

It's in the titan class: books written at tiptoe, with a strain that dislocates the writer, and exhausts the reader out of sympathy. Such can't help being failures, because the graceful thinkings are always those within our force: but, as you conclude, their cracks and imperfections serve an artistic end in themselves: a perfect picture of a real man would be unreadable."[9] While he was rewriting *Seven Pillars* he wrote to a friend: "Do you remember my telling you once that I collected a shelf of 'Titanic' books . . . *The Karamazovs, Zarathustra,* and *Moby Dick*. Well, my ambition was to make an English fourth. You will observe that modesty comes out more in the performance than in the aim!"[10] Lawrence could not escape the realization that his life and legacy would be in this book. And even long after he finished *Seven Pillars,* he found himself revealing the extent to which what he had subtitled "A Triumph" was at least partially a fiction. "I was on thin ice when I wrote the Damascus chapter," he told Robert Graves, "and anyone who copies me will be through it, if he is not careful. S[even]. P[illars]. is full of half truth: here."[11]

For all his achievements, the war had taken a heavy toll on Lawrence. He was frequently depressed, and overwhelmed by the complexity of civilian life and the conflict between the demands of fame and his need for privacy. An immaculate and stringently celibate man, he had been profoundly affected by the rape at Deraa,[12] his psyche so scarred that in 1923, while he was in the tank corps, he engaged a friend to whip him in the privacy of his home. The beatings, to the point of sexual orgasm, continued for more than a decade.[13] In the 1930s Lawrence finally retired with his books. He redesigned and carefully decorated the cottage at Clouds Hill in Dorset to reflect the precise demands of his life—privacy, simplicity, echoes of the ancient and desert worlds, and that firm sense of himself as "different" that had stuck with him since adolescence. In a way he had come full circle, back to the days at Oxford when his parents had built him a bungalow where he could close the curtains and escape the discipline of the ordinary world in books.

Lawrence died in a motorcycle accident in 1935. He was too iconic a figure not to inspire conspiracy theories about his death—that it had been arranged because of his spying (the French had always accused Lawrence of being a spy), or that it was a suicide because he was afraid of some revelation about his background—but there was never any evidence of foul play. He died as he had lived, driving fast and alone.

~

Aaron Aaronsohn's afterlife in Palestine and later Israel was more complicated. Aaronsohn never wrote a saga of his adventures. We know him through his diary, correspondence, and the powerful impressions he made on others. His scientific articles are still cited, and his pioneering work on dryland agriculture is still a model in Israel and elsewhere. The wild emmer he discovered did not become an answer to declining wheat yields—it was others, not he, who thought it would—but it recently has been cultivated in Italy as *farro* and used to make pasta sold in specialty and health-food stores. Without the emphatic persona that Lawrence's own writings evoked, and the iconic images of the "uncrowned king of Arabia" that Lowell Thomas created in his shows and books about Lawrence and that David Lean re-created in his 1962 film *Lawrence of Arabia,* Aaronsohn remained only a personal memory for those who knew him and had worked with him, with much that he had done hidden in the obscurity of British archives and in the papers, books, and specimens that escaped destruction in Zichron Ya'aqov. Ben-Gurion and generations of Zionist leaders under the British Mandate had quietly appropriated elements of Aaronsohn's model for Zionist development, but Aaronsohn's name and reputation, bound up with the spying activities of NILI and with his aggressive politics, were squelched by an official Zionist Labor ideology of moderate socialism and self-restraint. Nili eventually became a popular name for girls in Israel, but some continued to argue that the NILI organization had not been important in providing information to the British or in speeding the course of the war, even that a former insurance agent named Alter Levi had gotten more information for the British by extorting the clients of his chain of brothels.[14]

The Aaronsohns had not fared well in love. Aaron, Alex, and Rivka never married. Aaron seems not to have loved any woman after his romance with Sonia Suskin. Sarah's self-sacrificial and loveless marriage was childless. Rivka lived as an old maid after her unconsummated romance with Avshalom Feinberg. Alex alternately spent his later life being kept by the soap heiress Mary Fels and seducing young girls in Zichron. Perhaps as a family they had been too much in love with one another. If Sarah Lawrence had been overly strict in withholding her love from her middle son Ned, Malka and Ephraim Aaronsohn may have given their children such feelings of specialness that they were incapable of fully loving others.[15]

Aaronsohn's memorial was the house, books, and specimens that Rivka diligently preserved and cataloged. When Henrietta Szold visited Zichron a year after Aaronsohn's death, she found only "a handful of ruins! A few vestiges of his incessant work are left; and over these hovers his old father, broken-hearted but proudly resigned. His one prayer is that what is left may be preserved as a memorial of the son who was his pride."[16] Judge Mack, as part of his work for the Palestine Economic Corporation included an agricultural project at the newly established Hebrew University in memory of Aaronsohn, but the project was short-lived.[17] Brandeis visited Palestine in 1919, and made a pilgrimage to Zichron Ya'aqov, where a special gate was built in his honor; he even broke his lifelong habit of avoiding synagogues and went twice to the synagogue in Zichron.[18] Alex Aaronsohn tracked down the Turkish doctor who had been responsible for torturing Sarah and her father. Norman Bentwich, who had assured the British in Cairo that Aaronsohn was really there to spy for them and defeat the Turks, directed the prosecution against the doctor, arguing under Ottoman criminal code before a court composed of an English president and two Arab judges.[19] The doctor was convicted and sent to prison.

It was not until the Six Day War in 1967 that Israeli attitudes changed. After the conquest of the West Bank, Gaza, Sinai, and the Golan Heights—which brought Israeli-held territory close to the borders Aaron Aaronsohn had proposed almost fifty years before—Israeli troops were able to follow up Bedouin legends in the Sinai about a man who had been killed and buried in the desert. Local Bedouins identified a grave site near the town of Rafah marked by an unusual date palm; a forensic laboratory identified the remains exhumed from the grave as Avshalom Feinberg, and the legend arose that the palm had grown from a date in his pocket, picked off one of the trees Aaronsohn had planted on the road leading into the research station at Athlit. Feinberg was reburied on Mount Herzl in Jerusalem with the full honors accorded a hero of Israel. A frail Rivka Aaronsohn sat at the graveside for the ceremony.

Once Avshalom Feinberg was allowed to join the pantheon of Zionist heroes, the stories that had been kept alive in the writings of Aaron's brother Alexander and by those who remembered the Great War finally got their due publicity. Rivka, the gatekeeper of the legends, gradually allowed historians access to the papers, books, photographs, and specimens. As scholars and journalists began to explore the long-suppressed history of Aaron Aaronsohn and NILI, Aaron's house and his father's house next door were developed into an archive and museum, with exhibits showing the history of the agricultural research station and the NILI contributions in the war. A meteorological research station, using computer-controlled sensors, is tucked into a corner of the Aaronsohn house, carrying on the weather observation tradition that was so important to him and followed so scrupulously by Sarah. The old streets and many of the houses of the original settlers have been meticulously restored in Zichron. Tourists and Israeli schoolchildren in the equivalent of the fifth grade visit the museum and are taken on a tour of his house, where they are told the story of Aaron, NILI, and Sarah's martyrdom. One of Feinberg's poems to Sarah is a popular song in Israel.[20]

Tourists walk to the Zichron cemetery, where it is easy to find Sarah's grave. By Jewish tradition a suicide cannot be buried in the consecrated ground of a cemetery, and is usually buried outside, beyond a fence. At Zichron, the fence is around Sarah's grave, creating an easily identified island in the cemetery. Her gravestone, inscribed with the single word SARAH, is usually stacked with pebbles left by visitors.

The research station in Athlit was looted and destroyed by the Turks. By the early 1920s, it was already "a gaunt ruin . . . the shriveled fronds [of the palm trees] hung like mourning plumes," and the once-famous road was overgrown with poppies, thistles, daisies, and weeds "as though no one was so poor as to trouble to enter this graveyard of many high hopes." Camels and donkeys grazed the formerly lush fields, nibbling the leaves of what had been a fig orchard. Judah Magnes, one of the trustees of the research station, and later the first chancellor of the Hebrew University, visited Athlit in 1923 and wrote to Julius Rosenwald: "I am sending you two roses from Aaron Aaronsohn's 'grave.'" Magnes suggested that it would be fitting to pay off the debts of the research station to keep Aaronsohn's name and reputation clean. Rosenwald never patched up his differences with Aaronsohn, but he contributed generously to settle the debts of the station. When he died, a dozen years after Aaron Aaronsohn, the letter from Magnes was in his wallet.[21]

Today there is no sign pointing to the site of Aaronsohn's research station, but a visitor willing to push through the rough brush between the highway and the ruined crusader castle that Lawrence had visited, now restricted as an Israeli Defense Force experimental facility, can pick out two rows of tall palms trees. Nothing else is left of Aaron's grand experiment.

~

A year after Lawrence died, at the time of the 1936 rioting in Palestine, the writer Ladislas Farago had lunch at a California hotel with a journalist, a professor, and the professor's sixteen-year-old daughter. *Seven Pillars of Wisdom* had just appeared in a public edition, and the foursome began to speculate on the identity of the mysterious "S.A." to whom Lawrence dedicated the book. Lawrence never identified S.A., and gave only cryptic and confusing answers when asked, variously hinting at people and places. Some speculated that he was inviting comparison to the mysterious dedication of Shakespeare's sonnets.

That day at the hotel in California, the daughter of the professor mesmerized the three men by solving the mystery. She pointed out that Lawrence had visited the crusader castle at Athlit as a young man and could have met young Sarah Aaronsohn there, that there were opportunities for Sarah and Lawrence to meet while they were both spies during the war, that there had been no other woman in Lawrence's life, and that if he had fallen in love, it would surely have been with a woman whose spying feats were as daring and brave as his own. The mysterious S.A. of the dedication, she claimed, was Sarah Aaronsohn.

Lawrence was much in the news because of his recent death and the publication of *Seven Pillars of Wisdom,* and the journalist, sensing a scoop, set off for Palestine with the professor and his daughter. They made their way to Zichron Ya'aqov and found Rivka Aaronsohn living alone in her father's house. Rivka flatly denied that her sister, Sarah, had ever met, let alone had a romantic connection with, Lawrence. Farago also traveled to Palestine to explore the possible connection, and concluded that "Lawrence had never seen Sarah and hardly knew anything of her existence. Their romance is nothing but a mournful legend."

But with both the journalist and Farago among the many staying at the King David Hotel in Jerusalem to cover the Arab riots, the intriguing story of Sarah Aaronsohn and Lawrence made the rounds, and in 1938 a story appeared in the *Daily Express* in London under the headline WOMAN IN LAWRENCE OF ARABIA'S LIFE WAS A SPY, calling Sarah the head of the British secret service in Palestine and speculating about whether she and Lawrence had been lovers. The sensational story quickly faded. There was too much going on in the world in 1938.

Then in 1941, Abu Farid, the driver at the Jewish Agricultural Experiment Station in Athlit, who had driven Aaron before he left Palestine for England and Egypt, and had later driven Sarah on her dangerous information-gathering missions, gave an interview to the *Jerusalem Post*. Abu Farid was an old man, eager to get his story out before he died. He told the newspaper that British submarines had landed men at Athlit during the war, and that it had been his job to meet the boats they sent to the shore and to pick up the mail and gold they brought. One night, Abu Farid said, T. E. Lawrence had come ashore in one of the boats, and Aaron Aaronsohn introduced him, saying, "This is Abu Farid. He knows all our secrets and we can trust him." Lawrence had then said, "Take good care of Mr. Aaronsohn." The story, like the ones before, came and went. With the Second World War raging, the world was too busy even for a sensational spy romance.

In 1956, the story resurfaced once more when the *New Statesman* printed a letter from a Mr. Douglas V. Duff, who reported that outside Thear's Garage in Bridport, not far from Lawrence's cottage in Dorset, he had met Lawrence in the last few months of Lawrence's life. Lawrence had shown up on his motorcycle, insisting that he was not Colonel Lawrence but Mr. Shaw. Duff, born in Argentina, had written close to one hundred books, including three that he dedicated to Sarah Aaronsohn, "the martyr maid who died for Palestine and a world unworthy of her sacrifice." In his letter to the *New Statesman,* Duff said that Lawrence and he discussed the fact that they had both dedicated books to Sarah Aaronsohn. He quoted Lawrence as saying, "If she had had a man for a husband, she might have been the leader of a Hebrew return with glory."[22]

The oft-speculated relationship between Lawrence and Sarah Aaronsohn is intriguing. Sarah was a young girl in Zichron when Lawrence visited the castle at Athlit. She was independent of spirit, adventurous, given to exploring places like the crusader castle at Athlit on her own. Later, during the war, Lawrence met her brother Aaron many times between 1916 and 1918, when the two men were at the peak of their careers as spies and revolutionary leaders, larger-than-life men who seemed to have no fears of danger and no qualms about adventure.

But neither Lawrence nor Sarah ever wrote about meeting at Athlit or anywhere else. No contemporary of either of theirs, other than

Abu Farid, suggests that they ever met. Their paths never crossed during the war: Lawrence was not in western Galilee during the war, and when Sarah visited Cairo, Lawrence was not in Egypt. Abu Farid, much beloved as a driver and friend of Aaron's and Sarah's, was never entrusted with the highly secret information about when boats would land or with the mail pouches—only a tight circle of NILI members handled the messages and gold. No British submarines landed anyone at Athlit, there is no record of Lawrence's ever going to the coast of Palestine on the slow spy ships, and the regular delivery of secret messages and gold did not begin until after Aaron had left Palestine. Mr. Duff's books with their dedications to Sarah Aaronsohn were published *after* Lawrence died, making it unlikely that he and Lawrence discussed them. It's far more likely that Duff's invocation of Lawrence's name was a ruse to publicize Duff's own books. Although her initials fit, Sarah Aaronsohn almost certainly was not the S.A. of Lawrence's dedication.

But the lives of Aaron and Sarah Aaronsohn and T. E. Lawrence did streak across the same desert sky like blazing meteors, unexpected, blinding in their brilliance, demanding attention. Like meteors, they disappeared all too quickly, leaving behind only their ionized trails across the sky. For many, those trails seemed rainbows, illusionary paths to pots of gold. Is it surprising that to some the rainbows seemed to intersect?

ACKNOWLEDGMENTS

I have profited enormously from the counsel, contributions, and wisdom of friends and colleagues. Roni Levinger provided invaluable help with translations from Hebrew. Hadassah Davis loaned memoirs from her own collection. Itzik Levinger, Carmela Ben Moshe, Elia Manor, and Esther Dekel provided guidance in Israel. Hala Daloul was a good companion in Aqaba, Wadi Rum, Petra, and Damascus. Ross Kraemer, Brian Garfield, Katharina Galor, Jerrold Cooper, and Jacob Rosen answered questions and offered suggestions. David Jacobson, Maud Mandel, Jeffrey Lesser, the Brown University Judaic Faculty Seminar, and Jeremy Wilson provided perceptive and nuanced comments on the manuscript. Librarians and archivists at Brown, Yale, Harvard, the Bibliothèque Nationale, the British Library, the Aaronsohn Archive, the Public Record Office (Kew), and the Ministère des Affairs Étrangères (Paris) were generous with their time and advice. Wendy Strothman and Wendy Wolf were unflaggingly enthusiastic, demanding, and encouraging as agent and editor. Many individuals in Egypt, Israel, Jordan, Lebanon, Sinai, Syria, and Turkey were hospitable, patient, and helpful with unexpected and sometimes odd queries, and provided an invaluable background perspective on issues that still resonate in the Middle East today. Finally, my wife, Heather, accompanied me on long journeys to strange places, listened for years to excited tales, and ultimately shared my enthusiasm for Lawrence and Aaronsohn, and their intertwined stories.

The Rolls-Royce Enthusiasts' Club, the British Library, the Imperial War Museum, the Aaronsohn Archive, the National Portrait Gallery, the Central Zionist Archive (Jerusalem), the British Museum, and the National Archives Public Record Office graciously granted permission for the use of photographs.

NOTES

Epigraph

1. Négib Azoury, *Le réveil de la nation arabe dans l'Asie turque. Partie Asiatique de la question d'orient et programme de la Ligue de la patrie arabe* (Paris: Plon-Nourrit et Cie., 1905), 48–49.

2. Quoted in David Ben-Gurion to Paula Ben-Gurion, Oct. 25, 1938, David Ben-Gurion and Peninah Ben-Guryon, *Letters to Paula* (London: Vallentine Mitchell, 1971), 200.

Prologue

1. Bernard Lewis, *What Went Wrong? Western Impact and Middle Eastern Response* (New York: Oxford University Press, 2002), 133–36.

Chapter 1. The Road to the Savoy Hotel

1. Nov. 11, 1915, Aaron Aaronsohn, "Diary" (Aharonsohn Archive, Zichron Ya'aqov). Aaronsohn kept voluminous and detailed diaries, mostly in French, through much of his adult life. Portions from the war years have been published in Hebrew translation in Yoram Efrati, ed., *Yoman Aharon Aharonson (1916–1919)* (Tel Aviv: Karni, 1970). A much smaller selection of the wartime diaries is in Anthony Verrier, *Agents of Empire: Anglo-Zionist Intelligence Operations, 1915–1919: Brigadier Walter Gribbon, Aaron Aaronsohn and the Nili Ring* (London: Brassey's, 1995). Except where otherwise noted, I have relied on the original diaries in the Aharonsohn Archive at Zichron Ya'aqov.

2. T. E. Lawrence, *Seven Pillars of Wisdom,* ed. J. Wilson, complete 1922 "Oxford" edition (Fordingbridge, Hampshire: J. and N. Wilson, 2004), xv. Except where otherwise noted, references to *Seven Pillars* in the text or notes are to this edition. I have preserved Lawence's spellings of names and places in quotations, and his punctuation.

3. Oct. 17–22, 1916, Aaronsohn, "Diary"; Norman De Mattos Bentwich, *Judah L. Magnes: A Biography of the First Chancellor and First President of the Hebrew University of Jerusalem* (London: East & West Library, 1955), 73.

4. Eliezer Livneh, *Nili Toldoteyha Shel He'aza Medinit* (Tel Aviv: Schocken, 1961), 69.

5. Oct. 22, 1916, Aaronsohn, "Diary"; Eliezer Livneh, *Aharon Aharonson, Ha-Ish U-Zemano* (Jerusalem: Mosad Bialiḳ, 1969), 219.

6. Oct. 22, 1916, Aaronsohn, "Diary."

7. Lawrence, *Seven Pillars,* 187. The coincidence of their travel is noted in pencil on a loose typewritten schedule of Aaronsohn's travels that day, interleaved in his diary at the Aharonsohn Archive. Anthony Verrier mentions it in *Agents of Empire,* 186.

8. Leonard Woolley, Lawrence's closest companion for many years of archaeological research and on an expedition to Sinai shortly before the war, wrote that Lawrence would only walk in the desert and "might not have relished the idea of riding a camel." Leonard Woolley and T. E. Lawrence, *The Wilderness of Zin* (Winona Lake, IN: Eisenbrauns, 2003), xxv. See also Lawrence to Leeds, Jan. 24, 1914, T. E. Lawrence et al., *Letters to E. T. Leeds* (Andoversford, Gloucestershire: Whittington Press, 1988), 89; Lawrence, *Seven Pillars,* 63.

9. Lawrence, *Seven Pillars,* 97. "Wear an Arab headcloth when with a tribe. Bedu have a malignant prejudice against the hat, and believe that our persistence in wearing it . . . is founded on some immoral or irreligious principle." T. E. Lawrence, "Twenty-Seven Articles," Aug. 20, 1917, Robin Leonard Bidwell et al., *Arab Bulletin* (Gerrards Cross, Buckinghamshire, England: Archive Editions, 1986), II, no. 60, 350.

10. Lawrence, *Seven Pillars,* 43.

11. In *Seven Pillars of Wisdom* Lawrence wrote that going along on the mission was coincidence: "I took this strategic moment to ask for ten days' leave, saying that Storrs was going down to Jidda on business with the Grand Sherif, and that I would like a holiday and joyride on the Red Sea with him. They hated Storrs, and were glad to get rid of me for the moment." The last clause was probably true, but Clayton had a purpose in sending Lawrence.

12. Efraim Karsh and Inari Karsh, *Empires of the Sand: The Struggle for Mastery in the Middle East, 1789–1923* (Cambridge, MA: Harvard University Press, 1999), 175.

13. David Fromkin, *A Peace to End All Peace: Creating the Modern Middle East, 1914–1922* (New York: Holt, 1989), 219.

14. Sherif Hussein had withdrawn his objections to Christian aviators flying over the Hejaz (with the exception of the sacred precincts of Mecca and Medina), and also welcomed British aircraft to assist in attacks on the Turkish railway. Bidwell et al., *Arab Bulletin,* I, no. 13, 130.

15. Ronald Storrs, *The Memoirs of Sir Ronald Storrs* (New York: G. P. Putnam's Sons, 1937), 204.

16. T. E. Lawrence, "The Sherifs," Oct. 27, 1916, FO 882/5, fo. 401, in Jeremy Wilson, *Lawrence of Arabia: The Authorized Biography of T. E. Lawrence* (New York: Atheneum, 1990), 307; Storrs, *Memoirs,* 186.

17. "The foreigner and Christian is not a popular person in Arabia. However friendly and informal the treatment of yourself may be, remember always that your foundations are very sandy ones." "Twenty-Seven Articles," Bidwell et al., *Arab Bulletin,* II, no. 60, 349.

18. Lawrence, *Seven Pillars,* 69.

19. Ibid., 226–27.

20. Bidwell et al., *Arab Bulletin,* I, no. 1, 7.

21. T. E. Lawrence, "The Sherifs," Oct. 27, 1916, FO 882/5, fo. 41, in Wilson, *Lawrence,* 312; John E. Mack, *A Prince of Our Disorder: The Life of T. E. Lawrence* (Cambridge, MA: Harvard University Press, 1976), 162; Robert Graves and B. H. Liddell Hart, *T. E. Lawrence to His Biographers Robert Graves and Liddell Hart,* 2 vols., (Garden City, NY: Doubleday, 1963), I, 189. The subscribers' abridgement of *Seven Pillars of Wisdom* (1926) tones down some of the revealing comments about Faisal in the original (1922) edition. "My service of Faisal was mostly out of pity. He was such a brave, weak, ignorant spirit trying to do work for which only a genius, a great prophet, or a great criminal was fitted. A much-loved man must always be a little weak on some side; but Faisal was less than weak, he was empty:—only a great pipe waiting for a wind. A little breath rustled in him: while a full blast sounded a thundering organ note, as from the finest instrument, one which called for a great man to play on it. I was not great, for I could feel contempt, a thin motive of effort: and yet chance made me his player." Lawrence, *Seven Pillars,* 682.

22. Lawrence, *Seven Pillars,* 85.

23. Ibid., 80.

24. Ibid., 76.

25. "Syria: The Raw Material" (written in early 1915, but not circulated until later), Bidwell et al., *Arab Bulletin,* II, no. 44, 112.

26. Ibid., I, no. 32, 483.

27. T. E. Lawrence, "Military Notes," Nov. 3, 1916, FO 882/5, fos. 56–58, in Wilson, *Lawrence,* 314–15.

28. Nov. 8, 1916, Aaronsohn, "Diary."

29. Verrier, *Agents of Empire,* 35. The quote may be anecdotal; Djemal Pasha does not mention it in his memoirs. Ahmad Djemal, *Memories of a Turkish Statesman, 1913–1919* (London: Hutchinson, 1922).

30. Dec. 6, 1915, Aaronsohn, "Diary."

31. Frank E. Manuel, *The Realities of American-Palestinian Relations* (Washington: Public Affairs Press, 1949), 153; Aaron Aaronsohn, "Letter to Judge Julian M. Mack, New York, from Copenhagen" (typescript, Aharonsohn Archive, Zichron Ya'aqov), 7.

32. "It may be true that Galilee is smaller in size than Peraea, but it takes the palm for productivity; for the whole country is cultivated. . . . The country is watered by mountain torrents, and by perennial springs that suffice even in the dog-days when the torrents dry up." Flavius Josephus, *The Jewish War,* trans. G. A. Williamson (London: Penguin, 1970), 192.

33. Basil Thomson, *My Experiences at Scotland Yard* (New York: A. L. Burt, 1926), 225–26; Basil Thomson, *The Scene Changes* (Garden City, NY: Doubleday, 1937), 387–88.

34. Ross Mallett, *The Interplay Between Technology, Tactics and Organization in the First AIF* (Australian Defence Force Academy, 1999 [cited 2006]); available from unsw.adfa.edu.au/~rmallett/Thesis/Chapter6.html.

Chapter 2. Romania, Romania

1. David Vital, *The Origins of Zionism* (Oxford: Clarendon Press, 1980), 80.

2. Ibid., 92. From the opening speeches of local emigration societies in Focşani in southern Moldavia in late December 1881.

3. Unpublished diary of Major General Sir John Charles Ardagh, "Journey from Cairo to Damascus" (1883), quoted in Richard Andrews, *Der Spion des Lawrence von Arabien: Auf geheimer Mission für einem jüdischen Staat,* trans. Gabriele Herbst (Berlin: Aufbau-Verlag, 2004), 16; Simon Schama, *Two Rothschilds and the Land of Israel* (New York: Knopf, 1978), 60.

4. The blood-libel accusations were native to Europe and Russia; it was only with the increased communications of the last half of the nineteenth century that accusations appeared in the Ottoman lands and their successor states. See Ronald Florence, *Blood Libel: The Damascus Affair of 1840* (Madison, WI: University of Wisconsin Press, 2004).

5. Stones actually do "grow" on fields, as cultivation and the winter freeze-thaw cycle bring stones to the surface by the same mechanism that makes Brazil nuts rise to the top of a jar of mixed nuts. See Monte Basgall, "No Stone Unturned: Peter Haff Devotes 25 Years to Studying Nature's Desert Pavement" (2004 [cited Aug. 2004]); available from nicholas.duke.edu/dukenvironment/sp2004/f-nostone.pdf.

6. The phrase she used, *Mi-po ani lo zaz!* ("This is my home. From here I am not budging") became popular in Israel during the 2006 war against Hezbollah. Daniel Gordis, "The First War, All Over Again," July 21, 2006; available from danielgordis.org/Site/SiteViewDispatches.asp?id=7.

7. Hillel Halkin, *A Strange Death* (New York: Public Affairs, 2005), 20.

8. Ran Aaronsohn, *Rothschild and Early Jewish Colonization in Palestine: Geographic Perspectives on the Human Past* (Lanham, MD: Rowman & Littlefield, 2000), 69.

9. Schama, *Two Rothschilds,* 91.

10. Elie Scheid, *Mémoires sur les colonies juives et les voyages en Palestine et en Syrie* (1901), 121; quoted in ibid., 81.

11. Letters from the wife of Kalman Kantor, October–November 1889, and February 28, 1890, quoted in Deborah Bernstein, *Pioneers and Homemakers: Jewish Women in Pre-State Israel* (Albany, NY: SUNY Press, 1992), 35, 41.

12. Aaronsohn, *Rothschild and Early Jewish Colonization in Palestine,* 119.

13. Yizhar Hirschfeld and Adrian J. Boas, *Ramat Hanadiv Excavations: Final Report of the 1984–1998 Seasons* (Jerusalem: Israel Exploration Society, 2000).

14. Shmuel Katz, *Ha-Reshet: Ha-Haggadah Le-Vet Aharonson* (Tel Aviv: Miśrad ha-biṭaḥon, 2000), 44; Gerda Hoffer, *Zeit der Heldinnen: Lebensbilder aussergewöhnlicher jüdischer Frauen* (München: Deutscher Taschenbuch Verlag, 1999), 186.

15. Aaronsohn, *Rothschild and Early Jewish Colonization in Palestine,* 149, 151.

16. Schama, *Two Rothschilds,* 76.

17. Françoise Delfour, "L'école d'agriculture de Grignon, de 1867 à 1918" (2000 [cited Aug. 2004]); available from theses.enc.sorbonne.fr/document89.html.

18. Patrice Higonnet, *Paris: Capital of the World* (Cambridge, MA: Harvard University Press, 2002), 147.

19. Michael Stanislawski, *Zionism and the Fin de Siècle: Cosmopolitanism and Nationalism from Nordau to Jabotinsky* (Berkeley, CA: University of California Press, 2001), 13. Herzl's extensive reading in 1895 about Shabbetai Ẓevi and his mass followings may have been more important than the Dreyfus trial and conviction in forming his views. See Vital, *The Origins of Zionism,* 244.

20. Eliezer Livneh, *Aharon Aharonsohn, Ha-Ish U-Zemano* (Jerusalem: Mosad Bialiḳ, 1969), 20.

21. Katz, *Aharonson,* 36–38; Livneh, *Aharon Aharonsohn,* 28–29.

22. Halkin, *A Strange Death,* 28.

23. Katz, *Aharonson,* 44.

24. Quoted in ibid.

25. Livneh, *Aharon Aharonsohn,* 49–50.

26. Letter to David Fairchild, USDA, quoted in Heinz Reinhard Oppenheimer, "Florula Transiordanica; Révision critique des plantes récoltées et partiellement determinées," in *Reliquise Aaronsohnianse. Série de publications éd. par la famille Aaronsohn, I* (Genève: Imprimerie Jent s.a., 1931), 7–14.

27. Katz, *Aharonson,* 48–54.

28. Sonia Siskind to Aaron Aaronsohn, Nov. 20, 1913, quoted in ibid., 53.

29. Ibid., 59.

30. Palestine Exploration Fund, *Map of Western Palestine from Surveys Conducted for the Committee of the Palestine Exploration Fund by Lieuts. C. H. Conder and H. H. Kitchener* (London: 1882).

31. Norman De Mattos Bentwich, *Judah L. Magnes: A Biography of the First Chancellor and First President of the Hebrew University of Jerusalem* (London: East & West Library, 1955), 59.

32. Exodus 9:32 (". . . but the wheat and the emmer were not hurt, for they ripen late"); the Hebrew *ḳusemeth* is sometimes translated as "spelt," but there is no evidence of spelt from biblical times, unlike emmer, which has been found in ancient Egyptian tombs. David Fairchild, Elizabeth Kay, and Alfred Kay, *The World Was My Garden: Travels of a Plant Explorer* (New York: C. Scribner's Sons, 1943), 356; USDA, *Classification of Triticum Species and Wheat Varieties Grown in the United States.* Technical Bulletin 1287 (1997 [cited Aug. 2004]); available from hort.purdue.edu/newcrop/crops/wheat.html.

Chapter 3. Bastard

1. T. E. Lawrence to C. F. Shaw, April 14, 1927, in Jeremy Wilson, *Lawrence of Arabia: The Authorized Biography of T. E. Lawrence* (New York: Atheneum, 1990), 29, 983n.

2. John E. Mack, *A Prince of Our Disorder: The Life of T. E. Lawrence* (Cambridge, MA: Harvard University Press, 1976), 26–30.

3. Ibid., 5; Wilson, *Lawrence,* 942–43.

4. Mack, *A Prince of Our Disorder,* 21.

5. T. E. Lawrence to C. F. Shaw, April 14, 1927, quoted in Wilson, *Lawrence,* 32.

6. Mack, *A Prince of Our Disorder,* 10–11.

7. Robert Graves and B. H. Liddell Hart, *T. E. Lawrence to His Biographers Robert Graves and Liddell Hart,* 2 vols. (Garden City, NY: Doubleday, 1983), I, 64.

8. T. E. Lawrence, *Seven Pillars of Wisdom,* ed. J. Wilson, complete 1922 "Oxford" edition (Fordingbridge, Hampshire: J. and N. Wilson, 2004), 812.

9. T. E. Lawrence to D. Knowles, July 14, 1927, quoted in Wilson, *Lawrence,* 41.

10. A. T. P. Williams, "Lawrence in Oxford," *Oxford Magazine* 53, Feb.–June 1935, 696; A. G. Prys-Jones, "Lawrence of Arabia: Some Personal Impressions" (typescript), Jesus College, Oxford, both quoted in ibid., 43.

11. E. F. Hall, in A. W. Lawrence, *T. E. Lawrence, by His Friends* (Garden City, NY: Doubleday Doran, 1937), 46–47.

12. L. C. Jane to R. R. Graves, July 26, 1927, quoted in Wilson, *Lawrence,* 45.

13. Preface by A. W. Lawrence in T. E. Lawrence, *Crusader Castles* (New York: Oxford University Press, 1988), V. William Morris, who built Lawrence's special high-geared three-speed bicycle, became famous in the British automobile industry.

14. Robert Graves et al., *Lawrence and the Arabs* (London: Jonathan Cape, 1927), 18.

15. C. M. Doughty to T. E. Lawrence, Feb. 3, 1909, quoted in Wilson, *Lawrence,* 53–54.

16. T. E. Lawrence to his mother, Aug. 2, 1909, T. E. Lawrence et al., *The Home Letters of T. E. Lawrence and His Brothers* (New York: Macmillan, 1954), 98–99.

17. Ibid., 91–92.

18. T. E. Lawrence to his mother, Sept. 7, 1909, ibid., 107.

19. Nita and Michael Lange, "Diary (Sept. 27, 1910–Dec. 1, 1910)" (loaned by Hadassah Davis, Providence, RI), 37; Warwick P. N. Tyler, *State Lands and Rural Development in Mandatory Palestine, 1920–1948* (Portland, OR: Sussex Academic Press, 2001), 120.

Chapter 4. Fame

1. Eliezer Livneh, *Aharon Aharonsohn, Ha-Ish U-Zemano* (Jerusalem: Mosad Bialiḳ, 1969), 59.

2. Ibid., 102, 119.

3. Lange, "Diary," 41; Alexandra Lee Levin, *Vision: A Biography of Harry Friedenwald* (Philadelphia: Jewish Publication Society of America, 1964), 189.

4. Lange, "Diary," 41.

5. Leila Avrin and Colette Sirat, *La lettre hebraique et sa signification* (Paris and Jerusalem: Centre nationale de la récherche scientifique; Israel Museum Department of Judaica, 1981), provides examples and traces the provenance of Hebrew micrographic portraits of Herzl and Kaiser Wilhelm, among others.

6. Isaiah 1:27; Kathrin Ringger, "'An English Adventure': Diplomatic Efforts for a Home for the Jewish People, 1897–1922" in Heiko Haumann and Peter Haber, *The First Zionist Congress in 1897: Causes, Significance, Topicality* (Basel, New York: Karger, 1997), 273.

7. "The difference between myself and Shabbetai Ẓevi (the way I imagine him), apart from the difference in the technical means inherent in the times, is that Shabbetai made himself great so as to be the equal of the great of the earth. I, however, find the great small, as small as myself." Herzl, quoted in David Vital, *The Origins of Zionism* (Oxford: Clarendon Press, 1980), 244. On Herzl's narcissism, see Carl E. Schorske, *Fin-de-Siècle Vienna: Politics and Culture* (New York: Knopf, 1980).

8. Quoted in Walter Laqueur, *A History of Zionism* (New York: Holt, Rinehart and Winston, 1972), 96–97.

9. Quoted in ibid., 108.

10. Michael Stanislawski, *Zionism and the Fin de Siècle: Cosmopolitanism and Nationalism from Nordau to Jabotinsky* (Berkeley: University of California Press, 2001), 16.

11. See Saraya Antonius, *The Lord* (London: Hamilton, 1986), 177–78.

12. Menahem Sheinkin, in *Sefer Toldot Hahagana* (Tel Aviv, 1954), vol. I, 135, cited in Laqueur, *A History of Zionism,* 221.

13. Joseph Baratz, *The Story of Dagania* (Tel-Aviv: Omanuth, 1931), 52.

14. Ilan Pappé, *A History of Modern Palestine: One Land, Two Peoples* (New York: Cambridge University Press, 2004), 55.

15. [Aaron Aaronsohn], "Palestine. The Jewish Colonies," Bidwell et al., *Arab Bulletin,* II, no. 64, 388–92. The *Bulletin* does not identify Aaronsohn as the author of this rare essay by an outsider, only that it was by "one of the leaders of the Jewish movement." But he was the only person in Cairo at the time who would have been in contact with the group at the Arab Bureau, and who had the range of knowledge about the Jewish settlements in Palestine apparent in the report, and who would have expressed views like those in the article. The *Bulletin* notes that the article was submitted to another Zionist leader, an equal "authority," who took exception to the implication that Jewish purchasers sometimes found it necessary to expel dwellers on acquired lands. The latter argued that this was "never" the case, because the greater part of lands acquired were swampy, unhealthy, or reputed to be infertile, and hence must be uncultivated and uninhabited; as resident owners, therefore, the Jews had no fear of their claims being jumped by Arab cultivators.

16. Livneh, *Aharon Aharonsohn,* 163.

17. Hadassah F. Davis, "Dreams and Their Consequences: A Memoir of the Bentwich Family, 1880–1922" (typescript loaned by the author, Providence, RI: 2003), 53; Alexander Aaronsohn, *With the Turks in Palestine* (Boston, New York: Houghton Mifflin, 1916), 3–4.

18. Bidwell et al., *Arab Bulletin,* II, no. 64, 389.

19. Shmuel Katz, *Ha-Reshef: Ha-Haggadah Le-Vet Aharonson* (Tel Aviv: Miśrad ha-biṭaḥon, 2000), 65.

20. David Fairchild, Elizabeth Kay, and Alfred Kay, *The World Was My Garden: Travels of a Plant Explorer* (New York: C. Scribner's Sons, 1943), 356.

21. Ibid., 366.

22. M. R. Werner, *Julius Rosenwald: The Life of a Practical Humanitarian* (New York: Harper, 1939), 98.

23. Ibid., 96.

24. Daniel Boorstin, "Transforming the Charitable Spirit," in University of Chicago, *The Julius Rosenwald Centennial; the Julius Rosenwald Centennial Observance at the University of Chicago, October 15, 1962* (Chicago: 1963), 28–29.

25. Livneh, *Aharon Aharonsohn,* 131–32.

26. *Oakland Tribune,* Oct. 20, 1909; *Mountain Democrat* (Placerville, California), Aug. 14, 1909. On his reception, see, "Wheat Grows in Arid Soil," *Washington Post,* Jan. 3, 1910; "All Bars Let Down to Admit Desirable Plant Immigrants," *Sandusky Register,* Sept. 15, 1912; "Turning to the Holy Land for Food," *Mansfield News* (Mansfield, Ohio), Sept. 3, 1910.

27. Fairchild, Kay, and Kay, *The World Was My Garden,* 366.

28. Aaron Aaronsohn, *Agricultural and Botanical Explorations in Palestine,* U.S. Dept. of Agriculture, Bureau of Plant Industry, Bulletin no. 180 (Washington: GPO, 1910).

29. David Fairchild, "An American Research Institution in Palestine: The Jewish Agricultural Experiment Station at Haifa," *Science* XXXI, no. 793 (1911): 376–77.

30. After a personal crisis Szold visited Palestine in 1909, was shocked by the state of health care there, and turned her attention to the practical aspects of Zionism. Monika Häfliger, "Henrietta Szold," in Haumann and Haber, *The First Zionist Congress,* 262; Harry Barnard,

The Forging of an American Jew: The Life and Times of Judge Julian W. Mack (New York: Herzl Press, 1974), 110.

31. Livneh, *Aharon Aharonsohn,* 140–41, 153.

32. Katz, *Aharonson,* 22–23.

33. "Your stately form is like the palm . . . ," Song of Solomon, 7:8. "So she conceived him, and she retired with him into a remote place. And the labour pains came upon her at the trunk of a palm tree, and she said 'O that I had died before this, and been forgotten out of mind!' and he called to her from beneath her, 'Grieve not, for thy Lord has placed a stream beneath thy feet; and shake towards thee the trunk of the palm tree, it will drop upon thee fresh dates fit to gather.'" Sura 19:23.

34. See, for example, Ronald Storrs, *The Memoirs of Sir Ronald Storrs* (New York: G. P. Putnam's Sons, 1997), 177n.

35. Jemal Pasha, "La vérité sur la question Syrienne," (1916) in Bidwell et al., *Arab Bulletin,* III, 167.

36. Neville J. Mandel, *The Arabs and Zionism Before World War I* (Berkeley: University of California Press, 1976), 174.

37. The name is from the initial Hebrew letters of Isaiah 2:5: "O House of Jacob! Come, let us walk by the light of the Lord."

38. Avshalom Feinberg to Israel Feinberg, Oct. 14, 1907, Avshalom Feinberg, *Avshalom: Ketavim U-Mikhtavim,* ed. Aharon Amir (Jerusalem: Shikmonah, 1985), 174–75.

39. Quoted in Yosef Gorni, *Zionism and the Arabs, 1882–1948: A Study of Ideology* (New York: Oxford University Press, 1987), 56.

40. Katz, *Aharonson,* 66.

41. See, for example, Feinberg's journals of his tours, in Feinberg, *Avshalom: Ketavim U-Mikhtavim,* 181f.

42. Norman De Mattos Bentwich, *My 77 Years: An Account of My Life and Times, 1883–1960* (Philadelphia: Jewish Publication Society of America, 1961), 27.

43. The *dunam* as a measure of land area was used in the Ottoman Empire and is often used in Israel today. A *dunam* is one thousand square meters, which is one-tenth of a hectare, or approximately one-fourth of an acre.

44. March 15, 1913, quoted in Barnard, *The Forging of an American Jew,* 122–23; Felix Frankfurter and Joseph P. Lash, *From the Diaries of Felix Frankfurter: With a Biographical Essay and Notes,* 1st ed. (New York: Norton, 1975), 22.

45. Barnard, *The Forging of an American Jew,* 156–57.

46. Ibid., 168. "To Be a Jew," speech to the Young Men's Hebrew Association of Chelsea, Massachusetts, May 18, 1913, in Louis Dembitz Brandeis and Zionist Organization of America, *Brandeis on Zionism: A Collection of Addresses and Statements* (Washington, DC: Zionist Organization of America, 1942), 39–40. In "The Jewish Problem: How to Solve It," a June 1915 speech to a conference of Reform rabbis in New York, Brandeis repeats the story. Brandeis and Zionist Organization of America, *Brandeis on Zionism,* 30–31; Alpheus Thomas Mason, *Brandeis: A Free Man's Life,* anniversary ed. (New York: Viking Press, 1956), 442; Robert Burt, *Two Jewish Justices: Outcasts in the Promised Land* (Berkeley: University of California Press, 1988), 117–18; Aaron Aaronsohn, "Letter to Judge Julian M. Mack, New York, from Copenhagen" (Aharonsohn Archive, Zichron Ya'aqov), 19.

47. Barnard, *The Forging of an American Jew,* 184.

Chapter 5. The Archaeologist

1. Lawrence to his mother from Carchemish, June 24, 1911 in T. E. Lawrence, *The Diary of T. E. Lawrence, MCMXI,* ed. S. Lawrence (London: Corvinus Press, 1937), 93.

2. Lawrence to his mother, Aug. 1910, T. E. Lawrence et al., *The Home Letters of T. E. Lawrence and His Brothers* (New York: Macmillan, 1954), 110–11.

3. Quoted in Phillip Knightley and Colin Simpson, *The Secret Lives of Lawrence of Arabia* (New York: McGraw-Hill, 1970), 29.

4. John E. Mack, *A Prince of Our Disorder: The Life of T. E. Lawrence* (Cambridge, MA: Harvard University Press, 1976), 64–65.

5. Robert Graves and B. H. Liddell Hart, *T. E. Lawrence to His Biographers Robert Graves and Liddell Hart,* 2 vols. (Garden City, NY: Doubleday, 1963), I, 8.

6. Lawrence to his mother, late Aug. 1910, in Jeremy Wilson, *Lawrence of Arabia: The Authorized Biography of T. E. Lawrence* (New York: Atheneum, 1990), 68; Lawrence to Vyvyan Richards, Aug. 29, 1911, David Garnett, *The Letters of T. E. Lawrence,* 1st ed. (New York: Doubleday Doran, 1939), 87.

7. Graves, *T. E. Lawrence to His Biographers,* 3.

8. Lawrence to his family, Jan. 14 and Jan. 24, 1911, in Lawrence et al., *Home Letters,* 126, 130; Lawrence to Herbert Baker, Jan. 20, 1928, and Lawrence to R. V. Buxton, Sept. 22, 1923, in Garnett, *Letters,* 431, 568; Wilson, *Lawrence,* 74.

9. Hogarth to F. G. Kenyon, March 2, 1911, in Wilson, *Lawrence,* 80.

10. Lawrence to E. T. Leeds, March 27, 1911, Malcolm Brown, *The Letters of T. E. Lawrence* (London: J. M. Dent, 1988), 31–32.

11. Lawrence to his family, Dec. 1910, Lawrence et al., *Home Letters,* 115–16; Garnett, *Letters,* 89.

12. Garnett, *Letters,* 72.

13. There is a good collection of these photographs in Lawrence, *The Diary of T. E. Lawrence, MCMXI.*

14. Lawrence to his family, April 11, 1911, Lawrence et al., *Home Letters,* 148; Lawrence in the introduction to Charles Montagu Doughty, *Travels in Arabia Deserta* (New York: Random House, 1934).

15. Lawrence to his family, May 11, 1911, Lawrence et al., *Home Letters,* 206–7; Wilson, *Lawrence,* 992n, points out that the dating of the published version of this letter is incorrect. Lawrence to his family, April 11, 1911, quoted in Mack, *A Prince of Our Disorder,* 86. His brother thought this passage too damaging to include in the published correspondence. Lawrence to his family, Sept. 13, 1912, Lawrence et al., *Home Letters,* 232–33.

16. Lawrence to Leeds, June 2, 1911, in Wilson, *Lawrence,* 88.

17. Lawrence to his family, May 11, 1911, Lawrence et al., *Home Letters,* 161–62; Graves, *T. E. Lawrence to His Biographers,* 67–68.

18. Bell to her family, May 18, 1911, Gertrude Lowthian Bell and Florence Eveleen Eleanore Olliffe Bell, *The Letters of Gertrude Bell* (New York: Boni and Liveright, 1927), I, 305–6.

19. Margaret S. Drower, *Flinders Petrie: A Life in Archaeology* (Madison, WI: University of Wisconsin Press, 1995); Liddell Hart, *T. E. Lawrence to His Biographers,* 54.

20. Lawrence to his family, Jan. 31, 1912, Lawrence et al., *Home Letters,* 190–91.

21. Leonard Woolley, *Dead Towns and Living Men: Being Pages from an Antiquary's Notebook* (New York: Oxford University Press, 1929); Wilson, *Lawrence,* 102.

22. Woolley to Hogarth, Oct. 12, 1913, in Wilson, *Lawrence,* 127.

23. Woolley in Lawrence, *T. E. Lawrence, by His Friends,* 89. Though generally reliable as a source, Woolley may not be the ideal expert on sexuality. "His wife, Katharine Woolley, who always accompanied him, was a dominating and powerful personality of whom even at this time it is difficult to speak fairly. Her first marriage had been a disaster . . . and it was only with reluctance that she brought herself to marry Woolley—she needed a man to look after her, but was not intended for the physical side of matrimony. . . . Katharine, a

bad sleeper, sometimes needed attention from Leonard Woolley in the small hours, but as he was always whacked, no amount of calling could rouse him although he slept in an adjacent bedroom. To overcome this difficulty, a string was tied round Leonard's toe and violently tugged when his services were required in the night. Fortunately, this method of rousing him was only applied in emergencies." Max Mallowan, *Mallowan's Memoirs* (London: Collins, 1977), 36–37.

24. Woolley in A. W. Lawrence, *T. E. Lawrence, by His Friends* (Garden City, NY: Doubleday Doran, 1937), 89.

25. Lawrence to his family, June 24, 1912, Lawrence et al., *Home Letters,* 218–19.

26. July 29, 1911, in Lawrence, *The Diary of T. E. Lawrence, MCMXI.*

27. Leonard Woolley, *As I Seem to Remember* (London: Allen and Unwin, on behalf of Shaftesbury and District Society and Museum, 1962), 54.

28. Mack, *A Prince of Our Disorder,* 88.

29. Lawrence, *T. E. Lawrence, by His Friends,* 84, 91; Mack, *A Prince of Our Disorder,* 81; Wilson, *Lawrence,* 995n.

30. T. E. Lawrence, "Twenty-Seven Articles," Robin Leonard Bidwell et al., *Arab Bulletin* (Gerrards Cross, Buckinghamshire, England: Archive Editions, 1986), II, no. 60, 350.

31. Lawrence, *T. E. Lawrence, by His Friends,* 84; "Report by F. Willoughby Smith," Dec. 9, 1912, in Wilson, *Lawrence,* 945–48; Lawrence to his family, Oct. 22, 1912, Lawrence et al., *Home Letters,* 239.

32. Lawrence to Woolley, Jan. 25, 1913, in Wilson, *Lawrence,* 117; Lawrence, *T. E. Lawrence, by His Friends,* 106.

33. Lawrence to his family, March 13, 1913, and April 26, 1913, Lawrence et al., *Home Letters,* 249, 254; Lawrence to his family, June 15, 1913, ibid., 258; W. G. Lawrence to his family, Sept. 27, 1913, ibid., 447.

34. The British intelligence agents at the Arab Bureau were aware of this. See Bidwell et al., *Arab Bulletin,* III, no. 92, 194. See also Kathi Frances McGraw et al., *T. E. Lawrence: A 20th-Century Retrospective* (Summerduck, VA: Andrew Carvely, 1998), 11.

35. Lawrence to Richards, Dec. 16, 1913, Garnett, *Letters,* 160–61.

36. Leonard Woolley and T. E. Lawrence, *The Wilderness of Zin* (Winona Lake, IN: Eisenbrauns, 2003), xx, xxiii.

37. Lawrence to his family, Jan. 4, 1914, Lawrence et al., *Home Letters,* 280.

38. Lawrence to his family, Jan. 24, 1914, ibid., 283–84; Woolley to C. R. Watson, Feb. 17, 1914, in Wilson, *Lawrence,* 140; Woolley and Lawrence, *The Wilderness of Zin,* xxx, 170.

39. Woolley, *As I Seem to Remember,* 88, 91–93; David Hogarth, "War and Discovery in Arabia," *Geographical Journal,* LV, 6 (1920), 431; S. F. Newcombe and J. P. S. Greig, "The Bagdad Railway," *Geographical Journal,* XLIV, 6 (1914).

40. Hogarth to Woolley, July 6, 1914, in Wilson, *Lawrence,* 147.

Chapter 6. War

1. David Fromkin, *A Peace to End All Peace: Creating the Modern Middle East, 1914–1922* (New York: Holt, 1989), 61.

2. Avshalom Feinberg, "Rapport à Miss Henrietta Szold, October 1915" (typescript, Aharonsohn Archive, Zichron Ya'aqov), 21–22.

3. [Aaron Aaronsohn], Dec. 4, 1916, in Bidwell et al., *Arab Bulletin* (Gerrards Cross, Buckinghamshire, England: Archive Editions, 1986), II, no. 60, 505. See also Eliezer Livneh, *Nili Toldoteyha Shel He'aza Medinit* (Tel Aviv: Schocken Books, 1961), 33; Feinberg, "Rapport à Miss Henrietta Szold, October 1915," 23–25.

4. Feinberg, "Rapport à Miss Henrietta Szold, October 1915," 248.

5. Livneh, *Nili,* 22. Ahmad Djemal, *Memories of a Turkish Statesman, 1913–1919* (London: Hutchinson & Co., 1922), 88–89.

6. Livneh, *Nili,* 29.

7. Feinberg, "Rapport à Miss Henrietta Szold, October 1915," 32. Margaret FitzHerbert, *The Man Who Was Greenmantle: A Biography of Aubrey Herbert* (London: John Murray, 1983), 147.

8. Djemal, *Memories,* 157.

9. Bidwell et al., *Arab Bulletin,* I, no. 33, 504.

10. Alexander Aaronsohn, *With the Turks in Palestine* (Boston, New York: Houghton Mifflin, 1916), 7–27; Hillel Halkin, *A Strange Death* (New York: Public Affairs, 2005), 135–36, 305.

11. Livneh, *Nili,* 29.

12. Ibid., 37.

13. Louis H. Levin, "Distribution of Supplies on the *Vulcan* and on Conditions in Palestine," Confidential Report to the American Jewish Committee, 8–10, quoted in Alexandra Lee Levin, *Vision: A Biography of Harry Friedenwald* (Philadelphia: Jewish Publication Society of America, 1964), 437.

14. Joel 1:8. On the concept of mourning in anticipation of a catastrophe, see Saul M. Olyan, *Biblical Mourning: Ritual and Social Dimensions* (Oxford: Oxford University Press, 2004).

15. Feinberg, "Rapport à Miss Henrietta Szold, October 1915," 89.

16. Livneh, *Nili,* 56; Shmuel Katz, *Ha-Reshet: Ha-Haggadah Le-Vet Aharonson* (Tel Aviv: Miśrad ha-biṭaḥon, 2000), 76–77.

17. Aaron Aaronsohn, "Letter to Judge Julian M. Mack, New York, from Copenhagen, Oct. 9, 1916" (Beit Aharonsohn, 1916), 13.

18. Feinberg, "Rapport à Miss Henrietta Szold, October 1915," 52–76.

19. Unpublished memoirs of Liova Schneersohn, quoted in Anita Engle, *The Nili Spies* (London: Hogarth Press, 1959), 48–50; Livneh, *Nili,* 66–67.

Chapter 7. Cairo

1. Nov. 19, 1914, in Jeremy Wilson, *Lawrence of Arabia: The Authorized Biography of T. E. Lawrence* (New York: Atheneum, 1990), 154.

2. Sir Coote Hedley, head of the geographical section of the General Staff, which Lawrence joined in 1914: "[Lawrence] said he had been rejected for the Army as being too small." Robert Graves and B. H. Liddell Hart, *T. E. Lawrence to His Biographers Robert Graves and Liddell Hart,* 2 vols. (Garden City, NY: Doubleday, 1963), II, 193.

3. Wilson, *Lawrence,* 152.

4. David Fromkin, *A Peace to End All Peace: Creating the Modern Middle East, 1914–1922* (New York: Holt, 1989), 81. After the war Lloyd George refined his views of Kitchener: "No! he was like a great revolving lighthouse. Sometimes the beam of his mind used to shoot out, showing one Europe and the assembled armies in a vast and illimitable perspective, till one felt that one was looking along it into the heart of reality—and then the shutter would turn and for weeks there would be nothing but a blank darkness." Max Aitken Beaverbrook, *Politicians and the War, 1914–1916* (London: Collins, 1960), 175.

5. Carol Alfonso Nallino, *Appunti sulla natura del "Califfato" in genere e sul presunto "Califfato Ottomano"* (Italian Foreign Office, 1917), trans. R. R. Rodd, in Robin Leonard Bidwell et al., *Arab Bulletin* (Gerrards Cross, Buckinghamshire, England: Archive Editions, 1986), III, 287–88.

6. Ronald Storrs, *The Memoirs of Sir Ronald Storrs* (New York: G. P. Putnam's Sons, 1937), 206.

7. Fromkin, *A Peace to End All Peace,* 86; Elie Kedourie, *In the Anglo-Arab Labyrinth: The*

McMahon-Husayn Correspondence and Its Interpretations, 1914–1939 (Portland, OR: Frank Cass, 2000), 29.

8. Fromkin, *A Peace to End All Peace,* 86.

9. Dec. 20, 1914, in David Garnett, *The Letters of T. E. Lawrence,* 1st ed. (New York: Doubleday Doran, 1939), 190.

10. Lawrence to E. T. Leeds, Dec. 24, 1914, in Malcolm Brown, *The Letters of T. E. Lawrence* (London: J. M. Dent, 1988), 106.

11. Lawrence to D. G. Hogarth, April 20, 1915, Garnett, *Letters,* 197. "I spent three magnificent years in Cairo, and only went twice into a club—and then as some fellow's guest." Graves, *T. E. Lawrence to His Biographers,* 37; Lawrence to Robert Graves, undated, ibid., I, 36. The Savoy Hotel was torn down after the war and replaced by an apartment building; the square is now called Midan Talaat Harb. The former British Officers Club is now the Windsor Hotel. Groppi's is still there; the street is now called Sharia Adly. The Groppi's on the Midan Talaat Harb, across from where the Savoy Hotel used to be, was not built until after the war.

12. T. E. Lawrence to W. G. Lawrence, Jan. 21, 1915, T. E. Lawrence et al., *The Home Letters of T. E. Lawrence and His Brothers* (New York: Macmillan, 1954), 301; Yigal Sheffy, *British Military Intelligence in the Palestine Campaign, Cass Series: Studies in Intelligence* (London: Frank Cass, 1998), 45–47.

13. R. E. M. Russell, "Précis of conversation with Abd el Aziz el Masri, on 16th August 1914," Aug. 17, 1914, FO 371/2140, no. 46261, in Wilson, *Lawrence,* 158.

14. G. F. Clayton, report, Oct. 30, 1914, FO 371/2140, fos. 180–1, in ibid., 159–60.

15. P. Z. Cox to secterary to the government of India, Foreign and Political Department, telegram 82-B, Dec. 3, 1914, FO 371/2479, fo. 309, in ibid., 163.

16. Lord Kitchener to R. H. A. Storrs, for Sherif Abdullah, repeated in Foreign Office London to M. Cheetham, telegram 219, Sept. 24, 1914, FO 371/2768, fo. 76; Sherif Abdullah to Lord Kitchener and Lord Kitchener to M. Cheetham, repeated in M. Cheetham to Foreign Office, London, telegram 233, Oct. 31, 1914, FO 371/2139; both in ibid., 165.

17. See Kedourie, *In the Anglo-Arab Labyrinth,* 17–20; Wilson, *Lawrence,* 1003.

18. "Syria: The Raw Material" was written in the spring of 1915, but only printed in the *Arab Bulletin* in March 1917. Bidwell et al., *Arab Bulletin,* III, no. 44, 107–14.

19. A. N. H. M. Herbert, undated, cited in Margaret FitzHerbert, *The Man Who Was Greenmantle: A Biography of Aubrey Herbert* (London: J. Murray, 1983), 144; A. W. Lawrence, *T. E. Lawrence, by His Friends* (Garden City, NY: Doubleday Doran, 1937), 138; Storrs, *Memoirs,* 202.

20. S. F. Newcombe, 1927, in Wilson, *Lawrence,* 169.

21. Lawrence to D. G. Hogarth, Dec. 20, 1914, in Garnett, *Letters,* 190.

22. "The Alexandretta scheme . . . was from beginning to end, my invention, put forward necessarily through my chiefs (I was a 2nd. Lieut. of three months' seniority!)" The memos, dated Jan. 5, 1915, are cited in Wilson, *Lawrence,* 171–72; Liddell Hart, *T. E. Lawrence to His Biographers,* 17.

23. Feb. 20, 1915, Lawrence et al., *Home Letters,* 303.

24. To A. H. McMahon, telegram 91, Feb. 17, 1915, FO 371/2480, fo. 145, cited in Wilson, *Lawrence,* 179, 1005n.

25. Lawrence to D. G. Hogarth, March 22, 1915, Garnett, *Letters,* 193–96; Lawrence to E. T. Leeds, March 9, 1915, Lawrence et al., *Letters to E. T. Leeds,* 107; Lawrence to E. T. Leeds, April 18, 1915, ibid., 109.

26. Ronald Storrs, *Orientations* (London: Nicholson & Watson, 1943), 219.

27. Lawrence to his family and to his mother, April 4, 1915, and undated, Brown, *Letters,* 304.

28. Lawrence to C. F. Bell, April 18, 1915, ibid., 71–72. See also Newcombe's confirmation that many of the intelligence bulletins were written by Lawrence, in Wilson, *Lawrence,* 1006, note 1075.

29. Telegrams from Grey to McMahon and McMahon to Grey, May 14–15, 1915, FO 371/2486, fos. 7 & 9, in Wilson, *Lawrence,* 187.

Chapter 8. Sarah

1. Flavius Josephus, *The Jewish War,* trans. G. A. Williamson (New York: A. L. Burt, 1926), 521.

2. Avshalom Feinberg, *Avshalom: Ketavim U-Mikhtavim,* ed. Aharon Amir (Jerusalem: Shikmonah, 1985), 171.

3. Ayala Raz, "Fashion in Eretz-Israel: What We Were Wearing in the Early Days of This Century" (1999 [cited 2006]); available from mfa.gov.il/mfa/go.asp?MFAHodopo).

4. Anita Engle, *The Nili Spies* (London: Hogarth Press, 1959), 34.

5. Priska Gmür, "It Is Not Up to Us Women to Solve Great Problems," in Heiko Haumann and Peter Haber, *The First Zionist Congress in 1897: Causes, Significance, Topicality* (Basel, New York: Karger, 1997), 292.

6. Avshalom to Rivka Aaronsohn, March 14, 1912, Feinberg, *Avshalom: Ketavim U-Mikhtavim,* 91.

7. Engle, *The Nili Spies,* 35. Sarati was an endearment used by Sarah's family and by Avshalom; Saraleh is a Yiddish diminutive of her name.

8. Avshalom Feinberg to Sarah Aaronsohn, June 6, 1913, Feinberg, *Avshalom: Ketavim U-Mikhtavim,* 142. The heavy blue veil for the bride before marriage is a custom among the Jews of North Africa, Yemen, and Persia; Ashkenazi Jews like the Aaronsohns and the Feinbergs probably would not have followed the custom, but references to traditional Jewish rituals were fashionable among the Zionists.

9. Gerda Hoffer, *Zeit der Heldinnen: Lebensbilder aussergewöhnlicher jüdischer Frauen* (München: Deutscher Taschenbuch Verlag, 1999), 194.

10. Avshalom Feinberg to Sarah Aaronsohn, June 17, 1914, Feinberg, *Avshalom: Ketavim U-Mikhtavim,* 143–45.

11. Etan Belkind, *Kakh Zeh Hayah: Sipuro Shel Ish Nili* (Tel Aviv: Miśrad ha-biṭaḥon-ha-hotsa'ah le-or, 1977), 77–79. There are no entries in Aaron Aaronsohn's diary for this period.

12. Eliezer Livneh, *Nili Toldoteyla Shel He'aza Medinit* (Tel Aviv: Schocken Books, 1961), 59.

13. From Pirkei Avot, I: Mishna 14. Jabotinsky omitted the other half of Hillel's dictum: "When I am only for myself, what am I?" See Michael Stanislawski, *Zionism and the Fin de Siècle: Cosmopolitanism and Nationalism from Nordau to Jabotinsky* (Berkeley: University of California Press, 2001), 187–88.

14. Joseph B. Schechtman, *Rebel and Statesman: The Vladimir Jabotinsky Story,* 2 vols. (New York: Thomas Yoseloff, 1956), I, 86.

15. J. H. Patterson, *With the Zionists in Gallipoli* (New York: George H. Doran, 1916), 59–61.

16. Ronald Storrs, *Orientations* (London: Nicholson & Watson, 1943), 145.

17. Livneh, *Nili,* 69.

18. Feinberg, *Avshalom: Ketavim U-Mikhtavim,* 171.

19. *Bava Batra* 60b.

20. Nov. 25, 1915, Aaronsohn, "Diary."

21. Yigal Sheffy, *British Military Intelligence in the Palestine Campaign, Cass Series: Studies in Intelligence* (London: Frank Cass, 1998), 35; Dec. 7, 1915, Aaronsohn, "Diary."

22. Livneh, *Nili,* 72.

23. Ibid., 74.

24. Dec. 18, 1916 and June 21, 1917, Aaronsohn, "Diary"; Aaron Aaronsohn, "Letter to Judge Julian M. Mack, New York, from Copenhagen" (typescript, Aharonsohn Archive, Zichron Ya'aqov), 15. Many years later, Leonard Woolley wrote: "The Cairo people were very suspicious of Alex, and thought he might probably be an enemy agent. They therefore turned him down." Reported in a letter, June 11, 1957, in Engle, *The Nili Spies,* 54–55.

25. Feinberg to Henrietta Szold, 1915, in Engle, *The Nili Spies,* 56.

26. Avshalom Feinberg to Alex Aaronsohn, Jan. 2, 1914, Feinberg, *Avshalom: Ketavim U-Mikhtavim,* 159; Engle, *The Nili Spies,* 56; Feinberg, "Rapport à Miss Henrietta Szold, October 1915," 280.

27. Engle, *The Nili Spies,* 58.

28. Livneh, *Nili,* 78–79.

29. Eliezer Livneh, *Aharon Aharonsohn, Ha-Ish U-Zemano* (Jerusalem: Mosad Bialik, 1969), 162.

30. Ibid., 116.

31. Nov. 23, 1915, Aaronsohn, "Diary." Livneh, *Aharon Aharonsohn,* 203.

32. Weldon wrote in his memoirs that they had approached on December 2 and found no one waiting for them. Lewen Francis Barrington Weldon, *"Hard Lying": Eastern Mediterranean, 1914–1919* (London: Jenkins, 1925), 110–11; Dec. 13 and Dec. 14, 1915, Aaronsohn, "Diary."

33. Quoted in David Fromkin, *A Peace to End All Peace: Creating the Modern Middle East, 1914–1922* (New York: Holt, 1989), 35.

34. Sarah Aaronsohn to Zila Feinberg, Aug. 8, 1915, in Livneh, *Nili,* 90.

35. Dec. 16, 1915, Aaronsohn, "Diary"; Aaron Aaronsohn, "Pro Armenia" (typescript, Aharonsohn Archive, Zichron Ya'aqov).

36. Liova Yitzchak Schneersohn, "Diary," Jan. 1916, quoted in Yair Auron, *The Banality of Indifference: Zionism and the Armenian Genocide* (New Brunswick, NJ: Transaction Publishers, 2000), 179.

37. Nov. 23, 1915, Aaronsohn, "Diary."

38. Dec. 3, 1915, ibid.

39. Feinberg, *Avshalom: Ketavim U-Mikhtavim,* 252, 367.

Chapter 9. The Arab Bureau

1. Lawrence to E. T. Leeds, March 9, 1915, T. E. Lawrence et al., *Letters to E. T. Leeds* (Andoversford, Gloucestershire: Whittington Press, 1988), 107.

2. Lawrence to his family, Sept. 29, 1915, T. E. Lawrence et al., *The Home Letters of T. E. Lawrence and His Brothers* (New York: Macmillan, 1954), 308–9.

3. Ibid., 307; Lawrence to his family, Aug. 19, 1915.

4. Ronald Storrs, *Orientations* (London: Nicholson & Watson, 1943), 178. Kedourie argues that the Cairo staff ignored or twisted the intention of the Foreign Office in their reply to Hussein; others have raised questions about Kedourie's evidence for this assertion. Elie Kedourie, *In the Anglo-Arab Labyrinth: The McMahon-Hussein Correspondence and Its Interpretations, 1914–1939* (Portland, OR: Frank Cass, 2000), 69–71; Jeremy Wilson, *Lawrence of Arabia: The Authorized Biography of T. E. Lawrence* (New York: Atheneum, 1990), 1010n.

5. Kedourie, *In the Anglo-Arab Labyrinth,* 74. The demands of the secret coordinating committee are in "The Damascus Protocol," in George Antonius, *The Arab Awakening: The Story of the Arab National Movement* (Beirut, Lebanon: Khayats, 1961), 157–58.

6. Lawrence to A. B. Watt, Aug. 29, 1915, David Garnett, *Letters of T. E. Lawrence,* 1st ed. (New York: Doubleday Doran, 1939), 199–200.

7. Wilson, *Lawrence,* 205.

8. Abdul Latif Tibawi, *Anglo-Arab Relations and the Question of Palestine, 1914–1921* (London: Luzac, 1978), 76–81; Wilson, *Lawrence,* 1013n.

9. Liddell Hart, *T. E. Lawrence to His Biographers,* 2 vols, (Garden City, NY: Doubleday, 1963), II, 88.

10. Quoted in Wilson, *Lawrence,* 211–12.

11. Lawrence to his family, Oct. 19, 1915, Lawrence et al., *Home Letters,* 310; D. G. Hogarth, "Mecca's Revolt Againt the Turk," *Century Magazine* (1920) 78: 409.

12. Gertrude Bell to Lawrence, March 18, 1916, in Wilson, *Lawrence,* 258.

13. T. E. Lawrence, *Seven Pillars of Wisdom,* ed. J. Wilson, complete "Oxford" edition (Fordingbridge, Hampshire: J. and N. Wilson, 2004), 40; Deedes to Lawrence, March 26, 1916, in Wilson, *Lawrence,* 261.

14. Gertrude Bell to Florence Bell, April 9, 1916, Gertrude Lowthian Bell and Florence Eveleen Eleanore Olliffe Bell, *The Letters of Gertrude Bell* (New York: Boni and Liveright, 1927), I, 372; Lawrence to Clayton, April 9, 1916, in Wilson, *Lawrence,* 267.

15. Bruce Westrate, *The Arab Bureau: British Policy in the Middle East, 1916–1920* (University Park, PA: Pennsylvania State University Press, 1992), 89.

16. Lawrence, *Seven Pillars,* 38.

17. Lawrence to Leeds, Nov. 16, 1915, in Lawrence et al., *Letters to E. T. Leeds,* 78–79.

18. Sykes to Clayton, Dec. 28, 1915, in Wilson, *Lawrence,* 236.

19. Sherif Hussein to Sir A. H. McMahon, Jan. 1, 1916, ibid., 243–44.

20. June 6, 1916, Robin Leonard Bidwell et al., *Arab Bulletin* (Gerrards Cross, Buckinghamshire, England: Archive Editions, 1986), I, 7.

21. McMahon to Sherif Hussein, May 8, 1916, quoted in Wilson, *Lawrence,* 286.

22. Lawrence, *Seven Pillars,* 41.

23. Ibid., 238–40.

24. July 2, 1916, Lawrence et al., *Home Letters,* 327.

25. Lawrence, *Seven Pillars,* 43.

Chapter 10. Aaron Alone

1. "Journal," Jan. 30, 1914, Avshalom Feinberg, *Avshalom: Ketavim U-Mikhtavim,* ed. Aharon Amir (Jerusalem: Shikmonah, 1985), 220.

2. Jan. 1, 1916, Aaronsohn, "Diary."

3. Aaronsohn, "Letter to Judge Julian M. Mack, New York, from Copenhagen" (typescript, Aharonsohn Archive, Zichron Ya'aqov).

4. Eliezer Livneh, *Nili Toldateyha Shel He'aza Medinit* (Tel Aviv: Schocken Books, 1961), 83–86.

5. Nov. 26, Dec. 3, Dec. 7, and Dec. 8, 1915, Aaronsohn, "Diary."

6. Aaronsohn, "Letter to Judge Julian M. Mack, New York, from Copenhagen."

7. Nov. 23 and Dec. 8, 1915, Aaronsohn, "Diary."

8. Dec. 24, 1915, ibid.

9. Eliezer Livneh, *Aharon Aharonsohn Ha-Ish U-Zemano* (Jerusalem: Mosad Bialiķ, 1969), 209–10.

10. Aaronsohn, "Letter to Judge Julian M. Mack, New York, from Copenhagen"; Livneh, *Aharon Aharonsohn,* 211.

11. Dec. 23, 1915, and July 14, 1916, Aaronsohn, "Diary."

12. July 11, 1916, ibid.

13. Dec. 26, Dec. 27, and Dec. 31, 1915, ibid.

14. Aaronsohn, "Letter to Judge Julian M. Mack, New York, from Copenhagen."

15. July 12–14, 1916, Aaronsohn, "Diary."

16. Shmuel Katz, *Ha-Reshet: Ha-Haggadah Le-Vet Aharonson* (Tel Aviv: Miśrad ha-biṭaḥon, 2000), 99.

17. "Saïfna Ahmar, Ya Sultan!" *Atlantic Monthly,* CXVIII (August 1916), 188f. Later reprinted as Alexander Aaronsohn, *With the Turks in Palestine* (Boston, New York: Houghton Mifflin, 1916).

18. Livneh, *Nili,* 127.

19. Oct. 11 and Oct. 13, 1916, Aaronsohn, "Diary."

20. Sir Ralph later became ambassador to Brazil, and was a friend and confidant of Colonel Percy Harrison Fawcett, the explorer who disappeared in the Amazon in the 1920s while searching for the lost city of Z.

21. Livneh, *Aharon Aharonsohn,* 215.

22. Aaronsohn, "Letter to Judge Julian M. Mack, New York, from Copenhagen."

23. "As long as I was under the spell of Felix Frankfurter I could not even dream of writing a line: he is too spellbinding." Aaronsohn to Henrietta Szold, March 10, 1918, in Alexandra Lee Levin, *Vision: A Biography of Harry Friedenwald* (Philadelphia: Jewish Publication Society), 442.

24. Personal ("Dear Judge") letter, accompanying Aaronsohn, "Letter to Judge Julian M. Mack, New York, from Copenhagen."

25. Livneh, *Nili,* 100.

26. Oct. 17–19, 1916, Aaronsohn, "Diary."

27. Anita Engle, *The Nili Spies* (London: Hogarth Press, 1959), 77.

Chapter 11. At the Savoy Hotel

1. T. E. Lawrence, *Seven Pillars of Wisdom,* ed. J. Wilson, complete 1922 "Oxford" edition (Fordingbridge, Hampshire: J. and N. Wilson, 2004), xv.

2. Nov. 24, 1916, Aaron Aaronsohn, "Diary" (Aharonsohn Archive, Zichron Ya'aqov).

3. Robert Graves and B. H. Liddell Hart, *T. E. Lawrence to His Biographers Robert Graves and Liddell Hart,* 2 vols. (Garden City, NY: Doubleday, 1963), 84.

4. Oct. 27–28, 1916, Aaronsohn, "Diary."

5. Letter to Oubi [Rivka] and Lel [Alexander] Aaronsohn, Oct. 28, 1916, ibid.

6. Nov. 11, 1916, ibid.

7. Oct. 30, 1916, ibid.

8. Nov. 9, 1916, ibid.

9. Quoted in Anthony Verrier, *Agents of Empire: Anglo-Zionist Intelligence Operations, 1915–1919: Brigadier Walter Gribbon, Aaron Aaronsohn and the Nili Ring* (London: Brassey's, 1995), 208.

10. Aaronsohn learned on Oct. 28, 1916, that Woolley was a prisoner. Aaronsohn, "Diary."

11. Eliezer Livneh, *Aharon Aharonson, Ha-Ish U-Zemano* (Jerusalem: Mosad Bialiḳ, 1969), 226.

12. Nov. 7, 1916, Aaronsohn, "Diary."

13. Nov. 24, 1916, ibid.

14. Dec. 26, 1916, ibid.

15. March 13, 1915, quoted in Martin Gilbert, *Exile and Return: The Struggle for a Jewish Homeland* (Philadelphia: Lippincott, 1978), 83. The memo was addressed to Herbert Samuel, who would later become the first high commissioner in Palestine.

16. Dec. 8, 1916, Aaronsohn, "Diary."

17. Dec. 5, 1916, ibid.

18. Bentwich, *My 77 Years: An Account of My Life and Times* (Philadelphia: Jewish Publication Society of America, 1961), 43.

19. Dec. 18, 1916, Aaronsohn, "Diary."

20. Dec. 19, 1916, ibid.

21. Dec. 26, 1916, in Verrier, *Agents of Empire,* 229.

22. Dec. 29, 1916, Aaronsohn, "Diary."

23. Dec. 29, 1916, and Jan. 1, 1917, ibid.

24. Jan. 4, 1917, ibid.

25. Jan. 5, 1917, ibid.

26. Jan. 5 and Jan. 11, 1917, in Verrier, *Agents of Empire,* 230, ibid.

27. Jan. 15 and Jan. 17, 1917, Aaronsohn, "Diary."

28. Jan. 25, 1917, ibid.

29. Jan. 26, 1917, ibid.

30. Jan. 30, 1917, ibid.

31. C. E. Wilson to G. F. Clayton, Nov. 22, 1916, in Jeremy Wilson, *Lawrence of Arabia: The Authorized Biography of T. E. Lawrence* (New York: Atheneum, 1990), 331–32.

32. Lawrence, *Seven Pillars,* 115.

33. Lawrence to Arab Bureau, Dec. 5, 1916, in Malcolm Brown, *The Letters of T. E. Lawrence* (London: J. M. Dent, 1988), 92.

34. Lawrence, *Seven Pillars,* 103–4.

35. Lawrence, notebook, Jan. 23, 1917, quoted in Wilson, *Lawrence,* 352; Lawrence, *Seven Pillars,* 78.

36. J. C. Watson to GOC Middle East Brigade, Royal Flying Corps, Jan. 11, 1917, quoted in Wilson, *Lawrence,* 355–56.

37. Jan. 31, 1917, T. E. Lawrence et al., *The Home Letters of T. E. Lawrence and His Brothers* (New York: Macmillan, 1954), 334.

38. Lawrence, *Seven Pillars,* 100.

39. Ibid., 360.

40. [Aaron Aaronsohn], "Palestine. The Jewish Colonies," Robin Leonard Bidwell et al., *Arab Bulletin,* (Gerrards Cross, Buckinghamshire, England: Archive Editions, 1986), II, no. 64, 391.

41. Feb. 1, 1917, Aaronsohn, "Diary."

Chapter 12. Aqaba

1. Lawrence to Clayton, June 1917, British Library, Add. 45915, fo. 55.

2. Lawrence to C. E. Wilson, Aug. 1, 1917, in Jeremy Wilson, *Lawrence of Arabia: The Authorized Biography of T. E. Lawrence* (New York: Atheneum, 1990), 349.

3. Lawrence to Newcombe, Jan. 17, 1917, in Malcolm Brown, *The Letters of T. E. Lawrence* (London: J. M. Dent, 1988), 102–3.

4. T. E. Lawrence, *Seven Pillars of Wisdom,* ed. J. Wilson, complete 1922 "Oxford" edition (Fordingbridge, Hampshire: J. and N. Wilson, 2004), 167–68. In later editions Lawrence calls Brémond a "politician" instead of a crook.

5. Ibid., 666. Lawrence's declaration in the epilogue of *Seven Pillars* says only, "Fortunately I had early divulged the existence of this thing [the Sykes-Picot agreement] to Faisal" without giving a date. Jeremy Wilson argues convincingly that Lawrence told Faisal in early February at Wejh. Wilson, *Lawrence,* 1052–54.

6. Lawrence, *Seven Pillars,* 667.

7. Ibid., 237.

8. "Report on the Raiding Party sent to the Hejaz Railway line under Bimbashi Garland, February 1917," March 6, 1917, FO 882/6, fo. 40, in Wilson, *Lawrence,* 375.

9. Lawrence, *Seven Pillars,* 180.

10. Lawrence's unpublished notebook, March 10, 1917, quoted in Wilson, *Lawrence,* 381.

11. Lawrence, *Seven Pillars,* 200–1.

12. Ibid., 217–21.

13. Édouard Brémond, *Le Hedjaz dans la guerre mondiale: Collection de mémoires, études et documents pour servir à l'histoire de la guerre mondiale* (Paris: Payot, 1931), 9; David Holden and Richard Johns, *The House of Saud: The Rise and Rule of the Most Powerful Dynasty in the Arab World,* 1st American ed. (New York: Holt, Rinehart and Winston, 1982), 53.

14. Lawrence, *Seven Pillars,* 229–31, 385; Robin Leonard Bidwell et al., *Arab Bulletin* (Gerrards Cross, Buckinghamshire, England: Archive Editions, 1986), I, no. 57, 309. Auda went three months without teeth, making it impossible for him to eat meat, a desert staple, until after they had taken Aqaba; Sir Reginald Wingate sent his own dentist from Egypt to make Auda a set of Allied teeth.

15. Clayton to Wingate, May 29, 1917, FO 882/6, fo. 388, in Wilson, *Lawrence,* 397.

16. April 30, 1917, Bidwell et al., *Arab Bulletin,* II, no. 49, 193.

17. Lawrence, *Seven Pillars,* 234, 241.

18. Ibid., 263.

19. Ibid., 270–73.

20. Ibid., 291.

21. Ibid., 295–96. This passage in the 1922 edition does not appear in later editions.

22. May 13, 1917, Bidwell et al., *Arab Bulletin,* II, no. 50, 207.

23. Lawrence, *Seven Pillars,* 295.

24. Michael Asher, *Lawrence: The Uncrowned King of Arabia* (Woodstock, NY: Overlook Press, 1999), 259–60.

Chapter 13. Allenby

1. In a lecture at the Royal Military Academy, Woolwich, 1919. See mideastoutpost.com/archives/000177.html.

2. Feb. 16, 1917, Aaron Aaronsohn, "Diary" (Aharonsohn Archive, Zichron Ya'aqov).

3. Anita Engle, *The Nili Spies* (London: Hogarth Press, 1959), 85.

4. Feb. 13 and Feb. 15, 1917, Aaronsohn, "Diary."

5. March 3, 1917, ibid.

6. Feb. 19, 1917, ibid.

7. 1 Samuel 15:29. The story is sometimes told that they opened the Bible and pointed to a passage at random.

8. March 6, 1917, Aaronsohn, "Diary."

9. April 3, 1917, and scattered mentions in other entries, ibid.

10. April 21, 1917, ibid.

11. April 22, 1917, ibid.

12. April 19–20, 1917, ibid.

13. May 11, 1917, quoted in Martin Gilbert, *Exile and Return: The Struggle for a Jewish Homeland* (Philadelphia: Lippincott, 1978), 97.

14. April 4 and April 14, 1917, Aaronsohn, "Diary."

15. April 23–24, 1917, ibid.

16. April 27–28, 1917, ibid.

17. Isaiah Friedman, *Germany, Turkey, and Zionism, 1897–1918* (Oxford: Clarendon Press, 1977), 350–54.

18. April 21, 1917, Aaronsohn, "Diary."

19. Nov. 19, 1916, ibid.

20. Eliezer Livneh, *Aharon Aharonson, Ha-Ish U-Zemano* (Jerusalem: Mosad Bialik, 1969), 274–82.

21. April 21–22, 1917, Aaronsohn, "Diary."

22. May 23, 1917, ibid.

23. Richard Meinertzhagen, *Middle East Diary, 1917–1956* (London: Cresset Press, 1959), 5; T. E. Lawrence, *Seven Pillars of Wisdom*, ed. J. Wilson, complete 1922 "Oxford" edition (Fordingbridge, Hampshire: J. and N. Wilson, 2004), 429.

24. Meinertzhagen, *Middle East Diary*, 211.

25. April 23, 1917, Aaronsohn, "Diary."

26. Ibid., April 2, May 12, June 29, July 6, and July 7, 1917; Lewen Francis Barrington Weldon, *"Hard Lying"; Eastern Mediterranean, 1914–1919* (London: Jenkins, 1925), 174, 178, 184, 186.

27. June 30, 1917, Aaronsohn, "Diary."

28. July 1, 1917, ibid.

29. July 17, 1917, ibid.

30. Yigal Sheffy, *British Military Intelligence in the Palestine Campaign, Cass Series: Studies in Intelligence* (London: Frank Cass, 1998), 275.

31. Allenby apparently did not listen to Meinertzhagen's bizarre ideas, despite the claims of Meinertzhagen's diary and those who have subsequently believed him, like Yigal Sheffy, "Institutionalized Deception and Perception Reinforcement: Allenby's Campaigns in Palestine," in Michael I. Handel, *Intelligence and Military Operations* (London; Portland, OR: Frank Cass, 1990), 189–90. Recently, Meinertzhagen's invented autobiography has been exposed as a remarkable fraud; see Brian Garfield, *The Meinertzhagen Mystery* (Washington, DC: Potomac Books, 2006), especially Ch. 2, "The Haversack Ruse"; and John Seabrook, "Ruffled Feathers," *The New Yorker* (May 29, 2006), 56.

32. July 25, 1917, Aaronsohn, "Diary."

33. July 28, 1917, ibid.

34. July 26, 1917, ibid.

35. Lawrence, *Seven Pillars*, 348.

36. Lawrence to Clayton, July 10, 1917, David Garnett, *The Letters of T. E. Lawrence*, 1st ed. (New York: Doubleday Doran, 1939), 228–29. Lawrence also proposed Arab actions in parts of Lebanon in instructions he had given to Nesib Bey al Bekri. Garnett, *Letters*, 230–31.

37. Clayton memo, July 15, 1917, quoted in Jeremy Wilson, *Lawrence of Arabia: The Authorized Biography of T. E. Lawrence* (New York: Atheneum, 1990), 423.

38. Lawrence, *Seven Pillars*, 349.

Chapter 14. Athlit

1. Richard Meinertzhagen, *Middle East Diary, 1917–1956* (London: Cresset Press, 1959), 5.

2. For a fictional portrayal of an Aaronsohn family dinner, see Aharon Megged, *Mandrakes from the Holy Land* (New Milford, CT: Toby, 2005), 113–15.

3. Unpublished memoirs of Liova Schneersohn, Feb. 21, 1917, quoted in Anita Engle, *The Nili Spies* (London: Hogarth Press, 1959), 93–94.

4. Eliezer Livneh, *Aharon Aharonson, Ha-Ish U-Zemano* (Jerusalem: Mosad Bialik, 1969), 267–69.

5. Alexandra Lee Levin, *Vision: A Biography of Harry Friedenwald* (Philadelphia: Jewish Publication Society of America, 1964), 189.

6. Quoted in Engle, *The Nili Spies,* 103.

7. Lewen Francis Barrington Weldon, *"Hard Lying": Eastern Mediterranean, 1914–1919* (London: Jenkins, 1925), 166.

8. April 28, 1917, Aaron Aaronsohn, "Diary" (Aharonsohn Archive, Zichron Ya'aqov).

9. May 31, 1917, ibid.

10. June 11, 1917. See also June 9, and June 13, 1917, ibid.

11. Eliezer Livneh, *Nili Toldoteyha Shel He'aza Medinit* (Tel Aviv: Schocken, 1961), 271.

12. Aug. 2, 1917, Aaronsohn, "Diary"; Livneh, *Nili,* 263.

13. Livneh, *Aharon Aharonsohn,* 250.

14. July 27, 1917, Aaronsohn, "Diary."

15. Quoted in Engle, *The Nili Spies,* 165.

16. There is still a meteorology station at Beit Aharonsohn, now automated.

17. Yigel Sheffy, *British Military Intelligence in the Palestine Campaign, Cass Series: Studies in Intelligence* (London: Frank Cass, 1998), 160–61; Shmuel Katz, *Ha-Reshet: Ha-Haggadah Le-Vet Aharonson* (Tel Aviv: Miśrad ha-biṭaḥon, 2000), 175.

18. Engle, *The Nili Spies,* 105–6; Livneh, *Nili,* 254–57.

19. Message to Aaron Aaronsohn, n.d., quoted in Engle, *The Nili Spies,* 106.

20. Livneh, *Nili,* 262–63.

21. Engle, *The Nili Spies,* 108.

22. Ibid., 159.

23. Quoted in ibid., 166.

24. Steven Runciman, *A History of the Crusades,* 3 vols. (New York: Harper & Row, 1965), vol. 2, 93–94.

25. Sheffy, *British Military Intelligence in the Palestine Campaign,* 162; Livneh, *Nili,* 284, 298.

26. Engle, *The Nili Spies,* 169.

27. Livneh, *Aharon Aharonsohn,* 298.

28. Ibid., 244; Livneh, *Nili,* 242.

29. Engle, *The Nili Spies,* 178–79.

30. Weldon, *"Hard Lying,"* 194.

31. Dr. Neumann's unpublished memoirs, quoted in Engle, *The Nili Spies,* 185.

32. Ibid., 184.

Chapter 15. Deraa

1. T. E. Lawrence, *Seven Pillars of Wisdom,* ed. J. Wilson, complete 1922 "Oxford" edition (Fordingbridge, Hampshire: J. and N. Wilson, 2004), 684; Robert Graves and B. H. Liddell Hart, *T. E. Lawrence to His Biographers,* 2 vols. (Garden City, NY: Doubleday, 1963), I, 57.

2. Aug. 20, 1917, Aaron Aaronsohn, "Diary" (Aharonsohn Archive, Zichron Ya'aqov).

3. T. E. Lawrence to Mark Sykes, Sept. 9, 1917, quoted in Jeremy Wilson, *Lawrence of Arabia: The Authorized Biography of T. E. Lawrence* (New York: Atheneum, 1990), 443. The letter, which was enclosed with a letter from Lawrence to Clayton in the Clayton papers in Durham, seems not to have been sent. See also Eliezer Livneh, *Nili Toldoteyha Shel He'aza Medinit* (Tel Aviv: Schocken, 1961), 235.

4. T. E. Lawrence to Mrs. Lawrence, Aug. 2, 1909, T. E. Lawrence et al., *The Home Letters of T. E. Lawrence and His Brothers* (New York: Macmillan, 1954), 98–99.

5. Robin Leonard Bidwell et al., *Arab Bulletin* (Gerrards Cross, Buckinghamshire, England: Archive Editions, 1986), II no. 44, 107–14.

6. Aug. 20, 1917, Aaronsohn, "Diary."

7. T. E. Lawrence to Mark Sykes, Sept. 9, 1917, quoted in Wilson, *Lawrence,* 443.

8. Ibid., 442–43.

9. Ibid., 445.

10. Quoted in ibid., Clayton to Lawrence, Sept. 20, 1917.

11. William Yale, *The Near East: A Modern History* (Ann Arbor: University of Michigan Press, 1968), 243.

12. Lawrence to E. T. Leeds, Sept. 24, 1917, Malcolm Brown, *The Letters of T. E. Lawrence* (London: J. M. Dent, 1988), 124.

13. Lawrence, *Seven Pillars,* 430.

14. 449 Hogarth to Ormsby-Gore, Oct. 26, 1917, quoted in Wilson, *Lawrence.*

15. Lawrence, *Seven Pillars,* 430–31.

16. Ibid., 487.

17. George Lloyd, notes, undated (Oct. 25, 1917), quoted in Wilson, *Lawrence,* 1082n.

18. Lawrence, *Seven Pillars,* 492–93.

19. Ibid., 494.

20. The latest arguments in this line are from James Barr, *Setting the Desert on Fire: T. E. Lawrence and Britain's Secret War in Arabia, 1916–18* (London: Bloomsbury, 2006), who argues on the basis of electrostatic imaging of the pages of Lawrence's wartime diary that the missing pages that would have covered the Deraa episode included only the place-name Azrak, suggesting that Lawrence never left Azrak for Deraa. The same test was conducted on the pages in 1996 and failed to recover the word "Azrak." See J. N. Lockman, *Scattered Tracks on the Lawrence Trail* (Whitmore Lake, MI: Falcon Books, 1996), 128, fn 4. Whether the episode happened exactly as recounted by Lawrence, or at all, seems less important than Lawrence's psychological need to reveal or tell the story.

21. Lawrence to W. F. Stirling, June 28, 1919, Brown, *Letters,* 166.

22. Lawrence, *Seven Pillars,* 501–2.

23. Lawrence to his family, Dec. 14, 1917, Brown, *Letters,* 131.

24. Lawrence, *Seven Pillars,* 508.

Chapter 16. Sarah Alone

1. T. E. Lawrence, *Seven Pillars of Wisdom,* ed. J. Wilson, complete 1922 "Oxford" edition (Fordingbridge, Hampshire: J. and N. Wilson, 2004), dedication.

2. Frank E. Manuel, *The Realities of American-Palestinian Relations* (Washington: Public Affairs Press, 1949), 180–81.

3. Aaron to Alex Aaronsohn, Sept. 1917, hand carried by William Yale, quoted in ibid.

4. Ivria Lishinsky, Josef's daughter, witnessed the beatings. Eliezer Livneh, *Nili Toldoteyha Shel He'aza Medinit* (Tel Aviv: Schocken, 1961), 309; Alexander Aaronsohn, *Sarah: Shalhevet Nili* (Jerusalem: Ahi'asaf, 1942), 93.

5. Hillel Halkin, *A Strange Death* (New York: Public Affairs, 2005), 187 and passim; Aaronsohn, *Sarah: Shalhevet Nili,* 102.

6. Anita Engle, *The Nili Spies* (London: Hogarth Press, 1959), 199.

7. The letter is printed in Shmuel Katz, *Ha-Reshet: Ha-Haggadah Le-Vet Aharonson* (Tel Aviv: Miśrad ha-biṭaḥon, 2000), 322–24.

8. Hillel Yaffe's diary, cited in Engle, *The Nili Spies,* 201.

9. Quoted in ibid., 191.

10. Livneh, *Nili,* 344, 346; Katz, *Aharonson,* 287.

11. David Fromkin, *A Peace to End All Peace: Creating the Modern Middle East, 1914–1922* (New York: Holt, 1989), 317.

12. Chaim Weizmann, *Trial and Error: The Autobiography of Chaim Weizmann* (New York: Harper, 1949), 111.

13. Leonard Stein, *The Balfour Declaration* (Jerusalem: Magnes Press, 1983), 293.

14. When the Colonial Office tried to investigate the origins of the Balfour Declaration in 1922, Ormsby-Gore reported that "upon the origins of the Declaration little exists in the way of official records; indeed, little is known of how the policy represented by the Declaration was first given form." See his memo "Palestine," Dec. 24, 1922, quoted in David Vital, *Zionism: The Crucial Phase* (Oxford: Oxford University Press, 1987), 369–70.

15. Leopold Amery diary, Oct. 31, 1917, quoted in Martin Gilbert, *Exile and Return: The Struggle for a Jewish Homeland* (Philadelphia: Lippincott, 1978), 107–8.

16. Quoted in Kathrin Ringger, "'An English Adventure': Diplomatic Efforts for a Home for the Jewish People, 1897–1922," in Heiko Haumann and Peter Haber, *The First Zionist Congress in 1897: Causes, Significance, Topicality* (Basel, New York: Karger, 1997), 277. In other memoirs, Lloyd George gave other explanations, including the claim that the Balfour Declaration was a payoff to Weizmann for his synthesis of acetone for the British war effort.

17. Nov. 16, 1917, Aaron Aaronsohn, "Diary" (Aharonsohn Archive, Zichron Ya'aqov); Stein, *The Balfour Declaration,* 579.

18. Nov. 16, 1917, Aaronsohn, "Diary."

Chapter 17. The Desert Meeting

1. T. E. Lawrence, *Seven Pillars of Wisdom,* ed. J. Wilson, complete 1922 "Oxford" edition (Fordingbridge, Hampshire: J. and N. Wilson, 2004), 630.

2. Quoted in Ronald Storrs, *The Memoirs of Sir Ronald Storrs* (New York: G. P. Putnam's Sons, 1937), 93–94n.

3. Nov. 19, 1917 Aaron Aaronsohn, "Diary" (Aharonsohn Archive, Zichron Ya'aqov).

4. Nov. 1, 1917, ibid.

5. Harry Barnard, *The Forging of an American Jew: The Life and Times of Judge Julian W. Mack* (New York: Herzl Press, 1974), 164.

6. Simon Schama, *Two Rothschilds and the Land of Israel* (New York: Knopf, 1978), 54.

7. Eliezer Livneh, *Aharon Aharonson, Ha-Ish U-Zemano* (Jerusalem: Mosad Bialiḳ, 1969), 302.

8. Felix Frankfurter and Harlan B. Phillips, *Felix Frankfurter Reminisces* (New York: Reynal, 1960), 176.

9. Livneh, *Aharon Aharonsohn,* 304–6.

10. Lawrence, *Seven Pillars,* 510.

11. Djemal Pasha to Sherif Faisal, Nov. 1917, translated in Wingate to FO London, Dec. 25, 1917, quoted in Jeremy Wilson, *Lawrence of Arabia: The Authorized Biography of T. E. Lawrence* (New York: Atheneum, 1990), 469.

12. Lawrence, *Seven Pillars,* 665–66.

13. Lawrence to Leeds, Dec. 15, 1917, in Malcolm Brown, *The Letters of T. E. Lawrence* (London: J. M. Dent, 1988), 135.

14. Quoted in Wilson, *Lawrence,* 467, 1086n; Bruce Westrate, *The Arab Bureau: British Policy in the Middle East, 1916–1920* (University Park, PA: Pennsylvania State University Press, 1992), 177.

15. Lawrence, *Seven Pillars,* 520–21, 524.

16. Ibid., 518.

17. The essay was not published in the *Arab Bulletin,* which was seen by French officials, but in an "Arab Bulletin Supplementary Paper" with limited circulation. Westrate, *The Arab Bureau,* 160–61; Wilson, *Lawrence,* 472–75.

18. T. E. Lawrence et al., *Secret Despatches from Arabia* (London: The Golden Cockerel Press, 1939), 39–40.

19. Bidwell et al., *Arab Bulletin* (Gerrards Cross, Buckinghamshire, England: Archive Editions, 1986), III, no. 66, 1412–14.

20. Lawrence, *Seven Pillars,* 539, 545.

21. Feb. 12, 1918, Brown, *Letters,* 141.

22. Lawrence, *Seven Pillars,* 567–68.

23. Liddell Hart, *T. E. Lawrence to His Biographers,* 106.

24. Lawrence, *Seven Pillars,* 574.

25. Lowell Thomas, *With Lawrence in Arabia* (London: Hutchinson, 1925), vi–vii. The battle Thomas claimed to witness in Petra was actually in October 1917, six months before; neither Thomas nor Lawrence was there.

26. Paraphrase of an undated letter from Faisal to Djemal Pasha, in Wilson, *Lawrence,* 512.

27. Lawrence to William Yale, Dec. 11, 1929, David Garnett, *The Letters of T. E. Lawrence,* 1st ed. (New York: Doubleday Doran, 1939), 672.

28. Clayton to Sykes, Nov. 28, 1917, quoted in Wilson, *Lawrence,* 468.

29. In a coversation with William Yale, the American special agent in Egypt. Frank E. Manuel, *The Realities of American-Palestinian Relations* (Washington: Public Affairs Press, 1949), 164.

30. Lawrence, *Seven Pillars,* 667.

31. Clayton to Sykes, Feb. 4, 1918, and Lawrence to Clayton, Feb. 12, 1918, quoted in Wilson, *Lawrence,* 512.

32. March 10, 1918, Aaronsohn, "Diary."

33. March 22, 1918, ibid.

34. Ormsby-Gore to FO, Feb. 1918, in Martin Gilbert, *Exile and Return: The Struggle for a Jewish Homeland* (Philadelphia: Lippincott, 1978), 102–3; March 21, 1918, Aaronsohn, "Diary."

35. Livneh, *Aharon Aharonsohn,* 315.

36. [Aaron Aaronsohn], "Palestine Letter, April 2, 1918," Bidwell et al., *Arab Bulletin* III, no. 84, 109.

37. Weizmann to Balfour, in Chaim Weizmann, *The Letters and Papers of Chaim Weizmann* (London: Oxford University Press, 1968), vol. 8, 197–206.

38. P. C. Joyce, "Interview Between Dr. Weizmann and Sherif Faisal," June 5, 1918, quoted in Wilson, *Lawrence,* 513; Bidwell et al., *Arab Bulletin* III, no. 93, 208.

39. Weizmann to Vera Weizmann, in Weizmann, *The Letters and Papers of Chaim Weizmann,* VIII, 210; Doreen Ingrams, *Palestine Papers, 1917–1922: Seeds of Conflict* (London: J. Murray, 1972), 33.

40. Hart, *T. E. Lawrence to His Biographers,* 112.

41. Stewart Symes, *Tour of Duty* (London: Collins, 1946), 31–32.

Chapter 18. Damascus

1. Lawrence to Maj. C.C.J. Littleton, Oct. 14, 1918. (From a private collection, exhibited at the Imperial War Museum exhibit, "Lawrence of Arabia: The Life, the Legend," Oct. 14, 2005 to April 17, 2006.)

2. T. E. Lawrence, *Seven Pillars of Wisdom,* ed. J. Wilson, complete 1922 "Oxford" edition (Fordingbridge, Hampshire: J. and N. Wilson, 2004), 657.

3. Lawrence to V. W. Richards, July 15, 1918, David Garnett, *The Letters of T. E. Lawrence,* 1st ed. (New York: Doubleday Doran, 1939), 244–46.

4. Lawrence, *Seven Pillars,* 651–52.

5. Wingate to Foreign Office, telegram, June 16, 1918, in Jeremy Wilson, *Lawrence of Arabia: The Authorized Biography of T. E. Lawrence* (New York: Atheneum, 1990), 520, 1097n.

6. Bidwell et al., *Arab Bulletin* (Gerrards Cross, Buckinghamshire, England: Archive Editions), III, no. 96, 245–46.

7. Lawrence, *Seven Pillars,* 634.

8. Lawrence to Sherif Hussein, June 25, 1918, Malcolm Brown, *The Letters of T. E. Lawrence* (London: J. M. Dent, 1988), 147–49.

9. Lawrence, *Seven Pillars,* 641.

10. Hubert Young, *The Independent Arab* (London: J. Murray, 1933), 195f.

11. Lawrence, *Seven Pillars,* 698–99. Sherif Hussein's proclamation is translated in Bidwell et al., *Arab Bulletin* III, no. 104, 333.

12. Lawrence, *Seven Pillars,* 698–703.

13. Ibid., 722–23.

14. Dawnay to Joyce, undated [Sept. 20, 1918], and W. H. Bartholomew (chief of the General Staff, EEF) to Joyce, Sept. 21, 1918, both in Wilson, *Lawrence,* 549–50; Lawrence, *Seven Pillars,* 754.

15. *The Evening Standard,* Sept. 25, 1918.

16. Lawrence, *Seven Pillars,* 766–67.

17. Balfour telegram and statement, Sept. 23, 1918, in Wilson, *Lawrence,* 552–53.

18. Allenby to Sherif Faisal, Sept. 25, 1918, and "Special Instructions" (issued by General Staff Australian Mounted Division, signed by Major A. Chisholm), Sept. 29, 1918, in ibid., 555–56.

19. Lawrence, *Seven Pillars,* 776–78; "The Destruction of the Fourth Army," Bidwell et al., *Arab Bulletin* III, no. 106, 343–50.

20. Lawrence, *Seven Pillars,* 791.

21. Lawrence to W. F. Stirling, June 28, 1919, Brown, *Letters,* 165–66.

22. Alec Kirkbride, *An Awakening: The Arab Campaign, 1917–18* (Tavistock, England: University Press of Arabia, 1971), 92.

23. "Report by Lieutenant-General Sir H. G. Chauvel . . . on the Capture of Damascus, and the Arrangements Made for the Civil Administration Thereof," Oct. 2, 1918, in Wilson, *Lawrence,* 563.

24. Lawrence, *Seven Pillars,* 790; Wilson, *Lawrence,* 1107n.

25. War Office to General Headquarters, Egypt, telegram, Oct. 1, 1918, quoted in Wilson, *Lawrence,* 566.

26. Allenby to Lady Allenby, Oct. 7, 1918, quoted in Efraim Karsh and Inari Karsh, *Empires of the Sand: The Struggle for Mastery in the Middle East, 1789–1923* (Harvard University Press, 1999), 273.

27. Chauvel claimed he took notes of the meeting, but lost them, and later reconstructed the account he gave to the director of the Australian War Memorial in 1936. Alec Jeffrey Hill, *Chauvel of the Light Horse: A Biography of General Sir Harry Chauvel, G.C.M.G., K.C.B* (Carlton, Australia: Melbourne University Press, 1978), 242–43. Lawrence's version of the meeting is selective, recalling only the unintelligibility of the telegram and his request to Allenby to return to England. Lawrence, *Seven Pillars,* 810–11.

Chapter 19. Mapmakers

1. Daniele Varè, *Laughing Diplomat* (New York: Doubleday, Doran & Co., 1938), 157.

2. Quoted in Alexandra Lee Levin, *Vision: a Biography of Harry Friedenwald* (Philadelphia: Jewish Publication Society of America, 1964), 266.

3. Eliezer Livneh, *Aharon Aharonson, Ha-Ish U-Zemano* (Jerusalem: Mosad Bialik̦, 1969), 339, 318.

4. M. R. Werner, *Julius Rosenwald: The Life of a Practical Humanitarian* (New York: Harper, 1939), 101.

5. Nov. 28, 1918, Aaron Aaronsohn, "Diary" (Aharonsohn Archive, Zichron Ya'aqov).

6. Melvin I. Urofsky, *American Zionism from Herzl to the Holocaust,* 1st ed. (Garden City, N.Y.: Anchor Press, 1975), 222.

7. Robert Graves and B. H. Liddell Hart, *T. E. Lawrence to His Biographers Robert Graves and B. H. Liddell Hart,* 2 vols. (Garden City, NY: Doubleday, 1963), II, 165.

8. Malcolm Brown, *Lawrence of Arabia: The Life, the Legend* (London: Thames & Hudson, 2005), 139. "It [Curzon's tears] was horribly like a medieval miracle, a *lachryma Christi,* happening to a Buddha." Graves, *T. E. Lawrence to His Biographers,* 108.

9. The map, misfiled at the PRO in a 1920 folder, was discovered in September 2005 and first put on display at the Imperial War Museum exhibit, "Lawrence of Arabia: The Life, the Legend," Oct. 14, 2005, to April 17, 2006.

10. "The Reconstruction of Arabia," in David Garnett, *The Letters of T. E. Lawrence,* 1st ed. (New York: Doubleday, Doran, 1939), 268–69.

11. Adolph Baroni (Aaron Aaronsohn), "General Allenby in Palestine," *Asia Magazine* (November 1918), 896–906, quoted in Auron, *The Banality of Indifference,* 234. The Jabotinsky quote is from *Turkey and the War* (London: Unwin, 1912).

12. Margaret Macmillan, *Paris 1919: Six Months That Changed the World* (New York: Random House, 2002), 47.

13. "Pro Armenia," Nov. 16, 1916 (Aharonsohn Archive, 2C/13), 13; "On the Armenian Massacres: Memorandum Presented to the War Office, London, November 1916" (Aharonsohn Archive, 2C/14).

14. Nov. 29, 1918, Aaronsohn, "Diary."

15. Livneh, *Aharon Aharonsohn,* 332–34.

16. Édouard Brémond, *Le Hedjaz dans la guerre mondiale: Collection de mémoires, études et documents pour servir à l'histoire de la guerre mondiale* (Paris: Payot, 1931), 310–18; Maurice J. M. Larès, *T. E. Lawrence, la France et les Français* (Publications de la Sorbonne Imprimerie Nationale, 1980), 162–63.

17. David Hunter Miller, *My Diary at the Conference of Paris, with Documents* (New York: Printed for the author by the Appeal printing company, 1924), vol. 1, 74.

18. C. Weizmann, "Dr. Weizmann's interview with Emir Faisal and the Carlton Hotel, December 11, 1918. Colonel Lawrence acting as interpreter." FO 371/3420, in Wilson, *Lawrence,* 593.

19. George Antonius, *The Arab Awakening: The Story of the Arab National Movement* (Beirut, Lebanon: Khayats, 1961), Appendix E. Weizmann gives a shorter and more permissive translation of Faisal's proviso. Chaim Weizmann, *Trial and Error: The Autobiography of Chaim Weizmann* (New York: Harper, 1949), 308–9.

20. "Memorandum by the Emir Faisal," FO 608/80, fo. 122, in Wilson, *Lawrence,* 596.

21. Great Britain Foreign Office and E. L. Woodward, *Documents on British Foreign Policy, 1919–1939* (London: H.M. Stationery Off., 1946), vol. 1, no. 4, 340–41; Stephen Wentworth Roskill, *Hankey: Man of Secrets* (New York: St. Martin's Press, 1972), 28–29.

22. The quote, attributed to General Murray in the Robert Bolt screenplay for *Lawrence of Arabia,* is from *Seven Pillars of Wisdom:* "In my view if they [the Arab Revolt] did not reach the main battlefield against Turkey, it would have to confess to failure, and remain a side-show of a side-show." Lawrence, *Seven Pillars,* 237.

23. FO 608/97, fos. 445–7, in Wilson, *Lawrence,* 599. The note is in Lawrence's hand, but he was not at the meeting, so it is at best a secondhand report. See also Lawrence, "Diary of the Peace Conference" (fragment), Jan. 1919 in Garnett, *Letters,* 273–74.

24. David Lloyd George, *Memoirs of the Peace Conference* (New Haven: Yale University Press, 1939), vol. 2, 737.

25. T. E. Lawrence, *Seven Pillars of Wisdom,* ed. J. Wilson, complete 1922 "Oxford" edition (Fordingbridge, Hampshire: J. and N. Wilson, 2004), 4; Richard Meinertzhagen, *Middle East Diary, 1917–1956* (London: Cresset Press, 1959), 51. Lawrence specifies which chapters he wrote in Paris in the preface to the 1926 edition.

26. Livneh, *Aharon Aharonsohn,* 336.

27. Richard Andrews, *Der Spion des Lawrence von Arabien: Auf geheimer Mission für einem jüdischen Staat,* trans. Gabriele Herbst (Berlin: Aufbau-Verlag, 2004), 366–67. Lawrence, "Minutes on a letter from King Hussein to the Syrian Unity Party," March 10, 1919, FO 608/105, in Wilson, *Lawrence,* 607.

28. Felix Frankfurter and Harlan B. Phillips, *Felix Frankfurter Reminisces* (New York: Reynal, 1960), 155–56; Weizmann, *Trial and Error,* 308; Meinertzhagen, *Middle East Diary,* 15–16. Some Arab authors have argued that Faisal's letter was a forgery, despite the fact that it is in Israeli archives. See Maurice J.-M. Larès, "Colonel T. E. Lawrence: Initiator of Arab-Zionist Contacts," *T. E. Notes* 14, 1:4.

29. Norman De Mattos Bentwich, *My 77 Years: An Account of My Life and Times, 1883–1960* (Philadelphia: Jewish Publication Society of America, 1961), 59.

30. Livneh, *Aharon Aharonsohn,* 342; Shmuel Katz, *Ha-Reshet: Ha-Haggadah Le-Vet Aharonson* (Tel Aviv: Miśrad ha-biṭaḥon, 2000), 313.

31. Livneh, *Aharon Aharonsohn,* 343, 351.

32. See for example, Aaronsohn's letter to Bernard Flexner of the ZOA, in ibid., 345.

33. Katz, *Aharonson,* 315.

34. Ibid., 317.

35. Harry Barnard, *The Forging of an American Jew: The Life and Times of Judge Julian W. Mack* (New York: Herzl Press, 1974), 258; Felix Frankfurter and Joseph P. Lash, *From the Diaries of Felix Frankfurter: With a Biographical Essay and Notes,* 1st ed. (New York: Norton, 1975), 26.

36. Aaronsohn, "The Boundaries of Palestine," Jan. 27, 1919 (Zionist Archives), quoted in Aaron T. Wolf, "Hydrostrategic Decisionmaking and the Arab-Israeli Conflict," *Transformation of Middle Eastern Natural Environments: Legacies and Lessons,* ed. Jeff Albert, Magnus Bernhardsson, and Roger Kenna, *Yale School of Forestry and Environmental Studies Bulletin,* no. 103 (1998), 227–28.

37. "Zionist Organization Statement on Palestine," Feb. 3, 1919, Paris Peace Conference, jewishvirtuallibrary.org/jsource/History/zoparis.html.

38. Livneh, *Aharon Aharonsohn,* 340.

39. Feb. 4 and Feb. 16, 1919, Aaronsohn, "Diary."

40. Stephen Bonsal, *Suitors and Suppliants: The Little Nations at Versailles* (New York: Prentice-Hall, 1946), 56.

41. James Thomson Shotwell, *At the Paris Peace Conference* (New York: Macmillan, 1937), 129; Harold Nicolson, *Peacemaking 1919* (Boston: Grosset & Dunlap, 1965), 142.

42. Margaret Macmillan, *Paris 1919: Six Months That Changed the World* (New York: Random House, 2002), 418.

43. Aaronsohn to Weizmann, Feb. 16, 1919 (Weizmann Archives), quoted in Wolf, "Hydrostrategic Decisionmaking and the Arab-Israeli Conflict," 229.

44. Weizmann to Brandeis, March 3, 1919, in Livneh, *Aharon Aharonsohn,* 349. The three Zionist members—Jonas Friedenwald, a law clerk and friend of Brandeis's; Robert Szold, a lawyer and cousin of Henrietta Szold's; and Rudolf "Sonny" Sonnenborn, the son of a JAES founder—all had connections to Aaronsohn and the research station.

45. While in Rome, on his way to Palestine with the Zionist Commission, he wrote to Henrietta Szold: "Our collections, the work of 20 years of hardships and love are destroyed.

I have hastily bought in London and Paris the necessary scientific outfit . . . and shall start directly a new Herbarium, a new Geological Collection." March 10, 1918, in Levin, *Vision,* 442.

46. Andrews, *Der Spion des Lawrence von Arabien,* 397; Barnard, *The Forging of an American Jew,* 259.

Chapter 20. Endings

1. To Robert Graves, May 21, 1921, Robert Graves and B. H. Liddell Hart, *T. E. Lawrence to His Biographers Robert Graves and B. H. Liddell Hart,* 2 vols., (Garden City, NY: Doubleday, 1963), I, 15.

2. Weizmann to General Money, Jan. 26, 1919, Chaim Weizmann and Barnet Litvinoff, *The Letters and Papers of Chaim Weizmann* (New Brunswick, N.J.: Transaction Books, 1983), vol. 9, 150ff. Weizmann added: "There is a fundamental difference in quality between Jew and native."

3. Sir R. Rodd to Foreign Office London, telegram 346, May 18, 1919, FO 371/3809, and R. Cooper to Deputy Director of Air Intelligence, May 20, 1919, AIR 1/10102/204/5/1319, quoted in Jeremy Wilson, *Lawrence of Arabia: The Authorized Biography of T. E. Lawrence* (New York: Atheneum, 1990), 611–12.

4. Eliezer Livneh, *Nili Toldoteyha Shel He'aza Medinit* (Tel Aviv: Schocken, 1961), 412–13.

5. Allenby to Alexander Aaronsohn, July 14, 1919 (Aharonsohn Archives, Zichron Ya'aqov); Bullitt to Alexander Aaronsohn, June 9, 1920, in Alexander Aaronsohn, *Sarah: Shalhevet Nili* (Jerusalem: Ahi'asaf, 1942), 33; Felix Frankfurter to Alexandra Levin, June 7, 1916, in Alexandra Lee Levin, *Vision: A Biography of Harry Friedenwald* (Philadelphia: Jewish Publication Society of America, 1964), 442; Henrietta Szold, "Young Judean," June 1919, quoted in Irving Fineman, *Woman of Valor: The Life of Henrietta Szold, 1860–1945* (New York: Simon and Schuster, 1961), 289.

6. Tom Segev, *One Palestine, Complete: Jews and Arabs Under the British Mandate,* trans. Haim Watzman (New York: Henry Holt, 2000), 406; Elizabeth Monroe, *Philby of Arabia* (London: Faber and Faber, 1973), 99–100.

7. Wilson, *Lawrence,* 616.

8. Lawrence's mother, quoted in David Garnett, *The Letters of T. E. Lawrence,* 1st ed. (New York: Doubleday, Doran, 1939), 294; Wilson, *Lawrence,* 621.

9. T. E. Lawrence, letter to the editor, [London] *Times,* Sept. 11, 1919.

10. "Aide-mémoire in regard to the Occupation of Syria, Palestine, and Mesopotamia pending the decision in regards to Mandates," Sept. 13, 1919, FO 608/106, quoted in Garnett, *Letters,* 287.

11. Lawrence to Lloyd George (draft), Sept. 19, 1919, in Wilson, *Lawrence,* 1115n. Garnett associated the letter with the plans that William Yale claimed he had almost brought to fruition as a private citizen; Jeremy Wilson argues convincingly that Yale was exaggerating his own importance. See Evelyn Wrench, *Struggle, 1914–1920* (London: Nicholson & Watson, 1935), 363–64.

12. Malcolm Brown, *The Letters of T. E. Lawrence* (London: J. M. Dent, 1988), 283; A. W. Lawrence, *T. E. Lawrence, by His Friends* (Garden City, N.Y.: Doubleday, Doran, 1937), 213.

13. Lawrence to E. M. Forster, June 17, 1925, in Brown, *Letters,* 283.

14. Segev, *One Palestine, Complete,* 105–6; Elie Kedourie, *In the Anglo-Arab Labyrinth: The McMahon-Husayn Correspondence and Its Interpretations, 1914–1939* (Portland, OR: Frank Cass, 2000), 198–99.

15. Warwick P. N. Tyler, *State Lands and Rural Development in Mandatory Palestine, 1920–1948* (Portland, OR: Sussex Academic Press, 2001), 4, 13.

16. Yehoshua Porath, *The Emergence of the Palestinian-Arab National Movement, 1918–1929* (London: Cass, 1974), 70.

17. See, for example, "Report on the Political Situation in Palestine by Ormsby-Gore," Aug. 22, 1918, FO 371/3389, 147225, quoted in Chaim Weizmann, *Trial and Error: The Autobiography of Chaim Weizmann* (New York: Harper, 1949), 298; A. J. Sherman, *Mandate Days: British Lives in Palestine, 1918–1948* (Baltimore: Johns Hopkins University Press, 2001), 25.

18. David Lloyd George, *Memoirs of the Peace Conference* (New Haven: Yale University Press, 1939), vol. 2, 241.

19. Quoted in Bidwell et al., *Arab Bulletin* (Gerrards Cross, Buckinghamshire, England: Archive Editions, 1986), III, no. 90, 165.

20. This belief continued, even among British intelligence agents, after the war. See Kedourie, *In the Anglo-Arab Labyrinth,* 108.

21. The Wissotsky tea company still produces tea in Israel; the huge Brodsky sugar refinery was in Kiev.

22. *Illustrated Sunday Herald,* March 8, 1920.

23. Segev, *One Palestine, Complete,* 207–8.

24. David Fromkin, *A Peace to End All Peace: Creating the Modern Middle East, 1914–1922* (New York: Holt, 1989), 400. Lloyd George knew his Bible, but probably got the idea from a speech Curzon had given to the War Cabinet Eastern Committee in December 1918: "I imagine we shall all agree that we must recover for Palestine its old boundaries. The old phrase 'Dan to Beersheba' still prevails." Lloyd George, *Memoirs of the Peace Conference,* vol. II, 740.

25. T. E. Lawrence, *Seven Pillars of Wisdom: A Triumph* (London: Penguin, 1965), 15. This preface by A. W. Lawrence was based on a four-page leaflet, "Some Notes on the Writing of the *Seven Pillars of Wisdom* by T. E. Shaw" that Lawrence provided to those who bought or were presented with the 1926 edition.

26. Lawrence to E. Garnett, Aug. 26, 1922, Garnett, *Letters,* 360.

27. Lawrence, *Seven Pillars of Wisdom: A Triumph,* 16.

28. Graves, *T. E. Lawrence to His Biographers,* 110.

29. Liddell Hart, *T. E. Lawrence to His Biographers,* 143.

30. Graves, *T. E. Lawrence to His Biographers,* 112.

31. Lawrence to Robert Graves, May 21, 1921, and May 21, 1927, in ibid., 15, 112.

32. Ibid., 15.

33. Ronald Storrs, *Orientations* (London: Nicholson & Watson, 1932), 375.

34. Segev, *One Palestine, Complete,* 93–94; Sherman, *Mandate Days,* 73; Norman De Mattos Bentwich, *My 77 Years: An Account of My Life and Times, 1883–1960* (Philadelphia: Jewish Publication Society of America, 1961), 60.

35. Khalil Sakakini and Gideon Shilo, *Kazeh Ani Rabotai: Mi-Yomano Shel Halil Al-Sakakini, Bidayat* (Jerusalem: Keter, 1990), 47.

36. Segev, *One Palestine, Complete,* 124. A later version of his dying words was: "It is better to die for the homeland than to die for a foreign land, but it is better to live for the homeland."

37. Ibid., 126.

38. Baruch Kimmerling and Joel S. Migdal, *Palestinians: The Making of a People* (New York: Free Press, 1993), 79.

39. Quoted in Segev, *One Palestine, Complete,* 179.

40. On the changing attitudes toward pogroms, see Anita Shapira, *Land and Power: The Zionist Resort to Force, 1881–1948* (New York: Oxford University Press, 1992), 224.

41. Segev, *One Palestine, Complete,* 159.

42. Translated by David C. Jacobson, "Writing and Rewriting the Zionist National Narrative: Responses to the Arab Revolt of 1936–39 in Kibbutz Passover Haggadot," *Journal of Modern Jewish Studies* 6, no. 1 (2007, forthcoming).

43. "On the Slaughter" is not the same as the longer and better-known Bialik poem, "In the City of Slaughter," also about the Kishinev pogrom; for a translation of the former see ibid.; Kimmerling and Migdal, *Palestinians,* 96, 118.

Chapter 21. Legacies

1. Lawrence to Robert Graves, June 9, 1927, Robert Graves and B. H. Liddell Hart, *T. E. Lawrence to His Biographers Robert Graves and B. H. Liddell Hart,* 2 vols. (Garden City, NY: Doubleday, 1963), I, 58.

2. Quoted in Harry Barnard, *The Forging of an American Jew: The Life and Times of Judge Julian W. Mack* (New York: Herzl Press, 1974), 109.

3. "Twenty-Seven Articles," in Bidwell et al., *Arab Bulletin* (Gerrards Cross, Buckinghamshire, England: Archive Editions, 1986), II, no. 60, 347–53. General John Abizaid has posted portions of Lawrence's fifteenth article—"Better the Arabs do it tolerably than that you do it perfectly. It is their war, and you are to help them, not to win it for them"—at his Central Command headquarters in Qatar, and Lieutenant General David H. Petraeus, "Learning Counterinsurgency: Observations from Soldiering in Iraq," *Military Review* (Jan.–Feb. 2006), 3, offers his own fourteen observations, the first of which quotes from the same article: "Do not try to do too much with your own hands."

4. Lawrence to C. F. Shaw, Sept. 28, 1925, Malcolm Brown, *The Letters of T. E. Lawrence* (London: J. M. Dent, 1988), 289–90.

5. T. E. Lawrence, *Seven Pillars of Wisdom,* ed. J. Wilson, complete 1922 "Oxford" edition (Fordingbridge, Hampshire: J. and N. Wilson, 2004), 813.

6. Jeremy Wilson, *Lawrence of Arabia: The Authorized Biogrpahy of T. E. Lawrence* (New York: Atheneum, 1990), 652–54.

7. See Lawrence, *Seven Pillars,* 678.

8. Lawrence to Hogarth, June 27, 1923, David Garnett, *The Letters of T. E. Lawrence,* 1st ed. (New York: Doubleday, Doran, 1939), 426.

9. Lawrence to Vyvyan Richards [1922], Brown, *Letters,* 223–26.

10. Lawrence to Edward Garnett, Aug. 26, 1922, Garnett, *Letters,* 360. In another letter Lawrence wrote of "other great failures—*Moby Dick, Also Sprach Zarathustra, Pantagruel,*—books where the authors went up like a shoot of rockets, and burst. I don't mean to put mine into that degree of the class: but it is to me as *Zarathustra* was to Nietzsche, something bigger than I could do." Lawrence to A. P. Wavell, May 11, 1923, Brown, *Letters,* 234.

11. Graves, *T. E. Lawrence to His Biographers,* 104.

12. Lawrence wrote to his friend and collaborator Eric Kennington: "Celibacy is unnatural, in the real sense, and it overturns a man's balance: for it throws him either on himself (which is unwholesome, like sucking your own tail, in snakes) or on friendship to satisfy the urge of affection within . . . and such friendship may easily turn into sex-perversion. If I have missed all these things, as I hope and you seem to suggest—well then, I'm barrenly lucky. It has not been easy: and it leads, in old age, to misery." Sept. 15, 1927, quoted in Wilson, *Lawrence,* 705.

13. The beatings were revealed in articles by Colin Simpson and Phillip Knightley in *The Sunday Times* in 1968, and later published in their book *The Secret Lives of Lawrence of Arabia.* Their report was based on a confused and somewhat questionable story by John Bruce, who had served with Lawrence in the tank corps and claimed to have administered the beat-

ings. For a psychobiographical interpretation of the beatings, see John E. Mack, *A Prince of Our Disorder: The Life of T. E. Lawrence* (Cambridge, MA: Harvard University Press, 1976), 428–41.

14. Tom Segev, *One Palestine, Complete: Jews and Arabs Under the British Mandate,* trans. Haim Watzman (New York: Henry Holt, 2000), 14n.

15. Hillel Halkin, *A Strange Death* (New York: Public Affairs, 2005), 269.

16. Szold to her family, June 21, 1920, quoted in Marvin Lowenthal, *Henrietta Szold: Life and Letters* (New York: Viking Press, 1942), 140.

17. Barnard, *The Forging of an American Jew,* 307.

18. Philippa Strum, *Louis D. Brandeis: Justice for the People* (Cambridge, MA.: Harvard University Press, 1984), 244.

19. Norman De Mattos Bentwich, *My 77 Years: An Account of My Life and Times, 1883–1960* (Philadelphia: Jewish Publication Society of America, 1961), 44.

20. "Elef Neshikot" (A Thousand Kisses), sung by Yehoram Gaon.

21. M. R. Werner, *Julius Rosenwald: The Life of a Practical Humanitarian* (New York: Harper, 1939), 101–2; Norman De Mattos Bentwich, *Judah L. Magnes: A Biography of the First Chancellor and First President of the Hebrew University of Jerusalem* (London: East & West Library, 1955), 73.

22. Anita Engle, *The Nili Spies* (London: Hogarth Press, 1959), 233–38; R. Graves, "T. E. Lawrence and the Riddle of S.A.," *Saturday Review,* June 15, 1963; Ladislas Farago, *Palestine at the Crossroads* (New York: G. P. Putnam's Sons, 1937), 159–60; Cecil Bloom, "Was Lawrence of Arabia's S.A. a Palestinian Jewess?" *T.E. Notes* 15, no. 1 (2005); Cecil Bloom, "Immortal Beloved," *Jerusalem Post,* May 15, 2005.

INDEX

PHOTO-INSERT CREDITS

Page 1, top, by permission of the Aaronsohn Archive, Zichron Ya'aqov; middle, by permission of the Imperial War Museum; bottom, by permission of the Aaronsohn Archive, Zichron Ya'aqov.

Page 2, top left, by permission of the Aaronsohn Archive, Zichron Ya'aqov; top right, by permission of the Aaronsohn Archive, Zichron Ya'aqov; bottom, by permission of the Aaronsohn Archive, Zichron Ya'aqov.

Page 3, top, by permission of the Aaronsohn Archive, Zichron Ya'aqov; bottom left, by permission of the Aaronsohn Archive, Zichron Ya'aqov; bottom right, from Jeremy Wilson.

Page 4, top, by permission of the British Museum; bottom, by permission of the Aaronsohn Archive, Zichron Ya'aqov.

Page 5, top: by permission of the Aaronsohn Archive, Zichron Ya'aqov; bottom: by permission of the Aaronsohn Archive, Zichron Ya'aqov.

Page 6, top, by permission of the Imperial War Museum; bottom, by permission of the Imperial War Museum.

Page 7, top, by permission of the Aaronsohn Archive, Zichron Ya'aqov; bottom, by permission of the Aaronsohn Archive, Zichron Ya'aqov.

Page 8, bottom, by permission of the Central Zionist Archives, Jerusalem.

Page 9: by permission of the Imperial War Museum.

Page 10, top left, by permission of the Imperial War Museum; top right, by permission of the Aaronsohn Archive, Zichron Ya'aqov; bottom, by permission of the Aaronsohn Archive, Zichron Ya'aqov.

Page 11, top, by permission of the Central Zionist Archives, Jerusalem; middle, by permission of the Aaronsohn Archive, Zichron Ya'aqov; bottom, by permission of the Imperial War Museum.

Page 12, top: by permission of the Imperial War Museum; bottom: by permission of the Rolls-Royce Enthusiasts Club.

Page 13, top, by permission of the Imperial War Museum; bottom, by permission of the Imperial War Museum.

Page 14, middle, by permission of the Central Zionist Archives, Jerusalem; bottom, by permission of the Imperial War Museum.

Page 15, top, by permission of the Aaronsohn Archive, Zichron Ya'aqov; bottom, by permission of the Aaronsohn Archive, Zichron Ya'aqov.

Page 16: by permission of the British Museum.